Student Guide with Map Exercises

The Enduring Vision

A HISTORY OF THE AMERICAN PEOPLE

SIXTH EDITION

Boyer • Clark • Kett • Salisbury • Sitkoff • Woloch

Jay T. Nelson

DePaul University

Volume 1

Barbara Blumberg

Pace University

Volume 2

Houghton Mifflin Company   BOSTON   NEW YORK

Publisher: *Suzanne Jeans*
Senior Sponsoring Editor: *Ann West*
Marketing Manager: *Katherine Bates*
Senior Development Editor: *Jennifer Sutherland*
Senior Consulting Editor: *Jean L. Woy*
Editorial Assistant: *Nina Tamburello*

Printed in the U.S.A.

ISBN 13: 978-0-618-82108-2
ISBN 10: 0-618-82108-2

23456789-POO-11 10 09 08

Contents

PREFACE

This *Student Guide with Map Exercises to Accompany The Enduring Vision,* Sixth Edition, is intended to help you to master the history presented in *The Enduring Vision: A History of the American People.* It is *not* a substitute for reading the textbook. However, if used properly as a *supplement* to the text, it should assist you in focusing on the important events, issues, and concepts in American history, as well as on the well-known figures and ordinary people alike whose ideas and actions help us to understand the past. It is also designed to build your vocabulary, improve your knowledge of geography, and enhance your understanding of how the historian learns about the past.

Each chapter in the *Student Guide* corresponds to a chapter in *The Enduring Vision* and is divided into the following sections:

- *Outline and Summary.* This follows the outline of the textbook chapter and summarizes the material discussed under each text heading. You should read it quickly before reading the textbook chapter to give yourself an overview of the contents. Then carefully read the text chapter. After completing the text chapter, reread the outline and summary as a review.

- *Vocabulary.* In this section social science terms and other words used in the text chapter that may be new to you are defined. Look over the list before you read the textbook chapter. Familiarize yourself with any words that you do not already know.

- *Identifications.* Here you will find the important persons, laws, terms, groups, and events covered in *The Enduring Vision.* After reading the text chapter, test yourself by identifying who or what each item was and how this person or thing fits into the overall story. That is, what is its historical significance?

- *Skill Building.* In most of the chapters of the *Student Guide,* you will find either (a) a section designed to help you interpret charts and tables in the textbook or (b) a map exercise, asking you to locate places mentioned in the text chapter and to explain the historical significance of those geographical places. Some chapters contain both.

- *Historical Sources.* Too often we simply accept what we see in print as true and memorize it without stopping to ask how the author obtained the information and whether we should believe it. The purpose of the Historical Sources section found in most chapters is to explain where the historian gets his or her facts, and to assist you in evaluating the reliability of those sources and the conclusions based on them.

- *Multiple-Choice Questions, Short-Answer Questions, Essay Questions, and Answers to Multiple-Choice Questions.* After reading the corresponding chapter in *The Enduring Vision,* you should try to answer these questions. They are designed to help you review the significant material in the chapter; they will probably be similar to the kinds of questions and essays that your professor will give you to write on in papers, quizzes, and exams. Answers to the multiple-choice questions appear at the end of the *Student Guide.*

The last *Student Guide* chapter is intended to aid you in preparing for the final examination in your history course. It contains hints on studying, as well as multiple-choice and essay questions that ask you to consider and pull together the material presented in *all* of the chapters of *The Enduring Vision.*

For help in preparing the *Student Guide,* I would like to thank the authors of *The Enduring Vision* for writing a lucid, informative, political, social, and cultural history of the United States that is a pleasure to read and to write about. Second I appreciate the help of the editors at Houghton Mifflin who made valuable suggestions. Penelope Harper, professor of history at SUNY-Cortland, provided assistance in revising chapters 30-32. I am grateful to my husband, Alan Krumholz, and to my son, Mark, for their patience and support while I worked on this project.

    —Barbara Blumberg

Enduring Vision, Enduring Land

OUTLINE AND SUMMARY

I. Introduction

America's "enduring vision" includes (1) a vision of the land itself, a land which has offered a "haven for new beginnings" and opportunities, and (2) a search for a just social order in that land, a search that has constantly sought to balance individual freedom with obligations to the social group, or "community." Many times in our past we have not lived up to our ideals of freedom and social responsibility, but those who have tried to bring us back to the vision, along with most other Americans, have shared a hopefulness about progress.

II. The Continent and Its Regions

A. Introduction

North America's landscape evolved over the course of at least 3 billion years, ending with the last Ice Age. As the ice retreated, North America slowly warmed. The geological, geographical, and climatic diversity that followed has contributed to the regional cultural differences that have developed and to America's physical beauty, wealth of resources, and political preeminence.

B. The West

Lands in Alaska and Canada ranged from the treeless tundra of the Arctic to the heavily forested taiga of the subarctic. Farther south, the Pacific Northwest had a temperate, rainy climate and many resources, while the southern California coast offered a drier, warmer, Mediterranean climate. To the east of the fertile inter-mountain-range valleys and the Sierra Nevada lay the Great Basin, an arid, formidable desert. The backbone of western North America is formed by the Rocky Mountains. Beyond the Rockies' front range is the Continental Divide, the watershed separating rivers flowing eastward into the Atlantic from those draining westward into the Pacific. In the hot southwestern deserts of Arizona, southern Utah, western New Mexico, and southeastern California, Native Americans cultivated the first crops in what is now the United States.

C. The Heartland

North America's heartland extends from the Rocky Mountains to the Appalachians. Over the millennia, the Mississippi-Missouri-Ohio river system that drains it has carried so much silt down to the Gulf of Mexico that a fertile delta capable of providing food for a large population has been built up. Most of the eastern and northern sections of the heartland were once covered with thick forests. To the west, the trees give way gradually to grass-covered prairies. Beyond the Missouri River, these prairies become the Great Plains—treeless, an endless sea of grass, bitter cold in winter, blazing hot in summer, and often dry. In the nineteenth century, white settlers displaced the Indians in the American heartland, felled the trees, plowed up the grasses, and turned the Midwest into a breadbasket for the world, except during periodic droughts when it was subjected to severe dust storms.

D. The Atlantic Seaboard

East of the Appalachians lies the upland area known as the Piedmont, extending from Alabama to Maryland. Once blessed with rich, red soil, its fertility in modern times has been ruined by excessive cotton and tobacco farming. The northward extension of the Piedmont runs from Pennsylvania to southern New England. Its terrain, as well as that of upstate New York and most of New England, was sculpted by glaciation. Strewn with the rocks and boulders left behind by retreating ice, New England's soil is difficult to plow.

The fall line, a series of rapids in the rivers that block navigation upstream from the coast, separates the Atlantic coastal plain, or tidewater, from the interior. In the south the tidewater is cut by numerous small rivers. To the north, it narrows and flattens to form the New Jersey Pine Barrens, Long Island, and Cape Cod. North of Massachusetts Bay, the shoreline becomes mountainous. North America's true eastern edge, the continental shelf, is an area of relatively shallow water that extends as much as 250 miles into the Atlantic.

First the Indians and later Europeans found the northern Atlantic coastal region especially inviting for its abundant game and other food supply and for the excellent fishing in the Grand Banks and the coastal bays surrounding Cape Cod.

III. A Legacy and a Challenge

North America's fertile soils, abundant forests, and mineral deposits encouraged settlers to see their country's resources as boundless, and, therefore, they ruthlessly exploited those resources for personal gain. As a result, many of those resources have been exhausted and much of the environment polluted to the point of endangering human health. Today we face a challenge—how to stop the destruction of the very environment that has sustained us. Here we could well draw on the legacy of the Native Americans and reestablish a sense of historical and cultural continuity with our predecessors on the land. In this way we might recapture the Indians' sense "that the land—its life-sustaining bounty and its soul-sustaining beauty—is itself of inestimable value and not merely a means to the end of material growth."

VOCABULARY

The following terms are used in the Prologue. To understand it fully, it is important that you know what each of them means.

geology	the scientific study of the earth, rocks, and the changes that the earth has undergone or is undergoing
exploitation	the unfair or reckless use of people, animals, and/or the environment to profit materially from them
tundra	the nearly level, treeless plain with sparse, stunted vegetation of the kind found in the arctic regions of Europe, Asia, and North America
taiga	the evergreen forests of subarctic lands covering vast areas of northern North America and Eurasia
anchorage	harbor
steppe	dry, grassy land or plains
delta	a nearly flat plain of river-deposited silt and soil between diverging branches of the mouth of a river
bayou	a sluggish tributary or a swampy arm of a lake or river

IDENTIFICATIONS

After reading the Prologue, you should be able to identify and explain the historical significance of each of the following:

Precambrian era

Paleozoic era

Ice Age

Continental Divide

Breadbasket, dust bowl

fall line

continental shelf

Grand Banks

SKILL BUILDING: MAPS

1.   On the map of North America, locate each of the following and explain its geologic origins:

continental shelf

Appalachians

Pacific Coastal, Sierra Nevada, and Cascade mountain ranges

Rocky Mountains and Continental Divide

Great Lakes

Great Basin and Utah's Great Salt Lake

southwestern desert, Colorado River, and Grand Canyon

Mississippi Delta

Great Plains

tidewater region and fall line

Piedmont

North America

2.   On the map below, locate each of these major North American rivers, showing its point of origin and its mouth:

St. Lawrence

Hudson

Susquehanna

Potomac

Savannah

Mississippi

Missouri

Ohio

Snake

Columbia

Rio Grande

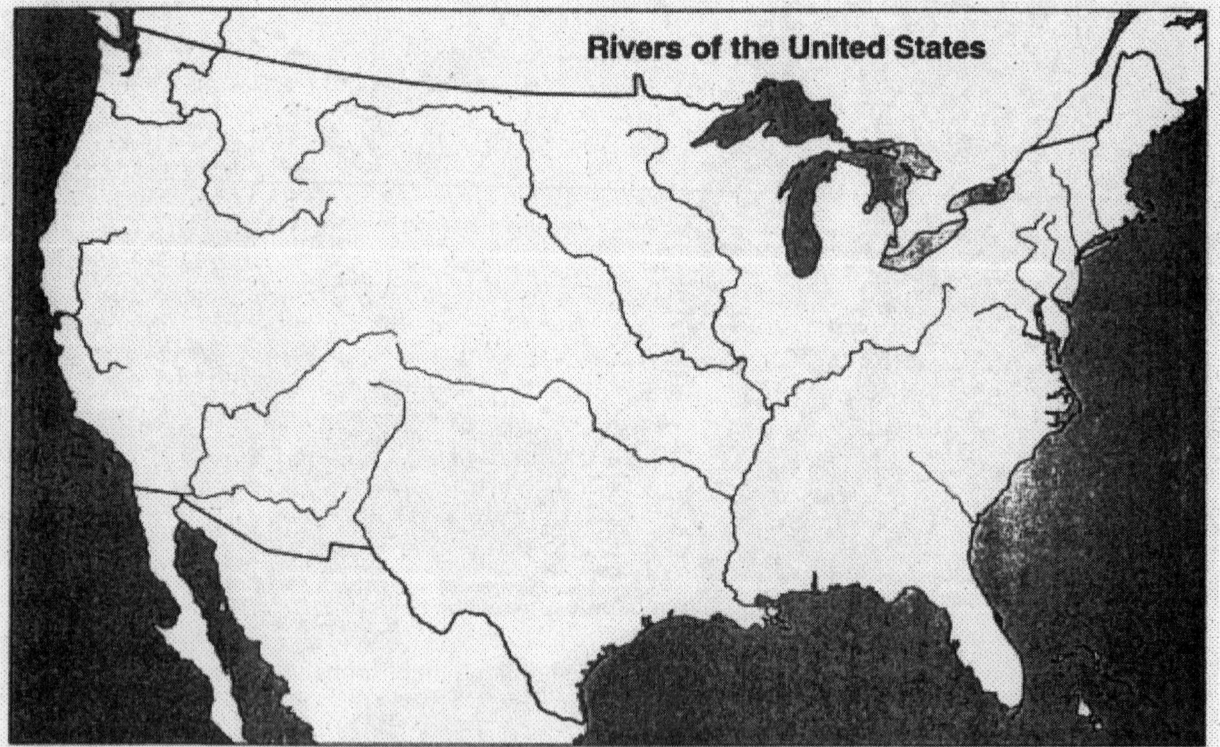

Multiple-Choice Questions

Circle the letter of the item that best completes each statement or answers the question.

1. The fall line is the
   a. edge of the continental shelf where the Atlantic Ocean suddenly becomes much deeper.
   b. mountain ranges of California over which Pacific air masses drop their moisture in the form of heavy rainfall.
   c. divide between the treeless Great Plains and the more forested Mississippi-Ohio Valley.
   d. series of rapids in rivers where hard continental rock meets the sedimentary plains along the Atlantic.
2. Agriculture was first practiced by the Indians of the
   a. Pacific Northwest.
   b. desert Southwest.
   c. midwestern heartland.
   d. Atlantic seaboard.
3. The Continental Divide is found in the
   a. Sierra Nevada.
   b. fall line.
   c. Ohio Valley.
   d. Rocky Mountains.
4. All of the following were created by glaciation *except*
   a. the Great Lakes.
   b. New England's rocky soil.
   c. the Grand Canyon.
   d. the coastline of Alaska.
5. Since the nineteenth century, the geographical region that has become America's breadbasket is the
   a. Midwest.
   b. Far West.
   c. Atlantic seaboard.
   d. Great Basin.
6. The region with the greatest annual temperature range in the United States is
   a. New England.
   b. the Southeast.
   c. the Pacific Northwest and Alaskan panhandle.
   d. the Great Plains.
7. All of the following states have a portion of the Piedmont running through them *except*
   a. Alabama.
   b. Pennsylvania.
   c. Rhode Island.
   d. North Carolina.

SHORT-ANSWER QUESTIONS

1. Describe the climate and terrain of each of the following regions: the West, the heartland, the Atlantic seaboard.

2. How was the fertile Mississippi Delta created?

3. Why was much of New England's soil rocky and difficult to plow?

ESSAY QUESTIONS

1. According to the Prologue, what has been the enduring vision of Americans? What have been some of the problems and contradictions within that vision?

2. "Geology, geography, and environment are among the fundamental building blocks of human history." Explain the meaning of this statement, and illustrate it with as many specific examples from the Prologue as possible.

ANSWERS TO MULTIPLE-CHOICE QUESTIONS

1. d
2. b
3. d
4. c
5. a
6. a
7. c

CHAPTER 1

Native Peoples of America, to 1500

OUTLINE AND SUMMARY

I. Introduction

American history began more than ten thousand years before Columbus's first voyage. Native Americans developed diverse cultures, but with much interaction among the many different groups.

This chapter focuses on these questions: (1) How did environmental change shape the transition from Paleo-Indian to Archaic ways of life?(2)What were the principal differences among the Native American cultures that emerged after 2500 B.C.? (3) Despite their diversity, what significant values and practices did North American Indians share?

II. The First Americans, c. 13,000-2500 B.C.

A. Peopling New Worlds

The two main theories about the origins of the people of the Americas are: (1) During the last Ice Age (c. 10,500 B.C.) bands of hunters from Siberia crossed the then-existing land bridge into Alaska and from there spread out over the Western Hemisphere. (2) As early as 13,000 B.C. people came by boat, settling at various spots along the western coast of the Americas. A majority of today's archaeologists believe that both theories are correct. In addition, around 7000 B.C. an Athapaskan-speaking people arrived in Alaska and northwestern Canada and gradually migrated to the southwest where they became the ancestors of the Apaches and Navajo. Even more recently, non-Indian groups (Eskimos, Inuits, and Aleuts) crossed the Bering Sea to Alaska.

These earliest Americans, called Paleo-Indians by archaeologists, lived in small hunting bands that moved constantly in pursuit of mammoths, mastodons, and other big game. About 9000 B.C. the mammoths and mastodons became extinct probably because of climatic warming. Groups of Paleo-Indians came together briefly at quarries, where they obtained flint for spear points and tools. By way of these encounters, the bands intermarried, traded, and exchanged cultural traits.

B. Archaic Societies

As the Earth's atmosphere warmed, a tremendous range of plants and animals flourished on the American continents and in their waters. This enabled archaic peoples (Native Americans of the period 8000 to 2500 B.C.) to broaden their diets to include small mammals, fish, and wild plants. Where the abundance was especially apparent larger groups of people lived in a smaller area and established permanent villages. Over time, these people distinguished between men's and women's roles: men hunted and fished; women harvested and prepared wild plants. As early as 5000 B.C. some Native Americans were starting to farm. In Mexico and Central America, Indians were growing squash, beans, and some fruit by 3000 B.C., and by 2500 B.C. maize cultivation had spread from Central America and Mexico as far north as New Mexico and as far south as the Amazon River basin.

III.   Cultural Diversity, c. 2500 B.C.–A.D. 1500
   A.   Introduction
         After about 2500 B.C. many Native Americans' way of life evolved from that of the Archaic
         period. The change was greatest among peoples who had started to farm, but, even among
         some who had not, extended religious and political systems and hierarchical states
         developed.

   B.   Mesoamerica and South America
         Farming societies in Mesoamerica (southern Mexico and Central America) and in South
         America greatly increased their food production between 2500 and 2000 B.C. Some of the
         most productive of these farming peoples, such as the Olmecs, established large urban
         centers after 1200 B.C. from which hereditary rulers imposed their will on small surrounding
         areas called "chiefdoms." Between A.D. 1 and 500 a few chiefdoms in Mesoamerica and
         South America grew into full-fledged states. The capital of one such state near present-day
         Mexico City, was Teotihuacan. At the height of its power (between the second and seventh
         centuries A.D.), this state had over 100,000 people. As this state declined in the eighth
         century, it was conquered and incorporated into still more powerful states, run first by the
         Mayans and later the Aztecs. These societies built huge engineering and public works
         projects, carried on extensive trade, and possessed sophisticated calendars and writing and
         number systems. The Aztec and Inca Empires were still expanding when the Spanish
         conquistadores arrived in the sixteenth century.

   C.   The Southwest
         In the Southwest (including the southwestern part of the United States and northern
         Mexico), water was often scarce. As a result, maize cultivation did not reach the area until
         2500 B.C. and full-time farming was common only after 400 B.C. With the coming of
         agriculture, new Indian cultures arose. By the third century B.C. the Hohokam people of
         southern Arizona had built extensive canal systems for irrigation, which allowed them to
         harvest two crops a year. They also resided in permanent villages of several hundred people.
         The Anasazi people of the Southwest lived primarily by farming, too. These ancestors of the
         Pueblo Indians dominated the Southwest for almost 600 years, founding confederations of
         towns such as Chaco Canyon, New Mexico, inhabited by about fifteen thousand persons.
         By the thirteenth century, however, the Anasazi and Hohokam cultures declined, and these
         peoples abandoned their large settlements, perhaps due to prolonged periods of drought. At
         roughly the same time the foraging Apaches and Navajo arrived in the Southwest.

   D.   The Eastern Woodlands
         Many tribes in the Eastern Woodlands (the area from the Mississippi Valley to the Atlantic
         coast) experimented with village life and political centralization even before they started
         farming. As early as 1200 B.C. five thousand people lived at Poverty Point on the shore of
         the Mississippi River in Louisiana. As Poverty Point declined in importance, a new mound-
         building culture, the Adena, emerged. Adena mounds, often containing graves, were built all
         over the Ohio Valley. In the second century B.C. Adena culture evolved into the more
         complex and widespread Hopewell civilization, which built more elaborate mounds.

         Agriculture did not become the primary source of food for Eastern Woodlands peoples until
         after the seventh century A.D. The first full-time farmers in the East lived on the flood plains
         of the Mississippi River, where, incorporating elements of Hopewell culture, they evolved
         into the still more sophisticated Mississippian civilization. Mississippian towns grew to have
         thousands of inhabitants. The largest town was Cahokia, near present-day St. Louis.
         Mississippian artists produced works of clay, stone, shell, and copper. Their religion was
         based on sun worship, and their political system was centralized and hierarchical. By the

thirteenth century, Mississippian culture had declined and most Eastern Woodlands Indians had abandoned large settlements and centralized political power. However, they continued to engage in agriculture, using the ecologically sound slash-and-burn method of land clearing to grow their corn and beans.

E.   Nonfarming Societies
Along the Pacific coast, from southern Alaska to northern California, Indians fished for salmon and learned to dry and store their catch year-round, making possible the establishment of permanent villages of several hundred people. Further south California Indians also resided in permanent villages and sustained themselves by collecting and grinding acorns into meal. Both groups engaged in trade and warfare and, as a result, united under the leadership of chiefs. On the Great Plains and in the Great Basin, the rainfall was too uncertain to allow permanent settlements. Instead, Indians there roamed over large areas, hunting a variety of animals, especially bison, and foraging for wild seeds and nuts. The Eskimos and Aleuts, arriving in western Alaska from Siberia, brought along advanced hunting tools, such as harpoons and spears. With these they hunted sea mammals and caribou. In time they spread across northern Canada all the way to Greenland, where in the period 980 to about 1100, they had limited contacts with Norsemen trying to colonize Greenland and Newfoundland. For the most part, though, the peoples of the Americas developed in isolation from those on other continents. In many ways the evolution of the American cultures paralleled those in Europe, Asia, and Africa.

IV.   North American Peoples on the Eve of Contact
A.   Introduction
By 1500 about 75 million people lived in the Western Hemisphere. Of these, 7 million to 10 million inhabited land north of Mesoamerica. These peoples were divided into several hundred nations and tribes and spoke diverse languages, but most shared certain characteristics: using bows and arrows and ceramic pottery; holding some common religious beliefs, practices and rituals; living in kinship-based communities; and agreeing to communal control of resources.

B.   Kinship and Gender
Kinship held Indian societies together. The kinship group, or extended family, was far more important than the nuclear family of husband, wife, and young children. In agricultural societies the women did the farming (except among the tribes of the Southwest, where both sexes were cultivators). There was fighting among kinship groups and tribes over scarce resources and other conflicts, but rarely did the combatants attempt to kill large numbers of the enemy.

C.   Spiritual and Social Values
Native Americans found all nature, including humanity, interrelated and suffused with spiritual powers or, in the language of the Algonquian, *manitou*. Indians sought to placate and be in tune with these spiritual forces. They did this through dreaming; altering their state of consciousness by acts of physical endurance and self-torture, such as the Sun Dance of the Plains Indians; and following the advice of medicine men and women. To smooth relations between persons of unequal status and power and hold their societies together, Indians relied on reciprocity, which included the giving of gifts and trading of goods in return for receiving prestige, submission, and authority. Indian communities generally demanded conformity and close cooperation of their members.

V.   Conclusion
Human history in the Western Hemisphere did not begin with the arrival of Columbus. For thousands of years before 1492 Native Americans hunted; gathered; farmed; built communities,

roads, and trails; and created complex societies. While not always good conservationists, Indians did, for the most part, respect the land and use it in ways that allowed natural resources to renew themselves. Europeans arriving in North America after 1500 showed no such self-restraint.

VOCABULARY

The following terms are used in Chapter 1. To understand the chapter fully, it is important that you know what each of them means.

archaeological

of or pertaining to the scientific study of any prehistoric culture by excavation and description of its remains

indigenous

native to a particular region

kiva

a large chamber, often wholly or partially underground, in a Pueblo Indian village; used for religious ceremonies and other purposes

hierarchy

a system of placing persons or things in a graded order, from lower to higher, in wealth, power, status, and so on

reciprocity

a system of mutual give-and-take, allowing individuals or social groups of unequal power, wealth, or status to get along while preserving unequal power relationships; also, a system by which human beings can coexist with nature and the powerful supernatural forces in which they believe

consensus

an agreement in opinion; collective opinion

IDENTIFICATIONS

After reading Chapter 1, you should be able to identify and explain the historical significance of each of the following:

Iroquois Confederacy

Paleo-Indians

Archaic peoples

chiefdoms

conquistadores

Hohokam culture

Anasazi and Pueblo cultures

Chaco Canyon

Poverty Point, mound-building culture, and Adena culture

Hopewell and Mississippian cultures

Eastern Woodlands peoples

Cahokia

nuclear families versus extended families

manitou

the Sun Dance

SKILL BUILDING: MAPS

On the map of Mexico, Central America, and South America, locate the regions where these Indian peoples and the sites associated with them existed:

Olmecs and Teotihuacan

Amazon Valley

Andes Mountains

Aztecs and Tenochtitlan

Mayas and Mesoamerica

Incas and Cuzco

On the map of North America on the following page, locate the regions where these Indian cultures and the sites associated with them existed:

Aleuts, Eskimos, and Arctic culture

Northwest Coast Indians

California Indians

hunting bands of the Great Basin and Great Plains

Hohokam culture

Anasazi and Pueblo cultures

Poverty Point

Adena culture

Hopewell and Mississippian cultures (Cahokia)

Eastern Woodlands culture (Iroquois Confederacy)

Central and South America
20°N
10°N
0°
10°S
20°S
30°S
40°S
50°S
105°W
90°W
75°W
60°W
45°W
30°W
15°W

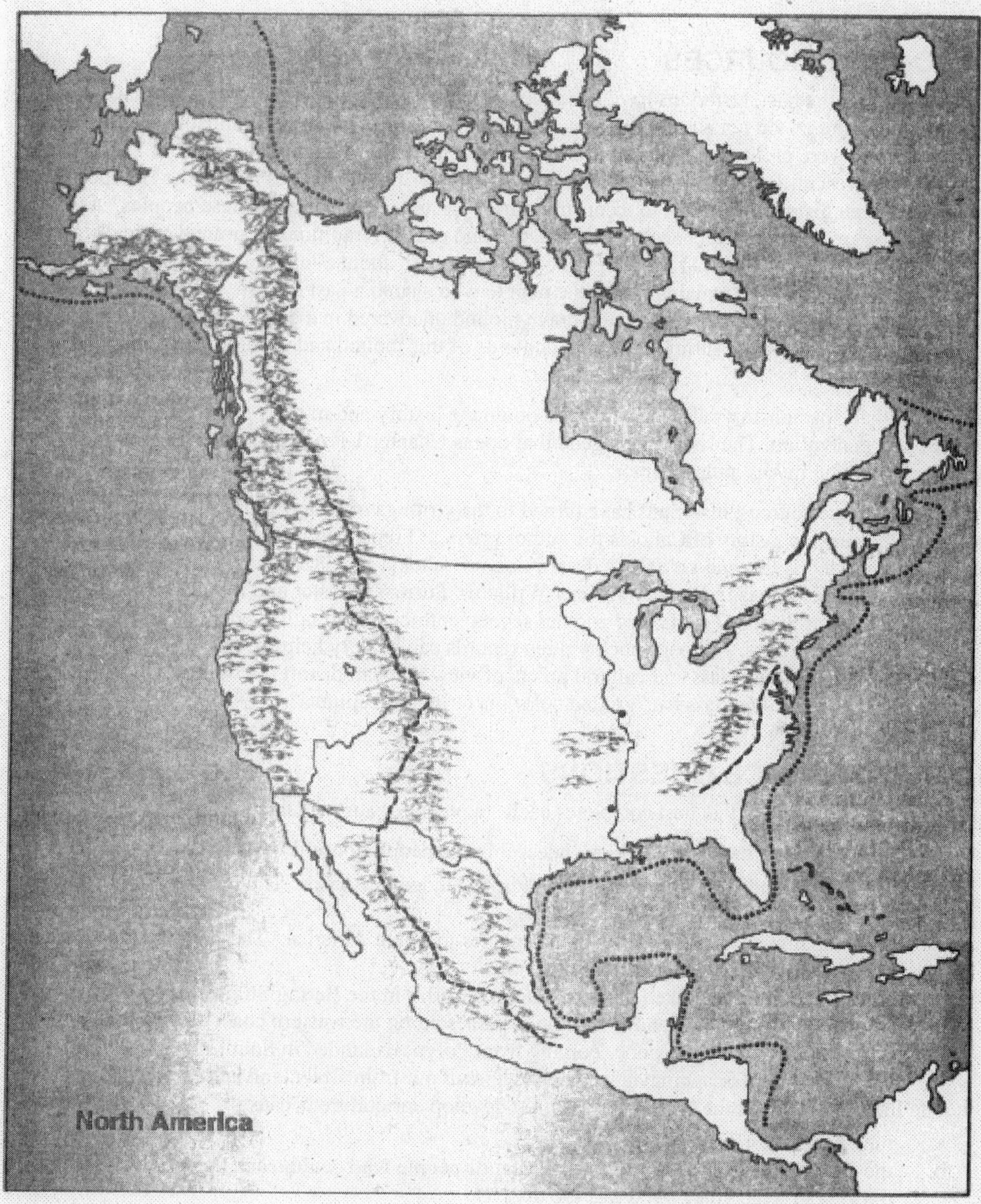

North America

HISTORICAL SOURCES

In learning about the past, historians have generally depended on written records as their major source. But written documents do not always exist for all places, groups, and times. For most of history the world's peoples were preliterate or illiterate and therefore left no written communication. The Indians inhabiting the present-day United States had not developed written languages before the Europeans arrived. How can historians attempt to reconstruct the lives and experiences of these peoples? As the author of Chapter 1 tells us, "archaeological evidence and oral . . . traditions examined critically are our principal sources of evidence." Archaeologists can detect much about a long-lost way of life by uncovering the artifacts and remains left by the people who shared a past culture. In "A Place in Time: Cahokia in 1200," there is a description of a grave mound uncovered in a dig. What was found at that site? What does the historian surmise from the contents of this mound and of other grave mounds in the same area?

Many tribes had special storytellers who handed down the history and myths of their people from generation to generation. The Hiawatha legend that opens Chapter 1 is one example. Find other references to Indian myths in the chapter.

In addition to these sources, historians have turned to the writings of early European explorers and settlers. In the capsule history of Cahokia the author refers to French explorers' accounts of Natchez Indian society in the 1600s and La Salle's description of Cahokia in 1682. What does the historian learn from these? At other places in Chapter 1 Roger Williams, Puritan minister and founder of Rhode Island, is quoted on Indian religious beliefs, and another seventeenth-century English colonist describes warfare among the Indians. Although such written records can be very helpful, scholars have to be aware of the biases and the class and cultural points of view that can distort the writers' accounts. How might a person's cultural or class background color his or her perceptions?

MULTIPLE-CHOICE QUESTIONS

Circle the letter of the item that best completes each statement or answers the question.

1. At present the main theory or theories concerning the peopling of the Americas are:
    a. Norsemen landed in Greenland and Eskimos landed in Alaska. Their descendents spread out all over North and South America.
    b. Humans first evolved from prehuman species in South America. These indigenous humans were later joined by migrants from Africa.
    c. Hunters from Asia walked across a glacial corridor in the Bering Straits, and others arrived from Asia by boat and landed at various places along the western coast of America.
    d. Fishermen in outrigger canoes coming from Polynesia landed in South America, while Norsemen from Scandinavia landed and spread out from Greenland and Newfoundland.

2. The Indian peoples of the Great Basin did *not* develop agriculture because
    a. they had no horses to pull plows.
    b. they had no contact with Eastern Woodlands people who could teach them how to farm.
    c. the area in which they lived was too dry.
    d. wild game and wild plants were so abundant that they had no need to do the hard work of farming to feed themselves.

3. Which one of these Indian cultures is *not* correctly matched to the geographical area in which it flourished?

    a.   Pueblo—Arizona and New Mexico
    b.   Woodlands—the Pacific Northwest and California
    c.   Hopewell—the Midwest
    d.   Hohokam—Arizona

4. All of the following helped shape Native Americans' social and cultural development before 1500 *except*

    a.   geographical isolation.
    b.   great climatic and geographical variations across America.
    c.   contact with Asian and African cultures, from which they adopted many practices.
    d.   long-term changes or cycles in weather, such as warming trends and extended droughts.

5. Which of the following tribes was the ancestor of the modern Pueblo Indians?

    a.   Adenas
    b.   Anasazis
    c.   Aleuts
    d.   Apaches

6. At the time of Columbus's first voyage to the New World, about how many Native Americans lived on the continent north of Mesoamerica?

    a.   7 million to 10 million
    b.   75 million
    c.   50,000 to 100,000
    d.   1 million to 2 million

7. All of these were characteristics of North American Indian cultures before contact with the Eastern Hemisphere *except*

    a.   strong kinship or extended family ties.
    b.   the belief that all nature was infused with spiritual power.
    c.   the belief that property ownership gave the owner perpetual and exclusive control over the land.
    d.   strong oral traditions but no written languages.

8. Cahokia was

    a.   located near present-day New York City and reached its peak of glory in the 1700s.
    b.   probably doomed by its primitive culture and lack of government institutions.
    c.   destroyed by French explorers, who burned it in 1682.
    d.   part of the mound-building Mississippian culture and grew to a population of 20,000 inhabitants.

9. Among North American Indians, women alone did the farming *except* among the tribes in the

    a.   Northeast.
    b.   Great Basin.
    c.   Southwest.
    d.   Mississippi Valley.

10. The term *Archaic peoples* refers to

    a.   Native Americans from about 8000 to approximately 2500 B.C.
    b.   the first nomadic hunters to reach North America.
    c.   the mound builders of the Mississippi Valley.
    d.   all Native Americans living here at the time of Columbus's voyage.

SHORT-ANSWER QUESTIONS

1. Where and when did the earliest direct contact between Europeans and Americans probably occur? What, if anything, resulted from the contact?

2. Where and how was agriculture first practiced in what is now the United States?

3. How did Native Americans' view of nature and land use differ from that of Europeans in the 1500s and 1600s?

ESSAY QUESTIONS

1. Compare and contrast the Native American societies that grew up in Mesoamerica and South America with those that developed in northern Mexico and the rest of North America. How do you account for some of the pronounced differences? Were there some similarities?

2. Compare and contrast the development and later decline of each of these major Indian cultures: Hohokam and Anasazi; Adena, Hopewell, and Mississippian.

3. Discuss the differing ways of life of the Native Americans living in the Arctic, the Pacific Northwest, California, the Great Basin, the Southwest, the Mississippi Valley, and the Eastern Woodlands. Explain how the physical environment influenced each way of life.

4. Because the Indian peoples of the present-day United States had not developed written languages before the coming of Europeans, how have historians attempted to reconstruct Native American history? Give as many specific examples from Chapter 1 as possible.

5. Compare and contrast the descriptions of Native American culture presented in Chapter 1 with the impressions offered in movies and television.

ANSWERS TO MULTIPLE-CHOICE QUESTIONS

1. c
2. c
3. b
4. c
5. b
6. a
7. c
8. d
9. c
10. a

CHAPTER 2

The Rise of the Atlantic World, 1400–1625

OUTLINE AND SUMMARY

I. Introduction

When Columbus and his crew landed on the island of San Salvador on October 12, 1492, the isolation of the Western Hemisphere from Europe and Asia ended. Henceforth, the Americas would become the area of encounter for Europeans, Africans, and Native Americans, and out of these interactions would emerge the Atlantic World.

Chapter 2 focuses on these questions: (1)What forces were transforming West Africa before the advent of the Atlantic slave trade? (2)How did European monarchs use commerce and religion to advance their nations' fortunes? (3)What role did the Columbian exchange play in the formation of an Atlantic world? (4) How did relations with Native Americans affect the success of early European colonizing efforts?

II. African and European Peoples

A. West Africa: Tradition and Change

In the grasslands south of the Sahara Desert and east of the West African coast, kingdoms arose that rivaled those in Europe in size and wealth. In the fourteenth century, one of these empires, the Mali, dominated the whole region and engaged in lucrative trade with Europe and the Middle East. Its leading city, Timbuktu, was an important center of Islamic learning. By the sixteenth century, however, most of Mali and the successor state, Songhai, had been conquered by Morocco. In the fifteenth century, the small states on the Guinea and Senegambian coast grew in population and importance because of the foreign demand for the gold that the Africans mined and traded. In the mid-1400s the Portuguese arrived on the coast, too, looking for gold and slaves. West African leaders ranged from powerful emperors, who claimed demigod status, to heads of small states, who ruled mainly by persuasion. Kinship groups formed the most important unit holding people together. Men could marry more than one woman, allowing high-status men to establish kinship networks with other important families through their several wives. Another driving force behind marriage was West Africa's high mortality rate, brought on by frequent famines and tropical disease epidemics. The shortage of people placed a high premium on the production of children.

These children contributed to the families' wealth by increasing its food production, important in West Africa because most of the food was obtained by farming, an activity in which both men and women engaged. They grew yams, rice, and other grains. By the fifteenth century a market economy had developed, with farmers trading surplus crops for artisan-made goods. Religion and spirituality permeated African culture and inspired artistic endeavors. West Africans developed sophisticated art and music, on which much of twentieth-century art and jazz are based. By the 1500s Islam was just starting to spread beyond the kings and upper class to the common people of the grasslands. Christianity, introduced by the Portuguese in the 1400s and 1500s, made limited headway until the nineteenth century.

B. European Culture and Society

At the time of Columbus's first voyage to America, Europe was at the height of a great cultural revival, the Renaissance. Scholars were trying to map the world and to understand natural science, including astronomy. European society was hierarchical; at the top were the kings who governed most states and had been consolidating their power for a century. Exploited peasants made up 75 percent of the people. Population increases in the sixteenth and seventeenth centuries made land in Europe scarce and valuable. That encouraged the upper classes to enclose more and more of the common fields, converting them to their private property, while displaced country people drifted to the small towns, which were crowded, dirty, and disease-ridden. Traditional European society, which like Native American and African cultures had been based on extended families and social reciprocity, was starting to change. Nuclear families were replacing kinship networks. In these nuclear families, according to the ideal, the father ruled over wife and children as the king ruled over his subjects. New business enterprises and organizations, like joint stock companies, broke the bonds of social reciprocity. Emerging entrepreneurs favored "unimpeded acquisition of wealth" and unregulated competition. They "insisted that individuals owed one another nothing but the money necessary to settle each market transaction."

C. Religious Upheavals

After the Spanish Reconquista only small pockets of Jewish and Muslim communities existed in Europe. And while some older, non-Christian beliefs still existed—namely astrological or belief in magic—most Europeans in 1492 were Christians. The Roman Catholic Church was headed by a pope whose authority was acknowledged everywhere except in Russia and the Balkan peninsula, and it was administered by a hierarchy of clergy who did not marry. By the fifteenth century this powerful institution was selling indulgences (blessings that would shorten the repentant sinner's time in purgatory) for donations to the church.

In 1517 a German Friar, Martin Luther, denounced indulgences and other corrupt practices, broke with the pope, and initiated the Protestant Reformation. Luther and other Protestants preached that one could not buy or earn salvation by good works (or donations to the church) and that priests had no special powers of intervention. God alone decided who was saved and who was damned, and Christians must have faith in his love and justice. French Protestant leader John Calvin and his followers went a step further, emphasizing the doctrine of predestination—God's foreknowledge of who was saved and who was damned.

The Protestant challenge led to the Counter-Reformation, in which the modern Roman Catholic Church was born. The renewed church aimed to clean out corruption and stimulate religious zeal, while attempting to suppress Protestantism. Thereafter, European countries divided into rival Protestant and Catholic camps.

D. The Reformation in England, 1533–1625

The Reformation began in England when King Henry VIII (ruled 1509–1547) asked the pope to annul his marriage to Catherine of Aragon, who had not given birth to a male heir. After the pope refused, Henry pushed through Parliament the laws of 1533–1534, which dissolved his marriage and declared the king head of the Church of England (Anglican).

Religious strife continued in England for more than one hundred years after Henry's split with the Catholic Church. Henry's son and successor, Edward VII, leaned toward Protestantism during his brief reign. He was followed by "Bloody Mary," who tried to restore Catholicism, often burning Protestants at the stake. This persecution turned her successor and half-sister, Elizabeth I (1558–1603), and the majority of the English people against Catholicism. But the English differed on how Protestant the Church of England should be. Those who wanted to remove all vestiges of Catholicism were called Puritans. These Calvinistic Puritans believed in predestination and felt that only the saved should belong to the church. They wanted each congregation to be self-governing and free from interference from bishops and a church hierarchy. Puritanism, with its message of righteousness and self-discipline, appealed particularly to England's landowning gentry, small farmers, university-educated clergy, intellectuals, merchants, shopkeepers, and artisans. Elizabeth managed to satisfy most English Protestants (Puritan and Anglican), but her successor, James I (1603–1625), the first of the Stuart kings, made clear his dislike of Puritans.

III.   Europe and the Atlantic World, 1400–1600
    A.   Portugal and the Atlantic, 1400–1500
        Portugal led the way in Europe's ocean expansion. Because of advances in maritime technology, such as the caravel and magnetic compass, Prince Henry the Navigator was able to send Portuguese sailors farther down the coast of Africa to fight Muslims and seek opportunities for profitable trade. Portugal established a gold-processing factory at Arguin, rounded Africa's Cape of Good Hope, and developed valuable commercial links with India. These Portuguese voyages brought Europeans face to face with black-skinned Africans and an entrance into the already flourishing slave trade.

    B.   The "New Slavery" and Racism
        Slavery existed in West Africa before the arrival of Europeans, but it was not based on racial differences between masters and slaves, and the slaves were often eventually absorbed into the owners' families. First Muslims from North Africa, then Europeans turned African slavery into an "intercontinental business." Generally, European slavers bought war captives from African slave-trading kings, thereby encouraging those rulers to engage in warfare with their neighbors, using the guns they had obtained from earlier slave sales. Nearly 12 million Africans were shipped across the Atlantic under horrific conditions to labor in the Western Hemisphere before the international slave trade finally ended, centuries later. The new slavery based on race would further dehumanize black Africans in the eyes of white Europeans, who regarded slaves as simply property, not persons.

    C.   To America and Beyond, 1492–1522
        Christopher Columbus insisted that Europeans could reach Asia and its rich trading opportunities by sailing westward across the Atlantic. He convinced the king and queen of Spain, who were anxious to break Portugal's monopoly of trade via the route around Africa, to finance his voyages of discovery. On his 1492 trip he landed on the island of Guanahaní in the West Indies, which he called San Salvador. On a subsequent voyage he claimed and colonized for Spain the island of Hispaniola (where today Haiti and the Dominican Republic are situated). Even after his last expedition across the Atlantic (1498–1502), Columbus did not realize he had discovered a new world. Nor did John Cabot suspect he was not in Asia when he explored and claimed the north Atlantic coast for England. Later explorers, when they did understand that a big landmass (which they named America) blocked the way to Asia, geared their efforts toward discovering a water route through or around the Americas to the beckoning trade of Asia. Balboa crossed the Isthmus of Panama and reached the Pacific in that quest. Magellan sailed around the tip of South America, getting as far as the Philippines before being killed. Verrazano explored the coast of North America, and Jacques Cartier sailed up the St. Lawrence, each looking for the supposed Northwest Passage to Asia.

    D.   Spain's Conquistadores, 1492–1536
        The early Spanish explorers soon became conquerors as well. Columbus exported Indian slaves from Hispaniola and gave grants to Spaniards to extract labor and other tribute from

the native population there. In 1519 Hernán Cortés landed in Mexico and subjugated the mighty Aztec Empire, and Francisco Pizarro conquered the Incas. Though often awestruck by the civilizations they encountered, Spanish conquerors fanned out over the Caribbean and the Americas from Mexico to Chile, subduing and enslaving the native peoples and enriching themselves and Spain. The Indian population was nearly decimated by forced labor, warfare, starvation, and, above all, alien diseases, particularly small pox. When shortages of Indian slaves developed, the Portuguese delivered African substitutes.

E.   The Columbian Exchange
The "Columbian exchange," that is the "biological encounter" of Europe, Africa, and America had tremendous impact on the peoples, animals, and plants of all three areas. The disease-causing microbes that Europeans and Africans brought with them wiped out whole tribes of Indians who lacked natural immunity, which in turn made it easier for Europeans to conquer and colonize. Europeans brought new animals—horses, cattle, sheep—to the Americas, as well as such plants as wheat, coffee, and sugar. Enslaved Africans introduced rice and yams. From the Americas, Europe and Africa received corn, potatoes, tobacco and many other plants, along with turkeys. Transplanted crops and animals enriched human diets but also caused environmental change and damage to the new habitats. Peoples, too, mingled. Since the 300,000 Spanish colonists who arrived in the Americas in the sixteenth century were 90 percent males, many of them took Indian wives and produced the *mestizo* populations of Mexico and Latin America. European planters begot mulatto children with enslaved African women. Children of mixed Indian-African ancestry were also common. The Americas produced fabulous wealth for Spain and her colonists in the sixteenth century. Gold and silver from Mexican and Peruvian mines, sugar cane from West Indian plantations, sheep and cattle from Mexican ranches all enriched Spain's kings, though their failure to use the wealth wisely limited the long-term benefit for their nation.

IV.   Footholds in North America, 1512–1625
A.   Spain's Northern Frontier
In the 1500s a number of Spaniards, searching for gold, silver, and slaves, penetrated areas that would one day be the United States. Cabeza de Vaca and Estevanico traveled from Florida to Texas to New Mexico; de Soto's party went from Tampa Bay to the Appalachians and then to Texas. The first lasting European post was established at St. Augustine. Although they found no gold, these and other expeditions spread European diseases that wiped out most of the surviving Mississippian communities, most before they even laid eyes on the newcomers. Coronado plundered pueblos and searched for riches from the Grand Canyon to Kansas. In 1598 Juan de Oñate proclaimed the royal colony of New Mexico, which barely survived Indian resistance and uprisings.

B.   France: Colonizing Canada
French attempts at planting permanent colonies in the St. Lawrence Valley in 1541, South Carolina in 1562, and Florida in 1564 all ended in failure. However, the French carried on a lucrative fur trade with the Indians from Newfoundland to Maine and along the St. Lawrence. Sensing the importance of this trade and determined to beat their rivals, the English and Dutch, to its profits, the French in 1608 sent explorer Samuel de Champlain to found Quebec, the first permanent French settlement in Canada. He wisely allied it with the local Hurons, Algonquins, and Montagnais.

C.   England and the Atlantic World, 1558–1603
By the late 1500s, intensifying conflicts with Catholic Spain were leading Protestant England to take an interest in the Western Hemisphere. Queen Elizabeth encouraged English "sea dogs" like Francis Drake to raid Spanish treasure ships and ports in the Western Hemisphere, and she split the rich plunder with them. Also, the English searched for the

Northwest Passage and scoured America for gold and colony sites. After an English colony in Newfoundland disbanded, Sir Walter Raleigh sponsored a settlement on Roanoke Island. The English colonists antagonized the initially friendly Indians and failed to plant crops to feed themselves. Their pleas to England for more supplies went unanswered because of the Anglo-Spanish war then raging. England's victory in that struggle, including her 1588 defeat of the Spanish Armada, established the English as a major power in the Atlantic. However, in 1590, when a relief ship did finally land in Roanoke, it found no Englishmen. To this day historians do not know what became of that "lost colony."

D.   Failure and Success in Virginia, 1603–1625
In May 1607 a party of 105 English people landed in Virginia and began the settlement of Jamestown. The venture was organized and financed by an English joint-stock company, the Virginia Company of London. The only role of the English government was to grant a charter to the company giving it the right to land anywhere from Cape Fear to the Hudson River. Many of the early arrivals were "gentlemen" who refused to farm, hoping instead to find gold. This failure to secure foodstuffs combined with the company's failure to adequately supply them, led to starvation and conflict with the Powhatans. During the first years the majority of the settlers died, and the survivors were on the verge of leaving several times. The discipline and forced work imposed for a while by Captain John Smith helped save the colony. Settler John Rolfe's development of a tobacco palatable to Europeans gave the colony the profitable export that ensured its financial success.

At first the stockholders in England treated the settlers as company employees, denying them any say in the colony's government or ownership of any of its land. To attract additional settlers and capital, the company started awarding land to people who paid their own and other people's passage to Virginia. This "headrights" system enabled planters who imported many indentured servants to acquire large estates. In 1619 the company also granted inhabitants the right to elect delegates to a legislative assembly, thus marking the beginnings of representative government in North America. An Indian attack in 1622 killed many of the English settlers. Charges of company mismanagement led King James I to revoke the charter in 1624, and Virginia became a royal colony. At that point Virginia had only about 500 colonists, most of whom were indentured servants who did not live long because of poor diet, diseases, and overwork.

E.   New England Begins, 1614–1625
In the winter of 1620, the *Mayflower* landed 102 English men and women at Plymouth Bay, where they founded Plymouth. The settlement was financed by some London merchants headed by Thomas Weston, who had received a patent from the Virginia Company of London to establish a colony. Weston had entered into an agreement with a group of English Separatists who had been living in Holland to escape Anglican persecution. The Separatists and other non-Puritan Englishmen who joined the expedition promised to send lumber, furs, and fish back to Weston for seven years in return for his investment.

Winter storms, however, blew the *Mayflower* off course, and the colonists landed outside the boundaries of Virginia and the jurisdiction of its government. Therefore, the adult males signed the Mayflower Compact, creating their own civil government and pledging to abide by its laws. Half the Pilgrims, as they came to be called, died during the first winter in Plymouth. Those still alive in the spring of 1621 were greatly helped by two friendly Indians, Squanto and Samoset, who taught them how to plant corn and arranged treaties with neighboring tribes. While Plymouth never grew wealthy or large, it was the vanguard of a mighty Puritan migration to New England in the 1630s and proved that a self-governing farm community could survive in New England.

F.   A "New Netherland" on the Hudson, 1609–1625
      In 1614, Dutch traders erected Fort Nassau, near present-day Albany, and established New
      Netherland. In 1626 local Munsee Indians allowed the Dutch to settle on an island at the
      mouth of the Hudson, the Dutch named it Manhattan and started the settlement of New
      Amsterdam. Most of the settlers lived by the fur trade, competing with the French. They
      dealt primarily with the Iroquois, the enemies of the French-backed Hurons.

V.   Conclusion
      In the 1500s an Atlantic world developed, connecting Europe, Africa, and the Americas. Through
      exploration, trade, and conquest, emerging Western European nation-states exploited for their
      benefit the peoples and resources of West Africa and the Americas, with often devastating effects
      on those populations. By 1600 the Spanish had planted their empire firmly in Mexico, the
      Caribbean, and Central and South America, but the Indian peoples north of Mexico still held back
      European conquerors and colonizers. Between 1600 and 1625 the Spanish made a few
      settlements to the north of Mexico to protect the borders of New Spain, while the French and
      Dutch established fur-trading colonies, and the English had begun farming on formerly Indian
      land in Virginia and Plymouth.

VOCABULARY

The following terms are used in Chapter 2. To understand the chapter fully, it is important that you
know what each of them means.

deference	the submission or yielding to the judgment, opinion, and/or will of another; respectful or courteous regard
hierarchy	a system of placing persons or things in a graded order, from lower to higher, in wealth, power, status, and so on
yeomen	free, landowning small farmers, below the gentry in status
capitalism	a system under which the means of production, distribution, and exchange are in large measure privately owned and directed and in which prices and wages are determined by supply-and-demand market forces
indoctrination	the teaching or inculcating of a doctrine or set of beliefs
Eucharist	the Christian sacrament of the Lord's Supper; communion; the sacrifice of the Mass; also the consecrated elements of the Lord's Supper, such as the bread
Gentry	landowners with substantial amounts of property and without aristocratic titles; considered "gentlemen" and therefore not to do manual labor; played an important role in English government
Caravel	a type of small, maneuverable ship developed by the Spanish and Portuguese in the 1400s
Astrolabe	an astronomical instrument for taking the altitude of the sun or stars, useful in solving problems in astronomy and navigation
Huguenots	French Protestants
patent	an official document conferring a right (such as the exclusive right to make use of or sell an invention) or a grant of land (such as the charter given to the Virginia Company of London)

IDENTIFICATIONS

After reading Chapter 2, you should be able to identify and explain the historical significance of each of the following:

"Crusades" versus jihad

English "Poor Laws"

enclose (enclosure movement)

joint-stock company

indulgences, Martin Luther, and the Protestant Reformation

John Calvin and the doctrine of predestination

Counter-Reformation

Separatists, Puritans, and Anglicans

conversion experience

Prince Henry the Navigator

Vasco da Gama

Treaty of Tordesillas

John Cabot

Vasco Núñez de Balboa

Ferdinand Magellan

Northwest Passage

conquistadores and *encomiendas*

Hernán Cortés and Francisco Pizarro

Juan de Oñate, Ácoma, and New Mexico

Samuel de Champlain

Spanish Armada, 1588

lost colony of Roanoke

Virginia Company of London

Captain John Smith

John Rolfe and Pocahontas

headrights

Thomas Weston, Pilgrims, and Plymouth

Mayflower Compact

SKILL BUILDING: MAPS

1. On the map of Africa and southern Europe on the following page, locate each of the following and explain its historical significance:

> Iberian peninsula
>
> Mediterranean Sea
>
> Morocco
>
> Sahara Desert
>
> Mali
>
> Songhai
>
> Timbuktu
>
> Benin
>
> Guinea
>
> Senegambia
>
> the Equator
>
> Cape of Good Hope
>
> Kongo

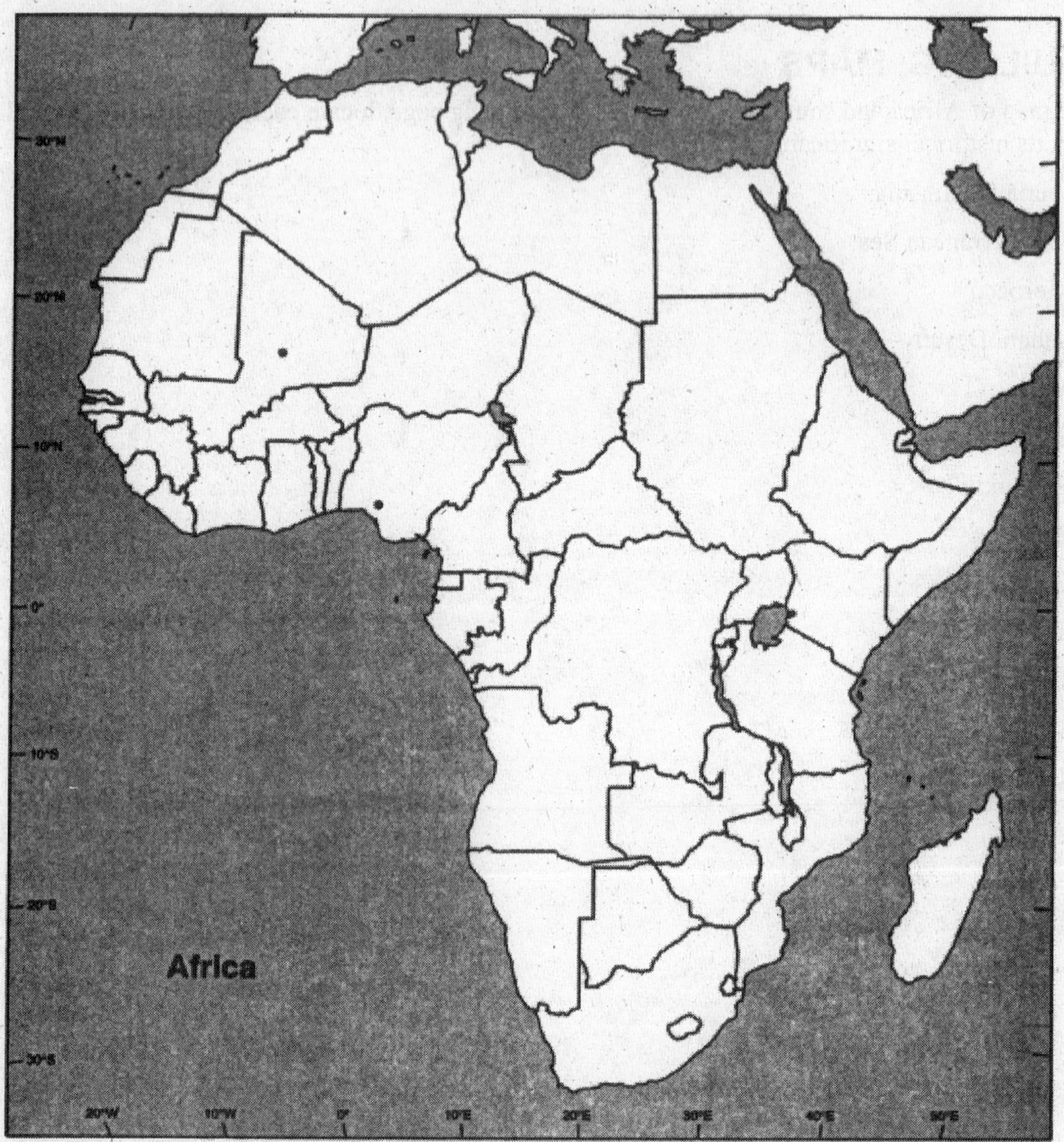

2.   On the map of Central and South America and the Caribbean, locate each of the following places and explain which European explorer and conqueror is associated with it:

San Salvador (Guanahaní)

Hispaniola (Haiti and the Dominican Republic)

Isthmus of Panama

Caribbean Sea

Pacific Ocean

Atlantic Ocean

Strait of Magellan

Tenochtitlán (Mexico City)

Puerto Rico

3.   On the map of North America, locate each of the following and indicate which European country had claimed and/or settled it by 1625:

       Great Lakes

       Mississippi River

       Great Plains

       Newfoundland

       Acadia (Nova Scotia)

       New Mexico

       St. Lawrence River

       St. Augustine, Florida

       Jamestown, Virginia, and James River

       Quebec

       Fort Nassau (later Albany, New York)

       New Amsterdam (later New York City)

       Roanoke Island (off the coast of North Carolina)

       Plymouth

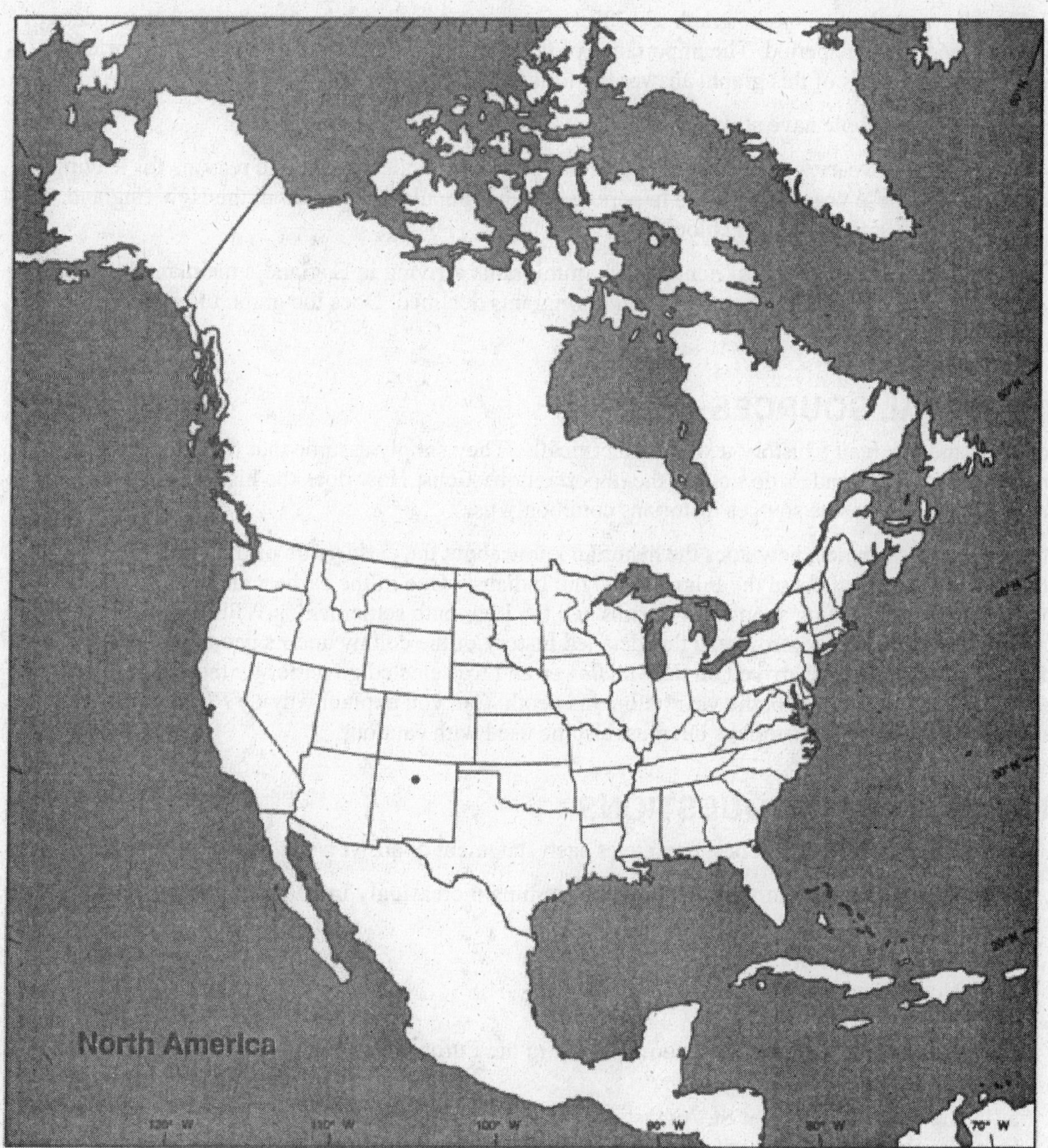

SKILL BUILDING: GRAPHS AND CHARTS

On page 29 in your textbook there is a line graph titled "Decline in Real Wages in England, 1500–1700." This graph shows the index of real wages, using 1500 as the base year. Real wages are not the amount of money a person earns but an estimate of what that amount of money at that time would allow the person to purchase. Economists derive these indexes by looking at the prices of a variety of goods and services offered in a given year and the actual wages earned by workers in the same period. Thus the index of real wages is a better indicator of people's standard of living than just the amount of their earnings. In the graph the real wages, or standard of living, of English workers in 1500 is represented as

100. By following the line on the graph to 1700, one can see at a glance by how much that standard of living declined over the period. The importance of this graph is the light it can throw on historical causation. On the basis of this graph, answer the following questions:

1.   Did English people have strong economic motives for emigrating?

2.   During which years would English people have had the greatest economic reasons for leaving home? Do these years correspond to periods of rapid population growth in the New England, Chesapeake, and Caribbean colonies?

3.   After 1700 the proportion of non-English immigrants arriving in England's mainland colonies increased and the proportion of English immigrants declined. Does the graph offer any clues as to why this occurred?

HISTORICAL SOURCES

Too often students read a history textbook uncritically. They simply assume that the information in print is correct. Such readers do not ask the important questions: How does the historian learn about the past? How reliable are the sources historians commonly use?

In Chapter 2, for instance, how does the historian know about the early years of the Plymouth settlement and the relations of the Pilgrims and the Indians? One of the earliest and best sources that historians have for learning about the Pilgrims and the Plymouth settlement is William Bradford's *Of Plymouth Plantation*. Bradford wrote this detailed history of the colony and its people between 1630 and 1650. A Separatist, he arrived on the *Mayflower* and was elected governor by the settlers over and over again from 1621 to 1656, the year before his death. Can you explain why *Of Plymouth Plantation* is an excellent source for historians but must also be used with caution?

MULTIPLE-CHOICE QUESTIONS

Circle the letter of the item that best completes each statement or answers the question.

1.   By the 1500s the nuclear family unit was becoming increasingly important among
     a.   Western Europeans.
     b.   South American Indians.
     c.   North American Indians.
     d.   West Africans.

2.   The beginnings of representative government in the European settlements in North America can be found in
     a.   the Spanish colony at St. Augustine, Florida.
     b.   the Dutch New Netherland, where the inhabitants were granted the right to elect their own legislature in the colony's charter.
     c.   Virginia, when, in 1619, the company provided for election of an assembly by the inhabitants.
     d.   the small Swedish fur-trading colony in the lower Delaware Valley.

3.   Which of the following statements about West African society at the time of first contact with Europeans is correct?
     a.   Slavery was unknown in Africa.
     b.   The majority of West Africans were either Muslims or Christians.
     c.   Agriculture had not yet developed. The majority of West Africans were hunters and gatherers.
     d.   Kinship groups were the most important units holding people together.

4. The financing of the Virginia settlement came from

    a. the English government.
    b. a joint-stock company.
    c. the Church of England.
    d. all of the above.

5. In which European settlement was fur trading with the Hurons and other tribes the primary economic activity?

    a. New Mexico
    b. Florida
    c. New France
    d. Virginia

6. The great majority of sixteenth-century Europeans were

    a. nobles.
    b. middle class.
    c. urban craftsmen and artisans.
    d. peasants.

7. The primary aim of the explorations of Balboa, Magellan, Verrazano, and Cartier was to find

    a. a water passage through the Americas and reach Asia.
    b. the fabled fountain of youth.
    c. the Seven Cities of Gold.
    d. favorable places for their respective nations to plant new colonies.

8. New technology in the production of which commodity had the most to do with stimulating the African slave trade in the 1500s?

    a. Sugar
    b. Tobacco
    c. Gold
    d. Indigo

9. All of the following statements about English Puritans are correct *except*

    a. they were Calvinists.
    b. they rejected the doctrine of predestination.
    c. they rejected bishops and a church hierarchy.
    d. their beliefs appealed to many small farmers, merchants, shopkeepers, and artisans.

10. Which of the following is *incorrectly* matched with his deeds?

    a. Hernán Cortés—conquered the Aztecs, built Mexico City
    b. Francisco Coronado—found the Grand Canyon, plundered the New Mexico pueblos
    c. Giovanni da Verrazano—founded Quebec
    d. Jacques Cartier—explored the St. Lawrence, made an early French attempt to colonize in North America

SHORT-ANSWER QUESTIONS

1. Explain what the Reformation and Counter-Reformation were. How did they lead to religious and political conflict in Europe?

2. Explain how the new learning and technology of the Renaissance facilitated European exploration and expansion.

3. Define the term *Columbian exchange* and give examples of the ways in which it affected the peoples, animals, and plants of Europe, Africa, and the Americas.

4.   Explain the beliefs of English Puritans. How did Elizabeth I and James I feel about those beliefs?

5.   Explain the various motives of the English for coming to America as settlers.

ESSAY QUESTIONS

1.   Compare and contrast the founding and early development of Virginia and Plymouth. Since both were English colonies, how do you account for their differences?

2.   Compare and contrast the early-seventeenth-century settlements in North America of the Spanish, French, Dutch, and English.

3.   Discuss the religious and political conflicts and the economic conditions in sixteenth- and early seventeenth-century England that made the English interested in exploration and colonization in the Western Hemisphere.

4.   "The Atlantic world brought few benefits to West Africans and Native Americans." Illustrate this statement by discussing the African slave trade and its impact, and the effects of European settlements in America on the indigenous peoples.

5.   Discuss the concept of social reciprocity. How did it operate in Native American, West African, and traditional European societies? In what ways was it breaking down in Western Europe by the sixteenth and seventeenth centuries?

ANSWERS TO MULTIPLE-CHOICE QUESTIONS

1. a
2. c
3. d
4. b
5. c
6. d
7. a
8. a
9. b
10. c

CHAPTER 3

The Emergence Of Colonial Societies, 1625–1700

OUTLINE AND SUMMARY

I. Introduction

By 1700 more than 250,000 people of European ancestry, mostly English, lived in what would one day be the United States. Also, during the seventeenth century about 300,000 West African slaves were brought to North America and the Caribbean, the majority to the West Indian sugar colonies and the remainder to the mainland. These great migrations from Europe and Africa resulted in the depopulation and uprooting of the native inhabitants.

This chapter attempts to answer four questions: (1)Why did Chesapeake planters shift from using white indentured servants as laborers to black slaves? (2)Why did colonial New Englanders abandon John Winthrop's vision of a "city on a hill"? (3)What were the most important differences between the Middle Colonies and other English colonial regions? (4)What factors distinguished French and Spanish colonies in mainland North America from those of England?

II. Puritanism in New England

A. Building a City upon a Hill, 1625–1642

When Charles I became king of England in 1625, he gave his blessings to a campaign to drive all Puritan influence out of the Anglican church. Nonconforming ministers and congregation members were fined and excommunicated. In response to this crack down on dissenters, in 1628, a group of Puritan merchants formed the Massachusetts Bay Company and obtained a charter from the king permitting them to establish a colony in North America. They decided that the company's officers and stockholders would emigrate along with the settlers. Thus, Massachusetts Bay would not be under the control of stockholders or proprietors back in England. In 1630 the company sent over eleven ships carrying seven hundred settlers under Governor John Winthrop. As the ships sailed westward, Winthrop delivered his lay sermon "A Model of Christian Charity," in which he articulated the Puritans' mission. They would create a godly community, "a city upon a hill" that would serve as an example for sinful England to emulate. Though Massachusetts was founded primarily for religious, rather than acquisitive, reasons, the Puritans did not object to material gain. However, they believed that moral and/or government restraint must limit ruthless exploitation and profiteering.

During the first severe winter in Massachusetts, 30 percent of Winthrop's party died. Nonetheless, within a year the colony was economically self-sufficient, and the population grew because heavy English immigration persisted through the 1630s. By 1642, 15,000 colonists lived in New England.

B. Towns, Families, and Farm Life

To ensure that colonists would settle in communities with congregations, all New England colonies provided for the establishment of towns. Families were granted no more land than was needed to support themselves, and they had to live in house lots near the town center.

"In a proper Puritan family, the wife, children, and servants dutifully obeyed the household's male head." Unlike Anglicans and Catholics, the Puritans allowed divorce, but it happened rarely. Because the Puritans believed healthy families were vital for the welfare of the community, the courts could and did discipline disobedient children, wives, and servants and irresponsible husbands. Puritans followed English common law in giving the wife no property rights independent of her husband's, yet she had significantly more rights than Englishwomen on such matters as spousal abuse and nonsupport.

Better living conditions resulted in a longer life expectancy in New England than in England. New Englanders also had larger families and therefore a faster rate of population growth. Most colonists had little or no cash, relying instead on the labor of their large, healthy families to sustain them. Rocky soil and a short growing season made it unlikely that anyone would become rich from agriculture. New Englanders seeking better opportunities turned to part- or full-time lumbering, fishing, rum distilling, and commerce. As they prospered, they became more worldly and materialistic and less preoccupied with religion.

C.   Economic and Religious Tension
In New England, Puritan leaders strove to enforce conformity to their religious views, or Puritan orthodoxy. All residents of the colony had to attend services and pay taxes for support of the church. Because the Puritans felt that everyone must be able to read the Bible to avoid Satan's snares, they required each town of fifty or more households to appoint a teacher for all children. To produce a continuing supply of learned Puritan ministers, they founded Harvard College in 1636. This early establishment of Harvard provided New England with a college-educated elite during the seventeenth century, which no other part of the English colonies possessed.

Each congregation was run by its male members and guided by its minister. Only those who could prove that they were saved through their public testimony about their conversion experiences were accepted as church members, although all residents had to attend services. Male church members were eligible to vote for and be elected members of the legislative body, at first called the General Court. In 1641 about 55 percent of adult males could vote under that church membership requirement, which was a higher percentage of the male population than was enfranchised in England or Virginia, where the vote and office holding were based on land ownership. The basic unit of local government, the town meeting, was generally open to participation by all male taxpayers (including non–church members).

Despite the efforts of the Puritans to enforce conformity to their religious mission and doctrines, there were dissenters. The first challenge came from Roger Williams, a devout Puritan minister who preached that church and state should be separate and that government must not interfere with private religious beliefs or compel church attendance. Because the Massachusetts civil authorities held that the purpose of government was to protect the true religion and prevent heresy, they banished Williams in 1635 for his subversive opinions. He fled southward, bought land from the Indians, and eventually established the colony of Rhode Island, which was the first to practice religious tolerance and separate church and state. Massachusetts also expelled Anne Hutchinson, who was regarded as a troublemaker for meddling in theology and questioning the clergy's moral authority. She and many of her followers also migrated to Rhode Island, and Massachusetts imposed greater restrictions on women. In the long run the challenge that most undermined the Puritan mission came from merchants who resented community regulation of their business practices.

Perhaps inevitably the founding fathers failed to pass on their intense religious fervor to the second and third generations. Declining church membership necessitated compromises like the Half-Way Covenant adopted in 1662.

D.   Expansion and Native Americans

At first Native Americans offered little opposition to Puritan colonization. But as the English pushed into the Connecticut Valley, the Pequots resisted. In 1637 the Puritans waged a bloody war of extermination against them. This cleared the way for Puritan settlement of Connecticut.

As European settlers increased and prospered, the Indian population declined. Many Native Americans died from diseases brought by the newcomers, such as diphtheria, measles, and tuberculosis. As Europeans cut down forests and cleared land to farm, they destroyed Indian hunting and gathering areas, reducing their food supply. New England's Indian population fell from 125,000 in 1600 to 10,000 by 1675. Demoralized, some Native Americans turned to alcohol; others agreed to convert to Christianity and live in the "praying towns" that the Puritans established for them. The last-ditch attempt of the Wampanoag chief Metacom (King Philip) to unite the remaining Indians and oust the English, in 1675–1676, ended in disaster. Metacom was killed, and many other Indians were captured and sold into slavery. King Philip's War reduced southern New England's Indian population by nearly 40 percent and ended all overt resistance to white expansion.

E.   Salem Witchcraft, 1691–1693

Economic resentments, the breakdown of the religious mission and sense of community, and resentment of economically independent and assertive women all may have contributed to the witchcraft hysteria that began in Salem in 1691 and engulfed Massachusetts until the end of 1692. It started with accusations by a group of young girls in Salem against a few residents of low standing. It escalated as more and more people made charges against others, including the wife of the governor. Twenty persons were convicted of witchcraft and executed, and hundreds more were in jail by the time the governor halted the trials and released the imprisoned.

The witchcraft hysteria was but an extreme expression of more widespread anxieties over social change in New England. The generation reaching maturity after 1692 would be far less willing to accept society's right to restrict their personal behavior and economic freedom.

III.   Chesapeake Society

A.   State and Church in Virginia

In 1619 the Virginia Company of London granted the settlers the right to elect a representative assembly. After Virginia became a royal colony, the settlers repeatedly petitioned the king to continue that right. In 1628 Charles I grudgingly agreed. The assembly eventually became a bicameral legislature composed of a House of Burgesses elected by landowners and an appointed Royal Governor's Council. Local government in Virginia, with most officials appointed rather than elected, was less democratic than in New England. The Anglican church was the established church, and all Virginians were required to pay fixed rates for its support. The role of religion in the daily life of Virginians had a much lower profile than it did for New Englanders.

B.   State and Church in Maryland

Maryland, the first proprietary colony, was founded by Cecilius Calvert, Lord Baltimore, on a tract of land given to him by Charles I. Lord Baltimore wanted to create a haven for fellow Catholics who could not worship in public, had to pay tithes to the Anglican church, and were barred from holding political office in England. However, Calvert remained in England, trying to govern as an absentee proprietor, and more Protestants than Catholics settled in Maryland. To protect the Catholic minority, Lord Baltimore drafted the Act of Religious Toleration and convinced the Maryland assembly to pass it in 1649. But in 1654 the Protestant majority disfranchised Catholics and repealed the act. An army was raised to restore religious toleration, but it was defeated. Thereafter, the Protestant-controlled legislature battled continuously with the proprietary Calverts and resisted any political role for the Catholic minority.

C.   Death, Gender, and Kinship
The constant demand for more laborers to grow tobacco brought more than 110,000 Englishmen to the Chesapeake area by 1700; 90 percent of them came as indentured servants. In the early decades in Virginia and Maryland, the life expectancy was twenty years shorter than that in New England and deaths exceeded births. Disease and overwork killed off perhaps 40 percent of indentured servants within six years of their arrival, and the shortage of women settlers prevented many men from marrying and starting families. The widows of the Chesapeake enjoyed greater property rights than women elsewhere. By the late 1600s, native-born residents acquired childhood immunities and deaths from epidemics began to lessen.

D.   Tobacco Shapes a Region, 1630–1670
Life in Virginia and Maryland was shaped by tobacco growing, the main occupation. The population spread out on farms and plantations near rivers. Few commercial centers or towns developed because ships from England came directly to riverfront docks built by the planters. There the ship captains sold their goods from Europe and bought the outgoing tobacco, with the planters serving as the middlemen for the surrounding small farmers. Some planters, taking advantage of the headright system, acquired huge estates and made great profits from exploiting their indentured servants to the hilt. For those indentured servants who survived their term of unpaid labor, acquiring their own farms was difficult because they lacked capital. Their chances of prospering as independent landowners shrank further after 1660, when depressed tobacco prices afflicted the Chesapeake region.

E.   Bacon's Rebellion, 16751676
Racism, depressed tobacco prices, and the resentments of the small farmers and landless toward the wealthy planters and the governing elite set the stage for Bacon's Rebellion. In 1676, economically hard-pressed farmers, under the leadership of Nathaniel Bacon, began a war of extermination against all remaining Indians in Virginia, with the intention of seizing their lands and crops and enslaving them. When the royal governor tried to restrain Bacon and his followers, they marched on Jamestown, burned it, and looted their enemies' plantations. The rebels dispersed, however, after Bacon's death later that year.

F.   From Servitude to Slavery
The first Africans arrived in Virginia in 1619 and may have been treated initially as indentured servants. During the period 1640–1660, the status of Africans deteriorated into that of lifelong slavery. After 1660 the Chesapeake colonies recognized the institution of African slavery with laws that defined the condition and rigidly controlled blacks. Still, as late as 1660 fewer than one thousand slaves lived in Virginia and Maryland. Heavy importation of African slaves began in the 1680s, and by 1700 black slaves constituted 22 percent of the Chesapeake population. The escalating replacement of white indentured servants by African slaves occurred for several reasons: (1) racism, (2) the desire of white planters to avoid class conflict with poor whites, (3) a falloff of white immigration from England as economic conditions improved there, and (4) more Africans being brought directly to the Chesapeake colonies as a greater number of companies entered the international slave trading business.

IV. The Spread of Slavery: The Caribbean and Carolina
    A.   Introduction
          Between 1630 and 1642 almost 60 percent of English migrants headed for the Caribbean, rather than the North American mainland. In the West Indies they developed a plantation-slave economy, concentrating on sugar growing. Some of these English colonists later resettled in the Chesapeake and Carolina colonies, bringing their slaves with them. By 1710 black slaves made up the majority of the Carolina inhabitants.

    B.   Sugar and Slaves: The West Indies
          The islands of the West Indies were colonized by each of the major North American European colonialist countries–Spain, France, England, and the Netherlands. Tobacco was the first export of the British West Indies, and it was raised primarily with the labor of white indentured servants. In the 1640s, however, most planters switched to sugar growing, which required more workers than tobacco did. Therefore, planters imported more and more slaves, until by 1713 blacks outnumbered whites by a margin of four to one.

    C.   Rice and Slaves: Carolina
          In 1663 King Charles II gave a group of his English supporters a grant of land in America, which they named Carolina in his honor. To attract colonists, the proprietors adopted the headright system. Most of the settlers came from other English mainland colonies and Barbados. There were also some French Huguenots (Protestants). The northern Carolinians cultivated tobacco and exported it, along with lumber and pitch. The southern Carolinians raised livestock. They carried on these economic activities primarily with their own family labor, using few black slaves.

          By the 1690s southern Carolinians had found a staple crop that would make them rich—rice. Those few who possessed sufficient capital to invest in the costly dams, dikes, and slaves necessary for large-scale rice production became fabulously wealthy, forming the only mainland elite that was as rich as the West Indian sugar planters. The humid rice patties were swarming with malaria-bearing mosquitoes, and large numbers of indentured English servants died rapidly. The planters' solution: import Africans who they believed were immune to these conditions, as well as experts on growing rice. As the rice planters imported ever more African slaves, the black population burgeoned, making South Carolina the only British mainland colony with an African majority. The southern Carolinian whites also allied themselves with the Yamasees and Creeks to capture Indians living in Spanish Florida and sell them into slavery, mostly in the West Indies.

V.   The Middle Colonies
    A.   Precursors: New Netherland and New Sweden
          The Dutch-founded fur-trading colony of New Netherland became America's first multiethnic society. Its population included Dutch, Germans, Swedes, Africans (free and slave), Protestants, Catholics, Jews, and Muslims. Eighteen different languages were spoken there. In 1655, New Netherland's governor Peter Stuyvesant took over and annexed the Swedish fur-trading settlement in the lower Delaware Valley. By 1664 New Netherland had 9,000 people and a thriving port city, New Amsterdam.

    B.   English Conquests: New York and New Jersey
          In 1664 Charles II presented the seized Dutch colony, New Netherland, to his brother James, Duke of York, who called it New York. Most of the Dutch settlers were allowed to keep their land and remained in the colony. When James became king in 1685, New York became a royal colony. The British royal governors rewarded their loyal followers with immense land grants, mostly along the Hudson River from New York City to Albany. These patroons,

or manor lords, grew almost as wealthy as the South Carolina rice planters on rents they collected from their tenant farmers.

James gave part of the former New Netherland, which came to be known as the Jerseys, to a group of proprietors, including Lord Berkeley and Sir Philip Carteret. The settlers, who were a mixture of New England Puritans, Quakers, Anglicans, Scottish Presbyterians, and Swedish Lutherans, quarreled continually with the absentee proprietors and with each other. In 1702 the king took over, and New Jersey became a royal colony.

C.   Quaker Pennsylvania

In 1686 Charles II, to repay a debt he owed the Penn family, gave a huge grant of territory in America to William Penn, a wealthy Englishman who had joined the much-persecuted Quakers. Penn hoped to found a colony based on Quaker principles that would offer a haven to his fellow worshipers, and, like other proprietors, he wanted to make a profit. In 1681 Penn laid out the city of Philadelphia and started the settlement. True to Quaker teachings against forced worship, he imposed no established church and allowed peoples of all faiths to settle. He also drafted a constitution, which created a legislative assembly to give residents a voice in running the colony. Relations with the Indians were favorable, for the most part, because Penn bought land from them on fair terms. The settlers prospered by growing grains on the fertile land and selling them to the West Indies. Indeed the trade made Philadelphia a major port by 1700. Since most of the colonists had come as families, the population quickly expanded through natural increase as well as immigration. Despite all their good fortune, some of the colonists resented the proprietor and his request for rents. The counties on the lower Delaware, inhabited by many Swedes and Dutch, gave Penn the most trouble. In 1704 they gained the right to elect their own legislature and separate from the rest of Pennsylvania, forming the colony of Delaware.

VI.   Rivals for North America: France and Spain

A.   France Claims a Continent

As the English colonies developed along the Atlantic coast, the French empire spread inland. In the 1660s and 1670s Louis XIV sent some six hundred settlers yearly, and French fur traders and missionaries fanned out over the Ohio Valley and explored the Mississippi from Wisconsin to the Gulf of Mexico. By the early 1700s the French claimed the entire Mississippi basin, called it Louisiana, and had erected forts and started fur-trading centers at Mobile, Alabama and Biloxi, Mississippi. Few Frenchmen lived in this vast empire but many of those who did mingled with the Indians, carrying on the all-important fur trade.

B.   New Mexico: The Pueblo Revolt

Spain attempted to strengthen her hold on New Mexico by subjugating the Pueblo Indians. Franciscan missionaries forced the natives to abandon their traditional way of life and convert to and practice Catholicism, and Spanish landowners compelled the Indians to labor on their *encomiendas*. By the 1670s Spanish exploitation and years of drought left many Indians starving, while diseases brought by Europeans decimated their numbers. Desperate, the natives, led by Popé, an Indian religious figure, endeavored to drive the Spanish out in the 1680 Pueblo Revolt. It was the most successful Indian uprising in American history. The Spanish were not able to quell the rebellion and reestablish control of New Mexico until 1700. And the Indians forced them to abolish the *encomiendas* and forced conversions.

C.   Florida and Texas

Spain's Florida colony also experienced grave troubles. The Guale, Timucua, and Apalachee Indians rebelled periodically against Spain's coerced labor and conversions. Then in the 1680s the situation further deteriorated when the English in Carolina and their Creek allies began invading Florida and carrying off Indians to sell in the slave trade. France's establishment of Louisiana further challenged the Spanish, who responded by founding the province of Texas (Tejas) in 1699, though white settlement did not begin there until 1716.

VII. Conclusion

By 1700, European nations had staked claims to most of the territory in the present-day United States east of the Mississippi River. Though the Spanish and French North American empires were larger in territory, the more compact English colonies along the Atlantic coast contained by far the most European settlers. The relatively low number of Spaniards precluded their development as a major center of colonization. The French, mainly residing in the St. Lawrence Valley, embarked on a commercial-agrarian economic plan on a much smaller scale than the English. In the English colonies different regions had emerged: New England had transformed from its religious beginnings to embrace a market economy based on trade and commerce. The Chesapeake revolved around tobacco-growing planters who had converted from dependence on a white indentured servant work force to one of enslaved Africans. In the West Indies, British sugar planters had imported huge numbers of enslaved Africans, who made up the majority of the population. Carolina rice growers followed the Caribbean pattern of plantation-slave economy and also created a black majority by 1700. Lastly, the middle colonies, built on Dutch and Swedish predecessors, displayed the greatest ethnic diversity and religious pluralism, and from the first built free market economies.

VOCABULARY

The following terms are used in Chapter 3. To understand the chapter fully, it is important that you know what each of them means.

tithes	taxes due for the support of the clergy and church, usually a tenth of one's income
established church	a church that is officially recognized and given legal and financial support by the government
dissent	object or disagree
Theocracy	a government by priests or clergy
Heresy	an opinion or doctrine at variance with established religious beliefs
subversive	tending to undermine existing or established institutions or doctrines; tending to cause the overthrow of existing governments or other established institutions
Bicameral	composed of two houses, chambers, or branches, as in a two-house legislative body
sacrament	any of seven rites that the historical Christian church considered to have been instituted by Jesus to convey divine grace (In Catholicism that includes matrimony, but not in Puritan doctrine.)
Proprietor	a person who has legal title to something; the owner or owner-manager of a business or other institution
proprietary colony	a settlement organized in territory granted by the crown to a proprietor or proprietors, like Maryland, the Carolinas, and later Pennsylvania and New York
blasphemy	any contemptuous or profane utterance, act, or writing concerning God; any word or deed meant to dishonor God or his works

IDENTIFICATIONS

After reading Chapter 3, you should be able to identify and explain the historical significance of each of the following:

John Winthrop and "A Model of Christian Charity"

Roger Williams

Anne Hutchinson and Antinomians

conversion relation

Massachusetts General Court

New England town meeting

Charles I and the English civil war

Oliver Cromwell

Stuart Restoration

Half-Way Covenant

"praying towns," "praying Indians"

King Philip's War

indentured servants

Virginia House of Burgesses and Royal Governor's Council

Cecilius Calvert (Lord Baltimore)

Maryland Act of Religious Toleration

Bacon's Rebellion

Anthony Ashley Cooper and John Locke

Peter Stuyvesant

William Penn and the Quakers

coureurs de bois

Popé and the Pueblo Revolt (1680)

SKILL BUILDING: MAPS

1. On the map of eastern North America and the Caribbean on the following page, locate each of the following and explain how its climate, soil, and other physical characteristics helped shape the economy and society there:

    Massachusetts

    Rhode Island

    Connecticut

    North Carolina

    South Carolina

    New York

New Jersey

Pennsylvania

Jamaica

the Bahamas

Barbados

Virginia

Maryland

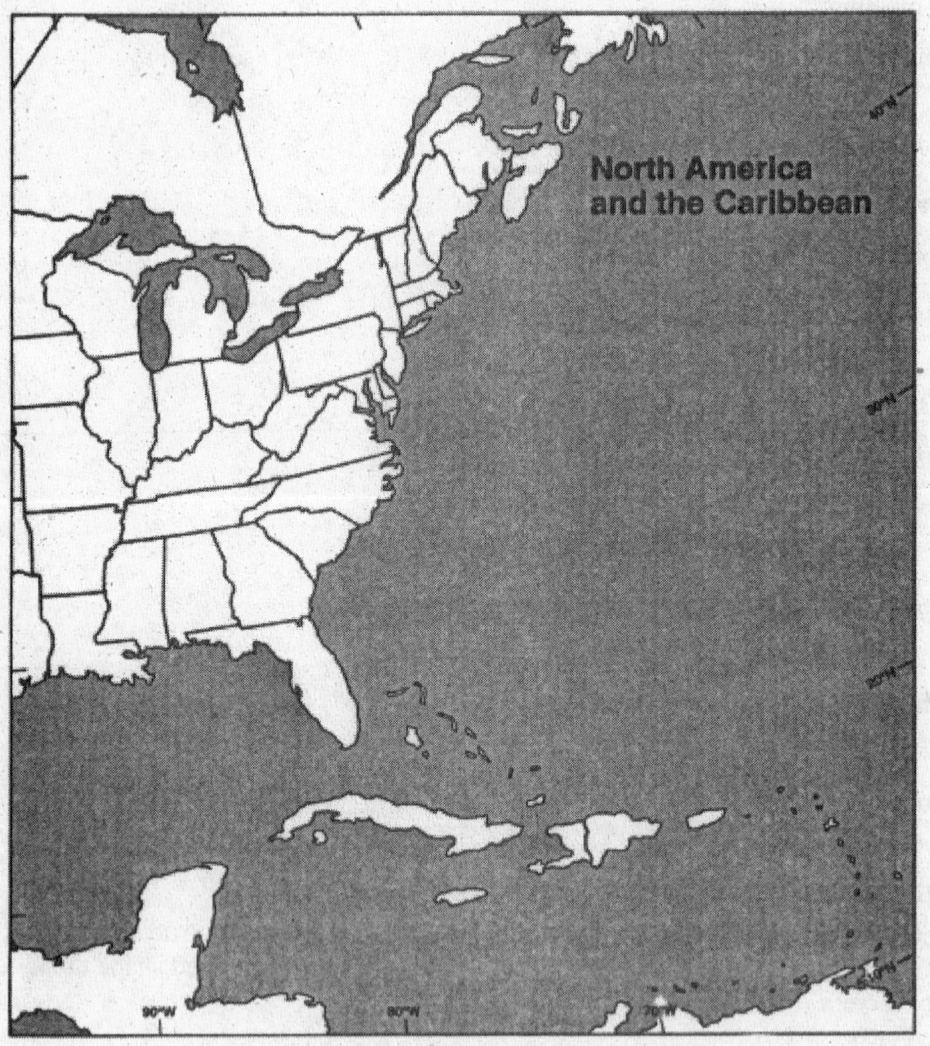

2. On the map of North America, locate each of the following and explain its significance in seventeenth-century American history:

    lands claimed by France

    Mississippi River

    Ohio River

    Gulf of Mexico

    Biloxi, Mississippi

    Mobile, Alabama

    lands claimed by England

    lands claimed by Spain

    Texas (Tejas)

    Taos

    Santa Fe

    Florida

    Great Lakes

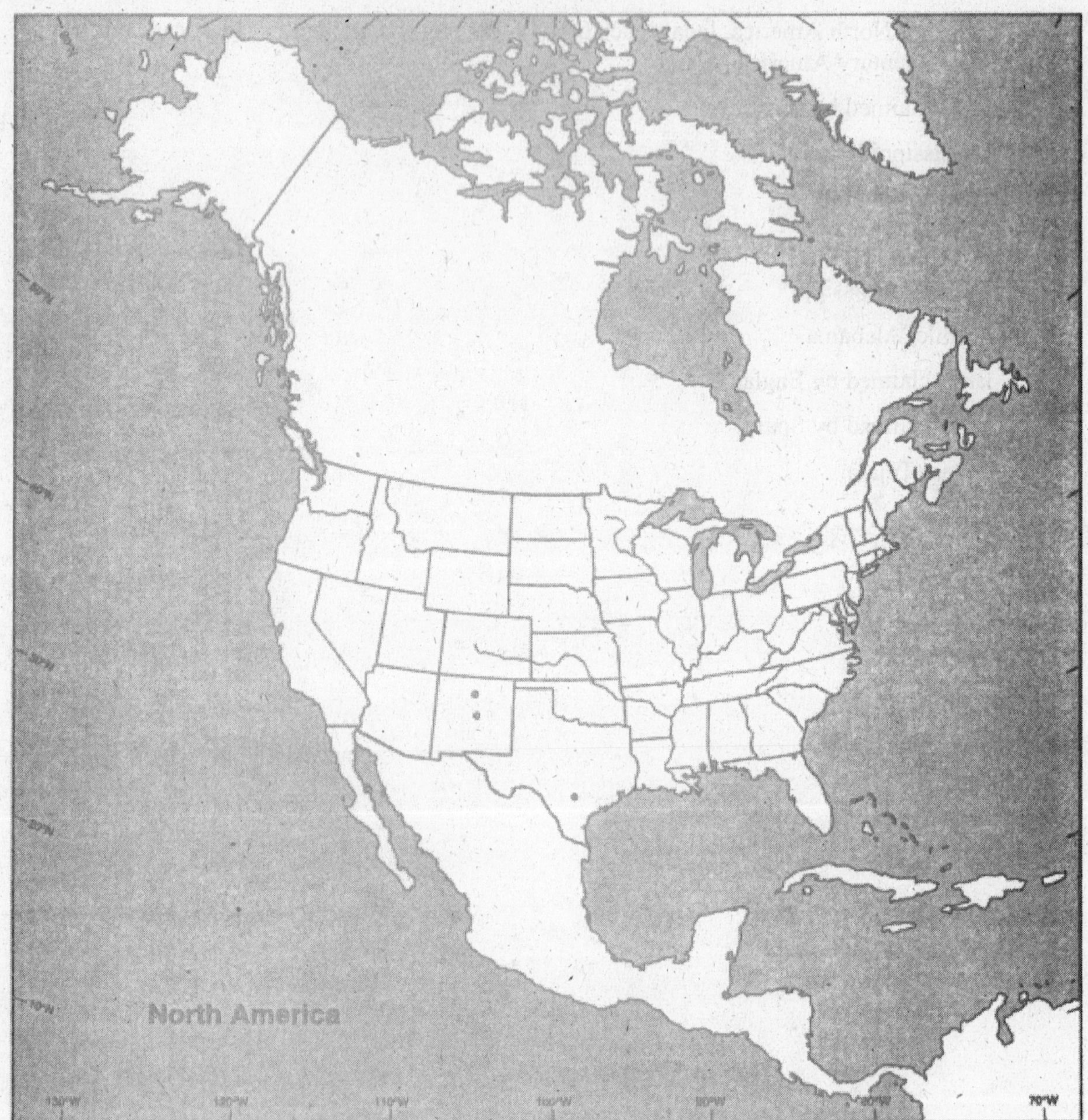

HISTORICAL SOURCES

In Chapter 3 the author tells us much about Puritan hopes, beliefs, religious practices, views on church and state, and family life. How did the historian discover this information? One useful historical source on New England Puritan thinking is the numerous sermons that ministers and lay leaders gave, many of which were carefully written down and preserved for posterity. Look at page 62, where you will see a reference to John Winthrop's lay sermon "A Model of Christian Charity." What does the historian learn about the Puritans' sense of their mission from it? Find other places in Chapter 3 where references are made to sermons. How is the author using the sermon or sermons mentioned in each case?

Another valuable source for gaining insight into past societies is their legal codes. For example, if the historian reads the code known as the Body of Liberties, adopted by the Massachusetts General Court in 1641, he or she finds there the guarantee that every man may participate in the town meeting. There are several sections of the Body of Liberties dealing with rights and duties of husbands, wives, children, and servants. Particularly revealing about the lack of separation of church and state is the part of the code titled "Capitall Laws." Here we see that religious or moral offenses, such as blasphemy, heresy, adultery, witchcraft, and "Carnall Copulation," were crimes for which civil authorities could impose the death penalty. As you review Chapter 3, look for other references to laws and legal codes. In each case what has the historian found from studying these statutes?

Of course, laws are not always fully enforced and at times do not reflect what is really happening in a society. Therefore, the historian often does research among old records of court cases as well as consulting statutes. For instance, on page 65 of the text we read that divorce was legal in Puritan Massachusetts, but we learn how rarely it happened from looking at court records: "Massachusetts courts allowed just twenty-seven divorces from 1639 to 1692." Similarly, on page 60 the author states that the first laws officially recognizing slavery in Virginia and Maryland were passed after 1660, but there is evidence that Africans were being treated as slaves by the 1640s and 1650s. Some of that evidence comes from court records.

Now look at "Technology and Culture: Native American Baskets and Textiles in New England." How has the writer used surviving material objects, such as textiles and baskets, as historical sources? What do these objects tell us about European-Indian relations in New England in the seventeenth century?

MULTIPLE-CHOICE QUESTIONS

Circle the letter of the item that best completes each statement or answers the question.

1.   The area that had the longest life expectancy and the fastest population growth through natural increase was

    a.   England.
    b.   New England.
    c.   the Chesapeake colonies.
    d.   the British West Indies.

2.   The first colony in English America that had separation of church and state and practiced religious tolerance was

    a.   Maryland.
    b.   Massachusetts.
    c.   Rhode Island.
    d.   Virginia.

3.   Harvard College was chartered in 1636 primarily to

    a.   train learned Puritan ministers.
    b.   produce an educated governing class.
    c.   educate lawyers who could defend the rights of the colonists.
    d.   teach Puritans how to farm the rocky New England soil.

4.   A man's right to vote for and be elected to the legislative body in seventeenth-century Massachusetts was based on

    a.   land ownership.
    b.   wealth.
    c.   length of residence in America.
    d.   church membership.

5. The greatest extremes of inequality in land ownership in the seventeenth century were found in

    a. New England.
    b. Maryland.
    c. the West Indies.
    d. Virginia.

6. The Half-Way Covenant was adopted because

    a. too few second- and third-generation Puritans were willing to testify publicly about their conversion experiences.
    b. Puritans believed that Indians were not capable of becoming fully Christian.
    c. Puritans wanted to justify enslavement of converted Indians and Africans.
    d. Puritans wanted to show Anglicans that they were willing to meet them halfway on resolving differences over religious doctrine.

7. Which colonies had the most ethnically, religiously, and racially diverse populations in North America?

    a. The Chesapeake colonies (Virginia and Maryland)
    b. The New England colonies (Massachusetts and Connecticut)
    c. North and South Carolina
    d. The Middle colonies (New York, New Jersey, Pennsylvania, and Delaware)

8. Which of the following statements about Maryland is correct?

    a. It was founded by a joint-stock company.
    b. Although it was intended as a haven for Catholics, they were often more persecuted there than were Catholics back in England.
    c. The dominant crop that shaped its economy and society was sugar cane.
    d. Unlike neighboring Virginia, Maryland never adopted the institution of African slavery.

9. The great majority of those arriving in Virginia between 1630 and 1700 were

    a. Africans.
    b. British gentry.
    c. non-English middle- and working-class people.
    d. British indentured servants.

10. Which of the following statements about Virginia is correct?

    a. Unlike Massachusetts, it had no established church.
    b. It was governed by an appointed royal governor and governor's council and a House of Burgesses elected by landowners.
    c. By 1640 the great majority of its plantation laborers were African slaves.
    d. The indentured servants' chances of upward social mobility improved in the second half of the 1600s.

SHORT-ANSWER QUESTIONS

1. In what ways was New England Puritanism different from Anglicanism? How did these differences affect life in Massachusetts?

2. Why did Massachusetts expel Roger Williams and Anne Hutchinson?

3. Explain the impact of sugar growing on British West Indian society and rice growing on South Carolina's evolution.

4. How did New Netherland turn into New York and New Jersey?

5.   Who was William Penn, and what were his motives for founding Pennsylvania?

6.   Describe the extent of the British, French, and Spanish empires north of Mexico in 1700 and how they differed from each other in settlement and economic patterns.

ESSAY QUESTIONS

1.   "In the course of the seventeenth century, New England evolved from a highly religious, community-oriented society to a region characterized by rising worldliness, individualism, and competitiveness." Discuss how and why this evolution took place.

2.   Compare and contrast the economies, social structures, and racial and ethnic compositions of New England, the Chesapeake colonies, the Carolinas, and the Middle colonies in the seventeenth century.

3.   Discuss the evolution and spread of slavery in the Chesapeake colonies in the seventeenth century. Why did African slavery develop there? How did the gradual shift from a plantation labor force of indentured servants to one of African slaves affect life in Virginia and Maryland?

4.   Discuss the course of European and Native American relations during the 1600s in the French, Spanish, and different regions of the British North American empires.

5.   Discuss the Salem witchcraft trials, telling first the known facts about what happened and then reviewing and evaluating the interpretation of the causes of the witchcraft accusations and hysteria offered in Chapter 3.

ANSWERS TO MULTIPLE-CHOICE QUESTIONS

1. b
2. c
3. a
4. d
5. c
6. a
7. d
8. b
9. d
10. b

CHAPTER 4

The Bonds of Empire, 1660–1750

OUTLINE AND SUMMARY

I.   Introduction

Chapter 4 attempts to answer the following questions: (1) How did the Glorious Revolution shape relations between England and its North American colonies? (2) What were the most important consequences of British mercantilism for the mainland colonies? (3) What factors explain the relative strengths of the British, French, and Spanish empires in North America? (4) What were the most significant results of the Enlightenment and Great Awakening in the British colonies?

II. Rebellion and War, 1660–1713

   A.   Introduction

Until the restoration of the Stuart kings in 1660, England made little effort to rule its overseas territories. However, with the accession of Charles II (ruled 1660–1685), the mother country sought to expand its empire and trade, impose royal authority on the colonies, and regulate their economic activities so as to benefit English commercial interests.

   B.   Royal Centralization, 1660–1688

The Stuart kings of the Restoration dreamed of becoming absolute monarchs like France's Louis XIV. They rarely called parliament into session and ignored the colonial legislatures. In 1684 Charles II revoked Massachusetts's charter. Between 1686 and 1688 his successor, James II, consolidated all the New England colonies, New York, and New Jersey into the Dominion of New England, abolished their assemblies, and placed full power into the hands of his arbitrary and dictatorial royal governor, Sir Edmond Andros. The colonists bitterly resented this denial of their rights. Tensions ran particularly high in Massachusetts and New York.

   C.   The Glorious Revolution, 1688–1689

In 1688–1689 James II's high-handed, pro-Catholic actions led to the Glorious Revolution in England. He was forced into exile. The throne went to William and Mary, who agreed to a limited monarchy and promised to summon Parliament annually and respect the civil liberties of English people. When news of the Glorious Revolution reached America in 1689, New Englanders rebelled against Andros and his councilors. Massachusetts and other colonies appealed to William and Mary for the return of their charters. The new monarchs dissolved the Dominion of New England and issued charters granting each colony the right to have a representative assembly. However, Massachusetts's new charter did not give it as much independence as it had formerly enjoyed. Its governors would be appointed by the crown, not elected, and it would have to tolerate and share power in the colony with Anglicans. Leisler's Rebellion in New York and John Coode's uprising in Maryland also were inspired by the Glorious Revolution.

   D.   A Generation of War, 1689–1713

Between 1689 and 1713, the British and French fought against each other in two wars, known in the colonies as King William's and Queen Anne's wars. The conflicts spread to North America, embroiling both natives and colonists. When peace returned in 1713,

France still controlled the North American interior, and the English colonists felt a heightened sense of British identity and dependence on their mother country's protection from their powerful neighbor.

III. Colonial Economies and Societies, 1660–1750
    A. Mercantilist Empires in America
The policies followed by Britain, France, and Spain toward their colonies in America were guided by the political-economic doctrine of mercantilism, which held that, to increase the nation's wealth in gold and silver, the country should produce within its own empire as much of what it needed as possible and its exports to foreign competitors should exceed its imports. To achieve these goals, the British Parliament passed a series of laws known as the Navigation Acts between 1651 and 1733. The laws required all trade to be conducted on British-owned ships; barred Americans from selling certain products, such as tobacco, rice, furs, indigo, and naval stores, to foreign countries unless they first passed through England; placed high taxes on products that Americans bought from outside the empire, like molasses from the French Caribbean; and forbade colonials from competing with British clothing manufacturers. Although Parliament intended these laws to benefit only England, the acts in practice did not unduly hamper the colonists. While the laws cut into the profits of rice and tobacco planters, the Navigation Acts also were beneficial. Colonials were considered English subjects, so the requirement that shipping be done on British vessels stimulated the growth of America's merchant marine, shipbuilding, and ports. The bounties paid to producers of hemp, lumber, and other items under the Navigation Acts encouraged the development of those industries in the colonies. The restrictions on large-scale manufacturing did little harm, since only home production and small workshops were economically feasible in America.

The French and Spanish colonies in North America did not develop nearly as robust economies as the British. New France's main export was furs, but by the eighteenth century these did not bring in much profit. In fact, the French government underwrote this money-losing trade with the Indians in order to keep on good terms with their Native American allies. Spain, which did little manufacturing but insisted her colonists buy finished goods only from her, simply drove her colonists into widespread smuggling of British and French products. Though all three mother countries followed mercantilist theories, those principles did not work well for France and Spain because they did not have the large merchant class with liquid assets to invest in the colonies and other commercial ventures that the British had.

    B. Population Growth and Diversity
The French and Spanish colonies in North America lagged behind the British in population growth as well as economic development. By 1750 British North America had 1,170,000 non-Indian inhabitants as compared to 60,000 in New France, and 19,000 in Spanish North America. While the British opened their colonies to all Europeans of whatever religion, the French and Spanish barred non-Catholics and made no effort to attract settlers from countries other than their own. Meanwhile the steady growth of the British colonies outpaced not only their European rivals, but also Britain itself.

After 1700 British North America grew rapidly from both natural increase and the arrival of newcomers. The eighteenth-century immigrants came less from England and more from other places, especially Africans brought on slave ships under horrible conditions, and Scots-Irish, Irish, and Germans, fleeing poverty. Many of the Europeans came as indentured servants. Consequently, the English colonies became more racially and ethnically diverse, a change sometimes resented by those of English extraction. Since most of the eighteenth-century white immigrants were too poor to buy land in the already developed coastal areas, they tended to push into the Piedmont region, which stretched along the eastern slope of the Appalachians. By 1750 one-third of the colonial population resided there.

From 1713 to 1754, the importation of slaves to the mainland was greatly increased, with the result that the black colonial population rose from 11 to 20 percent. Most slaves lived in the South, but 15 percent were in the colonies north of Maryland. The African-American population also multiplied through natural increase.

C.   Rural White Men and Women
Most rural families worked small farms and depended on the labor of their sons and the supplemental production of clothing, vegetables, and poultry of their wives and daughters. Few inherited much land from their parents since holdings were modest and families were large. Therefore, most young couples starting out had to work for others for a time and borrow money to buy their own farms.

D.   Colonial Farmers and the Environment
Colonial farmers rapidly cut down the forests to bring more land under cultivation. They used the timber for fences, fuel, and buildings. Farmers and planters also sold wood to townspeople. The resulting deforestation drove away large game and caused greater extremes in temperature and less dependable water levels in streams, which drastically reduced the amount of fish. It also dried and hardened the soil. As the farmers grew tobacco and other soil-depleting plants without fertilizer and without beneficial methods, such as crop rotation or letting fields lie fallow some years, the land lost its fertility and yields seriously diminished.

E.   The Urban Paradox
By 1740 about 4 percent of the colonists lived in cities. The four largest were Philadelphia, New York, Boston, and Charles Town (now Charleston). All were thriving ports that shipped the livestock, grain, and lumber that enriched the countryside, but each also had escalating problems of urban poverty, crowding, poor sanitation, and periodic epidemics of contagious diseases.

F.   Slavery
The economic progress of colonial America meant that most masters could afford to keep their slaves healthier. For the slaves, this meant heavier workloads and longer lives. Slaves worked harder and longer and had lower standards of living than whites. Masters generally spent 60 percent more to maintain their white indentured servants than their black slaves. As the number of slaves residing in cities mounted—they were 20 percent of New York's inhabitants and the majority in Charles Town and Savannah—urban racial tensions ran high, leading to incidents such as the 1739 Stono Rebellion in South Carolina and the 1712 and 1741 slave conspiracies in New York. All were brutally suppressed by frightened whites.

G.   The Rise of the Colonial Elites
In the eighteenth century, class differences were becoming more apparent in America. Wealthy rural gentry and urban commercial elites attempted to imitate the fashions and lifestyles of the European upper crust. They bought expensive chinaware, learned formal dances, studied foreign languages, and cultivated the manners of the gentry. Some even sent their sons abroad for study. This elitism would feed the growing taste for British consumer goods.

IV. Competing for a Continent, 1713–1750
A.   France and the American Heartland
After making peace in 1713 with its rivals, Britain and Spain, France resumed building its empire in North America. In 1718, the French founded New Orleans and made it the capital

of their province Louisiana. There settlers survived by a combination of farming, hunting, fishing, and above all trading with the Indians. The French managed to forge an alliance with the Choctaws in Louisiana and tried to win over Native American trading partners in the Ohio Valley and on the Great Plains. Several French posts in the Ohio Valley became sizable villages housing Indians, French, and mixed-ancestry métis. While generally more successful in getting along with the Indians than the British, the French also crushed tribes that stood in their way, such as the Natchez.

B.   Native Americans and British Expansion
British colonies, too, were expanding at the expense of Native Americans. The Carolinians met resistance from the Indian tribes on whose lands they were encroaching, culminating in the Tuscarora (1711–1713) and Yamasee (1715) wars, which drove those tribes from the area. The surviving Tuscarora moved to upstate New York and joined the Iroquois Confederacy. The Iroquois and several colonies forged a series of treaties known as the Covenant Chain, which aided the colonists' fight for lands while solidifying Iroquois power among Native Americans throughout the Northeast. Pennsylvania coerced the Delaware Indians into ceding their lands and moving into territory adjacent to that of the Iroquois. Other eastern tribes also were pushed westward, where they were used by the Iroquois as a buffer between themselves and the aggressive English.

C.   British Expansion in the South: Georgia
Georgia was the last of the original thirteen colonies to be established on the North American mainland and the only one to receive some financial support from the British government. James Oglethorpe, its founder and early guiding spirit, wanted it to be both a haven for English debtors who could rehabilitate themselves there and an outpost protecting the Carolinas from the Spanish empire to the south. Oglethorpe laid out the port city of Savannah in 1733, and by 1740 about 2,800 settlers had arrived. Most, however, were not English debtors. Nearly half were not even English, but German, Swiss, Scottish, and Jewish. To promote a society of industrious small farmers able to defend their homes from attack, Georgia banned African slavery and limited the size of landholdings. But once the settlers realized that their best chance of making their fortunes lay in rice cultivation, they chafed at these restrictions, which were dropped by 1750. Thereafter, Georgia attracted more settlers and developed a booming plantation-slave economy.

D.   Spain's Borderlands
While trying to fend off the Indians, French, and British, Spain spread its empire throughout the Southwest and part of the Southeast. The European population in New Mexico grew very slowly, but at least Navajo and Apache raids ceased. Instead, these tribes made an alliance with the Spanish against the Utes and Comanches, whom they all feared. In Texas the Spanish established outposts and missions, including the one later known as the Alamo. However, the Indians in Texas seemed more interested in trading with the French than in farming for the Spanish. Periodic raids on the province by the French and Comanches discouraged Hispanic settlement in Texas: as late as 1760, only 1,200 Spaniards lived there. The Spanish attempted to weaken the British Carolinas and Georgia by offering freedom to English-owned slaves who fled to their colony of Florida.

E.   The Return of War, 1739–1748
War among the imperial rivals for North America resumed in 1739. First the British and Spanish fought each other over the Florida-Georgia border. Then this Anglo-Spanish war merged into the larger War of the Austrian Succession, called King George's War (1740–1748) in British America. This third imperial conflict proved indecisive. Although New Englanders seized the French stronghold at Louisbourg for their mother country, in the peace treaty the British returned it in exchange for an outpost the French had taken in India.

Many Americans felt lingering resentment over how little England appreciated the lives they had sacrificed to gain Louisbourg.

V.   Public Life in British America, 1689–1750
    A.   Colonial Politics

The most important political result of the Glorious Revolution and the adoption of the English Bill of Rights in British America was the shift in power away from royal governors and appointed officials to the representative colonial assemblies. These legislative bodies exercised influence over the governors by controlling their salaries. The assemblies authorized spending and imposed taxes. The British Board of Trade, which could disallow laws passed by the assemblies, rarely did so prior to 1760. Thus, America, or at least its upper classes, became more and more self-governing, except for trade regulations, restrictions on printing money, and declaring war.

The wealthy elites dominated colonial politics. They were elected to the colonial assemblies and appointed to the governor's councils and to judgeships in the courts. Women, blacks, and Indians could not vote or hold office, and property qualifications probably excluded about 40 percent of white males from doing so. Still, the proportion of men who did have the vote was much higher than in England and Ireland for the same period.

    B.   The Enlightenment

American intellectuals, like Benjamin Franklin, were much influenced by the ideals of the eighteenth-century Enlightenment. Enlightenment thinkers emphasized reason, progress, science, and the capacity for human improvement. They were skeptical of beliefs not founded on science or strict logic. Centered in cities, followers of the Enlightenment circulated the latest European books, investigated nature and conducted experiments. The works of Newton and Locke were particularly prevalent. Some Enlightenment figures were Deists; that is, they believed in a god who created the universe and set it in motion according to natural laws discoverable by human intellect but who did not intervene thereafter with miracles.

    C.   The Great Awakening

Deists such as Franklin and Thomas Jefferson, while formally considering themselves Christians and attending church, disliked zealots who persecuted others in the name of religion. As such, enlightened intellectuals took a dim view of the emotional excesses of the 1740s Great Awakening, "an outpouring of passionate Christian revivalism" that swept through the thirteen colonies. Overcome by the fiery preaching of Jonathan Edwards, William Tennent, Theodore Frelinghuysen, and above all George Whitefield, thousands of colonists repented and flocked to churches and prayer meetings seeking salvation. The many Protestant denominations began another round of college founding to educate ministers for their faiths: the New Light Presbyterians' Princeton, the Anglicans' King's College (Columbia), the Baptists' Brown, and the Congregationalists' Dartmouth. The Great Awakening may also have had unintended political effects through its insistence on the equality of all born-again Christians in God's eyes and the corruption of "unsaved" upper-class leaders.

VI.   Conclusion

By 1750 the British mainland colonies had grown prosperous, had established representative governments, and had upper- and middle class intellectuals participating in the ferment of new ideas sweeping Europe known as the Enlightenment. However, Anglo-American society was also torn by class, race, and religious tensions. The imperial wars that Britain fought with the aid of the colonists between 1739 and 1748 both drew Americans closer to the mother country and spawned some resentment about British lack of appreciation for Americans' contributions.

VOCABULARY

The following terms are used in Chapter 4. To understand the chapter fully, it is important that you
know what each of them means.

manumission	the release of an individual from slavery or servitude
urbanization	the growth of cities
autonomous	self-governing; independent; subject to one's own will, choice, or law
dowry	the money, goods, or estate that a woman brings to her husband at marriage
paradox	a statement or condition that seems contrary to common sense, yet is perhaps true or the fact
artisans	persons skilled in industrial arts or crafts, for example, silversmiths, blacksmiths, cobblers, and printers
journeyman	A person who has learned a skilled trade and works at it for another person
libel	injuring a person's reputation by writing negative things about him; Zenger's acquittal introduced the principle that the writer or publisher is not guilty of criminal libel if he/she can prove the truth of what was written, no matter how damaging to the person's reputation

IDENTIFICATIONS

After reading Chapter 4, you should be able to identify and explain the historical significance of each of
the following:

Sir Edmond Andros and the Dominion of New England

the Glorious Revolution

English Bill of Rights, 1689

Leisler's Rebellion

John Coode

King William's War and Queen Anne's War

mercantilism and the Navigation Acts

James Oglethorpe

Francisco Menéndez

Stono Rebellion

King George's War

royal governors, colonial assemblies, and the Board of Trade

trial of John Peter Zenger

Enlightenment

Benjamin Franklin

American Philosophical Society

Royal Society

Deists

Great Awakening

Jonathan Edwards

George Whitefield

New Lights versus Old Lights

SKILL BUILDING: GRAPHS

Look at the pie graph titled "Distribution of Europeans and Africans Within the British Mainland Colonies, 1700-1755" on page 97 of the text. It visually presents important demographic data about the British mainland colonies. Was the population of the British mainland colonies more ethnically and racially diverse in the seventeenth or the eighteenth century? How might these demographic shifts affect Britain's relationship with its mainland colonies? By 1755 which group made up roughly one-fifth of the population? How do you account for the growth of that group between 1700 and 1755? For comparison, find out what portion of today's total U.S. population that group makes up.

HISTORICAL SOURCES

In Chapter 4 the author has gathered information from many sources, including travelers' accounts of life in America. In the eighteenth century a number of Europeans took extended trips through the colonies and then published books about their experiences. A fairly typical one was Andrew Burnaby's *Travels Through the Middle Settlements in North America in the Years 1759 and 1760* (London, 1798). Burnaby, an Anglican clergyman, filled his book with detailed observations about the dress; housing; religion; money; and ethnic, racial, and class composition of the colonies. Although Burnaby and other travelers give us wonderful eyewitness accounts, the historian has to be wary of the "facts" found in their books. Why?

Benjamin Franklin's autobiography, *Poor Richard's Almanack,* and other writings have long been a gold mine for historians of colonial America. In Chapter 4 look for the many references to Franklin, his observations, and his opinions. For what purposes has the author used these writings? Although Franklin was an astute observer of his world, he had his biases, as we all do. Can you tell what some of them were from the quotations from his writings that appear in Chapter 4?

In "A Place in Time: Mose, Florida, in 1740" the historian has used a number of sources to discover the story of the black community of former slaves who lived there. These include written documents: letters, treaties, and government papers. In addition, the historian has drawn on findings from archaeological excavations. What did these "digs" show?

MULTIPLE-CHOICE QUESTIONS

Circle the letter of the item that best completes each statement or answers the question.

1. Which of the following statements about the Anglo-American colonies in 1750 is correct?
    a. Colonists living in the port cities were much more prosperous than those in the countryside.
    b. Black slaves made up a greater proportion of the population than they had in 1700.
    c. More immigrants to the colonies were from England and fewer came from other parts of Europe than in the 1600s.
    d. The overall standard of living had risen little since 1700.

2. James Oglethorpe
   a. led the Stono Rebellion.
   b. encouraged the importation of African slaves to Georgia in order to promote profitable rice cultivation there.
   c. hoped Georgia would be a place for the rehabilitation of English debtors and a barrier to Spanish expansion northward.
   d. all of the above.

3. Which of the following statements concerning colonial government between 1700 and 1750 is correct?
   a. The royal governors and the Board of Trade frequently vetoed or disallowed laws passed by the colonial legislatures.
   b. All white men had the right to vote and hold office.
   c. The lower house of a colonial legislature was generally dominated by representatives of the lower and middle classes, whereas the upper house was dominated by the wealthy.
   d. The colonial legislatures became a powerful force in American government, controlling taxes, the budget, and executive salaries.

4. Which of the thirteen colonies was the last to be settled and the only one to receive some financial assistance from the British government?
   a. Georgia
   b. The Carolinas
   c. Pennsylvania
   d. Delaware

5. Which of the following statements about women in eighteenth-century America is correct?
   a. Women could not inherit their parents' land. Only sons could legally inherit family estates.
   b. Women could not choose their own husbands. The choice was made by their parents.
   c. Women in rural and urban families played an important part in helping to support their households.
   d. Women had legal control over their dowries and other property that they brought with them to marriage.

6. The Glorious Revolution in England touched off rebellions in all of the following colonies *except*
   a. Massachusetts.
   b. New York.
   c. Maryland.
   d. South Carolina.

7. Which of the following resulted from King William's and Queen Anne's wars?
   a. The French were driven from the North American continent.
   b. The Stuart kings were driven from power.
   c. The wars heightened Anglo-Americans' sense of their British identity and made them feel dependent on the mother country for protection.
   d. The British captured New Orleans and started to settle Louisiana.

8. The Dominion of New England was
   a. created by James II to consolidate his hold on the northern colonies and eliminate their colonial assemblies.
   b. welcomed by most New Englanders because it broke the dictatorial rule of the Massachusetts Puritans over the region.
   c. continued by William and Mary because the administrative consolidation made it easier to enforce the Navigation Acts.
   d. created as part of the reforms instituted after the Glorious Revolution.

9. The Navigation Acts
    a. prevented the development of American ports and shipping.
    b. required British-American colonists to ship their tobacco, rice, and naval stores to England.
    c. encouraged the development of clothing manufacturing in the American colonies.
    d. crippled the economic growth of British America in the 1700s.
10. All of the following institutions of higher learning were originally founded by religious denominations *except*
    a. the University of Pennsylvania.
    b. Princeton.
    c. Rutgers.
    d. Columbia.

SHORT-ANSWER QUESTIONS

1. What actions of the Restoration Stuart kings led to the Glorious Revolution in England and America?

2. What was the Dominion of New England? What happened to it in 1689?

3. What was Leisler's Rebellion? How did the British royal governor deal with it?

4. What impact did the practices of colonial farmers in the eighteenth century have on the environment of the Atlantic seaboard settlements?

5. Explain why the Spanish and French had more trouble attracting European settlers to their North American colonies than did the British.

6. What were the ideals of the eighteenth-century Enlightenment?

7. What was Deism? Name some American Deists.

ESSAY QUESTIONS

1. How much equality, liberty, and self-government existed in the American colonies in the period 1700–1750? Back up your assessment with as many specific facts as possible.

2. What was the Great Awakening? Who was attracted to it? Who was repelled by it? What impact did it have on religious, social, educational, and political developments in eighteenth-century America?

3. Discuss the racial and ethnic makeup and the social class structure of mid-eighteenth-century America.

4. Historians have long debated the impact of Britain's mercantilist economic policy on the colonies. Explain the mercantilist economic theory and show how Parliament incorporated it into the navigation system. According to Chapter 4, in what ways did that system hurt and benefit America? Does the author believe the harm outweighed the benefits?

5. "In the second quarter of the eighteenth century, no American more fully embodied the Enlightenment spirit than [Benjamin] Franklin." Discuss Franklin's life, beliefs, career, and achievements, and explain how they embodied the Enlightenment spirit.

ANSWERS TO MULTIPLE-CHOICE QUESTIONS

1. b
2. c
3. d
4. a
5. c
6. d
7. c
8. a
9. b
10. a

CHAPTER 5

Roads to Revolution, 1750–1776

OUTLINE AND SUMMARY

I. Introduction

Chapter 5 addresses these questions: (1) How did Britain and its colonies view their joint victory over France in the Seven Years' War? (2) How did colonial resistance to the Stamp Act differ from earlier opposition to British imperial measure? (3) In what ways did colonists' views of parliamentary authority change after 1770? (4) What led most colonists in 1776 to abandon their loyalty to Britain and choose national independence?

II. Triumph and Tensions: The British Empire, 1750–1763

A. A Fragile Peace, 1750–1754

Since neither power gained dominance in North America, the skirmishing in the Ohio Valley continued. In 1753, in an effort to drive colonial traders from the valley, the French began building a series of forts between the Ohio River and Louisiana. An expedition led by George Washington to block them misfired, leaving the Anglo-American frontier in danger. The attempt of seven colonies north of Virginia to forge an effective defensive union with the Albany Plan failed because the colonial legislatures refused to relinquish any of their authority over taxation.

B. The Seven Years' War in America, 1754–1760

After the Anglo-French clash in 1754, war broke out in America. Then in 1756, full-scale hostilities between Britain and France resumed in the Seven Years' War. At first British colonists fared poorly as France's Indian allies raided western settlements and the French seized key forts and threatened central New York and western New England. Unable to spare large British armies from the other military theaters where they were fighting the French, Prime Minister William Pitt offered British financial support to the colonials if they would do most of the fighting in America. Encouraged by the promise, colonials flocked to the struggle and drove the French from New York and much of the western frontier. Their success was aided by the decision of the Iroquois and other Ohio tribes to stop helping the French. After the fall of Quebec and Montreal, French resistance crumbled.

C. The End of French North America, 1760–1763

The 1763 Treaty of Paris officially ended the Seven Years' War. Under its provisions France ceded all of its North American territories east of the Mississippi River to Britain and all territories west of the river, as well as New Orleans, to Spain. During the war the British expelled many French Canadians from Acadia (Nova Scotia) because the English feared the Acadians were still loyal to France. Some of the exiles migrated to Louisiana, where their descendents became known as Cajuns. The British triumph in the Seven Years' War, while initially bonding colonists and mother country, soon sowed discord between them.

D. The Writs of Assistance, 1760–1761

To crack down on smuggling, mainly from the French, British customs officers began to employ writs of assistance, or blanket search warrants that permitted officials to enter any ship or building to search for smuggled goods and seize them. They proved quite effective.

But colonists protested that the writs violated traditional English guarantees against unreasonable search and seizure and that Parliament had violated their rights as Englishmen.

E.   Anglo-American Friction
After the Seven Years' War Britain tried to tighten control over its now much-expanded colonial empire and to finance its administration by imposing new taxes on Englishmen at home and overseas. These efforts aroused opposition on both economic and constitutional grounds. At about the same time (1760), George III became king. He was determined to govern more actively than his predecessors, but his shifting policies and frequent ministerial changes further upset British-American relations. British supremacy in eastern North America opened the door to conflict between the mother country and the colonists. The war left the British people staggering under a huge debt and heavy taxes. Why, they wondered, should the colonists be repaid for their war efforts, while they were left to suffer under their financial burdens?

F.   Frontier Tensions
The British were equally upset that they now had to expend more money and military effort to put down Indian uprisings caused by the western surge of colonists beyond the Appalachians. Hoping to pacify Chief Pontiac and his followers, the British issued the Proclamation of 1763, forbidding whites to settle beyond the crest of the mountains until the crown had negotiated treaties with the Indians under which they agreed to cede their lands. The colonists were angered by this interference with their western land claims. Since continuing to protect the frontier and consolidate control over the newly acquired territories would cost around 6 percent of the peacetime budget, British government officials saw no reason that the colonials should not be taxed to help defray the expense.

III.   Imperial Authority, Colonial Opposition, 1763–1766
A.   Introduction
After 1763 Anglo-American tensions centered on British efforts to finance its suddenly enlarged empire through a series of revenue measures and to enforce these and other measures directly rather than relying on local authorities. The reaction, a series of successful colonial protests, revealed the growing schism between British and colonial perceptions about the nature of their relationship.

B.   The Sugar Act, 1764
In 1764 Parliament adopted the Sugar Act, imposing import duties on sugar and other items to raise money for the British treasury. These taxes and a host of new regulations and restrictions burdened Massachusetts, New York, and Pennsylvania merchants particularly, but they also violated the long-standing guarantee of a fair trial. Accused smugglers were to be tried in vice-admiralty courts, without juries, by judges who had a financial stake in finding the defendants guilty.

C.   The Stamp Act Crisis, 1765–1766
Prime Minister George Grenville saw only that the Sugar Act brought in too little revenue to ease Britain's financial woes. He therefore proposed the Stamp Act and in 1765 convinced Parliament to pass it. It required colonists to purchase from government revenue agents special stamped paper for periodicals, customs documents, licenses, diplomas, deeds, and other legal forms. It also provided that violators would be tried in vice-admiralty courts. Since it was an internal tax, it touched many more colonials than the Sugar Act, which affected mainly merchants engaged in importing and exporting.

Colonists objected to Parliament's ability to impose on them internal or external taxes designed to raise revenue because they elected no representatives to that body. Their own colonial legislatures had sole authority to tax them. Colonists conceded that parliament might regulate trade within the empire, but there could be "no taxation without representation."

D.   Resisting the Stamp Act, 1765–1766

The Virginia House of Burgesses passed resolutions, proposed by Patrick Henry, denying Parliament's right to tax the colonies. Eight other provincial assemblies followed suit. In Boston a group of artisans, shopkeepers, and businessmen founded the Loyal Nine to fight the act. Similar organizations, usually called the Sons of Liberty, cropped up in other cities. The Loyal Nine and the Sons of Liberty directed outraged mobs in attacks on the homes and property of stamp distributors, causing all of them to resign their posts. In October 1765 representatives from nine colonies convened in the Stamp Act Congress in New York, where they reiterated the principle of no taxation without representation and no parliamentary denial of trial by jury and other English liberties. Most persuasive to the British, however, was the boycott of all English imports undertaken by American merchants. The decrease in their sales led British businessmen to plead for repeal of the Stamp Act.

E.   The Declaratory Act, 1766

In March 1766 Parliament revoked the Stamp Act, but at the same time it adopted the Declaratory Act, restating its right to tax and legislate for the colonies "in all cases whatsoever." The colonists ignored the latter, rejoiced at the repeal, disbanded the Sons of Liberty, and concluded that the mother country would return to its earlier limited governance.

F.   Ideology, Religion, and Resistance

Resistance to the Stamp Act had revealed a deep split in thinking between England and its colonists. Influenced by John Locke, the oppositionists, the eighteenth-century English radicals, and the classical philosophers, educated colonists saw in Parliament's actions a conspiracy of a corrupt government to deny them their natural rights and liberties. It was their duty as a free people to resist. Protestant clergymen, with the exception of the Anglicans and many pacifist Quakers, preached sermons to all classes of colonists backing these views. They declared that "solidarity against British tyranny and 'corruption' meant rejecting sin and obeying God."

IV.   Resistance Resumes, 1766–1770

A.   Opposing the Quartering Act, 1766–1767

In 1767 George III's new chancellor of the Exchequer, Charles Townshend, like Grenville before him, looked to the colonies for much-needed revenue. That same year, Parliament's angry reaction to New York's refusal to comply with the Quartering Act indicated that it was ready to crack down on colonial self-government.

B.   Crisis over the Townshend Duties, 1767–1770

Townshend pushed through Parliament the revenue Act of 1767 (the Townshend duties), which imposed taxes on glass, paint, lead, paper, and tea imported into the colonies. Townshend intended to set aside part of the tax money to pay the salaries of royal governors so that they would no longer be subject to pressure from the colonial assemblies that had been compensating them. John Dickinson's *Letters from a Farmer in Pennsylvania* expressed the American majority view that Parliament could use duties to keep trade within the empire but not to raise revenue, as the Townshend duties did. The Massachusetts legislature sent Samuel Adams's "circular letter" making the same point to the other colonial assemblies. In August 1768 Boston merchants adopted a nonimportation agreement that spread to other cities.

In 1770 Lord North, the new British Prime Minister, eliminated all of the duties with the exception of tea, the most profitable item for the royal treasury. In response, colonial leaders called for a policy of nonconsumption–refusal to drink British tea.

C.   Women and Colonial Resistance
White women's participation in public affairs had been widening slowly and unevenly in the colonies for several decades. The Daughters of Liberty played a part in defeating the Stamp Act. To protest the Revenue Act's tax on tea, more than three hundred "mistresses of families" in Boston denounced consumption of the beverage. Women bolstered the boycott by refusing to serve taxed tea and by organizing spinning bees to produce homespun apparel rather than buy British-made clothing.

D.   Customs "Racketeering," 1767–1768
Meanwhile the high-handedness and corruption of customs officials, who seized ships and cargoes for technical violations of the Navigation and Sugar acts and broke open sailors' chests to search for small amounts of undeclared merchandise, contributed to Americans' growing alienation from the mother country. Violent attacks by seamen and others on customs inspectors, like the *Liberty* incident in Boston, happened more frequently.

E.   "Wilkes and Liberty," 1768–1770
Although the boycott probably reduced imports only about 40 percent, this hurt many British merchants and artisans enough to make them again implore Parliament to rescind its taxes. Their appeal became part of a larger British protest movement against the domestic and foreign policies of George III and a Parliament dominated by a tiny elite of wealthy landowners. London journalist John Wilkes led the unrest. For this the government arrested him and denied him the seat in the House of Commons to which he had been elected. The government's actions prompted dissident Englishmen and American colonists to further question the authority of an unrepresentative Parliament.

V.   The Deepening Crisis, 1770–1774
The way in which British officials enforced Parliament's trade regulations made more and more colonials broaden their cry from no taxation without representation to no legislation at all without representation. The British, on the other hand, responded to the violence over the *Liberty* incident by sending another 4,000 soldiers to Boston, where their presence was hotly resented.

A.   The Boston Massacre
Tensions between the redcoats and the civilian population smoldered, ready to flare up. Then, on March 5, 1770, a group of British soldiers at a guardpost in front of the customs office fired into a disorderly crowd that was hurling dares, insults, and objects at them. Five civilians were killed and six more wounded in this so-called Boston Massacre. To defuse the situation, Massachusetts governor Thomas Hutchinson promised to try the soldiers, and the British removed their troops to a fortified island in Boston harbor. With John Adams as their lawyer, all but two of the redcoats were acquitted.

B.   The Committees of Correspondence, 1772–1773
In 1772 Lord North revived trouble when he prepared to implement Townshend's plan to pay royal governors' salaries out of customs revenue. Sam Adams and others responded by organizing committees of correspondence in each New England town to exchange information and coordinate activities in defense of colonial rights. In March 1773, Virginians also set up a committee of correspondence. Within a year every colony but Pennsylvania had such committees that linked Americans together in a communications web.

C. Conflicts in the Backcountry

Meanwhile, tensions in America among Indians, frontier settlers, and colonial authorities increased because of the relentless push of land-hungry whites westward. Colonial speculators and settlers ignored the Proclamation of 1763 and trespassed on Native Americans' lands. Settlers around Paxton, Pennsylvania, declared all Indians racial enemies. The Treaty of Fort Stanwix further reduced native lands, convincing many Indians that no policy of appeasement could stop colonial expansion. New Hampshire's Green Mountain Boys settled in Vermont, rejected New York's ownership of the area, and created a separate government and later new state. In North Carolina the frontier regulator movement rebelled against the eastern-dominated colonial legislature and was suppressed. These and others incidents demonstrated the readiness of the westerners to defy all established authority violently.

D. The Tea Act, 1773

The British East India Tea Company was on the verge of bankruptcy in 1773 because Americans were buying so little taxed tea. Parliament tried to save it with the Tea Act, which allowed the company to sell its tea directly to American consumers, cutting out all middlemen's profits. As a result, the company would be able to sell its product, even with the import duty still on it, at a lower price than Americans paid for smuggled tea. The committees of correspondence denounced the act because they saw it as an attempt to seduce colonists into paying a parliamentary-imposed tax and they knew Lord North planned to compensate the royal governors with the customs receipts. That would surely endanger colonial representative government. At most ports, when the company's ships arrived, no one accepted the cargo and the captains turned around and left. But the governor of Massachusetts insisted on Bostonians' receiving and paying the duties on the shipment that arrived there. On the night of December 16, 1773, Sam Adams convened a protest meeting, at the end of which a band of colonials disguised as Indians boarded the East India Company's vessel and dumped its tea into the harbor.

VI. Toward Independence, 1774–1776

A. Liberty for African-Americans

As tensions between England and her white colonists mounted, African-American slaves also demanded "Liberty." The Carolina government quickly arrested black freedom demonstrators in Charles Town in 1765. However, when a British court, in the case of James Somerset, seemed to indicate that slavery would not be enforced in England, American slaves began to look to the mother country as their potential liberator. In 1775, Virginia's governor, Lord Dunmore, proclaimed that any slave who "enlisted in the cause of restoring royal authority" would be set free. Before the white Virginians drove Dunmore out of the colony, a thousand blacks flocked to his side.

B. The "Intolerable Acts"

Infuriated by the Boston Tea Party, the British retaliated with a series of punitive laws, the Coercive Acts, which Americans dubbed the Intolerable Acts. These closed the Boston harbor, causing serious economic distress in Massachusetts; revoked the colony's charter and restructured its government to make it less democratic; banned the holding of more than one town meeting a year; provided for the housing of British troops in privately owned buildings; and permitted soldiers and other officials charged with killing colonials to be tried in England. General Thomas Gage, military commander in North America, took over as governor of Massachusetts. These measures and the unrelated Quebec Act, which provided no elected legislature for that province, convinced people in all the colonies that the British were out to destroy representative government and civil liberties in America.

C.   The First Continental Congress
      To resist the Intolerable Acts, all the colonies except Georgia sent representatives to a
      Continental Congress that convened in Philadelphia in September 1774. The Congress
      approved the Suffolk Resolves, which, among other things, advised colonials to begin
      arming themselves against attacks by royal troops. The Congress also created the
      Continental Association to enforce a total cutoff of trade with England and the British West
      Indies and sent a Declaration of Rights to George III, begging him to dismiss the ministers
      responsible for the Coercive Acts.

D.   From Resistance to Rebellion
      Committees of the Continental Association coerced wavering colonists into cooperating with
      the trade ban. Loyalists, or Tories, were intimidated. Volunteer militias, often calling
      themselves minutemen, drilled, and extralegal congresses met and tried to supplant the
      existing colonial assemblies headed by royal governors. On April 19, 1775, General Gage
      dispatched seven hundred soldiers to Lexington and Concord to seize the minutemen's
      weapon stockpiles and arrest key patriotic leaders. Forewarned by William Dawes and Paul
      Revere, the residents of Lexington and Concord challenged the redcoats arriving from
      Boston, and the first fighting of the Revolution broke out. As news of the battles at
      Lexington and Concord spread, twenty thousand New Englanders rushed to besiege Boston
      and oust the English. The British defeated the colonials at Breed's and Bunker Hills but
      suffered heavy casualties in doing so.

      Soon after Lexington and Concord the Second Continental Congress convened in
      Philadelphia. The majority of the delegates still hoped for reconciliation with England and
      sent the Olive Branch Petition to George III, pleading for a cease-fire at Boston, repeal of
      the Coercive Acts, and negotiations to establish American rights. The British ignored the
      plea and, in December 1775, declared the colonists in rebellion. The Second Continental
      Congress also established an American continental army and appointed George Washington
      to command it, although it was not yet ready to declare independence.

E.   *Common Sense*
      Loyalty to the king and hopes that he would restrain irritated ministers and members of
      Parliament lingered on through the summer and fall of 1775. Publication of Thomas Paine's
      pamphlet *Common Sense* in January 1776 did much to kill any remaining affection for
      monarchs. In his widely read pamphlet, Paine argued that monarchy was a corrupt,
      repressive institution that Americans should shun and instead should take the opportunity to
      create a new kind of nation based on republican liberty.

F.   Declaring Independence
      On June 7, 1776, Virginia delegate Richard Henry Lee proposed that Congress declare
      independence. The members first appointed a committee, including Thomas Jefferson, John
      Adams, and Benjamin Franklin, to draft a statement justifying the colonies' separation from
      England. Most of the writing was done by Thomas Jefferson. Much influenced by the
      Enlightenment natural rights philosophy, Jefferson's Declaration of Independence
      emphasized equality of all men and their universal rights to Life, Liberty, and the pursuit of
      Happiness. On July 2 Congress formally adopted Lee's independence resolution and created
      the United States of America. On July 3 it reviewed and revised Jefferson's Declaration,
      approving and signing it on July 4. While the equal rights for all championed by the
      Declaration of Independence did not exist in America in 1776, the document's ideals
      inspired the revolutionary generation and many who followed to bring the realities of
      American life closer to the Declaration's bold proclamation.

VII.　Conclusion

Triumphant over France in the Seven Years' War, Britain in 1763 was the world's leading power. However, her subsequent attempts to centralize imperial power and tax her colonies aroused American resistance. In the years between 1763 and 1776, the colonists strove to reestablish the colonial relationship as it had existed earlier when British supervision was minimal and colonial assemblies controlled taxes and internal legislation. They did this through peaceful protests of the Stamp Act, the Townshend duties, and finally the Tea Act. Different classes acted out of different motives: colonial elites resented erosion of their autonomy, merchants and middle-class colonists protested new economic restrictions, and the urban and rural poor questioned all authority— British and domestic elite as well. Unable to reconcile the mother country's and colonial's viewpoints and buoyed by Thomas Paine's *Common Sense,* the Americans finally severed their ties with England and declared independence.

VOCABULARY

The following terms are used in Chapter 5. To understand the chapter fully, it is important that you know what each of them means.

ceded	yielded or formally surrendered to another; given over, as by treaty
confederation	a government body formed by a number of states, societies, or other units, each retaining control of its own internal affairs
chasm	a split, gorge, gulf, gap
boycott	an organized refusal to buy or use products or to trade for the purpose of persuading, intimidating, or coercing
chancellor of the Exchequer	the minister of finance in the British government, similar to the U.S. secretary of the treasury
rhetorical	pertaining to the art of influencing the thought and conduct of one's hearers
allusions	passing references to something either directly or by implication
despotism	the situation of government exercising absolute power or control; tyranny
allegiance	the faithfulness or loyalty to any person or thing; obligation or duty of a citizen to the government
requisition	an act of requiring or demanding; authorities taking or demanding something for military or public needs
Tories	the name given during the Revolution to Americans who remained loyal to England
vigilantes	members of groups using extralegal means to control or intimidate

IDENTIFICATIONS

After reading Chapter 5, you should be able to identify and explain the historical significance of each of the following:

Albany Plan of Union

Acadians, Cajuns

Seven Years' War (French and Indian War)

Neolin, Pontiac's uprising, and the Proclamation of 1763

King George III

writs of assistance and James Otis

Sugar Act and vice-admiralty courts

George Grenville

Stamp Act and Stamp Act Congress

virtual representation

Patrick Henry

Loyal Nine and Sons of Liberty

Declaratory Act

Charles Townshend and the Townshend duties (Revenue Act of 1767)

John Wilkes

American Board of Customs Commissioners, customs racketeering

Samuel Adams

John Adams

spinning bees

Lord North

John Hancock

Crispus Attucks and the Boston Massacre

committees of correspondence

Tea Act and the Boston Tea Party

Lord Dunmore's proclamation

Coercive or Intolerable Acts and Quebec Act

Suffolk Resolves and Continental Association

minutemen, Paul Revere, and Lexington and Concord

Olive Branch Petition

Thomas Paine, *Common Sense*

Second Continental Congress and Declaration of Independence

SKILL BUILDING: MAPS

On the map of eastern North America on the next page, locate each of the following and explain its importance in the imperial wars between Britain and France or at the beginning of the American Revolution:

Nova Scotia (Acadia)

Ohio River and Ohio Valley

Albany, New York

Pittsburgh

Quebec

Montreal

British North America under the terms of the Treaty of Paris, 1763

Detroit

Halifax, Nova Scotia

Philadelphia

Boston

Lexington, Massachusetts

Concord, Massachusetts

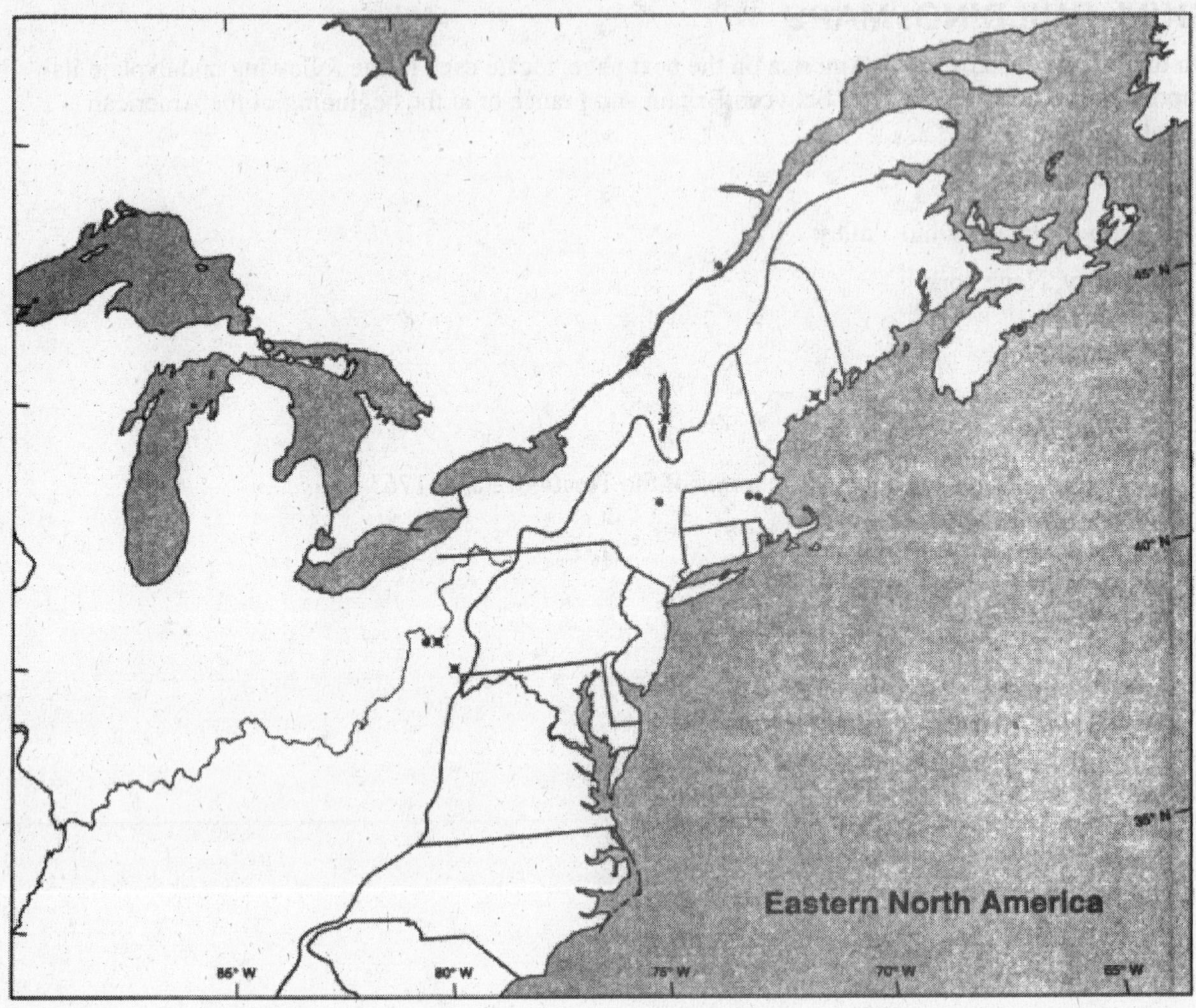

HISTORICAL SOURCES

The author of Chapter 5 has made considerable use of letters written by famous and ordinary people as historical sources. Letters dating from the 1760s and 1770s often contain colonial arguments against Parliament's actions and eyewitness accounts of riots, protest meetings, and other events, as well as expressions of the writers' fears, hopes, and opinions about the revolutionary situation that was brewing. Historians find letters in several places. The records of political leaders such as Benjamin Franklin, John and Sam Adams, Thomas Jefferson, and others frequently include letters that they wrote and received, some of which were intended for publication. Many were not for public consumption and therefore tend to be more candid. One also can read letters that were published in newspapers and periodicals. There are even private letters that were stolen or fell into the hands of others who disclosed them to the public, such as the letters of Massachusetts governor Thomas Hutchinson that Benjamin Franklin obtained and turned over to Sam Adams. There are abundant references to letters or information contained in letters in the chapter. In each case how has the author of Chapter 5 used these historical sources?

In addition to letters, the author of Chapter 5 has used newspapers and pamphlets printed during the revolutionary period and the records of proceedings kept by the various congresses, conventions, committees of safety, and committees of correspondence. Find places in Chapter 5 where material from newspapers, periodicals, and pamphlets is quoted. For what purposes does the author quote from these historical sources?

Now look at "Technology and Culture: Public Sanitation in Philadelphia." The author is telling us about Philadelphia's problems with pollution and clean water supply in the 1700s. He is indicating what technological solution to the problems were tried by whom and which classes benefited the least from the clean-up efforts. Where did the author find his information? Did he use letters and records of proceedings of government committees and boards?

MULTIPLE-CHOICE QUESTIONS

Circle the letter of the item that best completes each statement or answers the question.

1. Both the Proclamation of 1763 and the Quebec Act of 1774
   a. interfered with colonial claims to western lands.
   b. extended religious freedom to Catholics.
   c. were repealed after colonial protests.
   d. imposed new taxes on goods imported from Europe.

2. The Albany Plan of Union
   a. was vetoed by the British because it challenged royal authority.
   b. united Anglo-Americans in a loose confederation during the Seven Years' War, but fell apart after the French defeat.
   c. was not implemented because of opposition by colonial legislatures, but it set a precedent for future plans to unite the British mainland colonies.
   d. represented the earliest British attempt to suppress the colonial assemblies and exercise more imperial control.

3. Which of the following helped convince the delegates to the Second Continental Congress to vote for independence?
   a. The unexpected success of the colonists in clearing British troops out of New England
   b. Tom Paine's *Common Sense*
   c. The Boston Massacre
   d. John Dickinson's *Letters from a Pennsylvania Farmer*

4. In the Declaratory Act, Parliament stated that
   a. it had the right to legislate for the colonies in all matters, including taxes.
   b. the colonists were in rebellion and therefore subject to martial law.
   c. it would repeal all the Townshend duties except the one on tea.
   d. it would take over payment of the salaries of the royal governors and other colonial officials.

5. Which of these events occurred last?
   a. The Battle of Bunker Hill
   b. The fighting at Lexington and Concord
   c. The adoption of the Declaration of Independence
   d. The Boston Massacre

6. How did the French and Indian War differ from King William's, Queen Anne's, and King George's wars?
   a. In the French and Indian War, France rather than Spain was England's chief enemy.
   b. Americans participated only in the French and Indian War.
   c. The French and Indian War was the only one in which the Indians sided with the French rather than the British.
   d. As a result of the French and Indian War, France lost her empire in North America.

7. The chief reason for the repeal of the Stamp Act and the Townshend duties by Parliament was the
    a.   conviction that the colonists were on the verge of revolution.
    b.   pleas of Burke and Pitt to conciliate the colonists by recognizing their right to tax themselves.
    c.   harmful effects of colonial boycotts and nonimportation agreements on British business.
    d.   expectation that the colonial assemblies would voluntarily vote for higher taxes.
8. Americans objected to the Tea Act because
    a.   it would raise the price they had to pay for tea.
    b.   there was still a tax on tea and the customs duties collected on it would be used to pay the salaries of royal governors.
    c.   it forced them to drink tea when they preferred coffee.
    d.   it forced them to buy from the British East India Company, which sold low-quality, overpriced tea.
9. The Declaration of Independence was primarily written by
    a.   John Adams.
    b.   Patrick Henry.
    c.   John Hancock.
    d.   Thomas Jefferson.
10. John Adams, a key figure in the Revolution,
    a.   drafted a "circular letter" to colonial legislatures condemning the Townshend duties.
    b.   started committees of correspondence.
    c.   served as the lawyer for the soldiers tried for shooting civilians in the Boston Massacre.
    d.   convened the protest meeting at Old South Church that preceded the Boston Tea Party.

SHORT-ANSWER QUESTIONS

1. Explain why the colonists objected to writs of assistance and vice-admiralty courts.

2. Explain what the British meant by virtual representation and why the American colonists rejected the concept.

3. Why did the British pass the Coercive (Intolerable) Acts? What did the colonists think the laws showed about British intentions?

4. Where and when did the First Continental Congress meet? What actions did it take?

5. Why did General Gage send British troops to Lexington and Concord in 1775, and what happened as a result?

6. Why did the Second Continental Congress reverse itself on the question of independence between 1775 and 1776?

ESSAY QUESTIONS

1. In 1763 a French statesman predicted that England would rue the day she expelled France from North America. Did events prove the Frenchman right? How are the French and Indian War and its outcome related to the American Revolution? Discuss.

2. One historian has written, "The British ruled the colonies for one hundred and fifty years and lost them in twelve." Do you agree with this statement? Why or why not? Use as many specific facts in your answer as possible.

3. Another historian claims, "A salient feature of our Revolution was that its animating purpose was deeply conservative. The colonials revolted against British rule in order to keep things the way they were, not to initiate a new era." Do you agree? Use as many facts in your answer as possible.

4. Discuss the role of each of the following groups in the events that led to America's break with England: colonial merchants, Virginia planters, workers, sailors, artisans, frontier dwellers, and women.

5. Write an essay about the Declaration of Independence. Who wrote it? Why was it written and adopted? What political ideals did it express? How and why did the Second Continental Congress modify it before adopting it? How close to the political ideals it avowed was America in 1776? What importance has the document had in American and world history since 1776?

ANSWERS TO MULTIPLE-CHOICE QUESTIONS

1. a
2. c
3. b
4. a
5. c
6. d
7. c
8. b
9. d
10. c

CHAPTER 6

Securing Independence, Defining Nationhood, 1776–1788

OUTLINE AND SUMMARY

I. Introduction

Chapter 6 answers these questions: (1) What were the different conflicts contained within the American Revolution? (2) How did the Revolution affect relationships among Americans of different classes, races, and genders? (3) How did the state constitutions and Articles of Confederation reflect older political ideas? (4) How did the Constitution's proponents address Americans' concerns about concentrated political power?

II. The Prospects of War

A. Introduction

The Revolution was both a war of the American people against the British and a civil war between American supporters of independence and Americans who were opposed to breaking with the mother country.

B. Loyalists and Other British Sympathizers

About 20 percent of all whites opposed the Revolution. They called themselves loyalists, indicating their continued allegiance to the crown; the revolutionaries (patriots) named the loyalists "Tories" and hated them. The proportion of loyalists was greatest in New York and New Jersey, where the leading families had split between the two sides. Recent British immigrants and French Canadians tended to be loyalists. Thousands of southern slaves escaped to the royal army, while African-Americans in the North were more likely to support the Revolution. Indian tribes became deeply divided as well with many wanting to sit the conflict out. Neutrality was not an option, and the majority sided with the British.

C. The Opposing Sides

The British entered the war with major advantages: they outnumbered the Americans 11 million to 2.5 million, and they possessed the world's largest navy and one of the best professional armies. But they also had disadvantages. Because of their difficulty in recruiting soldiers, they had to employ twenty-one thousand loyalists and thirty thousand Hessian mercenaries. Supplying armies across 3,000 miles of ocean was a formidable task. Further, as the financial strain of the conflict mounted, English domestic support for it waned. The Americans mobilized their smaller population behind the war more effectively, and after 1778 they had French and Spanish assistance, centered on veteran European officers. They also were beset with problems: one-third of their population was either slaves or opposed to the Revolution, the state militias did well in guerrilla raids but lacked training for pitched battles, and there were few experienced officers to command the raw recruits of the Continental Army. Fortunately, the Americans did not have to conquer the redcoats; the rebels just had to keep resisting until the British public tired of the struggle.

George Washington, a Virginia tobacco planter who had sat in the House of Burgesses and the Continental Congress, was the logical choice as commander of the American army because of his military experience in the imperial wars with France. For much of the Revolution, America's fate depended on his ability to inspire his men to continue fighting despite numerous defeats.

III. War and Peace, 1776–1783

    A.   The War in the North, 1776–1778

The British evacuated Boston in March 1776 and moved into New York, where they greatly outnumbered Washington's army. In battles in and around the city, the British killed or captured a quarter of Washington's soldiers and forced him to make a hasty retreat across New Jersey and into Pennsylvania. During the winter of 1776–1777, Washington struck back at Trenton and Princeton. The redcoats pulled back to New York, and in New Jersey the Whigs forced loyalists remaining in the state to pledge allegiance to the Continental Congress.

Americans' best hope for victory lay in French diplomatic recognition and military alliance, but Louis XVI held back until he became convinced that the Americans had a chance of winning. When forces under General Horatio Gates foiled a major British offensive, surrounded General John Burgoyne's outnumbered army, and compelled the surrender of 5,800 British troops in October 1777 near Saratoga, New York, the French were impressed. By February 1778 France recognized the United States, and four months later she declared war on England. Subsequently the Spanish and the Dutch Republic also declared war on Britain. The formation of this coalition against the British proved to be the turning point in the war for independence.

In the fall of 1777, the British inflicted defeats on Washington's army at Brandywine Creek and Germantown, Pennsylvania, and occupied Philadelphia, compelling the Continental Congress to flee. While the royal army enjoyed the comforts of Philadelphia for the winter of 1778, Washington's men froze and drilled in nearby Valley Forge. In June the Continentals caught up with the British marching back to New York at the battle of Monmouth Court House, New Jersey. Badly mauled, the redcoats escaped to New York, where they sat under the protection of the British Navy, and Washington hovered across the Hudson keeping an eye on them.

    B.   The War in the West, 1776–1782

Although the number of people involved in the frontier battles was small, the skirmishes were deadly, as the British, the new country, and the Indians realized what was at stake— namely, who would control the area west of the Appalachians. The battles commenced in the South, where the Cherokees attacked from Virginia to Georgia. By 1777 the frontiersmen had crushed the Cherokees and forced them to cede much of their land in the Carolinas and Tennessee. Expeditions led by George Rogers Clark, John Bowman, and Daniel Brodhead inflicted heavy losses on hostile Ohio Indian tribes, who nonetheless kept up the struggle into the 1780s. Joseph Brant led the Iroquois on deadly raids against the western New York and Pennsylvania settlers until he was stopped at a battle near Elmira, New York. By the war's end the Iroquois population had dropped by a third. While not greatly influencing the outcome of the war, these battles played a major role in the development of the future American nation.

    C.   Victory in the South, 1778–1781

After 1778 the British shifted their attention to the South. They took Charles Town, South Carolina, in 1780, and General Charles Cornwallis led English forces into the Carolina backcountry. There he fought three major battles against American militiamen commanded by Nathaniel Greene. The British won all three encounters but suffered such heavy casualties that Cornwallis decided to leave the Carolina backcountry and head to Virginia.

Cornwallis established a new base on Virginia's Yorktown Peninsula, where he was later cut off and surrounded by American and French armies and a French fleet. On October 19, 1781, Cornwallis surrendered, and the fighting in the Revolutionary War ended.

D. **Peace at Last, 1782–1783**

John Adams, John Jay, and Benjamin Franklin represented America at the Paris peace negotiations that began in June 1782. Under the terms of the Treaty of Paris signed in 1783, the British recognized American independence and promised to remove all troops from American soil. The Mississippi River became the western boundary of the new nation, but New Orleans and the outlet of the river to the Gulf of Mexico, as well as East and West Florida, went to Spain. Notably absent from the Treaty was any reference to Native Americans, who in turn refused to acknowledge American sovereignty over their territories. Although the confederation agreed to compensate loyalists for their property losses and repay British creditors, several states later refused to comply. In retaliation, the British did not evacuate forts they still held in the Northwest. American victory had been costly: at least 5 percent of free males between sixteen and forty-five years of age died in the war. Many loyalists and former slaves fled to Canada, Britain, and the West Indies.

IV. **The Revolution and Social Change**

A. **Egalitarianism Among White Males**

Although there was no significant redistribution of wealth in America during the Revolution, the Declaration of Independence's bold assertion that "all men are created equal" did promote more egalitarian attitudes. The upper classes found it prudent to simplify their standard of living and treat common people with more respect. Ordinary folks were less likely to defer to their "betters" or automatically leave governing to them. Americans began to feel that political leaders should come from the "natural aristocracy"—men who demonstrated virtue, accomplishments, and dedication to the public good. The gains made through the advantage of family retreated before the republican principle of ability. However, the new egalitarianism did not include women, blacks, Indians, and landless white men.

B. **White Women in Wartime**

During the Revolution the assumptions about women barely changed; that is, women were dependent on fathers and husbands and had no public role to play. However, in the midst of war women took on added responsibilities and served visibly in support of the fighting men, raising money for the troops, some even serving incognito. The gains and rights they deserved for this and other social responsibilities would be up for discussion in the new republic.

C. **A Revolution for Black Americans**

In 1776 blacks accounted for 20 percent of the U.S. population, and almost all of them were enslaved. Five thousand blacks served in the Continental Army. The Declaration of Independence's words about equality made Whigs uneasy about slavery. The Quakers had taken the lead in attacking slavery. Then, between 1777 and 1810, all the northern states instituted gradual emancipation. No southern states, however, where the majority of blacks lived, outlawed bondage. Several did make the voluntary freeing of slaves easier, and by 1790 about 5 percent of Virginia and Maryland blacks had been freed. Most free blacks remained poor laborers, domestics, or tenant farmers. Some blacks and whites began to advocate the idea that freed slaves might be better off being returned to their homelands in Africa. Although most states granted freedmen certain civil rights, blacks continued in other respects to be treated as second-class citizens.

D. Native Americans and the Revolution
Regardless of which side they had fought on – or whether they had fought at all – Native Americans suffered worse than any group during the war. For many whites the republic's promise of equal opportunity meant moving west to obtain their own land, thus impinging on Indian territory. The tribes of the Ohio Valley were especially vulnerable because between 1754 and 1783 war and uprooting had reduced the Native American population east of the Mississippi by nearly 50 percent. Many Indians still living east of the river adapted some features of white culture, combined it with native customs, and created new lifestyles. But they insisted on their right to control their own communities and lives.

V. Forging New Governments
A. From Colonies to States
Certain beliefs inherited from the colonial era stood in the way of a thorough democratization of politics. Most Whigs believed that voting and office holding must be tied to property ownership. They frowned on political parties as strife-causing factions and did not see the need for apportioning seats in a legislature on the basis of population. Their revolutionary experience did, however, make them wary of unchecked executive authority, inclined to augment the role of elected legislatures, and interested in framing government institutions that would balance the interests of different classes to prevent any one group from gaining absolute power.

The first state constitutions reflected both the radical and traditional features of Whig thought. Except for Pennsylvania's, they did not provide for election districts that were equal in population. Nine of the thirteen states reduced property qualifications for voting, but none abolished them entirely. By 1784 all state constitutions included a bill of rights. They provided for frequent elections and stripped the governors of most of their powers. In the 1780s, however, many states revised their constitutions to strengthen the executive branch and increase the political power of wealthy elites. Most of the states also enacted social reforms. In Virginia, for example, Thomas Jefferson framed legislation abolishing primogeniture, entails, and the established church, as well as guaranteeing religious freedom.

B. Formalizing a Confederation, 1776–1781
In 1777 the Continental Congress drafted a constitution called the Articles of Confederation and sent it to the states for ratification. Because of numerous disputes among the states, especially over their claims to western lands and their representation in Congress, four years passed before the Articles of Confederation were ratified. There was a unicameral congress in which each state had one vote, but there was no national court system or executive. Financial, diplomatic, and military affairs were managed by congressional committees. The congress could request funds from the states but could not tax the people directly or regulate interstate and foreign commerce. The Articles affirmed the new nation's attachment to decentralized power when it reserved to each state full "sovereignty, freedom, and independence," leaving the national government severely limited in important respects.

C. Finance, Trade, and the Economy, 1781–1786
The confederation proved too weak to meet its greatest challenge, putting the country's finances on a sound basis. Unable to tax the people or force the states to contribute funds, the congress could not pay off its Revolutionary War debt or meet its operating expenses. Nor could the government under the Articles win diplomatic concessions from the British, who badly hurt New England shippers and merchants by shutting them out of the West Indian trade and imposing steep customs fees on goods entering England. Declining exports depressed the economies of both New England and the South. Its paper currency, the Continental, depreciated by 98 percent.

D.   The Confederation and the West, 1785–1787
The confederation also had to decide on the future of the trans-Appalachian west. The confederation was caught between speculators and settlers resolved to acquire these lands immediately and Native Americans determined to keep their homes. It responded by forcing Indian leaders to sign treaties ceding western lands, which the tribes, disputing the legitimacy of these American appointed Indian leaders, then repudiated. In addition, the congress passed the Ordinance of 1785 and the Northwest Ordinance of 1787. These laws set a successful pattern for surveying, selling, and administering western lands, as well as providing the way for territories to become states with the same powers and privileges as the original thirteen states. Equally important, the Northwest Ordinance for the first time banned slavery from a territory.

Meanwhile the British and Spanish governments made life difficult for western settlers. The British refused to evacuate seven forts in the Ohio Valley and supplied Indians in the region with arms and ammunition. The Spanish, too, sided with the Indians against American frontier families and closed off New Orleans to western farmers who wanted to ship their produce down the Mississippi and out to eastern cities and Europe through that port. Some westerners saw independent negotiations with Spain as the best resolution, and many predicted a new independent western country would break away from the weak confederation.

VI.   Toward a New Constitution, 1786–1788
A.   Shays's Rebellion, 1786–1787
Shays's Rebellion, in 1786 in Massachusetts, led some Americans to fear that the government was unable to protect even domestic law and order. Further, producers wanted a stronger government to regulate interstate and foreign commerce. Merchants and shippers desired a government that could secure foreign trade opportunities for them. Westerners hoped for better protection from the Indians. In 1786, an Annapolis, Maryland, meeting to promote interstate commerce instead called for a general convention of all the states to amend the Articles to create a more effective national government.

B.   The Philadelphia Convention, 1787
Fifty-five delegates from every state but Rhode Island gathered during the spring and summer of 1787 in Philadelphia. The majority of them were wealthy, had legal training, and shared a nationalist rather than a local perspective. In sessions closed to the press and the public, they decided to abandon the Articles and write a new constitution. The convention worked from a draft written by delegate James Madison. His Virginia Plan proposed a national government with broad powers to tax, legislate, and use military force against states. There would be a two-house congress, with representation in both chambers based on population. The small states, worried that they would always be outvoted, objected and countered with William Paterson's New Jersey Plan. It called for a unicameral congress in which each state, regardless of population, had an equal voice. The convention finally agreed to a compromise, with a two-chamber legislature: representation in the House based on population and representation in the Senate based on the principle of equality for each state.

The Constitution, finished in September 1787, vested in the federal government the power to levy and collect taxes, conduct diplomacy, and protect domestic order. It also granted to the national government (and denied to the states) authority to coin money and regulate interstate and foreign commerce. The Constitution carefully balanced state and federal power, the interests of one social group against another, and the authority of one branch of the national government versus another with its systems of federalism, separation of powers, and checks and balances. Many features of the Constitution were not democratic. It recognized and in some ways protected slavery and allowed direct election only of members of the House of Representatives. On the other hand, it acknowledged the people as the "ultimate source of political legitimacy" and, through the amendment process, opened the door for democratization of the government in the years ahead. Finally, the delegates provided for ratification of the Constitution by special state conventions composed of delegates elected by the people. As soon as nine conventions had approved the document, the new government would commence.

C. The Struggle over Ratification, 1787–1788
During 1787 and 1788 the country divided into proratification Federalists and opposing Antifederalists. Antifederalists feared that the Constitution concentrated too much centralized power in the hands of a national elite and that individuals' freedoms would be trampled because the document contained no bill of rights. But Antifederalists lacked the leadership stature of prominent Federalsits like George Washington and Benjamin Franklin. This respect, and the promise that they would amend the Constitution to provide a bill of rights once the new government was under way, led to a Federalist victory.

In an effort to win New Yorkers over to the Constitution, John Jay, Alexander Hamilton, and James Madison published a series of articles, later collected in a book called *The Federalist*. These articles still afford us a valuable commentary on the Constitution and insight into the political philosophy of the Founding Fathers.

VII. Conclusion
The final triumph of the nationalism born of the War of Independence came in late 1789 and early 1790, when the last two reluctant states, North Carolina and Rhode Island, ratified the Constitution and joined the new union. The Constitution did not create a democratic government for the United States, but it did establish the "legal and institutional framework within which Americans could struggle to attain democracy."

VOCABULARY

The following terms are used in Chapter 6. To understand the chapter fully, it is important that you know what each of them means.

mercenaries	hired soldiers serving in an army
Egalitarian	asserting the equality of all people
Confiscate	seize for public use; to take away property as a penalty
emancipation	freedom from slavery
deference	yielding to the opinions or wishes of another person, group or class (such as the upper-class elite)
sovereignty	the supreme or independent power or authority in government
republic	a government in which the supreme power rests in the body of citizens entitled to vote and is exercised by representatives chosen directly or indirectly by them; also, the head of government is nominated and/or elected rather than inheriting the position as a king
ideology	A body of doctrine, myth, and symbols of a social movement, institution, social class, or large group
agrarian	relating to farming, agricultural economy, or a rural way of life

connotations	secondary, implied, or associated meanings of a word or term rather than its dictionary definition
demagogue	A political leader who appeals to people's fears, prejudices, and emotions
entails	the legal requirements that prevent an heir and all his descendants from selling or dividing an estate
primogeniture	legal requirement that, in the absence of a will, only the eldest son inherits all a family's property
confederation	a league or alliance; a body of sovereign states more or less united for common purposes
interstate commerce	the business carried on in more than one state; transactions across state lines (as opposed to business done entirely within one state, or *intrastate* commerce)
anarchy	a state of society without government or law; political and social disorder due to absence of government control
ratification	the act of confirming by expressing formal consent or approval

IDENTIFICATIONS

After reading Chapter 6, you should be able to identify and explain the historical significance of each of the following:

Henry Knox

loyalists (Tories) versus patriots (Whigs)

Hessians

Marquis de Lafayette

General John Burgoyne, General Horatio Gates, and Saratoga

Frederick von Steuben

George Rogers Clark

Joseph Brant

Daniel Boone

Yorktown

John Adams, John Jay, Benjamin Franklin, and the Peace of Paris

"natural aristocracy"

Benjamin Banneker

Phillis Wheatley

Abigail Adams

Virginia Statute for Religious Freedom

the Articles of Confederation

Ordinance of 1785 and Northwest Ordinance of 1787

Continentals

Shays's Rebellion

Virginia Plan, New Jersey Plan, and Connecticut Compromise

checks and balances, functional separation of powers, and federalism

Federalists versus Antifederalists

John Jay, Alexander Hamilton, James Madison, and *The Federalist* papers

SKILL BUILDING: MAPS

1. On the map of eastern North America on the following page, locate each of the following and explain its importance in the Revolutionary War:

> Fort Ticonderoga
>
> Boston
>
> New York City
>
> Delaware River
>
> Trenton, New Jersey
>
> Princeton, New Jersey
>
> Albany
>
> Philadelphia
>
> Saratoga, New York
>
> Brandywine Creek and Germantown, Pennsylvania
>
> Valley Forge, Pennsylvania
>
> Monmouth, New Jersey
>
> Appalachians
>
> Tennessee
>
> Illinois
>
> Vincennes, Indiana
>
> Detroit, Michigan
>
> Ohio River
>
> Elmira, New York
>
> Savannah, Georgia
>
> Charles Town, South Carolina
>
> Yorktown, Virginia

2.   Draw on the map the boundaries of the United States as set by the Peace of Paris in 1783. Also draw the boundaries of the Northwest Territory created by the Ordinances of 1785 and 1787.

HISTORICAL SOURCES

The sessions of the Constitutional Convention were closed to the press and the public, and the delegates kept no official journal of their proceedings. How, then, do historians know what went on at the convention? How does the author of Chapter 6 know who said this or that about the Virginia Plan or the New Jersey Plan? How does he know about the "grand committee," or that Madison and the Virginians continued to fight against the Connecticut Compromise until they were overruled by the July 17, 1787 vote? Much of our information comes from detailed notes that James Madison took on the debates as he attended and participated in the sessions. He did not make these notes public during his lifetime, but after his death in 1836, Congress purchased Madison's papers that contained the notes. They were first published in 1840. While Madison's notes have proved a most valuable source of information, can you see why it is wise for historians also to look at any memoirs, letters, and comments they can find by other convention participants?

A way that historians have learned much about the thinking of Federalists and Antifederalists is by reading the articles and letters that they published in the press during the fight over ratification. John Jay, Alexander Hamilton, and James Madison wrote many essays, which appeared in such New York newspapers as the *Daily Advertiser* in 1787, arguing in support of the Constitution. New York governor Clinton, a leading Antifederalist, countered with letters attacking the proposed Constitution in the *New York Journal.* In addition to these newspaper pieces, historians can turn to the records of the speeches given for both sides at the state ratifying conventions.

As well as finding their sources, historians also have to decide which past events they will focus on. Traditionally, historians of the Revolutionary War concentrated on battles that Washington and the Continental Army fought or dramatic turning points in the struggle, such as Saratoga. In more recent decades historians, like the author of Chapter 6, have tried to offer a broader, or more balanced view of revolutionary fighting that includes the bitter clashes between white frontier settlers and Native Americans for control of the trans-Appalachian West. Look at "A Place in Time: Boonesborough, Kentucky in 1778." What light does it throw on the complex relations between whites and Indians and what motivated each side in the siege of Boonesborough?

MULTIPLE-CHOICE QUESTIONS

Circle the letter of the item that best completes each statement or answers the question.

1. Which of the following statements about the Revolutionary War is correct?
    a. The fighting ended with Cornwallis's surrender at Yorktown.
    b. Help from most Indian tribes enabled the Americans to win their independence from Britain.
    c. Most of the men who fought in the Continental Army were drafted and therefore had no choice but to serve.
    d. American victory at Boonesborough, Kentucky, turned the tide in the war in favor of the new nation.

2. Which statement about the men who wrote the U.S. Constitution is correct?
    a. Most of them doubted that a republic could effectively govern so large a nation as the United States.
    b. Most were wealthy men who were convinced that unless the national government was strengthened, the country would fall victim to foreign aggression or simply disintegrate.
    c. Most were men in their fifties and sixties who distrusted the younger revolutionaries.
    d. They wanted to get on with creating a democratic government that would enforce their belief that all men are created equal.

3. The Northwest Ordinance did all of the following *except*
    a. forbid slavery in the Northwest Territory.
    b. permit the citizens of a territory to elect a legislature and make their own laws.
    c. permit the citizens of a territory to write a state constitution and apply to Congress for admission as a new state.
    d. remove Native Americans and guarantee white settlers the right to buy land in the territory.

4. The British justified their refusal to evacuate their military forts in the Ohio Valley after the Revolution by pointing to America's failure to
    a. stop Indian attacks against Canada.
    b. pay for damage done to British shipping during the war.
    c. return or pay for loyalists' property and pay British creditors.
    d. allow British goods to enter the United States duty free.

5. Which of the following represented the most serious difficulty facing American commercial interests at the end of the Revolution?
    a. Loss of the protection of the British Navy
    b. British restrictions on trade with the West Indies
    c. Decreased demand for American goods in Europe
    d. France's refusal to sign a commercial treaty

6. Shays's Rebellion was provoked by
    a. retention of the northwest posts by Britain.
    b. the failure of the government to protect frontier settlements from Indian attacks.
    c. an excise tax imposed by Congress on whiskey.
    d. the heavy burden of taxes on the farmers of western Massachusetts.
7. Which of the following men was both an author of the U.S. Constitution and an outspoken supporter of its ratification?
    a. Thomas Jefferson
    b. Patrick Henry
    c. James Madison
    d. George Clinton
8. The greatest achievement of the Antifederalists was to
    a. force the Federalists to agree to add a bill of rights to the Constitution.
    b. convince New York and Virginia to turn over their western lands to the new national government.
    c. delay ratification of the Constitution until a section guaranteeing all white men the right to vote and hold office was added.
    d. force the Federalists to bestow citizenship under the new government to free blacks.
9. Who was the author of Virginia's Statute for Religious Freedom and bills abolishing entails and primogeniture?
    a. George Washington
    b. Richard Henry Lee
    c. Thomas Jefferson
    d. Patrick Henry
10. All of the following were true of the state constitutions adopted during the Revolution *except* they
    a. concentrated power in the popularly elected legislatures.
    b. all contained bills of rights.
    c. provided for weak executives and frequent elections.
    d. abolished property and tax-paying qualifications for voting.

SHORT-ANSWER QUESTIONS

1. Which groups of people tended to be loyalists, or British sympathizers, during the American Revolution?

2. Why is the Battle of Saratoga considered a turning point in the American Revolution?

3. In the Peace of Paris ending the Revolutionary War, what were the terms affecting America?

4. What was the relationship between Shays's Rebellion and the calling of the Constitutional convention?

5. Explain the differences between the Virginia plan and the New Jersey plan for the Constitution. In what ways was the Connecticut proposal a compromise between them?

6. What was the three-fifths controversy at the Constitutional convention? In what other ways did the Constitution recognize and deal with slavery?

7. Briefly describe the checks and balances and separation of powers in the U.S. Constitution. Give examples to illustrate.

8. Who were the Antifederalists, and what were their objections to the U.S. Constitution?

ESSAY QUESTIONS

1. Besides being a war for independence from Britain, the American Revolution was also a civil war of American against American and a war of Native Americans to defend their homelands. Discuss and illustrate this statement with as many facts as possible.

2. Discuss the advantages and disadvantages the British and the Americans each had in fighting the Revolutionary War. What do you think accounts for the Americans' ultimate victory?

3. Discuss the social, economic, and political changes within the thirteen states produced by the American Revolution. Be sure to consider things such as slavery, status of women, property distribution, voting rights, and religion.

4. Discuss the domestic and foreign difficulties the United States experienced under the Articles of Confederation. What were the accomplishments of the government under the Articles?

5. Discuss the backgrounds and political beliefs of the men who wrote the U.S. Constitution. What did they hope to accomplish by establishing this Constitution?

ANSWERS TO MULTIPLE-CHOICE QUESTIONS

1. a
2. b
3. d
4. c
5. b
6. d
7. c
8. a
9. c
10. d

CHAPTER 7

Launching the New Republic, 1788–1800

OUTLINE AND SUMMARY

I. Introduction
    Chapter 7 concentrates on these questions: (1) Which points in Hamilton's economic program were the most controversial and why? (2) What was the impact of the French Revolution on American politics? (3) What principal issues divided Federalists and Republicans in the election of 1800? (4) On what basis were some Americans denied full equality by 1800?

II. Constitutional Government Takes Shape, 1788–1796
    A. Introduction
        Although the Constitution had replaced the Articles of Confederation as the law of the land, the first test of its effectiveness was yet to come. It passed that test following the holding of the first national elections; the beginnings of legislative, executive, and judicial activity at the federal level; and the passage of a bill of rights.

    B. Implementing Government
        The first elections under the Constitution, in the fall of 1788, resulted in a Federalist sweep in Congress. An electoral college met in each state on February 9, 1789, with each elector voting for two presidential candidates. Electors in every state designated George Washington as one of their choices. The Constitution mentions executive departments only in passing. Through legislation Congress established the first cabinet. It consisted of four departments headed by secretaries of state, the treasury, and war and an attorney general.

    C. The Federal Judiciary and the Bill of Rights
        The Constitution authorized Congress simply to provide the federal courts below the level of the Supreme Court. This the lawmakers did by passing the Judiciary Act of 1789. It created a federal district court in each state.

        James Madison, who had been elected to the House of Representatives, led the way in drafting the first ten amendments, which became known as the Bill of Rights when they were ratified by the states in December 1791. The first eight protected individual rights, including freedom of speech, press, assembly and religion, and procedures for a fair trial and punishment. The Ninth and Tenth Amendments reserved to the people and the states powers not specifically granted to the federal government by the Constitution.

III. Hamilton's Domestic Policies, 1789–1794
    A. Hamilton and His Objectives
        Washington's secretary of the treasury, Alexander Hamilton, soon emerged as the leading figure in the administration. A strong nationalist, he had little faith in the common man. Hamilton advocated creating a strong central government and an economic environment attractive to investment. Private ambitions would serve the public welfare.

    B. Establishing the Nation's Credit
        Hamilton's "Report on the Public Credit," sent to Congress in January 1790, outlined a plan to establish the country's credit while at the same time wedding the upper classes to

government. He proposed that the federal government quickly pay off the outstanding foreign debt. Domestic holders of Revolutionary War bonds issued by the Continental Congress and the states could exchange them at full face value for new U.S. government bonds carrying 4 percent interest. Further, Hamilton urged Congress to maintain a perpetual debt, issuing new interest-bearing bonds as the old ones were retired. Hamilton hoped with these arrangements to provide former state creditors and other bondholders with a safe, attractive investment opportunity that would in turn give them a stake in the continued survival and economic health of the U.S. government. To pay for the interest on the domestic debt, Hamilton urged Congress to pass a tariff on imports and an excise tax on whiskey.

Repayment of foreign creditors aroused no opposition, but Hamilton's other proposals provoked bitter controversy. Most of the domestic Revolutionary War bond holders had long since sold their certificates to speculators for a fraction of their value. Now these speculators, mostly well-to-do northeasterners, stood to reap a fortune. The states that had already paid back their creditors also objected to the federal government's assuming the burden for states that had lagged in discharging their financial obligations, most of which were northern states, except South Carolina. James Madison led the southern congressional opposition to both proposals but was unable to defeat them. Hamilton garnered just enough southern votes to put through his assumption of state debt scheme by making a deal to round up northern votes for placing the nation's permanent capital on the Potomac, where the Virginians wanted it. Hamilton's measures dramatically improved America's credit rating but alienated many southerners.

C.   Creating a National Bank

Next Hamilton asked Congress to charter a national bank. The government would own one portion of its stock, and private individuals the rest. This bank would serve as a depository for federal tax receipts, make low-interest loans to the government, issue notes that would circulate as a national currency, regulate practices of state-chartered banks, and provide credit to expand the country's economy. The bank would, of course, further Hamilton's objective of tying rich businessmen to the federal government by affording them still another profitable investment.

Some government leaders began to see in Hamilton's bank and other proposals a disturbing pattern of favoring the interests of, and giving undue influence to, an elite group of investors. Led by Secretary of State Thomas Jefferson and Representative James Madison, opponents of the bank charter argued that it endangered the republic and was unconstitutional. When Congress passed the bill by a slim margin, a troubled President Washington asked Hamilton and Jefferson to advise him on the measure's constitutionality. The opinion each wrote presented the first clear-cut statements of the strict versus loose interpretations of the Constitution. Washington signed the bank bill into law.

D.   Emerging Partisanship

Beneficiaries of Hamilton's policies, including speculators, merchants, shippers, manufacturers, and other monied men of the port cities, rallied behind the administration in a budding political party calling itself Federalist. The Federalists had their strongest support in New England, New Jersey, and South Carolina. They also had many adherents in Pennsylvania and New York. But the agricultural interests of the South, West, and Middle Atlantic states saw no gains for themselves in Hamilton's programs. They began to coalesce in opposition to the administration and in favor of the "true principles" of republicanism, insinuating monarchical undertones existed in the Federalist camp. Washington appeared to remain above the factionalizing political landscape.

E.   The Whiskey Rebellion
To fund the assumption of state debts, Congress in March 1791 imposed a federal excise tax on domestically produced whiskey. Western Pennsylvania farmers who earned a little cash income by turning their surplus grain (which was too bulky to ship) into compact corn liquor for sale viewed the excise tax as an unfair levy. In July 1794 a mob of frontier farmers attacked U.S. marshals who had come west to serve summonses on sixty persons for nonpayment of the tax. Washington and Hamilton decided to crush this Whiskey Rebellion forcefully to demonstrate that citizens must obey federal law. Almost thirteen thousand militiamen marched west and rounded up rebellious farmers. Twenty were sent to Philadelphia for trial, and two received death sentences, but Washington later pardoned them.

IV.   The United States in a Wider World, 1789–1796
A.   Introduction
After 1793 the political polarization created by Hamilton's financial policies became even more pronounced as Americans argued over foreign policy.

B.   Spanish Power in Western North America
In the late eighteenth century Spanish ambitions to dominate much of North America revived. Spain built new presidios in what is now northern Mexico, New Mexico, and Texas and stationed more troops throughout the area. It also spread its settlements from Mexico up the coast of California. By doing so, Spain hoped to control trade with Asia and possess the Pacific Northwest, both of which were being challenged by the Russians, British, and Americans. What may have helped the most was the unwitting spreading of epidemic diseases, reducing native populations from about seventy-two thousand in 1770 to about eighteen hundred by 1830.

C.   Challenging American Expansion, 1789–1792
The greatest dangers to the United States in the trans-Appalachian west lay in British and Spanish assistance to Native Americans resisting settlers moving in and in the attempts of those foreign powers to detach the region from the rest of the United States. To counter this peril, the federal government, between 1791 and 1796, admitted Vermont, Kentucky, and Tennessee as new states. Both whites and Native Americans rejected Washington's efforts to "civilize" and integrate the eastern tribes into white society. The government instead continued to pressure the Indians to cede their lands and move farther west.

D.   France and Factional Politics, 1793
In 1789 the French Revolution began. Almost all Americans were initially sympathetic, but when the revolution became more radical and France went to war with Britain, Spain, and other European monarchies, opinion in this country divided. Western settlers and southern land speculators hoped a French victory would leave Britain and Spain too weak to keep stirring up Indians on America's frontier. However, northeastern merchants, shippers, and seamen were dependent on trade with England and feared a pro-French foreign policy would lead to British retaliation against U.S. commerce. These differences of opinion were voiced by the Republican and Federalist parties respectively. Meanwhile, the French ambassador, Edmond Genet, was actively recruiting Americans to fight for France. Instead of abiding by the 1778 treaty of alliance, however, Washington, in 1793, proclaimed U.S. neutrality.

E.   Diplomacy and War, 1793–1796
To discourage the pro-French activities of some Americans, the British began seizing U.S. merchant ships and impressing seamen, as well as stepping up their incitement of the Indians in the Ohio Valley. The Spanish also increased their incursion on American western lands. To halt the drift into war, Washington dispatched John Jay to England and Thomas Pinckney

to Spain. Jay's Treaty with England won few concessions except a British promise to evacuate their western forts, which owed much to Anthony Wayne's victory at the Battle of Fallen Timbers. Most southerners and westerners denounced Jay's Treaty, but a Federalist-dominated Senate ratified it to avoid war. Pinckney's dealing with Spain, which resulted in the Treaty of San Lorenzo, was more satisfactory, especially because it opened full use of the port of New Orleans to western farmers. Disagreements about foreign policy, especially ratification of Jay's Treaty, furthered the partisan split.

V. Parties and Politics, 1793–1800

   A.   Ideological Confrontation, 1793–1794

Horrified by the intensifying radicalism of the French revolution, the Federalists grew more suspicious of the common people and of unchecked democracy. But the Jeffersonian Republicans retained their sympathy for revolutionary France and did not fear popular participation in politics. Jefferson and Madison sought the support of ordinary citizens against Federalist policies by encouraging the publication of anti-administration newspapers like the *National Gazette*. They also approved of the democratic societies that were springing up in various locations.

   B.   The Republican Party, 1794–1796

By 1793 President Washington was clearly identified with the Federalists and Jefferson had resigned from the cabinet to lead the opposition. Republicans attacked the Federalists' pro-British leanings and won a slight majority in the House of Representatives. Federalist and Republican newspapers were engaged in a press war of exaggerated charges and countercharges. Stung by partisan criticism, Washington decided to retire after 1796. In his Farewell Address, he warned Americans to avoid political parties and entangling alliances with European countries. His decision not to run, however, opened the presidential election of 1796 to the first partisan contest.

   C.   The Election of 1796

The Republicans ran Thomas Jefferson; the Federalists, John Adams. The Federalists won control of Congress and the presidency by a narrow margin. As the second-highest vote-getter in the electoral college, Jefferson became the vice president (The Twelfth Amendment would later alter the process of the selection of vice presidents).

   D.   The French Crisis, 1798–1799

The French, angered by America's signing of Jay's Treaty with the British, began to seize U.S. merchant ships. Hoping to avoid war with France, President Adams sent a peace commission to Paris to negotiate. There, in what became known as the XYZ Affair, agents of the French government demanded a bribe as the price for negotiations. The affair outraged Americans and provoked an anti-French and anti-Republican backlash. Republican candidates were defeated in the 1798 congressional elections, and an undeclared naval war broke out with France.

   E.   The Alien and Sedition Acts, 1798

The Federalist-dominated Congress took advantage of the anti-French hysteria to push through a series of repressive measures known as the Alien and Sedition Acts, which aimed at silencing the opposition press and in other ways weakening the Republican Party. One measure attempted to rob the Republicans of the votes of their Irish-immigrant supporters by imposing a fourteen-year wait for citizenship. Under the Sedition Act, which made it a crime to speak, write, or print anything unfavorable about the government or the president that would bring him "into contempt or disrepute," the Federalists prosecuted and jailed a number of Republican journalists and political candidates. Madison and Jefferson fought back with the anonymously written Virginia and Kentucky Resolutions. Passed by the legislatures of those two states in 1798, the resolutions claimed that state governments could interpose themselves between their residents and the enforcement of unconstitutional federal laws such as the Alien and Sedition Acts. The resolutions set a precedent for the later states' rights position that states were the proper judges of federal actions and could nullify unconstitutional statues.

F.   The Election of 1800
The election took place in an atmosphere of tense and bitter partisanship. The Republicans nominated Jefferson and Aaron Burr for president and vice president. President Adams, running for a second term, greatly disappointed the "High Federalists" and hurt his own election prospects by reopening negotiations with France and thus quieting the war scare on which Federalist fortunes had thrived. The negotiations eventually patched things up with France and spared this nation an unnecessary war. The Republicans won the election, but Jefferson and Burr ended up tied for president because, under the Constitution as originally written, electors did not vote separately for president and vice president. The tie threw the election into the House of Representatives, which took thirty-six votes to name Jefferson president.

VI.   Economic and Social Change
A.   Producing for Markets
In colonial America the vast majority of whites lived and produced on small family-owned farms. Husbands, wives, children, and sometimes hired hands and/or servants grew and consumed their own food and made almost everything else they needed. Whatever little surplus the farm family accumulated, they traded with neighbors or merchants for items they could not fashion. By the 1780s, however, New England farms, with their thin, rocky soil, were insufficient to support burgeoning families. Grown sons and young couples moved west. Remaining daughters, wives, and sometimes husbands began supplementing their income by home manufacturing, for example, weaving cloth, sewing garments and shoes, and making nails. Merchants traveling into the countryside supplied them with the raw materials and later collected their output, paying them by the piece. This putting-out system was the forerunner of the industrial revolution. The merchants behind these innovations were also, in the 1780s and 1790s, opening the first banks and stock exchanges, preaching the need for the United States to industrialize, and supporting Hamilton's economic policies, which they saw as good for business.

B.   White Women in the Republic
The Revolution had brought little change in the status of women. However, the larger economic role that women began to play in the 1790s and the republican ideology did encourage a few advanced thinkers to call for women's equality. New Jersey briefly allowed women to vote. Women were generally permitted to choose their own husbands, and a small but increasing number of wives requested and were granted divorces. More educational opportunities opened for white women. These were justified by the argument that women had to be educated so they could inculcate republican virtues in their sons and daughters. But the organized fight for women's rights did not begin until the nineteenth century.

C.   Land and Culture: Native Americans
To halt the fraudulent land purchases obtained by many Americans, Congress enacted the Indian Trade and Intercourse Acts, which regulated the conduct of non-Indians on lands still under tribal control. But by 1795 eastern Indians had suffered devastating losses of land and population, and Indian culture was buckling under the strain of continual frontier warfare. Amongst the broken survivors, some sank into alcoholism while others simply moved or were absorbed into other Indian populations. Most still clung to their traditional ways.

Reformers, such as the Seneca prophet Handsome Lake, attempted to combat liquor and convince Iroquois men to become farmers. However, many Native Americans resisted further social change.

D.   African-American Struggles
As the revolutionary idealism that had eased out slavery in the North and won some rights for free blacks ebbed in the 1790s, the position of African-Americans deteriorated. In the late 1790s and early 1800s, states such as Delaware, Maryland, Kentucky, and New Jersey, which had earlier given freedmen the vote, rescinded it. Congress protected southern masters with the 1793 Fugitive Slave Law. White fears generated by the slave uprising in Saint Domingue and the 1800 Gabriel's Rebellion in Virginia further eroded sentiment for abolition and racial equality. The demand of the British textile industry for cotton and Eli Whitney's invention of the cotton gin in 1793 also revived southern plantation slavery, making the institution too profitable to question.

VII.   Conclusion
By 1801 the dangers of civil war and national disintegration had declined, if not disappeared. Two rival political parties had developed, but with the election of 1800 the nation managed a peaceful transfer of power from Federalists to Republicans. Slavery and racism, after some abatement, were again on the rise.

VOCABULARY

The following terms are used in Chapter 7. To understand the chapter fully, it is important that you know what each of them means.

speculator	a person trading in land, commodities, or stocks and bonds in the hope of profiting from changes in the market price; one who engages in business transactions involving considerable risk but offering large gains
secession	formal withdrawal from an association, as in states withdrawing from the union
entrepreneurs	persons who develop and carry out new economic enterprises
journeyman	a person who has served an apprenticeship in a trade and who works at it for another
tariff	a tax imposed on products imported from abroad
excise tax	a tax levied on goods and services manufactured, sold, or offered within the country
ex post facto law	a law criminalizing previously legal actions and punishing those who have been engaging in such actions
bill of attainder	a legislative act proclaiming a person's guilt and stipulating punishment without a judicial trial
insurrection	uprising; revolution
privateer	a privately owned and manned armed vessel commissioned by a government in time of war to fight the enemy, especially its commercial shipping

impress	force into service, as with a seaman; to seize or take for public use or service
constituents	the voters and residents of a district, state, or country whom an elected official represents
abomination	an object greatly disliked or hated; a horror
demagoguery	using the methods or practices of a demagogue, a leader who uses the passions or prejudices of the people for his or her own interests; using the methods or practices of an unprincipled popular orator or agitator
partisan	a supporter of a political party or cause; actions motivated by support of a political party or cause
cabal	a small group of secret plotters
libelous	writing that contains damaging or malicious misrepresentation
emoluments	profits or rewards arising from office, such as government service
ideology	body of beliefs
Sedition	the incitement of discontent or rebellion against the government; action or language promoting such discontent or rebellion

IDENTIFICATIONS

After reading Chapter 7, you should be able to identify and explain the historical significance of each of the following:

Judiciary Act of 1789

Bill of Rights

Hamilton's "Report on the Public Credit," 1790

James Madison

Hamilton's "Report on a National Bank"

Hamilton's Report on Manufactures

strict versus loose interpretation and the "necessary and proper" clause of the Constitution

Federalists versus Republicans

Whiskey Rebellion

citizen Edmond Genet

Jay's Treaty

Treaty of San Lorenzo (Pinckney's Treaty)

Washington's farewell address

XYZ Affair

Quasi-War with France

Alien and Sedition Acts, 1798

Virginia and Kentucky resolutions, 1798

interposition and nullification

election of 1800

Jefferson-Burr tie

"republican motherhood"

Handsome Lake

Richard Allen and Absalom Jones

Fugitive Slave Law, 1793

Saint Domingue (Haiti) slave uprising

Gabriel Prosser and Gabriel's Rebellion, 1800

Eli Whitney and the cotton gin

SKILL BUILDING: CHARTS AND GRAPHS

Look at the chart titled "Number and Percentage of Free Blacks, by State, 1800" on page 216 of the textbook. By studying that bar graph, you should be able to answer the following questions:

1. Had the revolutionary ideology of the Declaration of Independence resulted in the freeing of most African-Americans?

2. Had slavery been totally eliminated in any state by 1800?

3. Which northern states had made the least progress in eliminating slavery by 1800?

4. Which southern or border states had made the most progress in eliminating slavery by 1800? Which had made the least?

5. In which four states did the bulk of free blacks live in 1800?

HISTORICAL SOURCES

In Chapter 7 the author discusses the birth and development of opposing political parties. One source for historians writing on this topic is the newspapers that aligned themselves with either the Federalist or Republican Party, like the *Gazette of the United States* and the *National Gazette*. Early in the Washington administration, Alexander Hamilton helped set up John Fenno's *Gazette of the United States* to build public opinion behind the treasury secretary's financial program. James Madison countered in the 1790s by encouraging his friend Philip Freneau to establish the *National Gazette* to arouse the people against Federalist policies. How is the author of Chapter 7 using these historical sources? Can the historian rely on these newspapers for accurate, unbiased reporting of events in the 1790s? If not, why is the press of the 1790s still a valuable historical source?

On page 218 Gabriel's Rebellion of 1800 is discussed and a statement of one of the rebels is quoted. Where do historians gain this information? Gabriel Prosser and thirty-five of his followers were tried. James Monroe, then governor of Virginia, questioned Prosser about the uprising. Prosser would say little, but some of his codefendants did testify about their plans, motives, and intentions. These records are preserved in "Documents Relating to the Trial and Execution of Gabriel" in the Virginia State Historical Library. Such state historical archives afford historians much of the material they use to learn about the past.

MULTIPLE-CHOICE QUESTIONS

Circle the letter of the item that best completes each statement or answers the question.

1. The main purpose of the Alien and Sedition Acts was to
   a. publicize the activities of French revolutionaries in the United States.
   b. strengthen the policy of neutrality.
   c. strengthen the Republican Party.
   d. suppress the Republican opposition to Federalist policies.

2. Hamilton wanted the federal government to take over in full the Revolutionary War debt of the Continental Congress and the states because he believed that
   a. this would cause a heavy loss to speculators in certificates.
   b. the payment of all such obligations was guaranteed in the Constitution.
   c. this would cause well-to-do creditors to favor the new federal government and the extension of its powers.
   d. the states unanimously favored such a policy.

3. Hamilton's financial program was designed to do all of the following *except*
   a. gain the support of the commercial classes for the new national government.
   b. encourage the rapid industrialization of the United States.
   c. pay off the national debt as quickly as possible.
   d. establish the credit of the United States at home and abroad.

4. Hamilton's national bank
   a. provoked the first clear-cut argument over the strict versus loose interpretation of the Constitution.
   b. was a fully government-owned-and-operated institution.
   c. helped the United States retire its old revolutionary debt as quickly as possible.
   d. all of the above.

5. The XYZ Affair
   a. arose out of the French government's demand for a bribe as the price of negotiating.
   b. increased the popularity of the Republican Party and hurt the fortunes of the Federalists.
   c. was provoked by Hamilton to increase the popularity of the Washington administration.
   d. arose out of the Whiskey Rebellion.

6. The Virginia and Kentucky Resolutions
   a. attacked the Alien and Sedition Acts.
   b. were written by Madison and Jefferson.
   c. claimed the right of a state to protect its people from unconstitutional federal laws.
   d. all of the above.

7. Speculators were able to take advantage of which of these Federalist measures?
   a. The excise tax
   b. The refunding of the national debt by paying full face value of Revolutionary War bonds
   c. The tariff
   d. Placing the federal capital on land donated by Virginia and Maryland

8. Which action of President John Adams angered the "High Federalists"?
   a. His handling of the XYZ Affair
   b. His signing of the Alien and Sedition Acts
   c. His decision to improve relations with France in 1799–1800
   d. His request for a larger army

9. Which of these people would probably *not* be a supporter of Jefferson's Republican party?
   a. A Virginia planter
   b. A Boston merchant
   c. A western Pennsylvania farmer
   d. A recent Irish immigrant

10. Which of the following people scored a victory over the Indians that opened Ohio to white settlement and won a promise by the British to evacuate forts in the Northwest Territory?
    a. Gabriel Prosser
    b. Anthony Wayne
    c. Stephen Girard
    d. Matthew Lyon

SHORT-ANSWER QUESTIONS

1. What problems in the West faced the new federal government in 1789?

2. Briefly describe the drafting, content, and ratification of the Bill of Rights.

3. Explain Hamilton's reasoning in support of a loose interpretation of the U.S. Constitution and Jefferson's in defense of a strict interpretation.

4. Why did farmers in western Pennsylvania object to the excise tax on whiskey? How did the Washington administration deal with their rebellion? Why?

5. Why did President Washington make his Farewell Address? What advice did it offer his fellow citizens?

6. What happened to eastern Indians in the 1790s and early 1800s, and why?

7. Explain the reasons for heightened racism and declining abolitionist sentiment in the 1790s and early 1800s.

ESSAY QUESTIONS

1. Discuss the rise of political parties in the United States. Did the Constitution provide for political parties? If not, when and why did the first two parties develop? Who led and supported each party?

2. Discuss the economic and financial programs of Secretary of the Treasury Alexander Hamilton. What did they include? What was Hamilton trying to accomplish? How and why did his programs politically divide Americans?

3. Discuss the deteriorating positions of African-Americans and Native Americans in the post–Revolutionary War period. How do you account for the deterioration? What were the major changes or events that marked the declining status of each group?

4. Explain how differences over foreign policy in the period 1789–1800 encouraged the development of political parties and partisanship.

5. Discuss the dangers the nation faced during the Federalist era (1789–1800) and how it overcame or survived them. In your answer be sure to include conflict among social, economic, and sectional interest groups; challenges from foreign nations; and threats to individual liberties and the Bill of Rights.

ANSWERS TO MULTIPLE-CHOICE QUESTIONS

1. d
2. c
3. c
4. a
5. a
6. d
7. b
8. c
9. b
10. b

Jeffersonianism and the Era of Good Feelings, 1801–1824

OUTLINE AND SUMMARY

I.   Introduction

On March 4, 1801, Thomas Jefferson, without fanfare, walked to the Capitol and took the oath of office as president. His actions reflected his belief that the "pomp and circumstance" in which Washington and Adams had engaged ill-fitted republican government. Despite the partisan bitterness of the election of 1800, Jefferson, in his inaugural address, attempted to conciliate Federalists by emphasizing the principles on which most Americans agreed—federalism and republicanism.

The period 1801 to 1823 would see major changes, if not the reconciliation Jefferson hoped for. The Federalist Party would slowly die out, and the Republicans would be rent by factionalism. Renewed war in Europe would again endanger America and open opportunities. Taking advantage of these, the United States would acquire new territory that doubled its size. However, sectional strife over statehood for Missouri would nearly tear that expanded nation apart.

Chapter 8 addresses these questions: (1) How did Jefferson's philosophy shape policy toward public expenditures, the judiciary, and Louisiana? (2) What led James Madison to go to war with Britain in 1812? (3) How did the War of 1812 influence American domestic politics? (4) To what extent did Jefferson's legacy persist into the Era of Good Feelings?

II. The Age of Jefferson, 1801–1805

A.   Jefferson and Jeffersonianism

Thomas Jefferson; intellectual, scientist, architect, inventor, and statesman, was a complex, contradictory, and gifted individual. Author of the Declaration of Independence's bold statement about the equality of all men, he, nevertheless, doubted that blacks and whites could live side by side on terms of equality. Despite his opposition to racially mixing black and white blood, his political enemies charged that he himself had fathered the children of his slave Sally Hemings. Recent DNA evidence from Sally's male heirs appears to support the story.

Jefferson distrusted power concentrated in the federal government as a danger to republican liberty, preferring the state governments, which he saw as closer and more responsive to the people. Republican liberty could best be retained by a virtuous and vigilant citizenry that put the public good ahead of selfish private interests. To Jefferson, the group that displayed those qualities was educated small farmers. Cities and their landless inhabitants, on the other hand, were a potential menace to the republic.

B.   Jefferson's "Revolution"

Jefferson attempted to repeal Federalist measures that he felt were a danger to the simple republic, such as parts of Alexander Hamilton's economic program and the Alien and Sedition Acts. He reduced taxes and the national debt, primarily by slashing expenditures for the army and for the diplomatic establishment. In these ways he felt he was lifting an economic burden from hardworking farmers.

C.   Jefferson and the Judiciary
Although Jefferson was willing to cooperate with the moderate Federalists in many ways, he demanded that Congress repeal the Federalist-sponsored Judiciary Act of 1801 and remove the partisan Federalist judges that outgoing President Adams had appointed in his last hours as president. Jefferson had little success with impeachment of Federalist judges, however, gaining only one conviction and removal from the bench. The reason was that the majority in Congress apparently viewed the impeachment process as an inappropriate way to solve the problem of partisan judges. Jefferson's drive to keep additional Federalists out of the judiciary led to the landmark Supreme Court case of *Marbury* v. *Madison*. Chief Justice John Marshall used the case to significantly strengthen the power of the judicial branch. He claimed that federal courts had the right to review laws passed by Congress—the right of judicial review. For the first time, the Supreme Court declared a portion of a law passed by Congress unconstitutional. Jefferson did not oppose the concept of judicial review, but he believed that judges should not use it for partisan purposes.

D.   The Louisiana Purchase
Napoleon Bonaparte forced Spain to cede the Louisiana Territory to France. The French action alarmed Jefferson because it placed a major European power on the U.S. border and blocked the gradual expansion of the United States. The problem became especially pressing in 1802, when Spanish authorities, just before the territory's transfer to France, denied western farmers use of the port of New Orleans. Jefferson sent James Monroe and Robert R. Livingston to France with a request to buy the city. Napoleon, frustrated by uprisings in French Caribbean colonies, countered with an offer to sell the entire Louisiana Territory for $15 million. Since the Constitution did not explicitly give the federal government the power to acquire new territories and since Jefferson was wedded to strict interpretation, he briefly thought of first seeking an enabling amendment to the Constitution. His political acumen and desire to make land available to small farmers, the "backbone of the nation," won out, however, and he submitted the purchase treaty to the Senate, where it was quickly ratified.

E.   The Election of 1804
Republicans in Congress renominated Jefferson for president and dropped Aaron Burr in favor of George Clinton for vice president. The Federalists chose Charles C. Pickney and Rufus King. The successes of Jefferson's first term—doubling the size of the United States, maintaining peace, and reducing taxes and the national debt—won over many former Federalist voters, resulting in an overwhelming Republican victory.

F.   The Lewis and Clark Expedition
Jefferson requested funding from Congress for an expedition across the continent to explore the new Louisiana Purchase. They were charged with the difficult task of opening trade relations with unknown numbers of Indian tribes across the plains and northwest, bringing Americans into contact for the first time with the Mandan, Hidatsas, and Arikaras, as well as the powerful Sioux. The party, led by Meriwether Lewis and William Clark, left St. Louis in 1804; followed the Missouri, Snake, and Columbia rivers; crossed the Rockies; and reached the Pacific. They would not have returned safely if not for the priceless guidance and comfort offered by numerous Indian nations along the trail. The Corps of Discovery returned with a wealth of scientific information (and some misinformation), descriptions, and maps that stimulated interest in the West.

III.   The Gathering Storm, 1805–1812
    A.   Introduction
        Jefferson's second term as president was beset by problems caused by the breakdown of
        Republican Party unity and the renewal of the Napoleonic Wars.

    B.   Challenges on the Home Front
        Aaron Burr, Jefferson's first-term vice president, stirred up factionalism within the
        Republican Party. Jefferson believed that Burr was the chief plotter in a conspiracy to
        separate the western states from the Union. The president had Burr arrested and tried for
        treason. At the trial, over which John Marshall presided, the jury found the charges "not
        proved."

        Jefferson also was attacked by another faction of Republicans known as the Quids and led
        by John Randolph. They criticized the president's handling of the Yazoo land scandal and
        other actions that they saw as compromising "republican virtue".

    C.   The Suppression of American Trade and Impressment
        The British and French, at war with each other, forbade American ships from entering each
        other's ports and trading with the other side. Both powers seized U.S. ships, but the actions
        of the British caused greater harm because they had the larger navy and their warships often
        hovered just off the U.S. coast. Also, the British removed sailors on American ships and
        forced (pressed) them into service in the Royal Navy. When the British warship HMS
        Leopard attacked the American frigate USS *Chesapeake* near the Virginia coast and
        impressed four of its crewman, the country was outraged, but Jefferson still sought to avoid
        war.

    D.   The Embargo Act of 1807
        Jefferson persuaded Congress to pass an embargo as a means of "peaceable coercion. " He
        hoped that U.S. refusal to export any goods or to buy any products from abroad would put
        sufficient economic pressure on Britain and France to make them respect U.S. neutral rights.
        Unfortunately, the cutoff of trade did not hurt them enough to change their actions, but it
        proved disastrous to the U.S. economy. Seamen were unemployed; merchants and farmers
        who depended on foreign sales were ruined. The impact was hardest on New England. An
        unintended consequence of the embargo was to encourage the transfer of capital into
        domestic manufacturing, a development Jefferson had initially opposed.

    E.   James Madison and the Failure of "Peaceable Coercion"
        The unpopularity of the embargo, especially in New England, revived the Federalist Party.
        In 1808 it nominated Charles C. Pinckney to run against Republican James Madison.
        Although the Federalists carried much of New England, Madison won because of continued
        Republican strength in other sections.

        Just before Jefferson left office, Congress repealed the embargo and replaced it with the
        weaker Non-Intercourse Act. This law worked no better than the previous one. For the next
        year and a half, President Madison tried variations on the theme of peaceable coercion, such
        as Macon's Bill No. 2, but all failed to change British and French behavior.

        By 1810 Madison faced increasing pressure from Republican congressional representatives
        from the South and West who demanded a more aggressive policy toward Britain and
        France. These "war hawks" resented the insults to American honor and blamed the
        interference in trade for the economic recession hitting their home states.

F.   Tecumseh and the Prophet

The war hawks wanted the British to get out of Canada, partly because they believed the British were arming and inciting the Indians on the American frontier. Tecumseh and his brother Tenskwatawa, the Prophet, were two Shawnees attempting to unite the tribes of Ohio and Indiana against white settlers. They initially had no connection with the British, but after William Henry Harrison attacked the Prophet's town and won the battle at Tippecanoe, Tecumseh did join forces with England.

G.   Congress Votes for War

Madison, on June 1, 1812, asked Congress to declare war on England. The vote reflected party and sectional splits. Most of the no votes came from New England Federalists, while the majority of Republicans passed the declaration. The United States declared war in 1812 because of Britain's incitement of the Indians, the belief that continuing British restrictions on U.S. shipping were causing the recession in the South and West, and Madison's view that England intended to ruin America as a commercial rival.

IV.   The War of 1812

A.   On to Canada

In 1812 American attempts to conquer Canada failed. The British took Detroit and were routed only by Oliver H. Perry's victory on Lake Erie and William Henry Harrison's success in 1813 at the Battle of the Thames.

B.   The British Offensive

In 1814 the British landed on the shores of Chesapeake Bay and marched to Washington, which they captured and burned. After they failed to take Baltimore, they broke off the campaign.

C.   The Treaty of Ghent

U.S. and British commissioners met at Ghent, in Belgium, to make peace. The British, playing on their superior military position, demanded territory from the United States; when the Americans refused, the British, realizing that they no longer controlled the Great Lakes, backed down. In December 1814 they signed a treaty with the United States that restored the prewar status quo. The United States' resounding victory at the Battle of New Orleans, fought two weeks after the treaty was concluded, had no bearing on the terms of the Treaty of Ghent, but provided an uplifting ending for Americans.

D.   The Hartford Convention

The unpopularity of the war in the Northeast contributed to the revival of the Federalists. In the election of 1812, antiwar Republicans and Federalists supported De Witt Clinton for president against Madison. Although Madison won reelection, Clinton carried most of the Northeast. American military losses intensified Federalist discontent to the point that, in the fall of 1814, a group of party members from New England convened at Hartford, Connecticut, and passed resolutions aimed at strengthening their region's power within the Union. Their timing could not have been worse, coinciding with the end of the war and news of Jackson's victory in New Orleans silenced Federalist criticism. Public disapproval of the Hartford Convention led to the rapid demise of the Federalist Party. In the election of 1816, the Republican presidential nominee, James Monroe, scored an easy victory over his Federalist opponent. In 1820 Monroe won reelection with every electoral vote but one.

V.   The Awakening of American Nationalism

A.   Madison's Nationalism and the Era of Good Feelings, 1817–1824

The postwar period, characterized by a heightened spirit of nationalism and a new political consensus, has been called the Era of Good Feelings. As the Federalist party disappeared, the Republicans, to make the nation more economically self-sufficient, enacted many of the measures that the Federalists had earlier supported. Among these were the chartering of a new national bank and help for domestic manufacturing with a protective tariff. The sectional harmony started to break down almost immediately, however, because of the issue of slavery and its spread westward.

B. John Marshall and the Supreme Court
During the Era of Good Feelings, Chief Justice John Marshall wrote opinions that strengthened the power of the federal government at the expense of state sovereignty. Among these were *Dartmouth College* v. *Woodward,* which forbade state interference with contracts, and *McCulloch* v. *Maryland,* which favored the Hamiltonian broad interpretation of the Constitution and prohibited states from interfering with the exercise of federal powers.

C. The Missouri Compromise, 1820–1821
National harmony crumbled in the 1819 controversy over Missouri's application for statehood. For the first time, bitter sectional debate took place over the issue of the spread of slavery because the institution had become embroiled in political and economic issues dividing North and South. Admitting Missouri as a slave or free state would upset the balance of eleven free and eleven slave states that existed in 1819 and would give one section of the country a political advantage. The issue was settled for the time being when Congress in 1820 approved the Missouri Compromise: (1) Missouri entered the Union as a slave state; (2) Maine entered as a free state; (3) in the remainder of the Louisiana Territory slavery would be permitted only south of 36°30' latitude, the southern boundary of Missouri.

D. Foreign Policy Under Monroe
Under the leadership of President James Monroe and his able secretary of state, John Quincy Adams, the United States achieved several foreign-policy successes. Good relations with the British were cemented by the Rush-Bagot Treaty and the British-American Convention. In the 1819 Adams-Onís Treaty, Spain ceded East Florida to the United States and renounced its claims to West Florida.

E. The Monroe Doctrine
In December 1823 President Monroe proclaimed a policy later known as the Monroe Doctrine. Mostly written by John Quincy Adams, its purpose was to discourage European powers from helping Spain regain her lost colonies in the Americas while, at the same time, reserving the right of the United States to expand further in the Western Hemisphere. The Monroe Doctrine stated that (1) the United States would not become involved in strictly European affairs, (2) the American continents were not available for further European colonization, and (3) the United States would look upon any attempt by European countries to regain lost colonies or to interfere in the Americas as an "unfriendly act."

VI. Conclusion
In the election of 1800 the Republicans gained control of the federal government. President Jefferson in his first term cut government spending and taxes, protested Federalist stacking of the judiciary, and purchased Louisiana. His second term was beset by factionalism within his party and foreign difficulties as Britain and France, again at war, both violated U.S. neutral rights. When the policy of "peaceable coercion," initiated by Jefferson and followed by Madison, failed, Congress declared war on Britain. The War of 1812 caused sectional divisions. Federalist denunciation of the war at the Hartford Convention hastened the demise of the party. The remaining Republicans, anxious to make America economically self-sufficient, passed many of the nationalist measures once advocated by Hamiltonian Federalists: a new national bank, federally supported internal improvements, and protective tariffs. Even U.S. foreign policy,

especially the Monroe Doctrine, reflected assertive nationalism. However, national harmony shattered as Congress battled over the spread of slavery and Missouri's admission as a slave state.

VOCABULARY

The following terms are used in Chapter 8. To understand the chapter fully, it is important that you know what each of them means.

infidel	an unbeliever; one who does not accept a particular religion, such as Christianity
writ	a legal order in writing
Judicial review	the right of the federal courts to declare legislative acts unconstitutional
impeach	charge a public official, such as a judge or president, with misconduct in office; an impeachment is equivalent to an indictment, not to a conviction
Caucus	a meeting of political party members to nominate candidates and/or decide on other party actions
internal improvements	roads, canals, and other projects to improve transportation and communication
consensus	a general agreement

IDENTIFICATIONS

After reading Chapter 8, you should be able to identify and explain the historical significance of each of the following:

Tripolitan (Barbary) pirates

Judiciary Act of 1801

midnight judges

Marbury v. *Madison*

John Marshall

Lewis and Clark Expedition

Sacajawea

Aaron Burr and James Wilkerson conspiracy

British Orders in Council and Napoleon's Continental System

impressment

Chesapeake-Leopard Affair

Embargo and Non-Intercourse acts

war hawks, John C. Calhoun, and Henry Clay

Tecumseh and the Prophet

William Henry Harrison and the Battles of Tippecanoe and the Thames

Oliver H. Perry and the Battle of Lake Erie

Treaty of Ghent and the *status quo ante bellum*

Battle of New Orleans

Hartford Convention

Era of Good Feelings

Dartmouth College v. *Woodward*

McCulloch v. *Maryland*

Missouri Compromise

John Quincy Adams

Rush-Bagot Treaty and British-American Convention, 1818

Adams-Onís, or Transcontinental, Treaty

Monroe Doctrine

SKILL BUILDING: MAPS

On the map of the United States, locate each of the places listed below. How is each connected with one or more of the following historical events: U.S. treaties with Spain and France, Lewis and Clark expedition, War of 1812, sectional conflict and compromise?

East and West Florida

New Orleans

Louisiana Territory

Appalachian Mountains

Mississippi River

Missouri River

Snake River

Columbia River

St. Louis

Ohio River

Indiana Territory

Lake Erie and Lake Champlain

Chesapeake Bay

36°30' latitude

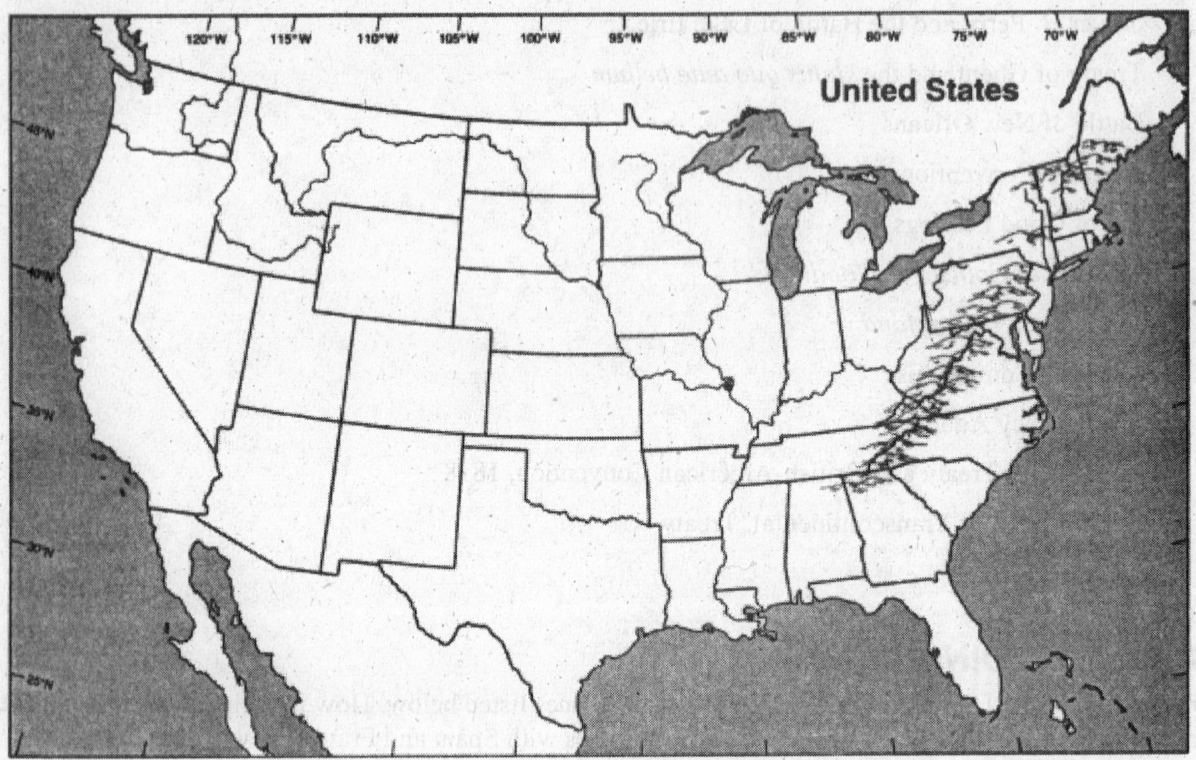

HISTORICAL SOURCES

The author of Chapter 8 discusses the reasons for America's declaration of war on England and the sectional controversies over that war. How does the historian know which congressional representatives from which states voted for war? How does the author know that John C. Calhoun and other southern and western representatives believed that British policy was damaging America's economy, or that President Madison attributed British actions to their desire to monopolize trade? The historian can read the speeches of senators and representatives and find the record of their votes in the *Debates and Proceedings in the Congress of the United States,* often cited as *Annals of Congress,* printed by the U.S. government. Madison's statement about British motives was part of his war message to Congress. Like all public communications of U.S. presidents, it is published in the multivolume *A Compilation of the Messages and Papers of the Presidents.*

Pages 227-229 of Chapter 8 give an account of the Lewis and Clark expedition. How did the author find out about the adventures of the party, the role of Sacagawea, and the mass of scientific information and some tall tales that Lewis and Clark brought back with them? Much of what we know about the expedition and its findings comes from the journals kept by Meriwether Lewis and William Clark, first published in 1814. Probably the definitive edition of the record of Lewis and Clark's trip is the eight-volume *Original Journals of the Lewis and Clark Expedition, 1804–1806*, edited by Reuben Gold Thwaites and published in 1904–1905. A single-volume, abridged version, *The Journals of Lewis and Clark*, edited by Bernard De Voto, is available for the general reader who would like to taste the flavor of this valuable historical source.

Now look at the section of Chapter 8 called "Mapping America," in which the author discusses how and why maps were made during the first quarter of the nineteenth century, including one of the Louisiana Territory drawn by William Clark. In this essay the author is using these early maps as historical sources. What historical insights can be gained from these maps?

MULTIPLE-CHOICE QUESTIONS

Circle the letter of the item that best completes each statement or answers the question.

1. Between 1800 and 1823, the United States did all of the following *except*

    a. fight a second war against Britain.
    b. extend the right to vote to women and blacks.
    c. double in territorial size.
    d. warn European powers not to claim new colonies in the Americas.

2. Thomas Jefferson believed that

    a. educated farmers were the most virtuous citizens and best upholders of republican liberty.
    b. state governments had too much power, and the federal government had not enough.
    c. the United States should develop prosperous cities, filled with new industries.
    d. the rich should pay heavier taxes so that government could provide more social services for the poor.

3. Chief Justice John Marshall's opinions backed

    a. a broad definition of treason that made it easier to convict the accused.
    b. a narrow interpretation of the Constitution, denying that the federal government had any powers beyond those enumerated in the document.
    c. the right of federal courts to declare acts of Congress unconstitutional.
    d. the doctrine that states could nullify illegal actions of the federal government.

4. The Embargo Act

    a. badly damaged the British economy.
    b. stimulated the growth of manufacturing in the United States.
    c. convinced the French to drop their trade restrictions against the United States.
    d. was favored by New England but resisted in the South.

5. By the terms of the Treaty of Ghent, ending the War of 1812,

    a. the United States gained Florida and some territory from Canada.
    b. the British agreed to stop impressment and other violations of U.S. neutral rights.
    c. neither the United States nor Britain gained territory or made concessions.
    d. the British agreed to evacuate New Orleans and compensate the United States for burning Washington.

6. The war hawks were

    a. mostly from New England.
    b. eager for war against Napoleon to gain the Louisiana Territory.
    c. supporters of Jefferson's and Madison's policy of economic coercion.
    d. Republicans from the West and South who wanted to take Canada from Britain and Florida from Spain.

7. Which of the following occurred during Madison's presidency?

    a. The United States sent a naval squadron against the Barbary pirates of North Africa.
    b. Congress chartered a second national bank.
    c. The United States bought Florida from Spain.
    d. Congress passed the embargo.

8. Secretary of State John Quincy Adams is associated with which of the following foreign-policy initiatives?

    a. Purchasing Texas from Mexico
    b. Purchasing Louisiana
    c. Formulating the Monroe Doctrine and purchasing Florida
    d. British sale of the Oregon Territory to the United States for $15 million

9. During the Era of Good Feelings
    a. the Federalist Party disappeared but the Republican Party adopted some of its policies.
    b. the United States won a war against England.
    c. sectional and partisan conflicts became more acute.
    d. President Monroe signed new treaties of alliance and friendship with Britain and France.
10. During the War of 1812,
    a. the United States successfully occupied Canada.
    b. the British captured Baltimore, Maryland.
    c. Tecumseh, the Prophet, and their Indian followers proved valuable allies to the Americans against the British.
    d. the northeastern states became increasingly unhappy about the war.

SHORT-ANSWER QUESTIONS

1. Explain what the Federalists were trying to accomplish with passage of the Judiciary Act of 1801 and appointment of the midnight judges.

2. Explain why Napoleon first forced Spain to cede Louisiana to France, and then turned around and offered to sell the territory to the United States.

3. Why did President Jefferson want to buy Louisiana from France? Why did the purchase pose a dilemma for him? How did he justify the purchase?

4. What happened at the Hartford Convention in 1814? What impact did it have on the Federalist Party? Why?

5. Why did Missouri's request for statehood touch off a sectional crisis? How was the crisis resolved, at least, in the short run?

ESSAY QUESTIONS

1. Compare and contrast the political and economic views of the Hamiltonian Federalists and the Jeffersonian Republicans. When, why, and how did the differences between the two parties blur?

2. Thomas Jefferson's first term as president was so successful that he overwhelmingly won reelection in 1804. His second term, in contrast, was marked by frustration and failure. Discuss the achievements of Jefferson's first term and the problems that beset his second.

3. Discuss the foreign-policy achievements of President James Monroe and his secretary of state, John Quincy Adams. How do those achievements still affect the United States and its foreign policy today?

4. Why did the United States engage in a nearly disastrous war against the British from 1812 to 1814? What, if anything, did the United States gain from that war?

5. Jefferson once wrote, "What is practicable must often control pure theory." In light of that statement assess Jefferson's actions as president. How much of his policies can be explained by his philosophy of government? How much by compromise with what was practicable?

ANSWERS TO MULTIPLE-CHOICE QUESTIONS

1. b
2. a
3. c
4. b
5. c
6. d
7. b
8. c
9. a
10. d

CHAPTER 9

The Transformation of American Society, 1815–1840

OUTLINE AND SUMMARY

I. Introduction

Chapter 9 discusses the economic and social changes that took place in the United States between 1815 and 1840. Some of the questions it attempts to answer are: (1) What caused the upsurge of westward migration after he War of 1812? (2) How did the rise of the market economy affect where Americans lived and how they made their living? (3) What caused the rise of industrialization? (4) What caused urban poverty in this period?

II. Western Expansion

A. The Sweep West

The sweep of population westward had by 1821 added the states of Vermont, Kentucky, Tennessee, Ohio, Louisiana, Indiana, Mississippi, Illinois, Alabama, Maine, and Missouri to the Union. Between 1790 and 1820 pioneer families clustered near the navigable rivers, but it was not until the coming of canals and railroads in the 1820s and 1830s they could afford to fan out a bit. Westerners also tended to settle near others who had come from the same region back east.

B. Western Society and Customs

Before 1830 life in the West was crude and difficult. Easterners often looked down on westerners' lack of refinement, and westerners in turn resented eastern pretensions to gentility.

C. The Far West

While most pioneers prior to 1840 settled between the Appalachian Mountains and the Mississippi River, a few adventurous souls traveled across the continent. New York merchant John Jacob Astor established a fur-trading post in the Oregon Territory as early as 1811, and hardy "mountain men" like Jedidiah Smith trapped animals on the Great Plains and beyond.

D. The Federal Government and the West

Midwestern settlement was encouraged by the Ordinance of 1785; the Northwest Ordinance; the Louisiana Purchase; the Transcontinental Treaty of 1819; the land warrants given to War of 1812 veterans; the extension of the National Road into Illinois by 1838; and the removal and declining strength of the Indians, who by 1820 no longer received Spanish and British aid.

E. The Removal of the Indians

By the 1820s the Cherokees, Creeks, Choctaws, and Seminoles of the South were under heavy pressure to cede their lands to whites. In 1830 Andrew Jackson pushed through Congress the Indian Removal Act, which granted the president the power to move all Native Americans, by force if necessary, west of the Mississippi River. The Creeks in Georgia and Alabama had already started to migrate by that point, and in 1836 the remainder were forced out. The Choctaws and Chickasaws suffered a similar fate. After losing a war of resistance that lasted from 1835 to 1842, most Seminoles also were expelled from Florida. The Cherokees, the most assimilated of the Indians, appealed to the U.S. Supreme Court for protection. Although Chief Justice John Marshall ruled in their favor, President Jackson ignored the court and compelled the tribe to cede its land and travel the "Trail of Tears" westward. After putting up some futile resistance in the Black Hawk War, the Sac, Fox, and other Midwest and Northeast Indians also had to move west of the Mississippi.

F.   The Agricultural Boom
The removal of the Indians and the high prices and escalating demand for wheat and corn drew more whites than ever into the old Northwest. Eli Whitney's invention of the cotton gin in 1793 and the boundless need of the British textile industry for raw cotton had similar results in the old Southwest. After the War of 1812, southeasterners poured into Alabama and Mississippi, driving land prices skyward and tripling the nation's cotton production. By 1836 cotton accounted for two-thirds of America's foreign exports.

III. The Growth of the Market Economy
A.   Introduction
High crop prices after the War of 1812 tempted more farmers than ever before to switch from subsistence to commercial agriculture. Commercial agriculture opened new opportunities for western farmers, but it also exposed them to greater risks. Many had to borrow money to buy land and to survive until they could sell their first crops. Once in debt, the commercial farmers were particularly vulnerable because they had no control over fluctuations in price, supply, and demand in world markets.

B.   Federal Land Policy
Jeffersonian Republicans introduced land policies aimed at a speedy transfer of the public domain to small farmers. Between 1800 and 1820, the government cut the minimum price per acre and the minimum number of acres that could be purchased. However, most government land was sold at auction, and speculators, believing it would soon shoot up in value, often bid the price up far above the minimum. The easy availability of credit encouraged this speculation.

C.   The Speculator and the Squatter
Many poor settlers who did not have the money to buy at auction simply squatted on government land. They exerted mounting pressure on Congress to grant them preemption rights over speculators and finally won their demand in 1841. Squatters, wanting to accumulate the cash to buy their farms, quickly turned to commercial agriculture. Many western farmers, after exhausting the soil's fertility growing cash crops, simply moved on to new land.

D.   The Panic of 1819
The land boom soon collapsed and crop and western land prices plummeted. Many speculators were ruined in the panic and depression of 1819. The National Bank tightened credit and called in the notes of the overextended western banks, many of which failed. The hard times experienced by agriculture and industry had long-term political effects. Many westerners hated the National Bank, blaming it for the crisis, and western farmers intensified their search for internal improvements that would cut transportation expenses for shipping their product to market.

E.   The Transportation Revolution: Steamboats, Canals, and Railroads
Before 1820 available transportation facilities were unsatisfactory. Existing roads were adequate for transporting people, but moving bulky loads over them by horse-drawn wagons was slow and costly. The great rivers west of the Appalachian Mountains that flowed north

to south became two-way streets for commerce when the steamboat, invented by Robert Fulton, was introduced to them. By 1855, 727 steamboats were providing regular ferry service on all the western rivers. However, rivers did not always exist where they were most needed for trade. Therefore, Americans in the 1820s began to build canals. Between 1817 and 1825, the State of New York constructed the 363-mile Erie Canal connecting Albany on the Hudson River with Buffalo on Lake Erie. The canal lowered freight rates to a fraction of what they had been and made New York City a leading outlet for midwestern produce. The Erie Canal's success encouraged dozens of other state-supported projects. The canal-building boom deflated with the depression of the late 1830s, but by 1840 some 3,000 miles of railroad track had been laid and trains were beginning to supplement and compete with canal shipping.

F.   The Growth of the Cities
This transportation revolution stimulated the development of towns and cities. First the coming of the steamboat to western waterways caused the growth of such river port cities as Pittsburgh, Cincinnati, Louisville, St. Louis, and New Orleans. Then the Erie Canal made the fortunes of lake port cities like Buffalo, Cleveland, Detroit, Chicago, and Milwaukee, while diminishing the importance of the river port cities. Overall, the period from 1820 to 1860 saw the most rapid urbanization in American history.

IV. Industrial Beginnings
A.   Introduction
Early industrialization also stimulated urbanization. The first cotton mill in the United States opened in Pawtucket, Rhode Island, when skilled mechanic Samuel Slater managed to sneak out of Britain and arrive in America with his ability to reproduce Richard Arkwright's spinning frame. Samuel Slater's first mill, opened in 1790, was soon joined by many others manufacturing textiles and shoes. The rapidity of industrialization varied from region to region, with New England leading the way and the South, where planters preferred to put their capital in land and slaves, lagging far behind. Industrialization began to change people's lives: it forced workers to regulate their labor by the clock and the pace of the machine and it downgraded the position of skilled artisans, but it also made cheaper machine made products available in greater profusion to working-class Americans.

B.   Causes of Industrialization
Industrialization was brought about by the Embargo Act of 1807, which induced merchants barred from foreign trade to divert their capital to founding factories. After the War of 1812 fledgling industries received protection from high tariffs, especially in the 1820s. Transportation improvements opened distant markets to manufacturers. Relatively high wages paid to American workers also made employers eager to adopt laborsaving techniques, like Eli Whitney's interchangeable parts, and new technology.

C.   Textile Towns in New England
New England was the first region to industrialize because its merchants were particularly hard hit by foreign trade disruptions and it had swift-flowing rivers for waterpower and excess female farm population for labor. Textile manufacturing became its leading industry. The Waltham and Lowell mills in Massachusetts, started by the Boston Associates, were the first to concentrate total cloth production within the factory. Originally 80 percent of the mill operatives were unmarried young women, who lived in company housing under the strict supervision of management. During the 1830s these Lowell women staged two of the largest strikes in American history to that date.

D.   Artisans and Workers in Mid-Atlantic Cities
In New York City and Philadelphia manufacturing of products such as shoes, saddles, or clothing was done in small shops as well as factories. Much of the work was still done by hand rather than by machine, but increasingly production was subdivided into small, specialized tasks performed by low-paid, semiskilled or unskilled laborers, often women. This resulted in a declining importance for skilled artisans, who, in protest in the late 1820s, formed trade unions and "workingmen's" political parties.

V.   Equality and Inequality
A.   Urban Inequality: The Rich and the Poor
The gap between the rich and the poor grew during the first half of the nineteenth century. The extremes were especially obvious in the cities, where the mansions of the wealthy lined the fashionable avenues while the poor crowded into noxious slums like New York's Five Points district. In Boston, in 1833, the richest 4 percent of the population owned almost 60 percent of the land. Contrary to the self-made-man, rags-to-riches myth, 90 percent of the very wealthy had started out with considerable means. At the other end of the scale, cities were developing a pauperized class consisting of the aged and infirm; widows; and destitute Irish immigrants, whose labor built the Erie and other canals in the North. Americans blamed the poor for being poor, and treated most with contempt, particularly the Irish, for being poor and Catholic, and free blacks, for being poor and black.

B.   Free Blacks in the North
Overwhelming discrimination kept most free blacks in poverty. They were generally denied the vote; educated in inferior segregated schools, if at all; forced to use separate and unequal facilities; and kept out of all but the lowest-paying, least skilled occupations. In response to this pervasive discrimination, northern blacks founded their own churches. Richard Allen, a freedman, started the first of these, the African Methodist Episcopal Church, in Philadelphia in 1816. By 1822 there were AME congregations all over the North. The black churches engaged in antislavery activities and ran schools and mutual-aid societies.

C.   The "Middling Classes"
The majority of white Americans were neither rich nor poor but belonged to what was then called the middling classes. For most people in that group the standard of living rose between 1800 and 1860, although members of the middle class experienced a lot of insecurity. And like other Americans, they also exhibited a high degree of transience, moving from neighborhood to neighborhood, city to city, and region to region.

VI.   The Revolution in Social Relationships
A.   The Attack on the Professions
One sign that economic changes were disrupting traditional relationships and forms of authority could be seen in the intense criticism of professionals such as lawyers, doctors, and ministers between 1820 and 1850. The denial that professionals had any special expertise was particularly prevalent on the frontier.

B.   The Challenge to Family Authority
Children became more inclined to question parental authority. Young men left home at an earlier age and struck out on their own. Young women increasingly made their own choice of whom to marry or even whether to marry.

C.   Wives and Husbands
Relations between spouses also were evolving. Wives continued to be legally subordinate to their husbands, but under the doctrine of separate spheres, middle-class women were demanding and winning greater voice in those areas where they were deemed to be

particularly competent: exerting moral influence on the family and creating within the home a calm refuge from the harsh, competitive world outside. As middle-class women gained more control over the frequency of their pregnancies, the size of white middle-class families declined markedly. However, the birthrate remained high among black and immigrant women.

D. Horizontal Allegiances and the Rise of Voluntary Associations
While the authority of fathers, husbands, professionals, and other social "superiors" waned, new relationships among persons in similar positions were forged through the proliferation of voluntary associations. Temperance and moral-reform societies of white middle-class women, union and workingmen's parties, and black fraternal and other clubs encouraged sociability among members and were attempts to enhance their influence on outside groups.

VII. Conclusion
After 1815 white Americans' westward movement speeded up due to a heightened European demand for agricultural products, especially cotton. Federal government policies, such as the removal of eastern Indians to west of the Mississippi River and the sale of land on more generous terms, also hastened western settlement. Improved transportation—introduction of the steamboat and building of canals and railroads—facilitated the shipment of western farmers' produce to eastern and European markets. This transportation revolution, in turn, encouraged the growth of cities, commerce, manufacturing, and industrialization. The economic transformations made some Americans wealthy and impoverished others and affected social relations within the family and society.

VOCABULARY

The following terms are used in Chapter 9. To understand the chapter fully, it is important that you know what each of them means.

mulatto	the offspring of one white and one black parent; a person of mixed black and white ancestry
public domain	the land owned by the government
subsistence agriculture	growing crops to feed and satisfy the needs of the farmer and his family, not cash crops for sale on the market
commercial agriculture	growing crops for sale on the market; farming as a business, big or small
squatter	one who settles on land, especially public or new land, without title or right
preemption	the act or right of purchasing before others or in preference to others
specie	gold, silver, or coined money (as opposed to paper)
capital	wealth (money) used or capable of being used in the production of more wealth
technology	the industrial arts; technical advances in production methods
antebellum	before the war; pre–Civil War

myth	a collective belief that is built up in response to the wishes of the group rather than having a base in fact
pauperism	the condition of being without means of support and living on public or private charity
transiency	moving frequently from place to place (as opposed to establishing permanent residency over long periods)

IDENTIFICATIONS

After reading Chapter 9, you should be able to identify and explain the historical significance of each of the following:

Alexis de Tocqueville, *Democracy in America*

John Jacob Astor

"mountain men": Kit Carson, Jedidiah Smith, and Jim Beckwourth

Five Civilized Tribes

Indian Removal Act, 1830

Cherokee Nation v. *Georgia* and *Worchester* v. *Georgia*

Trail of Tears

Black Hawk War

Eli Whitney, the cotton gin, and interchangeable parts

Panic of 1819

transportation revolution

Robert Fulton, the *Clermont,* and the Livingston-Fulton monopoly

Gibbons v. *Ogden*

Erie Canal

Samuel Slater

the out-work system and cottage industry

Boston Associates, Waltham and Lowell mills

New York's Five Points district

Richard Allen and the African Methodist Episcopal Church

middling classes

individualism

doctrine of separate spheres

Andrew Jackson Downing

SKILL BUILDING: MAPS

Using the map of the United States, do the following:

1.   Indicate the states that entered the Union between 1790 and 1821.

2.   Indicate the main area of western settlement between 1815 and 1840.

3.   Locate each of the following rivers or lakes and explain its economic importance to white Americans between 1815 and 1840:

>   Columbia
>
>   Missouri
>
>   Mississippi
>
>   Hudson
>
>   Ohio
>
>   Great Lakes

4.   Locate each of the following internal improvements and explain its economic and political impact on American life between 1815 and 1840:

>   National Road
>
>   Erie Canal
>
>   Baltimore and Ohio Railroad
>
>   Boston and Worcester Railroad
>
>   Massachusetts Western Railroad

5.   Indicate the areas from which the Five Civilized Tribes were removed and the areas in which they were resettled between 1820 and 1840.

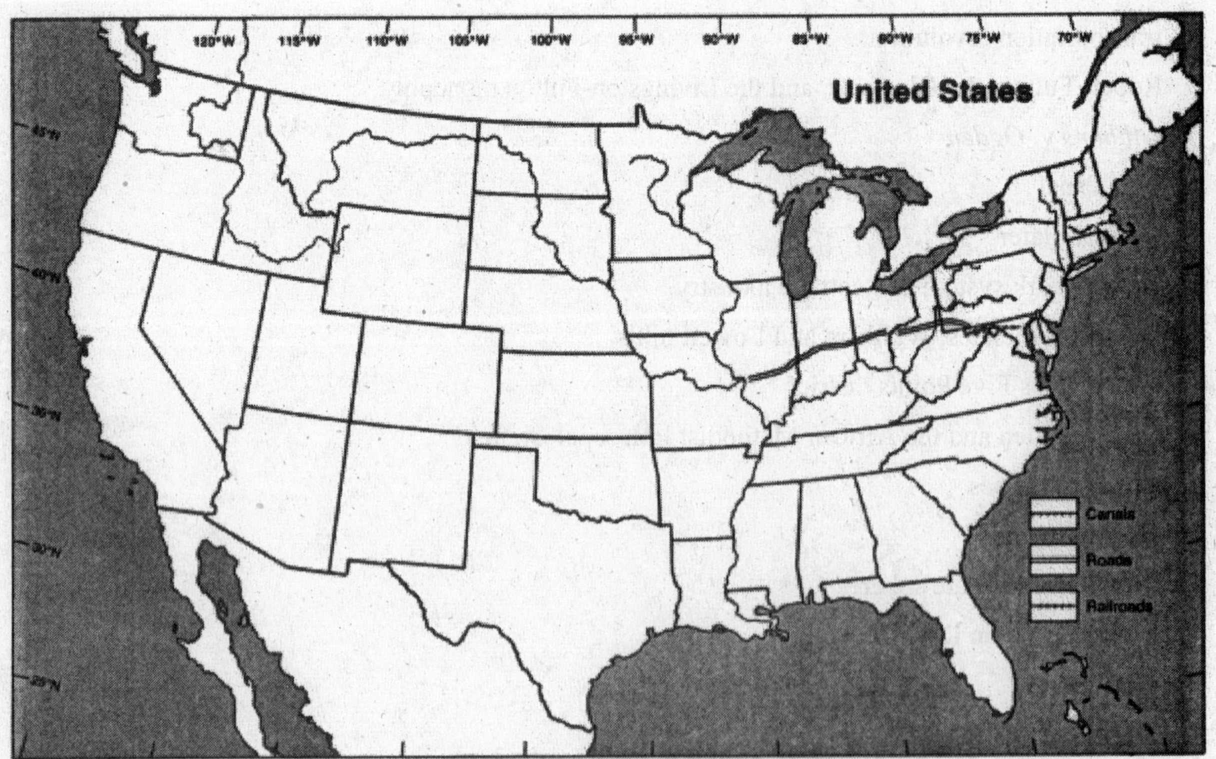

HISTORICAL SOURCES

The workers and working conditions in the Waltham and Lowell textile mills are described in Chapter 9. Where did the author find this information? There are numerous historical sources on Lowell and other New England mills, but they do not all paint the same picture. Lowell employees produced their own periodicals: *Operatives' Magazine* (1841–1842), *Lowell Offerings* (1840–1845), and *New England Offerings* (1848–1850). The articles appearing in these publications give quite a favorable view of conditions in Lowell. This makes it difficult to account for the walkout of eight hundred women in 1834 and fifteen hundred in 1836. A group of dissident workers denounced the *Lowell Offerings* as "a mouthpiece of the corporations," which had to approve all items that appeared in it. These unhappy laborers started rival publications, *Factory Tracts* and the *Voice of Industry,* that stressed the oppressiveness of life in the mills. In 1845 a Massachusetts legislative committee held public hearings on labor conditions in the textile mills. Female workers testified that the overly long workdays and insufficient pay had damaged their health. Management officials, on the other hand, spoke of the contented farm girls who worked a few years in the mills, saved hundreds of dollars from their pay, and then returned home to marry with this nest egg. In addition, European visitors and a Lowell Unitarian minister published accounts of life in the town and mills, which were mostly laudatory. But two thousand textile workers signed petitions sent to the Massachusetts House of Representatives pleading for a ten-hour-day law and other factory reforms. Obviously, such conflicting sources do not make the historian's task easy. In writing about the past, the historian, inevitably influenced by his or her own beliefs and predilections, weighs and evaluates evidence and chooses among available sources.

Now look at the account of the "Building of the Erie Canal." Like the opening of the Waltham and Lowell textile mills, the completion of this most expensive, difficult, and dramatic transportation project had a major impact on the lives of Americans. What were some of the effects of the canal on people living at the time?

MULTIPLE-CHOICE QUESTIONS

Circle the letter of the item that best completes each statement or answers the question.

1. Andrew Jackson's remark, "John Marshall has made his decision; now let him enforce it," refers to the president's intention to
    a. destroy the National Bank despite the Supreme Court ruling upholding its constitutionality.
    b. use force, if necessary, to make South Carolina obey federal laws that it thought unconstitutional.
    c. move the Cherokees west of the Mississippi River, regardless of Supreme Court rulings.
    d. disregard Chief Justice Marshall's ruling in *Gibbons* v. *Ogden.*
2. By 1840 about what portion of Americans lived between the Appalachian Mountains and the Mississippi River?
    a. One-quarter
    b. One-third
    c. One-half
    d. Two-thirds
3. Which of the following was most responsible for the spread of cotton growing into the old Southwest?
    a. The discovery of methods for getting sea-island cotton to flourish in the interior uplands
    b. The removal of the Five Civilized Tribes
    c. The adoption of a homestead law making the available land free to qualified settlers
    d. Eli Whitney's invention of the cotton gin

4. Which of the following statements about the Erie Canal is correct?

    a. It linked New York City through inland waterways to Ohio and made the city a major outlet for midwestern produce.
    b. It and the National Road were the only major internal improvements financed by the federal government before the Civil War.
    c. It contributed to the growing importance of Mississippi River cities such as New Orleans.
    d. It had little impact on shipping costs.

5. As a result of the Panic of 1819,

    a. western farmers returned to subsistence farming.
    b. many westerners hated the National Bank.
    c. westerners became reluctant to see federal tax monies spent on expensive internal improvements.
    d. industrialists denounced high U.S. tariffs for ruining their sales abroad.

6. In the 1820s and 1830s the majority of the workers in the Lowell and Waltham textile mills were

    a. children from poor immigrant families.
    b. Irish and French-Canadian immigrants.
    c. displaced artisans and skilled workers.
    d. young women from New England farms.

7. Which of the following statements about the professions in the late 1840s is correct?

    a. Lawyers, doctors, and clergymen were highly paid and respected.
    b. Women were entering the professions in significant numbers.
    c. No state required a person to have a medical education or a license to be a doctor.
    d. Increasing numbers of doctors, lawyers, and ministers moved to the West because they were most needed and valued there.

8. By the mid-1830s which of the following accounted for two-thirds of America's foreign exports?

    a. Wheat and corn
    b. Textiles
    c. Cotton
    d. Farm machinery

9. The transportation revolution in the years after the War of 1812 contributed to the growth of all of the following *except*

    a. industry in the Deep South.
    b. towns and cities in the North and West.
    c. new markets for northeastern manufacturers.
    d. commercial agriculture in the West.

10. Which of the following statements about African-Americans living in the North between 1815 and 1840 is correct?

    a. The great majority was still enslaved.
    b. They were the ones who did the backbreaking labor of digging the Erie and other northern canals.
    c. Their response to white imposed segregation and discrimination was to build their own separate institutions, such as the AME church.
    d. Black men, but not women, were generally allowed to vote and hold office.

SHORT-ANSWER QUESTIONS

1. Explain the developments between 1815 and 1840 that encouraged white settlement in the Midwest.

2. What stimulated northeastern manufacturing in the years after the War of 1812?

3. Explain why New England led the way in industrialization.

4. Compare and contrast manufacturing in New England with that in New York and Philadelphia.

5. In the period 1815–1840, how much truth was there to the rags-to-riches idea?

6. What changes occurred in the economic and social status of artisans and skilled workers in the period 1815–1840?

ESSAY QUESTIONS

1. Discuss the transportation revolution of the period 1815–1840. What changes took place? What was the impact of those changes on the country economically, politically, and socially?

2. Discuss the doctrine of separate spheres for women. What changes, if any, did the doctrine produce in the lives of white middle-class, white working-class, black, and immigrant women?

3. Alexis de Tocqueville in his *Democracy in America* was impressed by the "general equality of condition among the people." Writing about the same period, New York merchant Philip Hone stated: "[T]he two extremes of costly luxury in living, expensive establishments, and improvident waste are presented in daily and hourly contrast with squalid misery and hopeless destitution." How do you account for these very different assessments? Which man came closer to the truth? Why?

4. Discuss federal government policy toward Native Americans during the period 1815–1840.

5. Chapter 9 states that "the pre–Civil War period witnessed the widespread substitution of horizontal allegiances for vertical allegiances." What does this mean, and what evidence is offered in the chapter to support the claim?

ANSWERS TO MULTIPLE-CHOICE QUESTIONS

1. c
2. b
3. d
4. a
5. b
6. d
7. c
8. c
9. a
10. c

Democratic Politics, Religious Revival, and Reform, 1824–1840

OUTLINE AND SUMMARY

I. Introduction

After reading Chapter 10, you should be able to answer the following questions: (1) How was American politics democratized between 1800 and 1840? (2) Why was Andrew Jackson so popular with voters? (3) How and why did the Democratic and Whig Parties emerge? (4) What new assumptions about human nature did religious and reform leaders of the 1830s make?

II. The Rise of Democratic Politics, 1824–1832

    A. Introduction

In 1824 only one political party existed, the Republican, but it was fragmenting because of pressures produced by the industrialization of the Northeast, the spread of cotton growing in the South, and westward expansion. Out of this fragmentation grew two new political parties. On the whole, those who retained Jefferson's distrust of strong federal government and preferred states' rights became Democrats, while those who favored an active federal government that encouraged economic development became Whigs. Both Democratic and Whig politicians had to adapt to the democratic idea of politics as the expression of the will of the common man rather than "an activity that gentlemen conducted for the people."

    B. Democratic Ferment

Politics became more democratic as property qualifications for voting were eliminated, written ballots replaced voting aloud, appointive offices became elective, and presidential electors were chosen by the people. This broadening of suffrage was often brought about by competition between Republicans and Federalists in the 1790s and early 1800s. Each party sought to increase its voter base, increasing the number of eligible voters in the process.

    C. The Election of 1824

The fragmenting Republican Party could not agree on a single nominee for president. Instead, four Republicans ran. Andrew Jackson received the most popular and electoral votes, but not a majority. Therefore, as the Constitution requires, the House of Representatives had to choose among the three top contenders—Jackson, John Quincy Adams, and William Crawford. Henry Clay, who came in fourth, used his considerable influence with Congress to gain the selection of John Quincy Adams. President Adams in turn appointed Clay his secretary of state. Jackson supporters charged that a "corrupt bargain" had been made, and that charge hung like a cloud over the Adams administration. .

    D. John Quincy Adams as President

President Adams tried to encourage economic growth through federal internal improvement projects, but he remained aloof to the political games of the age, and his programs suffered a lack of support because of it. Idealistic as his view was, it guaranteed a single-term presidency.

E.   **The Rise of Andrew Jackson**
Andrew Jackson's victory over the British in the Battle of New Orleans in 1815 made him a popular hero. It was a time of "vague but widespread discontent" with Washington, in part because of the Panic of 1819. Jackson's position as political outsider also endeared him to the public and supporters, like Martin Van Buren, began to build a strong political organization that increasingly called itself the Democratic Party. The Democrats in 1828 nominated Jackson for president. Those who remained loyal to Adams called themselves National Republicans and renominated him in 1828.

F.   **The Election of 1828**
Although Jackson was a wealthy planter when he ran for president, the Democrats portrayed him as a man of the people opposing Adams the aristocrat. Jackson won the election with this common-man appeal. His victory also showed a clear sectional split, with the South and Southwest going heavily for Jackson and New England going mostly for Adams.

G.   **Jackson in Office**
Jackson immediately fired nearly half of the civil servants on the federal payroll, most in the Northeast, and replaced them with his supporters. Jackson did not initiate the spoils system, but he defended and practiced it on the grounds that frequent rotation in office gave more people a chance to serve. He also opposed federal support for internal improvements, as demonstrated in his Maysville Road veto. While southerners liked that stand and his Indian Removal Act of 1830, they resented his lack of action against the 1828 "Tariff of Abominations," which protected northern manufacturers and western farmers from foreign competition but raised the price that southerners had to pay for finished products.

H.   **Nullification**
The tariff issue prepared the way for a break between Jackson and his vice president, John C. Calhoun, who was becoming the chief spokesman for the southern planter class. Calhoun wrote and circulated the *South Carolina Exposition and Protest* in opposition to the Tariff of 1828. In it he argued that protective tariffs were unconstitutional and that states had the right to nullify federal laws that violated the U.S. Constitution.

In November 1832 South Carolina, acting on Calhoun's doctrine, nullified the Tariff of 1828 and the slightly less protectionist Tariff of 1832 and forbade the collection of customs duties at its ports. Jackson denounced the state's defiance and threatened to use the army and navy to enforce federal laws. A clash of arms was avoided only by the Compromise of 1833, proposed by Henry Clay. South Carolina rescinded its nullification, and Congress passed a new tariff law that gradually lowered duties over the next nine years.

I.   **The Bank Veto and the Election of 1832**
Jackson disliked all banks and the issuance of paper money, and he particularly hated the Second Bank of the United States. He regarded it as a privileged monopoly. This national bank, which controlled the nation's credit and was the depository for federal government monies, was run by its private stockholders, "Monied Capitalists," with little control from the federal government. In 1832 Nicholas Biddle, president of the Second Bank, applied for its recharter. The recharter bill passed Congress, but Jackson vetoed it, denouncing the bank for making "the rich richer and the potent more powerful."

In 1832, the Democrats named Jackson and Martin Van Buren for president and vice president, respectively, while the National Republicans ran Henry Clay. Clay opposed Jackson's record and advocated instead his American System of protective tariffs, rechartering of the national bank, and federally supported internal improvements. Jackson won easily and was ready to complete his destruction of the Second Bank.

III.   The Bank Controversy and the Second Party System, 1833–1840
    A.   The War on the Bank
        Jackson quickly tried to bankrupt the Second Bank by removing federal government deposits and distributing them to accounts in state-chartered banks. The "pet banks" that received the deposits, now having no restraint on them from the defunct national bank, extended much more credit and issued many more bank notes (paper money). Soon the number of state depositories ballooned beyond Jackson's expectations. This loosening of credit touched off a period of headlong economic expansion, reckless speculation, and rapid inflation.

    B.   The Rise of Whig Opposition
        During Jackson's second term, the National Republicans changed their name to Whigs. They began to attract broader support, including southerners angry over Jackson's denunciation of nullification; temperance and public-school reformers; anti-immigrant and anti-Catholic Protestants; followers of the Anti-Masonry movement; and the commercial community of merchants, manufacturers, and bankers.

    C.   The Election of 1836
        The Democrats ran Martin Van Buren for president in 1836; the Whigs, unable to agree on a single nominee, ran four candidates. The Democrats claimed the Whigs did this so that no man would receive a majority of the electoral votes, putting the choice into the House of Representatives, where one of their nominees might win. Yet Van Buren won a clear majority.

    D.   The Panic of 1837
        Just as Van Buren was inaugurated, the country's economy went into a severe depression. Its causes were both international and national. Jackson's bank policies had produced a wave of speculation and inflation that so alarmed him that in July 1836 he issued the Specie Circular, a proclamation that barred the purchase of government-owned land with anything but gold. This move burst the speculative bubble and contributed to the panic and depression that followed.

        President Van Buren, reflecting the antibank, hard-money stand, dealt with the depression by divorcing the federal government from banking. In 1840 he signed the Independent Treasury bill, which provided that federal government money would be kept in its own treasury instead of being deposited in banks.

    E.   The Election of 1840
        The Democrats renominated Van Buren in 1840. The Whigs chose the hero of Tippecanoe, William Henry Harrison, and ran John Tyler of Virginia for vice president. The Whigs adopted the popular appeal-to-the-common-man campaign techniques pioneered by the Democrats in the previous decade. These campaign tactics, along with Van Buren's unpopularity caused by the depression, gave the election to Harrison.

    F.   The Second Party System Matures
        Between 1836 and 1840, the number of people who voted increased by 60 percent. This rapid increase in voter interest was caused by popular campaign techniques, strong contrast and competition between rival parties, and controversial issues like tariffs and banking, all of which characterized the mature second party system.

IV.   The Rise of Popular Religion
    A.   Introduction
        In the 1820s and 1830s, Americans turned to preachers who rejected the Calvinist belief in predestination. Just as politics was becoming more democratic, so was religious doctrine.

The primary message was that any individual could be saved through his or her own efforts and faith. This democratic transformation was produced in part by a series of religious revivals known as the Second Great Awakening.

B.   The Second Great Awakening
From New England the Second Great Awakening moved rapidly to frontier areas where thousands gathered at religious camp meetings. These frontier revivals helped to promote law and order and diminish the violence prevalent in new western areas. The Methodists were the largest, most successful denomination on the frontier.

C.   Eastern Revivals
By the 1820s the center of religious revivals had moved east again and was particularly strong in an area of western New York known as the Burned-Over District. The revivalist leader Charles G. Finney preached that, rather than being naturally depraved, humans were capable of living without sin once they experienced an emotional religious conversion.

D.   Critics of Revivals: The Unitarians
In New England the educated and wealthy were often repelled by the emotional excesses of revivalism and turned instead to Unitarianism. This denomination preached that goodness should be cultivated by a gradual process of character building and by emulating the life and teachings of Jesus. Although the Unitarians were critical of the revivalists, both shared the belief that humans could shape their own destiny and improve their behavior.

E.   The Rise of Mormonism
Joseph Smith started Mormonism in the 1820s in the Burned-Over District. He and his followers founded a model city at Nauvoo, Illinois, but when they began the practice of polygyny, they were prosecuted by authorities and attacked by a mob that murdered Smith. The hostility that the Mormons encountered from others convinced Smith, before his death, and the leaders who succeeded him, that the Mormons must separate themselves from American society.

F.   The Shakers
Started by Mother Ann Lee, the Shakers also founded separate religious communities. While most of the religious revivalists encouraged their followers to get ahead economically and contribute to society, the Shakers rejected economic individualism and tried to withdraw from American society. They separated men and women, and banned marriage, relying on converts and adoption to keep their numbers up. They pooled their land and tools and labor, in the process creating remarkably prosperous villages.

V.   The Age of Reform
A.   Introduction
The reform movements were strongest in New England and in areas of the Midwest settled by New Englanders.

B.   The War on Liquor
The temperance movement began by preaching moderation in the use of liquor. With the formation of the American Temperance Society, however, the movement began to demand total abstinence and prohibition laws. Most members of temperance societies were middle class, though in the 1840s the Washington Temperance Societies attracted workers. The movement was successful in cutting per capita consumption of alcohol in half between the 1820s and 1840s.

C.   Public-School Reform
Secretary of the Massachusetts Board of Education Horace Mann advocated many educational innovations. These included state tax support of schools, grouping pupils into

classes by age and level of competence, longer school terms, use of standardized textbooks, and compulsory attendance laws. Despite opposition from various groups, many northern states adopted these reforms because they were backed by important constituencies: businesses that needed disciplined, literate workers; workingmen's groups that saw education as a road to social mobility; and reform-minded women, who realized school reform would open teaching careers to women. In fact, by 1900, 70 percent of public-school teachers were female.

D. Abolition

Opposition to slavery in the 1820s came mostly from black Americans. Not until 1831, when William Lloyd Garrison started publishing *The Liberator,* was there a militant white abolitionist movement. Most northern whites in the 1830s and 1840s, however, were hostile to the abolitionists. Moreover, the American Anti-Slavery Society, founded in 1833, suffered from internal quarrels between its Garrisonian wing and its New York and western wings. The main points of dispute were whether to support rights for women as well as blacks and whether to take abolitionism into politics. Despite hostility and internal division, the abolitionist movement kept the issue of slavery alive, put the South on the defensive, and gained supporters for the side issue of the constitutional rights of free expression and petition.

E. Women's Rights

Many of the women's rights leaders began their reform careers in the abolitionist movement. When women were denied full participation in that movement, Elizabeth Cady Stanton and Lucretia Mott in 1848 called a women's rights convention in Seneca Falls, New York. The convention adopted a Declaration of Sentiments, which launched the feminist movement. Thereafter, women gained a few rights, but they did not get the vote until 1920.

F. Penitentiaries and Asylums

In the 1820s and 1830s, religious revivalists and reformers came to believe that crime, poverty, and deviancy were caused by failures of parental guidance that could be mended by institutions providing the proper discipline and environment. Following that belief, reformers created penitentiaries and workhouses for criminals and the indigent. Dorothea Dix fought for the establishment of insane asylums to treat the mentally ill. These programs were tied to the belief that deviancy could be erased by settling the deviants in the right environment.

G. Utopian Communities

A few reformers founded "ideal" or "utopian" communities to demonstrate ways of life that they thought were superior to those prevailing in antebellum America. Among these model communities were New Harmony, Hopedale, and Brook Farm. Most of these settlements were short lived.

VI. Conclusion

In the 1820s and 1830s politics and religion responded increasingly to the common man. The enlarged electorate, seeing Andrew Jackson as the champion of the ordinary American, swept him into the presidency. However, Jackson's stands on federally financed internal improvements, protective tariffs, nullification, and the national bank divided citizens and led to the rise of the second party system—Democrats versus Whigs. The Panic of 1837 furthered the partisan split. Meanwhile reformers offered a variety of proposals to unleash the basic goodness of humans and perfect society. Though initially avoiding "corrupt" politics, reformers by the 1840s were starting to enter the political arena to advance their particular aims.

VOCABULARY

The following terms are used in Chapter 10. To understand the chapter fully, it is important that you know what each of them means.

suffrage	the vote; the right to vote
nullify	render or declare legally void or inoperative
itinerant	one who travels from place to place
utopian	founded on or involving perfection in law, politics, and human relations
deviancy	behavior differing from the normal, accepted behavior and/or morality of society
indigence	neediness, poverty

IDENTIFICATIONS

After reading Chapter 10, you should be able to identify and explain the historical significance of each of the following:

Henry Clay and the American System

second American party system

spoils system

"Tariff of Abominations," 1828

John C. Calhoun and the *South Carolina Exposition and Protest*

Compromise of 1833

Nicholas Biddle and the Bank of the United States

"pet banks"

Locofocos

Specie Circular

Long Cabin campaign, "Tippecanoe and Tyler too," and the election of 1840

Second Great Awakening

Burned-Over District

Charles G. Finney and "perfectionism"

William Ellery Channing and Unitarianism

Joseph Smith and Mormonism

Mother Ann Lee and the Shakers

Lyman Beecher and the American Temperance Society

Horace Mann

William Lloyd Garrison, *The Liberator,* and the American Anti-Slavery Society

Frederick Douglass

Sojourner Truth

James G. Birney and the Liberty party

Angelina and Sarah Grimké

John Quincy Adams and the "gag rule"

Elizabeth Cady Stanton, Lucretia Mott, the Seneca Falls convention, and the Declaration of Sentiments

penitentiaries and the "Auburn and Pennsylvania systems"

Dorothea Dix

Robert Owen and New Harmony

Transcendentalists, Brook Farm, and *The Dial*

John Humphrey Noyes and Oneida

SKILL BUILDING: MAPS

On the map of New York and New England, locate each of the places listed below. How is each connected with the religious and reform movements of the Age of Jackson?

Burned-Over District

Albany

Buffalo

Erie Canal

Hudson River

Lake Erie

Seneca Falls

Oneida

Boston

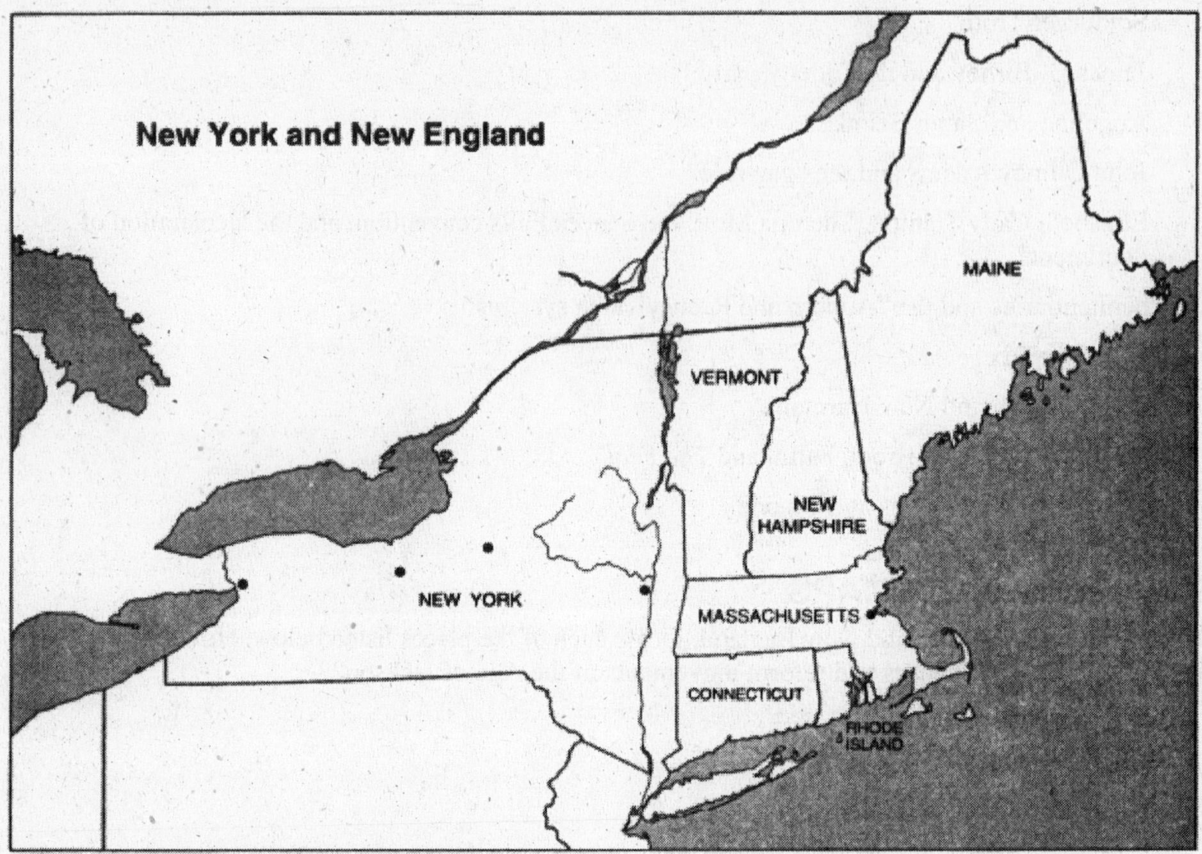

MULTIPLE-CHOICE QUESTIONS

Circle the letter of the item that best completes each statement or answers the question.

1. The immediate result of Jackson's distribution of federal funds to state banks was to

    a.   bring about rapid economic expansion, speculation, and inflation.
    b.   increase the power of the Second Bank of the United States.
    c.   make the purchase of land more difficult.
    d.   increase the effectiveness of the Specie Circular.

2. The *South Carolina Exposition and Protest* was drawn up in opposition to the

    a.   Missouri Compromise.
    b.   spoils system.
    c.   "Tariff of Abominations."
    d.   Compromise of 1833.

3. All of the following were founded as utopian communities *except*

    a.   New Harmony, Indiana.
    b.   Oneida, New York.
    c.   Brook Farm, Massachusetts.
    d.   Rochester, New York.

4. Which of the following statements about William Lloyd Garrison is *incorrect*?
    a. He favored the removal of freed blacks from the United States to colonies in Africa.
    b. He opposed abolitionists who wanted to start a political party and run candidates for office.
    c. He favored giving women equal positions and influence with men in the antislavery movement.
    d. He insisted that slavery was sinful and its continued existence unacceptable.

5. The "gag rule" was repealed in 1845 largely due to the efforts of
    a. Theodore Weld.
    b. Horace Mann.
    c. John Quincy Adams.
    d. Andrew Jackson.

6. Martin Van Buren did *not*
    a. create one of the first Democratic state party machines, the Albany Regency.
    b. sign the Independent Treasury Bill, which provided for deposit of federal funds in government vaults.
    c. serve as president during a severe economic depression.
    d. defect to the newly formed Whig party in protest over Andrew Jackson's handling of the nullification crisis.

7. Reformers of the antebellum period
    a. were usually Democrats rather than Whigs.
    b. were often inspired by the writings of Karl Marx.
    c. received their best response in New England and areas to which New Englanders had migrated.
    d. rarely advocated legal coercion to force people to live morally.

8. Revivalists and Unitarians were similar in
    a. the social classes they appealed to.
    b. their emotionalism.
    c. their belief that human behavior could be changed for the better.
    d. the cities and towns where most of their followers lived.

9. Which of the following quotations is *not* correctly paired with its source?
    a. "Our Union: It must be preserved." John C. Calhoun's *South Carolina Exposition and Protest*
    b. It makes "the rich richer and the potent more powerful." Andrew Jackson's veto message of the recharter of the Bank of the United States
    c. "I will not equivocate—I will not excuse—I will not retreat a single inch—AND I WILL BE HEARD." William Lloyd Garrison's *The Liberator*
    d. "All men and women are created equal." The Declaration of Sentiments of the Seneca Falls Convention

10. The Seneca Falls Declaration of Sentiments called for
    a. state tax support for public schools.
    b. equal rights for women.
    c. the immediate abolition of slavery.
    d. humane treatment of the mentally ill and the establishment of insane asylums for their care.

SHORT-ANSWER QUESTIONS

1. Explain the ways in which politics became more democratic in the 1820s and 1830s. What were the effects of greater popular participation in politics on parties and politicians?

2. Why were John Quincy Adams and Henry Clay accused of entering into a "corrupt bargain" in the election of 1824? How did that charge affect Adams's presidency?

3. Explain why the South disliked high tariffs and what John C. Calhoun proposed to do about such protective import duties.

4. Discuss the role Henry Clay played in the Compromise of 1833. Did the compromise settle the nullification question?

5. Why did Andrew Jackson hate the Second Bank of the United States? What actions did he take to destroy it?

ESSAY QUESTIONS

1. Andrew Jackson deserves to be ranked among America's greatest presidents. Accept or refute this statement and back up your position with a discussion citing specific examples of Jackson's policies and actions as president.

2. Discuss the origins and development of the second party system. Which parties were involved? Who supported each of them? What, if anything, did they stand for? What impact did their actions have on voter interest and participation in politics?

3. Discuss the reform movements of the antebellum period. Who participated? What inspired the reformers? What assumptions did they make? What were their aims and accomplishments?

4. Discuss the rise of "popular religion" in antebellum America. In what ways did religious doctrine become democratized? What assumptions did the new theologies make? How did these assumptions affect religious, social, and political life?

5. Compare and contrast the positions of the Jacksonian Democrats and the Whig supporters of Henry Clay's American System on the issues of the proper role of the federal government, protective tariffs, internal improvements, and banking. How do you account for their similarities and differences?

ANSWERS TO MULTIPLE-CHOICE QUESTIONS

1. a
2. c
3. d
4. a
5. c
6. d
7. c
8. c
9. a
10. b

CHAPTER 11

Technology, Culture, and Everyday Life, 1840–1860

OUTLINE AND SUMMARY

I.   Introduction

In the 1840s and 1850s most Americans believed God had ordained that man should progress, morally and materially. The means to progress of both kinds was through technology, which Americans defined as "the application of science to improve the conveniences of life." Chapter 11 covers the changes in the everyday lives of ordinary citizens brought about by the new technology of the period 1840–1860 as well as looking at the ways people responded to those transformations. After reading the chapter you should be able to answer the following questions: (1) How did technology transform the daily lives of middle-class Americans between 1840 and 1860? (2) How did American pastimes and entertainment change between 1840 and 1860? (3) How did Americans express their distinctiveness in their literature and art?

II. Technology and Economic Growth

    A.   Introduction

The steam engine, cotton gin, reaper, sewing machine, and telegraph transformed American life in the pre–Civil War decades. This new technology increased productivity and eased travel and communication, which in turn brought down costs and prices. As a result, most Americans between 1840 and 1860 enjoyed improved standards of living. But the new technology hurt other Americans. The cotton gin encouraged the expansion of the plantation-slave economy. Sewing machines and new manufacturing techniques rendered traditional crafts and the artisans who practiced them obsolete.

    B.   Agricultural Advancement

Between 1830 and 1860 settlers moved onto the grasslands of Indiana, Michigan, and Illinois, where John Deere's steel-tipped plow, developed in 1837, aided them in breaking the tough prairie sod. When Cyrus McCormick started to mass-produce mechanical reapers in 1847, farmers could harvest grain seven times faster than before, with half the labor. This made wheat the dominant crop of the Midwest. Although Americans quickly adopted these laborsaving inventions, they generally farmed wastefully, rapidly depleting the soil and then moving to virgin land. Only in the East did some farmers introduce fertilizers to increase their yields to the point where they could compete with those of the new western fields. The South, with its unpaid slave labor, had little incentive to invest in laborsaving machinery.

    C.   Technology and Industrial Progress

Americans of the antebellum period readily invested in new technology. A most important advance was Eli Whitney's principle of using interchangeable parts. Manufacturing such parts was greatly facilitated by improved machine tools. By 1851 Europeans were referring to interchangeable parts as the "American System of Manufacturing." Readiness to invest in innovations, interchangeable parts, and better machine tools resulted in rapid acceptance, mass production, and use of new inventions such as Samuel Colt's revolving pistol, Elias Howe's sewing machine, and Samuel F. B. Morse's telegraph.

D.   The Railroad Boom
By 1860 the United States had 30,000 miles of track, more than the rest of the world combined. Most of the new rail lines linked the East and Midwest. As a result, much of the produce of the Midwest, which had formerly been shipped downriver and out of the port of New Orleans, was now shipped via railroads radiating from Chicago eastward. These railroads stimulated the settlement of the Midwest and its growth of wheat farming, and at the same aided the development of cities, towns, and industry. Several states barred funding of the railroads, encouraging a shift toward private investment. As America's first big business the railroads pioneered new forms of financing in the 1850s, particularly the sale of stock and other securities. Many of the transactions were handled through Wall Street, making New York the nation's leading capital market.

E.   Rising Prosperity
Technological improvements reduced the price of commodities to consumers, which in turn contributed to an average 25 percent rise in the real income of American workers between 1840 and 1860. The increased annual income of working families also was attributable to the use of steam power, which allowed factories to operate in all seasons and therefore offer more work to laborers. Furthermore, the growth of towns and cities that accompanied industrialization opened new employment opportunities for women and children, who often had to work to supplement the inadequate wages of the husband and father. These economic opportunities, plus the comforts and conveniences of urban life, attracted a steady stream of Americans to cities.

III.   The Quality of Life
A.   Introduction
Technological advances improved the quality of life for those in the middle class. They now enjoyed luxuries formerly reserved for the rich, but these changes were slower to reach the poor, who increasingly came to congregate in cramped urban tenements. Medical knowledge lagged behind the strides made in industry and agriculture, leaving Americans to look to popular health fads for the prevention and cure of illness.

B.   Dwellings
In the cities the typical dwellings of the period were row houses. The row houses that the middle class lived in became increasingly elaborate, while the poor were forced into crowded row houses that were further subdivided by several families and boarders. On the frontier, one-room log cabins were common. These were replaced by the much more comfortable balloon-frame houses as the community matured and prospered.

The upper and middle classes, between 1840 and 1860, favored ornate home furnishings in the rococo style. The wealthy imported such furniture from Europe, but the middle class bought mass-produced imitations from new furniture manufacturing centers like Cincinnati and Grand Rapids.

C.   Conveniences and Inconveniences
Industrialization and improved transportation affected home heating, cooking, and diet. By the 1840s coal-burning stoves were replacing fireplaces for heating and cooking. Although these stoves were more convenient and made it possible to cook several dishes simultaneously, coal burning contributed to fouling the urban environment. Railroads brought fresh produce to city dwellers, but only the rich could afford fruits out of season. Because home iceboxes were rare before 1860, most Americans still ate meat preserved by salting rather than fresh meat.

By the 1840s and 1850s, cities such as New York began to construct aqueducts, reservoirs, and water works. These brought pure water to street hydrants, but the majority of houses were not yet hooked up to the water mains. As a result, Americans of the period bathed infrequently. Because few cities had sanitation departments and most people used outdoor privies, American cities often stank.

D.   Disease and Health
The transportation boom increased and widened the risks of epidemics. American cities were racked by recurring epidemics of cholera, yellow fever, and other diseases. The medical profession, which was divided and uncertain about the causes and cures of epidemic diseases, was held in low esteem. In the 1840s the development of anesthetics by Crawford Long and William T. G. Morton advanced the field of surgery, but the achievements of surgeons were still blighted by their failure to recognize the importance of disinfection.

E.   Popular Health Movements
Since neither public-health boards nor doctors seemed able to prevent disease, many Americans put their faith in various popular therapies, such as hydropathy and the Grahamite regimen.

F.   Phrenology
Phrenology was the most popular of the scientific fads of the antebellum period. Its claim that a skilled phrenologist could make an accurate analysis of an individual's character by examining the contours of his skull appealed to Americans for the same reason that they turned to popular cures. All promised to teach the principles of life and give the individual control over his or her own fate; science, like machines, was believed to be a tool to improve ones life.

IV. Democratic Pastimes
A.   Introduction
New technology transformed leisure as well as work in the years 1830–1860. Imaginative entrepreneurs used new inventions and advances in manufacturing to sell the kinds of entertainment they believed the public wanted.

B.   Newspapers
James Gordon Bennett, publisher of the *New York Herald,* was one of the first journalists to take advantage of new techniques in paper making and printing and the invention of the telegraph. He realized that a newspaper could make money by building mass circulation. He and other publishers slashed the price of their papers to a penny and used newspaper boys to sell hundreds of thousands of copies daily. The number of weeklies grew from 65 to 138 between 1830 and 1840. The penny papers filled their columns with human-interest stories of crime and sex. Bennett's *New York Herald* and Horace Greeley's *New York Tribune* also pioneered in modern financial and political reporting.

C.   The Theater
Antebellum theaters were filled with large, rowdy audiences from all social classes. People liked romantic melodramas best, although William Shakespeare's plays were performed more often than those of any other single dramatist.

D.   Minstrel Shows
Starting in the 1840s, minstrel shows—performances of songs, dances, and skits by white men in blackface—became popular with white working-class audiences. These shows catered to and reinforced the prejudices of whites by depicting blacks as stupid, comical, musical, and irresponsible.

E.   P. T. Barnum
P. T. Barnum, with his display of curiosities, flair for publicity, and development of the American Museum in New York, was the ultimate "entrepreneur of popular entertainment" in the antebellum period.

V.   The Quest for Nationality in Literature and Art
A.   Introduction
Europeans in the early nineteenth century looked down on American writing, while Americans pointed with pride to the achievements of Washington Irving, who by 1820 had published his famous stories "Rip Van Winkle" and "The Legend of Sleepy Hollow." After 1820, however, the United States had many more writers to boast of as the nation experienced "a flowering of literature" referred to as the "American Renaissance." Among its outstanding authors were James Fenimore Cooper, Ralph Waldo Emerson, Walt Whitman, Herman Melville, and others. In their writing some of these authors sought to develop a new, unique American literature. The painters of the Hudson River school and Frederick Law Olmsted in his landscape design also offered distinctively American visions.

B.   Roots of the American Renaissance
By the 1820s and 1830s two things transformed the writing of fiction in the United States: the transportation revolution, which opened a nationwide market for books, and the spread of the romantic movement. Romanticism, with its stress on feelings rather than learning, suited fiction well. For that reason, women, still not admitted to most colleges, could publish best-selling romantic novels, such as Harriet Beecher Stowe's *Uncle Tom's Cabin*.

C.   Cooper, Emerson, Thoreau, Fuller, and Whitman
In his novels, James Fenimore Cooper, the first of these new writers, introduced the particularly American character, the frontiersman Natty Bumppo. The essayist Ralph Waldo Emerson preached an American brand of romanticism known as transcendentalism. Rejecting the importance of education and reason in seeking truth, he contended that every individual is capable of knowing God, truth, and beauty by following his feelings. Therefore, young, democratic America had nothing to learn from Europe, but could produce its own great literature and art. Emerson's disciple Henry David Thoreau not only expressed his radical insights in his writing but also lived them. He went to jail rather than pay taxes to support what he considered the evil Mexican War and defended the right to defy unjust government policies in his essay "Civil Disobedience"(1849). Another Emerson adherent, Margaret Fuller, combined transcendentalism and feminism in her *Women in the Nineteenth Century* (1845). Walt Whitman, in *Leaves of Grass,* broke new ground with "lusty" and "bold" poetry in free verse that celebrated the American common man.

D.   Hawthorne, Melville, and Poe
These three authors did not answer Emerson's call to write about the American scene or distinctly American characters. Rather, they were more interested in analyzing moral dilemmas and probing psychological states. Unlike Emerson and Whitman, who were essentially optimistic, Hawthorne, Melville, and Poe shared an "underlying pessimism about the human condition" and explored universal questions of human nature.

E.   Literature in the Marketplace
Most nineteenth-century U.S. authors hoped to gain recognition and a living from their writings. Poe sold short stories to popular magazines. Emerson, Thoreau, and Melville made money by lecturing for lyceums. While most lyceum speakers were men, women could and did earn excellent livings by turning out sentimental novels, such as Susan Warner's *The Wide, Wide World.* Although neither the writers nor most of the female readers who

consumed the sentimental novels were active feminists, many of the works did illustrate the moral that "women could overcome trials and improve their worlds."

F. American Landscape Painting
American artists between 1820 and 1860 sought to depict their native land, especially in its primitive grandeur before pioneers deforested and plowed it. George Catlin, for example, in hundreds of pictures portrayed Indians as "noble savages" doomed by the "march of progress." Others, like Thomas Cole, painted allegorical scenes on themes of importance to a young republic.

Cole, Asher Durand and Frederic Church belonged to the Hudson River school. Their works, which subordinated realism to emotional effect, reflected the romanticism of the period. The designers of New York's Central Park, Frederick Law Olmsted and Calvert Vaux, also shared a romantic view of nature. In their plan they aimed to refresh the souls of harried urbanites by creating for them an idealized pastoral landscape in the midst of the city.

VI. Conclusion
New technology changed the lives of millions of Americans between 1840 and 1860. Advances in transportation and manufacturing improved the American diet, made a greater variety of necessities and luxuries available at lower prices, transformed leisure pursuits, and encouraged efforts to diffuse and popularize culture. Technological progress also produced negative effects. It increased the gap between the lifestyles of the reasonably affluent and the poor and between middle-class men and women. It led to assaults on America's beautiful natural environment. That despoliation troubled writers such as Thoreau and artists such as the painters of the Hudson River school. Nor did material progress and political democracy liberate man from the dark places in his own soul, Hawthorne's and Melville's fiction demonstrated.

VOCABULARY

The following terms are used in Chapter 11. To understand the chapter fully, it is important that you know what each of them means.

despoliation	stripping of riches or resources; ruining
machine tools	machines that shape metal products
real income (real wages)	how much one's income or wages will purchase, given the prices at the time
tenements	subdivided houses or apartments in the poorer, crowded parts of large cities
rococo	a style of architecture and decoration, originating in France about 1720, that was distinguished by abundant and elegant ornamentation
precepts	rules of action or conduct
stereotype	characteristics, usually negative, attributed to all members of a group
poll tax	a tax that must be paid to exercise the right to vote
allegory	a figurative or symbolic treatment of an abstract idea or spiritual concept

IDENTIFICATIONS

After reading Chapter 11, you should be able to identify and explain the historical significance of each of the following:

John Deere's steel-tipped plow and Cyrus McCormick's mechanical reaper

American System of manufacturing, or interchangeable parts

Samuel F. B. Morse

Catharine Beecher, *A Treatise on Domestic Economy*

contagion theory versus miasma theory

Crawford Long and William T. G. Morton

hydropathy

Sylvester Graham

phrenology

James Gordon Bennett, the *New York Herald,* and the penny press

Horace Greeley and the *New York Tribune*

Astor Place riot

minstrel shows

P. T. Barnum and the American Museum

Washington Irving

James Fenimore Cooper

Edgar Allan Poe

American Renaissance

Henry David Thoreau

Ralph Waldo Emerson and "The American Scholar"

transcendentalism

Margaret Fuller

Nathaniel Hawthorne

Walt Whitman

Herman Melville

Thomas Cole, Asher Durand, Frederic Church, and the Hudson River school

lyceums

Frederick Law Olmsted and Calvert Vaux

SKILL BUILDING: MAPS

1. Locate on the map each of the important railroad hubs and/or terminal cities listed below:

   Chattanooga, Tennessee

   Atlanta, Georgia

   Chicago, Illinois

   Buffalo, New York

   Pittsburgh, Pennsylvania

   Baltimore, Maryland

   Wheeling, Virginia (later West Virginia)

2. Trace on the map the routes of each of these main antebellum railroad lines:

   New York Central

   Erie

   Pennsylvania

   Baltimore and Ohio

   Illinois Central

3. What economic, social, and political effects did the building of these railroads have on the United States?

Eastern United States

HISTORICAL SOURCES

Chapter 11 contains a section that describes the deplorable sanitation and periodic epidemics that plagued America's antebellum cities. How do historians know about these conditions? Our most valuable sources on this are the investigative reports made to early municipal health boards by city inspectors. One of the most thorough of these, *The Sanitary Conditions of the Laboring Classes* (1845), was written by New York's crusading city inspector Dr. John H. Griscom.

Historians also try to learn about the attitudes, values, and interests of people in the past by reading what they read. Although many Americans today still read the works of Whitman, Hawthorne, Melville, and Poe, few but historians wade through the popular novels of the antebellum period, like Susan Warner's *The Wide, Wide World*. What did the author of Chapter 11 learn about American life and values from this and other popular novels, as well as the penny press and story newspapers?

Now look at the Technology and Culture feature "Guns and Gun Culture." How does the historian's account of new technology in the manufacturing of guns and new techniques in their sale throw light on antebellum American attitudes and values?

MULTIPLE-CHOICE QUESTIONS

Circle the letter of the item that best completes each statement or answers the question.

1. The 1840s and 1850s in the United States were characterized by all of the following *except*
   a. heightened literary and artistic output and inventiveness.
   b. advances in medical knowledge that lessened the danger and frequency of epidemics.
   c. improvements in transportation and increases in productivity that raised the standard of living for the middle class.
   d. building of municipal water works in many of the big cities to supply the needs of urban dwellers.

2. All of the following were inventions of the antebellum period that were mass-produced and/or widely used in the 1840s and 1850s *except*
   a. Alexander Graham Bell's telephone.
   b. Cyrus McCormick's mechanical reaper.
   c. Samuel F. B. Morse's telegraph.
   d. Elias Howe's sewing machine.

3. Which of the following cities declined in importance as a commercial center because of the railroad building that took place in the 1840s and 1850s?
   a. Atlanta
   b. Chicago
   c. Pittsburgh
   d. New Orleans

4. An urban middle-class home in the 1850s would probably *not* have
   a. several stories.
   b. indoor faucets supplying hot and cold running water.
   c. conspicuously ornamented furniture.
   d. a coal-burning stove for cooking and heating.

5.   James Gordon Bennett was the
   a.   founder of the American Museum.
   b.   inventor of the cylindrical steam-driven press.
   c.   founder of the penny press.
   d.   founder of the lyceums.

6.   Which of the following statements about transcendentalism is *incorrect*?
   a.   It was an American form of romanticism.
   b.   It claimed that knowledge of God and truth were born in each individual.
   c.   It claimed that great literature must conform to universal standards of form and beauty.
   d.   It claimed that a new democratic republic could produce art and literature as great as the old traditional societies of Europe.

7.   In designing New York's Central Park, Frederick Law Olmsted and Calvert Vaux
   a.   copied the layout of English formal gardens.
   b.   tried to create the look of the countryside and screen out the surrounding city.
   c.   celebrated the excitement and vitality of urban America by including museums, sports arenas, and other entertainment facilities.
   d.   catered to the tastes and interests of the upper class by making the park resemble the grounds of the Palace of Versailles.

8.   Which of the following writers introduced into fiction the character of the American frontiersman and the theme of conflict between primitive life in the wilderness and the advance of civilization?
   a.   Herman Melville
   b.   Edgar Allan Poe
   c.   James Fenimore Cooper
   d.   Nathaniel Hawthorne

9.   Which of the following writers defended the right to disobey unjust laws, criticized the materialism of American society, and doubted the beneficial effects of technological advances?
   a.   Walt Whitman
   b.   Henry David Thoreau
   c.   John Greenleaf Whittier
   d.   James Fenimore Cooper

10.   Which of the following statements about the Hudson River school of painters is *incorrect*?
   a.   Its members painted only landscapes of the Hudson River and its vicinity.
   b.   Its members subordinated realism to heighten emotional effect through the use of color and composition.
   c.   It included Thomas Cole, Asher Durand, Frederic Church, and about fifty other painters.
   d.   Its members sought to capture on canvas the natural grandeur of the American landscape.

SHORT-ANSWER QUESTIONS

1.   Why were interchangeable parts and improved machine tools extremely important in the growth of American manufacturing?

2.   How was most American railroad building in the 1850s financed? What role did New York City play in this financing?

3.   Why did Americans' real annual income increase between 1840 and 1860?

4.   Why did antebellum American cities make little headway against recurring epidemics of cholera, yellow fever, and other diseases?

5.   Explain the beliefs of American transcendentalists, such as Emerson and Thoreau.

ESSAY QUESTIONS

1. In the 1830s Ralph Waldo Emerson called for a probing exploration of American nationality in literature and art. To what extent did the writers and painters of the American Renaissance answer that call?

2. What technological advances were made in agriculture, industry, and transportation between 1830 and 1860? How did these affect the daily lives of antebellum Americans? What impact did these have on the environment?

3. "The bright possibilities rather than the dark potential of technology impressed most antebellum Americans." To what extent did Americans' lives and experiences between 1830 and 1860 justify that attitude?

4. Discuss the rise of popular culture in the period 1830–1860, including the penny press, the sentimental novel, theater and minstrel shows, and popular health and science movements. How did technological advances of the period affect popular culture?

5. How did new technology and an expanded marketplace affect artistic and intellectual life in the United States between 1840 and 1860? How did artists and intellectuals feel about these changes?

ANSWERS TO MULTIPLE-CHOICE QUESTIONS

1. b
2. a
3. d
4. b
5. c
6. c
7. b
8. c
9. b
10. a

CHAPTER 12

The Old South and Slavery, 1830–1860

OUTLINE AND SUMMARY

I.   Introduction
Nat Turner's rebellion (August 1831), in which more than sixty whites were killed, touched off panic among whites about slave insurrections. Whites took indiscriminate revenge on blacks, and the Virginia legislature, in the winter of 1831–1832, came close to passing an emancipation bill. After the failure of that bill, however, white opposition to slavery in Virginia and throughout the South gradually disappeared. The Upper South relied less on slavery and cotton growing than the Lower South and seceded from the Union more hesitantly, but from 1832 on, what united and created the region the "Old South" was its defense of slavery, its "peculiar institution."

Chapter 12 covers the economy and society of the Old South from 1800 to 1860. After reading it, you should be able to answer these questions: (1) How did the rise of cotton cultivation affect the society and economy of the Old South?(2) What major social divisions segmented the white South? (3) Why did nonslaveholding whites feel their futures were tied to the survival of slavery? (4) What were the distinctive features of African-American society and culture in the South?

II.   King Cotton
A.   Introduction
The main cash crop of the colonial South, tobacco, declined in the late eighteenth century. Cotton culture revived southern agriculture and encouraged its rapid expansion southward and westward. Cotton growing was stimulated by the growth of the British textile industry, development of the cotton gin, and removal of Indians from southern and western lands.

B.   The Lure of Cotton
The climate of the Lower South was ideal for growing cotton. Intense demand in Britain kept prices high, so cotton could be grown profitably on any scale, with or without slave labor. However, cotton cultivation and the institution of slavery did increase side by side. Cotton and corn were often grown together so that the South did not have to spend money on imported food.

C.   Ties Between the Lower and Upper South
The Upper South identified with the Lower South rather than with the free states because many Lower South residents had migrated from the Upper South; all southern whites benefited from the three-fifths clause in the Constitution; almost all southerners resented the criticism from northern abolitionists; and the residents of the Upper South enjoyed a large, profitable business in the sale of slaves to the Lower South.

D.   The North and South Diverge
While the North was rapidly industrializing and urbanizing, the South remained primarily rural and agricultural. Slaves could be and were employed in southern factories, but much of the South's capital was tied up in slave ownership and, therefore, not available for investment in industrial development. Southerners believed that raising cash crops through slave labor would continue to be profitable, and hence they lacked the incentive to switch their capital from land and slaves to financing industry.

The South's slave economy did not require a high rate of literacy; hence the Old South made less provision for public schools than the North. School attendance was not compulsory for southern whites, and the law forbade teaching slaves to read and write.

III. The Social Groups of the White South
    A. Introduction
In 1860 only one-quarter of southern whites owned slaves; 1 percent of southern whites owned one hundred or more slaves. The whites of the Old South fit into four classes (although there was considerable variation within each category): (1) planters, owners of twenty or more slaves; (2) small slaveholders; (3) yeomen, nonslaveholding small family farmers; and (4) people of the pine barrens.

    B. Planters and Plantation Mistresses
Characterized by a high degree of division of labor, the plantation was almost a factory in the field. The pursuit of profit led planters to look constantly for additional and more fertile land, organize their slave crews as efficiently as possible, and seek favorable merchant-banker connections. To supplement their income many opened their homes to visitors, the responsibility of hospitality falling to their already overburdened wives. Psychological strains that plantation agriculture placed on planters and their wives included physical isolation from other whites of their class; frequent moves; crude living conditions, especially for the many who lived on the new frontier; and the responsibilities of running a major economic enterprise. An additional stress on planters' wives was the sexual double standard that accepted illicit sexual relations between masters and their bondswomen, while demanding absolute sexual purity from white females.

    C. The Small Slaveholders
There were many more small slaveholders than planters. "In 1860, 88 percent of all slaveholders owned fewer than twenty slaves." In the upland regions, the small slaveholders tended to identify with the more numerous yeomen, while in the low country and delta, they identified with the planters and aspired to rise into that class, which they sometimes did.

    D. The Yeomen
These nonslaveholding family farmers were by far the largest group among southern whites. Those with the least fertile land tended to be subsistence farmers, but most yeomen grew at least some crops for sale. Their farms ranged in size from 50 to 200 acres. The yeomen farmers were congregated in the upland, hilly, and less fertile regions. They were, on the whole, a proud and self-sufficient group.

    E. The People of the Pine Barrens
They made up about 10 percent of the white population and owned neither slaves nor land. They typically squatted on unfenced land, on which they grazed hogs and cattle and grew corn for their subsistence. Able to survive in this manner, they refused to work as hired help for others.

IV. Social Relations in the White South
    A. Introduction
Southern white society showed a mixture of aristocratic and democratic elements. There were great differences in wealth between classes, but most whites did own land. Planters were overrepresented in state legislatures but did not always pass laws that only benefited themselves.

    B. Conflict and Consensus in the White South
Planters and yeomen inclined toward opposing political parties, the elite being Whigs, the small farmers, Democrats. Other characteristics of the Old South, however, minimized

conflict: the four main social groups clustered in different regions and often had little contact, both yeomen and planters were independent landowners, and whites rarely worked for other whites, though many worked side by side with their slaves. Although planters dominated state legislatures, all white men had the right to vote by the 1820s; therefore, the planters could not ignore the desires of the yeomen majority.

C.   Conflict over Slavery
There was a potential for conflict between slaveholders and nonslaveholders. The majority of nonslaveholding southerners, however, supported slavery. Why? Some hoped to become slaveholders; many feared freedmen would demand social and political equality with whites. Throughout the South, whites shared racist beliefs about blacks and feared that emancipation would be followed by a race war, which would endanger the lives of all whites.

D.   The Proslavery Argument
The proslavery argument also was used as a tool to unite southern whites behind the institution. The argument, which was constructed by southern intellectuals between 1830 and 1860, claimed that slavery was a positive good rather than a necessary evil. It claimed that slavery was sanctioned by history and the bible and that southern slaves were better treated than northern factory "wage slaves." By the 1830s most southern churches had adopted this proslavery position.

In addition to persuading themselves of the righteousness of their "peculiar institution," southerners increasingly suppressed all public criticism of slavery. They seized and destroyed abolitionist literature mailed to the South and smashed the presses of southern antislavery newspapers.

E.   Violence in the Old South
During the colonial and pre–Civil War periods, violence was more prevalent among southern whites than it was among the white people in the North. The murder rate was as much as ten times higher in the South, and physical prowess became a badge of honor.

F.   The Code of Honor and Dueling
Behind much southern violence was an exaggerated notion of personal pride. White men must "react violently to even trivial insults in order to demonstrate that they had nothing in common with slaves." Among gentlemen this pride took the form of a code of honor. Any intentional insult to one's reputation had to be redressed by a challenge to a duel.

G.   The Southern Evangelicals and White Values
The code of honor was potentially in conflict with the values preached by southern evangelical churches, such as humility and self-restraint. From the 1830s on, evangelical religion grew in influence to the point that some southern gentlemen, while clinging to the value of reputation in the eyes of others, did denounce drinking, gambling, and dueling as un-Christian practices. On the other hand, southern churches came partly to endorse the gentry's code of honor.

V.   Life Under Slavery
A.   Introduction
Slavery was an exploitative institution that took by force the life and labor of one race for the profit of another. Slaves could be found in cities or on farms, in the fields or around the house. As the central units of an economic institution slave life depended not only on the kindness or cruelty of masters but also on unseen market forces.

B.   The Maturing of the Plantation System
The institution of slavery changed between 1700 and 1830. In the earlier period, the majority of the black population was recent African or Caribbean arrivals, disproportionately young

males who spoke little English and were isolated on small farms. By 1830 there was a more even balance between males and females. Most were American born and English speaking and worked on large plantations. These changes facilitated a more rapid natural increase in the black population.

C.   Work and Discipline of Plantation Slaves
No other nineteenth-century Americans worked as many hours under as harsh discipline as slave field hands, who either worked in gang labor or under the task system. Slave craftsmen and domestics on the plantations had higher status and easier work but also were subjected at times to physical brutality.

D.   The Slave Family
The slave family was not recognized or protected by southern law. Husbands and wives, parents and children, were separated by sale. Sexual demands were made on black females by masters and other white men. Despite these hazards, the black family did not dissolve but evolved in ways that were different from those of middle-class whites. In the place of the nuclear family fictive kin networks allowed slaves to assimilate to new environments.

E.   The Longevity, Diet, and Health of Slaves
Slaves in the Old South lived longer and reproduced faster than those in Brazil or the Caribbean because of a more even sex ratio among U.S. blacks and a more adequate diet. On the other hand, southern slaves had a higher mortality rate than their white countrymen.

F.   Slaves off Plantations
Although the majority of slaves worked on plantations, the Old South also used slaves in mining, lumbering, manufacturing, and performing a variety of skilled artisan jobs in cities and villages.

G.   Life on the Margin: Free Blacks in the Old South
Not all blacks in the Old South were slaves; there were more than a quarter million free blacks in 1860. The position of the free blacks in the South deteriorated from the 1830s on. Southern law forbade teaching blacks, free or slave, to read. Obstacles were put in the way of manumission, and free blacks were barred from entering or remaining in many states. Nonetheless, many of the post–Civil War black leaders came from this group.

H.   Slave Resistance
Nat Turner's 1831 rebellion was the only one in which whites were killed. Two earlier planned insurrections, Gabriel Prosser's (1800) and Denmark Vesey's (1822), were betrayed before they got underway. On the whole, the Old South experienced far fewer uprisings than did South America and the Caribbean because slaves did not form a large majority anywhere in the South, whites had all the weapons and soldiers, blacks were reluctant to endanger their families, and blacks rarely had allies in southern Indians and never in nonslaveholding whites. An alternative way to freedom was to try to escape to the North. Black abolitionists such as Frederick Douglass, Harriet Tubman, and Josiah Henson were escaped former slaves, some of whom returned repeatedly to the South to help others escape, giving rise to the legend of the Underground Railroad. Relatively few slaves, however, made it to the North successfully. More than by either running away or violent revolt, blacks resisted slavery by furtive means: theft, negligence, arson, poisoning, and work stoppages and slowdowns.

VI.   The Emergence of African-American Culture
A.   Introduction
American blacks under slavery developed a distinctive culture that drew on African and American cultures but was "more than a mixture of the two."

B.   The Language of Slaves
During the colonial period verbal communication between slaves was difficult due to the variety of African languages they spoke. By the time most slave were American-born, they had developed their own language, a pidgin English. This was an indispensable tool for communication and a bridge to a distinctive black culture.

C.   African-American Religion
The first Africans brought to the South were Muslims or followers of a variety of indigenous African religions. By 1800 many had been converted to Christianity, especially as Methodists or Baptists. Masters hoped that by preaching Christian humility and acceptance to their slaves, they could make blacks docile and obedient. This did not necessarily work, since the rebels Gabriel Prosser, Denmark Vesey, Nat Turner, and many of their followers were devout Christians who were inspired by their interpretation of the Bible. While Christianity did not turn most slaves into revolutionaries, it did serve as a unifying force among blacks, as well as a source of hope and comfort.

D.   Black Music and Dance
Compared to the cultural patterns of upper-class whites in the Old South, the culture of blacks was "extremely expressive." Blacks expressed their feelings in shouts, music, and dance. They composed work songs and religious songs, later known as spirituals.

VII. Conclusion
Slavery is what unified the Old South. Though the majority of white southerners owned no slaves, they had become convinced that the perpetuation of the "peculiar institution" was in the best interests of the entire South. Northerners, on the other hand, believed that slavery made the South backward and bankrupt. Southern whites reacted to outside criticism by defending slavery as a benevolent way to handle the innate inferiority of the black race. Few slaves agreed. While most of them did not revolt or escape successfully, they did engage in covert resistance. White masters hoped black conversion to Christianity would render their slaves submissive. However, when blacks accepted Christianity, they read into it the message that slavery was a gross injustice.

VOCABULARY

The following terms are used in Chapter 12. To understand the chapter fully, it is important that you know what each of them means.

yeomen	nonslaveholding family farmers, the Old South's most numerous white class
Portico	a structure consisting of a roof supported by columns, usually attached to a building as a porch
social structure	the classes or groups that make up a society and their relations with each other
planters	large landholders, especially those who owned twenty or more slaves, who were a small elite class of the Old South
evangelical	referring to certain movements and/or denominations within the Protestant churches that stress the importance of personal experience of guilt for sin and of reconciliation to God through Christ
pidgin	a simplified language, with no original, native speakers, in which people of different native languages can communicate

IDENTIFICATIONS

After reading Chapter 12, you should be able to identify and explain the historical significance of each of the following:

Nat Turner's rebellion

debate in the Virginia legislature over slavery, 1831–1832

three-fifths clause of the Constitution

J. D. B. DeBow

Tredegar Iron Works

Whig party

Democratic party

Hinton R. Helper, *The Impending Crisis of the South*

proslavery argument

George Fitzhugh

southern code of honor

northern "character"

Gabriel Prosser

Denmark Vesey

Henry "Box" Brown

Frederick Douglass

Harriet Tubman

Josiah Henson

Underground Railroad

SKILL BUILDING: MAPS

On the map of the South, locate each of the areas listed below. In what states do you find these geographical areas? What was the historical significance of each?

Upper South

Lower (Deep) South

tidewater

pine barrens

Piedmont

Mississippi Delta

uplands

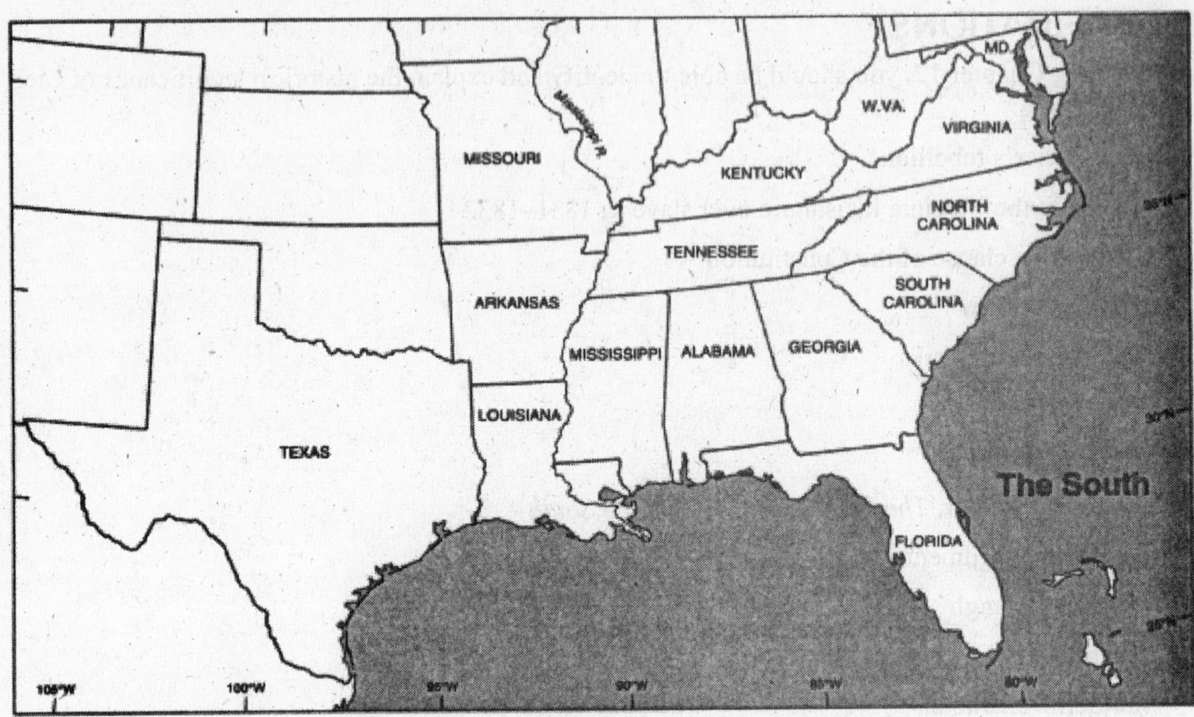

HISTORICAL SOURCES

The author of Chapter 12 has relied on many and varied historical sources to try to achieve a balanced and accurate account of life in the Old South. To see slavery as the bondsmen and bondswomen experienced it, the author has turned to accounts by former slaves, written or oral. Probably the most famous of the published narratives are those of black abolitionist, writer, and political leader Frederick Douglass, including his *Narrative of the Life of Frederick Douglass: An American Slave, Written by Himself* (1845); *My Bondage and My Freedom* (1855); and *Life and Times of Frederick Douglass* (1881). In this chapter, the works of Frederick Douglass are referred to and/or quoted. How has the author used these historical sources? Another of the well-known written narratives, Solomon Northup's *Twelve Years a Slave* (1854), also is quoted. What does the author of the chapter illustrate with this quotation? Northup was a free black living in New York who was kidnapped in 1841 and sold into slavery on a Louisiana cotton plantation. Find other places in the chapter where the memories of former slaves are cited. Many of these stories come from interviews that were conducted by unemployed writers and researchers who, during the depression in the 1930s, worked for the WPA Federal Writers Project. The government hired these persons to seek out elderly black people who had been slaves as children, ask them about their experiences, and record their answers. A sampling of these interviews, edited by Benjamin A. Botkin, was published in 1945 in a book titled *Lay My Burden Down*.

Historians have learned much about the life and attitudes of the planter class from letters and diaries. One of the most informative of these is the diary kept by Mary Boykin Chesnut, wife of a South Carolina planter. In Chapter 12, she is cited on the "sorrows of plantation mistresses," many of whom were reminded daily of their husbands' infidelities by the features of the mulatto children in the slave quarters. The historian can find confirmation of this charge against planters and see how one bondswoman felt about the unwanted advances of her master by looking at the narrative of escaped slave Harriet A. Jacobs, *Incidents in the Life of a Slave Girl, Written by Herself* (1861).

Chapter 12 also lets us see the Old South as it appeared to visitors from the outside. The author refers to and/or quotes from Frederick Law Olmsted's books *A Journey in the Seaboard Slave States* (1856), *A Journey Through Texas* (1857), and *A Journey in the Back Country* (1860). Olmsted, who later became one of America's foremost landscape architects and designer of New York's Central Park, took a fourteen-month tour of the slave states in the 1850s on a journalistic assignment from the *New York Times*. Olmsted's mostly critical observations about the Old South and its "peculiar institution" were different from the glowing defense of black slavery that historians encounter in the writings of its southern defenders. Chapter 12 cites the works of two such defenders, James Henry Hammond's "Letters on Slavery" in *The Pro-Slavery Argument* (1853) and George Fitzhugh's *Sociology for the South* (1854). What arguments did these books present in favor of black slavery?

Historians also conduct intensive studies of local records to gain insights into both regional and national history. Look at the account of the Edgefield District, South Carolina. What generalizations about the Old South does it seem to bear out?

MULTIPLE-CHOICE QUESTIONS

Circle the letter of the item that best completes each statement or answers the question.

1. The majority of white men in the antebellum South were
   a. planters.
   b. small slaveholders.
   c. nonslaveholding family farmers.
   d. merchants or shopkeepers.

2. All of the following were true of planters *except* they
   a. searched constantly for more and better land.
   b. were often in debt to Northern bankers and brokers.
   c. usually managed their own estates.
   d. almost always built mansions on their plantations for their families.

3. The yeomen farmers of the Old South
   a. were congregated in the upland and hilly regions.
   b. did not grow cash crops for market.
   c. did not have the right to vote.
   d. were generally tenants rather than landowners.

4. In 1857 a book calling on nonslaveholding southern whites to abolish slavery in their own interest was published by
   a. James Henry Hammond.
   b. Hinton R. Helper.
   c. George Fitzhugh.
   d. Gabriel Prosser.

5. As compared to the North, the Old South had a higher
   a. literacy rate.
   b. proportion of its people living in cities.
   c. murder rate.
   d. proportion of its white population working for other whites.

6. In 1860, what percentage of southern whites owned at least one slave?
   a. 25 percent
   b. 40 percent
   c. 50 percent
   d. 75 percent

7.   The black family under slavery

   a.   received no legal recognition or protection.
   b.   disintegrated.
   c.   copied the customs and patterns of white families.
   d.   was protected against separation of young children and mothers.

8.   Why weren't there more slave revolts in the Old South?

   a.   Blacks were outnumbered by whites almost everywhere in the South and lacked allies and guns.
   b.   Blacks had no strong desire for freedom, which they did not understand.
   c.   Blacks had no inspired leaders.
   d.   Blacks were restrained by strong bonds of loyalty to masters who treated them fairly.

9.   Most blacks in the antebellum South

   a.   rejected Christianity as the religion of their slave masters.
   b.   accepted the preaching of white clergy that slavery was divinely sanctioned.
   c.   drew from Christianity the view that slavery was an affliction to test their faith and for which masters would be punished.
   d.   became obedient and docile because of the Christian promise of reward in heaven for faithful servants.

10.   Which of the following statements about white people of the pine barrens is *incorrect*?

   a.   They generally "squatted" on their land rather than owned it.
   b.   They usually favored the institution of slavery, though they owned no slaves.
   c.   They usually worked for the planters as tenant farmers, sharecroppers, or overseers.
   d.   They carried on subsistence farming.

SHORT-ANSWER QUESTIONS

1.   Explain the differences between the Upper and Lower South. What tied them together?

2.   Explain why the Old South failed to industrialize.

3.   Summarize the proslavery argument developed by southern intellectuals to defend the "peculiar institution."

4.   Discuss the free black population of the Old South. How many were there by the eve of the Civil War? Where did most of them live? Under what economic and legal constraints did they exist?

5.   Describe the "furtive resistance" of slaves in the Old South.

ESSAY QUESTIONS

1.   Compare and contrast economic, social, and political developments in the North and South between 1800 and 1860. How do you account for the divergence between the two sections?

2.   Discuss the white social structure of the Old South. How egalitarian was it? What social classes or groups existed? What was their relationship to each other and to the institution of slavery?

3.   The great majority of white southerners never owned a single slave, yet the majority supported the institution of slavery. Write an essay explaining why.

4.   Was slavery in the South essentially a paternalistic institution in which most slaves were treated reasonably well, or was it primarily an exploitative institution? Back up your conclusions by citing as much evidence as possible.

5.   Discuss the emergence of African-American culture in the Old South. In what ways did it draw on African experiences? In what ways did it incorporate the American slave experience? How did it differ from white southern culture and values?

ANSWERS TO MULTIPLE-CHOICE QUESTIONS

1. c
2. d
3. a
4. b
5. c
6. a
7. a
8. a
9. c
10. c

CHAPTER 13

Immigration, Expansion, and Sectional Conflict, 1840–1848

OUTLINE AND SUMMARY

I. Introduction

Between 1845 and 1847, Brigham Young led some 20,000 Mormons into the Great Salt Lake Valley, then a part of Mexico. The Mormons purposely chose this remote desert area in hopes of isolating themselves from non-Mormon fellow Americans who were persecuting them. However, great numbers of their countrymen were also relentlessly pushing westward.

In the 1840s many Americans believed it was the "manifest destiny" of the United States to possess North America from coast to coast. Acting on that belief, the administration of James K. Polk, between 1845 and 1849, annexed Texas; divided the Oregon Territory with Great Britain; and fought the Mexican War, resulting in the conquest of California and New Mexico. Also, in the 1840s and 1850s a rising tide of new immigrants entered the country. Expansion and immigration were linked. The overwhelmingly Democratic immigrant vote helped elect President Polk, an ardent expansionist. Many Democratic Party leaders saw the acquisition of more land and a return to a republic of self-sufficient farmers as a way of relieving growing class, ethnic, and sectional conflicts; adding Oregon would please the North, Texas, the South. In fact, westward expansion had the opposite effect; it sharpened sectional strife, split the Democratic Party, and set the nation on the path to the Civil War. As you read about these events in Chapter 13, try to find the answers to the following questions: (1) How did immigration in the 1840s influence the balance of power between the Whig and Democratic Parties? (2) What economic and political forces fed westward expansion during the 1840s? (3) How did westward expansion threaten war with Britain and Mexico? (4) How did the outcome of the Mexican-American War intensify intersectional conflict?

II. Newcomers and Natives

A. Introduction

Between 1840 and 1860, 4.2 million immigrants entered the United States. The two biggest groups came from Ireland and the German states.

B. Expectations and Realities

Immigrants came in the hope of improving their economic condition. Few of the Irish immigrants possessed enough capital to acquire farms. Instead they settled heavily in northeastern cities, where they took jobs in construction and railroad building. Germans and Scandinavians, on the other hand, tended to concentrate in Illinois, Ohio, Wisconsin, and Missouri. Although more of them entered farming than the Irish did, they too were drawn to cities. By 1860 the Irish and Germans accounted for approximately 50 percent of the population of cities such as St. Louis, New York, Chicago, Cincinnati, Milwaukee, Detroit, and San Francisco.

C.   The Germans
The German immigrants were quite diverse, including people of different social classes and religions, but they were bound together by their common language and often settled in German neighborhoods. They prospered and built many ethnic institutions: German-language newspapers, voluntary associations, and schools. Native-born Americans criticized them for being clannish.

D.   The Irish
Between 1815 and 1844 almost 1 million Irish entered the United States, most of them Catholic, poor, and seeking greater economic opportunity. From 1845 to 1855, another roughly 2 million arrived, now overwhelmingly Catholic and fleeing the potato famine that was ravaging their homeland. They usually entered the urban work force at the bottom, competing for jobs with equally poor blacks. The competition led to animosity between the two groups and made most Irish hostile to abolition and abolitionists. Those Irish who rose to the level of skilled and semiskilled workers competed against native-born, white, Protestant mechanics, producing another level of hostilities, now ethnic and religious.

E.   Anti-Catholicism, Nativism, and Labor Protest
The antagonism of white, Protestant, native-born workers took the form of anti-Catholic and anti-immigrant outbursts and organizations. Such sentiments and organizations were behind the founding of the Know-Nothing (or American) Party, which played a significant political role in the 1850s. Labor also responded to low wages and job competition by advocating land reform (including free 160-acre homesteads in the West for all who wanted them) and by forming unions and waging strikes. Unions won a few gains, but their growth was limited by government and employer opposition and by the deep splits along ethnic and religious lines in the antebellum working class.

F.   Immigrant Politics
Almost all Irish and German immigrants became supporters of the Democratic Party. They saw it as an antiprivilege party, more sympathetic to the common man than the Whigs were. The Irish and Germans also resented Whig connections with the temperance movement and nativism. The Irish suspected the northern Whigs of antislavery views, and since the Irish feared economic competition from emancipated slaves, they wanted no part of abolitionism.

III.   The West and Beyond
A.   The Far West
In the 1820s, 1830s, and 1840s Texas and the present-day southwestern regions of the United States belonged to Mexico who, after independence, claimed all Spanish territories in the West. The Oregon Territory (including what are now the states of Oregon, Washington, and Idaho and parts of Wyoming, Montana, and Canada), ceded to the United States from Spain in the Adams-Onis Treaty, was under joint occupation by Britain and the United States.

B.   Far Western Trade
The earliest Americans to enter the Far West were fur trappers and traders. Some had sailed around South America and up the Pacific; others blazed overland trails, such as the Santa Fe. These traders introduced eastern manufactured goods in exchange for beaver pelts or Mexican silver and set up encampments and trading posts. They also spurred the interest of pioneer farmers with their tales of favorable climate and fertile soil in the Far West.

C.   The American Settlement of Texas, to 1835
In the 1820s the Mexican government gave generous land grants to Americans and encouraged their settlement in Texas as a way to guard against Indian attacks and hasten the

economic development of the province. So many came, primarily from the southern states, that the Mexican government in the 1830s attempted to end American immigration and prohibit slavery in Texas. Its efforts antagonized the Americans but failed to stop the flood of immigrants that by 1836 had raised the American population in Texas to thirty thousand whites and five thousand slaves. Meanwhile, in 1834 the new president-dictator of Mexico, Santa Anna, started to tighten his hold on Texas. The Americans in the province rebelled.

D.   The Texas Revolution, 1836
In the fall of 1835 Santa Anna led an army into Texas to suppress the uprising. The Mexicans defeated the Americans at the Alamo and at Goliad. However, in April, under the leadership of Sam Houston, the Americans routed the Mexicans at San Jacinto, took Santa Anna prisoner, and forced him to sign a treaty granting Texas independence. The Mexican government later refused to ratify the treaty, but Texas remained independent.

E.   American Settlements in California, New Mexico, and Oregon
The Mexicans also initially welcomed American colonists to California. By the 1840s a growing number were settling in the Sacramento Valley, where they lived apart from the Mexicans. In the 1830s American missionaries entered Oregon's Willamette Valley to attempt to convert the Indians there. The missionaries' glowing reports of the territory's climate and resources aroused keen interest back in the United States.

F.   The Overland Trails
In the 1840s, despite faulty maps and guidebooks, fears of Indian attacks, and other real and imagined dangers, more than fourteen thousand Americans joined wagon trains on the Overland Trail headed for Oregon or California. In contrast, the British could not effectively settle Oregon at all, and Mexican numbers in California were small and scattered.

IV.   The Politics of Expansion, 1840–1846
A.   Introduction
At the start of the 1840s western expansion was not an important political issue. Only after politicians failed to deal effectively with troubling economic issues did some of these leaders seize on expansion as a primary goal.

B.   The Whig Ascendancy
The Whig Party won the election of 1840 with William Henry Harrison. The party planned to enact Clay's American System of a new national bank, protective tariffs, and federal aid for internal improvements. These plans were thwarted, however, by Harrison's death after only one month in the White House. This brought Vice President John Tyler into office. Tyler, a states' rights Virginian, vetoed all the economic measures Congress, dominated by the Whigs, passed.

C.   Tyler and the Annexation of Texas
At odds with his party on economic issues, Tyler attempted to gain popularity by achieving success in foreign policy. He supported the U.S. annexation of Texas and appointed John C. Calhoun as his secretary of state to draw up a treaty. Calhoun wrote undiplomatically that one reason for annexation was to provide more territory for the expansion and protection of slavery. This added fuel to already existing northern suspicions that acquiring Texas was part of a southern conspiracy to expand slavery, and the Senate therefore rejected Tyler and Calhoun's annexation treaty.

D.   The Election of 1844
The annexation of Texas became an important issue in the 1844 election. The Whig nominee, Henry Clay, wavered on annexation, first opposing it as sectionally divisive, then softening his opposition, and finally opposing it again. His shifts lost southern votes to the

Democrats and northern antislavery votes to the Liberty Party. The Democrats nominated the ardently expansionist James K. Polk, who called for admitting Texas immediately. Many Irish and other recent immigrants voted for Polk because they disliked the Whigs' association with nativism, temperance, and anti-Catholicism. Polk won in a close election.

E.   Manifest Destiny, 1845
The election demonstrated, among other things, that expansionism had become a popular cause by the 1840s. Many expansionists repeated journalist John L. O'Sullivan's claim that it was the "manifest destiny" of the United States to spread its experiment in liberty and self-government from coast to coast. They eyed the excellent harbors of California and Oregon as the natural outlets for American trade with Asia. With Jeffersonian flair, expansionists argued that acquiring additional fertile soil would safeguard the U.S. future as a democratic republic of self-sufficient farmers and combat the social stratification and class strife that accompanied industrialization and urbanization. These ideas, carried in the penny press, strongly appealed to struggling immigrants in the cities.

F.   Polk and Oregon
In his 1844 presidential campaign, Polk had called for U.S. ownership of all the Oregon Territory as well as the annexation of Texas. Americans' spirit of Manifest Destiny placed Oregon squarely in their sights, though neither the British nor the United States wanted a war. They settled for a compromise treaty that split Oregon at the forty-ninth parallel. The Senate ratified the treaty in 1846.

V.   The Mexican-American War and Its Aftermath, 1846–1848
A.   The Origins of the Mexican-American War
In February 1845 Congress passed a joint resolution to annex Texas, although Mexico had never recognized the independence of the province. After Polk was inaugurated, he backed the Texan claim that its southern boundary was the Rio Grande as opposed to Mexico's contention that it was the Nueces River, 100 miles to the northeast. Polk's support encouraged Texas to accept annexation on July 4, 1845.

Polk also wanted to gain California and New Mexico, and he sent John Slidell to Mexico with an offer to buy them for $25 million. After Mexico refused, Polk ordered American troops under General Zachary Taylor into the disputed region south of the Nueces, hoping to provoke a war that would give the United States a chance to seize California and New Mexico. When Mexican troops clashed with Taylor's, Polk told Congress that Mexico had forced war with the United States.

B.   The Mexican-American War
In February 1847 Zachary Taylor defeated a Mexican army at the Battle of Buena Vista. Colonel Stephen Kearny took New Mexico, and California fell to combined naval and land assaults under commodores John D. Sloat and David Stockton and army officers Kearny and John C. Frémont. Mexico surrendered in September 1847 when an American force led by General Winfield Scott conquered Mexico City. Under the terms of the Treaty of Guadalupe Hidalgo, Mexico accepted the Rio Grande boundary and ceded to the United States almost all of the present-day U.S. Southwest in return for $15 million and a promise by the U.S. government to pay claims of U.S. citizens against Mexico.

C.   The War's Effects on Sectional Conflict
Despite the patriotism generated by the war, sectional conflict grew between 1846 and 1848. The Polk administration angered the North and West by lowering tariffs and vetoing federal aid for internal improvements. Most important, arguments began over the expansion of slavery into the Mexican cession. Northern Democrats worried that the western expansion of

slavery would close out opportunities for free laborers in the West and worsen class antagonism in the East.

D. The Wilmot Proviso
In 1846 a northern Democratic congressional representative, David Wilmot, tacked onto an appropriations bill an amendment that would bar slavery from the new territory acquired from Mexico. With much northern support, the so-called Wilmot Proviso passed the House but not the Senate. Extremist southerners led by Calhoun claimed it was unconstitutional for Congress to forbid slavery in any territory.

E. The Election of 1848
The Whigs nominated Zachary Taylor for president. The Democrats chose Lewis Cass, who tried to solve the sectional controversy by proposing popular sovereignty, giving the settlers who lived in a territory the right to decide whether to permit slavery. Not satisfied with this position, a faction of Democrats called Barnburners joined antislavery "conscience" Whigs and Liberty Party abolitionists to create the Free-Soil Party. It nominated Martin Van Buren, who ran on a platform opposing any further spread of slavery. Taylor, a military hero whose position on slavery was unknown, won the election. The good showing of the Free-Soilers in the North, however, demonstrated the popular appeal of keeping slavery out of the West and using it as a place of opportunity for poor white men.

F. The California Gold Rush
Just before the signing of the Treaty of Guadalupe Hidalgo, an American carpenter living in California discovered gold near Sacramento. The news, which soon reached the East, produced a rush of prospectors. California's population surged, and the weak military government proved unequal to containing the violence and disorder of the gold fields and mining boomtowns. Californians demanded a civilian state government. This brought to a head the issue of slavery in California and the rest of the Mexican cession.

VI. Conclusion
After winning the election of 1840, the Whigs were unable to enact their platform of national banking and protective tariffs because of the death of President William H. Harrison and his replacement by Vice President John Tyler, who espoused Democratic, not Whig, views. In the election of 1844, the ardently expansionist Democrat, James Polk was elected president. Polk, during his one term, nearly led the United States into a war against Britain and did fight Mexico. The issue of the spread of slavery into the territories taken from Mexico fanned sectional strife and split the Democrats, as many northern members joined others in 1848 in creating the Free-Soil party.

VOCABULARY

The following terms are used in Chapter 13. To understand the chapter fully, it is important that you know what each of them means.

steerage	the section of a ship, originally near the rudder, providing the cheapest accommodations for passengers
freethinker	one who has rejected authority and ritual, especially in religion, in favor of rational inquiry and speculation
nativism	dislike and suspicion of immigrants; the policy of protecting the interests of native inhabitants versus those of immigrants
secularize	transfer control or ownership of something from the church or religious authorities to civil authorities, such as the government

allegiance	a feeling of duty, obligation, or faithfulness to a person, idea, country, or government
dark horse	a little-known or unlikely political figure who unexpectedly wins nomination and/or election
proviso	a clause in a statute, contract, or the like, by which a condition is introduced; a stipulation or condition

IDENTIFICATIONS

After reading Chapter 13, you should be able to identify and explain the historical significance of each of the following:

Brigham Young and the Mormons

Know-Nothing, or American, Party

George Henry Evans

Commonwealth v. *Hunt* (1842)

Spanish missions and presidios

Stephen F. Austin and American *empresarios* in Texas

Antonio López de Santa Anna

the Alamo

Sam Houston

Overland Trail and the Donner party

John Tyler

John C. Calhoun

Henry Clay

James K. Polk

John L. O'Sullivan and Manifest Destiny

Zachary Taylor ("Old Rough and Ready")

Winfield Scott

John C. Frémont and the Bear Flag Republic

Treaty of Guadalupe Hidalgo

Wilmot Proviso

squatter or popular sovereignty

Martin Van Buren and the Free-Soil party

SKILL BUILDING: MAPS

On the map of the West on the following page, locate each of the following and explain its historical significance:

forty-ninth parallel

Great Plains

Rocky Mountains

Oregon Territory

54°40' latitude

St. Louis

Santa Fe

Santa Fe Trail

Texas and the Mexican cession

Sacramento Valley

Columbia River

Vancouver Island

Rio Grande

Nueces River

San Francisco

36°30' latitude

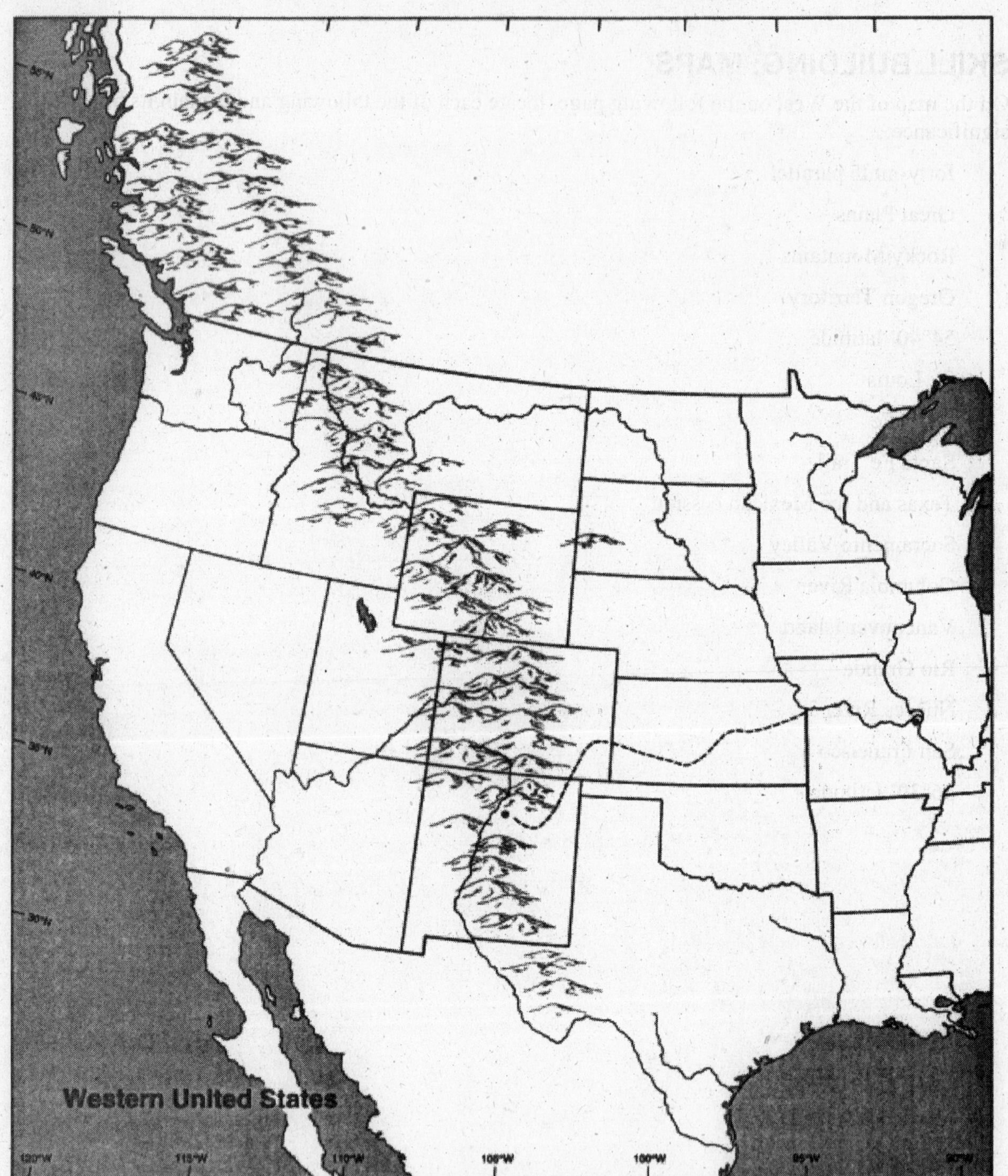
Western United States

MULTIPLE-CHOICE QUESTIONS

Circle the letter of the item that best completes each statement or answers the question.

1.   The two biggest sources of immigration to the United States between 1840 and 1860 were

   a.   Italy and eastern Europe.
   b.   China and Japan.
   c.   Ireland and the German states.
   d.   Britain and Scotland.

2.   In the case of *Commonwealth* v. *Hunt* (1842), the Massachusetts Supreme Court ruled that

   a.   slavery was unconstitutional in Massachusetts.
   b.   labor unions were not necessarily illegal combinations or monopolies.
   c.   Massachusetts tax money could not be used to support an unjust war against Mexico.
   d.   segregated schools for blacks in Massachusetts did not violate the U.S. Constitution.

3.   Squatter or popular sovereignty meant

   a.   allowing residents of a territory to decide whether to permit slavery there.
   b.   extending the right to vote to all male settlers in the Far West.
   c.   deciding the ownership of a territory by vote of its residents.
   d.   the right of the native Indian peoples to keep the lands they were already cultivating.

4.   Which of the following statements about President Polk's actions is *incorrect*?

   a.   He sent John Slidell to Mexico with an offer to buy California and New Mexico.
   b.   He ordered Zachary Taylor to keep his troops north of the Nueces River to avoid a confrontation with Mexico.
   c.   He agreed to split the Oregon Territory with the British at the forty-ninth parallel, although he had demanded all of it during his presidential campaign.
   d.   He signed a bill lowering the tariff and vetoed one giving federal aid for internal improvements.

5.   The expansionist term *Manifest Destiny* was first coined by

   a.   George Henry Evans.
   b.   Horace Greeley.
   c.   John C. Frémont.
   d.   John L. O'Sullivan.

6.   All of the following people or group were nativist and anti-Catholic *except*

   a.   the Know-Nothings.
   b.   Martin Van Buren.
   c.   Samuel F. B. Morse.
   d.   Lyman Beecher.

7.   The fate of the Donner party best illustrates the

   a.   hazards faced by pioneers traveling west on the Overland Trail.
   b.   lack of appeal of abolitionism to the majority of immigrants.
   c.   widespread lack of interest among Americans in Henry Clay's American System by the 1840s.
   d.   vicious attacks on Catholics and immigrants that took place in the 1830s and 1840s.

8. The Senate rejected the treaty annexing Texas that was drawn up by Secretary of State John Calhoun because
    a. he defended annexation as a way to protect and defend slavery.
    b. the Texans made it clear that they were not yet ready to give up their independence and join the United States.
    c. the British threatened to break off diplomatic relations if the United States took the territory without compensating them.
    d. Mexico threatened to declare war on the United States if it stole her province.

9. The Wilmot Proviso called for
    a. the annexation of Texas.
    b. prohibiting slavery in any territory acquired from Mexico.
    c. drawing the Missouri Compromise line of 36°30' to the West Coast.
    d. legislation to limit immigration into the United States.

10. Presidios were
    a. agents who contracted with the Mexican government to bring American settlers into Texas.
    b. Mexicans who owned huge ranches worked by enslaved Indians.
    c. Franciscan priests who endeavored to convert the Indians to Christianity.
    d. forts constructed by the Spanish to protect their missions in the Southwest.

SHORT-ANSWER QUESTIONS

1. In the antebellum period, why did Irish and German immigrants generally favor the Democratic Party over the Whig Party?

2. Why did Polk first demand all of the Oregon Territory from Britain and then agree to a compromise? What were the terms of that compromise?

3. Why did many northern Democrats who were not abolitionists favor the Wilmot Proviso?

4. What was the platform of the Free-Soil Party in the election of 1848? How well did the party do in the election? Why was its showing significant?

5. How were the clipper ships and the California gold rush related?

6. How did the California gold rush bring to a head the issue of slavery in the Far West?

ESSAY QUESTIONS

1. Discuss immigration to the United States in the 1840s and 1850s. Who came? Why did immigrants come? Where did they settle? What economic and political roles did they play?

2. Discuss the rise of anti-Catholic and nativist sentiment and movements in the United States in the 1840s. What caused them? Who supported such groups? What impact did these groups have on American politics?

3. What did expansionists mean by the term *Manifest Destiny*? What arguments did they use to justify expansion? To whom did these arguments appeal? Why?

4. Discuss the causes of the Mexican War. To what extent did the United States provoke the confrontation? Why did some members of Congress and the public oppose the war?

5. Explain the following statement with as much illustrative evidence as possible: "[E]xpansion brought sectional antagonism to the boiling point, split the Democratic Party in the late 1840s, and set the nation on the path to the Civil War."

ANSWERS TO MULTIPLE-CHOICE QUESTIONS

1. c
2. b
3. a
4. b
5. d
6. b
7. a
8. a
9. b
10. d

CHAPTER 14

From Compromise to Secession, 1850–1861

OUTLINE AND SUMMARY

I. Introduction
The decade of the 1850s opened with a compromise that was supposed to settle sectional differences, but it quickly came undone. Instead, the 1850s lurched from one sectional crisis to the next. The most devastating of those occurred on October 16, 1859, when John Brown and eighteen followers seized the federal arsenal and armory at Harpers Ferry, intending to arm southern white and black dissidents in a holy war against slavery. Brown's failed raid convinced southerners that they had barely survived a northern plot to get them all murdered in a slave insurrection. Northerners, while initially disavowing Brown, came, during his trial, to sympathize with him. The whole incident set the stage for civil war. As you read about the events of the 1850s in Chapter 14, try to find answers to the following questions: (1) How did the Fugitive Slave Act lead to the undoing of the Compromise of 1850? (2) Why did the Whig Party collapse after the Kansas-Nebraska Act while the Democratic Party survived? (3) How did the Republican doctrine of free soil unify northerners against the South? (4) Why did southerners conclude that the North was bent on extinguishing slavery in the southern states?

II. The Compromise of 1850
A. Introduction
When the treaty ending the Mexican War was signed in 1848, a delicate balance existed between free and slave states: there were fifteen of each. All the proposed solutions for handling slavery in the Mexican cession—whether to prohibit it, open the whole area to slaveholders, extend the Missouri Compromise line to the Pacific, or apply popular sovereignty—were controversial. Other issues also divided the North and South. Then, California and Utah asked Congress for admission to the Union as free states.

B. Zachary Taylor at the Helm
President Taylor had encouraged California to make this request for statehood. Believing that the majority of its residents opposed slavery, he urged Congress to welcome it into the Union as a free state. Southerners were horrified, however, at the prospect of losing the balance of power in the Senate by admitting California and perhaps next New Mexico as free states. In protest nine southern states sent delegates to a southern convention at Nashville.

C. Henry Clay Proposes a Compromise
Senator Clay proposed a compromise to settle the territorial problem and other sectional controversies.

1. Admit California as a free state.
2. Divide the rest of the Mexican cession into the New Mexico and Utah territories, with the future of slavery in each left up to its residents.
3. Settle the border dispute between Texas and New Mexico in New Mexico's favor.
4. Compensate Texas by having the federal government pay off the state's past public debt.

5. Allow slavery to continue in Washington, D.C., but ban slave trading there.
6. Pass and enforce a tough new fugitive slave law.

After heated debate and much maneuvering, the compromise passed.

D. Assessing the Compromise
The Compromise of 1850 did not settle the underlying differences between the sections. The one clear advantage that the South gained, the passage of the stringent Fugitive Slave Act, backfired.

E. Enforcement of the Fugitive Slave Act
The law was blatantly stacked against black people and sent federal marshals all over the country looking for runaways. This aroused widespread opposition in the North. Northern mobs attacked marshals to rescue arrested fugitives, vigilance committees helped runaways escape to Canada, and nine states passed personal liberty laws designed to interfere with enforcement of the act. Whereas the act embittered northerners against the South, southerners resented the North's refusal to live up to the terms of the compromise.

F. *Uncle Tom's Cabin*
The publication of Harriet Beecher Stowe's *Uncle Tom's Cabin* and the many dramatizations of it further aroused antisouthern feelings and sympathy for slaves in the North. By 1853, 1.2 million copies had been sold.

G. The Election of 1852
The Whigs nominated war hero General Winfield Scott to run against Democrat Franklin Pierce for president. The Democrats rallied behind the Compromise of 1850 and popular sovereignty in the territories. Pierce and the Democrats trounced the Whigs, whose northern and southern wings were being torn apart by the sectional controversy.

III. The Collapse of the Second Party System, 1853–1856
A. Introduction
During Pierce's administration the second party system—Whig against Democrat— collapsed. In the 1850s the issues that had been the main focus of partisan politics (banking, internal improvements, tariffs, and temperance) were pushed from center stage by the debate over slavery's extension. The Whig Party, more internally divided on the question than the Democrats, disintegrated when Stephen A. Douglas's Kansas-Nebraska bill threw the future of slavery in the territories wide open.

B. The Kansas-Nebraska Act
Passage of this act in 1854 dealt a shattering blow to the second party system and renewed the sectional strife that Clay's compromise had aimed to quiet. Stephen A. Douglas was eager to advance the settlement of Kansas and Nebraska and to promote the building of a transcontinental railroad through the area. To accomplish these goals, he needed to organize a territorial government for the region, but he was running into southern opposition because the area was north of the Missouri Compromise line and would therefore be free. To gain southern support, Douglas introduced the Kansas-Nebraska bill, which repealed the Missouri Compromise, organized two territories, and left the question of slavery in both Kansas and Nebraska up to popular sovereignty. That gave the South a chance to gain at least Kansas (adjacent to the slave state of Missouri) for the "peculiar institution."

C. The Surge of Free-Soil
Douglas was surprised at the angry reaction in the North, where many regarded the law as part of an atrocious southern plot to spread slavery into Kansas, the rest of the Louisiana Territory, and even into the North. Free-soil sentiment had grown tremendously in the North, not primarily because of sympathy for black slaves—many free-soilers were racists—

but because northerners wanted the territories to be the place where upwardly mobile, enterprising, poor Americans could become independent, self-employed farmers and businessmen. If slavery invaded the territories, it would discourage and drive out free labor.

D.   The Ebbing of Manifest Destiny
Enthusiasm for expansion, which had unified the Democratic Party, waned in the free states as northerners saw in each southern move to acquire territory a plot to gain additional slave states. This northern attitude became so pronounced that President Pierce had to repudiate southern-backed plans to buy or seize Cuba.

E.   The Whigs Disintegrate, 1854–1855
Southern Whigs had joined Democrats in voting for the Kansas-Nebraska Act. Northern "conscience" Whigs, led by Senator William Seward, and free-soil Democrats reacted angrily against both of the major parties. In the elections of 1854 and 1855 many of the disaffected Whigs turned first to the American, or Know-Nothing, Party and later increasingly to the new Republican Party. As a result of these moves, the Whig Party fell apart.

F.   The Rise and Fall of the Know-Nothings, 1853–1856
The American Party (Know-Nothings) evolved out of a secret nativist society called the Order of the Star-Spangled Banner. In the North the party combined hatred of Catholics, immigrants, and slavery-extension. It took a conspiratorial view of the world in which the Pope and Slave Power were both plotting to extinguish the American democratic republic. In 1854 and 1855 the Know-Nothings scored major victories in northern states such as Massachusetts. However, the party declined rapidly thereafter because, like the major parties, it was pulled apart by the slavery-expansion issue. Its southern adherents supported the Kansas-Nebraska Act, a position unacceptable to northern nativists, who deserted to the emerging Republicans.

G.   The Republican Party and the Crisis in Kansas, 1855–1856
The Republican Party first appeared in several northern states in protest against the Kansas-Nebraska Act. As the Know-Nothings waned by 1856, the Republicans became the main opposition party to the Democrats. The Republicans were basically a coalition of former northern Whigs and Democrats who wanted to restore the Missouri Compromise, Liberty Party abolitionists, and free-soilers. Little united them at first except their opposition to the Kansas-Nebraska Act. However, the subsequent fighting in Kansas between proslavery and antislavery forces greatly strengthened the party and its free-soil stand.

Both proslavery and antislavery settlers rushed to Kansas. In 1855, when the first election for a territorial legislature took place, thousands of proslavery Missourians invaded Kansas for the day and voted illegally. This fraud produced a rabidly proslavery legislature, which from its capital in Lecompton, Kansas, passed repressive laws aimed at squelching the free-soilers. The free-soilers, considering the Lecompton legislature a sham, organized a rival government in Topeka. After the sack of Lawrence and John Brown's Pottawatomie massacre, civil war broke out in Kansas between the two governments and their followers. Popular sovereignty had not worked. Instead it caused angry debate between Pierce, who recognized the fraudulent Lecompton government, and northern Democrats and Republicans, who decried the outcome as a sham. It also spread violence to Congress with Preston Brooks's attack on Senator Charles Sumner.

H.   The Election of 1856
The Republicans nominated John C. Frémont, whose platform called on Congress to exclude slavery from all remaining territories. The Democrats nominated James Buchanan and backed popular sovereignty. Millard Fillmore ran as a Know-Nothing. Buchanan won, but

the Republicans did remarkably well in the North. Had Frémont carried Pennsylvania and either Illinois or Indiana, he would have been elected despite receiving almost no southern votes.

IV.   The Crisis of the Union, 1857–1860
   A.   The Dred Scott Case, 1857
   Two days after Buchanan's inauguration, the Supreme Court entered the controversy over slavery in the territories with its *Dred Scott* decision. The Court, composed mostly of southerners, ruled that blacks, slave or free, were not citizens of the United States and that the Missouri Compromise had always been unconstitutional because Congress had no right to exclude slavery from any territory. To do so violated the Fifth Amendment protection of property and property holders. The Republicans denounced the decision and prepared to ignore it.

   B.   The Lecompton Constitution, 1857
   In Kansas the proslavery Lecompton legislature proposed a state constitution that protected slaveholders and gave the settlers the right to vote only on whether to allow more slaves into Kansas. President Buchanan backed the Lecompton constitution and called on Congress to grant Kansas statehood under it. Stephen Douglas, author of the Kansas-Nebraska Act, broke with Buchanan and denounced the actions of the Lecompton legislature, claiming it undermined the original intent of popular sovereignty. Northern Democrats and Republicans applauded Douglas; southern Democrats applauded Buchanan.

   C.   The Lincoln-Douglas Debates
   In 1858 Douglas ran for reelection to the Senate. His lesser-known Republican opponent, Abraham Lincoln, challenged Douglas to a series of debates. In the debates Lincoln attacked slavery as morally evil but denied that Congress had the right to abolish it in the South or that he favored equality for blacks. Rather, he stuck to his position of barring slavery from the territories. Lincoln also forced Douglas into making his Freeport Doctrine statement, which pleased northern Democrats but made Douglas and his views unacceptable to the South. Although Douglas won the Illinois Senate seat, the election further split the Democratic Party. It also made Lincoln "famous in the North and infamous in the South."

   D.   The Legacy of Harpers Ferry
   John Brown's raid touched off a wave of fear and hysteria in the South. Southerners believed Brown had the backing of abolitionists and Republicans who were plotting to incite more slave rebellions. These fears played into the hands of southern extremists.

   E.   The South Contemplates Secession
   Southerners began to speak of secession as the only way to protect themselves. They regarded northern opposition to the Fugitive Slave Act and to slavery in Kansas as unconstitutional and an offense to the South, which wounded southern pride. Some argued that separation from the Union would also permit the South to seize more territory in the Caribbean and the West for slavery.

V.   The Collapse of the Union, 1860–1861
   A.   The Election of 1860
   The Republicans broadened their appeal in the free states in 1860 by supporting a protective tariff, federal aid for internal improvements, and a homestead act. For president, they nominated the Illinois moderate Lincoln. The northern and southern Democrats, unable to agree on a platform, split. Northern Democrats nominated Douglas, who still advocated popular sovereignty. Southern Democrats selected John C. Breckenridge, who insisted that Congress must pass laws protecting slavery in all territories. The Constitutional Union Party, with appeal mostly in the border states and Upper South, ran John Bell. Lincoln, who's

name did not appear on southern ballots, won a majority in the electoral college, but only 39 percent of the popular vote.

B.   The Movement for Secession
Believing that a Republican president would unleash more John Browns on them, the states of the Deep South began to secede even before Lincoln took office. South Carolina led the way in December 1860, followed by Alabama, Mississippi, Florida, Georgia, Louisiana, and Texas. On February 4, 1861, delegates from these seven states met in Montgomery, Alabama, to form the Confederate States of America.

C.   The Search for Compromise
Kentucky senator John Crittenden proposed a compromise to bring the Deep South back into the Union. It included constitutional amendments that guaranteed the federal government would never interfere with slavery in the South and that drew the Missouri Compromise line across the remaining territories, with slavery permitted south of the line in all present and future U.S. territory. Lincoln rejected the Crittenden plan because he would not abandon the free-soil promise on which he had been elected. He regarded the plan as an invitation to the South to seize territory in the Caribbean for slavery. He also felt that he had won an honest election and that giving in to a losing minority would damage the American tradition of majority rule.

D.   The Coming of War
The Confederacy began to take over federal forts within its region. Soon after Lincoln's inauguration, it bombarded Fort Sumter in Charleston's harbor, thus firing the first shot in the rebellion that became the Civil War. Lincoln responded by proclaiming that a rebellion existed in the Lower South and calling for 75,000 militia volunteers from the loyal states to subdue it. Rather than send their troops to fight against sister southern states, Virginia, North Carolina, Arkansas, and Tennessee seceded and joined the Confederacy. The North was now aroused and ready to fight to save the Union, though not yet ready to abolish slavery.

VI.   Conclusion
At no time prior to the Civil War did the majority of Americans call for the end of slavery in the South. Rather, in the decade of the 1850s the gulf between North and South widened over the spread of slavery into the territories. Northerners believed their freedom to pursue economic opportunity would be denied if they had to compete against slave labor in the West. Southerners claimed that to curtail slavery in the territories violated their constitutional right to use their property (slaves) as they saw fit. Attempts to enforce the Fugitive Slave law, the Kansas-Nebraska Act's repeal of the Missouri Compromise, the subsequent fighting in Kansas, the *Dred Scott* decision, and John Brown's raid all further embittered intersectional conflict. National political parties collapsed under the strain: the Whigs disintegrated; the Democrats divided into northern and southern wings. A new strictly northern party, the Republican, emerged. By the end of the 1850s northerners were convinced the South meant to impose slavery throughout the nation. Southern states were ready for secession as the only way to protect their "peculiar institution" from a North that they saw as intent on destroying slavery even in the South.

VOCABULARY

The following terms are used in Chapter 14. To understand the chapter fully, it is important that you know what each of them means.

omnibus bill	a bill including numerous items or subjects
stalwart	a steadfast or uncompromising political party supporter
conspiracy	a secret agreement to perform an evil or unlawful act; a secret plot
naturalization	the legal process that confers the rights and privileges of citizenship on an immigrant
capital crime or offense	a crime or offense punishable by death
doughface	in the 1850s, a northern politician whose views were acceptable or even sympathetic to the South
bombastic	pretentious language, overblown speech
plaintiff	one who brings suit in a court
referendum	the procedure of submitting legislative measures directly to the voters for approval or rejection
insurrection	an armed uprising or other open resistance against a government or other established authority; a revolt
lynch	put a person to death for some alleged offense by the actions of a mob or group having no legal authority
vigilantes	members of extralegal citizen groups organized to maintain order and punish offenses

IDENTIFICATIONS

After reading Chapter 14, you should be able to identify and explain the historical significance of each of the following:

John Brown's raid on Harpers Ferry

William H. Seward and irrepressible conflict

popular (squatter) sovereignty

Daniel Webster

Henry Clay's omnibus bill and the Compromise of 1850

Millard Fillmore

Fugitive Slave Act of 1850, Anthony Burns, and personal-liberty laws

Harriet Beecher Stowe, *Uncle Tom's Cabin*

American (or Know-Nothing) Party

Stephen A. Douglas and the Kansas-Nebraska Act

free-soil and free labor

Gadsden Purchase

John A. Quitman, William Walker, and filibustering

Ostend Manifesto

"Bleeding Kansas"

Lecompton versus Topeka legislature and the Lecompton constitution

sack of Lawrence and Pottawatomie massacre

Charles Sumner and Preston Brooks

John C. Frémont

James Buchanan

Roger B. Taney and *Dred Scott* v. *Sandford*

Lincoln-Douglas debates and Douglas's Freeport Doctrine

Panic of 1857

John C. Breckenridge

John Bell and the Constitutional Union Party

Jefferson Davis and the Confederate States of America

Crittenden compromise

Fort Sumter

SKILL BUILDING: MAPS

On the map of the United States, locate and draw in each of the following. How is each related to sectional conflict and the coming of the Civil War?

Missouri

Kansas and Nebraska territories

36°30' latitude

New Mexico Territory

Utah Territory

California

Gadsden Purchase

states that seceded by February 1861 (Lower South)

states that seceded after fighting at Fort Sumter (Upper South)

border slave states that did not secede

Charleston, South Carolina

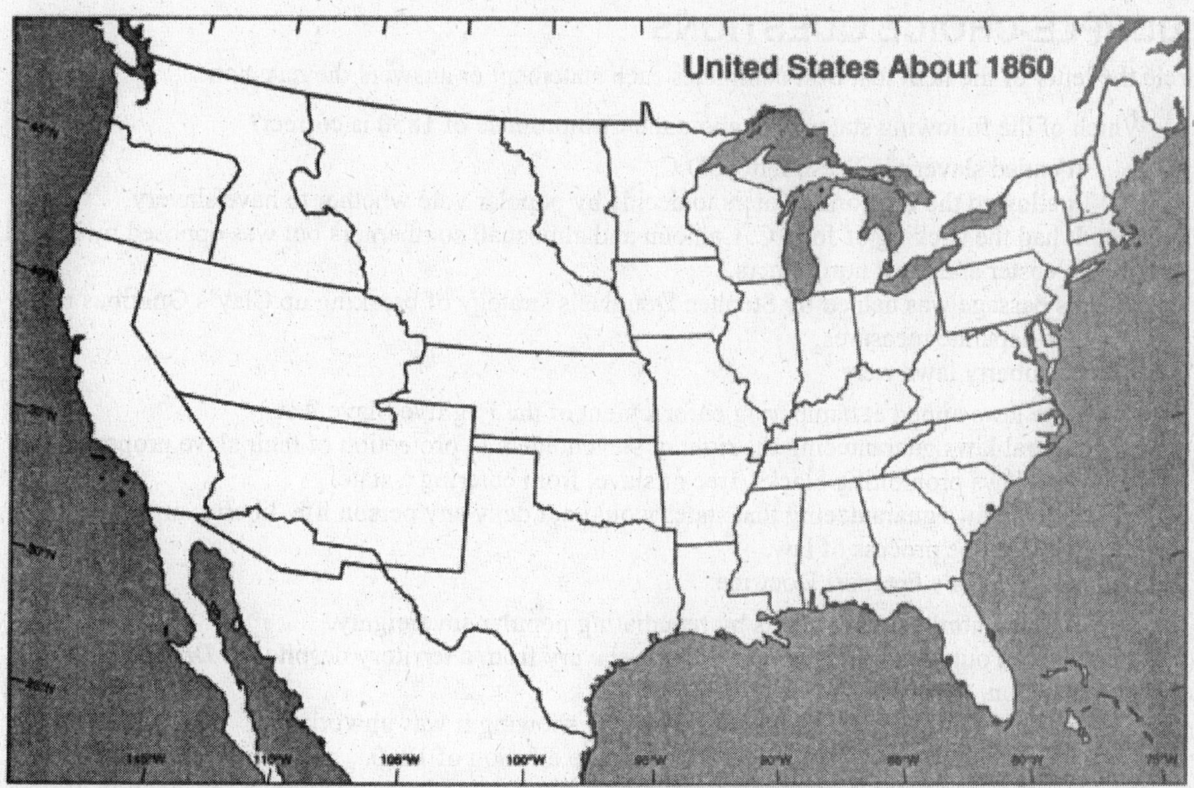

HISTORICAL SOURCES

Chapter 14 concentrates on the widening gulf between North and South on the questions of slavery and its extension into western territories. How do historians attempt to understand what northerners and southerners felt and believed in the 1850s? One historical source that the author of Chapter 14 uses is literary works published during the period, as well as the letters and comments of well-known poets and novelists. The most famous and influential piece of fiction in the 1850s was Harriet Beecher Stowe's *Uncle Tom's Cabin.* Look at the discussion of the novel on pages 402-403. By analyzing that novel, what does the historian learn about its emotional appeal to antebellum northerners? How did it touch their family values? Despite its abolitionist position, how did the book reflect the negative stereotypes about blacks that were prevalent among white northerners?

The historian can see the differing reactions to the novel in the North and South by reading reviews of it that appeared in northern and southern periodicals. For example, in December 1852 in a magazine called the *Southern Literary Messenger,* the historian can read a scathing denunciation of *Uncle Tom's Cabin,* which, according to the reviewer, criminally prostitutes the "high functions of the imagination to the pernicious intrigues of sectional animosity, and to the petty calumnies of willful slander."

The author of Chapter 14 also quotes a poem by John Greenleaf Whittier on page 401. Why does the author cite this 1850s writer? The historian can read an equally impassioned defense of the southern way of life and its planter elite in the poems, letters, and novels of the South Carolinian writer William Gilmore Simms.

Another way to gauge feelings in the Deep South on the eve of the Civil War is by taking a close look at a single city of the region. Turn to "A Place in Time: Charleston, South Carolina, 1860–1861." How does this description of Charleston add to our understanding of the southern mood in 1860 and the reasons why the Lower South seceded? What does this selection illustrate about the interplay of social class and race in the antebellum South?

MULTIPLE-CHOICE QUESTIONS

Circle the letter of the item that best completes each statement or answers the question.

1. Which of the following statements about the Compromise of 1850 is correct?

   a.   It ended slavery in Washington, D.C.
   b.   It allowed the California voters to decide by popular vote whether to have slavery.
   c.   It had the backing of John C. Calhoun and almost all southerners but was opposed by Daniel Webster and most northerners.
   d.   Its passage was helped by Stephen Douglas's strategy of breaking up Clay's Omnibus bill into separate measurcs.

2. Personal-liberty laws were

   a.   state laws aimed at hampering enforcement of the Fugitive Slave Act.
   b.   federal laws guaranteeing the right of slaveholders to protection of their slave property.
   c.   state laws prohibiting blacks, free or slave, from entering a state.
   d.   federal laws guaranteeing that states would not deny any person life, liberty, or property without due process of law.

3. Stephen Douglas's Freeport Doctrine

   a.   angered northern Democrats by repudiating popular sovereignty.
   b.   pointed out how settlers could exclude slavery from a territory despite the *Dred Scott* decision.
   c.   undermined Lincoln's free-soil position by showing it was unworkable.
   d.   helped to unify the Democratic Party for the election of 1860.

4. Which is the most valid statement describing the Republican Party position in the election of 1860?

   a.   There should be immediate, complete emancipation of slaves in the South.
   b.   A program of gradual, compensated emancipation should be started.
   c.   There should be no further extension of slavery into the territories.
   d.   The principle of popular sovereignty should be applied honestly in the remaining territories.

5. What did the South gain from the Compromise of 1850?

   a.   A stronger fugitive slave law
   b.   A slave code for the territories
   c.   The right to bring slaves into all territories taken from Mexico
   d.   A lower tariff

6. The Lecompton constitution would have provided

   a.   a policy for the Supreme Court to follow in cases involving slavery.
   b.   an independent country in Africa for freed slaves.
   c.   a permanent compromise on slavery for future states.
   d.   a proslavery government for Kansas.

7. The Ostend Manifesto pertained to

   a.   Cuba.
   b.   California.
   c.   Mexico.
   d.   Florida.

8. The *Dred Scott* decision declared that Congress could *not*

   a.   admit new slave states.
   b.   prohibit slaveholders from taking slaves into northern states.
   c.   bar slavery in the territories.
   d.   pass a fugitive-slave law.

9.   The secession of southern states began immediately after

    a.   the announcement of the *Dred Scott* decision.
    b.   civil war began in Kansas.
    c.   Lincoln's inauguration.
    d.   Lincoln's election.

10.   The Crittenden compromise was not acceptable to Lincoln for all of the following reasons *except* he

    a.   would not abandon the promise of free soil on which he had been elected.
    b.   had decided soon after his election to issue the Emancipation Proclamation.
    c.   believed that loyal southerners would soon overturn secession.
    d.   thought the plan would encourage southerners to seize more territory for slavery in the Caribbean.

SHORT-ANSWER QUESTIONS

1.   Discuss the provisions of the Fugitive Slave Act of 1850. How did northerners attempt to prevent its enforcement?

2.   What were the provisions of the Kansas-Nebraska Act? Why did it anger and alarm many northerners?

3.   What brought about civil war in Kansas in 1856?

4.   Explain Lincoln's position on slavery when he ran for the Senate in 1858 and for president in 1860.

5.   Explain the impact of John Brown's Harpers Ferry raid on the South's mood and thought.

6.   Discuss the political impact of the Confederacy's seizure of Fort Sumter.

ESSAY QUESTIONS

1.   Imagine that you are a Virginia cotton planter or planter's wife. Compose a letter to a friend in New York explaining why your state has just seceded from the Union.

2.   Repeated sectional compromises in 1820, 1833, and 1850 held the Union together and averted civil war. Why did compromise fail in 1860–1861?

3.   Although the Compromise of 1850 postponed secession and civil war for a decade, it also contributed to embittered feelings in each section toward the other. Discuss and illustrate this statement.

4.   Discuss the birth of the Republican Party. How and why did it come about? Who supported it and why? What did it stand for? How and why did it broaden its appeal in the late 1850s?

5.   Discuss the demise of the second party system. How is its breakdown related to immigration, nativism, slavery, and the spread of slavery into the West?

ANSWERS TO MULTIPLE-CHOICE QUESTIONS

1. d
2. a
3. b
4. c
5. a
6. d
7. a
8. c
9. d
10. b

CHAPTER 15

Crucible of Freedom: Civil War, 1861–1865

OUTLINE AND SUMMARY

I.   Introduction

Immediately after Fort Sumter's fall, volunteers flocked to the Union and Confederate armies. Filled with loyalty and patriotism for their respective sides, neither soldiers nor politicians foresaw the long, bloody war ahead. As the Civil War dragged on and on and one out of every five soldiers who fought in it died, both the Union and Confederate governments were forced to impose the draft and adopt other coercive policies not dreamed of in 1861. Most important, the Union, which entered the fray with no objective beyond stopping secession, discovered that in order to win the war it also had to emancipate the slaves. As you read about the Civil War in Chapter 15, try to answer these questions: (1) What advantages did each combatant, Union and Confederate, possess at he start of the Civil War? (2) How successfully did the governments and economies of the North and South respond to the pressures of war? (3) How did the issue of emancipation transform the war? (4) What factors determined the military outcome of the war? (5) In what lasting ways did the Civil War change the United States as a nation?

II. Mobilizing for War

A.   Recruitment and Conscription

North and South alike were unprepared for war. In the spring of 1861 the Union had a small army of 16,000, mostly in the West. One-third of Union army officers resigned to join the Confederacy, which in April 1862 was the first to pass a conscription law. The act exempted from the draft people in several occupations, including those who owned or oversaw twenty or more slaves. The 20-Negro law led nonslaveholders to complain that this was "a rich man's war but a poor man's fight." The South managed to procure the arms it needed but was less successful in providing its troops with food and clothing. Therefore, in 1863 it imposed the Impressment Act, which allowed government agents to take food supplies from farmers at a set price and seize slaves to work for the army. This law was hated even more than the Conscription Act.

In 1863 the North passed the Enrollment Act, making all able-bodied white males aged twenty to forty-five eligible for the draft. The northern law also granted exemptions. Most resented were the provisions that permitted men to buy substitutes to serve in their places and excused those who paid the government a $300 commutation fee. By war's end, 2.8 million men served on either side.

B.   Financing the War

Both sides sold war bonds and printed unbacked paper money. The Union's greenbacks did not depreciate unduly in value because the federal government made greenbacks legal tender and imposed stiff new taxes to keep the government solvent. The South, which was reluctant to impose and collect new taxes and tried to pay its bills by printing more and more paper money, saw its currency depreciate drastically. The North also passed the National Bank Act, permitting federally chartered banks to issue national bank notes, backed by the federal government.

C.   Political Leadership in Wartime
Lincoln faced opposition from northern Democrats, who disliked the National Bank Act, the draft, and the emancipation of slaves, as well as from the Radical Republicans. Led by Salmon Chase, Charles Sumner, and Thaddeus Stevens, the Radicals pressed Lincoln to end slavery and, after 1863, criticized his lenient reconstruction plans. In the face of this opposition, Republicans rallied behind Lincoln and coalesced into a strong political entity that would rule federal elections for years. Jefferson Davis, president of the Confederacy, was less successful in containing factionalism. He was embroiled in destructive fights with his vice president, Alexander Stephens, and other states' rights southern leaders. The absence of an opposition party in the South further contributed to the factionalism of the southern Democrats. Davis lacked the support to pass any measures he supported, and governance in the South was often at a standstill.

D.   Securing the Union's Borders
Because loss of the border states to the Confederacy would endanger Washington, D.C., and make fighting the war tougher, Lincoln took extraordinary measures. He occupied those states militarily and suspended the writ of habeas corpus there, arresting prosecession supporters without charge. The Supreme Court in *Ex parte* Merryman ruled Lincoln's actions unconstitutional, but he defied the Court and, with his emergency measures, kept Maryland, Delaware, Kentucky, and Missouri in the Union.

III.   In Battle, 1861–1862
A.   Armies, Weapons, and Strategies
Northern advantages over the South included a larger population, many more white men of fighting age, and control of 90 percent of the country's industry and two-thirds of its railroad track. The South's advantages were fighting a defensive war on its home territory and, with a slave labor force to carry on nonmilitary activities, being able to use a larger percentage of its white men for fighting.

The improved bullets and Springfield or Enfield rifles used during the Civil War increased the infantry's firepower, which in turn reduced the effectiveness of cavalry, encouraged the digging of trenches, and put a premium on the element of surprise in an attack.

At the start of hostilities the Union adopted the Anaconda plan, which called for sealing off the South with a blockade of its coastline and cutting it in two by gaining control of the Mississippi River. In 1861 the Union did not yet have enough ships and troops to carry out this plan. Instead, west of the Appalachians, Union soldiers occupied Kentucky and moved southward into Tennessee, while in the eastern theater the North made repeated, futile attempts to capture Richmond.

B.   Stalemate in the East
After the Confederates routed the Union at the first Battle of Bull Run (First Manassas), General George McClellan tried to take Richmond from the South, moving his army up the York Peninsula. Robert E. Lee's smaller Confederate army stopped McClellan, and Lincoln called off the Peninsula campaign. Then Lee and Stonewall Jackson headed north, defeated the Union at the Second Battle of Bull Run (Second Manassas), and continued into western Maryland. Lee hoped with this invasion to seize needed food; threaten Washington, D.C.; increase peace sentiment in the North; and convince Britain and France to recognize the Confederacy. At the bloody Battle of Antietam (Sharpsburg) in September 1862, Union forces under McClellan halted Lee's advance and forced him to retreat southward. After Antietam, Lincoln issued his preliminary Emancipation Proclamation. Another Union attempt to take Richmond, under General Burnside, failed miserably at the Battle of Fredericksburg.

C. The War in the West

The western theater saw important Union victories. In 1861–1862 Ulysses S. Grant secured control of Missouri and Kentucky and then moved into Tennessee, capturing two key forts. Next he headed south toward Mississippi. Confederate attempts failed to stop him at the bloody Battle of Shiloh in southern Tennessee. Meanwhile a naval force under Admiral David G. Farragut captured New Orleans and pushed northward up the Mississippi. A second Union flotilla moving southward captured Memphis. By 1863 the North controlled the entire river except for a 200-mile stretch between Port Hudson, Louisiana, and Vicksburg, Mississippi.

Fighting also broke out in the trans-Mississippi West, where northern and southern forces were joined by Mexican-Americans and Indians. After defeating the Confederates, much of the Union army in the Southwest and on the Great Plains turned to the final conquest of Native Americans.

D. The Soldiers' War

The typical Civil War soldier, whether in the Union or Confederate army, was a volunteer who came from a farm or small town and ended up serving in the infantry. He usually enlisted with visions of military glory and proving his "manhood." His real war experiences soon stripped away romantic illusions. Life in army camps was tedious; the food was bad in the Union army and scarce in the Confederate. Confederate soldiers also often lacked blankets, clothes, and shoes. Poor sanitation in the camps of both armies produced high rates of disease and meant soldiers in blue and in gray had to contend with lice, flies, ticks, and rats. The casualty rates in battles, such as Shiloh and Antietam, were horrendous. In their letters home, Confederate soldiers often claimed to be fighting for southern rights and to protect slavery. Union soldiers at first said little about abolishing slavery, but mentioned the need for emancipation more often as the war continued, either for humanitarian reasons or as the best way to defeat the South.

E. Ironclads and Cruisers: The Naval War

The Union gradually tightened its blockade. It further disrupted foreign trade vital to the Confederacy by capturing its ports and coastal areas. Confederate attempts to break the stranglehold with an ironclad ship led to the battle of the *Merrimac* and the *Monitor,* the first clash of ironclads, but did not disrupt the blockade. The South inflicted serious damage on northern shipping with commerce raiders, but this did not hinder the Union's winning the war.

F. The Diplomatic War

The Confederacy tried to convince France and Britain that it was in their interests to extend diplomatic recognition. Hoping to establish a colonial empire in Mexico, Napolean III of France had grounds to welcome a permanent division in the United States. The South expected active help from the British, who, desperate for the South's cotton, might be counted on to break the Union blockade. There was tension between the Union and the British over the *Trent* affair and over the commerce raiders and rams built for the Confederacy in England, but the South's "cotton diplomacy" failed. The British had stockpiles of cotton on hand at the start of the war and then found alternative sources of supply. Lincoln's Emancipation Proclamation, which turned the struggle into a war against slavery, won British sympathy for the Union.

IV. Emancipation Transforms the War, 1863

A. From Confiscation to Emancipation

In his inaugural address, Lincoln proclaimed that he had no intention of interfering with slavery in the South. Whenever Union armies approached, however, slaves fled to them.

Some commanders, calling these people contraband of war, refused to return them to their masters. In August 1861 Congress backed this policy with the First Confiscation Act but stopped short of freeing the slaves. Lincoln at first resisted calls for emancipation because he did not want to push the border slave states into secession; further, he knew many northerners feared that freedmen might come north and compete for jobs. Radical Republicans, however, demanded immediate emancipation and pointed out that the South's use of slave labor was helping it militarily. After early Union defeats, many northerners agreed that it was necessary to strike a blow against slavery to beat the Confederacy. In July 1862 Congress passed the Second Confiscation Act, which authorized freeing slaves who came within Union lines and using blacks as soldiers. Lincoln hesitated a while longer to enforce this law, but when he failed to persuade Union slave states to accept federally compensated abolition, he drafted his Emancipation Proclamation. The proclamation stated that, as of January 1, 1863, all slaves in areas then in rebellion were "forever free." Since it applied only in areas not controlled by the Union, the proclamation at first freed no slaves, but issuing it was a masterful move. It satisfied Radical Republicans, appealed to antislavery sentiment in Britain and France (forestalling their recognition of the Confederacy), and encouraged slaves to run away and join the Union army.

B.   Crossing Union Lines
By 1865 about half a million former slaves were in Union-held territory. Some worked for the army. Others worked for loyal planters or on abandoned plantation lands. Many Union soldiers were bitterly prejudiced against blacks but began to change their attitudes as black spies and scouts helped them. Freedmen's aid societies in the North sent agents into the South to distribute relief and open schools. In March 1865 Congress created the Freedmen's Bureau to educate, dispense relief to, and find employment for the former slaves. Congress also stipulated that 40 acres of abandoned property or confiscated land could be leased to each freedman with an option to buy after three years.

C.   Black Soldiers in the Union Army
After Lincoln issued the Emancipation Proclamation, large numbers of blacks were accepted in the Union army. By 1865, 186,000 blacks had served, making up approximately one-tenth of all Union soldiers. The black troops suffered much discrimination. Placed in segregated regiments and commanded by white officers, they received less pay and suffered a higher mortality rate than whites. Despite unfair treatment, they served the Union well. Black soldiers captured by the South were not treated as prisoners of war, but were sent back to their states to be re-enslaved or even executed.

D.   Slavery in Wartime
Southerners attempted to maintain control over their slaves by stepping up patrols, telling slaves horror stories about the Yankees, and moving slaves far from Union lines. Nonetheless, blacks ran to Union camps. Others remained on the plantation doing little or no work. Near the end of the war the Confederate congress passed a bill to arm three hundred slave soldiers, though the plan was never put into effect.

E.   The Turning Point of 1863
In the summer and fall of 1863 the Union scored important victories. Lee's invasion of the North was turned back at Gettysburg in July. Simultaneously, Grant took Vicksburg, and Port Hudson fell to another Union force. The North then controlled the whole Mississippi River. In September the North also routed the Confederacy from Chattanooga, clearing the way for Union troops to invade Georgia.

V.   War and Society, North and South
  A.   The War's Economic Impact: The North
       War-related industries and the railroads boomed. The Republican-dominated Congress
       enacted measures that encouraged further business development: raising tariffs, chartering
       and granting land and loans to the Union Pacific and Central Pacific railroad corporations to
       build a transcontinental line, and creating a new national banking system. Other legislation
       benefited the West particularly, such as the Homestead and the Morrill Land Grant Acts
       (1862). Everyone did not benefit equally from the rising economy. While manufacturers and
       speculators made fat profits, workers' wages lagged behind inflation. Women, who
       increasingly replaced drafted men, received even less pay than males. Workers protested
       their economic lot by forming national unions.

  B.   The War's Economic Impact: The South
       The war destroyed the South's economy, wrecking its railroads and cutting its cotton and
       food production. Food shortages worsened the South's already rampant inflation and caused
       such hardships for soldiers' families that many Confederates deserted to try to provide for
       their wives and children. Some food was supplied through a flourishing cotton trade with
       the enemy North.

  C.   Dealing with Dissent
       The Union and the Confederacy both faced internal dissent. In the South nonslaveholders
       with Unionist sentiments and states' rights politicians denounced Jefferson Davis's
       government. On the whole the Confederate government took little action against these
       dissidents. In the North peace Democrats (Copperheads) criticized the Emancipation
       Proclamation and demanded an immediate peace settlement with the South. Peace
       Democrats had their strongest following in the border states, in the Midwest, and among
       immigrant workers in northeastern cities. Attempts to begin drafting men in July 1863
       sparked riots in New York City that had to be quelled by federal troops. Lincoln suspended
       the writ of habeas corpus and imposed martial law more frequently than Jefferson Davis did.
       Lincoln's actions lead to the Supreme Court case *Ex parte* Milligan (1866), in which the
       justices ruled that civilians cannot be tried by military tribunals when the regular civil courts
       are open.

  D.   The Medical War
       Northern citizens formed the U.S. Sanitary Commission, a civilian organization that raised
       money for medical supplies and distributed extra food and medicine to army camps. Some
       3,200 women volunteered their services as nurses to either the Union or Confederate army,
       among them Dorothea Dix and Clara Barton, later founder of the American Red Cross.
       Nevertheless, limited medical knowledge about sanitation and germs led to a frightful death
       toll from disease and infected wounds. Conditions in prisoner-of-war camps were
       particularly grim. The Confederate prison camp at Andersonville, Georgia, was the most
       notorious.

  E.   The War and Women's Rights
       Women's rights leaders hoped that the war would win equality for women as well as blacks.
       Elizabeth Cady Stanton and Susan B. Anthony organized the National Woman's Loyal
       League in 1863 to campaign for amendments ending slavery and granting blacks and women
       the vote. The Civil War, however, did not change women's inferior political status.

VI. The Union Victorious, 1864–1865
  A.   The Eastern Theater in 1864
       In 1864 Lincoln put Grant in command of all Union armies. Grant moved his headquarters
       to the eastern theater and proceeded to attack Lee in Virginia. At the same time, he ordered

Sherman to invade Georgia. Despite heavy casualties at the Battles of the Wilderness, Spotsylvania, and Cold Harbor, Grant pressed forward, forcing Lee to pull back to trenches outside Petersburg and Richmond. Grant dispatched another Union force under Philip Sheridan, which devastated and conquered the Shenandoah Valley.

While Grant battled Lee in the Wilderness, Sherman advanced relentlessly into Georgia. Confederate forces had to evacuate Atlanta, which fell to Sherman in September 1864.

B.   The Election of 1864
Lincoln faced a tough election fight first from the Radical Republicans, who would have preferred to nominate Salmon Chase, and then from the peace Democrats, who nominated George McClellan. To win the votes of prowar Democrats, Lincoln and the Republicans nominated a prowar Tennessee Unionist, Andrew Johnson, for vice president. Sherman's capture of Atlanta in September clinched Lincoln's victory in November. Following the election, Congress passed the Thirteenth Amendment, which was ratified by the end of 1865.

C.   Sherman's March Through Georgia
After burning much of Atlanta, Sherman marched across Georgia to Savannah. His army lived off the countryside and seized or destroyed everything of possible military value. In December 1864 Sherman took Savannah and turned north to South Carolina. The destruction visited on that state was even greater and was climaxed with the gutting of its capital, Columbia. Sherman then continued into North Carolina.

D.   Toward Appomattox
While Sherman swung north, Grant closed in on Lee's army. By spring 1865 Confederate morale had broken and men were deserting in droves. On April 3 Grant entered Richmond. Lee made a last attempt to escape from the Union armies but soon after surrendered to Grant at Appomattox Courthouse. Within a month all remaining Confederate resistance ended. On April 14 John Wilkes Booth shot Lincoln, who died the next day, bringing Andrew Johnson to the presidency.

E.   The Impact of the War
The Civil War killed some 620,000 Americans, more than any other war the nation has fought. It ruined the southern economy but stimulated industrialization and capital investment in the North. While the Civil War did not wipe out the states' rights doctrine, it did greatly strengthen the federal government: there would be no more attempts at secession. The war ended slavery, but it left undecided the future of 3.5 million freedmen.

VII. Conclusion
Historians still debate the question of why the North won the Civil War. Certainly the North had great advantages over the Confederacy in manpower, industry, and railroads, but it also had a much tougher task than the Confederacy. To win, the North had to invade and conquer the South and destroy its armies and resources. The South had only to fight a defensive war on its home ground, keeping its territory and armies intact until the Union tired of the struggle and accepted secession. Some historians attribute the North's victory primarily to the Confederacy's internal weaknesses. Still others say the North prevailed because it won key battles, but often not by much. Therefore, chance played an important part in the outcome. Whatever the reasons for the Union's triumph, the legacy of the Civil War is clearer. It ended slavery, forged a stronger federal government, weakened states' rights, and heightened nationalism.

VOCABULARY

The following terms are used in Chapter 15. To understand the chapter fully, it is important that you know what each of them means.

conscription	the compulsory enrollment of men for military or naval service; the draft
gross national product (GNP)	the sum, measured in dollars, of all goods and services produced in a given year
writ of habeas corpus	a formal order requiring that an arrested person be brought before a judge or court and either charged with a specific crime or released (The right to such a writ is guaranteed in the U.S. Constitution.)
reconnaissance	a search in the field to uncover useful military information
flotilla	a group of small naval vessels; a subdivision of a fleet
emissaries	agents sent out on a mission, sometimes of a secret nature
belligerent	when used as a diplomatic term, as in this chapter, a state or nation at war
bigotry	intolerant attachment to a particular belief, prejudice, or opinion
dissent	disagree with the opinions and policies of the government, church, or social majority
martial law	the law imposed on an area by military forces when civil authority has broken down or been pushed aside
crucible	an ordeal; severe, searching test

IDENTIFICATIONS

After reading Chapter 15, you should be able to identify and explain the historical significance of each of the following:

20-Negro law and Impressment Act

Enrollment Act, 1863, and bounty jumpers

Legal Tender Act and greenbacks

National Bank Act, 1863, and national bank notes

Jefferson Davis and Alexander Stephens

Charles Sumner, Thaddeus Stevens, and the Radical Republicans

Ex parte Merryman, 1861, and *Ex parte* Milligan, 1866

Winfield Scott and the Anaconda plan

First and Second Battles of Bull Run (First and Second Manassas)

George B. McClellan

Thomas "Stonewall" Jackson

Robert E. Lee

Battle of Antietam (Sharpsburg)

Ulysses S. Grant

William T. Sherman

ironclads and the battle of the *Merrimac* and the *Monitor*

Trent affair

Charles Francis Adams, the *Florida, Alabama,* and Laird rams

cotton diplomacy

First and Second Confiscation Acts and Emancipation Proclamation

Freedmen's Bureau

Fort Pillow massacre

Gettysburg

Vicksburg

Homestead Act, 1862

Morrill Land Grand Act, 1862

Copperheads and Clement L. Vallandigham

New York City draft riot

Elizabeth Cady Stanton, Susan B. Anthony, and the National Woman's Loyal League

National Union party and Andrew Johnson

surrender at Appomattox Courthouse

SKILL BUILDING: MAPS

On the map of the South on the following page, locate each of the areas or places listed below. What is the political and/or military importance of each in the Civil War?

western theater

eastern theater

Appalachian Mountains

Mississippi River

Montgomery, Alabama

Richmond, Virginia

Washington, D.C.

Shenandoah Valley

Maryland

Missouri

Kentucky

Memphis, Tennessee

Vicksburg, Mississippi

Gettysburg, Pennsylvania

Atlanta, Georgia

route of Sherman's march to the sea

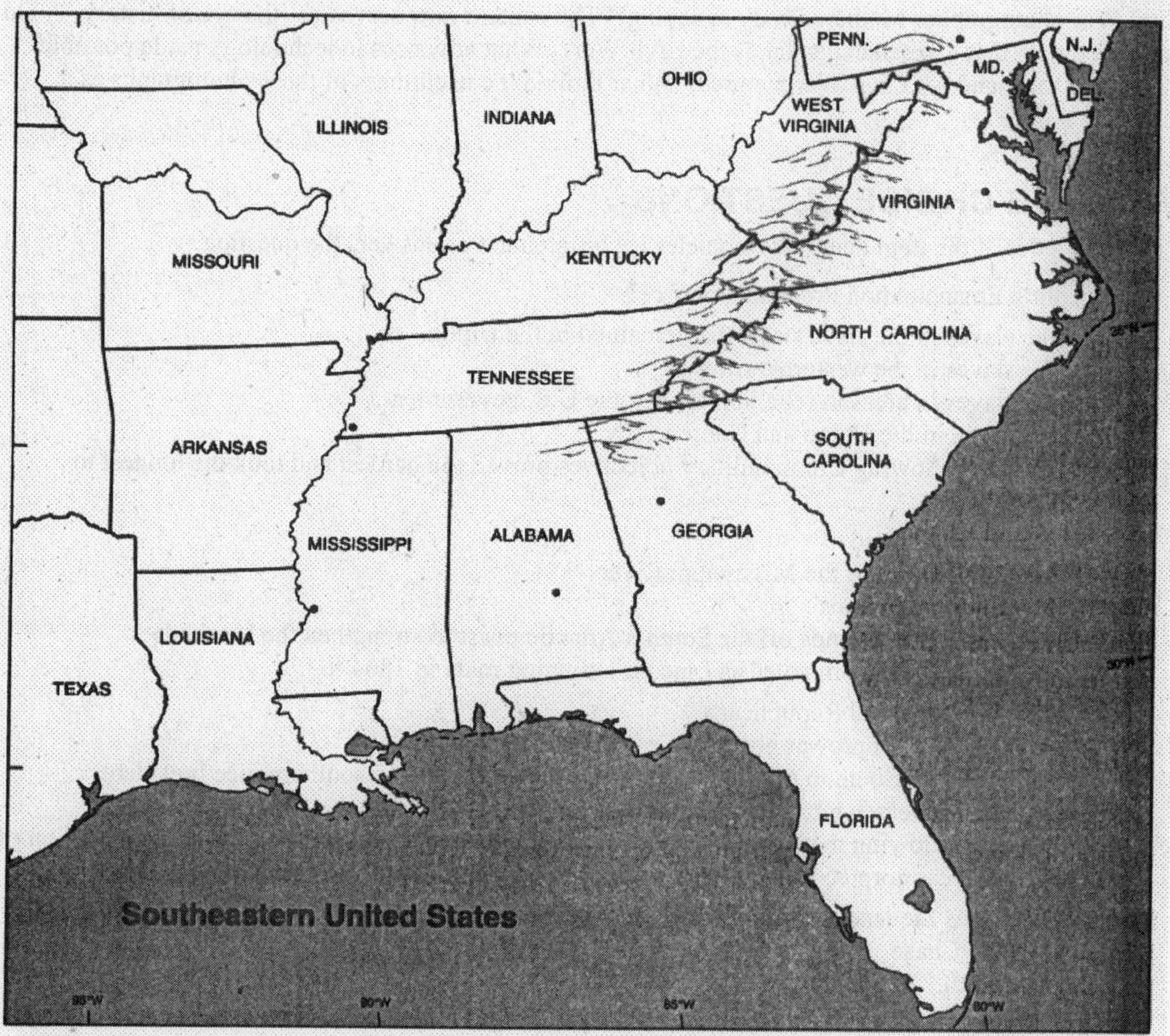

HISTORICAL SOURCES

Among the many historical sources used in Chapter 15 there are three particularly interesting ones: published personal narratives of participants in the Civil War; letters written by Union and Confederate soldiers and their families; and photographs, for the Civil War was the first conflict to be extensively captured by the camera.

On page 443 the author quotes from Thomas W. Higginson's *Army Life in a Black Regiment*. Who was Higginson? What does the author intend to show by using his book? Why is Higginson's book a valuable historical source? Was Higginson an "objective" observer? Would there be any danger in a historian's relying on this source alone to learn about black soldiers in the Civil War?

In many places in Chapter 15, letters of soldiers and their families are quoted. Find some of these and show how the historian uses them. Would these letters tend to duplicate what the historian can learn from William T. Sherman's *Memoirs*? Why or why not?

Now look at "Culture and Technology: The Camera and the Civil War." In that piece the author quotes Civil War photographer Mathew Brady as saying, "The camera now served as 'the eye of history.'" Do you agree with that assessment as far as the Civil War? What advances in technology made possible the tens of thousands of Civil War pictures? What limited the usefulness of these photographs as a historical source?

MULTIPLE-CHOICE QUESTIONS

Circle the letter of the item that best completes each statement or answers the question.

1. Lincoln's Emancipation Proclamation freed
   a. the slaves in the slave states that remained in the Union.
   b. the slaves in the western territories.
   c. the slaves in areas in rebellion against the U.S. government.
   d. all slaves in the Union and Confederacy.

2. Which of the following Union military objectives proved the hardest and took the longest to accomplish?
   a. Taking Richmond
   b. Gaining control of the Mississippi River
   c. Taking New Orleans
   d. Seizing the sea islands off the South's Atlantic coast to strengthen the blockade

3. Andrew Johnson was nominated as Lincoln's running mate in 1864 to
   a. please the Radical Republicans.
   b. win the votes of prowar northern Democrats.
   c. influence the South to rejoin the Union, since he would be a southern vice president.
   d. reward Tennessee for remaining loyal to the Union.

4. Which of the following men, denouncing Lincoln's Emancipation Proclamation and suspension of the writ of habeas corpus, called for immediate peace with the Confederacy?
   a. Thaddeus Stevens
   b. Salmon Chase
   c. Clement L. Vallandigham
   d. Charles Sumner

5. Union capture of Vicksburg and Port Hudson was strategically important because it
   a. opened the way to Richmond.
   b. completed Union control over the Atlantic coast.
   c. gave Lincoln the victories he was waiting for to issue the Emancipation Proclamation.
   d. gave the North control over the whole Mississippi River.

6. The Supreme Court ruled in *Ex parte* Milligan that
   a. civilians could not be tried by military tribunals when the civil courts were open.
   b. Lincoln had no constitutional right to free slaves in the Confederacy.
   c. the Union had no right to confiscate the property of rebel leaders.
   d. Congress rather than the president had the right to direct the reconstruction of the South.

7. Slaves during the Civil War

    a. mostly remained loyal to their masters and the South.
    b. often served as officers in the Union army over other blacks.
    c. ran to Union lines when they could and worked for or fought for the North.
    d. were never allowed to enlist as soldiers in either the Union or the Confederate army.

8. By 1865, African-Americans constituted about what portion of the Union army?

    a. 1/10
    b. ¼
    c. ¾
    d. 1/20

9. Which of the following statements about women in the Civil War is correct?

    a. Women were *not* allowed to enter army camps to nurse soldiers.
    b. Women replaced draftees in many of the industrial jobs in the North.
    c. Loyal Unionist women were allowed to vote and run for political office.
    d. Northern missionary and freedmen's aid societies refused to use women volunteers.

10. Which of the following statements is correct?

    a. Both the Union and the Confederacy printed unbacked paper money to help finance their war efforts.
    b. The Union had to resort to conscription to get enough soldiers, but the Confederacy recruited enough volunteers to avoid imposing the draft.
    c. Neither the Union nor the Confederacy exempted the wealthy from the draft.
    d. Both the Union and the Confederacy ruthlessly suppressed all internal dissent for the duration of the war.

SHORT-ANSWER QUESTIONS

1. Explain how President Lincoln kept the four border slave states in the Union.

2. Why didn't the British recognize the Confederacy as a nation? What help did the British give the South?

3. Who were the Radical Republicans? On what grounds did they criticize Lincoln during the Civil War?

4. How were African-Americans in the Union army discriminated against?

5. What caused the 1863 New York City draft riot?

ESSAY QUESTIONS

1. In his inaugural address in 1861 Lincoln said, "I have no purpose, directly or indirectly, to interfere with the institution of slavery in the states where it exists." In September 1862 he issued his preliminary Emancipation Proclamation. Explain why and how this marked change of policy took place.

2. Discuss the military advantages and disadvantages of each side at the start of the Civil War. Considering that the preponderance of advantages belonged to the Union, why did it take the North four years to defeat the South?

3. Compare and contrast the economic impact of the Civil War on the Union and the Confederacy.

4. The Civil War has been called a second American Revolution that significantly transformed the social, economic, and political fabric of the nation. Write an essay agreeing or disagreeing with that assessment and offer as much evidence as possible to back up your position.

5.   Pretend that you are one of the following: a northern woman or young man working in a factory, the wife of a Confederate soldier, or a rank-and-file Confederate soldier. Write a journal or letter, based on the content of Chapter 15, explaining your attitudes, experiences, hardships, aspirations, and gripes.

ANSWERS TO MULTIPLE-CHOICE QUESTIONS

1. c
2. a
3. b
4. c
5. d
6. a
7. c
8. a
9. b
10. a

CHAPTER 16

The Crises of Reconstruction, 1865–1877

OUTLINE AND SUMMARY

I. Introduction

The ending of the Civil War and the Reconstruction period that followed constituted a "crucial turning point" in American history. Vital problems had to be solved, above all, how and under what conditions the South should be readmitted to the Union and what the rights and status of the 3.5 million freedmen should be. Chapter 16 discusses the challenges facing the nation between 1865 and 1877 and how those challenges were met or failed to be met. While reading the chapter you should consider the following questions: (1) How did the Radical Republicans gain control over reconstructing the South, and what was the impact of their program on the ex-Confederates, other white southerners, and black southerners? (2) How did freed blacks remake their lives after emancipation? (3) What political and economic developments occurred in the North during the Reconstruction Era?   (4) What brought about the end of reconstruction?

II. Reconstruction Politics, 1865–1868

A. Lincoln's Plan

Differences between President Lincoln and Congress on reconstruction of the Confederate states began as early as 1863. In December Lincoln issued a plan that would allow the formation of a new state government when as few as 10 percent of the state's voters took an oath of loyalty to the Union and recognized the end of slavery. This plan said nothing about votes for the freedmen. Lincoln hoped to win over southern Unionists with this plan and draw them into the Republican Party. Republicans in Congress thought the plan inadequate and passed the Wade-Davis bill instead. This bill required that at least 50 percent of the voters take an oath of allegiance, and it excluded from participation in government all those who had cooperated with the Confederacy. Lincoln pocket-vetoed the bill, and at the time of his death he and Congress were at an impasse.

B. Presidential Reconstruction Under Johnson

President Andrew Johnson, who was unconcerned about the blacks but wished to promote the interests of the poorer whites in the South, announced his Reconstruction plan in May 1865. Johnson required whites to take an oath of allegiance to the Union, after which they could set up new state governments. These had to proclaim secession illegal, repudiate Confederate debts, and ratify the Thirteenth Amendment (abolishing slavery). Whites who had held high office under the Confederacy and all those with taxable property of $20,000 or more could not vote or hold office until they applied for and received a special pardon from the president. During the summer, Johnson undermined his own policy of excluding planters from leadership by handing out pardons to them wholesale. The new governments created under Johnson's plan were soon dominated by former Confederate leaders and large landowners. Some of the Johnson governments refused to ratify the Thirteenth Amendment, and all showed their intention of making black freedom only nominal by enacting "black codes." Horrified by such evidence of continued southern defiance, the Republican-dominated Congress, in December 1865, refused to recognize these governments or to seat the men they sent to the House and Senate.

C. Congress Versus Johnson
The Radical Republicans, who wished to give black men the vote and transform the South into a biracial democracy, were in a minority in 1866. The majority moderate Republicans wanted only to get rid of the black codes and protect the basic civil rights of blacks. The moderates attempted to accomplish these limited goals by continuing the Freedmen's Bureau and passing the Civil Rights Act of 1866. When Johnson vetoed both of these measures, he drove the moderates into an alliance with the Radicals, and together they overrode his vetoes. The now radicalized Republicans also moved to protect the provisions of the Civil Rights Act by embodying them in a constitutional amendment.

D. The Fourteenth Amendment, 1866
With the Fourteenth Amendment, the federal government for the first time defined citizenship and intervened to protect persons from state governments. The amendment stated that all persons born in the United States or naturalized were citizens. No state could deny any person's rights without due process of law or deny equal protection of the law. States that refused black men the vote could have their representation in Congress reduced. Former Confederate officials were excluded from voting and officeholding until pardoned by a two-thirds vote of Congress. The southern states, except for Tennessee, refused to ratify the amendment and Johnson denounced it, but in the congressional elections of 1866 the Republicans won huge majorities, giving them a mandate to force ratification of the Fourteenth Amendment and proceed with congressional Reconstruction of the South.

E. Congressional Reconstruction, 1866–1867
In 1867 and 1868 Congress enacted its Reconstruction program over Johnson's vetoes. The earlier Johnson governments, black codes, and all other laws the southern states had passed were invalidated. All the former Confederate states except Tennessee, which had been readmitted, were divided into districts under the temporary rule of the military. Each state was required to write a new constitution enfranchising black men and to ratify the Fourteenth Amendment. When these things were done, Congress could readmit the state to the Union. Congressional Reconstruction was more radical than Lincoln's or Johnson's, since it enfranchised blacks and temporarily disfranchised many whites. It did not, however, go as far as the Radicals wanted, since it failed to confiscate southern land and redistribute it to blacks and poor whites. Johnson, as Commander in Chief of the army, dragged his feet in enforcing congressional Reconstruction, thus convincing Republicans that he had to be dealt with.

F. The Impeachment Crisis, 1867–1868
In March 1867 Congress passed the Tenure of Office Act aimed at reducing the president's power. Johnson violated it by firing Secretary of War Edwin Stanton, at which point the Republicans in Congress began impeachment proceedings. Some Republicans wavered, however, fearing that removal of Johnson would upset the constitutional balance of power. As a result, the vote to convict and remove the president fell one short of the necessary two-thirds of the Senate.

G. The Fifteenth Amendment and the Question of Woman Suffrage, 1869–1870
Congress passed a final amendment to complete its Reconstruction program. The Fifteenth Amendment stated that the right to vote could not be denied because of race, color, or previous condition of servitude. The Republicans hoped with this amendment to protect southern blacks, extend suffrage to northern blacks, and gain many new voters for their party. When Congress refused to include woman suffrage, some feminists denounced the amendment and its Republican sponsors. By 1870 the three new amendments—ending slavery, guaranteeing the rights of citizens, and enfranchising black men—were a part of the

Constitution and Congress had readmitted all the former Confederate states. Thereafter congressional efforts at Reconstruction weakened.

III. Reconstruction Governments
    A. A New Electorate
        The Reconstruction laws of 1867–1868 created a new electorate in the South by enfranchising blacks and temporarily disfranchising 10 to 15 percent of the whites. This new electorate put in power Republican governments that were made up of a coalition of carpetbaggers (northerners who had come south for a variety of reasons), scalawags (cooperating southern whites), and blacks.

    B. Republican Rule
        The Republican Reconstruction governments democratized southern politics by abolishing property and racial qualifications for voting and officeholding, redistricting state legislatures, and making formerly appointive offices elective. They undertook extensive public works, offered increased public services, and established the South's first public schools. All of this cost money, and therefore taxes rose. Southern landowners bitterly resented the increased taxes and accused the state governments of corruption and waste. Some of their charges were true, but many were exaggerated. In no state was the land of ex-Confederate planters confiscated and redistributed to freedmen.

    C. Counterattacks
        White southern Democrats refused to accept black voting and officeholding and launched a counterattack to drive the Republican Reconstruction governments from power. White vigilante groups began a campaign of violence and intimidation against blacks, Freedmen's Bureau officials, and white Republicans. Congress investigated this reign of terror and attempted to suppress it with the Enforcement Acts, but only a "large military presence in the South could have protected black rights" and preserved the black electorate. By the 1870s Congress and President Grant were no longer willing to use military force to remake the South.

IV. The Impact of Emancipation
    A. Confronting Freedom
        Freedmen, usually lacking property, tools, capital, and literacy, left the plantations where they had been enslaved and searched for family members from whom they had been separated. Once reunited, many took the first opportunity to legalize their marriages so that they could raise their children and live an independent family life.

    B. African-American Institutions
        The desire to be free of white control also led blacks to establish their own institutions. Most important were the black churches, which played major religious, social, and political roles. Many black schools were started with the help of the Freedmen's Bureau and northern philanthropists, including the earliest black universities: Howard, Atlanta, and Fisk. Segregation of all facilities in the South became a way of life despite Charles Sumner's Civil Rights Act of 1875, which was unenforced and later invalidated by the Supreme Court.

    C. Land, Labor, and Sharecropping
        Above all, freedmen wanted to become landowning, independent farmers, but few did because the Republicans believed that property rights were too sacred to be violated by confiscation and redistribution of the white planters' lands. Besides, blacks did not have the capital to buy land and agricultural tools. With the end of slavery, the planters continued to own the land but had no work force. Therefore, landless laborers and landholding planters developed the form of tenantry known as sharecropping. Many white small farmers also lost

their land and became sharecropping tenants. By 1880, 80 percent of the land in the cotton states was worked by landless tenants.

   D.   Toward a Crop-Lien Economy
Rural merchants (often themselves landlords) sold supplies to sharecroppers on credit—with a lien on the tenants' share of the crop as collateral. Because interest rates were exorbitant, cotton prices low, and merchants often dishonest, sharecroppers fell deeper and deeper into debt. Southern law prohibited their leaving the land until they had fully repaid their debts. Thus sharecroppers were locked into poverty and indebtedness.

V.   New Concerns in the North, 1868–1876
   A.   Grantism
The popular Civil War hero Ulysses S. Grant won the presidency in 1868 on the Republican ticket. His administration was marred by rampant corruption, as were many state and local governments of the time. In 1872 Republicans, disgusted by the scandals, broke with Grant and formed the Liberal Republican Party.

   B.   The Liberals' Revolt
The Liberal Republicans nominated Horace Greeley for president, and the Democrats endorsed him as well. The regular Republicans renominated Grant, who won the 1872 election, but the split in the Republican ranks seriously weakened Republican efforts to remake the South.

   C.   The Panic of 1873
During Grant's second term the nation suffered a financial panic and a severe economic depression. These produced business failures, mass unemployment, heightened labor-management conflict, and disputes over the country's currency system, all of which further diverted Republican attention from Reconstruction.

   D.   Reconstruction and the Constitution
The Supreme Court in the last quarter of the nineteenth century also undermined Republican Reconstruction. In a series of decisions, the Court interpreted the Fourteenth and Fifteenth Amendments in a way that made them all but useless for protecting black citizens. It declared the Civil Rights and Enforcement Acts unconstitutional and upheld state segregation laws.

   E.   Republicans in Retreat
By the 1870s the Republicans were abandoning their Reconstruction policy. Most of them were more interested in economic growth than in protecting black rights. The Radicals who were committed to biracial democracy in the South were dead or had been defeated in elections. Many northerners wanted to normalize relations with the white South. They shared the racial belief that blacks were inferior to whites, and the federal government could not force equality.

VI.   Reconstruction Abandoned, 1876–1877
   A.   Redeeming the South
After 1872 congressional pardons restored voting and officeholding rights to all ex-Confederates. These men and the South's rising class of business entrepreneurs led the Democratic Party in a drive to redeem the South from Republican rule. Using economic pressure, intimidation, and violence, the Democrats had regained control of all the southern states but South Carolina, Florida, and Louisiana by 1876. Once in power the Democrats cut taxes and public works and services and passed laws favoring landlords over tenants. Some blacks responded to the deteriorating situation by migrating from the South, but most were trapped where they were by debt and poverty.

B.   The Election of 1876

The Republicans nominated Rutherford Hayes, the Democrats, Samuel Tilden. Tilden won in the popular vote, but because of fraud and intimidation at the polls, the electoral votes in four states were disputed. A special electoral commission, stacked in favor of the Republicans, awarded all the disputed votes to Hayes. The Democrats refused to accept the finding until a compromise deal was worked out by southern Democrats and Republican supporters of Hayes. In exchange for southern acceptance of Hayes as president, the Republicans promised (1) to let Democrats take over the last Republican Reconstruction governments in Louisiana and South Carolina, (2) to remove the remaining troops from the South, (3) to give more federal patronage to southern Democrats, and (4) to provide federal aid for building railroads and for other internal improvements in the South. This so-called Compromise of 1877 struck the final blow to Radical Reconstruction and ended all federal protection for the freedmen.

VII. Conclusion

By the end of the Reconstruction era the Republicans had firm support in the Northeast and Midwest; the Democrats were solidly entrenched in the South and would remain so for nearly a century. Many historians today look back on Reconstruction as a democratic experiment that failed partly because Congress did not redistribute land to freedmen, and without any property they were too economically vulnerable to hold on to their political rights. The Republicans also were unwilling to continue using military force to protect blacks and remake southern society. Reconstruction did, however, leave as a lasting legacy the Fourteenth and Fifteenth Amendments. During that brief era, southern blacks reconstituted their families, created their own institutions, and for the first time participated in government.

VOCABULARY

The following terms are used in Chapter 16. To understand the chapter fully, it is important that you know what each of them means.

suffrage	the vote; the right to vote
enfranchisement	the giving of the rights of citizenship and voting (the taking away of these rights is called disfranchisement)
allegiance	faithfulness and obligation to a person, idea, country, or government
amnesty	a general pardon for offenses against a government
yeomen	nonslaveholding, small-landowning farmers
referendum	the procedure of submitting legislative measures to the voters for approval or rejection
mandate	instruction about policy given or supposed to be given by the voters to a legislative body or government
confiscate	seize private property by government authority
impeachment	the charging of a public official, such as a judge or president, with misconduct in office
vigilantes	members of extralegal citizens' groups organized to maintain order and punish offenses
electorate	the body of persons entitled to vote in an election

stereotype	a characteristic or set of characteristics, usually negative, attributed to all members of a group
coalition	a combination or alliance between different groups, parties, or states in support of a particular cause, individual, or purpose
mulatto	the offspring of one white and one black parent; a person of mixed black and white ancestry
mobilization	putting forces or resources into active service for a cause
writ of habeas corpus	a formal order requiring that an arrested person be brought before a judge or court and be charged with a specific crime or released; the right to such a writ is guaranteed in the U.S. Constitution
capital	wealth (especially money) that can be used to produce more wealth
segregation	the act of separating or setting apart from others, especially on the basis of race (the undoing of such separation is called desegregation or integration)
collateral	security or property pledged for the payment of a loan
speculator	one who trades in commodities, securities, or land in the hope of making a profit from changes in their market value; one who engages in business transactions that involve considerable risk but offer the chance of large gains
filibuster	use delaying tactics, such as long speeches, to prevent a vote or action by a legislative body

IDENTIFICATIONS

After reading Chapter 16, you should be able to identify and explain the historical significance of each of the following:

Charles Sumner, Thaddeus Stevens, and the Radical Republicans

black codes

Freedmen's Bureau

Reconstruction Act of 1867

Tenure of Office Act

carpetbaggers and scalawags

Ku Klux Klan, Enforcement Acts (Ku Klux Klan Act)

Civil Rights Act of 1875

Liberal Republicans and Horace Greeley

greenbacks and the Greenback party

Mississippi Plan and redemption

SKILL BUILDING: CHARTS

1. Look at the table titled "The Duration of Republican Rule in the Ex-Confederate States" on page 494 in the textbook.

   a. For how many years on average did Republicans control the governments of the ex-Confederate states?

   b. Can you explain why Republican rule lasted less than a decade in every ex-Confederate state?

   c. Which state was readmitted to the Union before the start of congressional Reconstruction? After reading the chapter, can you explain why?

   d. In what three states did Republicans hold power the longest? Can you explain what brought about the return of the Democrats to power in those three states?

2. Look at the table titled "Percentage of Persons Unable to Write by Age Group, 1870–1890, in South Carolina, Georgia, Alabama, Mississippi, and Louisiana" on page 484 of the textbook.

   a. What percentage of whites in each age group were unable to write in 1870? After reading the textbook, can you explain why these figures are so high?

   b. Did the educational levels of whites improve by 1890? Can you explain why it did or did not?

   c. Was the educational level of blacks higher or lower than that of whites in 1870? What about 1890? How might a critic of Republican Reconstruction of the South use these figures?

   d. After reading the text, can you explain the reasons for the differences between whites and blacks?

HISTORICAL SOURCES

Among the many historical sources used in Chapter 16 there are three that are often useful to historians writing political history: (1) law codes, statutes, and constitutional amendments passed by the states and the federal government; (2) records of congressional speeches, remarks, and votes, as found in the *Congressional Globe,* later named the *Congressional Record;* and (3) records of congressional hearings and investigations that are printed and made public by the federal government.

The text refers to laws known as black codes passed by the ex-Confederate states. By studying these laws, what does the historian learn about the intentions and attitudes toward blacks among the governing whites? What other conclusions does the textbook come to on the basis of this source?

Find at least three places in Chapter 16 where remarks of congressmen or important votes in the House or Senate are discussed. In each example, analyze what the author is illustrating or proving with this evidence.

The text uses testimony about vigilante violence in the South that was given before a joint congressional committee. Why are records of hearings and investigations by congressional committees a rich source for historians? Could a historian get a distorted or biased view of a past situation by relying solely on such a source? Why or why not?

MULTIPLE-CHOICE QUESTIONS

Circle the letter of the item that best completes each statement or answers the question.

1. Lincoln's plan of reconstruction
   a. required southern states to enfranchise blacks.
   b. required that 50 percent or more of white voters in an ex-Confederate state take an oath of allegiance to the Union before a new state government could be established.
   c. was intended to gain the support of southern unionists and attract them to a southern Republican Party.
   d. was eventually accepted by Congress.

2. Which of the following statements about Andrew Johnson is *incorrect*?
   a. He wanted to exclude planters from political leadership in the South, but then he undermined his intention by granting many pardons to this group.
   b. He cared deeply about obtaining just treatment for the freedmen.
   c. He was a lifelong Democrat with no interest in building the strength of the Republican Party.
   d. He vetoed all of the congressional Reconstruction acts, only to have Congress override his vetoes.

3. "Exodusters" were
   a. former scalawags who switched from the Republican to the Democratic Party in the 1870s.
   b. the Democratic redeemers who drove out the Republican Reconstruction governments by violence, intimidation, and economic pressure.
   c. carpetbaggers who left the South in the 1870s and returned to the North.
   d. southern blacks who migrated to Kansas to homestead in the 1870s.

4. All of the following were corruption scandals linked to the Grant Administration *except*
   a. the $13 million Tweed Court House.
   b. Jay Gould's and Jim Fisk's cornering of the gold market.
   c. the "whiskey ring."
   d. the Credit Mobilier's skimming of Union Pacific railroad profits.

5. Andrew Johnson was impeached but not convicted because
   a. he proved that he had not violated the Tenure of Office Act.
   b. he resigned before the Senate voted on his guilt.
   c. seven Republicans, fearing that removal of the president would upset the balance of power among the three branches of government, voted "not guilty" with the Democrats.
   d. the Supreme Court ruled that he had not engaged in misconduct in office.

6. Which of these women was indicted, convicted, and fined for going to the polls and voting and urging other women to do the same in the election of 1872?
   a. Lucy Stone
   b. Susan B. Anthony
   c. Elizabeth Cady Stanton
   d. Lucy Hayes

7. In the Republican Reconstruction governments of the South, the group that held the most political offices consisted of
   a. carpetbaggers.
   b. scalawags.
   c. blacks.
   d. the planter elite.

8.   The Republican Reconstruction governments of the South
    a.   gave the region the most honest, efficient governments it had ever had.
    b.   excluded almost all whites from officeholding and were run almost exclusively by blacks.
    c.   created public-school systems, built and repaired roads and bridges, and opened institutions to care for orphans and the disabled.
    d.   cut taxes and passed laws favoring the interests of landlords over those of tenants and sharecroppers.
9.   The sharecropping and crop-lien systems that developed in the post–Civil War South
    a.   contributed to soil depletion, agricultural backwardness, and southern poverty.
    b.   reduced the portion of southern land owned and controlled by the planter elite.
    c.   forced most black people out of agriculture and into southern cities.
    d.   tied white planters and black tenants together economically but had no effect on white small farmers.
10.   Most historians today view Radical Reconstruction as a democratic experiment that failed because it
    a.   left blacks without property and failed to defend their rights with sufficient military force.
    b.   relied on excessive military force instead of political persuasion.
    c.   was unrealistic in its expectation that illiterate blacks could be turned into responsible citizens overnight.
    d.   was overly vindictive and harsh toward all white southerners.

SHORT-ANSWER QUESTIONS

1.   What actions of President Johnson drove moderate Republicans in Congress into cooperation with Radical Republicans?

2.   What are the major provisions of the Thirteenth, Fourteenth, and Fifteenth Amendments to the U.S. Constitution?

3.   Why did Elizabeth Cady Stanton, Susan B. Anthony, and some other feminists oppose the Fifteenth Amendment?

4.   Why did the Liberal Republicans break with President Grant? What impact did the split have on Republican Reconstruction?

5.   Explain how Supreme Court decisions in the 1870s and 1880s undermined Republican Reconstruction.

6.   What were the terms of the Compromise of 1877? Which of the terms were actually carried out after the inauguration of Rutherford B. Hayes?

7.   Explain briefly why the freedmen's dream of "forty acres and a mule" never came to pass.

ESSAY QUESTIONS

1.   Compare and contrast Lincoln's, Johnson's, and Congress's plans of reconstruction (as represented by the Reconstruction Acts of 1867–1868 and the Fourteenth and Fifteenth Amendments). What were the objectives of each plan? Why did each fail to achieve its goals?

2.   Discuss the transformation of southern agriculture during the Reconstruction period. Why did the sharecropping and crop-lien systems evolve? What were the consequences of those systems for the economy of the South and for white and black farmers?

3. Discuss the achievements and failures of the Republican Reconstruction governments in the South. Who supported and who opposed them? Why? Why and how were they driven from power?

4. Imagine that you are a Freedmen's Bureau agent in the South during the Reconstruction period. Using the information in Chapter 16, write an account of what you have seen black people doing and experiencing. As such an agent, how have you been involved with the blacks in your district?

5. Write an essay discussing the Grant administration. What were its policies on Reconstruction and the freedmen? What was meant by "Grantism?" What successes and failures did the administration have in foreign policy? Why did the Liberal Republicans break with Grant?

ANSWERS TO MULTIPLE-CHOICE QUESTIONS

1. c
2. b
3. d
4. a
5. c
6. b
7. b
8. c
9. a
10. a

CHAPTER 17

The Transformation of the Trans-Mississippi West, 1860–1900

OUTLINE AND SUMMARY

I.   Introduction

Chapter 17 addresses the following questions: (1) How and why did Native American life on the Great Plains change between the 1850s and 1900? (2) What roles did the army and the railroads play in the settlement of the West? (3) How did Anglo-Americans displace Spanish-speaking people in the Southwest? (4) How did the Wild West image of cowboys and Indians originate? (5) Why did some Americans wish to conserve the natural resources and beauty of the West, and how did this lead to creating the national parks?

II.   Native Americans and the Trans-Mississippi West

A.   The Plains Indians

In the mid-nineteenth century, the Sioux, Blackfoot, Cheyenne, Arapaho, Crow, and other Native American tribes roamed the northern Great Plains. In the central and southern Plains lived the Five Civilized Tribes and the Comanches, Kiowas, Pawnees, and others. Many of the Plains Indians, among them the Lakota Sioux, Crow, and Cheyenne, hunted the migrating buffalo herds. They ate the meat and used the hides for tepees and clothing. In the 1860s the demand for buffalo hides in the eastern markets grew so great that white hunters, sometimes aided by the Indians, became professional buffalo killers. One such hunter, "Buffalo Bill" Cody, in 1867-1868, killed over 4,000 animals to feed the crews building the first transcontinental railroad. By the 1880s hunting had reduced the once huge herds to only a few thousand animals and doomed the nomadic, buffalo-centered way of life of the Plains tribes.

B.   The Assault on Nomadic Indian Life

By the time of the Civil War, the government was pressuring Plains tribes to surrender their vast hunting grounds and settle as farmers on restricted reservations. Some tribes, such as the Pueblos and Crows, accepted the change peacefully, but from the 1860s to 1890, some 100,000 Native Americans of the Sioux, Cheyenne, Arapaho, Kiowa, Comanche, and other tribes engaged in almost constant warfare with the army over possession of the Great Plains and the Southwest. In this struggle, atrocities, such as the Chivington Sand Creek massacre, occurred. In 1867–1868 the government signed peace treaties with many of these tribes, which assigned most of them to two large reservations, one in present-day Oklahoma (then known as the Indian Territory) and the other in present-day South Dakota (the Great Sioux Reserve). However, many of the tribes rejected a sedentary farming way of life. They, therefore, left the reservations and harried white pioneers. The army retaliated by attacking any bands off their reservations, even if those groups did not happen to be the ones that had committed hostile acts. After the Red River war in the 1870s, the southern Plains tribes gave up. By 1886, when Geronimo surrendered, the southwestern tribes also capitulated.

C.   Custer's Last Stand, 1876
When the Sioux refused to report to the government-run agencies on their reservation and to sell the Black Hills part of their reserve,, the army made war against them. The most famous casualties in that campaign were Colonel George A. Custer and his Seventh Cavalry, which the Sioux annihilated at the battle of the Little Bighorn in 1876. Despite their brief triumph, the Sioux were subsequently forced to settle near the government agencies and to surrender the Black Hills. In the late 1870s the army crushed brief resistance by Chief Joseph's Nez Percé and Chief Dull Knife's northern Cheyennes.

D.   "Saving" the Indians
Humanitarian reformers in the East began to cry out against government mistreatment of the Indians. In 1881 Helen Hunt Jackson's *A Century of Dishonor* called attention to the sorry record. These reformers thought the best way to end the injustice was to assimilate Indians quickly into mainstream white society. Therefore, well-intentioned reformers, as well as whites who were interested only in seizing more Indian land, supported the 1887 Dawes Severalty Act. The law ended collective tribal ownership of land and split the reservation into 160-acre farms that were assigned to the head of each Indian family. Any remaining reservation land was sold to whites. At the end of twenty-five years, the Indians were to receive full title to their farms and U.S. citizenship. The government also attempted to suppress tribal languages and culture. The new policies proved disastrous for most Indians. By 1934 the total acreage owned by Indians had fallen by 65 percent. What was left in Indian hands was often too dry or infertile to be farmed.

E.   The Ghost Dance and the End of Indian Resistance on the Great Plains, 1890
Desperate because of their plight, the Sioux and other tribes turned to the Ghost Dance movement. The army's decision to stop the movement led to the death of Sitting Bull, the last battles between whites and Indians, and the 1890 Wounded Knee massacre of 300 Sioux. By 1900, most of the remaining 100,000 Plains Indians lived in poverty on their reservations, dependent on government support to survive. The Navajo of the Southwest, on the other hand, adjusted more readily to reservation life and by 1900 had increased their land and livestock holdings.

III.   Settling the West
A.   The First Transcontinental Railroad
With the meeting of the Union Pacific and Central Pacific tracks at Promontory Point, Utah, in 1869, the United States completed its first transcontinental railroad. Construction had been authorized by the Pacific Railroad Act of 1862, and much of the labor was performed by Chinese and Irish immigrants, as well as Mexican-Americans and African-Americans. Because the government granted land to the companies for every mile of track laid, the railroads emerged as the biggest landlords in the West. By the end of the 1800s, nine major railroads linked the country, making westward travel and shipping much faster and easier.

B.   Settlers and the Railroad
To encourage railroad companies to lay track across the country, state and federal governments granted them millions of acres of land. Eager both to sell these lands and to create future customers for rail service, the companies made all-out efforts to attract settlers. They opened land bureaus, sent agents to the East Coast and Europe, and offered easy credit and free transportation out west to potential purchasers. Between 1870 and 1900, railroads helped to recruit whole families, single women, and over 2 million European immigrants to farm the Trans-Mississippi West. The railroads wielded great economic and social influence over western development. Their pressure for quick payment from land buyers pushed

western farmers into concentrating on producing a single cash crop, such as wheat or corn, which made them very vulnerable to price fluctuations on the world market.

C.   Homesteading on the Great Plains
Settlers also were drawn to the Great Plains by the Homestead Act, which provided a free 160-acre farm to anyone who would live on and improve it over a five-year period. This offer was especially attractive to immigrants from western and northern Europe, where land was extremely expensive. Some 400,000 families registered claims under the Homestead Act between 1862 and 1900, although there were flaws in the provisions and implementation of the law that allowed the most valuable western land to end up in the hands of railroads, land speculators, lumber companies, and big ranchers. Homesteading pioneers on the Great Plains had to cope with major trials: isolation, backbreaking work, extreme weather conditions, and living in sod houses due to the lack of trees for lumber. Many gave up and left their farms, but for those who persisted for ten years or more, generally their lives became more comfortable.

D.   New Farms, New Markets
Railroads, improved farm machinery, and mounting eastern demand for food, all led to the development of millions of new farms and soaring American agricultural production between 1870 and 1900. However, starting a new farm on the Great Plains was a risky business. Most settlers had to go heavily into debt to acquire horses, machinery, and seed even if they obtained free land. To meet debt payments to railroads and banks, farmers specialized in growing cash crops, which made them vulnerable to world market conditions and dependent on the railroads to reach the markets. Uncertain rainfall and severe weather conditions added to the farmers' problems.

E.   Building a Society and Achieving Statehood
Out of crude frontier settlements, "civilized" communities began to develop. Churches and Sunday schools were usually the earliest institutions to emerge. Residents drew up state constitutions, and one after another, Kansas, Nevada, Nebraska, and Colorado entered the Union in the 1860s and 1870s. Most of the northern portions of the Great Plains achieved statehood in the late 1880s and the 1890s. With the entrance to the Union of Oklahoma, Arizona, and New Mexico early in the twentieth century, the trans-Mississippi West completed its transition from frontier territories to states. Although most western governments were conservative, they did lead the eastern states in granting woman suffrage. By 1910 Idaho, Wyoming, Utah, and Colorado women had full voting rights.

F.   The Spread of Mormonism
Persecuted in the East, the Mormons, led by Brigham Young, migrated to the Great Salt Lake Valley, starting in 1847. They declared their territory the independent country of Deseret, attracted many converts from the East and Europe, created a church-directed government, and practiced polygyny. In the 1860s the federal government began outlawing their practices and in the 1870s won backing for repressive and coercive measures from the federal courts. Under pressure, the Mormons renounced polygyny and church involvement in government in 1890 and applied for statehood. Utah was admitted to the union in 1896.

G.   Southwestern Borderlands
After the Mexican War, American ranchers and settlers in the Southwest took over the territorial governments and forced most of the Spanish-speaking population off the land. The Mexican minority tended to become low-paid day laborers who faced discrimination and periodic violent attacks. Mexican-Americans fought back by organizing groups such as *Las Gorras Blancas* (the White Caps), but they had little success. The Hispanic struggle for justice and equality would continue throughout the twentieth century.

IV. Exploiting the Western Landscape
   A.   The Mining Frontier
        Starting with the California gold rush in 1849, a series of mining booms swept the West. In
        the 1850s gold rushes took place in the Sierra Nevada and in British Columbia. New gold
        and silver strikes followed in Nevada, Colorado, Idaho, Montana, Wyoming, South Dakota,
        and Alaska. Each new discovery brought a rush of eager prospectors who believed in the
        get-rich-quick myth of the West. Infamous boomtowns such as Virginia City, Nevada,
        sprang up and then declined into ghost towns when the mines were depleted. Although a few
        individual prospectors with picks, shovels, and strainers did make their fortunes, most barely
        earned a living. The real profits from the mining frontier went to large mining companies
        backed by European and eastern capital. They had the expensive equipment necessary to
        mine the gold and silver deposits deep underground. While these mining companies
        stimulated U. S. economic growth with the millions of ounces of gold and silver they dug
        from the earth, they also ravaged the landscape and filled the surrounding area with smoke
        and chemicals from their smelters.

   B.   Cowboys and the Cattle Frontier
        Confinement of the Plains Indians on reservations, extension of the railroad into Kansas, and
        the construction of new stockyards at railheads such as Abilene made possible the open-
        range cattle industry. Railroad promoters enticed thousands of people to enter the business
        by predicting great profits. For a time open-range ranchers did make fortunes, although this
        was not true for the ordinary cowboys who tended the cattle on the long drives to the
        railheads. Most cowboys were poorly paid young men, about one-fifth of them black or
        Mexican. The open-range cattle bonanza reached its peak in the years 1880–1885.
        Thereafter the industry declined rapidly because of overgrazing, fencing of the open range
        by farmers, and freezing winters in 1885 and 1886 that killed 90 percent of the steers in
        some regions. The open range and great cattle drives disappeared, although cattle ranching
        continued.

   C.   Cattle Towns and Prostitutes
        The open-range cattle industry produced the legendary cattle towns, such as Abilene,
        Kansas. These towns were generally less lawless and violent than they have been portrayed
        in novels, films, and on television, but they did have many saloons and prostitutes to serve
        the single young men who rode the range and drove the cattle into town. The prostitutes
        came from many different class and ethnic backgrounds.

   D.   Bonanza Farms
        Believing that enormous profits could be made in large-scale wheat growing, speculators in
        the late 1870s and the 1880s established ten-thousand-acre farms and invested heavily in the
        latest equipment. For a while these bonanza farms did reap handsome profits, but
        overproduction, poor weather conditions, and falling wheat prices sent most of the
        enterprises into bankruptcy by 1890. Large-scale farming did best in California, where big
        growers irrigated their land and cooperatively marketed their citrus fruit under the "Sunkist"
        trademark.

   E.   The Oklahoma Land Rush, 1889
        The federal government initially set aside Oklahoma as a reservation for various Native
        American tribes, but as pressure from land-hungry farmers mounted, the government
        reconsidered. In 1889 Congress opened some 2 million acres in the heart of the Indian
        Territory to white settlers. Within weeks Oklahoma pioneers filed six thousand homestead
        claims.. In the following years, under the provisions of the Dawes Act, more and more
        Oklahoma land passed into the hands of whites, and by 1898 Congress in the Curtis Act
        proclaimed the end of the Indian Territory.

V.　The West of Life and Legend

    A.　The American Adam and the Dime-Novel Hero

Writers in the middle of the nineteenth century often presented the West as a place to escape from the corruptions of civilization, as seen in Mark Twain's *Huckleberry Finn*. In the 1860s and 1870s eastern dime-novel writers created the western novel, with its frontiersman hero who fights Indians and "bad guys" for right and justice. One of the novelists, Ned Buntline, made Buffalo Bill so famous that his real-life model, William F. "Buffalo Bill" Cody, cashed in on the fame by founding a Wild West touring show that became extremely popular.

    B.　Revitalizing the Frontier Legend

The dime novels and Wild West shows caught the fancy of three young members of the eastern elite: Theodore Roosevelt, Frederic Remington, and Owen Wister. The three visited the West and made it the subject of their histories, art, and novels. In doing so they fostered the frontier legend of the West as a testing ground in which the fittest and best survived and as the home of the cowboy, who embodied the essence of manly virtue.

    C.　Beginning a National Parks Movement

The frontier legend aroused some public interest in protecting the West's natural beauty and wonders. Also, in response to the work of John Wesley Powell, Henry D. Washburn, George Perkins Marsh, and John Muir, the nation created its first national parks (Yellowstone and Yosemite), and Muir became president of the first organization dedicated to conservation, the Sierra Club.

VI.　Conclusion

As Americans struggled to adjust to the disruptive changes brought by industrialization and urbanization, they embraced the myth of the West as a paradise where life was simple, moral right and wrong were clear-cut, and opportunity abounded. That myth was created by popular writers, journalists, artists, railroad publicists, and politicians; however, it ignored the darker elements of westward expansion: the use of the army to destroy the way of life of the Native Americans and force them onto reservations; the heedless exploitation of the environment; and the fact that the individual prospectors, ranchers, and homesteaders were increasingly overtaken by big eastern-financed companies in mining, ranching, and agribusiness. It was also true that the creation of new western settlements enhanced the image of the United States as a land of opportunities; fostered certain democratic ideas, such as extending the vote to women; and gave birth to the conservation movement. The development of the vast western resources made the nation one of the world's richest powers by 1900.

VOCABULARY

The following terms are used in Chapter 17. To understand the chapter fully, it is important that you know what each of them means.

entrepreneur	one who owns, launches, manages, and assumes the risks of a business venture
in perpetuity	forever
severalty	the legal situation in which property, such as land, is held or owned by separate or individual right, as opposed to collective ownership
polygyny	the practice of having more than one wife at one time

bonanza   a rich mass of ore, as in mining; a sudden find of wealth

ethnocentric   seeing one's own ethnic group and its culture as superior to or more important than other groups and their cultures

IDENTIFICATIONS

After reading Chapter 17, you should be able to identify and explain the historical significance of each of the following:

John M. Chivington and the Sand Creek Massacre

Geronimo

George Armstrong Custer

Chief Joseph

Chief Dull Knife

Wounded Knee

Pacific Railroad Act, 1862

the Oklahoma land rush and the "sooners"

Ned Buntline and William F. "Buffalo Bill" Cody

SKILL BUILDING: MAPS

1. On the outline map of the Great Plains and the Far West, identify each state and indicate the decade in which it entered the Union.

2. Each of the following places was significant in the history of the frontier West. Locate each and explain its importance.

    100th meridian

    Sierra Nevada

    Rocky Mountains

    Virginia City, Nevada

    Denver, Colorado

    Missouri River and Great Sioux Reserve

    Indian Territory (Oklahoma)

    Black Hills, South Dakota

    Little Big Horn, Montana

    Wounded Knee, South Dakota

    Abilene, Kansas

    Chisholm Trail

    Promontory Point (near Ogden, Utah)

    Colorado River

Yellowstone National Park

Yosemite National Park

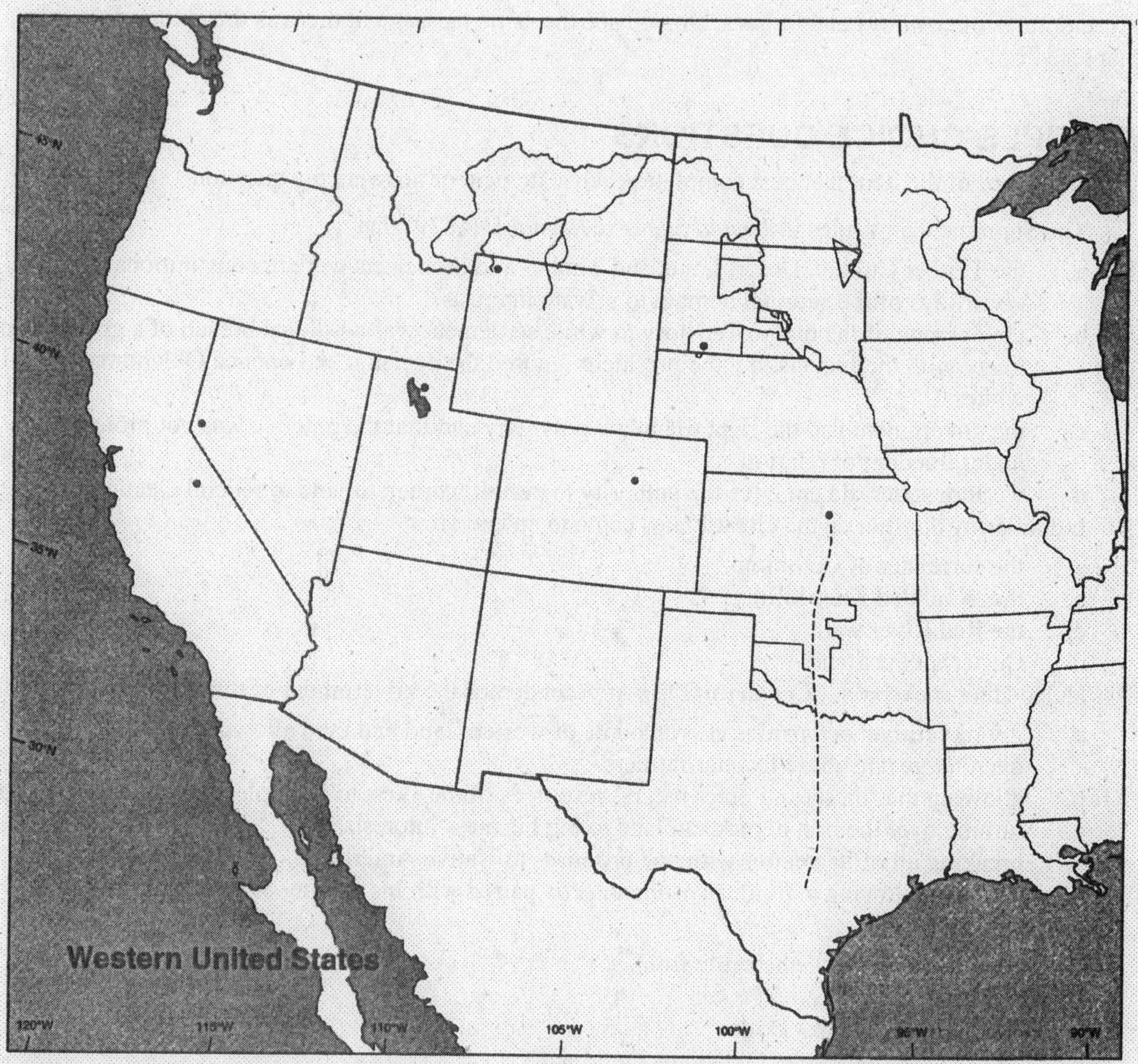

HISTORICAL SOURCES

Historians try to discover not only what life was like for different groups of people living in the past but also what those people believed, valued, and perceived. Unless we know these things, it is difficult to understand motivation, to answer the question, why did people do what they did?

In Chapter 17 the author uses popular novels published in the last forty years of the nineteenth century to shed some light on beliefs, values, and perceptions. An example is Ned Buntline's *Buffalo Bill: King of the Border Men* (1869), cited on page 526. What does this popular novel try to convey to the reader? Why are popular novels good historical sources? How can we know whether their readers shared the values and perceptions of their authors?

While these novels may be historical sources, they have little lasting literary merit. In Chapter 17 the author also uses the works of more gifted writers and artists as historical sources. Page 526 refers to a book by Mark Twain, one of the best nineteenth-century writers, and mentions the paintings and sculptures of Frederick Remington, the fine western artist. How does the author use the work of Twain and Remington? What is illustrated in each case? Look at some reproductions of Remington paintings and sculptures of cowboys and Indians. Do you see the same message in them as the author does in Chapter 17?

MULTIPLE-CHOICE QUESTIONS

Circle the letter of the item that best completes each statement or answers the question.

1. The Supreme Court ruled in *United States* v. *Reynolds* (1879) that

    a. the Timber Culture, Desert Land, and Timber and Stone acts were unconstitutional giveaways of the national domain to private interests.

    b. the opening of the Indian Territory to white settlement was an illegal breach of a government treaty with the Indians, but the president ignored the decision and opened Oklahoma to whites.

    c. the government had the right to outlaw polygyny and that the practice was not protected under freedom of religion.

    d. western states did not have the authority to permit women to vote in federal elections.

2. Indian-army conflict on the Great Plains came to an end after

    a. the surrender of Geronimo.

    b. the Wounded Knee killings.

    c. the Red River war.

    d. Custer's Last Stand.

3. Helen Hunt Jackson's *A Century of Dishonor* condemns the government of the United States for

    a. giving railroad companies vast amounts of western land and then allowing them to overcharge and abuse frontier farmers.

    b. allowing the forests and other natural resources of the West to be exploited for private greed.

    c. turning over the best homestead land to big business interests.

    d. breaking all of its treaties with and promises to Native Americans.

4. Which of the following individuals is *incorrectly* paired with his writing or activity in the trans-Mississippi West?

    a. Joseph G. McCoy—the cattle frontier

    b. Owen Wister—*The Virginian*

    c. Wovoka—the Ghost Dance

    d. Henry Comstock—the Oklahoma land rush

5. In the latter half of the nineteenth century, the federal government attempted to confine all Plains Indian tribes on two big reservations located in

    a. Texas and Arizona.

    b. California and Oregon.

    c. Nebraska and Kansas.

    d. Oklahoma and South Dakota.

6. The first transcontinental railroad was

    a. financed entirely by private capital, with no government subsidy.

    b. built primarily with the forced labor of Sioux, Cheyenne, and Comanche prisoners of war and black slaves.

    c. completed in 1869 with the joining of the Union Pacific and Central Pacific tracks in Utah.

    d. chartered originally by the Confederacy, in its hopes to take over the West, and then continued by the Union after the South's defeat.

7. Although the new state governments in the West were generally conservative, the one area in which they were ahead of the eastern states was in

    a.   granting woman suffrage.
    b.   ending all discrimination on the basis of race.
    c.   enacting legislation against prostitution.
    d.   desegregating public education.

8. Whose campaign to protect the wilderness led to establishing Yosemite National Park and the founding of the Sierra Club?

    a.   Joseph G. McCoy
    b.   Hamlin Garland
    c.   Owen Wister
    d.   John Muir

9. The days of the open range and great cattle drives came to an end after 1886 for all of the following reasons *except*

    a.   overgrazing and crowding of the range.
    b.   severe winters and dry summers in 1885 and 1886.
    c.   a decline in the demand for beef.
    d.   expansion of the railroads throughout the West.

10. He was the Indian leader who helped defeat Custer at the Little Big Horn, traveled with Buffalo Bill's Wild West show, and was killed in 1890 by reservation agents trying to suppress the Ghost Dance.

    a.   Chief Joseph
    b.   Chief Dull Knife
    c.   Geronimo
    d.   Sitting Bull

SHORT-ANSWER QUESTIONS

1. Explain the meaning of Richard Pratt's motto "Kill the Indian in him and save the man."

2. What were the provisions of the Dawes Act? Why did humanitarian reformers promote the law? Whom did it end up favoring? Why?

3. What were the provisions of the Homestead Act (1862)? Why did the law prove to be less beneficial to the poor, hoping to become independent landowners, than Congress had intended?

4. Explain what attracted farmers to the Great Plains and some of the difficulties they faced in making a living from their farms.

5. What happened to the Hispanic population of the Southwest after 1848?

6. What was Frederick Jackson Turner's "frontier thesis"? How do today's historians regard it?

7. Discuss the beginnings of the national parks and conservation movement. Who were some of its early advocates? What were their motives?

8. In what ways were the lives of the U.S. cowboy, the Mexican *vacquero*, and the Argentine *gaucho* similar? Compare the popular mythic image of each group to its real-life experiences.

ESSAY QUESTIONS

1. One historian has written a book about the Plains Indians in the period 1840–1900 titled *The Long Death*. Drawing on the material in Chapter 17, decide whether you think this is an appropriate title. Include in your discussion the impact of the slaughter of the buffalo, the reservation policy, the Dawes Act, and the attempts of government and reformers to "civilize" and assimilate the Indians. Consider also the responses of Native Americans to the actions and policies of whites and the government.

2. The railroads, more than any other agency, stimulated settlement of the Great Plains and shaped the pattern of development there. Discuss this statement, explaining why and how railroads helped shape the West.

3. The myth of the frontier celebrated the economic opportunities that the West offered to everyone. Judging from the material in Chapter 17, how much truth was there in that myth? (Cite as much specific evidence as possible.)

4. According to the author of Chapter 17, "Although westerners attributed their economic achievements to American individualism and self-reliance, the development of the trans-Mississippi West depended heavily on the federal government." Write an essay agreeing or disagreeing with this statement and giving as much historical evidence as possible to support your position.

5. "Unlike earlier westward expansion, almost every aspect of the settlement of the final frontier was influenced by the transformation occurring within American industry and the American economy." Explain and illustrate this statement with material about the development of farming, mining, and cattle raising found in Chapter 17.

ANSWERS TO MULTIPLE-CHOICE QUESTIONS

1. c
2. b
3. d
4. b
5. d
6. c
7. a
8. d
9. c
10. d

CHAPTER 18

The Rise of Industrial America, 1865–1900

OUTLINE AND SUMMARY

I. Introduction

As you read Chapter 18, try to answer the following questions: (1) What brought about prodigious industrial growth and the rise of giant corporations in the period 1865–1900? (2) How did some business leaders, such as Andrew Carnegie and John D. Rockefeller, overwhelm competitors and dominate their industries? (3) How and why did southern industrialization patterns differ from northern ones? (4) How did workers respond to the changes resulting from rapid industrialization and the growth of big business? (5) In the labor-management clashes of the period, why did management almost always win?

II. The Rise of Corporate America

A. The Character of Industrial Change

Rapid industrial expansion was made possible by using America's vast coal deposits for cheap energy and adopting new technology, which enabled manufacturers to cut production costs and employ low-paid unskilled and semiskilled workers. Ruthless competition among businesses lowered commodity prices and ruined weaker companies, leaving fewer huge corporations in control of each industry. The unrelenting competition also drove business to brutally exploit labor and heedlessly pollute the environment. Though prices fell, interest rates remained high and credit tight because of the failure of the money supply to keep up with the expansion of the economy.

B. Railroad Innovations

By 1900 the United States had more rail miles tying the country together than did all of Europe, including Russia.   Building this extensive railroad system opened a vast internal market to American industry. The railroad companies also led the way in developing accounting, financial, and managerial practices that made large-scale corporate enterprise possible, such as the sale of stocks and bonds to raise needed capital. Railroad management innovations became the model for other businesses trying to sell products in a national market.

C. Consolidating the Railroad Industry

A group of innovative and unscrupulous railroad entrepreneurs, including Collis P. Huntington, Jay Gould, and James J. Hill, bought out their smaller competitors one by one. By the 1890s they had established great trunk lines that controlled most of the track. These integrated lines, with their standardized equipment and track gauge, carried goods all over the country much more efficiently than had been done formerly. However, the railroad companies abused their powers. They bribed politicians with free passes and other favors and gave rebates and kickbacks to big shippers while overcharging small businesses and farmers.

Suffering from these railroad abuses, small shippers demanded legislation to curb the unfair practices. In the 1870s many midwestern states outlawed rate discrimination, but these laws were ruled unconstitutional when the Supreme Court said states could not regulate interstate commerce. In 1887 Congress passed the Interstate Commerce Act, which forbade pools, rebates, and other monopolistic practices and established the Interstate Commerce Commission (ICC) to investigate complaints and unreasonable rates. The legislation proved ineffective for several reasons, among them federal court decisions, which nearly always sided with the railroads and the ICC's lack of power to set railroad rates.

In the early twentieth century, under the guidance of investment bankers, such as J. P. Morgan, railroad consolidation proceeded still further. By 1906 seven giant corporations controlled two-thirds of all the track.

D.   Applying the Lessons of the Railroads to Steel
Andrew Carnegie's career illustrates the close connection between railroad expansion and the growth of heavy industry. Carnegie's best customers were the railroad companies. From his early experiences working in the railroad industry, he learned the organizational, accounting, and managerial innovations that he later applied to his steel business. He also copied the railroad practice of consolidating small enterprises into fewer and fewer huge companies. Carnegie integrated his business both vertically and horizontally. When J. P. Morgan's Federal Steel and Carnegie Steel combined in 1901 to form U.S. Steel, it was the world's first corporation capitalized at over $1 billion and contained 200 member companies.

E.   The Trust: Creating New Forms of Corporate Organization
By 1900 the consolidation process that had placed the railroad and steel businesses in the hands of a few corporate giants had also taken place in the oil, sugar, meatpacking, and many other industries. In the oil-refining business, John D. Rockefeller led the way toward consolidation. His Standard Oil Company, like Carnegie Steel, was quick to adopt the latest technology. He made deals with the railroads to get special shipping discounts, engaged in deception and aggression to ruin competitors, and created the first trust and later holding company to extinguish all competition in oil refining.

The growth of trusts, oligopolies, and monopolies in one industry after another led to public pressure for government intervention. In 1890 Congress passed the Sherman Anti-Trust Act, which outlawed all contracts and combinations that were in restraint of trade in interstate commerce. The law proved ineffective in stopping the growth of trusts because it was vaguely worded, presidents rarely brought suits against companies under it, and the Supreme Court in the *E. C. Knight* case (1895) interpreted the meaning of interstate commerce so narrowly as to prevent the law's use against manufacturing corporations. After that, large-scale consolidations in industry accelerated.

III. Stimulating Economic Growth
A.   The Triumph of Technology
The invention and patenting of new machines in the period 1860–1900 also brought about the growth of huge corporations. For example, Alexander Graham Bell's invention of the telephone in 1876 gave rise to Bell Telephone, which by 1900 had installed some 800,000 phones in the United States. Thomas A. Edison, with the founding of his Menlo Park laboratory, perfected the light bulb and invented the phonograph, microphone, motion-picture camera, and over a thousand other items. These men proved that new inventions could be the foundation of profitable big business.

B.   Specialized Production
Manufacturers of specialized products, such as locomotives, furniture, and women's clothing, also greatly expanded their output between 1865 and 1900, although their work was not necessarily done in huge factories.

C.   Advertising and Marketing
Aggressive advertising and marketing were effective in expanding sales and beating out competitors in the late nineteenth century. Procter and Gamble, American Tobacco, and Eastman-Kodak all built huge demand for their products this way.

D.   Economic Growth: Cost and Benefits
By 1900 the chaos of thousands of small companies competing for the national market had been replaced by an economy dominated by a small number of enormous corporations offering a dazzling array of new products. The price of these accomplishments was the crushing of thousands of small- and medium-sized business, the exploitation of millions of workers, and the fouling of the environment.

IV.   The New South
A.   Obstacles to Economic Development
The South industrialized more slowly than the North and until 1900 lagged far behind it. The reasons for this included the destruction of the South's credit system by the Civil War and its subsequent shortage of capital. Other factors were federal government policies that hurt the South economically, such as high protective tariffs, and the South's poor educational facilities and high rate of illiteracy.

B.   The New South Creed and Southern Industrialization
In the 1870s southern newspaper editors, planters, and businessmen began to preach the "New South Creed"—the region must industrialize. Eager to attract northern capital, southern states offered tax exemptions for new businesses that would locate there. They also held industrial fairs, leased convicts from state prisons as cheap labor, and practically gave away land, forests, and mineral rights to northern corporations. Iron and steel production expanded dramatically around Birmingham, Alabama, and Chattanooga, Tennessee. The iron and steel mills hired many unskilled blacks.

C.   The Southern Mill Economy
Unlike the iron and steel industry, where factories were usually in or near urban areas, southern textile mills opened in the countryside, and towns and villages were created around them. Most of the textile mills were located in the Piedmont region of Virginia, the Carolinas, Georgia, and Alabama. The southern mills combined northern technical expertise with southern rural paternalism. They recruited workers from the poor white farm population of the Piedmont, hiring whole families, including many women and children. The owners, despite substantial profits, paid the laborers 30 to 50 percent less than New England mills did. The textile companies dominated life in the mill towns they started. They provided their employees with housing, stores, schools, and churches. Because the mills underpaid their workers and overcharged for rent and supplies, the employees often fell into debt to companies, just as sharecroppers were indebted to their landlords and creditor-merchants.

D.   The Southern Industrial Lag
Despite impressive advances, southern industrialization occurred on a small scale and at a slower pace than in the North. Furthermore, the southern economy remained essentially in a colonial status, with industry being owned largely by northern firms. U.S. Steel, for example, controlled the foundries in Birmingham.

V.   Factories and the Work Force
A.   From Workshop to Factory
As the number of industrial workers in the United States climbed from 885,000 to 3.2 million by 1900 and the trend toward large-scale, increasingly mechanized production accelerated, the nature of work changed markedly. There were fewer artisans, and the remaining skilled workers had less control over their work and derived less satisfaction from

it. Factories hired more low-skilled, low-paid women and children to do jobs that had become simple, machine-paced, repetitive, and boring.

B.   The Hardships of Industrial Labor
Already by the 1880s almost one-third of the labor force in the steel and railroad industries were unskilled workers. Common laborers drifted from city to city and from industry to industry, working for wages that were one-third of those paid to skilled artisans. In the expanding factories and on railroads, workers were exposed to a variety of industrially induced diseases, such as black and brown lung. They also had appallingly frequent accidents resulting in permanent disability or death. The excessive hours of work and the presence of many child laborers contributed to the high rate of industrial accidents. Employers rarely paid compensation to injured workers and opposed passage of state health and safety codes.

C.   Immigrant Labor
More and more, immigrants filled the least skilled, lowest-paid, dirtiest, and most dangerous jobs in the expanding mines, factories, and railroads. Impoverished French Canadians crossed the border to work in the New England textile mills; the Chinese constructed railroads and mined ore in the West. If immigrant workers stayed healthy, they often lived better than they had in their homelands. Although most of the immigrants worked very hard, they did not adjust easily to the fast pace and monotony of factory work or to the rigid discipline management tried to impose on them.

D.   Women and Work in Industrial America
Since women could be paid even less than men and could do unskilled industrial jobs just as well, management hired more and more women. Married, working-class women and their children often spent hours finishing garments, rolling cigars, and performing other labor for manufacturers in their tenement apartments. Young, single women readily took jobs in factories because they preferred them to domestic service, almost the only alternative for uneducated females. Immigrant parents regularly sent their daughters into the mills and factories to supplement inadequate family incomes. By 1900 women made up 17 percent of the labor force. In the late nineteenth and early twentieth centuries, women also began to obtain clerical positions. Office work paid better and offered more prestige than factory jobs, but women clerical workers had almost no chance of moving up to managerial positions. Despite the increase in female wage earners, women's work outside the home was viewed as temporary. A woman's career was that of housewife and mother.

E.   Hard Work and the Gospel of Success
Newspapers and magazines preached the gospel that, for male workers, America was the land of opportunity and hard work led to success. The papers were filled with rags-to-riches stories of poor immigrant boys such as Andrew Carnegie who rose to become heads of major corporations. In fact, Carnegie was the exception. Ninety-five percent of executives of big corporations came from middle- and upper-class families. There was some opportunity, however, for skilled workers to move into ownership and management of small businesses. For unskilled immigrant laborers, there was less mobility. At best they moved from unskilled to semiskilled or skilled industrial jobs, and they remained in the working class. A huge gulf existed between the rich and poor. By 1890 America's richest families, the top 10 percent, owned 73 percent of the country's wealth. At the other extreme, better than 50 percent of all industrial laborers earned incomes that placed them below the poverty line.

VI. Labor Unions and Industrial Conflict

    A. Organizing the Workers

In response to the unfavorable changes that rapid industrialization was forcing on them, workers turned to labor unions. In 1866 William H. Sylvis recruited workers from several trades into the National Labor Union. As it declined in membership in the 1870s, it was overshadowed by the Knights of Labor, led by Terrence V. Powderly. The Knights called for advanced social and economic reforms, including equal pay for men and women; abolition of child labor; inclusion of black workers in unions; a graduated income tax; and cooperative ownership of factories, mines, and other businesses. Despite their egalitarian ideals, the Knights and other labor groups favored immigration restriction. Labor opposition to the Chinese, whom they accused of working so cheaply that they undercut native-born workers, was especially strong. The federal government responded to anti-Chinese sentiment by passing the Chinese Exclusion Act in 1882. When the Knights won a series of strikes in the 1880s, workers rushed to join, swelling its membership to 700,000. In the late 1880s, however, the Knights suffered setbacks: it lost several big strikes, its craft unions broke away to form a separate American Federation of Labor (AFL), and its membership declined.

The AFL, led by Samuel Gompers, did not attempt to organize unskilled workers, and it dropped the far-reaching social-reform goals of the National Labor Union and the Knights. Instead, the AFL concentrated on winning short-term improvements in wages and hours for its skilled members. The AFL grew, but by 1900 less than 5 percent of America's workers belonged to it or any other union. The development of unions was seriously impeded by splits in the labor force between skilled artisans and common laborers, religious and ethnic divisions, and differences among labor leaders concerning goals and tactics.

    B. Strikes and Labor Violence

Between 1881 and 1905 almost 37,000 strikes took place, involving nearly 7 million workers. In many of these, violence erupted as strikers attacked employers' property and the scab laborers hired to replace them. Some of the biggest and most violent confrontations were the railroad strikes of 1877, the eight-hour strikes of 1886, the Haymarket Square bombing (for which four anarchists were unjustly convicted and executed), the Homestead steel strike, and the Pullman strike.

To combat labor unrest, employers forced workers to sign yellow-dog contracts and hired their own private police forces. Because of the violence, the public regarded strikers as dangerous radicals. The federal government intervened repeatedly on the side of management, using the army to quell disturbances and injunctions to order union members back to work. When injunctions were disobeyed, union officers like Eugene Debs, leader of the Pullman strike, were thrown in jail. As a result of employer, public, and government hostility, strikes almost always failed and unions languished.

    C. Social Thinkers Probe for Alternatives

The growing extremes of poverty and wealth and the violent clashes between labor and management troubled middle-class Americans. A number of social commentators tried to explain these developments and put forward their own solutions. Social Darwinists, like Andrew Carnegie and William Graham Sumner, believed that labor's misery was an inevitable product of the constant struggle for survival that weeded out all but the fittest. They opposed any government interference with the workings of these natural laws. On the other hand, Lester F. Ward, Henry George, and Edward Bellamy attributed the social problems to a human-made economic system that placed private property and unrestrained profit seeking above all else. They called, respectively, for government regulation, tax reform, and a cooperative commonwealth. Tiny socialist and anarchist groups preached that only the overthrow of the capitalists and the government that protected them would make possible a just and humane society.

VII. Conclusion

Industrialization had brought great benefits to America: international power status, lower-cost goods, more jobs, and a tremendous array of new consumer products. But the price had been high. Shoddy business practices and polluted factory sites abounded. Much of the industrial work force lived in urban slums and grinding poverty. Exploited laborers periodically vented their rage and frustrations in violent outbursts and strikes. Middle-class Americans were ambivalent about the new industrial order. They wanted to keep the benefits but somehow alleviate the accompanying social evils.

VOCABULARY

The following terms are used in Chapter 18. To understand the chapter fully, it is important that you know what each of them means.

capitalist	an owner of a large business; person who has extensive capital (money) invested in business enterprises
rebate	a return of part of an original amount paid for some service or merchandise
pool	an agreement among formerly competing companies to set uniform prices and divide the business among themselves according to a predetermined formula; the purpose is to maximize profits by ending competition
vertical integration	the organization of a single corporation to control all stages of manufacturing, from obtaining raw materials to marketing the finished product
horizontal integration	the organization of a single corporation, through consolidation measures, to gain broad control over all manufacturing of a particular product
oligopoly	a market situation in which a few giant companies can control price and levels of production in an entire industry; near monopoly
"bread-and-butter" unionism	(also trade unionism "pure and simple") the union practice of concentrating on issues of immediate concern to its members, such as reducing hours and raising wages, rather than promoting broad social reforms
yellow-dog contract	an agreement that employers forced employees to sign swearing that they would not join unions or strike
anarchist	a person who advocates the overthrow of all established governments and of capitalist economic institutions
injunction	a court order requiring a person to do or not do a particular thing
laissez-faire	the doctrine that government should intervene as little as possible in economic affairs, such as regulating business

IDENTIFICATIONS

After reading Chapter 18, you should be able to identify and explain the historical significance of each of the following:

Thomas A. Edison

William H. Sylvis and the National Labor Union

Terence V. Powderly and the Knights of Labor

Mother Jones

Chinese Exclusion Act, 1882

Samuel Gompers and the American Federation of Labor

railroad strikes of 1877

Homestead strike, 1892

Eugene Debs

Henry George, *Progress and Poverty*

Marxist socialists

SKILL BUILDING: MAPS

Locate each of the following sites and explain why each was important in the rise of industrial America from 1860 to 1900:

Pittsburgh, Pennsylvania

Homestead, Pennsylvania

Mesabi range, Minnesota

Titusville, Pennsylvania

Birmingham, Alabama

Piedmont region of Virginia, the Carolinas, Georgia, and Alabama

Menlo Park, New Jersey

Chicago, Illinois

Pullman, Illinois

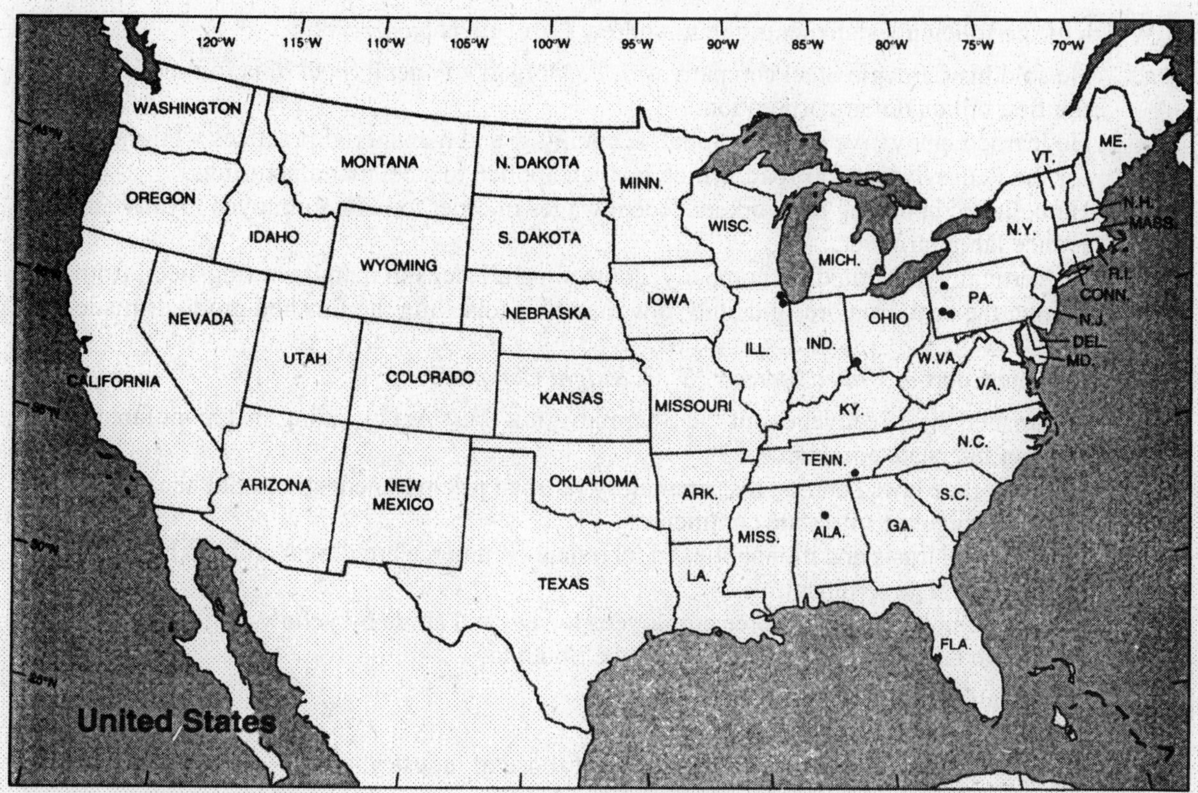

MULTIPLE-CHOICE QUESTIONS

Circle the letter of the item that best completes each statement or answers the question.

1. Rapid industrial development in the United States between 1860 and 1900

    a. increased the demand for and importance of skilled artisans.
    b. produced by 1900 an economy dominated by enormous corporations.
    c. increased the opportunities by 1900 for small- and medium-sized companies to succeed.
    d. reduced by 1900 the use of women and child laborers in mines and mills.

2. Why did the South's industrialization lag behind the North's?

    a. The post–Civil War South lacked capital and technically trained personnel.
    b. Southern industry paid higher wages than northern factories and therefore could not compete effectively with northern plants.
    c. The South had almost no natural resources.
    d.   Southern states taxed factories and mills heavily, thereby discouraging new enterprises.

3. Which of the following entrepreneurs is *incorrectly* matched with the industry he dominated?

    a. Collis P. Huntington—railroads
    b. J. Pierpont Morgan—banking
    c. James B. Duke—tobacco
    d. Jay Gould—steel

4.   Which of the following statements about Andrew Carnegie is *incorrect*?

    a.   He sold his Carnegie Steel company to J. P. Morgan's Federal Steel; this formed U.S. Steel, the first billion dollar corporation.

    b.   He learned innovative organizational, accounting, and managerial practices while working for the Pennsylvania Railroad, which he then applied to steel manufacturing.

    c.   He believed in paying his workers decent wages in order to build employee loyalty and reduce labor turnover.

    d.   He vertically integrated his company, controlling all steps in manufacturing steel, from mining the coal, iron ore, and other raw materials to selling the finished products made of steel.

5.   The Supreme Court in *United States* v. *E. C. Knight Company*

    a.   diminished the effectiveness of the Sherman Anti-Trust Act by ruling that manufacturing was not interstate commerce.

    b.   declared state laws banning discriminatory railroad pricing unconstitutional because states could not regulate interstate commerce.

    c.   ruled that all trusts and monopolies in interstate commerce are illegal and can be broken up by the federal government.

    d.   held that employers could force employees to sign and abide by yellow-dog contracts.

6.   The New South Creed preached the need for the South to

    a.   industrialize.

    b.   combat racial prejudice.

    c.   promote the interests of agriculture ahead of those of industry.

    d.   match its wage scale to that prevailing in the North.

7.   Studies of top managers in large corporations in the late nineteenth century show that

    a.   the majority of them rose from the ranks of skilled workers.

    b.   the majority of them started out as poor but ambitious immigrant boys like Andrew Carnegie.

    c.   the great majority of them came from middle- and upper-class families.

    d.   women were beginning to make their way into executive positions.

8.   Which of the following men is incorrectly paired with what he preached?

    a.   Alexander Berkman—anarchism

    b.   Henry George—the single tax

    c.   William Graham Sumner—Social Darwinism

    d.   Edward Bellamy—laissez-faire capitalism

9.   Which of the following people argued that poverty was *not* the result of unchangeable natural laws and could be eliminated by government intervention and social planning?

    a.   William Graham Sumner

    b.   Lester Frank Ward

    c.   Andrew Carnegie

    d.   John D. Rockefeller

10.   Four anarchists were wrongfully charged with murder and executed for the

    a.   1886 Haymarket Square bombing.

    b.   burning of Union Depot and the Pennsylvania Railroad roundhouse in the railroad strikes of 1877.

    c.   killing of three Pinkerton detectives in the 1892 Homestead strike.

    d.   blowing up of a mill in Coeur d'Alene, Idaho, in 1892.

SHORT-ANSWER QUESTIONS

1. Explain how the building of the nation's railroad network stimulated American industrialization and the growth of large corporations.

2. What were the provisions of the 1887 Interstate Commerce Act? Why was it passed? Why was it ineffective in regulating railroad rates and stopping railroad abuses of small shippers for the first twenty years of its existence?

3. John D. Rockefeller "integrated the petroleum industry both vertically . . . and horizontally. . . . " Briefly explain the meaning of this statement and explain how Rockefeller achieved his goal of eliminating almost all "wasteful" competition in the oil industry.

4. What were the provisions of the Sherman Anti-Trust Act? Why did it prove ineffective in halting trusts, consolidation, and other monopolistic practices?

5. How were the objectives of the American Federation of Labor different from those of the earlier National Labor Union and Knights of Labor?

6. What caused the 1894 Pullman strike? Why did the workers ultimately lose the strike?

7. What was the theme of Horatio Alger's novels? How realistic were these books in terms of late-nineteenth-century American experience?

8. Explain what a Social Darwinist believed that government should do about poverty and exploitation of labor. How did the Social Darwinist justify such recommendations?

9. By 1898, "the United States had established itself as a world leader in electrical technology." Explain briefly what brought this about.

ESSAY QUESTIONS

1. Discuss the reasons for rapid industrial expansion and the growth of huge corporations between 1860 and 1900. What were some of the benefits the American people reaped from these developments? What were some of the social and economic costs or problems produced by industrialization and the growth of big business?

2. Discuss the impact on labor of industrial development in the post–Civil War period. In your answer include the effects on skilled, unskilled, southern, immigrant, and women workers.

3. Discuss the contemporary intellectual response to late-nineteenth-century industrialism and the social problems that accompanied it. Be sure to include in your answer the ideas of the Social Darwinists, such as William G. Sumner, and their opponents, including Lester F. Ward, Henry George, and Edward Bellamy.

4. Discuss the industrialization of the South in the post–Civil War period. Why did the South lag behind the North? How much had the South's industry grown by 1900? In what ways was southern industrial development different from that in the North? Why?

5. Between 1881 and 1905, there were almost 37,000 strikes, and workers made numerous attempts to unionize. Yet by 1900 less than 5 percent of the labor force belonged to any union, and workers lost most strikes. What obstacles stood in the way of unionization and successful strikes?

ANSWERS TO MULTIPLE-CHOICE QUESTIONS

1. b
2. a
3. d
4. c
5. a
6. a
7. c
8. d
9. b
10. a

CHAPTER 19

Immigration, Urbanization, and Everyday Life, 1860–1900

OUTLINE AND SUMMARY

I.   Introduction

As you read Chapter 19 you should look for answers to the following questions: (1) How did immigrants help shape the cities? (2) What were political bosses, and why did they gain power in post–Civil War cities? (3) Why did tensions develop between civic reformers and the urban poor? (4) How did new consumer products and greater leisure time reinforce awareness of class and ethnic differences? (5) What was "Victorian morality," and why was it under attack by the late nineteenth century? (6) How did economic and educational transformations affect the social roles of women?

II.   The New American City

A.   Introduction

In the post–Civil War years, the United States experienced rapid urbanization. By 1900 New York, Chicago, and Philadelphia each had more than 1 million inhabitants, and 40 percent of all Americans lived in cities. Because they offered work and other opportunities, cities attracted thousands from the surrounding rural districts and most of the 11 million immigrants who arrived in the nation between 1870 and 1900. The runaway population growth swamped municipal services, caused terrible housing and sanitary conditions, and aggravated class differences and conflicts. The physical deterioration, ethnic diversity, and social instability alarmed native-born reformers who tried to clean up cities and quickly "Americanize" immigrants.

B.   Migrants and Immigrants

In the post–Civil War years thousands of young people, especially women, moved from farms to cities to find employment. Also between 1860 and 1890 some 10 million Northern European immigrants, mostly German, English, and Irish, settled in East Coast and midwestern cities. In the late nineteenth century, these earlier immigrants were joined by the "new immigrants" from southern and eastern Europe—Italians, Slavs, Greeks, and Jews—as well as Armenians from the Middle East. By 1890 the foreign-born and their children accounted for four-fifths of the population of greater New York. Most who disembarked on the East Coast came through the immigration reception centers at Castle Garden (1855–1890) or Ellis Island (1892 on) in New York. After 1910, Angel Island in San Francisco served as the main West Coast reception center. German and Scandinavian newcomers, bringing a little capital with them, tended to migrate to midwestern cities and to farms on the prairie beyond. Italians and Irish, usually without cash, took the first jobs they found in eastern cities.

C.   Adjusting to an Urban Society

To ease their adjustment, immigrants clustered together in ethnic neighborhoods where they could speak their native language, buy their traditional foods, and celebrate traditional holidays with compatriots and even persons from the same village or district. The various immigrant groups improved their social and economic status at different rates. Those who came with a skilled trade or spoke some English generally did well. The Irish came in such great numbers that they were able to dominate the Democratic Party and Catholic church leadership in New York and Boston, where they accounted for 16 and 17 percent of the population, respectively. Nationality groups that had high rates of return to their homelands, such as Italians and Chinese, experienced slower upward mobility and assimilation. By the end of the nineteenth century, resentment of the newcomers, from whatever country, was growing.

D.   Slums and Ghettos
Neighborhoods deteriorated into slums as landlords packed more and more people into their buildings. The poorer the residents, the greater the crowding and the faster the area declined. Ethnic slum neighborhoods became ghettos when discrimination and law kept members of the minority group, whether racial or immigrant, from obtaining housing elsewhere, even if they had the money to do so. For example, black ghettos grew in Chicago and Philadelphia, Mexican in Los Angeles, and Chinese in San Francisco. Because slums and ghettos were usually adjacent to industrial districts, they were filled with soot, coal dust, noise, and foul orders. Pollution and crowding were especially hard on the young, with such neighborhoods having frightful infant mortality rates.

E.   Fashionable Avenues and Suburbs
In contrast to slums, grand millionaires' mansions lined Fifth Avenue in New York, Commonwealth Avenue in Boston, and fashionable boulevards in other cities. The wealthy and the middle class also moved to newer, more desirable suburbs on the edges of the old, compact cities. Thus, American cities became increasingly segregated along class as well as ethnic and racial lines.

III.   Middle- and Upper-Class Society and Culture
A.   Manners and Morals
The nineteenth-century Victorian worldview preached that, to make personal and national progress, an individual must work hard, exercise self-discipline, display good manners, and cultivate an appreciation of literature and the arts. To the highly moralistic Victorians, status was conferred by possessing these attributes, especially knowledge of proper etiquette for all occasions, along with possessing abundant amounts of the right material goods. Thus, the Victorian code served to heighten the visible gap between classes.

B.   The Cult of Domesticity
Victorian morality assigned a special place to women. Whereas men tended to business and public affairs, women used the domestic sphere to provide the genteel, sensitive, and spiritual influences that moved society toward higher civilization. They decorated their homes as richly and artistically as their means permitted and fostered the family's sense of cultural appreciation. At no time, however, were all middle-class women satisfied with devoting their whole life to this cult of domesticity.

C.   Department Stores
Innovative entrepreneurs, such as Rowland H. Macy, John Wanamaker, and Marshall Field, developed urban department stores that appealed particularly to the Victorian outlook of the upper and middle echelons. These giant emporiums advertised high-quality goods at low cost and encouraged buyers to believe that owning the right material possessions contributed to civilized living. The department stores were designed to look like palaces, with marble staircases, sparkling chandeliers, and thick carpets. For the middle and upper classes shopping "became an adventure, a form of entertainment, and a way to affirm their place in society."

D. The Transformation of Higher Education

Higher education was still restricted to the upper and upper-middle classes. As late as 1900 only 4 percent of youths between eighteen and twenty-one years of age were enrolled in colleges or universities. Indeed, these institutions were seen as the training schools for the future business and professional elites. Wealthy capitalists, such as John D. Rockefeller and Leland Stanford, made large donations to already existing universities or started new ones. With private contributions and state support, more than 150 additional colleges and universities were founded between 1880 and 1900. Higher education for upper- and upper-middle-class women also grew impressively. Some eastern elite universities—Columbia and Harvard—established affiliated schools for women—Barnard (1889) and Radcliffe (1894), respectively. Additionally, more all-female colleges were founded, Wellesley, Smith, and others. By 1900, women made up one-third of the nation's college students. In this period, the research university was developed and major reforms were instituted in medical and other professional training.

IV. Working-Class Politics and Reform

A. Political Bosses and Machine Politics

Urban political machines, headed by powerful political bosses, emerged to govern the unwieldy cities with their many competing interests. The machines gave tax breaks and awarded contracts to favored businessmen in return for payoffs and gathered the votes of poor immigrants by providing them with relief, legal help, and city jobs. New York's Boss William Marcy Tweed and his Tammany Hall machine were typical. Between 1869 and 1871, Tweed gave $50,000 to the city's poor and built new schools, hospitals, and other facilities, but he and his ring also cost taxpayers some $70 million through graft and padded contracts. He was finally toppled from power with the help of Thomas Nast's political cartoons in *Harper's Weekly*. By the late nineteenth century middle- and upper-class good-government reformers had begun their drives against the bosses. The bosses and machines, in turn, attempted to hold on to power by providing more public services and improved urban facilities, such as better sewer systems and more parks.

B. Battling Poverty

Middle-class reformers also set out to relieve poverty. They often tended to blame the problem on character flaws of the poor and "self-destructive" cultural practices of the immigrants. Therefore, reformers concentrated on moral uplift and Americanization campaigns among the needy. Typical were Robert M. Hartley's New York Association for Improving the Condition of the Poor (AICP) and Charles Loring Brace's New York Children's Aid Society. Brace founded dormitories, reading rooms, and workshops for indigent boys and sent thousands of them to live with and work for families in the Midwest. In addition, the Young Men's and Young Women's Christian Associations offered rural young people arriving in the cities temporary housing, recreation, and moral strictures against alcohol and other vices.

C. New Approaches to Social Reform

By the 1880s the Salvation Army and Josephine Shaw Lowell's Charity Organization Society (COS) had joined the fight against poverty. Lowell's group preached a tough-minded approach to charity, insisting that the needy must meet the standards of responsibility and morality set by the COS's "friendly visitors" to receive aid. Critics charged, with some justification, that the COS was more interested in "controlling the poor than in alleviating their suffering."

D. The Moral-Purity Campaign

Middle- and upper-class reformers attacked what they considered urban vice. Crusaders such as Anthony Comstock and Charles Parkhurst demanded that city officials close down gambling dens, saloons, and brothels and censor obscene publications. In 1894 the nonpartisan Committee of Seventy elected a New York City mayor committed to moral purification, but within three years the effort failed, and the more tolerant political machine was back in power.

E. The Social Gospel

The Social Gospel movement developed in the 1870s and 1880s among a small group of Protestant clergymen. Founded by Washington Gladden, a Congregational minister, the movement preached that urban poverty was caused in part by actions of the rich and well-born and "that true Christianity commits men and women to fight social injustice head on, wherever it exists." Walter Rauschenbusch, a Baptist pastor in New York's "Hell's Kitchen" slums, made the clearest statement of the movement's philosophy, and his advocacy of Christian unity led to the founding of the Federal Council of Churches.

F. The Settlement-House Movement

Like the Social Gospel ministers, the settlement-house founders blamed poverty not on the poor but on social and environmental causes. Settlement-house leaders, such as Jane Addams, believed that middle-class relief workers must reside among the immigrant masses and learn what services they needed by firsthand experience. At Hull House, for example, Addams ran a day-care nursery, gave legal and health aid, helped find employment, and offered classes in English and other subjects for her immigrant Chicago neighbors. Settlement-house workers also published studies of the terrible housing and sanitation they encountered, and they lobbied legislators for improved services and corrective laws. By 1895 more than fifty settlement houses in various cities were training a generation of young college students, many of whom would become state and local government officials applying the lessons they had learned. Florence Kelley, for example, a former Hull House worker, became factory inspector for Illinois in 1893.

V. Working-Class Leisure in the Immigrant City

A. Streets and Saloons

The neighborhood streets, especially in summer, served as the arena of social life and free entertainment for shop girls, laborers, and poor immigrant families. For workingmen the saloons offered male companionship, reinforced group identity, and were centers for immigrant politics.

B. The Rise of Professional Sports

Americans were the first to turn what had been a children's game into the professional sport of baseball. The earliest teams were the New York Knickerbockers and the Cincinnati Red Stockings. Team owners organized the National League in 1876, and by the 1890s, baseball had become big business. It appealed to members of all social groups, particularly workers. Horse racing was often a social event for the rich, while boxing contests drew spectators from all social levels, but especially appealed to workingmen. The most popular sports hero of the nineteenth century was heavyweight boxing champion John L. Sullivan.

C. Vaudeville, Amusement Parks, and Dance Halls

Vaudeville shows, amusement parks like New York's Coney Island, and dance halls were popular with working-class women as well as men.

D. Ragtime

Although the middle class preferred hymns or songs that carried a moral lesson, the masses became fans of ragtime, which originated with black musicians in the saloons and brothels of the South and Midwest. In the 1890s, honky-tonk piano players introduced its syncopated rhythms to a wide national audience.

VI. Cultures in Conflict
  A. The Genteel Tradition and Its Critics
      In the 1870s and 1880s a group of upper-class writers and magazine editors, among them Charles Eliot Norton and E. L. Godkin, attempted to set standards for fine writing and art. They insisted that literature must avoid sexual allusions, vulgar slang, disrespect for Christianity, and depressing endings. High-toned journals like *The Century* and the *North American Review* upheld this genteel standard by banishing from their pages authors who violated these rules. Many emerging writers refused to fit into the mold. The works of regionalists like Sara Orne Jewett, realists like William Dean Howells, and naturalists like Stephen Crane all violated the cannons of the genteel tradition in one way or another. Mark Twain's *Adventures of Huckleberry Finn* (1884) and Theodore Dreiser's *Sister Carrie* (1900), among the best novels of the period, were both condemned by proponents of Victorian ideals.

      Social scientists such as Thorstein Veblen and W. E. B. Du Bois criticized the business elite and challenged middle-class notions about the link between moral worth and economic standing. The depression and labor unrest of the 1890s further undermined the smug Victorian outlook and its genteel culture.

  B. Modernism in Architecture and Painting
      Some architects and artists began questioning Victorian ideals of beauty. Modernist architects William Holabird, John Wellborn Root, Louis Sullivan, and Frank Lloyd Wright refused to copy European design. Rather, they looked to their vision of the future for inspiration and argued that a building's form should follow its function. Winslow Homer and Thomas Eakins rejected sentimentality in favor of tough realism in their paintings. Mary Cassatt was one of the first American artists to paint in the French Impressionist style.

  C. From Victorian Lady to New Woman
      Although Frances Willard and her Woman's Christian Temperance Union (WCTU) did not openly challenge the cult of domesticity, they broadened the scope of women's social responsibilities. The WCTU, with a membership of 150,000 by 1890, became America's first mass organization of women. Through its crusade against liquor, women gained experience as lobbyists, organizers, and lecturers. Middle- and upper-class club women founded the General Federation of Women's Clubs in 1892 and were getting involved in social welfare projects and tenement reform by the end of the century. The so-called new woman broke Victorian restraints about dress and exercise, and the most advanced thinkers, such as Charlotte Perkins Gilman, advocated women's economic independence from men through work outside the home. However, the new-woman emphasis on economic and social independence and equality had little impact on the lives of working-class women.

  D. Public Education as an Arena of Class Conflict
      Starting in the 1870s, middle-class reformers, such as federal commissioner of education William Torrey Harris, campaigned to expand public schools, bring them under central control, and make attendance mandatory. Harris viewed the public schools as instruments for indoctrinating the masses with middle-class values and outlook. By 1900, as a result of the work of education advocates, thirty-one states had passed laws requiring school attendance for all children from eight to fourteen years of age, the illiteracy rate had dropped significantly, and more than half a million students were attending some five thousand high schools. Centralized urban public-school systems, however, aroused opposition from various quarters. Poor immigrant parents, who needed the wages of their children to survive, objected to laws that kept youngsters in school beyond the elementary level. Catholics disliked the Protestant orientation of the public schools and organized their own

> parochial school systems, and upper-class parents preferred to send their offspring to exclusive, private academies.

VII. Conclusion

Between 1860 and 1900 class and ethnic conflicts appeared in almost every area of city life. To distinguish themselves from the exploited working class immigrants, whom the upper classes viewed as racially inferior, native-born elite and middle-class Americans embraced Victorian moral codes. The upper and middle classes, with their genteel Victorian morality and ideals, were dismayed by the raucous, vibrant culture of the working masses. "Respectable" people periodically attempted to suppress "indecent" lower-class enjoyments such as gambling; gathering in dance halls, saloons, and amusement parks; listening to ragtime; attending Sunday baseball games and bare-knuckle prizefights. However, Victorian standards of decency were weakening by the 1890s as they came under attack from younger middle-class writers, artists, social scientists, and "new women," as well as the working and immigrant masses. By 1900 the two cultural traditions were reaching an accommodation that blended elements of both. National pastimes became highly commercialized and working-class amusements of the nineteenth century evolved into the mass culture of sports spectaculars, movies, and other entertainments of modern America.

VOCABULARY

The following terms are used in Chapter 19. To understand the chapter fully, it is important that you know what each of them means.

compatriots	fellow countrymen and countrywomen; persons from the same country
protocol	proper etiquette
ghetto	any neighborhood or quarter in which a minority group is required to live by law or discrimination (originally, Jews in Venice, Italy)
prototype	the original or model from which other things are formed
ethos	the dominant assumptions of a people or period; the fundamental spiritual characteristics of a culture
caustic	sarcastic, sharp, biting
platitudes	flat, dull, or trite remarks, especially when uttered as if they were fresh and profound
mores	customs
congenial	agreeable, pleasing
lobbyist	one who tries to influence legislators

IDENTIFICATIONS

After reading Chapter 19, you should be able to identify and explain the historical significance of each of the following:

Scott Joplin and ragtime

"pull factors" and "push factors"

Castle Garden, Ellis Island, and Angel Island

cult of domesticity and "the woman's sphere"

Rowland H. Macy, John Wanamaker, and Marshall Field

Tammany Hall, William Marcy Tweed, and Thomas Nast

Charles Parkhurst

Jane Addams and Hull House

John L. Sullivan

the new woman

Mark Twain (Samuel Langhorne Clemens)

Stephen Crane, *Maggie: A Girl of the Streets*

Thorstein Veblen, *The Theory of the Leisure Class*

William Torrey Harris

MULTIPLE-CHOICE QUESTIONS

Circle the letter of the item that best completes each statement or answers the question.

1. Which of these writers came the closest to fulfilling the guidelines for serious literature as laid down by such supporters of the genteel tradition as Richard Watson Gilder and E. L. Godkin?
    a. Henry James
    b. Stephen Crane
    c. Sarah Orne Jewett
    d. Mark Twain

2. By 1900 all of the following U.S. cities had populations of over 1 million *except*
    a. New York.
    b. Chicago.
    c. Los Angeles.
    d. Philadelphia.

3. Which of the following statements about American cities between 1860 and 1900 is *incorrect*?
    a. Runaway growth of urban population swamped municipal services and facilities.
    b. Terrible housing and sanitary conditions developed in them.
    c. By 1900 the majority of the American people lived in them.
    d. Their neighborhoods became increasingly segregated along class, ethnic, and racial lines.

4. The majority of the "new immigrants" arriving in the United States between 1890 and 1920 came from
    a. Asia.
    b. northern and western Europe.
    c. the Middle East.
    d. southern and eastern Europe.

5. In the late nineteenth century, middle- and upper-class Americans generally frowned on
    a. flaunting their wealth by wearing expensive clothes and lavishly decorating their homes.
    b. women from good families going outside their homes to shop in downtown department stores.
    c. women taking an interest in literature and fine arts.
    d. saloons, vaudeville, and ragtime as immoral, low class, and vulgar.

6.   All of these were advocates and preachers of Victorian morality *except*

   a.   Henry Ward Beecher.
   b.   Catherine Beecher.
   c.   Theodore Dreiser.
   d.   Anthony Comstock.

7.   All of the following reformers tried to help the poor but also tended to blame their poverty on their moral deficiencies *except*

   a.   Florence Kelley.
   b.   Jacob Riis.
   c.   Charles Loring Brace.
   d.   Josephine Shaw Lowell.

8.   Jane Addams and her coworkers at Hull House did all of the following *except*

   a.   establish a day-care nursery for children of working mothers.
   b.   pressure Congress to restrict the flow of poor immigrants to the United States.
   c.   pressure legislators to enforce sanitation regulations and pass laws protecting the urban poor.
   d.   run classes, a laundry, an employment bureau, and recreation programs.

9.   "Prairie-school" houses featuring low silhouettes and rejecting the bulk and clutter of the typical Victorian home were the creation of

   a.   John L. Sullivan.
   b.   Thomas Eakins.
   c.   Andrew D. White.
   d.   Frank Lloyd Wright.

10. Compulsory education at urban public schools in the late nineteenth century was fought by

   a.   Catholic immigrants because of the Protestant orientation of the public schools.
   b.   poor working-class families who needed to send youngsters over age ten to work.
   c.   upper-class parents who did not want their children mingling with the immigrant masses.
   d.   all of the above.

SHORT-ANSWER QUESTIONS

1.   Explain the reasons for conflict between immigrants and native-born reformers in the late nineteenth century.

2.   Who founded the Social Gospel movement? What did Social Gospel ministers preach and do?

3.   How did department stores in the period 1860 to 1900 try to appeal to consumers?

4.   In what ways did the settlement-house movement prepare the way for progressive reform in the early twentieth century? Who was Florence Kelley? How did her career illustrate the connection between settlement houses and the progressive reform movement?

5.   Why did Theodore Dreiser's *Sister Carrie* shock guardians of genteel culture in the Victorian Age?

6.   How did the middle and upper classes in the Victorian period explain why they were more economically successful than the working class?

7.   What was modernism in the arts? Give three examples of painters and/or architects whose work was modernist, and state what made their work modern.

8.   What new inventions made possible indoor bathrooms with flush toilets? This technology was in place by the 1870s, and yet as late as 1920, 80 percent of American homes still did not have flush toilets. Why?

ESSAY QUESTIONS

1. Explain the Victorian genteel tradition in the arts. Discuss the writers, painters, architects, and social scientists who broke with it in the late nineteenth century.

2. Between 1870 and 1900 nearly 11 million immigrants entered the United States. Discuss who came, why they came, where they settled, how they fared, and the impact they had on urban America.

3. Discuss the rise of the urban political machines and bosses. Why did they emerge? What roles did they play? Who supported them and why? Who fought them and why?

4. Discuss the Victorian view of the role of women. How did the so-called new woman of the late nineteenth century challenge the Victorian ideal? Which women were the most affected by the new-woman patterns? Which were least affected by the changes?

5. Discuss the varied responses of nineteenth-century middle-class reformers to urban ethnic diversity, poverty, and crime.

ANSWERS TO MULTIPLE-CHOICE QUESTIONS

1. a
2. c
3. c
4. d
5. d
6. c
7. a
8. b
9. d
10. d

Politics and Expansion in an Industrializing Age, 1877–1900

OUTLINE AND SUMMARY

I. Introduction

Chapter 20 covers national politics between 1877 and 1900 and U.S. participation in the Spanish-American War and the race for empire. After reading the chapter, you should be able to answer these questions: (1) What were the issues and the political spoils that the Democrats and Republicans fought over? (2) What caused the rise of the Grange, Farmers' Alliances, and the Populist Party? (3) What was at stake in the election of 1896, and what was its outcome? (4) Why did the United States go to war with Spain in 1898 and what resulted from the American victory?

II. Party Politics in an Era of Upheaval, 1877–1884

A. Contested Political Visions

The Republicans and Democrats differed on tariffs and money supply, but the majority of politicians of both parties held that the federal government had no right to regulate business or protect workers' welfare. They were, however, willing to subsidize and in other ways encourage corporate growth. People looked to state and local governments to address their economic and social problems, not Washington.

B. Patterns of Party Strength

Male voter turnouts were high, and the two political parties—Democratic and Republican—were closely matched in strength. The main Democratic support came from the solid South, states that bordered the South, recent immigrants in the big cities, and most Catholics. The Republicans generally won the votes of people in rural and small-town New England, Pennsylvania, and the upper Midwest and of native-born Protestants.

C. Regulating the Money Supply

The nation split on the questions of how much money the government should issue and what should back it. Bankers, creditors, most businessmen, economists, and politicians all believed that, to maintain economic stability and avoid inflation, the money supply must be limited to what the government could back with its holdings of gold. Debt-ridden southern and western farmers wanted a larger money supply, including retention of the unbacked Civil War currency (greenbacks), the issuing of notes backed by silver and gold, and the minting of silver coins. They believed this larger money supply would raise falling farm prices and make it easier to pay off debts. In the 1870s the Greenback Party tried to further this program. Even after the party's demise, debtor groups continued to demand a larger money supply and got a little help from the 1890 Sherman Silver Purchase Act.

D. Civil-Service Reform

The spoils system had operated since the days of Andrew Jackson. A group of reformers, including Carl Schurz and E. L. Godkin, saw its defects and demanded a "professional civil service based on merit."

After a crazed job seeker assassinated President James A. Garfield, the civil-service reformers were finally able to convince Congress in 1883 to pass the Pendleton Act. It created a civil-service commission to prepare competitive examinations for federal jobs, and it prohibited politicians from asking government employees for campaign contributions. Gradually it began to raise the honesty and competence of the federal bureaucracy.

III.   Politics of Privilege, Politics of Exclusion, 1884–1892
   A.   A Democrat in the White House: Grover Cleveland, 1885–1889
In 1884 the Republicans nominated James G. Blaine, who was tainted by the corruption of the Grant era and was identified with the spoils system. When the Democrats chose Grover Cleveland, who had a reputation for fighting the spoilsmen, a number of Republican civil-service reformers bolted their party to support him. This Mugwump switch helped Cleveland win the presidency.

Cleveland, a believer in laissez-faire, had little understanding of the social problems caused by industrialization. He did, however, attempt to lower the tariff, arguing that reduced rates would remove a potentially corrupting government surplus of funds, reduce prices for consumers, and slow the growth of trusts. Lower tariffs appealed to farmers and many Democrats from the West and South but alarmed manufacturers and those Republican politicians who looked out for their interests. Cleveland also angered Civil War veterans when he halted wholesale granting of disability pensions to them.

   B.   Big Business Strikes Back, Benjamin Harrison, 1889–1893
The tariff became a major issue in the election of 1888. The Democrats renominated Cleveland; the Republicans chose Benjamin Harrison and stood behind high protective tariffs. Industrialists contributed heavily to the Republicans. Although Cleveland received more popular votes than Harrison, he lost in the Electoral College. In 1890 the victorious Republicans passed the McKinley Tariff, raising rates to an all-time high. They also rewarded Civil War veterans with generous pensions.

   C.   Agrarian Protest and the Rise of the People's Party
When prices of wheat and other agricultural products dropped in the 1870s, debt-burdened farmers fell on hard times. They responded by forming the first nationwide agricultural organization, the Patrons of Husbandry, or Grange, led by Oliver H. Kelley. The Grange tried to help farmers economically by organizing cooperatives to market their crops and buy supplies. It also lobbied state legislatures to regulate the railroads, which were overcharging farmers, giving discounts to large shippers, and bribing state officials. A number of states did pass Granger Laws, but they were bitterly attacked by the railroads as unconstitutional. At first federal courts upheld state regulation, but in the *Wabash* case (1886) the Supreme Court ruled that states could not regulate interstate railroads. Congress stepped into the void by passing the Interstate Commerce Act (ICA, 1887), which created the Interstate Commerce Commission (ICC) to investigate and oversee railroad practices. The ICA did little to curb railroad abuses, but the law and the ICC set a precedent for future federal regulation of interstate commerce. The failure of the Granger Laws and the Grange's other efforts to help farmers economically led to the organization's decline after 1878.

Farmers believed that the federal government was unresponsive to their needs. Western and southern farmers suffered from falling agricultural prices, a tight money supply, and high interest rates. They were heavily in debt and were overcharged by industrial trusts, grain elevator operators, and railroads. Earlier, farmers had turned to the Grange and the Greenback Party to redress their grievances. When these failed, farmers joined the Southern, National Colored Farmers', and Northwestern Alliances. The alliances called for tariff reduction, a graduated income tax, public ownership of railroads, and "free silver," among other things. In 1892 the alliances founded the People's, or Populist, Party and wrote a platform based on their program. They also endorsed the direct election of senators and other electoral reforms and nominated James B. Weaver for president.

D. African-Americans After Reconstruction
After Reconstruction white Democrats in the South increasingly deprived black southerners of the right to vote. At first the whites used intimidation and terror, but after 1890 they found even more effective means in poll taxes, literacy tests, and grandfather clauses. Southern blacks also were victimized by segregation laws, the convict-lease system, and lynching. Some southern Populists attempted to combat prejudice and encourage white and black farmers to unite against their exploiters, but the southern Democratic elite purposely inflamed racial antagonism to keep poor farmers divided.

The federal government did nothing to protect black rights. The Supreme Court gave its stamp of approval to segregated but equal facilities in *Plessy* v. *Ferguson* (1896). It also upheld poll taxes and literacy tests (1898).

Blacks responded to these abuses in several ways. Some fled the South only to find de facto segregation in the North. Booker T. Washington advised fellow blacks to accept their second-class status for a time and concentrate on getting ahead economically and educationally. The old abolitionist Frederick Douglass still called on blacks to demand full equality. With the disenfranchisement of blacks and the defeat of southern populism, the South became a one-party region, always controlled by the Democrats.

IV. The 1890s: Politics in a Depression Decade
A. 1892: Populists Challenge the Status Quo
In 1892 the Democratic candidate, Grover Cleveland, regained the presidency from the incumbent Republican, Benjamin Harrison. Populist James B. Weaver received more than a million votes, but few of them came from the urban Northeast. The Populists also gained less than one-quarter of the votes of the agricultural South, largely because of the race issue.

B. Capitalism in Crisis: The Depression of 1893–1897
Soon after Cleveland was inaugurated, the nation suffered a financial panic that ushered in a severe depression.

During the depression thousands of banks and businesses failed; between 20 and 25 percent of the labor force was unemployed; and agricultural prices fell more than 20 percent, completing the ruin of many farmers already in economic difficulty. Hard times increased the appeal of the Populists and spawned strikes and protests. In 1894 Jacob Coxey led a march of the unemployed on Washington to demand a public-works program to create jobs. He was arrested, and the demonstration was broken up. The heightened unrest frightened the middle class.

C. Business Leaders Respond
Cleveland, in keeping with laissez-faire doctrine, opposed government help for victims of the depression. His use of force against the Pullman strikers and Coxey's marchers appeared heartless. He angered farmers when, in defense of the gold standard, he induced Congress to repeal the Sherman Silver Purchase Act. Cleveland's actions split the party, as Democrats from agricultural states began to favor free silver. Hard times also led many Americans to question the laissez-faire doctrine.

D. 1894: Protest Grows Louder
The voters repudiated Cleveland in the 1894 midterm elections. Congress went Republican, and the vote for Populist candidates climbed more than 40 percent above their 1892 tallies.

The issue of free silver came to symbolize the deep split between economic classes. Creditors feared that abandonment of a strictly gold standard would cause runaway inflation and ruin. Debt-ridden farmers saw silver as the panacea that would raise farm prices and return prosperity.

E.   Silver Advocates Capture the Democratic Party
At the 1896 Democratic convention, western and southern delegates gained control, wrote a platform calling for free silver, and nominated silver advocate William Jennings Bryan. The Republicans nominated William McKinley, who promised to maintain the gold standard and raise the protective tariff. The Populists, though not completely satisfied with the Democratic platform, feared that if they ran their own candidate, they would split the farm vote, ensuring the election of McKinley. The Populists, therefore, endorsed Bryan but nominated one of their own, Tom Watson, for vice president.

F.   1896: Republicans Triumphant
McKinley received huge campaign contributions from businessmen who feared Bryan. Besides having less money, Bryan was handicapped by the lack of appeal of free silver to factory workers and the urban middle class. They realized that it would probably bring about higher food prices. McKinley won the election, carrying the Northeast, Midwest, and most cities. His party also kept its majority in Congress. As promised, McKinley and the Republicans maintained the gold standard and raised the tariff to an all-time high. These policies aroused little opposition, however, because prosperity returned, more gold became available with new discoveries, and farm prices began to rise. McKinley easily beat Bryan for a second term in the election of 1900. Indeed, the elections of 1894 and 1896 ushered in a long period of Republican dominance in U.S. politics that lasted almost unbroken until the 1930s. The Populist Party disintegrated after 1896, but many of the reforms it had advocated were enacted by Progressives after 1900.

V.   Expansionist Stirrings and War with Spain, 1878–1901
A.   Roots of Expansionist Sentiment
In the late nineteenth century the United States showed heightened interest in overseas empire. The example of European nations and Japan, which were seizing colonies in Asia and Africa, stimulated U.S. expansionism. During the depression of 1893–1897 American businessmen and politicians argued that the United States must capture overseas markets to maintain prosperity. Inspired by Alfred T. Mahan's *The Influence of Sea Power upon History* and by Social Darwinist ideas, Republican politicians—including Theodore Roosevelt, Henry Cabot Lodge, and John Hay—claimed that, to be a great power, the United States must build up its navy and obtain far-flung colonies in which to establish fueling stations and bases and exercise its influence in the world as a superior country. Combining religion and Social Darwinist racism, Josiah Strong's *Our Country* (1885) told Americans that, as members of the superior Anglo-Saxon race, they were destined to spread Christianity and civilization to "inferior" peoples.

B.   Pacific Expansion
Expansionist enthusiasm led the United States to establish a joint protectorate with Germany and Great Britain over the Samoan Islands. American sugar plantation owners overthrew the government of Queen Liliuokalani in Hawaii and asked the United States to take over the islands. President Cleveland, who was not an expansionist, declined to do so. The next president, William McKinley, an expansionist urged on by sugar interests, requested Congress to annex Hawaii, which it did in 1898.

C.   Crisis over Cuba
The Cubans revolted against Spanish rule in 1895, and the Spanish authorities brutally attempted to suppress the rebellion. Public opinion in the United States turned against the Spanish as William Randolph Hearst's *Journal* and Joseph Pulitzer's *World,* using yellow-journalistic sensationalism, featured daily accounts of atrocities. President McKinley did not want to intervene, but he sent the battleship *Maine* to Havana to protect the lives and property of Americans on the island. On February 15, 1898, an explosion on the *Maine* killed 266 of its crewmen. The yellow press immediately accused the Spanish of blowing up the ship, and the public demanded revenge. Bending to popular pressure, McKinley asked Congress to declare war on Spain, which it did in April 1898. It also passed the Teller Amendment proclaiming that the United States had no designs on Cuba and would leave the island as soon as its independence was ensured.

D.   The Spanish-American War, 1898
The fighting against Spain lasted less than four months. Admiral George Dewey attacked the Spanish fleet in the Philippines and American troops took Manila Bay in August. By July 1898 the Spanish were driven from Cuba. The defeated Spanish recognized Cuba's independence and ceded to the United States the Philippines, Puerto Rico, and Guam.

Contrary to the Teller Amendment, the United States occupied Cuba from 1898 to 1902, then withdrew its forces only after Cuba agreed to the conditions set forth in the 1901 Platt Amendment. This amendment limited Cuba's sovereignty by, among other things, reserving to the United States the right to intervene in Cuba and to maintain a naval base there. Although the Platt Amendment was abrogated in 1934, the United States still retains the base at Guantanamo Bay in Cuba.

E.   Critics of Empire
Some Americans were horrified by their nation's actions in the Spanish-American War. Among these people were civil-service reformers Carl Schurz and E. L. Godkin, agricultural spokesmen such as William Jennings Bryan, settlement-house founder Jane Addams, and writers and intellectuals such as Mark Twain and William James. They founded the Anti-Imperialist League, which pointed out that imposing U.S. rule on other peoples by military force violated the principles of human equality and liberty championed in our own Declaration of Independence. Despite the League's efforts, the Senate ratified the treaty annexing the Philippines, and in 1900 pro-expansionist McKinley again defeated anti-imperialist Bryan for the presidency.

F.   Guerrilla War in the Philippines, 1898–1902
President McKinley was persuaded that the United States should keep the Philippines by the arguments of the expansionists and the desire of businessmen to use the islands as a way of penetrating nearby Chinese markets. That U.S. decision led to a war against Filipino independence fighters. To crush the guerrilla resistance of the Filipinos, the United States used brutal tactics and lost many more solders than it had in the Spanish-American War. The United States ruled the Philippines until 1946, when it finally granted the country its independence.

VI.   Conclusion
Between 1877 and 1896 the two major political parties—Democrats and Republicans—were closely matched in strength. Each party had loyal followers: Democrats, the South and new immigrants in cities; Republicans, rural and small town native-born Americans in the Northeast and Midwest. Both parties ignored the pressing economic problems of the country's farmers, who turned successively to the Grange, the Farmers' Alliances, and the Populist Party. In 1896, when the Populists joined the Democrats in backing William Jennings Bryan, big business used its

financial might to turn back the Populist challenge and elect McKinley president. McKinley's victory marked the start of a long period of Republican dominance in national politics. The McKinley administration soon led the United States into the Spanish-American War and an imperialist foreign policy. However, this burst of expansionism in the late nineteenth and early twentieth centuries never fully diverted U.S. attention from domestic issues. The Populist Party, though it was defeated in 1896, left behind the feeling that government must free itself from business domination and play a more active role in solving the economic and social problems arising from industrialization. After the turn of the century, the Progressive movement would build on that new attitude.

VOCABULARY

The following terms are used in Chapter 20. To understand the chapter fully, it is important that you know what each of them means.

disenfranchisement	depriving persons of the right to vote
spoils system	the practice whereby the victorious political party rewards its supporters with appointments to government jobs, regardless of their qualifications for the positions
patronage	the control of appointments to public office or of other political favors
agrarian	rural, agricultural
lynch	kill a person for some alleged offense without due process of law, usually in reference to hanging by a mob
caveat	a warning or caution
de facto	in fact; in reality (as opposed to de jure, according to law or required by law)
reactionary	extremely conservative; favoring a return to the social or political conditions of a past time
panacea	a remedy for all ills or difficulties; a cure-all
dark-horse candidate	a little known or unlikely political figure who unexpectedly wins nomination
jingoism	an aggressive, bellicose spirit or foreign policy that advocates seizing new territories and/or securing national advantages by use of force
sovereignty	independence; self-government or authority of a nation or state
imperialism	the policy of extending the rule or authority of an empire or nation over foreign countries or of acquiring and holding colonies and dependencies
protectorate	the relationship of a strong state toward a weaker state or territory that it protects and partly controls
subjugate	conquer; bring under complete control

IDENTIFICATIONS

After reading Chapter 20, you should be able to identify and explain the historical significance of each of the following:

laissez-faire doctrine

greenbacks and the Greenback Party

Carl Schurz, E. L. Godkin, and civil service reform

Interstate Commerce Act, 1887

Southern, Northwestern, and National Colored Farmers' Alliances

Tom Watson, Mary E. Lease, and the Populist Party

separate but equal doctrine

Jacob Coxey

free silver

Alfred T. Mahan, *The Influence of Sea Power upon History*

Josian Strong, *Our Country*

Social Darwinism

Henry Cabot Lodge, John Hay, Theodore Roosevelt

William Randolph Hearst, the *Journal,* and yellow journalism

Joseph Pulitzer and the *World*

Anti-Imperialist League

SKILL BUILDING: MAPS

On the map of Asia and the Pacific, locate each of the following. Explain the significance of each on late-nineteenth-century and early-twentieth-century U.S. foreign policy.

Samoa

Hawaiian Islands, Honolulu, Pearl Harbor

Philippines, Manila Bay, Manila, Luzon

Guam

China, Manchuria, Beijing (Peking)

Japan

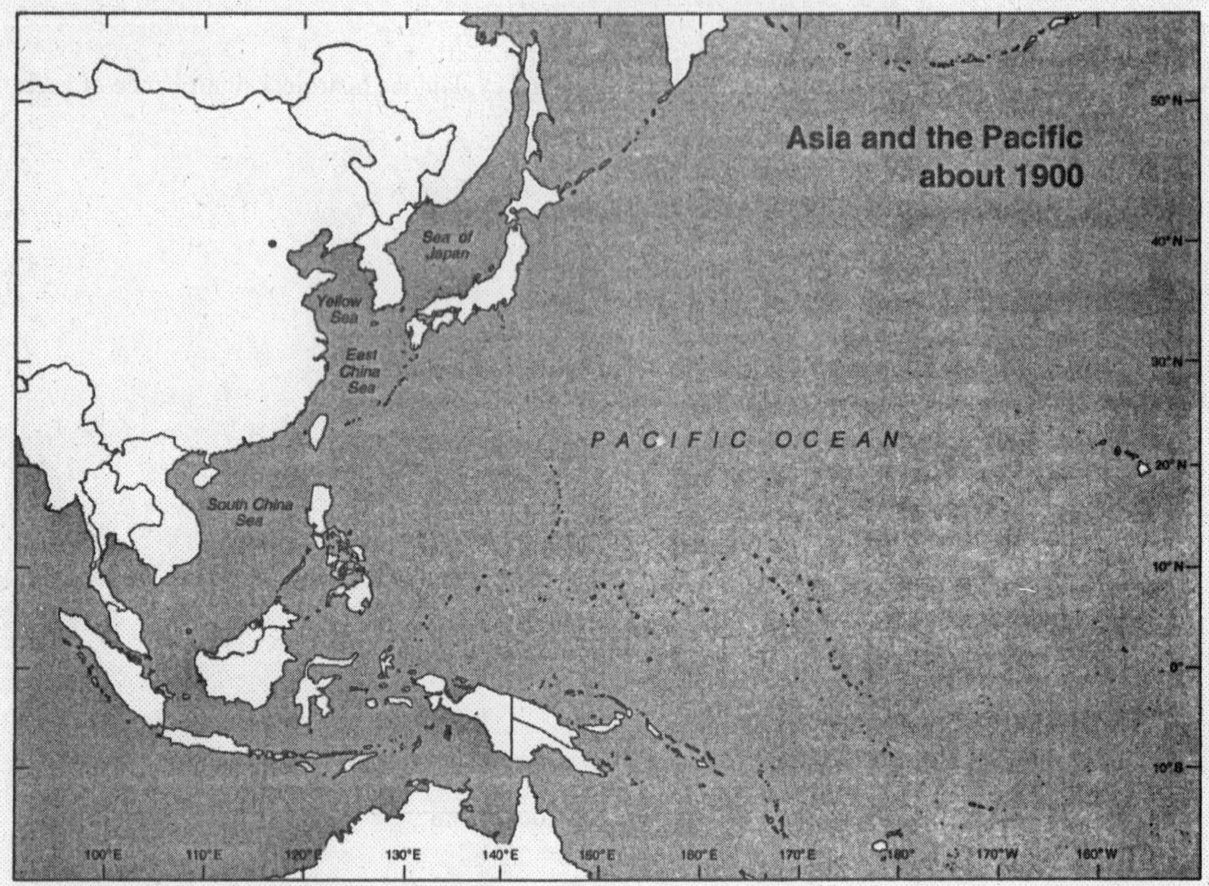

SKILL BUILDING: GRAPHS

Look at the line graph titled "Consumer Prices and Farm-Product Prices, 1865–1913" on page 605 of the text. After studying this graph you should be able to answer the following questions:

1. Was the period 1875–1897 one of overall economic inflation or deflation?

2. During that period, which generally dropped lower: total cost of living for consumers or prices of farm products?

3. During which years did farmers' income fall the farthest below their expenditures? Based on what you have read in this chapter, would you say that those years corresponded to the periods of greatest agrarian political unrest?

MULTIPLE-CHOICE QUESTIONS

Circle the letter of the item that best completes each statement or answers the question.

1. The Pendleton Act provided for
   a. civil-service reform.
   b. using silver as well as gold to back paper currency.
   c. separate but equal facilities for blacks and whites.
   d. higher protective tariff rates.

2. In which election did the presidential candidate who won in the popular vote lose in the Electoral College?

    a. 1896—Bryan won the popular vote, but lost to McKinley in the electoral vote.
    b. 1884—Blaine won the popular vote, but lost to Cleveland in the electoral vote.
    c. 1888—Cleveland won the popular vote, but lost to Harrison in the electoral vote.
    d. 1900—Bryan won the popular vote, but lost to McKinley in the electoral vote.

3. All of the following were anti-imperialists, who opposed U.S. subjugation of the Philippines *except*

    a. Mark Twain.
    b. Alfred T. Mahan.
    c. Samuel Gompers.
    d. Jane Addams.

4. American imperialists argued that U.S. participation in the race for colonies would do all of the following *except*

    a. cause lower taxes in the United States.
    b. provide bases for the U.S. Navy.
    c. provide the United States with new markets.
    d. bring civilization to backward peoples.

5. In the case of *Wabash* v. *Illinois* (1886), the U.S. Supreme Court ruled that

    a. states cannot regulate interstate railroads.
    b. the Interstate Commerce Act was unconstitutional.
    c. the Granger Laws were a legitimate use of the state's police powers.
    d. separate but equal facilities on railroads are constitutional.

6. The free-silver position of the Democrats and Populists in 1896 failed to win much support from urban labor because

    a. it would destroy labor unions.
    b. factory workers were relatively prosperous in the 1890s.
    c. workers liked Grover Cleveland and laissez-faire.
    d. workers feared it would result in higher food prices.

7. The Teller Amendment was later partially repudiated by

    a. the Platt Amendment.
    b. the Hay–Bunau-Varilla Treaty.
    c. *Plessy* v. *Ferguson*.
    d. the Sixteenth Amendment.

8. The yellow journalism of William R. Hearst's *Journal* and Joseph Pulitzer's *World* probably contributed to

    a. Bryan's defeat in 1896.
    b. Cleveland's election in 1884.
    c. the passage of poll taxes, literacy tests, and grandfather clauses.
    d. the United States' declaration of war on Spain.

9. The Mugwumps were

    a. supporters of James G. Blaine for president in 1884 because of his call for an expansionist foreign policy.
    b. reformers who left the Republican Party in 1896 to support the Democratic and Populist candidate, William Jennings Bryan, and free silver.
    c. Republicans who refused to support the spoilsman James G. Blaine for president in 1884 and switched their backing to the Democratic nominee, Grover Cleveland.
    d. the reform Democrats and Republicans who gathered in Omaha, Nebraska, in 1892 to found the Populist Party.

10. Which of the following statements about Booker T. Washington is correct?
    a. He urged African-Americans to get a college education in order to improve their economic opportunities and fight for their rights.
    b. He secretly backed legal cases challenging disenfranchisement and segregation, but publicly advised African-Americans to accept the loss of the vote and segregation.
    c. He joined Frederick Douglass in urging African-Americans to demand full equality and fight violence with violence.
    d. He advised southern blacks to migrate to the North, where they could still exercise their right to vote and where there were no segregation laws on the books.

SHORT-ANSWER QUESTIONS

1. Discuss the causes of agrarian discontent in the period 1870 to 1897.

2. What was the Grange, or Patrons of Husbandry? What were the Granger Laws? Why did they prove ineffective? Why did the Grange decline by the late 1870s?

3. Why did American farmers between the 1870s and 1897 generally favor issuing greenbacks and adopting free silver?

4. Since the Fifteenth Amendment clearly states that no one shall be denied the right to vote because of race, color, or previous condition of servitude, how did the South manage to disenfranchise almost all black voters by 1900?

5. Why did the Populists decide to endorse the 1896 Democratic presidential candidate, William Jennings Bryan, instead of nominating a member of their own party to run?

6. Why did William Jennings Bryan lose to William McKinley in the election of 1896?

7. How, why, and when did the United States acquire the Hawaiian Islands?

8. Secretary of State John Hay called the fight with Spain "a splendid little war." Why did he think that? Why might many of the troops who served in the Spanish-American War disagree with him?

9. Explain the relationship the United States established with Cuba after the Spanish-American War.

ESSAY QUESTIONS

1. Discuss what happened to African-Americans in the post-Reconstruction South. How did the federal government react to these developments? What impact did these developments have on national politics?

2. Write an essay on the rise of populism in the 1890s. How and why was the Populist Party founded? What did it hope to accomplish? Why did it fail to become a major party and gain control of the federal government? Did it accomplish anything?

3. Discuss the economic depression of 1893–1897. What caused it? Whom did it particularly hurt? How did the Cleveland administration deal with it? What were its effects on national politics?

4. In 1898 the United States declared war on Spain, although there seemed to be little provocation. Why did the majority of Americans and most government leaders favor war?

5. With the annexation of the Philippines, the United States for the first time imposed its rule on a distant people by military force. How can you account for this change in U.S. foreign policy? What pressures and groups led the nation in this imperialistic direction? Were there countergroups trying to prevent this course? If so, why were they unsuccessful?

ANSWERS TO MULTIPLE-CHOICE QUESTIONS

1. a
2. c
3. b
4. a
5. a
6. d
7. a
8. d
9. c
10. b

CHAPTER 21

The Progressive Era, 1900–1917

OUTLINE AND SUMMARY

I. Introduction

Chapter 21 covers the economic and social changes and problems caused by industrialization and urbanization and how the Progressive reform movement emerged to wrestle with these. As an example, the unsafe and unsanitary conditions in which millions of workers labored produced tragedies, such as the 1911 Triangle Shirtwaist fire, in which 141 sweatshop employees perished. Afterward, aroused Progressives convinced New York State to enact many labor protective laws. As you read the chapter, consider these questions: (1) How did intellectuals and writers prepare the way for Progressive reform? (2) What conditions in the cities and states bothered Progressives, and what did they hope to do about them? (3) How did Progressive reform reach national politics, and which leaders and issues were involved? (4) What impact did Progressive reform have on the lives of women, immigrants, the urban poor, and African-Americans? (5) Did progressivism alter people's views on the proper role of government in America's society and economy?

II. Progressives and Their Ideas

A. The Many Faces of Progressivism

Progressive reformers included much of the new urban middle class (mostly white, native-born Protestants). Middle-class women, often college educated, working through settlement houses and private organizations, such as the National Consumers' League, played an important role in Progressive reform. Urban, immigrant political machines and workers began to demand improved labor conditions. Unlike the rural-based Populist movement, the Progressives were strongest in the cities and attracted much more support from middle-class professionals and intellectuals than the earlier movement. Most Progressives accepted the capitalist system; they merely wanted to reform the worst abuses that had developed under it. There was never one unified movement, but many different groups of reformers. Some preached regulation of big business; others concentrated on passing laws to protect workers. Still others thought the way to cure social ills was to curtail immigration. Progressives generally attempted to be "scientific" in their approach, backing their demands for change with scholarly studies of deplorable conditions to be remedied.

A. Intellectuals Offer New Social Views

Many intellectuals criticized unrestrained, brutal capitalist competition and called for an activist government that would regulate business practices and protect the economically vulnerable. These intellectuals included economist Thorstein Veblen, journalist Herbert Croly, pragmatic philosopher William James, and settlement-house leader Jane Addams.

New educational and legal ideas paved the way for the Progressive movement. John Dewey preached that schools must foster in students respect for the values of democracy and cooperation. Supreme Court justice Oliver Wendell Holmes, Jr., attacked conservative judges for being guided entirely by legal precedent. He insisted that the "law must evolve as society changes."

B.   Novelists, Journalists, and Artists Spotlight Social Problems
Muckraking journalists and novelists played an important role in stimulating the Progressive movement by exposing to middle-class Americans political corruption and corporate wrongdoing. Muckraking journalists included Lincoln Steffens, who wrote about urban political machines and bosses, and Ida Tarbell, who revealed the cutthroat competitive practices of Standard Oil Company. Magazines such as *McClure's* and *Collier's* specialized in muckraking articles. Novelists Frank Norris in *The Octopus* and Theodore Dreiser in *The Financier* also told tales of business abuses and political corruption. Meanwhile, "Ashcan School" artists and photographers such as Lewis Hine depicted the harsh world of the immigrants, factory workers and child laborers.

III.   State and Local Progressivism
A.   Reforming the Political Process
The earliest signs of the Progressive movement appeared in cities where municipal reformers battled corrupt political machines and elected activist mayors dedicated to change. Reform mayors such as Hazen Pingree of Detroit and Samuel Jones of Toledo generally brought honesty to municipal government, provided city dwellers with improved municipal services and facilities, and forced transportation and utility companies to lower rates and pay their fair share of taxes. Other municipal reformers experimented with commission and city-manager forms of government.

The reform efforts soon moved up to state government. Progressives attempted to democratize politics by establishing secret balloting, the direct primary, the initiative, the referendum, and recall. In practice these measures fell short of producing the democratic results that their Progressive authors had hoped for.

B.   Regulating Business, Protecting Workers
After 1900 the growth of huge business corporations speeded up. For example, in 1901 J. P. Morgan consolidated hundreds of independent steel makers to form the U.S. Steel Company, which controlled 80 percent of production in the nation. This trend alarmed many Americans. The real wages of industrial laborers rose after 1900 but were still so inadequate that in many families the mothers and children had to work to make ends meet. In 1910 at least 1.6 million youngsters between ten and fifteen years of age worked full-time. Industrial laborers spent on average nine and a half hours a day in mills and shops that were often hazardous to their health and safety. Employers, inspired by efficiency experts such as Frederick W. Taylor, tried to get even more work out of their employees.

Under Progressive influence, state governments started to impose regulations on railroads, mines, and other business corporations. The pioneer was Wisconsin, under Governor Robert La Follette. Between 1901 and 1906 he convinced the legislature to create a state railroad commission, increase corporate taxes, and limit business contributions to political campaigns. He and the legislature also introduced political reforms such as the direct primary. These Progressive measures and La Follette's method of relying on the expertise of academics at the state university became known as the "Wisconsin Idea." States passed important labor laws as well: maximum number of hours per workday for female employees, such as Oregon's ten-hour law; factory safety codes, such as the one enacted in New York after the Triangle Shirtwaist fire; workers' compensation acts; and bans on child labor.

C.   Making Cities More Livable
Cities grew rapidly between 1900 and 1920 as rural Americans and millions of immigrants moved into them. Overwhelmed and often corrupt municipal governments failed to provide the newcomers with adequate services and public facilities. Progressive reformers began to beautify cities with more parks and playgrounds, broad boulevards, and impressive

municipal buildings. State legislatures passed housing codes to upgrade living conditions in tenements and slum neighborhoods. Cities and states improved garbage collection, street cleaning, and water and sewer systems, as well as requiring higher standards of cleanliness and quality from sellers of food and milk. These Progressive reforms significantly decreased infant mortality and tuberculosis deaths. There were, in addition, attempts to reduce air pollution, but business fought these vigorously and the continued reliance on coal as the chief energy source, left cities smoky and sooty.

IV.   Progressivism and Social Control
   A.   Moral Control in the Cities
Some reformers tried to guard morality by inducing cities to censor movies and outlaw prostitution. A wave of hysteria over white slavery (young women tricked into a life of prostitution) led to passage of the federal Mann Act (1910) and the close of red-light districts in several cities.

   B.   Battling Alcohol and Drugs
Prohibition became the biggest moral crusade of the Progressive Era. Due to the efforts of the Anti-Saloon League, the Woman's Christian Temperance Union, and various church groups, many localities enacted bans on liquor sales and the national prohibition movement grew stronger. Progressives also campaigned against the then-widespread use of such addictive drugs as morphine, heroin, and cocaine. Their efforts led to passage of the federal Narcotics Act (1914) outlawing the distribution of heroin, morphine, and cocaine except by doctors' prescriptions.

   C.   Immigration Restriction and Eugenics
As 17 million immigrants, primarily from southern and eastern Europe, poured into the country between 1900 and 1917, many native-born Americans became fearful. They often believed that immigrants caused poverty and immorality. In 1894 Senator Henry Cabot Lodge and other prominent Bostonians founded the Immigration Restriction League. In 1917, over President Wilson's veto, Congress excluded illiterate immigrants.

Eugenicists claimed that humans and society could be improved by controlled breeding. Inspired by their ideas, some states passed laws during the Progressive Era allowing forced sterilization of criminals, mentally deficient persons, and sex offenders. Pseudo-scientific racism was spewed by some so-called progressive writers, such as Madison Grant in *The Passing of the Great Race* (1916).

   D.   Racism and Progressivism
In 1900 the majority of the 10 million African-Americans were still in the rural South, mostly living as sharecroppers. To escape from poverty, disfranchisement, Jim Crow laws, and violence, they began migrating to cities and to the North. In the North they encountered de facto segregation and discrimination. Under these difficult circumstances, African-Americans developed their own communities and culture. Racism in American society reached a peak during the Progressive Era. Many progressives either ignored racial discrimination or were themselves racists. Southern Progressives such as James K. Vardaman and Ben Tillman combined advocacy of economic and political reform with vicious attacks on African-Americans. The two Progressive-reformer presidents of the era, Theodore Roosevelt and Woodrow Wilson, compiled sorry records on racial justice. Roosevelt ordered the unwarranted dishonorable discharge of an entire regiment of African-American soldiers in the Brownsville, Texas, incident, and Wilson praised the racist movie *Birth of a Nation* and condoned the introduction of racial segregation in all federal government agencies and departments. On the other hand, white progressives such as Lillian

Wald and Mary White Ovington decried racial injustice and helped found the National Association for the Advancement of Colored People (NAACP).

V. African-Americans, Women, and Workers Organize
  A. African-American Leaders Organize Against Racism
   Booker T. Washington, America's best-known black leader between 1890 and 1915, advised blacks to concentrate on economic advancement through vocational education and, for the time being, accept the South's Jim Crow and disfranchisement laws. Northern African-American intellectuals and professionals—William Monroe Trotter, Ida Wells-Barnett, and W. E. B. Du Bois—urged African-Americans to fight for economic, political, and educational equality. In 1905 Du Bois and other African-American critics of Washington formed the Niagara Movement. In 1909 Du Bois and other members of the Niagara Movement joined with white Progressives in organizing the NAACP, which rejected Booker T. Washington's accommodationist advice and began the long fight for racial justice.

  B. Revival of the Woman-Suffrage Movement
   A new group of feminists emerged to revitalize the women's movement. Carrie Chapman Catt, who became president of the National American Woman Suffrage Association in 1900, led her members in lobbying, distributing literature, and demonstrating. They convinced several states to grant women the vote. Impatient with the pace of change, however, Alice Paul organized the National Woman's Party to bring direct pressure on the federal government for passage of a constitutional amendment enfranchising women.

  C. Enlarging "Woman's Sphere"
   Feminists challenged the assumption that the only proper roles for women were those of wife, mother, and homemaker. Women like Florence Kelley, Alice Hamilton, and Margaret Sanger led the Progressive drives to abolish child labor, protect the health of workers and consumers, and establish birth-control clinics.

  D. Workers Organize; Socialism Advances
   To improve their lot, workers kept trying to unionize. However, their right to strike was frequently curtailed by conservative court decisions such as *Danbury Hatters*, and employers often hired recent immigrants as scabs when employees struck. Because of these obstacles, the AFL craft unions grew primarily in the skilled trades, leaving most factory workers unorganized. Two unions attempted to help semiskilled and unskilled workers: the International Ladies' Garment Workers' Union, which led successful strikes in the needle trades, and the Industrial Workers of the World (IWW). The IWW signed up western miners, lumberjacks, and migratory farm workers and won a major strike in 1912 in the textile mills of Massachusetts. Government repression of the IWW during World War I, however, caused the decline of the organization.

   The Socialist Party of America, which hoped to end capitalism through the ballot box rather than revolution, was gaining followers. When party leader Eugene Debs ran for president in 1912, he received 900,000 votes.

VI. National Progressivism—Phase I: Roosevelt and Taft, 1901–1913
  A. Roosevelt's Path to the White House
   Theodore Roosevelt, who entered the White House in 1901 after an anarchist assassinated William McKinley, became the United States' first Progressive president. A believer in strong executive leadership, Roosevelt enlarged the powers of the presidency, turning the office into both an effective public forum and the center of legislative initiative.

B. Labor Disputes, Trustbusting, and Railroad Regulation
Unlike earlier presidents who used troops to break strikes, Roosevelt, in the coal miners'
strike of 1902, induced management and the United Mine Workers to submit the dispute to
arbitration by a commission that he appointed. The commission granted the miners increased
pay and reduced hours.

Roosevelt did not want to attack big business, but he preached that corporate giants must
obey the law and serve the public interest. When he believed that firms like the Northern
Securities Company had violated the Sherman Anti-Trust Act, he prosecuted them. Despite
his trustbusting, he stayed on good terms with big business, which contributed heavily to his
1904 campaign. In that election he easily won a second term over his conservative
Democratic opponent, Alton B. Parker. In 1906 Roosevelt strengthened corporate regulation
when he signed the Hepburn Act, which gave the Interstate Commerce Commission (ICC)
the power to set maximum railroad rates and examine railroads' financial records.

C. Consumer Protection
Responding to public concern generated by Upton Sinclair's *The Jungle,* Roosevelt
persuaded Congress to pass the Pure Food and Drug Act and the Meat Inspection Act.

D. Environmentalism Progressive Style
Roosevelt made his most enduring reforms in conservation. Years of exploitation for private
gain had damaged and depleted America's natural environment. By the 1890s land use had
become a political issue, pitting business interests, preservationists, and conservationists
against each other. While entrepreneurs wanted to continue unrestricted development for
private enrichment, preservationists such as John Muir and the Sierra Club wished to save
large wilderness tracts for their beauty and spiritual worth. Roosevelt's Forest Service chief
Gifford Pinchot, father of the conservation movement, sought government scientific
management to make the public domain best serve the resource needs of the nation of his
day and in the future. At times, the preservationists and the conservationists engaged in
bitter combat. An example was in the 1913 fight over the building of a dam in a beautiful
part of Yosemite National Park to provide water and hydroelectric power for San Francisco.
In this instance the conservationists won. Roosevelt used the presidency to popularize both
conservation and preservation. He signed the Newlands Act (1902), which was of great
importance in economic development of the West, and, in cooperation with Pinchot, set
aside some 200 million acres of forest and mineral-rich lands for government-managed use
rather than for sale to business. Roosevelt approved the Antiquities Act and created new
national parks. In 1916, during President Wilson's administration, Congress established the
National Park Service to protect and run the national historic sites, monuments, and parks.

E. Taft in the White House, 1909--1913
With Roosevelt's backing, his secretary of war, William Howard Taft, won the Republican
nomination and election as president in 1908 over third-time Democratic nominee William
Jennings Bryan. Pledged to continue Roosevelt's Square Deal, Taft prosecuted more trusts
than Roosevelt had, but Taft lacked Roosevelt's activism, flair for publicity, and political
skill.

In the fight shaping up between the progressive (Insurgent) and conservative wings of the
Republican party, Taft sided with the conservatives. When he signed the tariff-raising
Payne-Aldrich bill, backed conservative Speaker of the House Joseph Cannon, and fired
conservationist Gifford Pinchot, Taft alienated progressive Republicans. They joined with
Theodore Roosevelt, who returned from a trip abroad in 1910, in denouncing the
conservatives and campaigning for revived Progressive reform.

F.   The Four-Way Election of 1912
In 1912 Theodore Roosevelt challenged Taft for the Republican nomination. When the convention chose Taft, Roosevelt's backers walked out, founded the rival Progressive Party, and nominated Roosevelt. The Democrats gave the nod to Woodrow Wilson, reform governor of New Jersey, and the Socialists ran Eugene Debs. Roosevelt campaigned on his New Nationalism program of accepting big business as inevitable but building a powerful, activist federal government to regulate the corporate giants. Wilson's New Freedom, on the other hand, rejected big government in Washington and called for a return to an economy composed of small, competing enterprises. Roosevelt did well, but the split in Republican ranks gave Wilson and the Democrats control of the White House and Congress.

VII.   National Progressivism—Phase II: Woodrow Wilson, 1913–1917
A.   Introduction
Wilson had been a political science professor and president of Princeton University before becoming New Jersey governor. He could be a skilled and flexible politician, but at other times he was intolerant and self-righteous. Despite Wilson's stated preference for small business and limited government in the 1912 election, he as president led the effort to "use government to address the problems of the new corporate order."

B.   Tariff and Banking Reform
Wilson convinced Congress to pass the 1913 Underwood-Simmons Tariff, which reduced import duties by roughly 15 percent. Also in 1913 he signed the Federal Reserve Act, which kept banking a private enterprise but imposed public regulation over it. The twelve regional Federal Reserve banks were empowered to expand the nation's credit and money supply by issuing Federal Reserve notes under the supervision of the Federal Reserve Board, appointed by the president.

C.   Regulating Business; Aiding Workers and Farmers
Wilson pushed through Congress the Federal Trade Commission law and the Clayton Antitrust Act. The Federal Trade Commission was a federal regulatory agency with the power to uncover unfair methods of business competition and then issue cease and desist orders against the perpetrators. The Clayton Act supplemented the vague and general Sherman Anti-Trust Act by defining and listing specific illegal practices.

Wilson endorsed the clause in the Clayton Act exempting union strikes, boycotts, and picketing from prosecution under the antitrust laws. He signed the Keating-Owen child labor law (later declared unconstitutional), the Adamson Act providing for an eight-hour day for railroad workers, and the Workmen's Compensation Act for federal employees. Other legislation he signed helped farmers obtain loans at lower interest rates.

D.   Progressivism and the Constitution
Wilson nominated to the Supreme Court Progressive Jewish attorney Louis Brandeis. Although conservatives and anti-Semites objected, Wilson persuaded the Senate to confirm Brandeis. The Progressive Era also saw four amendments added to the U.S. Constitution: the Sixteenth (authorizing a federal income tax), Seventeenth (providing for popular, direct election of senators), Eighteenth (establishing the power of the federal government to impose prohibition), and Nineteenth (granting women the right to vote).

E.   1916: Wilson Edges Out Hughes
In 1916 the Democrats renominated Wilson, who ran against Charles Evans Hughes, the candidate of the now-reunited Republicans. In a close race Wilson won a second term.

VIII. Conclusion

Although some Progressive reforms did less good than their backers had hoped, and despite progressivism's repressive and intolerant elements, the movement as a whole left a legacy of government intervention to regulate destructive corporate practices, protect the economically vulnerable, and ameliorate social problems arising from industrialization. It was a precedent on which the New Deal would later build.

VOCABULARY

The following terms are used in Chapter 21. To understand the chapter fully, it is important that you know what each of them means.

capitalism	a system under which the means of production, distribution, and exchange are mostly privately owned and directed
socialism	a system under which the means of production, distribution, and exchange are owned by the community as a whole and administered by the government
pragmatism	the philosophy that truth is not determined by fixed universal laws but by the practical test of what works (It comes from philosopher William James's 1907 book *Pragmatism*.)
direct primary	an election in which the registered members of a political party vote on who their party nominees for office should be
initiative	a procedure by which a specified number of voters may propose a law and compel a popular vote on its adoption
referendum	a procedure by which voters can express their views on proposed state legislation, either approving or killing the measure
recall	the right to remove a public official from office by a vote of the people taken on petition of a specified number of the registered voters
eugenics	the manipulation of reproductive processes to improve the characteristics of a plant or animal species, especially human beings
arbitration	the hearing and deciding of a dispute between parties by a person or persons agreed to by the disputing parties
nostrums	patent medicines
adulterated	doctored, having foreign substances mixed in
workers' compensation law	a law requiring employers to take out an insurance policy on their employees so that if a worker is hurt on the job, the insurance company will pay medical and living expenses until the worker can return to work (in case of the worker's death, the payments are made to his or her dependents)

cease and desist order

an order by a court or government regulatory agency to stop and refrain thereafter from actions that the agency believes are illegal (if the order is complied with, no punitive action is taken)

IDENTIFICATIONS

After reading Chapter 21, you should be able to identify and explain the historical significance of each of the following:

Triangle Shirtwaist fire

Jane Addams

Lincoln Steffens, Ida Tarbell, and the muckrakers

Hazen Pingree and the Progressive reform mayors

International Ladies' Garment Workers' Union

Eugene Debs and the Socialist Party of America

Theodore Roosevelt and the Square Deal

Pure Food and Drug Act and Meat Inspection Act

Federal Trade Commission

Clayton Antitrust Act

Louis Brandeis and *Muller* v. *Oregon*

constitutional amendments of the Progressive Era: Sixteenth, Seventeenth, Eighteenth, and Nineteenth

SKILL BUILDING: TABLES

Look at the table "Children in the Labor Force, 1880–1930" on page 637 of your textbook. In what year did the problem of child labor seem to be most severe? Judging from the data in this chart, do you think the Progressive movement had any impact on child labor in the United States? Can you offer any other explanations for the percentage differences between 1880 and 1930?

SKILL BUILDING: GRAPHS

Look at the line graph titled "Immigration to the United States, 1870–1930" on page 641 of the text. After studying the graph, you should be able to answer the following questions:

1. During which years did the United States receive the greatest number of immigrants? Was there any year in which more than 1 million persons arrived?

2. During the peak period of immigration, were the majority of newcomers from western and northern Europe or from southern and eastern Europe?

3. Just from looking at the graph, can you tell what impact the Immigration Act of 1921 had on how many immigrants arrived and where they came from?

4. What were the effects of major economic depressions in the United States (1873–1879 and 1893–1897) and of World War I (1914–1918) on immigration to this country?

HISTORICAL SOURCES

If the historian writing about the Progressive Era is to understand why many Americans of the period favored reform, he or she needs to view the problems facing society as citizens living at the time perceived them. In the years 1890–1917 many middle-class people who did not personally experience exploitation learned about it from books, articles, and studies written by reformers. Examples include John Spargo's 1906 book *The Bitter Cry of Children*, dealing with the evils of child labor, and Lincoln Steffens's *The Shame of the Cities* (1904), focusing on municipal corruption. Novelists joined in the move to expose social ills, and because they offered plots with adventures and love stories along with their social message, they reached many more readers than Spargo's or Steffens's nonfictional accounts. Muckraking novels of the period include Upton Sinclair's *The Jungle* (1906), Frank Norris's *The Octopus* (1901), and Theodore Dreiser's *The Financier* (1912). The historian who wants to understand why Americans called for laws to prohibit child labor, protect consumers, regulate railroads and big business, and clean up graft can read these books. While these works make excellent historical sources, can you see any dangers in the historian's reliance on them as the only or main source of information about the period 1890–1917?

MULTIPLE-CHOICE QUESTIONS

Circle the letter of the item that best completes each statement or answers the question.

1. Which of the following muckrakers is correctly paired with the evils he/she exposed?
    a. Ida Wells-Barnett—lynching and racism
    b. Ida Tarbell—railroad abuses of small shippers and farmers
    c. Lincoln Steffens—banking and financial abuses
    d. David Graham Phillips—government corruption in New York and many other cities
2. The moral crusades of Progressive reformers led to
    a. the closing down of red-light districts in many cities.
    b. passage of the Mann Act (1910).
    c. creation of city and state film censorship boards.
    d. all of the above.
3. All of the following federal legislation was aimed at regulating railroads and other big business corporations *except* the
    a. Clayton Act.
    b. Hepburn Act.
    c. Payne-Aldrich Act.
    d. Federal Trade Commission Act.
4. Which of the following statements about the Niagara Movement is correct?
    a. It was founded and led by Booker T. Washington to promote his accommodationist message and combat the newly formed National Association for the Advancement of Colored People (NAACP).
    b. It brought together W. E. B. Du Bois, Ida Wells-Barnett, William Monroe Trotter, and other African-Americans who rejected Washington's leadership and called for militant resistance to racism.
    c. It was founded by a group of white Progressive reformers, led by Oswald Garrison Villard and Mary White Ovington, who wished to guide the African-American struggle for equality.
    d. It was founded by southern and northern white racists, including Madison Grant and Ben Tillman, to counter the militant demands for full equality coming from the recently established NAACP.

5. Which of the following Progressive Era laws aimed at protecting workers was declared unconstitutional by the U.S. Supreme Court?

    a. Adamson Act
    b. Oregon's Ten-Hour Law
    c. Keating-Owen Act
    d. Federal Workmen's Compensation Act

6. Which of the following statements about the National American Woman Suffrage Association is correct?

    a. It was led by Alice Paul who concentrated on putting pressure on Congress to pass a constitutional amendment enfranchising women.
    b. Its membership was made up almost entirely of white, middle-class, native-born women.
    c. It succeeded in its goal of winning the vote for women everywhere in the United States just before the country entered World War I.
    d. All of the above.

7. Which of the following was *not* an electoral reform designed to give people a more direct voice in politics and government?

    a. Initiative and referendum
    b. Seventeenth Amendment
    c. Eighteenth Amendment
    d. Direct primary

8. Which statement about the Progressive movement is correct?

    a. Progressives wanted to use the powers of government to restrain big business and protect the economically vulnerable.
    b. Most Progressives rejected the capitalist system, preferring one based on cooperation for the good of the whole community.
    c. Like the earlier Populist movement, the Progressive movement was primarily agrarian based.
    d. Progressives respected civil liberties so highly that they rejected any legislation that dealt with personal morals, such as sexual activities, drinking, and choice of entertainment.

9. All of the following promoted racism during the progressive era *except*

    a. Mary White Ovington.
    b. Madison Grant.
    c. D. W. Griffith.
    d. James K. Vardaman.

10. Which of these progressive women activists is *incorrectly* paired with the reform she fought for?

    a. Margaret Sanger—birth control
    b. Florence Kelley—banning child labor
    c. Carrie Chapman Catt—woman suffrage
    d. Elizabeth Gurley Flynn—temperance

SHORT-ANSWER QUESTIONS

1. Explain the ways in which the Populist and Progressive reform movements were similar. In what ways were they different?

2. Explain how the muckrakers helped to stimulate the Progressive reform movement. Cite three examples.

3. What were the records of Presidents Theodore Roosevelt and Woodrow Wilson on treatment of African-Americans?

4. Which groups of people were attracted to the Socialist Party of America and/or the Industrial Workers of the World in the period 1900–1917? Why?

5. Who founded the National Association for the Advancement of Colored People (NAACP)? Why? How did the founders of the NAACP differ in their ideas from Booker T. Washington?

6. What were some of the political and economic-social reforms enacted by state governments under the leadership of Progressive governors such as Robert La Follette? What was the Wisconsin Idea?

7. How did Theodore Roosevelt's handling of the 1902 coal miners strike differ from the actions of earlier presidents toward labor and strikes? Did the mineworkers benefit from Roosevelt's intervention?

8. Discuss the contributions of Theodore Roosevelt and his U.S. Forest Service chief, Gifford Pinchot, to the conservation movement. Why did Pinchot and the conservationists sometimes clash with John Muir and the preservationists? Was Roosevelt a preservationist? Which of his actions indicate he was or was not?

9. Explain the reasons for the break between President Taft and the Insurgent (progressive) Republicans. What were the political consequences of this break?

10. What were the main provisions of the Federal Reserve Act? How was it a compromise between those who favored government-owned and controlled banking and those who wanted to keep banking a private enterprise? Why is this law considered "Wilson's greatest legislative achievement"? What functions in the nation's economy today does the Federal Reserve serve?

ESSAY QUESTIONS

1. Discuss the roles played by women in the Progressive movement or movements.

2. One historian claims that "on the issue of racial justice," the record of the Progressives was "generally dismal." Do you agree with this statement? Why or why not? (Support your position with as many relevant examples as possible on the actions of various progressives.)

3. In Chapter 21 the author concludes that the "Progressive Era stands as a time when American politics seriously confronted the social upheavals caused by industrialization." But progressivism also had its illiberal and coercive side. Write an essay either agreeing or disagreeing with this assessment. Support your positions with as much specific evidence as possible.

4. The author of Chapter 21 asserts that "Progressive reform was not an American invention." U.S. progressives drew ideas from European and British Commonwealth nations, and overseas reformers learned from their American counterparts. Write an essay illustrating the interactions of progressive reformers in various countries in the late nineteenth and early twentieth centuries as they attempted "to cope with the social impact of rapid industrialization and urban growth."

5. One historian has written this about progressive reform: "The Roosevelt Era . . . had been a period of beginnings, of a scattering of pioneer legislation. . . . The Wilson Era, building on this foundation, was a period of sweeping achievement." Do you agree with this statement? Why or why not? Support your position with as much specific evidence as possible about the legislation passed during each president's administrations and the actions of each president.

ANSWERS TO MULTIPLE-CHOICE QUESTIONS

1. a
2. d
3. c
4. b
5. c
6. b
7. c
8. a
9. a
10. d

Global Involvements and World War I, 1902–1920

OUTLINE AND SUMMARY

I. Introduction

Chapter 22 focuses on U.S. foreign policy from 1902 to 1920, concentrating especially on U.S. involvement in World War I. After reading the chapter, you should be able to answer the following questions: (1) What objectives underlay U.S. foreign policy in Asia and Latin America? (2) Why did the United States enter World War I in 1917? (3) How did U.S. participation in World War I affect Americans at home? (4) During the war, how did the role of government in the U.S. economy and in people's lives generally change? (5) What part did President Wilson play in creating the League of Nations, and why did the U.S. Senate reject U.S. membership in the organization?

II. Defining America's World Role, 1902–1914

    A. The "Open Door": Competing for the China Market

American businessmen who dreamed of penetrating the Chinese market became alarmed at developments there. European powers were forcing the weak Chinese government to lease that country's ports to them, and then they closed those ports to trade and investment by business of any country but their own. U.S. secretary of state John Hay attempted to aid American business by sending his 1899 Open Door notes to the European powers involved, asking them to keep their leased Chinese ports open to trade and investment from all countries on equal terms. He received noncommittal replies. Soon thereafter the United States joined the European countries involved in China in putting down a Chinese uprising against foreign imperialists, known as the Boxer Rebellion. Some of the countries wanted to use the rebellion as an excuse for carving China into colonies for themselves. Hay announced U.S. opposition to this plan in his 1900 Open Door notes. He asked all countries to respect the territorial integrity of China and repeated the demand for equal trading and investment opportunities there. The Open Door notes became a cornerstone of U.S. policy in Asia and helped shape this country's response to the Japanese drive to conquer China in the 1930s.

    B. The Panama Canal: Hardball U.S. Diplomacy

For commercial and strategic reasons, the United States wanted to build a canal across the Isthmus of Panama. In 1902 the United States negotiated a treaty leasing a canal zone from Colombia, the country that owned the isthmus at the time. However, the Colombian senate, hoping for more money, rejected the treaty. An infuriated President Roosevelt conspired with the directors of a bankrupt French company that had been trying earlier to build a canal and hoped to profit from the United States' taking over its land lease. Philippe Bunau-Varilla, an official of the company, fomented revolution in Panama, and Roosevelt sent a U.S. warship in 1903 to see to it that the uprising succeeded. The United States then recognized Panama's independence and negotiated a treaty leasing the land, with Bunau-Varilla appointed to speak for Panama. The canal, a great engineering feat by the U.S.

Army, opened in 1914, but the imperialistic methods Roosevelt used to seize the area created lasting ill will toward the United States in Latin America.

C. Roosevelt and Taft Assert U.S. Power in Latin America and Asia
Theodore Roosevelt and his successor, William Howard Taft, believed that the United States had to play an active role in world affairs and protect American interests in Latin America and Asia. Taft concentrated particularly on promoting U.S. commercial interests abroad, a foreign policy referred to as dollar diplomacy.

In response to a threat that European nations might invade the Dominican Republic to collect debts owed their citizens on which that country had defaulted, Roosevelt, in 1904, announced his Roosevelt Corollary to the Monroe Doctrine. It warned European nations not to intervene in the Western Hemisphere. Instead, the United States would act as policeman in Latin America, keeping order there and seeing that finances were handled properly and debts repaid. Citing his corollary, Roosevelt had U.S. officials take over the Dominican Republic's customs service and manage its foreign debt. Taft, also using the corollary, sent marines into Nicaragua to protect U.S. investors there and keep in power a government friendly to U.S. business interests. The marines occupied Nicaragua from 1912 until 1933.

As part of his Asian policy, Roosevelt mediated an end to the Russo-Japanese War and used his influence to obtain a peace settlement that maintained the balance of power in Asia. Afterward, he tried to improved U.S. relations with Japan by negotiating a gentlemen's agreement under which Japan would limit emigration of its people to the United States. Roosevelt hoped this would cool American prejudice, but discrimination against Japanese immigrants in the western states continued anyway.

D. Wilson and Latin America
Despite criticizing Republican expansionism, Democratic president Woodrow Wilson proved just as interventionist in Latin America as Roosevelt and Taft. To keep order and create a favorable climate for American investors, Wilson ordered marines to occupy the Dominican Republic and Haiti. The marines stayed to supervise those governments until 1924 and 1934, respectively. Wilson repeatedly intervened in Mexico during its revolution, trying to bring to power leaders who were liberal, democratic, and friendly to capitalistic enterprise. U.S. foreign policy in Asia and Latin America between 1900 and 1914 showed that the United States was willing to become involved in foreign affairs to keep order, encourage the kinds of governments the United States approved of, and protect U.S. economic interests. These same tendencies would later pull the country into World War I.

III. War in Europe, 1914–1917
A. The Coming of War
A system of rival military alliances, imperialist expansion, and aggressive nationalism were all underlying causes of World War I in Europe. When, in June 1914, a Bosnian Serb nationalist assassinated Austrian Archduke Franz Ferdinand, Austria declared war on Serbia. Russia, bound by a secret agreement to protect Serbia, mobilized, and by the fall of 1914 the web of alliances had pulled all of the major European powers, except Italy, into "The Great War." Abandoning her earlier pact with Germany and Austria, Italy entered the war on the side of the Allies in 1915.

B. The Perils of Neutrality
As soon as the war began in Europe, President Wilson proclaimed U.S. neutrality and asked the American people to be neutral "in thought as well as in action." Most Americans agreed with Wilson that the United States should not fight, but few had neutral feelings. Wilson and the majority of Americans had emotional bonds with England.

Despite his initial proclamation of neutrality, Wilson asked Congress to declare war on Germany in 1917. What accounts for this turnabout? First, Wilson became convinced that, for the United States to shape the postwar settlement, it must participate in the fighting. Second, Wilson's handling of the issue of neutral rights on the high seas pulled the country into a war with Germany. The British violated our rights to trade by mining the North Sea and stopping ships and goods bound for Germany. Wilson's protests were not vigorous enough to prevent the British from ending almost all German-American trade. Germany retaliated with unrestricted submarine warfare. This led to injuries and the deaths of civilians, including Americans, in the sinking of Allied ships such as the *Lusitania* and the *Sussex*. In ever more threatening notes, Wilson warned Germany to stop unrestricted submarine warfare or the United States would break off diplomatic relations. Some congressional representatives, Secretary of State Bryan, and the founders of the Woman's Peace Party believed Wilson's policies would pull the country needlessly into the armed conflict. Finally, American citizens between 1914 and 1917 developed a large economic stake in an Allied victory, making neutrality much more difficult. U.S. trade with the Allies increased greatly, and American investors lent them $2.3 billion to finance these purchases, on which the United States' continued prosperity depended.

Between 1914 and 1917 the war on the Western Front in Europe degenerated into a bloody stalemate. British propaganda in the United States charged that the Germans were committing atrocities.

The war was a major issue in the 1916 election. Because the Democrats sensed the American public's desire for peace, Wilson ran for reelection reminding voters he hadn't gone to war. Charles Evans Hughes, the Republican candidate, sometimes called for a tougher stand against Germany and other times criticized Wilson for having been too threatening. Wilson's close victory seemed to indicate that the majority of Americans still hoped to avoid participation in the conflict.

C. The United States Enters the War
Because Germany decided that full use of its submarines would contribute more to its victory than keeping the United States out of the war, it fully unleashed its U-boats in January 1917. Wilson responded by breaking off diplomatic relations. During February and March, German U-boats attacked five American ships, and the United States learned of the Zimmermann telegram. On April 2, 1917, Wilson asked Congress to declare war on Germany, which it did after a short, bitter debate. Three important factors produced this declaration: German attacks on American shipping, U.S. economic investment in the Allied cause, and American cultural links to the Allies.

IV. Mobilizing at Home, Fighting in France, 1917–1918
A. Raising, Training, and Testing an Army
After declaring war on Germany, Congress passed the Selective Service Act, under which nearly 3 million men were drafted. Both volunteers and draftees were sent to home-front training camps, where the War Department monitored their behavior, warning them of the dangers of sex and drink. Psychologists administered their newly developed IQ tests, which, in fact, measured educational attainment rather than intelligence. The 12,000 Native Americans serving in the army were integrated with white troops, but the 260,000 African Americans were assigned to all-black units. The navy used blacks only in menial positions, while the marines excluded them entirely. Racist civilians provoked clashes with African-American soldiers stationed in Houston.

B.   Organizing the Economy for War
To mobilize the economy behind the war effort, the federal government imposed an unprecedented amount of regulation on American business. It did this by creating thousands of special wartime agencies. The most powerful of these, the War Industries Board, allocated scarce materials, established production priorities, and introduced more efficient production practices. The Food Administration encouraged farmers to increase output, while exhorting civilians to conserve food and fiber. The U.S. Railroad Administration consolidated all the privately owned rail lines into one, unified, government-operated system for the duration of the war. This government regulation, mostly dismantled after the armistice, did not prevent soaring wartime profits and encouraged corporate mergers.

C.   With the American Expeditionary Force in France
The American Expeditionary Force (AEF) sent some 2 million soldiers to France in 1917 and 1918. They arrived at a critical time for the Allies. After the Bolsheviks came to power in Russia, that country dropped out of the war, which freed the German armies on the Eastern Front to fight in the west. With these reinforcements, Germany launched an offensive in the spring of 1918 that brought its troops within 50 miles of Paris. American soldiers were rushed to the front, where they helped to stop the German advance. About 16,500 women also served with the AEF in such noncombat positions as nurses, telephone operators, and clerical workers.

D.   Turning the Tide
By July 1918 U.S. troops were participating in the Allied counteroffensive that, through the summer and fall, drove the Germans out of much of France. Among them were several African-American regiments that served with distinction; one received the French *Croix de Guerre*. In the often brutal fighting, soldiers lost their illusions about war being a great adventure. An influenza epidemic that swept Europe and the United States in 1918 added to the suffering and death.

V.   Promoting the War and Suppressing Dissent
A.   Advertising the War
Wilson believed that the federal government must promote unanimous support for the war. Secretary of the Treasury William G. McAdoo pioneered in using advertising techniques and propaganda to sell war bonds. With posters, parades, and movie stars as sales promoters, McAdoo was able to sell enough bonds to finance approximately two-thirds of the war costs. The remainder was paid for with increased federal income and other taxes. The main job of popularizing the war fell to George Creel's Committee on Public Information. It created posters, advertisements, news releases, and films and sent seventy-five thousand speakers around the nation. Many progressive reformers, muckrakers, teachers, and religious leaders supported the war, echoing Wilson's assertion that we were in a struggle to spread liberalism, democracy, and other American values.

B.   Wartime Intolerance and Dissent
The Creel committee's propaganda produced a wave of anti-German hysteria and hatred of anyone who questioned America's participation in the war. As fear and intolerance mounted, German-Americans where victimized, and antiwar radicals were verbally and physically attacked.

C.   Opponents of the War
Despite all the "patriotic" pressure, some Americans continued to oppose the war. These included some German-Americans and religious pacifists. A minority of women's rights and progressive leaders, such as Jane Addams, and Randolph Bourne, pointed out that the war was killing reform and unleashing reaction and intolerance. Many socialists branded the war

a crusade to protect capitalists' profits and saw no reason for workers to die to enrich their bosses. There was also considerable resistance to the draft in the rural South.

D. Suppressing Dissent by Law
The government attempted to silence these dissenters with the repressive Espionage and Sedition Acts. These made it a crime to criticize the war, government, Constitution, or armed forces. Some fifteen hundred people were convicted and jailed; the Socialist Party of America's leader, Eugene Debs, among them. The Supreme Court upheld the constitutionality of the laws with the "clear and present danger" doctrine.

VI. Economic and Social Trends in Wartime America
A. Boom Times in Industry and Agriculture
Stimulated by war, the American economy boomed. The real income of farmers and unskilled workers rose significantly. Thousands of workers streamed into industrial centers to take jobs in war plants. The influx created terrible housing, school, and other shortages in these cities.

B. African-Americans Migrate Northward
Reduced immigration and soaring war production created labor shortages in northern industry. From labor recruiters, African-American-owned newspapers, letters, and word of mouth, southern African-Americans learned of these new job opportunities. Hoping to escape southern racism and find good jobs, an estimated half a million African-American people migrated to the North. In northern cities whites resented the African-American newcomers, who competed for jobs and housing. In places such as East St. Louis, Illinois, race riots broke out.

C. Women in Wartime
Many women's rights activists hoped that the war would lead to equality for women. During the war, thousands of women served in the military and in volunteer organizations. About 1 million took jobs in industry. Arguing that women should be rewarded for their major contributions to winning the war, the woman-suffrage movement finally got the Nineteenth Amendment added to the Constitution in 1920. Aside from the vote, women lost many of their wartime gains after the armistice. Those holding well-paying jobs in industry generally were replaced by men returning from wartime service.

D. Public Health Crisis: The 1918 Influenza Pandemic
In the midst of war, a worldwide outbreak of influenza killed some 30 million people. Six times as many Americans (555,000) died of the flu as were slaughtered in battle in France. Army camps and cities were particularly hard hit.

E. The War and Progressivism
The war strengthened the prohibition movement. The antiliquor forces argued that the "unpatriotic" German-American brewers should be put out of business and that grain used to manufacture whiskey and gin would be better used to feed the armed forces and our allies. In this atmosphere, the Eighteenth Amendment, banning the manufacture, transportation, or sale of alcoholic beverages, was ratified by 1919. The war also boosted the Progressive Era antiprostitution campaign and produced a brief flurry of protective labor laws, but in most other areas the intolerant, repressive war atmosphere stifled progressivism.

VII. Joyous Armistice, Bitter Aftermath, 1918–1920
A. Wilson's Fourteen Points; the Armistice
Wilson presented his fourteen-point peace plan in a speech to Congress in January 1918. It included self-determination, impartial adjustment of colonial claims, freedom of the seas, reduced armaments, and a world association of nations, among other proposals. Whether

Wilson could get these ideas incorporated in the treaties signed at the end of the war remained to be seen. In October 1918 the Kaiser's government asked Wilson for an armistice based on the Fourteen Points. Almost immediately afterward revolutionaries in Germany deposed the Kaiser and proclaimed a republic. Representatives of the new republic signed the armistice with the Allies on November 11, 1918.

B.   The Versailles Peace Conference, 1919
Wilson personally headed the American delegation to Versailles. He appointed no prominent Republicans to the delegation, a political mistake since a Republican-controlled Senate would have to ratify any treaty signed. At the conference Wilson had to compromise with the Allied leaders; David Lloyd George, Georges Clemençeau, and Vittorio Orlando, who had no faith in his Fourteen Points. The Treaty of Versailles that they produced contained some of Wilson's points, such as independence for Poland and the Baltic states, but overall the treaty was harsh and punitive and aroused resentment and desire for revenge in Germany. Wilson and the Allied leaders also attempted to overthrow the Bolsheviks in Russia and to isolate and weaken that Communist-controlled nation.

C.   The Fight over the League of Nations
Dismayed at the treaty's punitive features, Wilson concentrated his hopes on the League of Nations part of it. In July 1919 Wilson submitted the Treaty of Versailles to the Senate for ratification. There it ran afoul of Republican reservationists, led by Henry Cabot Lodge, and isolationists. Out of a mixture of partisanship and fear that U.S. participation in the league would embroil the country in future European wars, the Republicans demanded changes in the treaty. Had Wilson been willing to accept the modifications (reservations) that Lodge proposed concerning the league, the treaty would have been approved. Wilson, however, refused to compromise, and in votes on the treaty and league in November 1919 and March 1920, the Senate failed to ratify by the necessary two-thirds.

D.   Racism and Red Scare, 1919–1920
The war-generated intolerance and antiradical hysteria reached a peak in 1919–1920. Lynch mobs killed seventy-six blacks, and race riots broke out in more than twenty-five cities; the bloodiest occurred in Chicago. A rash of postwar strikes and a series of bombing incidents convinced many Americans that the country was on the verge of a communist uprising. To protect against this supposed danger, the Justice Department, under A. Mitchell Palmer, raided the homes and meeting places of suspected radicals and arrested more than four thousand of them, although there was no evidence that they had committed any crime. Aliens suspected of radicalism were deported.

E.   The Election of 1920
The election of 1920 came in the midst of the violence and repression. The Democratic candidate, James Cox, was soundly defeated by Republican Warren G. Harding, who appealed to the public with his promise of a return to "normalcy." Harding's victory ended any chance for U.S. membership and participation in the league.

VIII. Conclusion
World War I brought death to 10 million people worldwide, including 112,000 Americans. The war transformed American society, helped finally to pass the Eighteenth and Nineteenth amendments, and gave the country its first taste of active government regulation of the economy. Although Washington retreated from activism in the 1920s and Progressive reform seemed dead, during the Great Depression of the 1930s some of these World War I regulatory agencies and social programs would serve as models for the New Deal of Franklin D. Roosevelt. In the short run, however, the intolerance and repression that grew during the war arrested further Progressive reform.

VOCABULARY

The following terms are used in Chapter 22. To understand the chapter fully, it is important that you know what each of them means.

belligerent	a country at war
territorial integrity	the condition of a country being whole, entire, and self-governing rather than broken up into colonies of other countries
liberal	favorable to progress and reform in economic and political affairs and to individual self-expression and liberty; associated with representative government rather than aristocratic, authoritarian, or dictatorial rule
coup	the act of a small group in bringing about a sudden change of government illegally and/or by force
armistice	a truce; a suspension of fighting by agreement of the parties so they can discuss peace terms
dissent	the disagreement with the majority opinion and/or that of the authorities, such as the government
sedition	the incitement of resistance or rebellion against the government; action or language promoting such resistance
self-determination	the freedom of a people or nationality to decide for itself the form of government it shall have
convoy	a group of ships moving together, guarded by warships for their protection
abdicate	give up power and the right to govern
reparations	compensation in money, material, labor, and the like, by a defeated nation for damage done to civilian populations and property during war
mandate or trusteeship	a commission given to one nation by an associated group of nations (such as the League of Nations) to administer the government and affairs of a people in a territory judged not yet ready for self-government and independence

IDENTIFICATIONS

After reading Chapter 22, you should be able to identify and explain the historical significance of each of the following:

gentlemen's agreement

dollar diplomacy

U-boats and unrestricted submarine warfare

National Security League and preparedness

Bernard Baruch and the War Industries Board

Herbert Hoover and the Food Administration

Vladimir Lenin, Leon Trotsky, and the Bolsheviks

George Creel and the Committee on Public Information

East St. Louis race riot, 1917; Chicago race riot, 1919

Wilson's fourteen-point peace plan

Treaty of Versailles and Covenant of the League of Nations

Henry Cabot Lodge, Reservationists, and Irreconcilables

SKILL BUILDING: MAPS

1. On the world map on the next page, locate the following places and explain how each of them was connected with U.S. foreign policy between 1902 and 1917:

    Panama

    Panama Canal

    Colombia

    Dominican Republic

    Mexico

    China

    Japan

    Haiti

    Manchuria

    Korea

    Russia

    Nicaragua

2. On the map of Europe during World War I, (1) indicate the Allied powers, the Central powers, and the neutral countries; (2) indicate the areas and names of the countries occupied by the Central powers at the time of their greatest success; (3) locate Sarajevo, and explain its significance; (4) locate the Marne and Meuse Rivers, the Argonne Forest, and Verdun, and explain their significance in the war on the Western Front; and (5) draw in the Armistice Line of November 11, 1918.

3. On the post–World War I map of Europe, (1) indicate the territories taken from Germany, (2) indicate the territories taken from Russia, (3) indicate the new nations created at the end of the war, (4) show what remained of Austria.

World Map About 1900

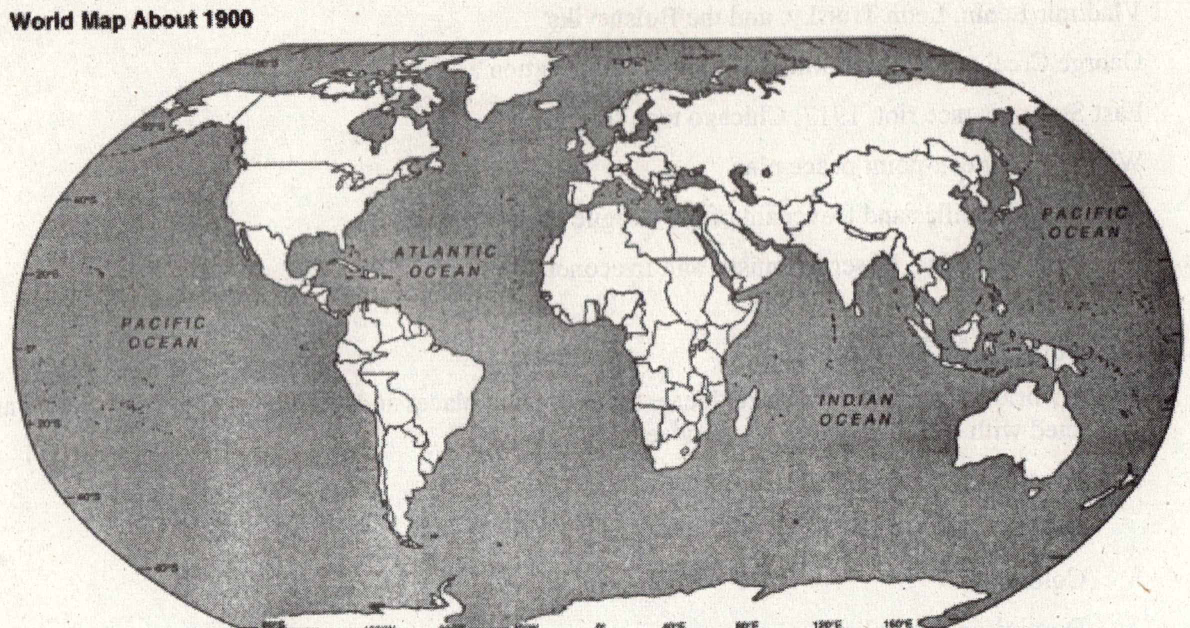

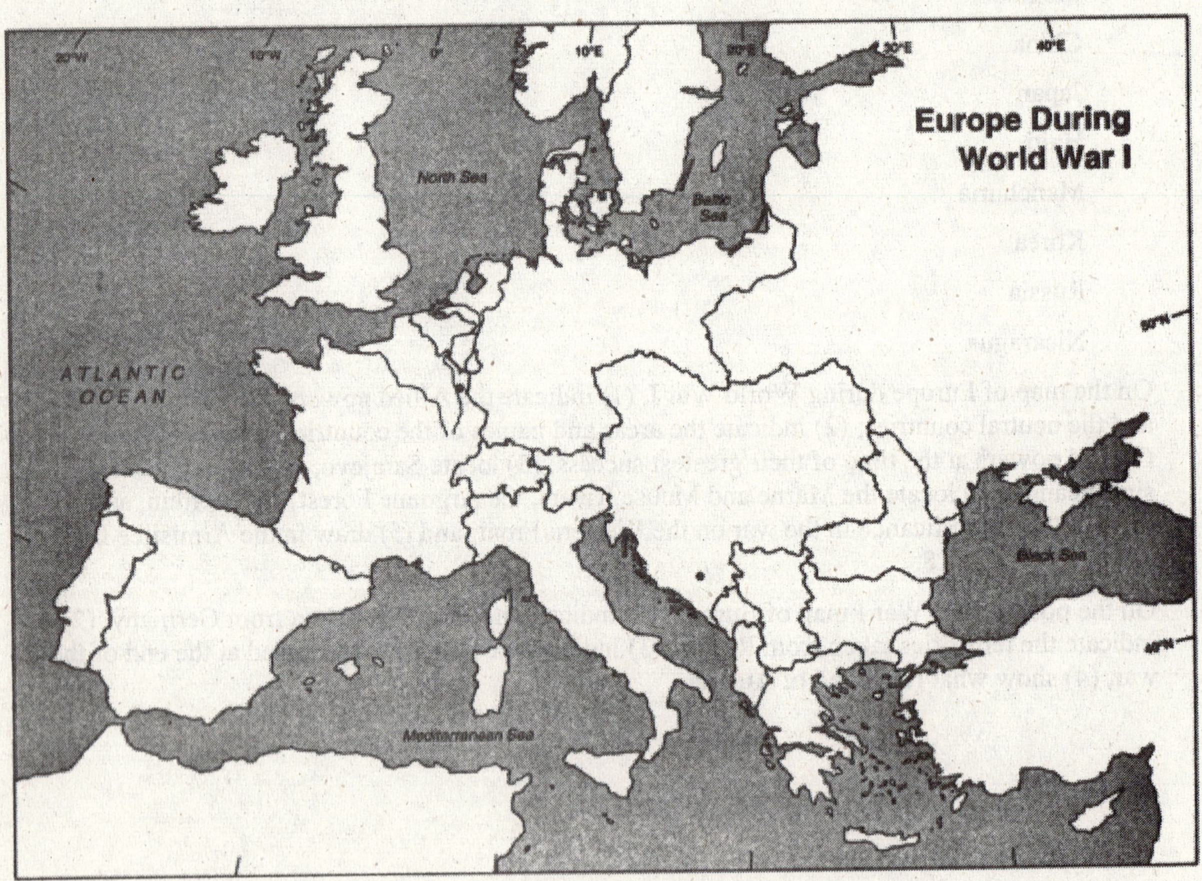

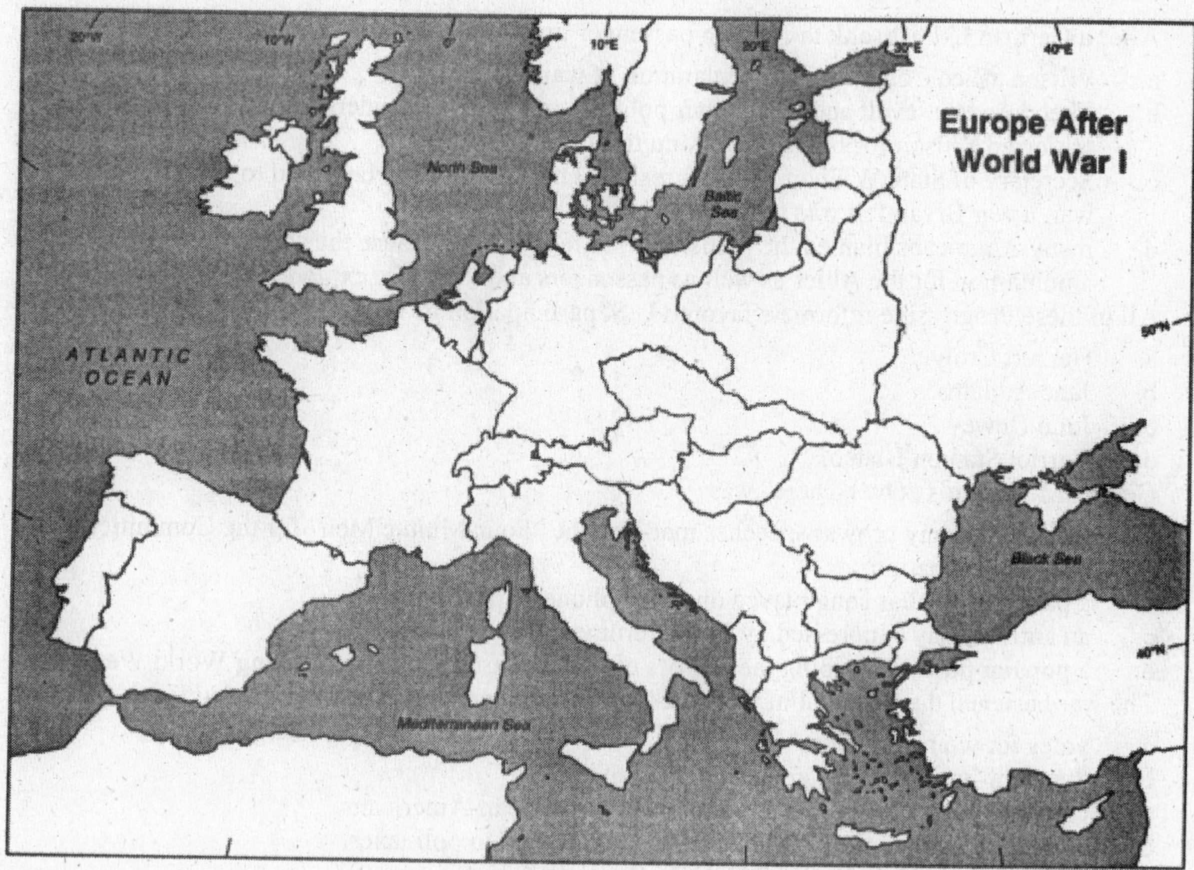

MULTIPLE-CHOICE QUESTIONS

Circle the letter of the item that best completes each statement or answers the question.

1. Who was responsible for largely eradicating yellow fever from Panama?
   a. Walter Reed
   b. John Hay
   c. John J. Pershing
   d. Philippe Bunau-Varilla

2. In the first seventeen years of the twentieth century, the United States intervened with military force in all of the following places *except*
   a. Nicaragua.
   b. Mexico.
   c. Jamaica.
   d. Haiti.

3. After a German U-boat sank the British passenger liner, the *Lusitania,*

    a. Wilson asked Congress for a declaration of war on Germany.
    b. Theodore Roosevelt and some other political and business leaders called for war and criticized Wilson for being "too proud to fight."
    c. Secretary of State William J. Bryan resigned because Wilson hesitated to ask Congress for war, a war Bryan felt was more than justified.
    d. many Americans blamed the British for the loss of life because the ship was carrying ammunition for the Allies as well as passengers and therefore exploded and sank quickly.

4. All of these Progressive reformers favored U.S. participation in World War I *except*

    a. Herbert Croly.
    b. Jane Addams.
    c. John Dewey.
    d. Harriot Stanton Blatch.

5. George M. Cohan's "Over There" was

    a. one of the many prowar speeches made by the "Four-Minute Men" for the Committee on Public Information.
    b. a patriotic popular song played on many phonographs.
    c. an antiwar play suppressed by the government during World War I.
    d. a popular poem describing the horrors of trench warfare in France during World War I.

6. The war hastened the approval of two constitutional amendments. These provided for

    a. votes for women and prohibition.
    b. the eight-hour workday and an end to child labor.
    c. equal pay for men and women and votes for African-Americans.
    d. direct popular election of U.S. senators and an end to poll taxes.

7. In the case of *Schenck* v. *United States,* the Supreme Court

    a. held that the U.S. Railroad Administration had acted unconstitutionally in taking over privately owned rail lines.
    b. upheld convictions under the Espionage Act on the grounds that free speech could be curtailed when it presented a "clear and present danger" to the country.
    c. ruled that segregated facilities for whites and African-Americans were acceptable as long as the accommodations were equal.
    d. held that the federal government did *not* have the right to propagandize its own people as George Creel's Committee on Public Information was doing.

8. Which of the following statements is *not* true of the Wilson administration during World War I?

    a. It took over and ran the railroads and imposed greater federal regulation over the economy than ever before in U.S. history.
    b. It set up a federal agency to build public support for the war with news releases, posters, speakers, and other propaganda.
    c. It interned all Japanese-Americans in ten guarded camps until the war was won.
    d. It sold millions of dollars worth of government bonds to Americans through techniques learned from advertising and public relations.

9. The Treaty of Versailles

    a. resembled for the most part Wilson's fourteen-point peace plan.
    b. turned over to Russia large blocks of territory in eastern Europe.
    c. disarmed Germany and stripped her of her colonies.
    d. failed to create an association of nations as Wilson had promised it would.

10. In the two years immediately after World War I, the United States
    a. enjoyed improved relations and cooperation between labor and management.
    b. joined the League of Nations and began to play a larger role in world affairs.
    c. showed a renewed interest in progressive reform and elected an administration promising to carry on Wilson's New Freedom.
    d. experienced heightened racial violence and antiradical hysteria.

SHORT-ANSWER QUESTIONS

1. Why did Secretary of State John Hay write his Open Door Notes of 1899 and 1900? What did they say? With what country did the United States increasingly conflict in the 1930s and early 1940s in our attempt to uphold the Open Door policy?

2. Theodore Roosevelt said, "I took the Canal Zone." Explain how he took it. What were the consequences of his actions for the United States?

3. What was the Roosevelt Corollary to the Monroe Doctrine? Why did Roosevelt issue it? Where did he first apply it?

4. After a German submarine sank the *Sussex*, a French passenger ship, in 1916, what did Wilson threaten to do? How did the Germans respond to this *Sussex* threat? Did it appear that Wilson had stopped unrestricted submarine warfare by diplomacy? When and why did the submarine crisis with Germany flare up again?

5. What effect did the Zimmermann telegram and the March 1917 revolution in Russia have on Wilson's and the American public's willingness to go to war with Germany? Why?

6. Discuss the experiences of African-Americans in the U.S. armed forces during World War I.

7. Discuss the people who opposed U.S. entry into World War I. Who were they? Why did they oppose participation?

8. How did World War I help gain passage and ratification of the Eighteenth and Nineteenth Amendments?

9. Wilson claimed one of the reasons for U.S. entry into World War I was to make the world safe for democracy, but, ironically, government policies during and for a time after the war nearly killed democracy in the United States. Explain and illustrate this statement.

10. What caused the Red Scare of 1919–1920? What actions did U.S. attorney general A. Mitchell Palmer take during the scare?

ESSAY QUESTIONS

1. The author of Chapter 22 claims that between the 1890s and 1920 "America's dealings with Asian and Latin American nations . . . were shaped by both economic and ideological considerations." "U.S. policy makers wanted to expand corporate America's access to foreign markets and raw materials. . . ." They also wanted to spread democracy, freedom, and law and order. Write an essay on U.S. foreign policy in Latin America and Asia from 1899 to 1920 in which you support or refute this statement with as much specific evidence as possible.

2. In 1914 Woodrow Wilson proclaimed U.S. neutrality and asked the American people to be neutral in thought as well as action. In April 1917 Wilson asked Congress to declare war on Germany. What caused this turnaround in U.S. policy toward World War I?

3.   During World War I how did the U.S. government attempt to mobilize the economy, influence public opinion, and silence all dissent?

4.   Discuss the impact of World War I on the home front. Include in your answer the effects of the war on business, labor, agriculture, African-Americans, women, and the Progressive reform movement.

5.   Woodrow Wilson wanted to reach a liberal settlement at the end of the war that would ensure peace and democracy for generations thereafter. What prevented the realization of his plans? (In your answer consider the obstacles presented by the leaders of the other allied powers, the actions of the U.S. Senate, and how his own behavior may have contributed to the failure of his plans.)

ANSWERS TO MULTIPLE-CHOICE QUESTIONS

1. a
2. c
3. b
4. b
5. b
6. a
7. b
8. c
9. c
10. d

CHAPTER 23

The 1920s: Coping with Change, 1920–1929

OUTLINE AND SUMMARY

I. Introduction

In many ways modern America began in the "Roaring Twenties." It was a time of rapid economic growth, technological advances, and changing social and cultural values. With millions of cars coming off Detroit's assembly lines, Americans took to the roads. They were entertained by movies and radio programs, and they bought an array of new consumer products. All of these new developments in society stimulated great artistic creativity, but also contributed to social tensions, fears, and culture wars.

As you read Chapter 23, ponder the following questions: (1) Why was the economy so prosperous in the 1920s, and how were different social groups affected by the economic boom? (2) What were the dominant political values of the 1920s, and how did the Republican presidents of the period represent them? (3) What was the new popular culture of the decade, and which Americans did it barely touch? (4) What developments in the period contributed to both the social tensions and the artistic flowering?

II. A New Economic Order

A. Booming Business, Ailing Agriculture

Demobilization following World War I disrupted the economy, causing a sharp recession. By 1922 recovery had set in, and for the rest of the decade the economy grew rapidly and prospered. Development of the electric appliance (refrigerators, washing machines, and vacuum cleaners) and automobile industries contributed to this economic growth and prosperity. Mass production of cars created hundreds of thousands of jobs and stimulated a host of related industries, such as rubber, oil, steel, and highway construction. American business also invested heavily abroad during the 1920s, and loaned money to European nations to help them repay war debts. However, high protective tariffs in the 1920s tended to suppress international trade. Although wages rose overall during the decade, many workers did not share in the pay increases. Southern, African-American, Mexican-American, recent immigrant, and female workers clustered at the bottom of the wage scale.

American farmers did well during World War I, but after the armistice, both the European and domestic markets contracted, and prices plunged. Farmers, hard pressed to repay loans and meet mortgage payments, tried to compensate by growing more. This created surpluses that drove down produce prices further. Agriculture remained a depressed sector of the economy throughout the decade.

B. New Modes of Producing, Managing, and Selling

Introduction of the assembly line and other technological advances brought more than a 40 percent increase in productivity between 1919 and 1929. This led to bigger profits and a wave of corporate mergers. By 1930 one hundred corporations controlled almost half the business done in the United States. Competition also disappeared as corporations joined together in trade associations to fix prices and divide markets, and networks of chain stores displaced small, independently owned retail stores. Big business successfully boosted sales and profits by introducing installment buying and relying more heavily than ever on advertising. Business influence and values pervaded all areas of American life in the 1920s: big businessmen became the new cultural heroes, politicians vied to serve business, and organized religion tried to copy its selling techniques.

C.   Women in the New Economic Era
The proportion of women working outside the home stayed at about 24 percent throughout the decade. Working women earned less than men holding similar jobs. The growth of large corporations increased the need for secretaries, typists, and filing clerks, and most of these positions were taken by women. Few women, however, broke into management or the professions, other than the traditionally female ones, such as teaching and nursing.

D.   Struggling Labor Unions in a Business Age
The 1920s were an unsuccessful time for organized labor. Union membership fell from 5 million in 1920 to 3.4 million in 1929. Management discouraged the growth of unions by intimidation, violence, insistence on the open shop, use of scab labor during strikes, and the introduction by some companies of benefits such as stock purchase plans. Employers often charged, even when it was not true, that unions and strikes were Communist led.

III.   The Harding and Coolidge Administrations
A.   Stand Pat Politics in a Decade of Change
A conservative-controlled Republican convention in 1920 nominated Warren G. Harding for president. He then won handily over his Democratic opponent, James M. Cox. The Harding administration was riddled with corruption. Veterans' Bureau chief Charles Forbes stole bureau funds. Attorney General Harry Daugherty and his Justice Department underlings sold influence and immunity from prosecution. Secretary of the Interior Albert Fall leased government oil reserves at Teapot Dome, Wyoming, and other locations to favored businessmen in exchange for bribes. On Harding's death, Coolidge assumed the presidency.

B.   Republican Policy Making in a Probusiness Era
In the Coolidge administration corruption lessened, but the probusiness attitudes continued. High tariffs protected domestic manufacturers from foreign competition. Espousing the "trickle down" theory, Secretary of the Treasury Andrew Mellon convinced Congress to lower federal taxes for the wealthy. Under Chief Justice William Howard Taft, a Harding appointee, the Supreme Court declared the federal child labor law unconstitutional.

While promoting government assistance to business, Coolidge opposed federal aid to all other groups. He refused to extend relief to 1927 flood victims and twice vetoed the McNary-Haugen bill, which proposed to have Washington buy up surplus farm commodities at good prices.

C.   Independent Internationalism
In the 1920s, the United States followed an independent internationalism, protecting what it saw as U. S. global interests alone, rather than joining the League of Nations and the World Court. When a new arms race began, Harding's Secretary of State, Charles E. Hughes, called an international naval arms conference in Washington, D.C., in 1921. Out of the conference emerged treaties that imposed a ten-year moratorium on battleship construction and pledged the major powers to respect each other's territorial possessions in the Pacific. The 1920s Republican administrations also insisted that the World War I allies repay a portion of their war debts to the United States, and then made it difficult for them to do so by curtailing their sales in the United States with high protective tariffs.

D.   Progressive Stirrings, Democratic Party Divisions
Progressive reform sentiment did not completely disappear in the 1920s. A coalition of labor and farm groups in 1924 revived the Progressive Party and nominated Robert La Follette for president. A Democratic Party badly split between its urban and rural wings nominated an unappealing compromise candidate, John W. Davis. With the economy booming, the Republican incumbent, Calvin Coolidge, won the presidency easily.

E.   Women and Politics in the 1920s: A Dream Deferred
Ratification of the Nineteenth Amendment granting women the vote had less impact on politics in the 1920s than many women's rights advocates had predicted. During this period the women's movement splintered: some feminists backed an equal rights amendment; others feared it would undermine laws protecting female workers.

IV.   Mass Society, Mass Culture
A.   Cities, Cars, Consumer Goods
This was the first decade in which the majority of Americans lived in cities. Throughout the 1920s city life-styles and values spread to more and more of the population. The new consumer goods were most readily available to city dwellers. New electric appliances transformed household duties, as did the rise of supermarkets and commercial bakeries. Automobiles had the biggest impact on American culture. Traffic jams, parking problems, mounting accidental deaths, reduced parental supervision of young adults, and the spread of suburbs are examples of the changes brought about by cars.

B.   Soaring Energy Consumption and a Threatened Environment
The mass production and sales of automobiles and electric appliances took a heavy toll on the environment and natural resources. Generating enough electricity to power the new appliances consumed millions of tons of coal, but the most voracious users of oil and gasoline were the millions of automobiles. Not only did the nation waste and heedlessly deplete fossil fuels, but cars, power plants, steel mills, and other industries supplying the ever-growing demand for energy polluted the atmosphere. Cars also made it easier for people to visit wilderness areas, but tourists' demands for good roads, hotels, and other amenities in pristine areas soon threatened to ruin them. A few groups protested, but Americans on the whole were indifferent to the environmental threat.

C.   Mass-Produced Entertainment
As assembly-line production made work less fulfilling and time-consuming, Americans turned increasingly to mass-produced entertainment for gratification. Popular magazines, such as *Reader's Digest,* built massive circulations. All over the United States people listened to the same radio programs and watched the same movies, thus producing a more homogeneous national culture. However, the new standardized culture did not permeate all segments of the United States. In rural areas evangelical Christians denounced much of it as godless. Mexican-Americans and African-Americans in the rural South and the urban ghettoes maintained most of their own vibrant ethnic folkways.

D.   Celebrity Culture
Mass communication made possible by radio and film created nationwide heroes and media events. Americans loved sports celebrities like Babe Ruth, Ty Cobb, and Jack Dempsey and showered wild acclaim on Charles A. Lindbergh for his solo flight across the Atlantic.

V.   Cultural Ferment and Creativity
A.   The Jazz Age and the Postwar Crisis of Values
In the so-called Jazz Age, some young people rejected the values of their elders on sexual matters, dress, and decorum. The ideas of Sigmund Freud became popular. Women asserted

their freedom by discussing sex openly, wearing makeup, smoking, and shortening their skirts and their hair. This upheaval in manners and morals primarily affected the urban middle class. Most farmers, African-Americans, industrial workers, and recent immigrants were more concerned with economic survival than experimenting with new life-styles.

B.   Alienated Writers
The decade saw the emergence of many talented writers, including Sinclair Lewis, Ernest Hemingway, and F. Scott Fitzgerald. They were often critical of both the narrow-minded, small-town values of prewar America and the materialistic business culture of the twenties. Some felt so uncomfortable with 1920s America that they spent much of the decade abroad, and yet they cared deeply about finding and creating an "authentic" American culture through their works.

In his *American Mercury* magazine, Henry L. Mencken championed the works of these new writers and kept up a steady barrage of ridicule of American politics and society.

C.   Architects, Painters, and Musicians Confront Modern America
American cities in the 1920s were filled with skyscrapers, an architectural trend applauded by many and denounced by others. More than ever, American artists painted the American scene, urban and rural, past and present. Some of the most talented were Thomas Hart Benton, Edward Hopper, Joseph Stella, and Georgia O'Keeffe. New classical composers appeared, such as Aaron Copland, but the unique contribution of America to the musical world was jazz. In the twenties composers and performers such as George Gershwin, Jelly Roll Morton, Louis Armstrong, and Duke Ellington gained national and international recognition.

D.   The Harlem Renaissance
In the 1920s, the growing African-American population in northern cities, especially New York, stimulated a flowering of creative activity known as the Harlem Renaissance. The concentration in New York of recording companies, book and magazine publishers, theater productions, and African-American civil-rights organizations, such as the NAACP headquarters, drew African-American artists, writers, composers, musicians, and intellectuals from all over the United States and the West Indies to Harlem. Whites flocked to Harlem's jazz clubs to hear these musicians. All-black stage shows played on Broadway. White-owned publishing houses printed the novels and short stories of Langston Hughes, Claude McKay, and other African-American writers who explored the African-American experience in their works. Some sympathetic whites also produced works portraying African-American life, such as George Gershwin's musical *Porgy and Bess*. However, many whites held romanticized and stereotyped views of Harlem and African-Americans.

VI. A Society in Conflict
A.   Immigration Restriction
The United States, in 1924 and 1929, passed restrictive laws that drastically cut the total number of immigrants permitted to enter the country and established quotas for each nationality. Reflecting the fears and intolerance of the time, the laws excluded Chinese and Japanese entirely, and eastern and southern Europeans received small quotas. As a result of these restrictive laws, total immigration into the United States fell from the average 1 million a year in the period 1900–1914 to 280,000 in 1929. This discriminatory, national-origins quota system remained in U.S. law until 1965.

B.   Needed Workers/Unwelcome Aliens: Hispanic Newcomers
The 1920s National Origins Act did not curtail immigration from Western Hemisphere countries, which continued to be heavy in the 1920s. By 1930, about 2 million Mexicans had arrived in the United States. Most lived in the Southwest and worked in agriculture.

While agribusiness wanted their cheap labor, the Mexicans experienced bitter resentment from nativist Americans.

C.   Nativism, Anti-Radicalism, and the Sacco-Vanzetti Case
The Sacco-Vanzetti case further illustrates the intolerance and divisions in society in the 1920s. Nicola Sacco and Bartolomeo Vanzetti were Italian immigrants who were convicted of robbery and murder. The evidence was circumstantial, but the prosecution probably prejudiced the jury against them by stressing their ethnic origin and political radicalism. Throughout the decade, conservatives successfully opposed the attempts of liberals to win a new trial for the pair, and they were executed in 1927.

D.   Fundamentalism and the Scopes Trial
Several states passed laws prohibiting the teaching of any scientific theory that contradicted the account of human origin given in the Bible. When John T. Scopes, a high school teacher in Dayton, Tennessee, challenged his state's law, the American Civil Liberties Union hired a team of distinguished lawyers, headed by Clarence Darrow, to defend him. William Jennings Bryan assisted the prosecution. Although Scopes was convicted, the fundamentalist religious position was ridiculed in the courtroom and in the national press. Nonetheless, flashy evangelists like Billy Sunday and Aimee Semple McPherson attracted huge audiences throughout the 1920s. More states passed anti-evolution laws, and textbook publishers deleted mention of Darwin's theories to appease local school boards.

E.   The Ku Klux Klan
Another indication of social conflict and intolerance in the twenties was the rise of the Ku Klux Klan. Preaching hatred toward blacks, Jews, Catholics, immigrants, and the new urban values, the Klan grew to an estimated 5 million members. For a time it exerted real political power in a few states, including Oregon and Oklahoma. It threatened, intimidated, beat, and murdered those it considered to be dangerous to a "purified" America.

F.   The Garvey Movement
Disillusioned to find the North almost as racist as the South, many poor urban African-Americans in the 1920s became followers of Marcus Garvey and his Universal Negro Improvement Association (UNIA). Garvey preached black pride, black "economic solidarity," and a return to Africa. At its peak the UNIA had 80,000 members and became the first mass movement among African-Americans.

G.   Prohibition: Cultures in Conflict
Prohibition split Americans. Its supporters were generally native-born, fundamentalist Protestants, especially those in rural areas. Its opponents included liberals, intellectuals, rebellious youths, and big-city immigrants. Enforcement of prohibition broke down almost immediately because many Americans did not believe in it and organized crime was busy supplying the demand for illegal liquor. Prohibition became a big issue in the 1928 election. Democrat Alfred E. Smith called for its repeal; Republican Herbert Hoover praised it as a "noble experiment."

VII. Hoover at the Helm
A.   The Election of 1928
Herbert Hoover won the election by a landslide over Alfred Smith. Many rural, fundamentalist Protestants would not vote for Smith because he was a Catholic and a "wet" and he came from New York City, but the biggest reason for Hoover's victory was economic prosperity and Republican promises that things would get even better.

B.   Herbert Hoover's Social Thought

Hoover encouraged voluntary cooperation among corporate leaders to raise wages, plan production and marketing, and standardize products. He believed that kind of self-regulation by business, rather than government intervention, would ensure economic growth and a better life for all. After the depression set in, his clinging to voluntarism and reluctance to use government power would greatly handicap his ability to deal with a sick economy.

VIII. Conclusion

In the 1920s Americans tried to adjust to the mass production, mass culture, and urban society that had emerged. The decade's political leadership was for the most part conservative and backward looking. Those who found this new world unfamiliar and threatening often reacted with repression and hate, like the champions of prohibition, the fundamentalists, and the Klansmen. Others embraced the new life-styles made possible by radios, cars, movies, and electric appliances. The social ferment also produced an outpouring of creative energy: the Harlem Renaissance, jazz, and American literature.

VOCABULARY

The following terms are used in Chapter 23. To understand the chapter fully, it is important that you know what each of them means.

scabs	workers who take strikers' jobs
isolationist	one who favors a policy of nonparticipation in international affairs
reactionary	Favoring return to an earlier political or social order or policy
suffrage	the vote
materialistic	more devoted to accumulating products and possessions than to spiritual needs and considerations
expatriates	persons who have withdrawn themselves from residence in their native country
nativism	the policy of protecting the interests or ways of native inhabitants against those of immigrants; prejudice against or dislike for immigrants
hedonism	way of life devoted to pleasure
fundamentalism	a movement in American Protestantism that preaches that everything in the Bible is literally true and rejects any historical account or scientific theory that differs from biblical statements
speakeasies	places where liquor was illegally sold and consumed

IDENTIFICATIONS

After reading Chapter 23, you should be able to identify and explain the historical significance of each of the following:

Gastonia, North Carolina, and other textile mill strikes, 1929

the open shop and the "American Plan"

Andrew Mellon and the "trickle down" theory

the flapper and the "New Woman"

F. Scott Fitzgerald

Ernest Hemingway

Georgia O'Keeffe

Edward Hopper

George Gershwin

Duke Ellington

Sacco and Vanzetti

Marcus Garvey and the Universal Negro Improvement Association

Volstead Act, "wets," and "drys"

Alfred E. Smith versus Herbert Hoover

SKILL BUILDING: GRAPHS AND CHARTS

Graphs and charts allow us to convey important historical information and trends in visual shorthand. Look at the graphs and charts in Chapter 23 as examples. First, glance at the line graph "Economic Expansion, 1920–1929" on page 699. What does it indicate about industrial production in the 1920s as compared to production in the prewar years? During which years of the 1920s did the economy go into a short-lived but sharp recession?

Next turn to page 707 and look at the line graph "The Automobile Age: Passenger Cars Registered in the United States, 1900–2003." Roughly how many cars were registered in this country in 1910, 1920, 1925, and 1930? Did the number of registered vehicles rise more sharply during the twenties or thirties? How do you account for this?

Finally, look at the table on page 724 dealing with the elections of 1924, 1928, and 1932. What does it indicate about American ethnic group voters and the Democratic Party? Which was the only ethnic group that did not vote primarily Democratic by 1932? Why do you suppose that was?

HISTORICAL SOURCES

Chapter 23 uses as a source an in-depth community study of Muncie, Indiana, in the 1920s, conducted by two famous sociologists, Robert and Helen Lynd. Their findings, published in 1929 under the title *Middletown,* are referred to on page 706. What generalizations about American society is the historian making from the findings reported in *Middletown*? Muncie, Indiana, was a medium-sized, midwestern town. Can we be certain that the attitudes, values, and lifestyles that the Lynds found there were similar or identical to the ones that prevailed in huge eastern cities such as New York or in small communities in the Far West or Deep South? Does the text claim that a fairly homogeneous national culture emerged in the 1920s?

Look at "Beyond America—Global Interactions: The 'New Woman' in the 1920s." There the author makes the point that the "New Woman" phenomenon and the alarm it caused in conservative circles were not confined to the United States, but could be seen in Europe, Latin America, Canada, and other places. As evidence the author cites novels and newspaper articles. What other historical sources can you find that the author employs?

MULTIPLE-CHOICE QUESTIONS

Circle the letter of the item that best completes each statement or answers the question.

1. By 1930, what percentage of the African-American population lived in cities?

    a.   80 percent
    b.   50 percent
    c.   40 percent
    d.   20 percent

2. All of the following contributed to the general prosperity of the 1920s *except*

    a.   the development of new consumer-goods industries, especially home electric appliances.
    b.   federal minimum-wage laws that ensured that workers were well paid and thus had additional purchasing power.
    c.   the growth of the automobile industry.
    d.   a marked increase in productivity due to new technology and industrial techniques, such as the moving assembly line.

3. U.S. foreign policy toward Europe during the 1920s was characterized by

    a.   a willingness to forgive and forget the World War I debts owed to the U.S. government by former allies.
    b.   a desire to lead and dominate the League of Nations.
    c.   unilateralism, except for a willingness to enter into a treaty to curtail a naval arms race.
    d.   a refusal to participate in the League of Nations but a willingness to join the World Court and abide by its decisions.

4. Secretary of the Treasury Andrew Mellon was a believer in the "trickle down" theory of economics. In keeping with that theory he

    a.   advised Coolidge to sign the McNary-Haugen bill into law.
    b.   favored and advised Congress to pass the Flood Control Act (1928).
    c.   denounced the Supreme Court's decision that the federal child labor law was unconstitutional.
    d.   urged Congress to lower federal income taxes for the rich.

5. In the election of 1924,

    a.   Catholicism and prohibition were the two main issues.
    b.   the Democratic candidate, John W. Davis, won by a narrow margin over Republican Calvin Coolidge.
    c.   labor, farm, and reform groups revived the Progressive Party and ran Robert La Follette for president.
    d.   the Democratic Party nominated William Jennings Bryan for president for the fourth time.

6. Whose novels did much to spread the popular image of the 1920s as the "Jazz Age" of wild parties, drinking, sex, and materialism?

    a.   F. Scott Fitzgerald
    b.   Langston Hughes
    c.   Ernest Hemingway
    d.   Willa Cather

7. The largest group of immigrants entering the United States in the 1920s came from

    a.   China and Japan.
    b.   Mexico and other Western Hemisphere countries.
    c.   the countries of the British Commonwealth.
    d.   eastern and southern Europe.

8.   Marcus Garvey's Universal Negro Improvement Association

   a.   appealed to the small class of African-American professionals but never to the masses of poor urban African-Americans.
   b.   preached that African-Americans should remain in the rural South and specialize in farming.
   c.   started African-American-owned business ventures and called for a return to Africa.
   d.   gained its main following in the South among sharecroppers.

9.   Which of the following statements about the Scopes trial is *inaccurate*?

   a.   The American Civil Liberties Union hired Clarence Darrow to defend Scopes and challenge the constitutionality of Tennessee's anti-evolution law..
   b.   As a result of the Scopes trial, fundamentalist beliefs were discredited and anti-evolution laws were repealed.
   c.   Three-time Democratic presidential candidate William Jennings Bryan headed the prosecution team in the Scopes trial and argued that the people of Tennessee had the right to protect their children from godless scientific theories.
   d.   The trial was broadcast on the radio and became a media event.

10.   All of the following were popular types of entertainment in the 1920s *except*

   a.   going to the movies.
   b.   watching baseball games.
   c.   listening to the radio.
   d.   watching television.

SHORT-ANSWER QUESTIONS

1.   President Warren G. Harding remarked, "I have no trouble with my enemies . . . , but . . . my goddamn friends . . . keep me walking the floor nights." Why did Harding say that? Who were the friends and what were they up to?

2.   What happened to the trade union movement in the 1920s? Why?

3.   Why did Secretary of State Charles Evans Hughes call the Washington Naval Arms Conference? What was accomplished at that conference?

4.   In what ways did industrial and technological developments in the 1920s increase environmental dangers and the rapid use and waste of natural resources? Was government in the 1920s interested in either conservation or preservation?

5.   Explain the economic and social impact of the booming automobile industry on the United States in the 1920s.

6.   What was the Harlem Renaissance? Briefly discuss three writers and their works associated with the Harlem Renaissance. In the 1920s, how did whites react to the Harlem Renaissance? Was the white image of African-American life in 1920s Harlem accurate?

7.   Why did Congress pass the National Origins Act of 1924? What were its provisions? What impact did it have on the numbers and origins of the immigrants arriving in the United States from 1924 to 1965?

8.   What caused the rise of the Ku Klux Klan in the 1920s? What did it stand for? Who was attracted to it? Why? What caused its decline in the second half of the 1920s?

9.   How effective was prohibition in reducing excessive drinking? Why wasn't it more successful? What were some of prohibition's socially harmful effects on American society?

10.   Discuss Herbert Hoover's social thought. How did his outlook hinder him in fighting the depression that began during his presidency?

ESSAY QUESTIONS

1. What accounts for the economic growth and prosperity of the 1920s? Who benefited most from that prosperity? Who did not share in it and why?

2. Federal policies under Presidents Harding and Coolidge reflected the probusiness attitudes of the 1920s. Write an essay discussing and illustrating this statement with specific examples.

3. Discuss the impact of the economic, cultural, and social changes of the 1920s on the lives of American women. Were the changes felt by working-, middle-, and upper-class women?

4. Sharp social conflicts existed in American society in the 1920s. These conflicts produced fear, intolerance, and attempts to "purify" the country by legislation and coercion. Write an essay discussing these conflicts and the attempts of government and private groups to bring back a more traditional and homogeneous America.

5. The 1920s were a time of changing manners and morals and of cultural ferment. Write an essay discussing the changes that took place in popular culture and among artists and intellectuals.

ANSWERS TO MULTIPLE-CHOICE QUESTIONS

1. c
2. b
3. c
4. d
5. c
6. a
7. b
8. c
9. b
10. d

CHAPTER 24

The Great Depression and the New Deal, 1929–1939

OUTLINE AND SUMMARY

I. Introduction

Franklin D. Roosevelt, elected president in 1932 in the midst of the United States' worst depression, dominated national politics until his death in 1945. His programs, aimed at relief, recovery, and reform, are called the New Deal. In the course of the 1930s, the New Deal went through two phases. During 1933–1935, the first New Deal attempted to unite all Americans behind relief and recovery measures. In 1935, under attack from radicals and conservatives, Roosevelt initiated the second New Deal. More radical than the first, it tried less to conciliate business, imposing greater government regulation instead. It introduced legislation to benefit workers, farmers, sharecroppers, and others at the bottom of the economic ladder. A superb politician, Roosevelt won the love of the have-nots and the hatred of many of the financially privileged.

As you read Chapter 24 you should answer these questions: (1) What were the causes of the 1929 stock market crash and of the depression that followed? (2) What was the social and political impact of the crash and depression? (3) What strategy did the first New Deal employ, and what specific measures were passed to implement it? (4) Why did Roosevelt turn to a second New Deal in 1935, and what major legislation expressed the shift? (5) How did the depression and New Deal affect farmers, workers, women, and minorities? (6) Which New Deal programs failed and why? Which programs still have an impact on the nation and why? (7) How did the economic hard times affect American arts and popular culture?

II. Crash and Depression, 1929–1932

    A. Black Thursday and the Onset of the Depression

In 1928 a wave of wild speculation started. As 9 million Americans played the market in hope of quick profits, they drove stock prices to dangerously inflated levels. Worse yet, they often speculated on borrowed money; that is, they bought on margin. Low taxes for the rich engineered by Secretary of the Treasury Andrew Mellon and the easy-credit policy of the banks contributed to the speculation. The optimistic buyers ignored warning signs such as the falloff of new construction. Then on October 24, 1929, Black Thursday, the speculative bubble burst; stock prices plummeted as panicked shareholders rushed to sell. On the following Tuesday the plunge continued. This stock market crash triggered the worst depression in U.S. history.

Between 1929 and 1933, the nation sank deeper and deeper into depression. Farm prices declined by 60 percent; more than 5,500 banks failed. Unemployment climbed to 25 percent of the labor force. What were the causes of the Great Depression? Many economists point to the structural weaknesses in the economy: (1) Workers' wages did not rise sufficiently during the 1920s to allow them to buy all of the consumer goods coming off the factory assembly lines. By 1929 there was an overproduction crisis with more houses, automobiles, electric appliances, and other consumer items for sale than there were Americans who could afford to buy them. (2) The 1920s depressed agricultural sector further weakened the economy. (3) The collapse of European economies under the weight of World War I debt repayments and the unfavorable balance of trade with the United States caused our foreign sales to fall sharply. The monetarist school of economists claims it was not these structural weaknesses of the economy but the tight-money policy of the Federal Reserve Board in the early 1930s that caused the depression. Contracted credit denied businessmen the capital they needed to start new ventures and get the economy rolling again.

B. Hoover's Response

President Herbert Hoover's ideological commitment to private-sector initiative, limited government intervention, and balanced federal budgets severely handicapped him in dealing with the depression. Hoover asked business leaders not to lay off any more workers or impose further wage cuts. Although businessmen initially agreed, they later broke their pledges because they could not sell their products. Hoover preached that private charity and local government must handle relief for the jobless, but private philanthropy and city and county governments were soon overwhelmed by the numbers needing help. Hoover signed legislation creating the Reconstruction Finance Corporation, which was empowered to lend money to failing business corporations, but he held out until July 1932 against using federal funds to assist states in helping the unemployed. His pronouncements in favor of self-help and local initiative made him seem indifferent to the suffering of depression victims.

C. Mounting Discontent and Protest

Millions of people lost their jobs. They and their families, often unable to feed themselves or pay rent, wandered the country looking for work and lived in shantytowns like New York's "Hoover Valley" in Central Park. Everywhere banks foreclosed on farmers and homeowners who could not meet mortgage payments. The spreading mood of despair and confusion resulted in a burgeoning suicide rate.

As conditions worsened, protests escalated. Midwestern farmers tried to raise agricultural prices by halting the shipment of food to cities. Destitute veterans marched on Washington demanding immediate cash payment of their bonuses for World War I service. Rather than explain to them why he opposed payment, Hoover ordered the army to remove the "bonus marchers" from the capital. The sight of armed troops expelling peaceful veterans convinced the public of Hoover's callousness. Writers in the early thirties reflected the despair and disillusionment with life in capitalist America in such novels as John Dos Passos's *The 42nd Parallel*, James T. Farrell's *Young Lonigan*, and Jack Conroy's *The Disinherited*.

D. The Election of 1932

The Republicans renominated Hoover, who stuck by his failed antidepression measures. The Democrats nominated Franklin D. Roosevelt. How he would fight the depression was not clear. Nonetheless, the anti-Hoover sentiments of the people carried FDR and the Democrats to lopsided victories in the presidential and congressional elections.

III. The New Deal Takes Shape, 1933–1935

A. Roosevelt and His Circle

The promise of government action and the mood of optimism in FDR's inaugural address lifted people's spirits. The relief, recovery, and reform measures that followed, known as the New Deal, were forged by many contributors. A circle of Roosevelt advisers called the "brain trust" devised broad programs of "federal economic planning." Eleanor Roosevelt and her social worker and women reformer friends pushed for legislation to assist the economically disadvantaged and minority groups. Old-time Progressives, university professors, and able young lawyers joined the Roosevelt administration to contribute ideas and administer new programs.

B. The Hundred Days
Between March 9 and June 16, 1933, the administration introduced and Congress passed an unprecedented volume of legislation. These laws had the overall effect of greatly increasing federal involvement in the economy. The Federal Deposit Insurance Corporation (FDIC) insured bank accounts up to $5,000. The Civilian Conservation Corps (CCC) employed jobless young men on conservation projects. The Home Owners Loan Corporation and the Farm Credit Administration refinanced mortgages and thus saved the homes and farms of millions of Americans. Other important laws imposed regulation on the stock market and established the Tennessee Valley Authority (TVA) and the Public Works Administration (PWA). Washington entered the field of relief with the creation of the Federal Emergency Relief Administration (FERA). The Agricultural Adjustment Act (AAA) and the National Recovery Administration (NRA) aimed at reviving agriculture and business. The former guaranteed prices for agricultural produce and paid farmers for not growing crops that were in surplus. The NRA helped business draft and enforce codes to eliminate cutthroat competition, price-cutting, and the use of child labor in exchange for management promises to bargain with unions chosen by their employees.

C. Problems and Controversies Plague the Early New Deal
Complaints concerning the NRA multiplied. Management resented government regulation. Small businesses claimed that the codes helped only the big firms. The NRA bogged down in supervising code making in every possible industry. In 1935 a case challenging the constitutionality of the NRA reached the Supreme Court, and the justices struck it down in a unanimous decision.

Drought and the AAA reduced price-depressing surpluses, and as a consequence overall farm income rose by 50 percent between 1933 and 1937. However, the AAA did nothing for landless farm laborers, and it hurt tenants and sharecroppers. Landlords kicked many tenants and sharecroppers off their property and pocketed the government subsidy checks for withdrawing the land from production. Poor farmers also fell victim to the vast dust storms that rolled over the Upper South and Great Plains, destroying the crops in their paths. Ruined by nature and the AAA, many poor farmers, tenants, and sharecroppers headed for California, where they struggled to survive as migratory farm laborers. Between 1933 and 1935 New Dealers were split between whether the government should concentrate on pulling up the agricultural sector as a whole or on helping the rural poor. It was not until 1935 that legislation aiding farm laborers, tenants and sharecroppers was passed.

Harold Ickes, the careful PWA administrator, thoroughly checked each project to be underwritten by his agency. As a result the projects eventually built with PWA funds were enduring. In the short run, however, the PWA was slow to get work under way and slow to put money into the hands of the unemployed. Harry Hopkins, the less meticulous head of the FERA, quickly dispensed millions of dollars to the destitute. President Roosevelt, anxious for fast economic recovery, relied more and more heavily on Hopkins, transferring funds from the PWA to Hopkins's FERA and its work projects arm, the Civil Works Administration (CWA). Even after the CWA was terminated in the spring of 1934, Hopkins rather than Ickes dominated federal relief policy making.

D. Challenges from Right and Left, 1934–1935
When the first phase of FDR's New Deal did not end the depression, frustration with and criticism of Roosevelt began. In 1934 there were thousands of strikes, some led by communists. Business leaders and conservatives, charging that the New Deal was radical and socialistic, formed the American Liberty League to defeat New Dealers at the polls. However, the president and his policies retained the support of most Americans. This was demonstrated in the 1934 midterm congressional elections in which the Democrats greatly

increased their majorities in the House and Senate. Despite this electoral vote of confidence, demagogic extremists, who attacked the New Deal and proposed instead various radical plans for ending the depression, were gaining followings. These included Charles Coughlin and his National Union of Social Justice, Francis Townsend and his elderly supporters, and Huey Long and his "Share Our Wealth" movement. In 1935, Roosevelt, hoping to still the discontent and steal the thunder of the extremists, proposed to Congress a second burst of reform, relief, and recovery legislation.

IV. The New Deal Changes Course, 1935–1936

  A. Introduction

Roosevelt took a swing to the left. In 1935 he proposed to Congress a new package of reform measures, known as the Second New Deal, with the emphasis now on aiding the disadvantaged, rather than trying to appeal to all classes.

  B. Expanding Federal Relief

At Roosevelt's request, Congress in 1935 passed the Emergency Relief Appropriation Act, granting nearly $5 billion for expanded work-relief programs. The largest part of the money went to the newly created Works Progress Administration (WPA), headed by Harry Hopkins. Between 1935 and 1943 the WPA employed more than 8 million people in various construction, clerical, professional, and arts endeavors. Thanks to the WPA, thousands of roads, bridges, schools, hospitals, post offices, and other public facilities were constructed and/or repaired; and millions of Americans enjoyed free or low-cost plays and concerts, saw murals and paintings, and received instruction in the arts. A second new agency, the National Youth Administration, provided part-time jobs for students, allowing thousands of young people who otherwise could not have afforded it to go to and remain in college. Ickes's PWA shared in the money, too, using it for major construction projects. The large amount spent on these work-relief programs caused mounting federal budget deficits. According to British economist John Maynard Keynes, such deficit spending was a positive way to pump funds into the economy and combat the depression. Roosevelt never endorsed Keynesian economics, but he tolerated deficit spending as a short-term necessity to relieve suffering.

  C. Aiding Migrants, Supporting Unions, Regulating Business, and Taxing the Wealthy

The massive relief programs and other laws of the Second New Deal were not intended to please all social classes. They openly aimed at serving the needs of labor and the rural and urban poor. The Resettlement Administration, created in May 1935, resettled and/or made loans to small farmers, tenants, and sharecroppers to turn them into farm owners on productive land. Although the Resettlement Administration aided the rural poor, agriculture as a whole suffered a blow when the Supreme Court in 1936 declared the AAA unconstitutional. The pro-union National Labor Relations (Wagner) Act of July 1935 stimulated the growth of organized labor. It required employers to recognize and bargain with their employees' unions and established the National Labor Relations Board to act as watchdog in labor-management relations. The Revenue Act of 1935 (which the wealthy called the "Soak the Rich" law) boosted taxes on corporations and upper-income Americans.

  D. The Social Security Act of 1935; End of the Second New Deal

The Social Security Act of 1935, drafted by a committee headed by Secretary of Labor Frances Perkins, provided for old-age pensions, survivors' benefits for families of deceased workers, unemployment insurance, and aid to dependent mothers and children and the handicapped. The 1935 law did not cover farmers and domestic workers, but " it established the principle of federal responsibility for social welfare and laid the foundation for a vastly expanded welfare system in the future." Social Security and the other Second New Deal laws went a long way toward reducing the appeal of extremist demagogues and saving the capitalist system by reforming its excesses and addressing the social injustices it spawned. While in the 1920s business had dominated government, Roosevelt's New Deal now concerned itself more fairly with the needs of other segments of the population: workers, farmers, poor mothers and children, and sharecroppers. Roosevelt's vigorous leadership also had the long-term effect of strengthening the powers of the presidency and broadening Americans' expectations of the role that the nation-state should play in society.

E. The 1936 Roosevelt Landslide and the New Democratic Coalition
The Republicans nominated Alfred Landon of Kansas to run against Roosevelt, whom the Democrats enthusiastically renominated. Roosevelt swept every state but Maine and Vermont, and the Democrats increased their large majorities in Congress.

The victories resulted from a new Democratic coalition that had emerged, consisting of the South, urban immigrants, industrial workers, farmers, African-Americans, and women. African-American voters were attracted to the Democratic party by Roosevelt's aid to the poor and his stepped-up appointments of African-Americans to responsible government positions. The Roosevelt administration also made careful efforts to cultivate women's votes.

F. The Environment and the West
The New Deal achieved an impressive record in conservation. The CCC built hiking trails, thinned forests, and planted thousands of trees. The Departments of Agriculture and the Interior taught farmers soil-conservation practices and stopped overgrazing on public lands. The TVA's dams controlled earth-eroding floods. Congress created three more national parks, and the president heeded the lobbying of the Wilderness Society, established in 1935, by setting aside 160 new wildlife refuges. The West was the region perhaps most aided by New Deal projects. Highways linking it to the rest of the nation were repaired and upgraded. The great western dams—Boulder, Shasta, Grand Coulee, and others—provided the West with hydroelectric power, flood control, irrigation, and soil conservation. The PWA and WPA also supplied western states with thousands of public structures, ranging from bridges to post offices to ski lodges.

V. The New Deal's End Stage, 1937–1939
A. FDR and the Supreme Court
In February 1937 FDR proposed a court reform bill that would allow the president to appoint a new Supreme Court justice to serve alongside each member of the Court who had reached seventy years of age and would not retire. Roosevelt requested this change because the aging, conservative majority on the Supreme Court had been declaring reform and recovery laws such as the NRA and AAA unconstitutional and seemed likely to invalidate the Social Security and Wagner Acts that would soon be brought before it in test cases. Congress killed the president's "court-packing plan." FDR did, however, influence a number of the elderly, conservative judges to modify their views or retire. The Supreme Court upheld the Wagner Act, and between 1937 and 1939 Roosevelt was able to fill four Court vacancies with liberal New Dealers.

B. The Roosevelt Recession
Roosevelt suffered another blow when the economy turned sharply downward in August 1937. The causes of this so-called Roosevelt recession included (1) a reduction in consumer spending power because of social-security deductions, (2) a tightening of money supply when the Federal Reserve Board raised interest rates, and (3) cutbacks, to try to balance the budget, in New Deal work and relief programs. Faced with rising unemployment and slumping industrial output, Roosevelt had to ask Congress for new appropriations to revive and expand the PWA, WPA, and other programs, which restarted economic recovery.

C.   Final Measures; Growing Opposition
In Roosevelt's second term, Congress passed only a few reforms. These included the
Housing Act of 1937; the Fair Labor Standards Act; the 1937 Farm Tenancy Act, which
replaced the Resettlement Administration with the Farm Security Administration; and a
second Agricultural Adjustment Act. A coalition of conservative, southern Democrats and
Republicans blocked further reform. Roosevelt attempted to break up this anti–New Deal
coalition by asking voters to defeat conservatives in the 1938 elections. The people instead
elected more conservatives. Thereafter, FDR switched his attention to foreign affairs and
proposed no additional domestic reform, and the New Deal ended.

VI.   Social Change and Social Action in the 1930s
A.   The Depression's Psychological and Social Impact
The depression imposed tremendous suffering. Even with all the New Deal programs, the
unemployment rate never fell much below 14 percent during the thirties. A quarter of all
farm families had to accept relief to survive, as did 1 million elderly citizens. The hard
times brought both physical and emotional distress to millions. According to one historian,
the depression stamped on many living through it "a dull misery in the bones."

During the depression women workers suffered about a 20 percent unemployment rate; were
often displaced by men in teaching, social work, and librarianships; were usually paid less
than men; and were often told that if they were married, they would be dismissed. Some
women workers were helped by unions and by the Fair Labor Standards Act, but many of
the occupations in which women predominated were not covered by either. Despite all these
disadvantages, the proportion of women, including married women, in the labor force
continued to grow. Hard times brought changes in family life and population trends.
Marriage rates and birthrates declined, while desertion increased. Population growth
slowed. If the depression broke up some families, it produced in others greater solidarity
and promoted a spirit of cooperation among people.

B.   Industrial Workers Unionize
In 1933 fewer than 3 million workers belonged to unions. Management in the steel,
automobile, textile, and other mass-production industries had defeated all previous attempts
to organize their employees. In the 1930s the combination of hard times and the prolabor
attitude of government revived interest in unions. At first the American Federation of
Labor, committed to protecting the narrow interests of its skilled craft-union affiliates, failed
to grasp the new opportunities. But some of its more activist leaders, including John L.
Lewis and Sidney Hillman, in November 1935 established the Committee for Industrial
Organization (later renamed the Congress of Industrial Organizations [CIO]) and sent
hundreds of organizers to the steel, rubber, car, and textile factories to sign up members in
industry-wide unions. In March 1937 Lewis convinced U.S. Steel to sign a contract
recognizing the steelworkers' union and granting pay increases and a forty-hour workweek.
When General Motors refused to negotiate, Walter Reuther and other United Automobile
Workers (UAW) officials led sit-down strikes that halted all production for six weeks.
President Roosevelt and the governor of Michigan refused to use the army or militia to
dislodge the strikers, and the occupiers beat back the attack of local police. Thus General
Motors had no alternative but to sign a contract recognizing the UAW.

Henry Ford and Tom Girdler, leader of Republic and other "Little Steel" companies, refused
to deal with unions and fought them with violence, as in the beating of Walter Reuther and
other UAW organizers and the Memorial Day shooting of striking steel workers. Even they,
however, finally recognized and bargained with unions by 1941. The textile workers of the
South; agricultural laborers; domestics; and most women, African-American, and recent
immigrant workers remained unorganized. Nonetheless, the labor movement in the thirties

scored a major breakthrough, raising union membership to more than 8 million. Powerful corporations gave in to unionization because of workers' militancy and the refusal of the New Dealers to put the power of government on the side of business against strikers. The 1930s labor unity was more apparent, however, than real. Many of the union leaders were radicals who wished to get rid of capitalism. The rank-and-file members just wanted improved wages, hours, and conditions. In the anticommunist atmosphere of post-World War II, the unions expelled many of the leftist organizers and became much less militant.

C.   African- and Hispanic Americans Resist Racism and Exploitation
The Depression slowed the movement of rural African-Americans to cities and to the North. In 1940, 75 percent of the 12 million African-Americans still lived in the South. African-Americans in agriculture and industry had even higher rates of displacement and unemployment than whites, and they were often denied equal protection of the law, as demonstrated by lynchings and the case of the Sottsboro boys. The NAACP battled against lynchings, segregation, and disfranchisement; while other African-American leaders organized "don't shop where you can't work" campaigns. Resentment against employment and other types of discrimination touched off a major race riot in Harlem in 1935.

The Depression was equally hard on more than 2 million Hispanics. Many of the Mexican immigrants were migratory farm laborers who competed for jobs with the "Okies" arriving in the Southwest. With a surplus of farm workers, employers and relief officials put pressure on Hispanics to return to Mexico, and half a million did during the 1930s. Those who remained either drifted to the barrios of southwestern cities or worked for miserably low wages on large farms. Mexican-Americans struck for better pay and were sometimes successful. Asian-American farmers and agricultural workers also suffered from discrimination and efforts to remove them from the country.

D.   A New Deal for Native Americans
The 330,000 Indians were the poorest of all Americans. By 1933 they had lost to whites two-thirds of the land they had owned in 1887, the year the ill-conceived Dawes Act was passed. John Collier, a reformer, became Roosevelt's commissioner of Indian affairs. He used New Deal agencies to create jobs and build much-needed facilities on Indian reservations. He also proposed legislation to end the Dawes Act, stop all further sale of Indian lands, grant self-government to the tribes, and encourage the revival of Native American culture. After much opposition, Collier saw part of his program embodied in the 1934 Indian Reorganization Act, which did at least reverse the steady loss of Indian lands and set the stage, by restoring tribes as legal entities, for later law suits by Native Americans to regain rights and land promised in long-violated treaties.

VII.   The American Cultural Scene in the 1930s
A.   Avenues of Escape: Radio and the Movies
Listening to the radio was an extremely popular activity in the 1930s. The comedy of Jack Benny and George Burns and Gracie Allen and the melodrama of the soap operas gave people an escape from bleak economic reality. Mass culture became even more standardized than it had been in the twenties. Movies, too, were enormously popular. A few documentaries and some dramas dealt with contemporary social problems. But most Hollywood films offered escape from a troubled world. Americans flocked to see gangster movies like *Little Caesar,* musicals like *Gold Diggers of 1933,* and the Marx Brothers comedies. Hollywood films of the thirties presented most characters as stereotypes.

B.   The Later 1930s: Opposing Fascism; Reaffirming Traditional Values
Writers and artists in the latter half of the 1930s found much to admire in America's history and its people, though not necessarily in its capitalist economic system. Several things

account for this upsurge in cultural nationalism: (1) The rise of aggressive fascism abroad threatened all the democratic and humanitarian values our country claimed to uphold. (2) The communists, between 1935 and 1939, praised New Deal America and advocated a Popular Front of all left-wingers and liberals against fascism: the Loyalists' struggle against Francisco Franco's fascist rebels in the Spanish Civil War (1936–1939) especially awakened American liberals and intellectuals to the fascist menace. (3) The WPA art projects encouraged appreciation of America's heritage. John Steinbeck's *The Grapes of Wrath* and James Agee and Walker Evans's *Let Us Now Praise Famous Men* paid tribute to the endurance of America's rural poor. Composers Aaron Copland and George Gershwin used American folktales and racial minorities in their works. American jazz and swing blossomed. Regional writers, such as Zora Neal Hurston and William Faulkner, and painters, such as Thomas Hart Benton, depicted their home sections. American folk art and historical museum and novels became popular.

C.   Streamlining and a World's Fair: Corporate America's Utopian Vision
The look of material objects surrounding Americans in the 1930s began to change as business, hoping to boost sales, adopted the industrial design known as streamlining. Corporate attempts to show the public that capitalism could bring the nation a prosperous, modern, streamlined future reached a high point at the New York World's Fair in 1939.

If Americans felt more positive about their society in the late thirties, they also experienced growing apprehension about the gathering war clouds. That may be why so many people overreacted to Orsen Welles's 1938 radio dramatization of *War of the Worlds*.

VIII. Conclusion
Economists believe the Great Depression was caused by weaknesses in the 1920s economy: low farm prices, uneven income distribution, tight credit, and contracted money supply, among others. The depression affected different groups in different ways, but it touched all aspects of American life. Roosevelt's New Deal did not fully lift the country out of the depression; only World War II accomplished that. However, the New Deal brought about major reforms, among them the Social Security and Wagner Acts, and introduced tougher regulation of big business. It set a precedent for greatly expanded federal government involvement in the economy and society, the wisdom of which people would debate for the next half-century. In one of the country's darkest times, Roosevelt's experimental approach and determined optimism served the nation well.

VOCABULARY

The following terms are used in Chapter 24. To understand the chapter fully, it is important that you know what each of them means.

buying stock on margin	purchasing stock partly with one's own money and partly with money borrowed from a bank or broker specifically for the purpose of buying the stock
foreclosure	the legal action by which a bank repossesses the house or farm of a borrower for failure to keep up regular payments on the mortgage
nostrums	quack cures or questionable medicines
pump priming	government spending (often to the point of creating a budget deficit) for the purpose of stimulating the economy
demagogue	an unprincipled political leader; one who leads people by playing on their prejudices, passions, and fears

panacea	a remedy for all ills; a cure-all
anti-Semitic	prejudiced against or intolerant of Jewish people
deficit spending	government expenditure in excess of its tax receipts and other revenues
collective bargaining	negotiation between employers and union representatives concerning wages, hours, and conditions of work
sacrosanct	sacred; not to be violated
militancy	aggressiveness, combativeness
barrios	Hispanic urban neighborhoods
repatriation	the bringing or sending back of a person to his or her own country
streamlining	eliminating all extraneous design features in favor of smoothly flowing surfaces (ones that are often teardrop shaped and offer the least resistance in passing through the air)
utopia	a place of perfection

IDENTIFICATIONS

After reading Chapter 24, you should be able to identify and explain the historical significance of each of the following:

First New Deal, Second New Deal

brain trust

Bank holiday, Emergency Banking Act, and Federal Deposit Insurance Corporation (FDIC)

Civilian Conservation Corps

Harry Hopkins

Tennessee Valley Authority

Federal Securities Act and the Securities and Exchange Commission

Works Progress Administration (WPA) and the Federal Arts Projects

John Maynard Keynes and Keynesian economics

resettlement and Farm Security administrations

National Labor Relations (Wagner) Act

Revenue Act of 1935 ("Soak the Rich" law)

Mary McLeod Bethune and the "black cabinet"

Housing Act of 1937

John L. Lewis, Sidney Hillman, and the Congress of Industrial Organizations (CIO)

Walter Reuther, the United Automobile Workers (UAW), and the sit-downs

Scottsboro boys

Benny Goodman, Count Basie, and swing

Zora Neal Hurston, *Their Eyes Were Watching God*

SKILL BUILDING: MAPS

On the map of the United States below, locate each of the places listed:

the seven-state region covered by the Tennessee Valley Authority

the areas affected by the dust storms (dust bowls) of the 1930s

Olympic National Park

Shenandoah National Park

Kings Canyon National Park

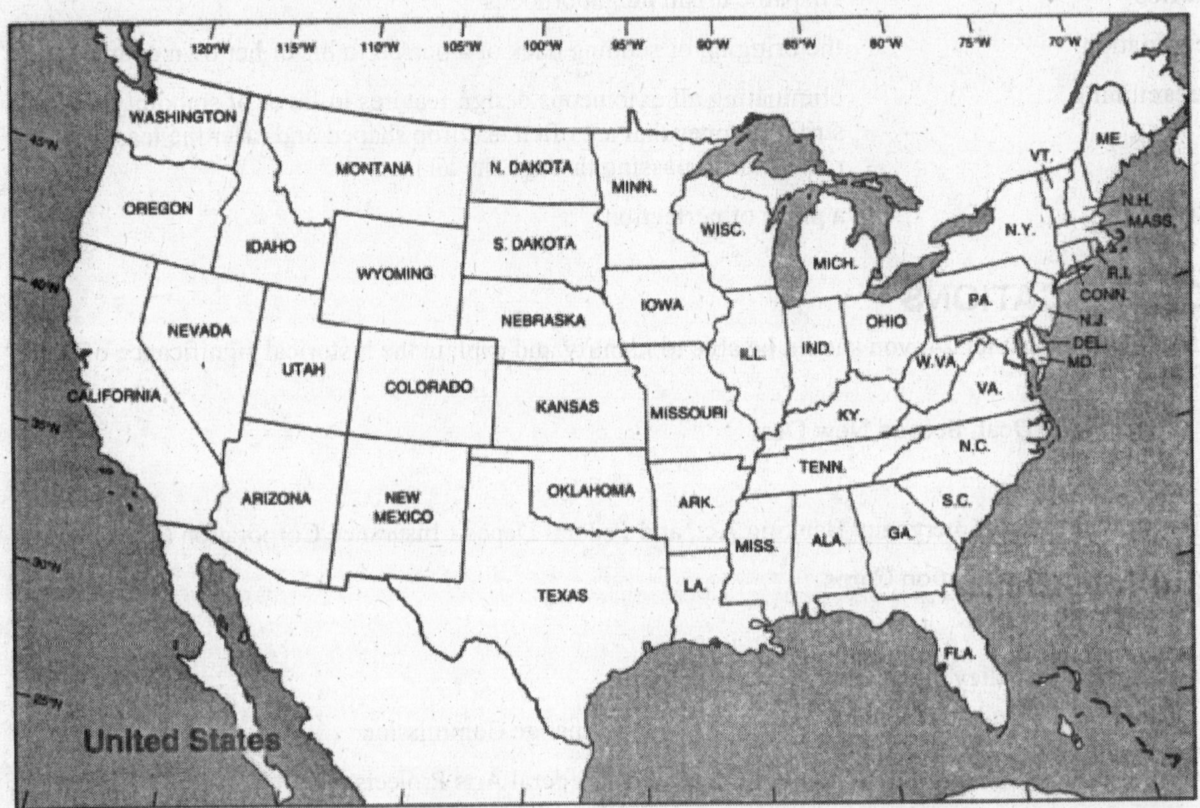

SKILL-BUILDING: GRAPHS

Look at the line and bar graphs on page 732 under the title "The Statistics of Hard Times." From these you should be able to learn the answers to many questions about the Great Depression and the New Deal. For example:

1. Judging from the statistics on personal income, unemployment rate, stock prices, and building construction, did the New Deal succeed in reviving the economy to 1929 levels at any point prior to the United States' 1941 entry into World War II?

2. What was the impact of World War II on economic recovery?

3. Judging from all of the statistics shown in the graphs, which was the worst year of the depression?

4. During his presidency, Herbert Hoover kept predicting that prosperity was just around the corner. Is there anything in these graphs that would support his forecast? The Roosevelt administration claimed that it had made considerable headway in improving the economy by 1939. Do the graphs confirm that assertion?

HISTORICAL SOURCES

The sources of information that historians use to learn about the personalities, feuds, hopes, fears, and intentions of the men and women who wield power in each presidential administration are the memoirs, diaries, and histories those individuals write. Find the places in Chapter 24 that discuss Hugh Johnson, Frances Perkins, Eleanor Roosevelt, Harry Hopkins, and Harold Ickes. Part of what the historian knows about them comes from books that each published: Hugh Johnson, *The Blue Eagle from Egg to Earth;* Francis Perkins, *The Roosevelt I Knew;* Eleanor Roosevelt, *This I Remember;* Harry Hopkins, *Spending to Save;* and *The Secret Diary of Harold L. Ickes.* Why are such books good historical sources? Why is it important that historians check any "facts" they obtain from these memoirs, diaries, and histories against several other sources before relying on them?

In the Culture and Technology section of Chapter 24, the author uses another valuable twentieth-century historical source: movies. All of the movies referred to in that essay are available for viewing in film museums and archives. Some, such as *Gone With the Wind*, the *Wizard of Oz*, and *Snow White and the Seven Dwarfs*, have been copied onto videotapes and DVDs. What insights into the time period in which the movie was made can the historian gain from viewing these old films? How does the author account for the fact that despite the very limited budgets on which many people lived in the 1930s, they still went to the movies regularly? How did new technological advances affect "box office appeal" and "the economics of the film industry"?

MULTIPLE-CHOICE QUESTIONS

Circle the letter of the item that best completes each statement or answers the question.

1. In 1932 President Hoover used the army to expel which of the following protest groups from Washington, D.C.?
    a. Farmers demanding that government support agricultural prices
    b. Women demanding equal treatment from relief officials
    c. World War I veterans demanding immediate payment of their bonuses
    d. African-Americans demanding passage of a federal antilynching law
2. All of the following attacked Roosevelt and the New Deal for not going far enough in fighting the depression and urged the adoption of more radical measures *except*
    a. Huey Long and the "Share Our Wealth" movement.
    b. Francis Townsend and the Townsend clubs.
    c. Charles Coughlin and the National Union for Social Justice.
    d. Al Smith and the American Liberty League.
3. Which of the following best characterizes Herbert Hoover's handling of the depression?
    a. He followed the advice of Secretary of the Treasury Andrew Mellon to do nothing and wait for economic recovery to occur naturally.
    b. His efforts were limited by his fears of unbalancing the federal budget and concentrating too much power and responsibility in Washington.
    c. He refused to have the federal government help failing business corporations.
    d. He initiated vast new programs to employ the jobless, control farm surpluses, and regulate banking and the stock exchange.

4. Which of the following statements about Frances Perkins is *incorrect*?

   a. She was the first woman to serve in a president's cabinet.
   b. She chaired the committee that drafted the Social Security Act.
   c. She headed both the Federal Emergency Relief Administration and the WPA.
   d. She used her influence as Secretary of Labor to insist that the NRA codes drafted by industries ban child labor.

5. The 1935 Social Security Act provided for all of the following *except*

   a. Medicare and Medicaid for the elderly and poor.
   b. unemployment insurance.
   c. old-age pensions and survivors' benefits.
   d. welfare for the disabled and mothers of young children without a bread winner.

6. During the New Deal, which interest group exercised less influence over the federal government than it had in the 1920s?

   a. Organized labor
   b. Farmers
   c. Business
   d. Social workers

7. The New Deal agency which built the Triborough Bridge in New York and major hydroelectric dams in the West (Hoover, Grand Coulee, Bonneville, and others) was the

   a. PWA.
   b. CCC.
   c. NYA.
   d. RFC.

8. Which of the following agencies was created during Hoover's administration to help failing business corporations and continued to be active through the New Deal years?

   a. Federal Emergency Relief Administration
   b. Tennessee Valley Authority
   c. Federal Deposit Insurance Corporation
   d. Reconstruction Finance Corporation

9. John Maynard Keynes's economic theory

   a. suggests that deficit spending by the government can stimulate economic recovery.
   b. was closely followed by Franklin Roosevelt and his New Deal.
   c. stresses the importance of government's maintaining a balanced budget at all times.
   d. was proved wrong by the United States' experience in the 1930s.

10. The Marx Brothers were

    a. gifted comedians who made zany movies in the 1930s.
    b. African-American teenagers sentenced to death by an all-white jury for allegedly raping two white women.
    c. the main characters in Clifford Odets's 1934 play, *Waiting for Lefty*.
    d. the leaders of the 1937 sit-down strike against General Motors.

11. The Fair Labor Standards Act (1938) did all of the following *except*

    a. ban child labor.
    b. guarantee workers' right to join a union.
    c. set minimum wage.
    d. set maximum hours.

12. In the 1930s the Congress of Industrial Organizations made major strides in unionizing workers in all of these industries *except*
    a. steel.
    b. automobiles.
    c. textiles.
    d. rubber.

SHORT-ANSWER QUESTIONS

1. What caused the huge stock market boom in 1928–1929 and its subsequent crash in October 1929? How did the practice of buying on margin contribute to both boom and bust?

2. Why were the Agricultural Adjustment Act and the National Industrial Recovery Act passed during the Hundred Days? What were the main provisions of each law? What did each law accomplish? What problems did each law create? What finally happened to each law?

3. What were the dust bowls? What caused the dust storms? Who were the "Okies"? What novel of the 1930s depicted the dust storms and the people who fled them?

4. What New Deal for Native Americans did Roosevelt's Indian Commissioner John Collier try to carry out? Why was his program controversial even among Indian tribes? What, if anything, did the Indian Reorganization Act accomplish?

5. Which groups made up the new Democratic coalition that reelected Roosevelt by a landslide in 1936? Why was each group attracted to the New Deal?

6. What was the Popular Front? How was it related to the Spanish Civil War and Francisco Franco? Whose 1940 novel has a protagonist who volunteers to fight for the Loyalists against Franco's fascists in Spain? Why did "enthusiasm for joining with communists under the antifascist banner" vanish in August 1939?

7. Discuss the record of the New Deal on conservation and the environment.

8. "On racial-justice issues . . . the New Deal's record was mixed at best." Do you agree with this statement? Why or why not?

9. Describe Roosevelt's court-packing plan. Why did he propose it? Did he win or lose the fight to remake the Supreme Court? Why?

10. What caused the "Roosevelt recession"? What did the New Deal do to combat it?

11. What brought about the end of the New Deal in 1939?

ESSAY QUESTIONS

1. Discuss the causes of the depression of the 1930s. Consider both the structural weaknesses and the monetarist explanations.

2. Compare and contrast President Hoover's and President Roosevelt's attempts to deal with the depression and its victims. Why did each president follow his particular course?

3. The author of Chapter 24 states "The New Deal's importance . . . lies not only in specific laws, but also in the way it redefined the scope of the presidency and, more broadly, the social role of the state." Write an essay explaining this statement and illustrating it with as much specific historical evidence as possible.

4. One historian has written, "When Franklin D. Roosevelt faced the newly elected Congress in 1935, the result promised to be a fresh outburst of reform and recovery legislation which would surpass even that of the Hundred Days." Explain what movements and events in America in 1934 and 1935 were pushing Congress and Roosevelt toward this new "outburst of reform." What were some of the most important laws passed during this second "outburst of reform"?

5. In 1933 fewer than 3 million workers belonged to unions; by 1941 more than 8 million did. How and why did this "unionization of vast sectors of America's industrial work force" come about? Which workers were still almost totally unorganized in 1941?

6. Discuss the impact of the depression and the New Deal on the lives of women, African-Americans, Hispanics, and Indians. How much progress was made in raising each group to full political and economic equality with white males?

7. Discuss American culture in the 1930s. How did popular culture and the fine arts respond to the political and economic events and conditions of the depression decade?

ANSWERS TO MULTIPLE-CHOICE QUESTIONS

1. c
2. d
3. b
4. c
5. a
6. c
7. a
8. d
9. a
10. a
11. b
12. c

CHAPTER 25

Americans and a World in Crisis, 1933–1945

OUTLINE AND SUMMARY

I. Introduction

Chapter 25 focuses on U.S. foreign policy between 1933 and 1945 and participation in World War II. As you read Chapter 25, consider these questions: (1) How did President Roosevelt's Good Neighbor Policy affect U.S.-Latin American relations? (2) How did the American people and their government respond to the international crises of the 1930s? (3) How did President Roosevelt and Congress mobilize the country for war? (4) What impact did the war have on the U.S. economy? (5) How did the war change American society and affect minorities and women? (6) What were the different goals of the United States, Britain, and the Soviet Union, and how did these goals affect their combat strategies? (7) Why did President Truman decide to drop atomic bombs on Japan, and was he justified in doing so?

II. The United States in a Menacing World, 1933–1939

A. Introduction

During FDR's first two terms, he improved relations with Latin America. Meanwhile, aggressive, militaristic fascist regimes came to power in Italy, Germany, and Japan. The United States reacted to these developments abroad ambivalently, torn between dislike of fascism and an even stronger desire for peace.

B. Nationalism and the Good Neighbor

Roosevelt announced the Good Neighbor policy. His administration applied this policy in Latin America by agreeing that no state has the right to intervene in the affairs of another. FDR withdrew U.S. troops from Haiti and the Dominican Republic, ended the Platt Amendment, and refrained from using force against left-wing governments in Cuba and Mexico. The administration did, however, apply economic pressure to influence events in those two countries. Roosevelt's restraint in using military force improved U.S.-Latin-American relations.

C. The Rise of Aggressive States in Europe and Asia

Benito Mussolini and his fascist followers took control of Italy in 1922. In 1933 the Nazi leader Adolf Hitler became chancellor of Germany. Preaching racism, aggressive nationalism, and anti-Semitism, Hitler quickly established an absolute dictatorship over Germany, began persecuting the Jews, and embarked on military buildup and conquest. In 1936 his troops reoccupied the Rhineland; in 1938 he annexed Austria. Meanwhile, Mussolini invaded Ethiopia. Germany grabbed the Sudetenland from Czechoslovakia without firing a shot when, in 1938, at the Munich Conference, the British and French agreed to the transfer to appease Hitler. On the other side of the world, Japanese imperialists seized the Chinese province of Manchuria and in 1937 began a war of conquest to take over all of China.

D. The American Mood: No More War

Americans disliked these actions but were determined not to be pulled into another war. The majority in this country now viewed our participation in World War I as a mistake. The revelations of the Nye Committee about the roles played by bankers and weapons suppliers in that war reinforced that belief. In the thirties novelists and playwrights condemned war in their works; and Congress passed the Neutrality Acts, prohibiting the United States from making loans or selling arms to belligerents and banning Americans from traveling on the ships of nations at war.

E. The Gathering Storm, 1938–1939
In 1939 Hitler seized the remainder of Czechoslovakia, threatened to attack Poland, and signed the German-Soviet Non-Aggression Pact to ensure Russian neutrality during the planned German invasion of Poland.

Many Americans grew alarmed and started to feel that the United States should take a more active role. FDR agreed. After the fascist conquest of Czechoslovakia and Albania, the president sent messages to Hitler and Mussolini asking them to pledge not to invade any other nation. The two dictators responded with ridicule. Roosevelt also asked Congress to appropriate much more money to build up U.S. defenses.

F. America and the Jewish Refugees
Throughout the thirties German persecution of the Jews intensified. In 1935 the Nuremberg Laws stripped German Jews of citizenship and rights. On *Kristallnacht* in 1938 the Nazis unleashed a wave of violence against Jews, attacking them in their homes, synagogues, and businesses. As the outrages and threats increased, tens of thousands of European Jews fled, seeking countries that would admit them. Among them were distinguished musicians, architects, writers, and scholars who enriched the cultural life of their adopted nation. Such refugee physicists as Leo Szilard and Enrico Fermi played key roles in developing the atomic bomb for the United States.

Congress would not amend discriminatory immigration laws, however, to offer a haven to the hundreds of thousands of additional Jews desperately needing a safe home, nor would Roosevelt exert pressure on the lawmakers to do so. The majority of Americans opposed letting in more Jews, apparently because of isolationist, anti-immigrant, and anti-Semitic attitudes. In 1939 the United States even stopped the *St. Louis*, a ship carrying Jewish refugees, and forced it to return to Europe. There the countryless refugees were soon murdered by the Nazis.

III. Into the Storm, 1939–1941
A. The European War
World War II began on September 1, 1939, when Hitler attacked Poland. Britain and France, committed by treaty to defend Poland, declared war on Germany. Soon after, the United States revised the Neutrality Acts to permit sales of weapons to belligerents on a cash-and-carry basis. Most Americans favored this move as a way to help Britain and France without having to fight. In April 1940 German armies turned on Denmark and Norway; in May they conquered the Netherlands and Belgium; by mid-June France capitulated. The Germans then began terror bombing raids over the cities of England. During this Battle of Britain, Prime Minister Winston Churchill appealed to President Roosevelt for help. The majority of Americans favored stepped-up weapons shipments to bolster Hitler's one remaining opponent, but an articulate minority feared that such aid would weaken U.S. defenses and needlessly pull us into war.

B. From Isolation to Intervention
Because of the menacing situation in Europe, Roosevelt decided to run for a third term. His Republican opponent, Wendell L. Willkie, held foreign-policy views similar to Roosevelt's. During the campaign Roosevelt underlined his interventionist position by signing an executive agreement with Winston Churchill to give Britain fifty overage U.S. destroyers in

exchange for leases on air and naval bases in British possessions in the Western Hemisphere. In protest, isolationists organized the America First Committee, which preached that we must not give any aid to belligerents or become involved in the struggle against Hitler. However, in apparent support of Roosevelt's actions, the voters elected him to an unprecedented third term.

When FDR learned that Britain was running out of dollars to buy the war supplies she desperately needed, he proposed the Lend-Lease bill. It would permit the president to lend or lease military equipment to any country whose defense he thought vital to American security. Although this would certainly be an unneutral act, the majority of the public favored it, and Congress passed it in March 1941. When Hitler attacked the U.S.S.R. in June 1941, Roosevelt gave lend-lease aid to the Soviets as well as to the British. Unfortunately, the supplies often ended up at the bottom of the Atlantic because of the constant sinkings by German submarines. To prevent such losses, the United States began convoying British ships as far as Iceland, tracking German submarines, and notifying the British of their location. These actions inevitably led to conflict between German and American vessels. By the fall of 1941 the two countries were engaged in an undeclared naval war. Meanwhile Roosevelt and Churchill moved closer to an alliance when they met off the coast of Newfoundland in the summer of 1941 and issued the Atlantic Charter.

C.   Pearl Harbor and the Coming of War
With Europe at war, Japan expanded its aggression from China to the resource-rich British, Dutch, and French colonies in Southeast Asia. Japan's drive to dominate all of Asia (the Greater East Asia Co-Prosperity Sphere) clashed directly with the Open Door policy of the United States. Though not wanting a war, the Roosevelt administration attempted to change Tokyo's course by applying economic pressure. By July 1940 Washington prohibited the sale of aviation gasoline to Japan. When Tokyo occupied northern Indochina and signed the Tripartite Pact with Germany and Italy, Roosevelt placed an embargo on all items Japan needed. In July 1941, in response to Japan's seizure of the rest of Indochina, Washington froze Japanese assets in the United States, ending all trade. Japanese prime minister Hideki Tojo decided to make a last-ditch effort to persuade Washington to reopen trade and recognize Japan's conquests. If that failed, Japan would attempt to destroy the U.S. Pacific fleet with a surprise attack on Pearl Harbor, leaving the United States too weak to thwart Japan's imperial dreams. Washington knew its refusal would provoke an attack somewhere in the Pacific. Nonetheless, the Roosevelt administration would not yield and sent warnings to all base commanders. On December 7, 1941, the Japanese struck Pearl Harbor, and the next day Congress recognized that a state of war existed with Japan. On December 11, Japan's two allies, Germany and Italy, declared war on the United States, and the U.S. reciprocated.

In the months after Pearl Harbor the United States faced a bleak situation. Nazi submarines prowled off our east coast and took a heavy toll on Allied ships. Hitler's armies had pushed to the outskirts of Leningrad and Moscow and were launching new offensives in the Crimea and Caucasus. Other German armies landed in North Africa and headed toward the vital Suez Canal. Japan followed the raid on Hawaii with conquests of the Philippines, Malaya, Thailand, Hong Kong, Guam, Wake, Singapore, the Dutch East Indies, and most of the island chains in the Western Pacific.

IV.   America Mobilizes for War
A.   Organizing for Victory
To plan the military effort, FDR created the Joint Chiefs of Staff and the Office of Strategic Services, predecessor of the Central Intelligence Agency. To mobilize the economy, Roosevelt established hundreds of special wartime agencies, such as the War Production

Board, which allocated scarce materials, limited manufacture of civilian goods, and awarded military production contracts. Under this government direction, the United States produced more armaments than Germany, Italy, and Japan combined. Government contracts guaranteed handsome profits to the giant corporations that received most of the defense contracts. Federal authority and the federal budget grew rapidly, as did the influence of the military and big corporations on American life.

B.   The War Economy
Between 1941 and 1945 the U.S. government spent nearly twice as much as it did from 1789 through 1940. Fueled by this expenditure, the economy boomed. During the war the purchasing power of industrial workers went up by about 50 percent, corporate profits climbed by 70 percent, and unemployment vanished as 17 million new jobs were created. Many of the poor moved into the middle class. Most labor leaders gave no-strike pledges, but John L. Lewis led his miners on repeated work stoppages. An increasingly conservative Congress retaliated with the antilabor Smith-Connally Act. To curb inflation the Office of Price Administration imposed price controls and rationing. As a result the cost of living during the last two years of World War II rose by only 8 percent. The government raised the huge sums needed to fight the war with the sale of bonds, which provided half the money, and with steeply increased federal taxes, which provided the rest.

C.   "A Wizard War"
The government also employed thousands of scientists in the drive for victory. The secret Manhattan Project to beat the Germans in the race to develop nuclear weapons was the greatest of the government-sponsored scientific endeavors. Led by physicist J. Robert Oppenheimer, the Manhattan Project spent some $2 billion. On July 16, 1945, it catapulted the world into the atomic age when it tested the first nuclear bomb over the New Mexico desert.

D.   Propaganda and Politics
To unify Americans and prevent dangerous security leaks, Roosevelt established the Office of War Information and the Office of Censorship.

Full employment and prosperity led to a politically conservative trend. More Republicans and conservative Democrats were elected to Congress in 1942. They cut welfare programs, abolished New Deal agencies, and halted any further reforms. At the same time, the role of the federal government in people's lives grew ever larger, as government supervised the economy, funded research, and molded public opinion.

V.   The Battlefront, 1942–1944
A.   Liberating Europe
The British and Americans concentrated on beating Hitler first, Japan afterward. Stalin pressed his two allies to launch an invasion of Europe across the English Channel as quickly as possible. Churchill convinced Roosevelt they should postpone this second front and land instead in North Africa, where by May 1943, they had defeated large German and Italian armies. Meanwhile the Soviets turned the tide of battle in the east by winning at Stalingrad, holding out at Leningrad, and attacking the German invaders along a thousand-mile front. Again postponing the cross-channel invasion, the British and Americans captured Sicily and started a slow march up the Italian peninsula. There they encountered stiff opposition from German troops who were rushed in after Mussolini was deposed and the Italian government surrendered. In 1944–1945 the Soviets cleared the Germans out of the U.S.S.R. and pursued them across eastern Europe. The British and Americans finally landed on the beaches of Normandy in June 1944 and fought their way toward Germany. The Nazis temporarily

stopped the Allied drive in the Battle of the Bulge, but by early 1945 the Americans and British had reached the Rhine.

B.   War in the Pacific

The Japanese advances in the Pacific were first halted in the spring and summer of 1942 at the Battles of the Coral Sea and Midway. Thereafter, the U.S. Navy and Army assaulted Japanese strongholds in the Solomon, Gilbert, Marshall, and Mariana Islands, and the U.S. Navy largely destroyed what was left of the Japanese fleet at the Battles of the Philippine Sea and Leyte Gulf.

C.   The Grand Alliance

The Grand Alliance of Britain, the U.S.S.R, and the United States was forged out of military necessity, but the three had different goals for the postwar period. Roosevelt wanted to defeat fascism and establish a new world order strong enough to keep the peace, open trade, and protect national self-determination. Churchill hoped to keep the British colonial empire and maintain a balance of power in Europe against the Soviets. Stalin intended to weaken Germany permanently and to protect his country against any future attack from the west by imposing Soviet domination over eastern Europe. FDR attempted to reconcile and paper over these differences with personal diplomacy. He held top-level wartime conferences with the Allied leaders at Casablanca, Cairo, and Tehran. At Tehran, the first meeting of Churchill and Roosevelt with Stalin, details of the Normandy invasion were worked out and other military and political problems discussed.

Roosevelt had to divert his attention from wartime diplomacy long enough to win reelection in 1944. The Democrats nominated him for a fourth term but dropped Vice President Henry Wallace in favor of Harry S Truman. The Republicans nominated Thomas E. Dewey. In November Roosevelt won an unprecedented fourth term by the smallest margin of his career.

VI.   War and American Society

A.   Introduction

Some 15 million Americans served in the armed forces, and another 15 million moved from one place to another. More women than ever before went into the paid labor force.

B.   The GIs' War

GIs saw death and brutality all around them. Some troops in all of the armies committed atrocities. Some suffered lasting psychological damage; others became hardened and cynical. For many, however, their war service opened new vistas. Young people who had never ventured far from home experienced foreign cities and countries. In the army they lived and died with and learned to be more tolerant of Americans of different religions, classes, ethnicity, and regions. About 1 million of them married women they met overseas.

C.   The Home Front

Along with the 15 million Americans who left their homes to serve in the armed forces, another 15 million moved from one location to another for family and economic reasons. People left rural areas to seek jobs in war-production centers, especially in the West. Terrible shortages of housing and other facilities developed in these cities, contributing to urban blight and many social problems.

High school enrollment dropped as more teenagers quit to take full-time jobs. On the other hand, the armed forces sent nearly a million people to college campuses for special training. Americans went to the movies to watch films that entertained them, and the public gobbled up war news from periodicals and from the reports of radio correspondents.

Drawn by high wages, patriotism, and government encouragement, millions of women went to work in defense plants. By 1945 women constituted over one-third of the labor force. They took on such formerly male-dominated work as welding, riveting, operating cranes, and running lathes, although they earned only about 65 percent of what men received in the same fields. More than one-third of the women had children under fourteen years of age. Because there were few day-care centers, youngsters were often left on their own. Juvenile delinquency increased alarmingly. Marriage, birth, and divorce rates also soared. Some 300,000 women joined the armed forces. After 1945 most women left these wartime occupations but the experience gave them a new sense of their own capabilities.

D.   Racism and New Opportunities
During World War II African-Americans demanded that the nation fight racism at home as well as abroad. The NAACP and the Congress of Racial Equality led the struggle for civil rights. To forestall a massive march on Washington organized by A. Philip Randolph, FDR in 1941 signed an executive order prohibiting racial discrimination in hiring and promotion by government agencies and defense contractors. The Fair Employment Practices Commission he created had little power, but wartime labor shortages opened many new jobs to African-Americans. Roughly 1 million African-Americans served in the armed forces, generally in segregated outfits commanded by white officers. They experienced other forms of discrimination as well. In civilian life, tensions developed between African-Americans demanding equality and resistant whites. Race riots erupted in Detroit and dozens of other places. More than 700,000 African-Americans left the South to settle in cities of the North and West. The move opened up greater opportunities and potential political power for African-Americans.

E.   War and Diversity
Twenty-five thousand Native Americans served in the armed forces; another 50,000 left reservations to work in defense industries. With assimilation impeded by prejudice against them, many Native Americans returned to their reservations after the war. Conditions there had deteriorated badly because Congress had slashed appropriations for Indian programs.

Hundreds of thousands of Mexicans entered the United States, legally and illegally, during the war to work on the big farms in the western states. At the same time many Mexican-Americans left migratory farm labor to seek better jobs in cities. In Los Angeles Anglo-American prejudice against Chicanos exploded in the zoot-suit riot. Some 350,000 Mexican-Americans served in the armed forces, and as with homosexual, African-American, and Native American veterans, they emerged from the experience with a heightened consciousness and demands for equality.

F.   The Internment of Japanese-Americans
The government's treatment of Japanese-Americans during World War II was one of the worst violations of civil liberties in U.S. history. In an atmosphere of hysteria over Pearl Harbor, fear of Japanese invasion of the mainland, and traditional prejudice against Asian-Americans, the government uprooted 112,000 Japanese-Americans living on the West Coast and locked them in internment camps in remote interior regions. Unwilling in wartime to question claims of military necessity, the Supreme Court in the 1944 *Korematsu* case upheld the constitutionality of evacuation. In the 1980s the government finally admitted that its actions had been unjustified, apologized to Japanese-Americans, and agreed to pay compensation to them for the property losses they suffered when they were detained.

VII. Triumph and Tragedy, 1945
    A.   The Yalta Conference
          Roosevelt, Churchill, and Stalin conferred for the last time at Yalta in February 1945. Since the Red Army occupied most of eastern Europe at that point and the United States wanted to secure Soviet help in defeating Japan, Roosevelt and Churchill had to make concessions to Stalin. In return for Stalin's promise that the U.S.S.R. would declare war on Japan shortly after Germany's surrender, the Western leaders agreed to Russia's regaining the territory Japan had wrested from it in 1905. Roosevelt and Churchill settled for Stalin's vague promise to allow free elections in Poland and other eastern European nations. Stalin endorsed plans for the United Nations founding conference in April 1945.

    B.   Victory in Europe
          In April 1945 American and Russian troops met at the Elbe River, and Hitler committed suicide. On May 2, Berlin fell to the Soviets, and on May 8, Germany unconditionally surrendered. Roosevelt did not live to see V-E day. On April 12 he died suddenly, bringing Harry S Truman to the presidency.

          Truman distrusted the Soviets and soon accused them of breaking their Yalta promise to allow free elections in Poland. Stalin responded angrily and tightened his hold on eastern Europe. At the San Francisco conference that framed the United Nations Charter (April–June 1945) tensions among the United States, Britain, and the U.S.S.R. were already apparent. By the time Truman, Churchill, and Stalin met at Potsdam in July, the Grand Alliance had disintegrated so badly that the three could agree on little.

    C.   The Holocaust
          When the first reports of Nazi genocide toward the Jews reached this country in 1942, most Americans did not believe them. Though the Roosevelt administration confirmed the existence of the extermination camps and the mass murders and torture going on in them, it chose to concentrate on winning the war as quickly as possible rather than divert bombers to destroying the camps. The U.S. government's other efforts to rescue European Jews before the Nazis could kill all of them were also feeble because Congress and much of the public did not want to admit large numbers of Jewish refugees to the country, and the United States' ally, Britain, did not wish to offend the Arabs by opening Palestine to fleeing European Jews. By 1945, the Nazis had murdered 6 million Jews and several million gypsies, communists, homosexuals, and others they deemed inferior. As the Allies liberated the death camps in the last months of the war, reported the scenes of horror they saw, and took pictures, the American public finally realized the truth of the early news of the Holocaust.

    D.   The Atomic Bombs
          The fighting in the Pacific continued. In 1945, after suffering heavy casualties, the United States captured Iwo Jima and Okinawa. In July the United States successfully tested an atomic bomb at Alamagordo, and Truman issued the Potsdam Declaration, calling on Japan to surrender unconditionally or face "prompt and utter destruction." When Japan rejected that warning, Truman ordered use of the nuclear bombs. On August 6 the first fell on Hiroshima; on August 9 the second hit Nagasaki, following which Japan surrendered. Since then, historians and others have probed the motives of the United States and debated whether it was justified in dropping atomic bombs on Japanese cities. Fifty million people died in World War II, more than half of them civilians. The Soviet Union alone lost 20 million. Much of Europe and Asia lay in ruins. While the United States was physically undamaged, profound changes had occurred in American life during the war, and some 400,000 U.S. servicemen were dead.

VIII. Conclusion

The response of the U.S. government and the American people to the aggressions of Germany, Italy, and Japan through most of the 1930s was to retreat into isolationism. Only after Japan attacked Pearl Harbor, did Congress vote for war on it, and only after Hitler and Mussolini declared war on the United States, did our government reciprocate. Once in the struggle, the country engaged in total war. The powers of the federal government, and especially of the president, expanded mightily to mobilize the American economy fully. It became more productive and prosperous than ever before in our history. As the depression ended, full employment returned, the majority of the people earned good money, and Allied armies defeated the enemy, Americans' faith in "capitalism and democratic institutions" rebounded. Confident and optimistic about the future and our national power, America almost immediately after winning "the greatest war in history" locked horns with its former ally, the Soviet Union, in a Cold War.

VOCABULARY

The following terms are used in Chapter 25. To understand the chapter fully, it is important that you know what each of them means.

appeasement	making concessions to pacify, quiet, or satisfy the other party
belligerent	a country at war
blitzkrieg	lightning war; swift waging of war by use of aircraft, tanks, and other powerful weapons, as practiced by Hitler's armies between 1939 and 1941
convoying	using destroyers or other armed naval vessels and/or planes to escort and protect cargo ships and troop transports
hegemony	great influence or domination of one nation over others
embargo	a prohibition of commerce by government order
braceros	Mexican farm laborers brought into the United States under contract for seasonal work who are then expected to return to their country
Chicanos	Mexican-Americans
the Holocaust	the name given to the systematic effort of the Nazis to annihilate all European Jews
kamikaze	Japanese pilot who attacks a target by crashing suicidally into it
pogrom	government sanctioned and encouraged physical attacks by mobs on a minority group

IDENTIFICATIONS

After reading Chapter 25, you should be able to identify and explain the historical significance of each of the following:

Nye Committee hearings

Neutrality Acts

German-Soviet Non-Aggression Pact, 1939

St. Louis

Henry Wallace

Wendell L. Willkie

the America First Committee

Greater East Asia Co-Prosperity Sphere versus the Open Door policy

Hideki Tojo

Leo Szilard, Enrico Fermi, Albert Einstein, the Manhattan Project, and J. Robert Oppenheimer

the second front

Dwight D. Eisenhower

Battle of the Bulge

Battles of the Coral Sea and Midway

Douglas MacArthur

"Rosie the Riveter"

pachucos, sailors, and the Los Angeles zoot-suit riot

Korematsu case (1944); *Personal Justice Denied* (1982)

SKILL BUILDING: MAPS

1. On the map of Europe and North Africa in the 1930s, on the following page, locate each of the following and explain its significance in the coming of World War II:

    Spain

    Soviet Union

    Italy

    Germany

    Rhineland

    Ethiopia

    Austria

    Sudetenland

    Munich

    Czechoslovakia

    Albania

    Danzig

    Poland (area occupied by the Soviet Union; area occupied by Germany under the terms of the 1939 German-Soviet Pact)

2. On the map of the European theater of war, 1939–1945, locate and explain the military and/or political importance of each of the following:

    areas overrun by the German offensive between April and June 1940 (Denmark, Norway, Netherlands, Belgium, Luxembourg, and France)

    English Channel

    Dunkirk

    Iceland

    Leningrad

    Moscow

    Stalingrad

    Crimean Peninsula (Yalta)

    Caucasus Mountains

    North African campaign (Mediterranean Sea, Egypt, Suez Canal, Morocco, Algeria, Tunisia, Libya, and Allied landing areas)

    Sicily

    Casablanca

    Cairo

    Rome

    eastern European countries occupied by the Soviet Union in 1944–1945 (Romania, Bulgaria, Yugoslavia, Hungary, and Czechoslovakia)

    Tehran, Iran

    Normandy

    Paris

    Ardennes Forest (Battle of the Bulge)

    Rhine River

    Berlin

    Vienna

    Elbe River

3. On the map of the Far Eastern theater of war, 1941–1945, locate and explain the military and/or political importance of each of the following:

    areas attacked and/or occupied by Japan prior to or on December 7, 1941 (Manchuria, parts of China, Indochina, Thailand, and Pearl Harbor)

    Dutch East Indies

    Burma and the Burma Road

    Malaya

    Philippines (Manila)

Guam

Wake

Battle of the Coral Sea

Battle of Midway

Solomon Islands (Guadalcanal)

Mariana Islands

Battle of the Philippine Sea

Leyte Gulf

Kurile Islands

Sakahalin Island

Iwo Jima

Okinawa

Hiroshima and Nagasaki

Europe and North Africa, 1930s

European Theater,
1939–1945
ATLANTIC OCEAN
North Sea
Baltic Sea
Black Sea
Mediterranean Sea
Red Sea

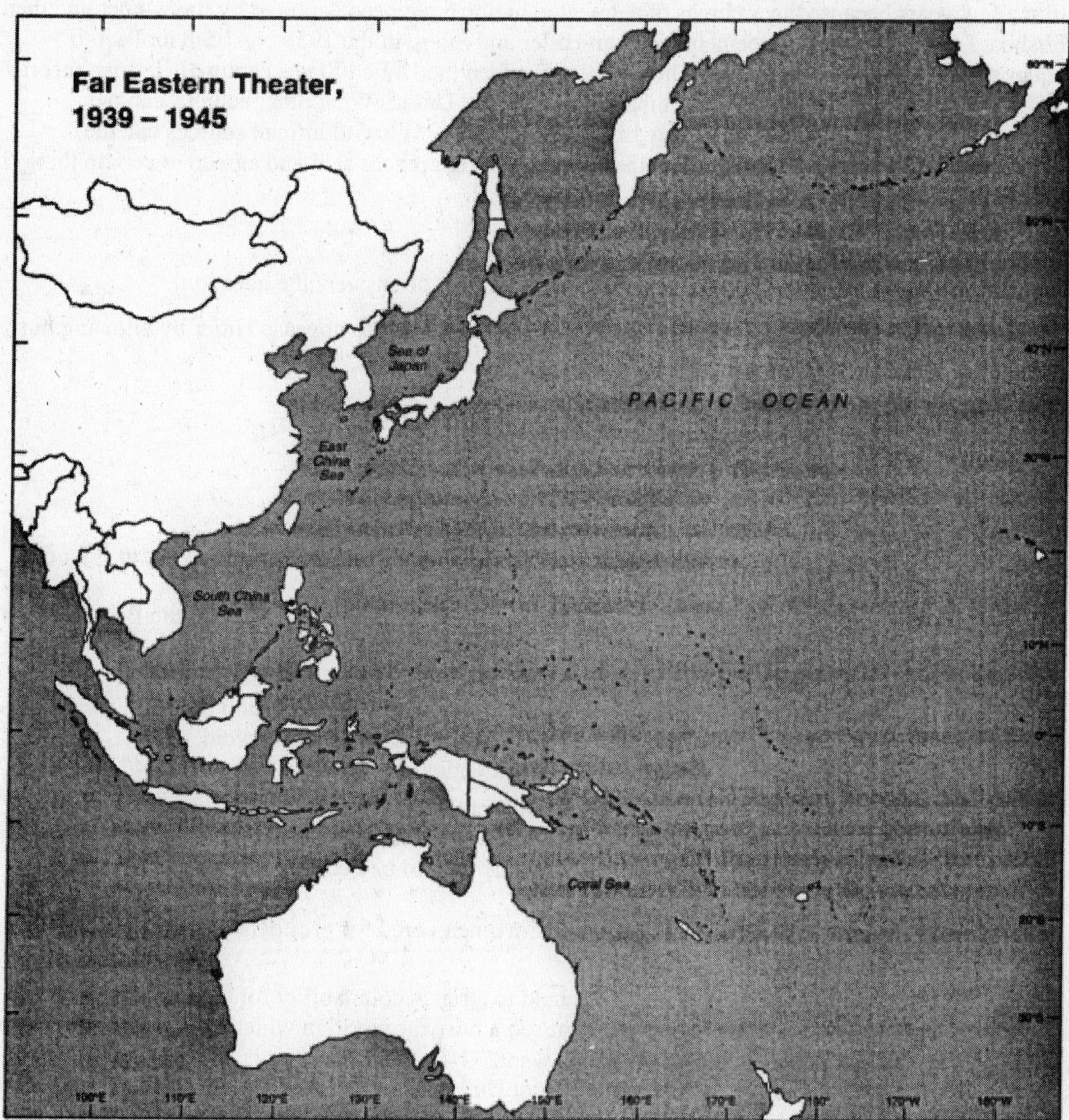

HISTORICAL SOURCES

Look at the discussions of the decisions made at the wartime conferences held at Casablanca, Cairo, Tehran, Yalta, and Potsdam. How do historians know what was said and done at these conferences? Surely Roosevelt, Churchill, and Stalin did not announce to the world as they left Tehran that they had agreed to an Allied landing in France in May or June 1944 to coincide with a Soviet offensive on the Eastern Front. The historian learns what secret decisions were made at which diplomatic conferences some years later (the wait can be twenty-five years or more) when the records from those meetings, held in the archives of the U.S. State Department and the foreign-service offices of other countries, are opened to researchers. In the United States in recent decades, historians have been able to shorten the wait occasionally by bringing court cases under the Freedom of Information Act to force government agencies to declassify secret documents. In other instances secret diplomatic deals have been exposed within a few years because the archives of a defeated nation have been captured by the winner and then published. For example, the agreement between Hitler and Stalin in the 1939 Nazi-Soviet Pact to conquer and divide Poland became public knowledge when the United States captured German records in 1945 and quickly published them to embarrass the Soviet Union. What other sources can the historian use to double-check the accuracy of archival records? What additional sources can the historian consult to find out why the participants in these conferences said and agreed to certain things?

MULTIPLE-CHOICE QUESTIONS

Circle the letter of the item that best completes each statement or answers the question.

1. At the 1938 Munich Conference Britain and France attempted to appease Hitler by allowing him to
    a.   take the Sudetenland from Czechoslovakia.
    b.   reoccupy the Rhineland.
    c.   annex Austria.
    d.   take back Danzig and the Polish Corridor.

2. Lend-lease
    a.   was favored by isolationists as a way to prevent the United States from having to fight in World War II.
    b.   favored the Germans because they were considered better credit risks than the British and Soviets.
    c.   was extended to both Britain and the Soviet Union to help them defeat the Nazis.
    d.   was one of the most unpopular policies of the Roosevelt administration because it was pulling the country into a war the majority of Americans wished to avoid.

3. Which of the following was unique about the presidential elections of 1940 and 1944?
    a.   A candidate was elected president for a third term and a fourth.
    b.   The Democratic incumbent ran with no real opposition from the Republicans.
    c.   The contests were both so close that the winner had to be decided by a House of Representatives vote.
    d.   They were the first two elections in which women voted for president.

4. The Potsdam Declaration
    a.   warned Hitler that Germany would be held to strict accountability for the Holocaust.
    b.   issued by Churchill and Roosevelt promised a postwar world in which all peoples "may live out their lives in freedom from fear and want."
    c.   was issued by Stalin proclaiming the Soviet Union's right to a sphere of influence in eastern Europe.
    d.   warned Japan to surrender unconditionally or face "prompt and utter destruction."

5. American troops first fought German and Italian soldiers
    a.   in the Battle of the Bulge.
    b.   at Stalingrad.
    c.   in North Africa.
    d.   in Normandy.

6. The battle that ended the Japanese offensive and forced her to revert to defending what she had earlier occupied was the
    a.   Battle of Midway.
    b.   Battle of the Bulge.
    c.   Battle of the Philippine Sea.
    d.   battle for Iwo Jima.

7.   Franklin D. Roosevelt's Good Neighbor Policy

   a.   was applied primarily in Asia in the 1930s where the United States tried very hard to improve relations with Japan.
   b.   ended all U.S. interference in Latin American affairs.
   c.   did not keep the United States from sending the marines to Cuba to oust a left-wing government there in 1934.
   d.   resulted in improved relations with Latin American countries and paid off during World War II when most of those countries lined up behind the United States.

8.   Which of the following did *not* occur during World War II?

   a.   The federal government imposed wage and price controls and rationing to combat inflation.
   b.   The federal government took over many industries and strictly limited the profits of others.
   c.   The federal government raised the income tax and introduced the payroll-deduction system to collect it more efficiently.
   d.   Farm income soared, unemployment disappeared, and real wages increased.

9.   Which of the following happened during World War II?

   a.   Marriage, birth, and divorce rates rose rapidly.
   b.   Women were denied the right to serve in the armed forces.
   c.   High school and college attendance increased greatly because families had the money to keep their youngsters in school.
   d.   The majority of preschool children were placed in child-care centers as their mothers worked in defense-industry jobs.

10.   The "Double V" campaign referred to the

   a.   effort of Japanese-Americans to win release from internment camps as well as their effort to help beat Japan.
   b.   demand of African-American leaders to make World War II a victory over racism at home as well as over the Nazis abroad.
   c.   demand of labor unions that workers gain as much from the wartime economic boom as big industrial corporations did.
   d.   effort of American women to fight sexual discrimination at home while supporting the war effort against the sexist ideas of the Axis powers.

SHORT-ANSWER QUESTIONS

1.   What actions did Nazi Germany take against the Jews in the 1930s? What were the Nuremberg laws (1935)? What was *Kristallnacht*?

2.   What contributions to American culture and science did the Jewish and other antifascist refugees admitted to the United States between 1933 and 1941 make?

3.   Who was A. Philip Randolph? What did he call on African-Americans to do in the summer of 1941? How did President Roosevelt respond to Randolph's demands and plans?

4.   Who issued the Atlantic Charter? What did it state were the war aims of the United States and Great Britain?

5.   Explain the purpose of the Office of Price Administration (OPA). How did it try to accomplish its mission? Did it prove effective in achieving its mission?

6.   What were Operations Torch and Overlord? Why was each launched? How well did each succeed?

7.   Explain the issues discussed, the controversies that arose, and the decisions made at the Yalta conference.

8. What was Nazi Germany's "final solution" to the Jewish problem? Why didn't the U.S. government do more during World War II to stop the killing and rescue the victims?

ESSAY QUESTIONS

1. In what ways did Hitler defy the terms of the Treaty of Versailles and commit acts of aggression between 1933 and 1939? What aggressions did Germany's ally, Italy, commit during those same years? How did Britain, France, and the United States react to these aggressive moves? Why?

2. Discuss the actions of President Roosevelt and Congress between 1939 and 1941 to help Great Britain and the Soviet Union fight Nazi Germany. Did the majority of Americans support these moves? Why or why not? Which group did not approve of Roosevelt's policies? Why?

3. Discuss the conflicts between the United States and Japan that led to the Japanese attack on Pearl Harbor. What did Japan hope to accomplish with that attack?

4. Discuss the major strategy, campaigns, and battles of the United States and its allies in the European war theater between 1942 and 1945.

5. Discuss the major strategy, campaigns, and battles of the United States in the Asian war theater between 1942 and 1945.

6. Discuss the effects of World War II on U.S, business, labor, and government.

7. Discuss the effects of World War II on African-Americans, Mexican-Americans, Native Americans, and Japanese-Americans.

8. Discuss the impact of World War II on American women, marriage, and the family.

9. Discuss the formation of and strains in the Grand Alliance of the United States, Britain, and the Soviet Union during World War II. How was the second-front controversy related to those strains?

10. Why did the United States drop atomic bombs on Hiroshima and Nagasaki? What explanations have been offered? Do you feel the United States' actions were justified? Why or why not?

ANSWERS TO MULTIPLE-CHOICE QUESTIONS

1. a
2. c
3. a
4. d
5. c
6. a
7. d
8. b
9. a
10. b

CHAPTER 26

The Cold War Abroad and at Home, 1945–1952

OUTLINE AND SUMMARY

I.   Introduction

Chapter 26 deals with the onset of the Cold War and its impact on American life at home and on the nation's foreign policy. The Cold War refers to the "state of mutual hostility short of direct armed confrontation" that developed between the United States and the Soviet Union as each superpower struggled to shape the postwar world in a way that "served its own national interests." As you read the chapter, consider the following questions: (1) How did President Truman's and Soviet leader Joseph Stalin's policies contribute to the Cold War? (2) What was the containment policy, and how did the U.S. government implement it between 1947 and 1952? (3) Why did New Deal liberalism weaken after World War II, and what effects did its decline have on Truman's administration? (4) What caused the red scare following World War II, and why did Americans become so frightened of Communism? (5) What impact did the Cold War have on civil rights for African-Americans? (6) What were the effects of the GI Bill of Rights on the postwar economy and society?

II.   The Postwar Political Setting, 1945–1946

    A.   Demobilization and Reconversion

In response to popular demand, the Truman administration rapidly demobilized the armed forces, which dropped from 12 million men in 1945 to 1½ million by 1948. Many veterans had trouble readjusting to civilian life. They were faced with severe housing shortages, disappearing defense plant jobs, and reestablishing family bonds. Over a million marriages made during the war ended in divorce by 1950. Women lost their wartime industrial employment and were told by society that they should find fulfillment in marriage and motherhood. Many followed the advice, but others took new lower-paying jobs as office workers and saleswomen. By 1950, more women were in the paid labor force than had been during World War II.

    B.   The GI Bill of Rights

In 1944 Congress passed the Servicemen's Readjustment Act, or GI Bill, to reward the men and women who fought for the country in World War II and help them adjust to civilian life when it was over. It provided returning GIs with low-interest government-backed loans to start their own businesses or buy homes or farms. Some 4 million veterans bought homes with their GI loans, which greatly stimulated the postwar construction industry, economy, and suburbanization. Uncle Sam also offered to pay tuition and expenses for four years of college or professional training for any veterans who wanted it. Eight million veterans accepted the offer. By 1947, over half of the nation's college students were GI Bill veterans. Enrollments soared and many new two- and four-year colleges were founded to meet the demand. These generous government benefits assisted a generation of working class Americans to rise into the middle class.

    C.   The Economic Boom Begins

By late 1946, the U.S. economy was booming. The money the government gave veterans for education, homes, and businesses under the GI Bill certainly stimulated growth. With most of its industrial rivals weakened by the war, the United States enjoyed a favorable position in world trade. Its advantage was heightened by the workings of the new International Monetary Fund and World Bank, which this country mainly controlled and funded. Further, wartime advances in science and technology made possible the development of whole new industries, such as electronics and synthetic materials. Consumers, who had accumulated some $135 billion in savings between 1941 and 1945, went on a postwar buying spree, grabbing up homes, cars, electric appliances, and televisions.

D. Truman's Domestic Program

There was little support after World War II for resuming New Deal reform. Congress passed the watered-down Employment Act of 1946 but balked at Truman's other domestic-reform proposals. With the OPA and price controls terminated, inflation soared. Escalating prices led to an unprecedented number of strikes in 1946 as workers demanded higher wages to keep up with the cost of living. Truman wavered between getting tough with strikers and giving in to their demands. Shortages of housing and consumer goods continued as reconverting industries struggled to catch up with consumer purchases. Americans blamed Truman for inflation, strikes, and shortages, and in November 1946 they elected Republican majorities to Congress for the first time since 1928. There was also much public uneasiness about the atomic arms race that was beginning.

III. Anticommunism and Containment, 1946–1952

A. Polarization and Cold War

After defeating their common enemy Hitler, the United States and the Soviet Union began to argue over Eastern Europe, especially Poland. To secure his nation against future attacks from the west, Stalin insisted that friendly communist governments must be installed on the Soviet borders. While the Red Army occupied these countries, Stalin broke his Yalta promise to allow free elections and saw to it that communist regimes came to power in Poland, Bulgaria, and Romania. President Truman would not accept Soviet domination of Eastern Europe because it violated the principles of national self-determination that the United States had espoused in the Atlantic Charter and Yalta Declaration. Further, Truman believed the spread of communism threatened American economic interests in Eastern Europe and elsewhere. Also, he realized that opposition to Soviet intervention would be popular at home with conservatives and voters of Eastern European extraction.

B. The Iron Curtain Descends

Truman's denunciation of Soviet actions induced Stalin to tighten his grip on Eastern Europe. Nonetheless, the president became more convinced that he should "get tough with the Russians," and he received encouragement. George F. Kennan, a State Department expert on the U.S.S.R., advised that the United States should apply "long-term, patient, but firm and vigilant containment of Russian expansive tendencies." Former British prime minister Winston Churchill, in his iron curtain speech, condemned Stalin's behavior and called for an anticommunist alliance of the English-speaking peoples. Truman threatened to use U.S. naval and land forces if Stalin did not withdraw his troops from Iran and offered a nuclear arms control plan that Russia rejected. When the United States objected to a Soviet counterplan, both sides plunged ahead with developing and stockpiling ever-deadlier weapons. In their emerging Cold War, the United States and the Soviet Union would use economic pressure, nuclear threats, propaganda, and subversion against each other, but they would not engage in direct military combat.

C. Containing Communism

In March 1947 Truman asked Congress to appropriate millions of dollars to help the Greek and Turkish governments fight communist rebel movements and Soviet influence in their countries. The president declared that this was part of a new U.S. commitment to support peoples all over the world who were threatened by Soviet aggression and/or internal communist uprisings. The Republican-controlled Congress endorsed this Truman Doctrine when it voted to appropriate the money in May. Truman and his secretary of state, George C. Marshall, also worried about the situation elsewhere in Europe. Postwar economic collapse was causing impoverished Western Europeans to vote for Communist Party candidates. To curtail the appeal of communism, Marshall and Truman proposed massive U.S. assistance to rebuild European economies. Congress appropriated $17 billion for this Marshall Plan. By 1952 that money had revived Western Europe economically. Communist popularity there had waned, and American business boomed with increased sales to now prosperous European customers.

D.   Confrontation in Germany
In 1947–1948 Stalin broadened his sphere of influence in Eastern Europe as communist regimes took over Hungary and Czechoslovakia. When the United States, Britain, and France announced that they would unite their zones of occupation in Germany into a rearmed West German state, including the Western-occupied parts of Berlin, the Soviets reacted with the Berlin blockade. Stalin prevented all ground movement of goods and people between West Germany and West Berlin. He hoped to halt the establishment of the West German republic or at least force the Western powers out of Berlin. Instead Truman instituted the Berlin airlift and intimated to Stalin that if Russia shot down any supply planes, the United States would retaliate with atomic bombs. In May 1949 Stalin ended his unsuccessful Berlin blockade, and the West German Federal Republic (West Germany), including West Berlin, was established. Also that year the United States joined with ten European nations and Canada in an anticommunist military alliance called the North Atlantic Treaty Organization (NATO). The Soviets responded by establishing the German Democratic Republic (East Germany), developing their atomic bomb, and in 1955 joining with their satellites in the Warsaw Pact military alliance. Thus the two superpowers divided Europe into rival armed camps.

E.   The Cold War in Asia
The United States and the U.S.S.R. also contended for economic and military influence in Asia. The United States pulled a rebuilt Japan into its economic orbit, occupied much of Japan's former Pacific island empire, crushed a communist movement in the Philippines, and aided the French in their attempt to hold on to their empire in Indochina. But American military and economic assistance to Jiang Jieshi did not save his unpopular Nationalist government from overthrow by Mao Zedong. In 1949 the communist takeover of China and Soviet testing of an atomic bomb led to hysteria in the United States and a search for disloyal elements at home to blame for these events. Stung by Republican charges that Truman had lost China, the administration decided to develop the hydrogen bomb and recommended great increases in military spending. The Soviets built hydrogen bombs, too, and the thermonuclear terror increased.

F.   The Korean War, 1950–1953
In 1945 the U.S.S.R. and the United States liberated Korea from Japanese rule. The Soviets set up a communist-governed People's Democratic Republic of Korea north of the thirty-eighth parallel; the United States helped create the pro-Western Republic of Korea to the south. Eager to reunite Koreans under its rule, the Democratic People's Republic of Korea invaded the South in 1950. Truman, without consulting Congress, sent U.S. forces under General Douglas MacArthur to South Korea to repel the invasion. The United Nations also dispatched a token army to fight under MacArthur. U.S., U.N., and South Korean troops soon pushed the North Koreans back to the thirty-eighth parallel, but Truman and

MacArthur decided to conquer the North and place it in the hands of the South Korean government. When MacArthur's armies neared the Yalu River, the boundary between North Korea and China, Mao Zedong warned that he would not "stand idly by." MacArthur, ignoring the threat, was caught off guard by the thirty-three Chinese divisions that hurled his troops deep into South Korea. After months of bloody fighting, MacArthur's forces again reached the vicinity of the thirty-eighth parallel. Truman then ordered the general to hold that position while the United States sought to negotiate a settlement. MacArthur protested, swearing that he could achieve total victory if only Truman would allow him to atomic-bomb and blockade China. When the general would not desist, the president removed him from command to uphold the principle of civilian control over the military. By the time the truce talks concluded in 1953, the border between the two Koreas was set in nearly the same place it had been before 1950, and the United States had expended some fifty-four thousand lives and $54 billion. Between 1950 and 1953 defense spending climbed from one-third to two-thirds of the entire federal budget. The United States also began aiding France against an independence revolt in Indochina and created an anticommunist military alliance with Australia, New Zealand, and other countries in Asia, SEATO.

IV.　The Truman Administration at Home, 1945–1952
　　A.　The Eightieth Congress, 1947–1948
　　　　The Republican-controlled Congress refused to pass further reforms and began to undo the New Deal. Over Truman's veto, it passed the Taft-Hartley Act, which was far less favorable to unions than the Wagner Act had been. Truman courted liberal, labor, and Jewish votes for the next election by condemning the reactionary Congress and recognizing the new state of Israel.

　　B.　The Politics of Civil Rights and the Election of 1948
　　　　In 1946 Truman created the President's Committee on Civil Rights to investigate racism and suggest ways to protect minorities. The committee recommended that Congress pass antilynching, anti–poll tax, and other civil-rights bills. When Truman encountered strong resistance from southern Democrats, he failed to submit specific proposals to the lawmakers. At the 1948 Democratic National Convention, liberals and urban politicians, who needed the northern African-American vote, forced the party to adopt a strong civil-rights plank, committing Truman to press for the measures recommended by his civil-rights committee. This platform induced many southern Democrats to found the rival States' Rights Democratic (Dixiecrat) Party and nominate South Carolina segregationist J. Strom Thurmond for president.

　　　　The Democrats ran Truman; the Republicans, Governor Thomas E. Dewey. Truman's defeat seemed likely because of the Dixiecrat split and the defection of some left-wing Democrats to Henry A. Wallace, the candidate of the new Progressive Party. During the campaign Truman secured the northern African-American vote by issuing executive orders against discrimination in government employment and segregation in the armed forces. With the support of northern African-Americans and most of the Roosevelt New Deal coalition, Truman scored an unexpected victory. Neither Thurmond nor Wallace had drained off enough Democratic votes to defeat him.

　　C.　The Fair Deal
　　　　Truman then asked Congress to pass a package of social and economic reforms he called the Fair Deal. The Eighty-first Congress extended several older New Deal programs, such as increasing the minimum wage and social-security benefits and undertaking slum clearance and public-housing construction. But a conservative coalition of southern Democrats and Republicans blocked all civil-rights and most Fair Deal measures. Truman increasingly turned his attention from domestic reform to the Cold War and the Korean War.

V.   The Politics of Anticommunism
   A.   Loyalty and Security
        Truman, concerned by Republican accusations that he was not protecting internal security, established the Federal Employee Loyalty Program in March 1947. It provided for checks on all government workers to root out any disloyal personnel. Between 1947 and 1951 more than 500 persons were fired and thousands of others resigned, often because they had espoused unpopular ideas, not because they had committed unlawful acts.

   B.   The Anticommunist Crusade
        The loyalty program stimulated more fear of subversion. Magazines published stories about the "red" menace. Thirty-nine states passed laws requiring their employees to take loyalty oaths. Teachers, union leaders, and public officials hesitated to advocate reform lest they be suspected of being procommunist. In 1947 the House Un-American Activities Committee (HUAC) began hearings on communist influence. Witnesses who refused to testify about their own and other people's past political activities and views were cited for contempt of Congress and lost their jobs. After HUAC investigated the entertainment industries, Hollywood studios and radio networks blacklisted employees they considered left-wing. The Truman administration prosecuted the leaders of the Communist Party for conspiracy to preach the overthrow of the government, and the Supreme Court upheld the convictions on the grounds that First Amendment freedoms may be restricted to protect national security. All of this ignored the fact that danger from the 30,000 American Communists was minimal.

   C.   Alger Hiss and the Rosenbergs
        In 1950 former State Department official Alger Hiss was convicted of perjury for lying about providing classified documents to the Soviets. This case heightened public alarm, as did the Rosenberg trial. Ethel and Julius Rosenberg were found guilty of conspiracy to commit espionage as part of a spy ring that had stolen atomic secrets for the Soviets. The Rosenbergs insisted they were innocent, but the judge, reflecting anticommunist hysteria, imposed the death sentence. Secret Soviet documents that became available in the 1990s indicate Hiss and Julius Rosenberg may have been guilty. Republicans claimed these cases proved that the Democratic administrations had been honeycombed with communist traitors.

   D.   McCarthyism
        Of all Republicans, Senator Joseph McCarthy exploited the theme of communist traitors among the Democrats most blatantly. Without supporting evidence, McCarthy loudly accused Democratic senators, members of the Truman administration, and other public officials of either being or harboring communist agents. He won a following among insecure and/or discontented groups, and he frightened political leaders into rigid anticommunist stances on complex issues that required open minds and discussion. Congress also passed the repressive McCarran Internal Security Act and the McCarran-Walter Immigration and Nationality Act.

   E.   The Election of 1952
        The Democrats nominated Adlai Stevenson for president; the Republicans, the popular military hero Dwight D. Eisenhower. McCarthyist labeling of the Democrats as the party of treason, public frustration over the stalemate in Korea, and Eisenhower's pledge to go to that country to end the war, all combined to win the Republicans control of the White House and Capitol Hill.

VI.   Conclusion
   World War II was followed by a period of economic boom. The GI Bill of Rights contributed significantly to that prosperity and the rise of a generation of working-class veterans into the middle class.   Millions of GIs used the benefits and loans to attend college, start businesses, and

buy homes. The election of 1952 ended the first phase of the postwar era and twenty years of Democratic control of the presidency. In pursuit of its Cold War containment of communism, the United States, between 1947 and 1952, extended aid to Greece and Turkey, enacted the Marshall Plan, carried out the Berlin airlift, facilitated the founding of the West German republic, organized NATO, and fought the Korean War. At home, Truman's anticommunist rhetoric and government loyalty program contributed to a red scare that silenced dissenters and weakened Democratic liberalism, as did the economic prosperity. While Republicans could not undo popular New Deal programs, they did block most Fair Deal initiatives.

VOCABULARY

The following terms are used in Chapter 26. To understand the chapter fully, it is important that you know what each of them means.

polarization	moving to opposite or contrasting positions
subversion	working to undermine or overthrow existing institutions, such as the government, especially by secret means
intransigence	unwillingness to compromise
insurgent	one who engages in armed resistance to the established government; a rebel or revolutionary
oligarchy	a form of government in which power is vested in a few or in a dominant class or clique; the members of that class or clique
closed shop	a factory or other workplace in which new workers must join the union before they can be employed
exacerbate	make more violent, bitter, or severe
espionage	spying
red herring	something to divert attention

IDENTIFICATIONS

After reading Chapter 26, you should be able to identify and explain the historical significance of each of the following:

Jackie Robinson

Bretton Woods Agreement, International Monetary Fund, and World Bank

Yalta Declaration of Liberated Europe

North Atlantic Treaty Organization and Warsaw Pact

National Security Council and NSC-68

Taft-Hartley Act

To Secure These Rights

House Un-American Activities Committee

Federal Employee Loyalty Program

Smith Act and *Dennis* v. *United States*

Alger Hiss, Whittaker Chambers, and Richard M. Nixon

Ethel and Julius Rosenberg

Joseph R. McCarthy and McCarthyism

McCarran Internal Security Act

McCarran-Walter Immigration and Nationality Act

Adlai Stevenson

SKILL BUILDING: MAPS

1. On the map of Europe on the following page, locate and explain the historical significance, during the period 1945–1952, of each of the following:

   communist-bloc nations of Eastern Europe (Soviet Union, Bulgaria, Hungary, Romania, Albania, Yugoslavia, Poland, and Czechoslovakia)

   Iran

   Black Sea

   Greece and Turkey

   Mediterranean Sea

   Berlin

   German Federal Republic (West Germany)

   German Democratic Republic (East Germany)

   North Atlantic Treaty Organization members in Europe

   Warsaw Pact members

2. On the map of Asia that follows, locate and explain the historical significance, during the period 1945–1952, of each of the following:

   Japan

   Manchuria

   Democratic People's Republic of Korea (North Korea)

   Republic of Korea (South Korea)

   thirty-eighth parallel

   Seoul

   Yalu River

   Philippines

   French Indochina (Cambodia, Laos, and Vietnam)

   Taiwan (Formosa)

   People's Republic of China

   Marshall Islands

Europe, 1945–1952
ATLANTIC OCEAN
North Sea
Baltic Sea
Black Sea
Mediterranean Sea
Red Sea

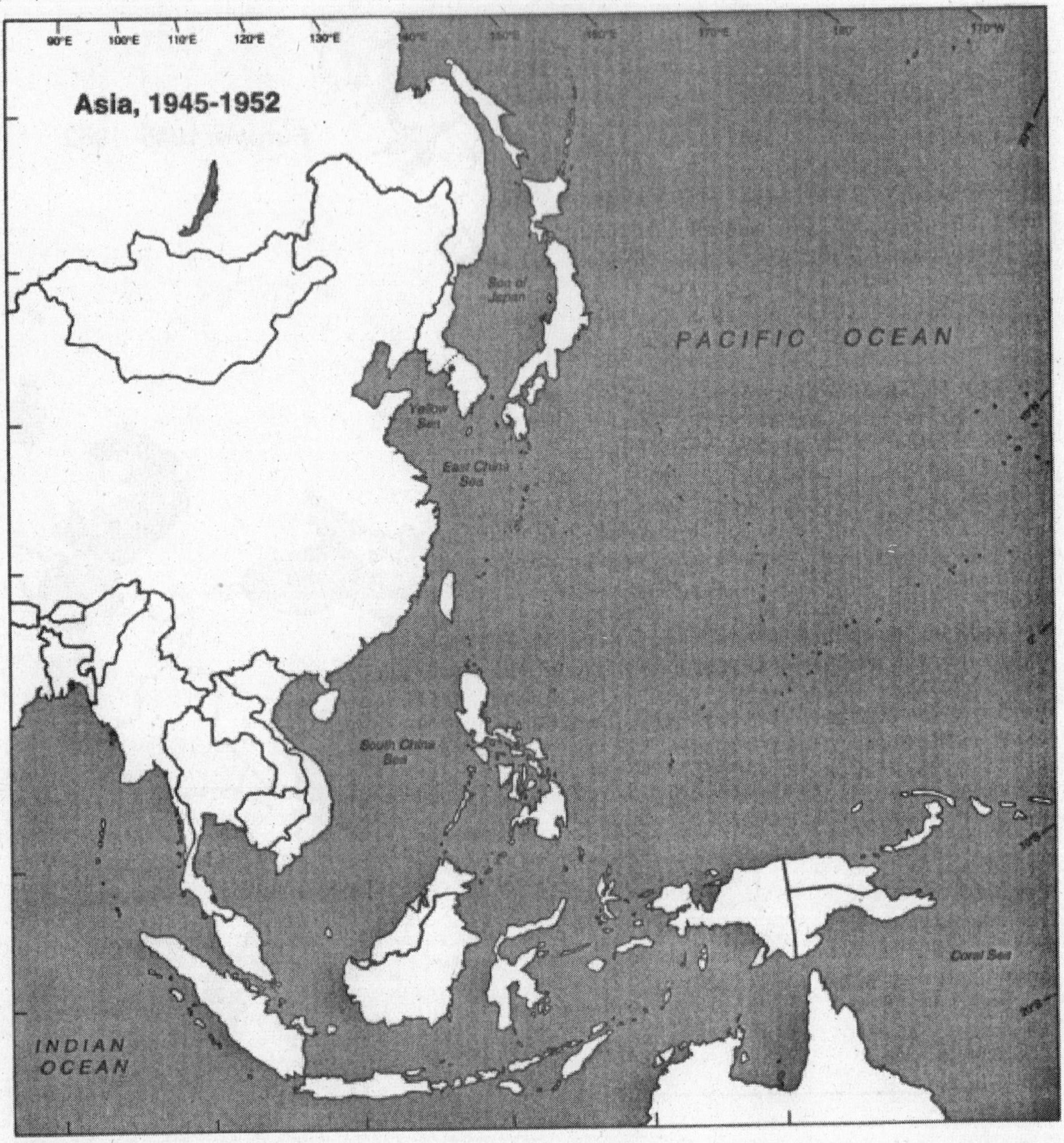

Asia, 1945-1952
90°E
100°E
110°E
120°E
130°E
140°E
150°E
160°E
170°E
180°
170°W
PACIFIC OCEAN
Sea of Japan
Yellow Sea
East China Sea
South China Sea
INDIAN OCEAN
Coral Sea

HISTORICAL SOURCES

In Chapter 26 the author has used as historic sources two significant public speeches: (1) Winston Churchill's iron curtain speech delivered at Westminster College in Fulton, Missouri, in March 1946 and (2) President Truman's address to a joint session of Congress in March 1947, in which he announced the Truman Doctrine. The historian can find the contents of these speeches in the *Congressional Record* and in newspapers such as the *New York Times,* which published the full text. How does the author use these speeches? What does he learn from them about the thinking that shaped U.S. foreign policy? What do they tell about the origins of the Cold War? Furthermore, historians of the Cold War now have more U.S. government documents and Russian ones as well to research. After the fall of the Soviet Union, Russia opened many secret files from the communist period. What new information on the Hiss and Rosenberg cases has been uncovered from these files?

The historian writing about postwar history has available particularly valuable source material in movies and television. Television and motion picture cameras recorded for millions of viewers the images of "the rumpled" Whittaker Chambers and "the elegant" Alger Hiss. Millions watched as the House Un-American Activities Committee questioned film directors, screenwriters, movie stars, and other "friendly" and "unfriendly" witnesses about their political views. Today the historian can read the printed transcripts of these hearings and also view the film footage. How does the author use these printed and visual records in Chapter 26? Do visual images from television and movie cameras tell their own story, or must the historian still interpret what he or she sees?

MULTIPLE-CHOICE QUESTIONS

Circle the letter of the item that best completes each statement or answers the question.

1. Who held up a laundry list and claimed, "I have here in my hand a list of 205 names known to the Secretary of State as being members of the Communist party and who nevertheless are still working and shaping policy"?
    a. Richard M. Nixon
    b. George C. Marshall
    c. Joseph R. McCarthy
    d. Whittaker Chambers
2. At the 1955 Bandung Conference,
    a. Third World nations denounced colonialism and proclaimed their neutrality in the Cold War.
    b. many Asian nations lined up behind the United States, creating the South East Asia Treaty Organization (SEATO).
    c. twenty-nine nations met and endorsed the Balfour Declaration of 1917.
    d. the Soviet Union led twenty-nine Asian and African nations in denouncing the United States as the chief imperialist nation in the world.
3. In which of these cases did the Supreme Court rule that Congress could curtail freedom of speech to protect national security?
    a. The *Rosenberg* case
    b. The Alger Hiss trial
    c. *Morgan* v. *Virginia*
    d. *Dennis* v. *United States*

4.   Which of Truman's Fair Deal proposals did the Eighty-first Congress pass?

   a.   An increased federal minimum wage
   b.   Federal aid to education
   c.   Repeal of the Taft-Hartley Act
   d.   A strong civil-rights law

5.   The president announced his Truman Doctrine to Congress when he asked the lawmakers to

   a.   appropriate $1.3 billion for military assistance to NATO nations.
   b.   appropriate $400 million in military assistance to Greece and Turkey.
   c.   create the Central Intelligence Agency (CIA) to "engage in covert activities in support of the nation's security."
   d.   fund the Berlin airlift for however long it took to counter the Soviet blockade.

6.   In the election of 1948, Truman

   a.   lost the South to the Dixiecrats and J. Strom Thurmond.
   b.   lost most of the liberal vote to Henry A. Wallace and the Progressive Party.
   c.   gained most of the northern African-American vote by issuing an executive order desegregating the armed forces.
   d.   lost to Republican Dwight D. Eisenhower because he appeared "soft on Communism" and lost the labor vote for signing the Taft-Hartley Act.

7.   The National Security Act of 1947 provided for all of the following *except*

   a.   combining the War and Navy Departments into the new Department of Defense.
   b.   establishing the National Security Council (NSC).
   c.   starting the Central Intelligence Agency (CIA).
   d.   instituting the Federal Employee Loyalty program.

8.   In which of these conflicts did American and Soviet troops clash on the battlefield?

   a.   The Korean war
   b.   The efforts to get supplies to Berlin despite the Russian blockade
   c.   The Indochinese war in which Ho Chi Minh's communists tried to oust the French
   d.   None of the above

9.   Alger Hiss was accused of

   a.   giving secret State Department documents to an agent working for the Soviet Union in the 1930s.
   b.   preaching the overthrow of the U.S. government by force and violence.
   c.   helping the communists come to power in China in 1949 by sending them information on Jiang Jieshi's secret military plans.
   d.   opposing U.S. development of the hydrogen bomb in the early 1950s because of his Communist sympathies.

10.   The Korean War

   a.   ended Soviet occupation of the Korean peninsula.
   b.   reunited North and South Korea.
   c.   set a precedent for U.S. participation in undeclared wars not approved by Congress.
   d.   permanently moved the border of South Korea to the Yalu River.

SHORT-ANSWER QUESTIONS

1.   What were the provisions of the GI Bill of Rights (Servicemen's Readjustment Act of 1944)? Briefly explain the impact of the GI Bill on America's postwar economy and society.

2.   Why did the U.S. economy enjoy a boom after World War II rather than slide back into depression?

3. What did George F. Kennan say in his 1946 long telegram to the State Department? How did Truman react to Kennan's call for "long term, patient but firm and vigilant containment of Russian expansive tendencies"?

4. What did Winston Churchill accuse Stalin of in his iron curtain speech? What did he suggest Great Britain and the United States must do to stop Russian expansionism?

5. Explain why the president expounded the Truman Doctrine to Congress. What was Truman proposing? Why did Congress go along with the doctrine?

6. Why did Secretary of State George C. Marshall propose the Marshall Plan (European Recovery Plan)? What was the plan? Did Congress agree to it? Did it accomplish what Marshall and Truman had hoped it would?

7. Why did the Soviet Union impose the Berlin blockade, and how did President Truman respond to it?

8. Why were the communists able to take over China in 1949? How did conservative Republicans explain communist success in China?

9. Briefly explain the impact of the Cold War on the struggle of African-Americans at home for civil rights. Illustrate with three actions of President Truman concerning civil rights for African-Americans.

10. What was the second Red Scare? What impact did it have on American politics and society?

11. Who supported Senator Joseph McCarthy and McCarthyism, and why?

12. What accounts for the victory of Eisenhower and the other Republicans in the election of 1952?

ESSAY QUESTIONS

1. One historian has argued that President Truman was at least partly responsible for McCarthyism and the popular obsession with communist subversion that gripped the United States in the late 1940s and 1950s. Discuss your reasons for either agreeing or disagreeing with that charge.

2. Another historian observed, "If the Truman years represent an era of progress, however limited, in civil rights [for African-Americans], they represent an era of retrogression in civil liberties [free exercise of the rights guaranteed in the First Amendment]." Discuss the statement and support or refute it with specific evidence from Chapter 26.

3. Discuss the origins of the Cold War.

4. What was the containment policy? How did the Truman administration implement it in Europe and Asia?

5. Discuss the differences between President Truman and General Douglas MacArthur on how to conduct the Korean War. Was the president justified in firing the general? Why or why not?

6. Discuss the decolonization which followed World War II and the ways in which it became embroiled in the Cold War that the United States fought against the Soviet Union.

ANSWERS TO MULTIPLE-CHOICE QUESTIONS

1. c
2. a
3. d
4. a
5. b
6. c
7. d
8. d
9. a
10. c

CHAPTER 27

America at Midcentury, 1952–1960

OUTLINE AND SUMMARY

I. Introduction

Chapter 27 explores the realities of and contradictions in American life in the 1950s. As you read the chapter, answer the following questions: (1) Did President Dwight D. Eisenhower practice the "politics of moderation"? (2) Did Eisenhower essentially continue or modify Truman's containment policy? (3) What were the objectives, successes, and failures of the 1950s civil-rights movement? (4) What impact did television and suburbanization have on American life in the 1950s? (5) Were the 1950s a decade of conservatism and conformity? (6) How did the discontent of some young people and minorities foreshadow the social ferment to come in the 1960s?

II. The Eisenhower Presidency

A. "Dynamic Conservatism"

Popular as the World War II commander of Allied forces in Western Europe, Dwight Eisenhower became president of the United States in 1953. He exercised executive authority with restraint; seldom took a public, forceful role in lawmaking; and delegated much responsibility to subordinates. At times, however, he could be an active and "ruthless" politician.

Eisenhower called his approach to governing "dynamic conservatism" or "modern Republicanism." He staffed his administration with corporate executives and expected them to run it with business efficiency. He resisted right-wing pleas to dismantle the New and Fair Deals but tried to restrain further growth of federal activities. Eisenhower's pragmatism led him, despite his dislike of unbalanced budgets, to increase federal spending to combat economic recessions in 1953 and 1957. He signed the Interstate Highway Act of 1956 and legislation to raise the minimum wage, extend social-security coverage, and create the Department of Health, Education and Welfare. In 1956 Eisenhower was renominated by the Republicans and again beat his Democratic opponent, Adlai Stevenson.

B. The Downfall of Joseph McCarthy

Although Eisenhower hated McCarthy, the president did not speak out against him and his reckless accusations. Senator McCarthy's 1954 televised hearings, during which he accused the army of protecting communist spies, finally led to his downfall. The Senate censured him, and thereafter the media and public officials ignored him. Fears of internal subversion remained, however, as the House Un-American Activities Committee continued its endless hunt for communists. Right-wing groups such as the John Birch Society warned against the "creeping socialism" of Truman and Eisenhower.

C. Jim Crow in Court

Conservatives were especially upset at the liberal direction Supreme Court decisions started to take after 1953, when Earl Warren became chief justice. Not only did the Court reverse the convictions of some Communist Party leaders under the Smith Act, but in 1954 in *Brown* v. *Board of Education,* it ruled that racially segregated schools violated the Fourteenth Amendment. Eisenhower's failure to back the *Brown* decision and his regret at having appointed Warren encouraged southern resistance. White Citizens Councils, the Ku Klux Klan, and congressional signers of the Southern Manifesto, all fought school integration, with the result that no progress toward desegregation had been made in the South by the end of 1956.

D.   The Laws of the Land
Southern defiance of the *Brown* ruling reached a high point in September 1957 when mobs of angry whites and Governor Orval E. Faubus blocked the entry of nine African-American students into Little Rock, Arkansas's all-white Central High School. Eisenhower eventually ordered the U.S. Army into Little Rock to enforce federal authority and protect the African-American students. Still, resistance continued so fiercely that by 1960 less than 1 percent of African-American students in the Deep South attended integrated schools. Eisenhower's use of troops, no matter how reluctant, raised African-American hopes and won approval from 90 percent of northern whites. Eisenhower also signed the Civil Rights Acts of 1957 and 1960, which did little to protect the right of African-Americans to vote but did establish a permanent federal civil-rights commission with broad investigative powers.

III.   The Cold War Continues
A.   Introduction
The Eisenhower administration signed an armistice that ended the fighting in Korea in July 1953. The settlement left Korea divided between communist North and anticommunist South near the same thirty-eighth parallel border that had existed prior to hostilities.

B.   Ike and Dulles
Right-wing Republicans were not satisfied with simply containing the spread of communism. To placate them, Eisenhower appointed the aggressive John Foster Dulles secretary of state. Dulles advocated liberating the Eastern European countries from communism and insisted the West should risk war rather than back down in a crisis. Eisenhower ignored Dulles's advice, however, and essentially continued the containment policy.

Eisenhower tried to achieve "peaceful coexistence" with the U.S.S.R. by meeting Soviet leaders at the 1955 Geneva summit conference. The gathering produced no nuclear-arms control plan, but subsequently the two powers independently stopped their atmospheric atomic tests. Meanwhile, the United States relied increasingly on its nuclear weapons to deter Soviet aggression, and Dulles committed the United States to defending many Third World countries. In the 1950s the United States also admitted two new states: Alaska and Hawaii.

C.   CIA Covert Actions
In its effort to secure anticommunist regimes, the Eisenhower administration relied more and more on covert actions, including assassinations and overthrow of governments, by the Central Intelligence Agency (CIA), led by Allen Dulles. During the 1950s the CIA helped install pro-Western autocratic governments in Iran, the Philippines, and Guatemala. Its role in placing the pro-U.S. Shah Reza Pahlavi on the throne and keeping him there spawned festering hatred of the United States among Iranians.

D.   The Vietnam Domino
The CIA carried on its most extensive secret operations in Vietnam. After the Vietnamese overthrew French rule, the CIA blocked elections to unify the country and pushed into power the dictatorial Ngo Dinh Diem in South Vietnam. Eisenhower claimed Diem had to remain in office to prevent Vietnam's fall to the Communists, which would be followed by communist takeovers in all of the surrounding countries in Asia. This came to be known as the "domino theory."

E.   Troubles in the Third World
When England, France, and Israel invaded Egypt in 1956 to reclaim the Suez Canal from Gamal Abdel Nasser, Eisenhower demanded that they withdraw because they had not consulted with the United States in advance. He feared the Suez expedition might lead to a war with the Soviets, who were backing Egypt. After the aborted Suez venture, the president committed the United States to keeping communism out of the Middle East with his 1957 Eisenhower Doctrine, and in July 1958 he sent 14,000 marines into Lebanon to help its pro-Western government squash a rebellion.

Eisenhower's support for pro-Western dictators led to anti-U.S. demonstrations in Latin America and Japan and hostility from the new revolutionary government led by Fidel Castro in Cuba. The president's hope for improving Soviet-American relations with a 1960 summit conference was dashed when the U.S.S.R. shot down an American U-2 reconnaissance plane that had been spying on Soviet military installations.

F.   The Eisenhower Legacy
President Eisenhower ended the fighting in Korea, kept the peace thereafter, and initiated small steps toward relaxing Soviet-U.S. tensions. On the other hand, he speeded up the nuclear-arms race, expanded the Cold War, and gave the CIA the go-ahead to subvert foreign governments that the United States disliked. At home Eisenhower followed a middle-of-the-road course that pleased neither right-wingers nor liberals. Liberals criticized his failure to denounce McCarthy and racism. Conservatives faulted him for not repealing the New and Fair Deals. Eisenhower left office warning his countrymen about the growing influence of the "military-industrial complex" over American society.

IV.   The Affluent Society
A.   Introduction
In the 1950s the United States enjoyed a broad-based, unprecedented level of prosperity. By 1960, 60 percent of American families owned homes and 75 percent had cars. The prosperity was slightly marred by three brief recessions and worry over a mounting national debt.

B.   The New Industrial Society
Greatly increased government expenditures partly accounted for the prosperity and the national debt. Some of the federal money financed public works and other domestic programs, but the majority of it (about 10 percent of the GNP) went into military buildup. The government also underwrote much scientific research, as did large corporations. New technology from this research fueled the growth of industry, made possible increasing automation, and supplied a host of consumer products. The western states profited particularly from government-financed research and development. Most westerners and Americans generally paid little heed to the environmental toll taken by all of the expanded economic activity, especially the spiraling use of petroleum, both domestic and imported. No one paid attention when as early as 1953, a physicist warned that burning so much oil was "warming up the Earth."

C.   The Age of Computers
The development of computers was a key component of the postwar technological revolution. Starting with the Mark I calculator in 1944, the manufacturing of ever more complex electronic computers became a billion-dollar business, and the devices transformed the U.S. economy and way of life.

D.   The Costs of Bigness
Technological advances accelerated the long-term trend toward fewer and larger economic enterprises controlling the United States' industry and agriculture. A new middle class of

professionals and administrators arose to manage these corporate giants. The big corporate farms increased their yields and profits by heavy use of chemical fertilizers, herbicides, and pesticides. Until the 1962 publication of Rachel Carson's *Silent Spring,* most Americans ignored the dangers of these toxic substances to the environment. Not until the 1960s and 1970s did states and the federal government begin to ban the use of DDT.

E.   Blue-Collar Blues
Union membership and power reached its peak in the early 1950s. The AFL and CIO merged into a single federation in 1955 and won for some of the 36 percent of nonagricultural workers who were unionized benefits such as guaranteed annual wages and health-care plans. Thereafter, the union movement declined, as its successes quieted labor militancy; the number of blue-collar laborers fell; and the growing portion of workers in public, white-collar, and service employment proved difficult to organize. By 1960, only 31 percent of workers were union members.

F.   Prosperity and the Suburbs
Rising purchasing power, expanding credit, and burgeoning advertising stimulated avid consumerism. During the 1950s Americans purchased 58 million cars, which improved mobility but contributed to increased highway fatalities, air pollution, and the movement of whites to the suburbs. Government highway building, loans, and tax credits also made it possible for former city dwellers to purchase homes in suburbia. The construction industry built 2 million new homes a year, 85 percent of them in suburbs. Twenty million Americans moved to the suburbs, so that by 1960 the suburban population of the United States equaled that of the central cities. People and industry also moved increasingly from the Northeast to the Sun Belt states of the South and West. By 1963, California had become the state with the largest population, and by 1980 more Americans lived in the South and West than in the North and East. The shift of population to the usually more conservative regions of the nation would soon boost the political fortunes of the Republicans.

V.   Consensus and Conservatism
A.   Togetherness and the Baby Boom
In the 1950s Americans married younger and produced more babies than the previous generation had. The increased birthrate and medical advances that cut infant mortality resulted in the largest population growth of any decade in U.S. history. By 1960, one-third of the U.S. population was under fourteen years of age. The huge size of this baby boom generation made middle-class Americans very concerned about childcare. Dr. Benjamin Spock's *Common Sense Book of Baby and Child Care*, a best seller in the 1950s, preached to women the need to be stay-home moms to rear the young properly.

B.   Domesticity
In the midst of this baby boom, educators, psychologists, and the media all delivered the message that women were most contented when they fulfilled their "natural" roles of wife, mother, and homemaker. Fewer women than men attended college in the 1950s, and almost two-thirds of the females dropped out before graduating. The numbers of working women continued to grow. By 1960, they made up one-third of the labor force, but most were trapped in low-paying, dead-end positions.

C.   Religion and Education
There were signs of renewed interest in religion in the 1950s, such as the popularity of films and books with religious themes, growing church attendance, and the inclusion of the words *under God* in the Pledge of Allegiance and "IN GOD WE TRUST" on the currency. School and college enrollments reached all-time peaks in the 1950s, but much of the education

promoted social and psychological adjustment rather than mathematics, science, and other academic subjects.

D. The Culture of the Fifties
American fiction of the fifties slighted social issues in favor of exploring the personal yearnings of alienated characters. The most significant novels tended to be by southern, African-American, and Jewish writers, such as William Faulkner, Eudora Welty, James Baldwin, and Philip Roth. Hollywood films portrayed Americans as white and middle class, while ignoring minorities and the poor. Women were usually shown as "cute helpmates" or "dumb blondes." Moviegoing declined as Americans watched more television.

E. Television Culture
The influence of television on the nation's economy and culture grew phenomenally during the 1950s. In 1946 it was rare for a family to possess a television; by 1960, 90 percent of all households owned at least one. The three major networks (ABC, NBC, and CBS) monopolized the airwaves and by 1960 were taking in over $1.5 billion in advertising revenue. TV commercials influenced what people read, ate, and wore.

The TV industry both reflected and influenced the values and perceptions of the country. Due to McCarthyism-generated fear and the desire to please a mass audience, television programs avoided controversial or complex issues. Instead, TV fed the public a steady diet of "soaps, unsophisticated comedies, and violent westerns." These programs fostered consumerism, conformity, complacency, and racial and gender stereotypes. TV also impacted politics. A politician's TV image became extremely important. McCarthy's negative one in the televised Army-McCarthy hearings contributed to his downfall, while John F. Kennedy's "telegenic" image helped win him the presidency in 1960. TV greatly escalated the cost of campaigning, thereby encouraging the sixty-second sound bite rather than serious political discussion.

VI. The Other America
A. Poverty and Urban Blight
Few white, middle-class Americans realized that more than one-fifth of their compatriots still lived below the poverty line. The poor included the elderly, migratory agricultural workers, Native Americans, Appalachian whites, African-Americans, and Hispanics concentrated in city slums. In the cities the crying need for low-cost housing went unmet as only a small portion of the public housing provided for in the Housing Act of 1949 was actually built.

B. African-Americans' Struggle for Justice
The struggle of southern African-Americans for social justice entered a new phase of nonviolent, direct action with the 1955 Montgomery bus boycott, sparked by Rosa Parks and led by Martin Luther King, Jr. After their success in Montgomery, King and other African-American ministers organized the Southern Christian Leadership Conference to continue the campaign against discrimination.

C. Latinos and Latinas
The Hispanic population of the country was also, for the most part, poor and discriminated against. By 1960 almost 1 million Puerto Ricans lived in New York's East Harlem *barrio*, where they struggled with low-paying jobs, poor housing, inadequate schools, inability to speak English, and disruption of family ties in a new culture. Mexican-Americans in the Southwest fared no better. The reinstated *bracero* program, which brought temporary agricultural workers in from Mexico, kept wages for farm laborers low and competition for the jobs keen. Increasing numbers of Mexican-Americans moved to cities: in the 1950s the Mexican population of Los Angeles, Denver, El Paso, Phoenix and San Antonio doubled.

During the decade, Latinos and Latinas, too, began to organize and protest against discrimination.

D.   Native Americans
Native Americans were the poorest group in the country. In the fifties the government terminated all special federal services for Indians and encouraged the breakup of the reservations. These policies resulted in the transfer of more than 500,000 acres of Indian land to whites and the further impoverishment and demoralization of Native Americans. Some transplanted Indians prospered and assimilated in cities, but most could not obtain jobs and survived on welfare. One-third returned to their depleted reservations. The National Congress of American Indians condemned the termination policy.

VII. Seeds of Disquiet
A.   Sputnik
Russia's launching of Sputnik in 1957 shook American confidence and complacency. In a rush to catch up, the United States created the National Aeronautics and Space Administration (NASA), launched its own missiles, and greatly increased federal spending on education, with an emphasis on turning out more engineers, scientists, and mathematicians to put us ahead of the Soviet Union in the Cold War of arms research and development.

B.   A Different Beat
Many teenagers expressed mild cultural rebellion in their manner of dress and enthusiasm for rock and roll and its most popular performer, Elvis Presley.

C.   Portents of Change
By the late 1950s the first signs of the "youth movement that would explode in the 1960s" could be seen in the emergence of the Beat writers, such as Allen Ginsberg and Jack Kerouac, and in college student protests against the House Un-American Activities Committee, racial segregation, and the nuclear-arms race.

VIII. Conclusion
The 1950s were a complex time. On the whole, Americans in that decade were conformist, complacent, and prosperous. Eisenhower's policies, while friendlier toward big business than Truman's, were otherwise not that different from his predecessor's. Eisenhower did not dismantle New Deal reforms and even expanded some social welfare programs. He, too, engaged in Keynesian deficit spending to combat recessions and continued the containment of communism abroad. The tendency of U.S. foreign policy to back repressive, dictatorial rulers, as long as they were anticommunist became more pronounced. Both government and the majority of middle-class Americans largely ignored persistent poverty, urban decay, and racial injustice. However, there were glimmers of protest and progress. Beat writers, social scientists, and disaffected youths started to question middle-class values and assumptions. African-Americans began their nonviolent struggle for full equality and made some gains through Supreme Court decisions and the passage of two civil-rights laws.

VOCABULARY

The following terms are used in Chapter 27. To understand the chapter fully, it is important that you know what each of them means.

pragmatic	concerned with or guided by the practical consequences of a given action
Jim Crow	the practice or policy of racial segregation
oxymoron	a combination of contradictory words
coup	a sudden overthrow of a government
proletariat	the industrial working class
autocratic	acting like a dictator; exercising absolute, unchecked power
automation	the operating or controlling of a mechanical process by highly automatic means, such as electronic devices
oligopoly	situation in which a few large companies dominate a whole industry
conglomerates	huge business corporations created by the merger or takeover of many companies in unrelated fields of industry
mores	customs of central importance accepted without question by a group, people, or social class and embodying their fundamental moral views

IDENTIFICATIONS

After reading Chapter 27, you should be able to identify and explain the historical significance of each of the following:

"dynamic conservatism" or "modern Republicanism"

Interstate Highway Act, 1956

"new conservatives," or radical Right

the Warren Court

Ho Chi Minh, the Vietminh, and the National Liberation Front

Mark I, ENIAC, and Silicon Valley

Rachel Carson, *Silent Spring*

David Riesman, *The Lonely Crowd*

Michael Harrington, *The Other America*

Rosa Parks, Martin Luther King, Jr., and the Montgomery bus boycott

Southern Christian Leadership Conference

Native Americans and federal termination and relocation policies

National Aeronautics and Space Administration (NASA)

National Defense Education Act, 1958

rock and roll

Allen Ginsberg, Jack Kerouac, and the Beats

SKILL BUILDING: MAPS

1.   On the map of Asia, locate and explain the historical significance of each of the following in U.S. foreign policy at midcentury:

> North Korea
>
> South Korea
>
> thirty-eighth parallel
>
> Philippines
>
> North Vietnam
>
> South Vietnam
>
> seventeenth parallel
>
> Thailand
>
> Burma
>
> Indonesia

2.   On the map of the Middle East, locate each of the following and explain its significance in U.S. foreign policy in the 1950s:

> Egypt
>
> Suez Canal
>
> Mediterranean Sea
>
> Gulf of Suez
>
> Israel
>
> Syria
>
> Jordan
>
> Lebanon

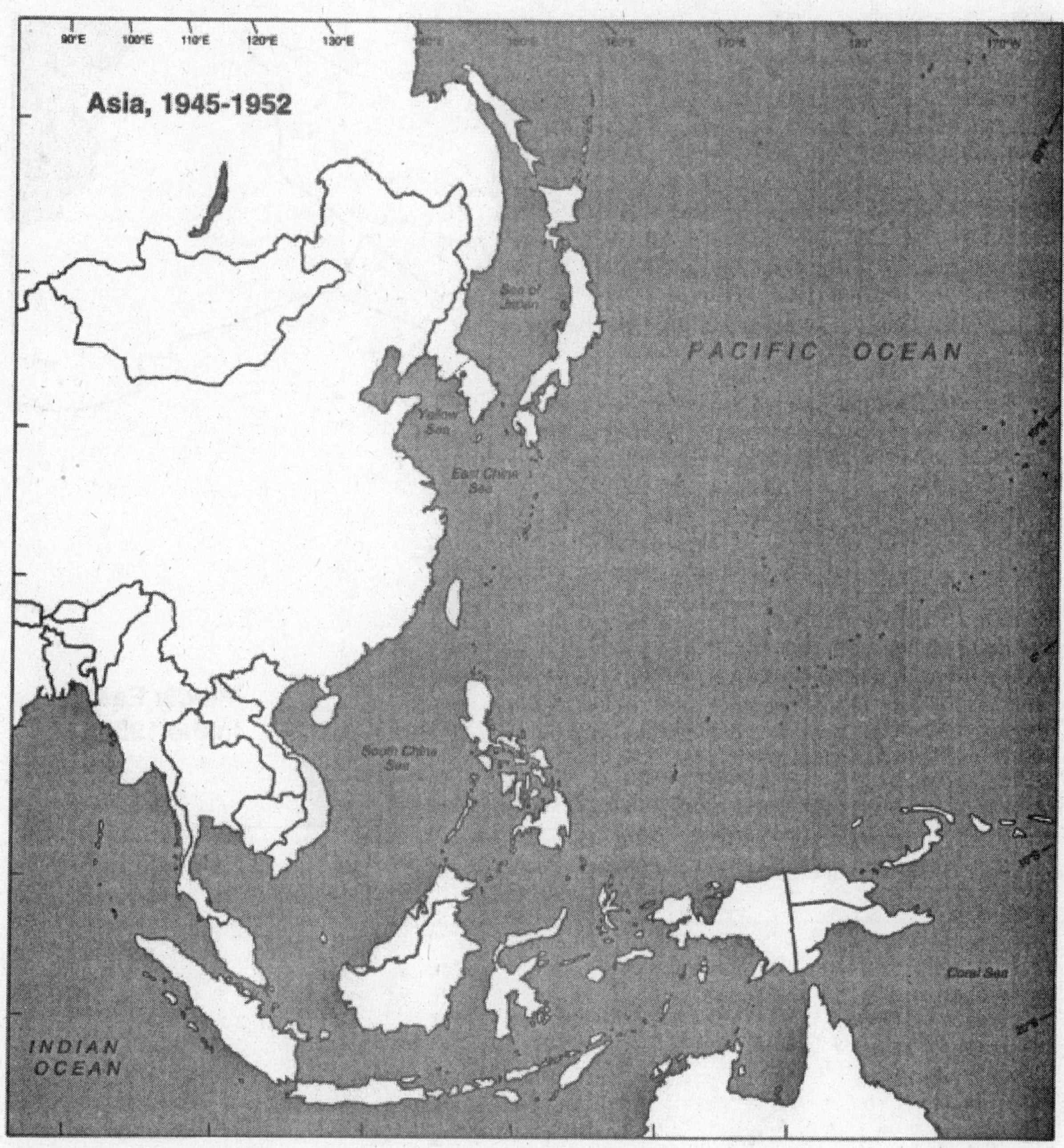
Asia, 1945-1952
Sea of Japan
PACIFIC OCEAN
Yellow Sea
East China Sea
South China Sea
INDIAN OCEAN
Coral Sea
90°E
100°E
110°E
120°E
130°E

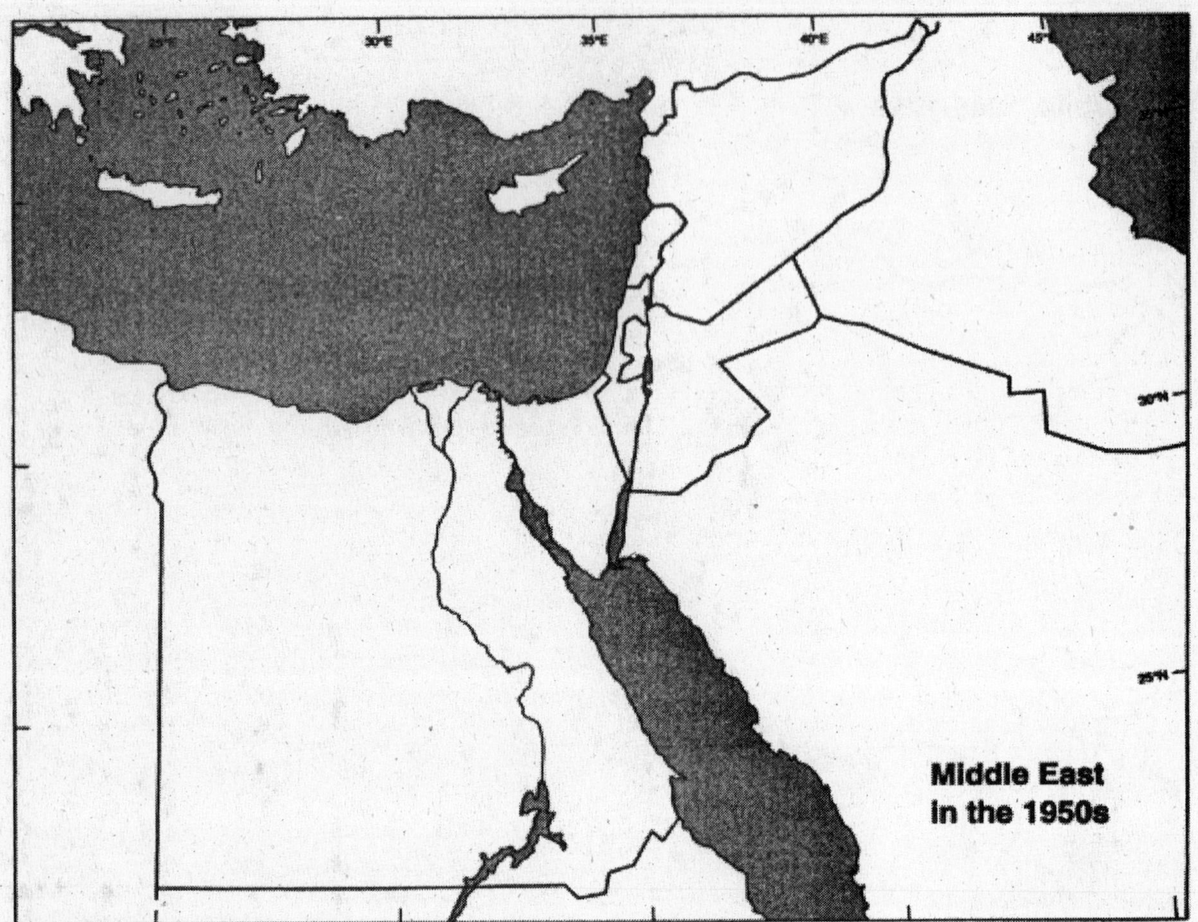
Middle East
in the 1950s

SKILL-BUILDING: GRAPHS AND CHARTS

Look at the pie charts under the title "Urban, Suburban, and Rural Americans, 1940–1960" on page 842. These charts indicate some of the most significant population shifts in those years. After studying them, you should be able to answer the following questions:

1. Between 1940 and 1960 which area of the United States—cities, suburbs, or rural small towns—declined in its percentage of total population?

2. What happened to the percentage of Americans living in suburbs during that period?

3. Historians tell us that most of the population growth in suburbs came from white, middle-class families moving out of central cities. Yet the pie charts show the central cities containing slightly less than one-third of the population in 1940, 1950, and 1960. Who was moving into the central cities to replace the white middle class migrating to the suburbs?

HISTORICAL SOURCES

In Chapter 27 the author has learned much about the recent past by looking at items of popular culture and entertainment: television programs, Hollywood films, hit songs, most admired movie and rock stars, and the best-selling books of the period. The chapter opens with a commentary on the most popular TV program of the fifties, "I Love Lucy." On pages 847-848 the author describes some of the other most watched television shows. There is a section devoted to Elvis Presley and a reference on page 854 to Dick Clark's *American Bandstand*. On page 845 the author discusses the book that sold more copies than any other but the Bible in the 1950s: Benjamin Spock's *Baby and Child Care*. How does the author use each of these examples of popular culture? In each case what does the author claim it shows about American society and values at midcentury? Using the same sources, could you come to different conclusions about 1950s America?

Look at "Technology and Culture: The Interstate Highway System." This is a capsule history of the biggest public works project ever undertaken by the federal government. How was its being built related to the Cold War? According to the author, what was its impact on American society, both positive and negative?

MULTIPLE-CHOICE QUESTIONS

Circle the letter of the item that best completes each statement or answers the question.

1. President Eisenhower once said "the biggest damn fool mistake I ever made" was

    a. appointing Earl Warren as chief justice of the Supreme Court.
    b. not denouncing Joseph McCarthy and McCarthyism publicly in 1952 and 1953.
    c. appointing John Foster Dulles as secretary of state and allowing him to practice "brinksmanship."
    d. giving the CIA a free hand to conduct covert actions to undermine foreign governments it didn't approve of.

2.   Which of these actions did President Eisenhower take in response to the Suez crisis?

   a.   He ordered 14,000 marines into Egypt to protect the canal from Soviet infiltrators.

   b.   He joined in an invasion staged by France, Britain, and Israel to overthrow Gamal Abdel Nasser.

   c.   He forced Britain, France, and Israel to withdraw their armies from Egypt and announced the Eisenhower Doctrine.

   d.   He asked the United Nations to internationalize the Suez Canal and send in a peace keeping force to protect it.

3.   The Southern Manifesto, signed by more than one hundred members of Congress,

   a.   called on the Ku Klux Klan, White Citizens Councils, and other southern resistance groups to cease violent opposition to desegregation.

   b.   denounced Governor Orville Faubus for complying with court orders to desegregate Little Rock public schools.

   c.   pledged southern white and African-American lawmakers to work together to end segregation in their area gradually.

   d.   denounced *Brown* v. *Board of Education* and pledged unending opposition to desegregation.

4.   President Eisenhower advanced his domino theory to justify U.S. intervention in the internal affairs of

   a.   Guatemala.

   b.   Vietnam.

   c.   Korea.

   d.   Egypt.

5.   Which of the following statements about women in the 1950s is correct?

   a.   Women generally married later and had fewer children than they had in the 1930s and 1940s.

   b.   Almost two-thirds of female college students dropped out before graduating.

   c.   The proportion of married women who were employed declined.

   d.   A greater proportion of women became involved in the feminist movement than ever before.

6.   The 1950s government policies of termination and relocation proved disastrous for

   a.   Native Americans.

   b.   African-Americans.

   c.   Mexican-Americans.

   d.   Puerto Ricans.

7.   Which of these 1950s novels is *incorrectly* paired with its subject matter?

   a.   James Baldwin, *Go Tell It on the Mountain*—the black experience in America

   b.   Bernard Malamud, *The Assistant*—Jewish immigrant experience in New York City

   c.   Eudora Welty, *The Ponder Heart*—southern small town life

   d.   Ralph Ellison, *Invisible Man*—white middle class discontent and conformity

8.   Which did *not* occur in the 1950s?

   a.   The total number of farms declined as large-scale agribusiness increasingly dominated farming.

   b.   Less than 1 percent of American businesses earned more than half of all corporate income.

   c.   The portion of the labor force belonging to unions increased from roughly one-quarter to almost one-half.

   d.   More than half of the federal budget each year went to finance military preparedness.

9. About what portion of the American people lived in poverty during the prosperous 1950s?
    a. One-third
    b. One-fifth
    c. One-half
    d. One-tenth
10. Which of the following is *not* correctly paired with an organization or his concern?
    a. Benjamin Spock—baby and childcare
    b. Jackson Pollock—the New York art scene and abstract expressionism
    c. Billy Graham—the Southern Christian Leadership Conference
    d. Allen Dulles— the Central Intelligence Agency

SHORT-ANSWER QUESTIONS

1. What brought about the downfall of Joseph McCarthy? Did his eclipse end excessive fears of Communist subversion?

2. What did the Supreme Court decide unanimously in the *Brown* v. *Board of Education of Topeka* case? On what grounds did it reach its decision? How did the court somewhat weaken the decision in 1955?

3. Discuss briefly President Eisenhower's record on civil rights for African-Americans. Include his response to *Brown* v. *Board of Education*, his actions in Little Rock, and his connection to the Civil Rights Acts of 1957 and 1960.

4. Explain the roles in U.S. foreign policy of Secretary of State John Foster Dulles and his brother, CIA director Allen Dulles.

5. What did President Eisenhower mean when he warned Americans to be wary of the military-industrial complex?

6. Describe the economic changes that occurred in American agriculture in the 1950s. What impact did those changes have on the environment?

7. Why did union membership and influence decline in the second half of the 1950s?

8. Describe at least three major demographic changes that occurred in America in the 1950s. What social and political impact would these developments have on the nation?

9. Discuss briefly America's growing Latino and Latina population in the decade of the fifties. Where did they come from? Where did they settle? Why did they come to the mainland United States? What problems did they face? How did the *bracero* program affect Mexican Americans?

10. What were the effects on American life of Russia's launching of *Sputnik*?

ESSAY QUESTIONS

1. "Eisenhower pursued a centrist course in domestic affairs." Write an essay either agreeing or disagreeing with this assessment. Back up what you say with as many specific facts as possible.

2. Discuss the Eisenhower legacy in foreign policy. How successful was he in keeping the peace and easing tensions with the Soviets? In what ways did his policies expand the Cold War and accelerate the nuclear-arms race?

3. "A booming, broad-based prosperity made the 1950s a period of economic abundance without historical parallel." Explain the developments and circumstances that produced the prosperity and abundance. What role did government policies play in encouraging economic activity?

4. The section of Chapter 27 dealing with American society and culture in the 1950s is titled "Consensus and Conservatism." Is this an apt title? Discuss major trends in American family life, religion, education, the arts, and entertainment during the fifties to illustrate why this is or is not an appropriate title.

5. Discuss "the other America." What does the term refer to? Which groups made up the other America in the 1950s? Why were they shut out of the unprecedented economic prosperity of that decade?

ANSWERS TO MULTIPLE-CHOICE QUESTIONS

1. a
2. c
3. d
4. b
5. b
6. a
7. d
8. c
9. b
10. c

CHAPTER 28

The Liberal Era, 1960–1968

OUTLINE AND SUMMARY

I.   Introduction

Starting in February 1960, in Greensboro, North Carolina, a wave of sit-ins to desegregate lunch counters and other public places swept through the South. The courage of the African-American students who initiated these demonstrations emboldened their elders and energized the struggle for racial equality. It also broke the conservative complacency of the 1950s, paving the way for crusading authors like Ralph Nader and Betty Friedan to arouse the nation to the dangers for the consumer and to the pervasive sexism. The rhetoric of John Kennedy's New Frontier and Lyndon Johnson's Great Society attracted young, progressive Americans with their promise of an end to these wrongs. But assassinations of key leaders, widespread racial strife, and escalation of the war in Vietnam produced a white, conservative backlash and curtailed reform. The decade closed in discord and disillusionment.

As you read Chapter 28, answer these questions: (1) How successful was President Kennedy's New Frontier in domestic and foreign policy? (2) Did Lyndon Johnson have the same goals as his predecessor, and did he achieve more or less than Kennedy? (3) How did the Great Society program raise unrealized expectations and therefore produce some violent reactions? (4) How much progress did the civil-rights movement make toward achieving economic, political, and social equality for African-Americans, and why did African-Americans become more militant between 1964 and 1968? (5) What caused deepening U.S. involvement in the Vietnam War, and why did President Johnson follow that course?

II. The Kennedy Presidency, 1960–1963

A.   Introduction

Son of a wealthy and ambitious father, John F. Kennedy was a liberal who believed in an activist federal government that could both improve life at home and carry on the Cold War abroad. Helped by his father's money and connections, Kennedy first won a seat in Congress in 1945 from a Boston district. Though his record in the House was unimpressive, Massachusetts voters elevated him to the Senate in 1952 and reelected him in 1958. In 1960, having acquired a Pulitzer Prize for his *Profiles in Courage,* mostly ghostwritten by a staff member, Kennedy captured the Democratic nomination for president. The youthful, just forty-two year-old candidate summoned America to a New Frontier.

B.   A New Beginning

Richard M. Nixon, the Republican presidential nominee, identified himself with the still popular Eisenhower and his "middle way," although liberals never forgot Nixon's McCarthyist background. John F. Kennedy, the lesser known Democratic candidate, challenged his opponent to a series of televised debates. The four debates enhanced the popularity of the telegenic Kennedy and marked the beginning of television's domination in American presidential politics. Kennedy won in the closest contest since 1884.

Unlike Eisenhower, whose cabinet was top-heavy with businessmen, Kennedy surrounded himself with liberal intellectuals. He appointed his closest confidant and adviser, his brother

Robert Kennedy, as attorney general. The president gave his administration a cultural tone by inviting artists and writers to the White House, and he used television to broaden his popular appeal. Knowing little of his personal weaknesses, Americans responded warmly to JFK's carefully crafted public image.

C.   Kennedy's Domestic Record
Despite Kennedy's call for a New Frontier, he pushed little reform legislation through Congress. Rather than press the fight with Congress, the president concentrated on promoting economic growth through increased military spending and tax incentives to business. At the time of Kennedy's assassination, the economy was booming thanks to defense spending. Indeed, by 1963, defense expenditures reached the largest portion of the total federal budget that they ever assumed during the Cold War period. Because of Rachel Carson's *Silent Spring* and other warnings, Americans were beginning to worry about the polluted environment. In response Congress passed the 1963 Clean Air Act.

D.   Cold War Activism
Kennedy, much more vigorous in foreign affairs than domestic, greatly stepped up military spending. He also convinced Congress to fund the Peace Corps. By 1963, there were 5,000 volunteers aiding Third World people in forty countries.

Kennedy approved a plan formulated under Eisenhower to help anticommunist Cuban exiles in the United States who wanted to invade the island and overthrow Fidel Castro. The Bay of Pigs landing failed miserably, but Kennedy persisted in backing plots to assassinate or depose Castro. Kennedy also took a tough line with the U.S.S.R. in defense of Western occupation rights in Berlin. Unable to dislodge U.S. forces from West Berlin, the Soviets walled it off from their zone.

E.   To the Brink of Nuclear War
In October 1962 the Soviet Union and the United States came to the verge of nuclear war over the Cuban missile crisis. Kennedy and U.S.S.R. premier Nikita Khrushchev stepped back from the brink at almost the last moment with an agreement that the Soviets would remove the rockets they had installed in Cuba in exchange for Kennedy's promise not to invade that country. (Later Kennedy quietly removed U.S. missiles from Turkey as Khrushchev had earlier demanded.) After this brush with disaster, the United States and the Soviet Union moved toward détente, a determination on both sides to avoid direct, armed conflict in settling their differences. A "hot line" was installed between the White House and the Kremlin to facilitate communication. The two powers signed a treaty banning atomic tests in the atmosphere and the oceans. But the nuclear- and conventional-arms race escalated.

F.   The Thousand-Day Presidency
On November 22, 1963, in Dallas, Texas, Lee Harvey Oswald shot President Kennedy to death, bringing Vice President Lyndon Baines Johnson to the Oval Office. Kennedy left his successor a mixed legacy. He had compromised in Laos but intensified U.S. entanglement in Vietnam. While praising disarmament and détente, he had pushed a massive arms buildup. In domestic matters, the New Frontier accomplished little. Congress did not act on the majority of Kennedy's reform proposals. His idealistic rhetoric aroused the hopes of reformers, the poor, the powerless, and the young, but he also left behind a hopeless entanglement in Vietnam that would make the fulfillment of rising domestic expectations next to impossible.

III.   The Struggle for African-American Equality, 1961–1968
    A.   Introduction
    Following the lunch counter sit-ins, African-Americans attempted to convince Kennedy to support civil rights vigorously. He would not do so because he feared splitting the Democratic Party, touching off filibusters in the Senate, and losing reelection. While he appointed many African-Americans to federal offices, he also placed on the bench a number of white segregationists. He took two years to fulfill his campaign promise to issue an executive order against segregation in federally funded housing. It was only the militancy of the civil-rights activists and the answering fury of southern racists that finally forced the president's hand.

    B.   Nonviolence and Violence
    Kennedy finally sent federal marshals into the South after white mobs in Anniston, Birmingham, and Montgomery, Alabama, savagely attacked Congress of Racial Equality (CORE) freedom riders who were defying the unconstitutional segregation imposed on interstate travelers. It took still more freedom rides to convince the president that the Interstate Commerce Commission would have to enforce the Supreme Court ruling against segregated interstate transportation. Racist violence also eventually forced Kennedy to dispatch federal troops to the University of Mississippi campus to protect James Meredith, the first African-American student enrolled there.

    C.   The African-American Revolution
    In 1963, to expose the viciousness of southern racists and compel Kennedy to act, Martin Luther King, Jr. led marches, sit-ins, and pray-ins in Birmingham, Alabama. Police chief Eugene "Bull" Conner, in front of television cameras, sent his police with electric cattle prods, high-pressure water hoses, and attack dogs against the peaceful demonstrators. The televised brutality aroused international indignation and prompted Kennedy to convince Birmingham's leaders that they must desegregate stores and upgrade African-American employees. The concessions won in Birmingham encouraged "Freedom Now!" protests in hundreds of other southern towns and cities. Kennedy began to realize that if the federal government did not commit the nation to "peaceful and constructive" reform of race relations, African-Americans in their frustration might follow leaders who preached the need for violence. Therefore, the president quickly forced segregationist governor George Wallace to allow two African-American students to enter the University of Alabama, and in June 1963 Kennedy proposed a broad civil-rights bill.

    D.   The March on Washington, 1963
    On August 28, 1963, Martin Luther King, Jr. addressed a throng of 250,000 who had marched on Washington to persuade Congress to pass Kennedy's proposed civil-rights bill. Though King gave a great political speech calling on Americans to live up to his dream of "true brotherhood," he failed to move Congress. Southern white terrorism against African-Americans continued in September with the Ku Klux Klan's bombing of an African-American church in Birmingham, which killed four young girls attending Sunday school. The last of the perpetrators was not tried and convicted until 2002.

    E.   The Civil Rights and Voting Rights Acts
    After Kennedy's assassination, President Johnson maneuvered through Congress the tough 1964 Civil Rights Act. It banned segregation and/or discrimination in public facilities, federally funded programs, schools, and employment. It created the Equal Employment Opportunity Commission (EEOC) to investigate and stop job discrimination based on race, religion, national origin, or gender. But the law did not guarantee voting rights.

In 1964 the Student Nonviolent Coordinating Committee (SNCC) and CORE organized the Mississippi Freedom Summer Project, sending thousands of college student volunteers into the South to run freedom schools and register African-Americans to vote. Their efforts were stymied by the violence of the Ku Klux Klan and local police officials. To dramatize the problem of continuing disfranchisement, Martin Luther King, Jr., organized mass demonstrations in Selma, Alabama. When a national television audience saw Sheriff Jim Clark and his troopers viciously attack peaceful protesters, the public demanded federal action. President Johnson urged Congress to pass a voting rights law. The resulting Voting Rights Act of 1965 authorized federal examiners to register qualified voters and suspend discriminatory literacy tests. For the first time since Reconstruction, African-Americans, through the ballot box, achieved significant power in southern politics.

F.   Fire in the Streets
The summers of 1965 through 1968 saw the outbreak of race riots in cities around the country, causing some $500 million worth of property damage, 7,000 injuries, and 200 deaths. The Kerner Commission, appointed by President Johnson to investigate, found the causes of the trouble to be persisting "white racism" that had subjected African-Americans to poverty, slum housing, poor education, and police brutality. The Kerner report recommended more federal aid to poor, urban African-Americans. However, Johnson and Congress, noting the white backlash against further federal assistance to African-Americans, did not act on the proposals.

G.   "Black Power"
The Black Power movement, influenced by the teachings of Malcolm X, emerged from the civil-rights campaign in 1966. It preached race pride and self-determination, rejected Martin Luther King, Jr.'s nonviolence, and questioned the value of integration. After 1966 both CORE and SNCC changed from being interracial, integrationist civil rights organizations to all-black, militant separatists willing to engage in violent confrontations. The Black Panthers preached the same black power message and became embroiled in shoot-outs with the police.

IV.   Liberalism Ascendant, 1963–1968
A.   Introduction
Kennedy's assassination brought to the White House Lyndon Baines Johnson. At first distrusted by liberals and disparaged by Kennedy loyalists, Johnson soon proved himself a master at "wooing allies, neutralizing opponents, building coalitions, and achieving results." In the term he inherited from Kennedy and in the one he was elected to in 1964, Johnson pushed through Congress a prodigious amount of liberal legislation, even exceeding Roosevelt's New Deal record.

B.   Johnson Takes Over
Johnson urged Congress to approve Kennedy's tax-cut and civil-rights proposals as a memorial to the fallen president. In February 1964 taxes were sliced by $10 billion, and the resulting increase in consumer spending and employment brought in more revenue, thus reducing the federal deficit. That same year Congress also passed a major civil-rights bill. Inspired by Michael Harrington's *The Other America*, Johnson and Congress declared war on poverty with the Economic Opportunity Act of 1964, which founded the Office of Economic Opportunity, the Job Corps, VISTA, Head Start, and the Community Action Program. As the 1964 election approached, Johnson said his purpose with these measures and more to come was to create the Great Society, free from poverty and racial injustice, where the quality of life would be improved for all.

C.   The 1964 Election
The Democrats nominated President Johnson. Conservatives thoroughly disliked his Great Society promise of more federal spending on domestic welfare. Southern segregationists and some white industrial workers resented Johnson's backing of the civil-rights movement. At the Republican convention, these forces and other right-wing elements gained control, nominating ultraconservative Senator Barry Goldwater of Arizona. Goldwater, repudiating moderate Republicanism, advocated ending the War on Poverty, the Tennessee Valley Authority, and social security. He hinted that he might use nuclear weapons against Cuba and North Vietnam to bring them into line with U.S. wishes. Johnson won a landslide victory and brought with him huge Democratic majorities on Capitol Hill. The stage seemed to be set for completing the liberal agenda. Despite Goldwater's resounding defeat, his candidacy marked the emergence of the "new conservatism," which would increasingly gain control of the Republican Party and transform it from a moderate party dominated by eastern business interests to one run by right-wing southerners and westerners.

D.   Triumphant Liberalism
During 1965 Johnson sent to Congress a steady stream of social-welfare and reform proposals and got most of them enacted. These included Medicare and Medicaid, federal assistance to education, the Voting Rights Act, a liberalized immigration law, the establishment of the departments of Transportation and Housing and Urban Development and funding of major programs for them to run, creation of the National Endowments of the Arts and Humanities, additions to and protection of the national parks, and tougher antipollution measures. The new, less discriminatory immigration law allowed millions of Asians and Hispanics to come to the United States, making the American population and culture much more diverse. Great Society measures significantly benefited the poor and disadvantaged. The proportion of Americans living below the poverty line fell from 22 percent in 1960 to 13 percent in 1969. The percentage of African-Americans who were poor was cut in half. But by 1966 the president's attention and more and more of the nation's resources were diverted from building the Great Society to fighting the war in Vietnam. The dashed hopes of liberals, African-Americans, and the poor produced urban race riots and anger at LBJ. The riots, in turn, alienated white, middle-class Americans. Democratic losses in the 1966 congressional elections reflected the disappointment and ended most reform efforts.

E.   The Warren Court in the Sixties
With Johnson's appointment of two more liberals to the Supreme Court, including Thurgood Marshall, the first African-American justice, the already liberal Warren Court became even more liberal. In the 1960s it handed down decisions banning prayer in public schools, limiting press and film censorship, and requiring equal-sized election districts and due process for persons accused of crimes. Liberals applauded. Conservatives railed that the judges were undermining law and order.

V.   Voices of Protest
A.   Introduction
The civil-rights and Black Power movements set an example for Native Americans, Hispanic Americans, and women. They began to organize to raise group pride and fight for redress of their grievances.

B.   Native American Activism
In 1961 representatives from many tribes gathered to denounce the termination policy. There followed demands for Indians to be included in the War on Poverty programs. President Johnson responded by ending the termination policy, endorsing Native American

self-determination, and creating the National Council on Indian Opportunity, which directed more federal monies into improving conditions on reservations than ever before. However, because of persisting poverty and discrimination, militant young Native Americans organized the American Indian Movement (AIM) in 1968, called for "Red Power," and occupied Alcatraz Island for a year and a half.

C.　Hispanic Americans Organize
César Chávez's and Dolores Huerta's United Farm Workers union started organizing the mostly Mexican American agricultural laborers of California and the Southwest. They sought support for the union and its strikes (*La Causa*) by promoting consumer boycotts of grapes and other produce, aligning themselves with the civil-rights movement and appealing to Mexican American identity and pride. Meanwhile, young Hispanics began referring to themselves as Chicanos or Chicanas and demonstrating for Hispanic studies programs and bilingual education in the schools. In Colorado, Rodolfo "Corky" Gonzales founded the Crusade for Justice, in Texas Hispanics launched the political party *La Raza Unida,* and Puerto Rican New Yorkers established the Young Lords.

D.　Asian American Activism
Asian Americans, too, displayed heightened ethnic consciousness and put forth demands for recognition and respect. In 1968, Filipino, Chinese, and Japanese-American students organized the Asian American Political Alliance to protest the war in Vietnam and demand Asian American studies courses at their colleges and universities.

E.　A Second Feminist Wave
The growing unhappiness of middle-class white women with the 1950s emphasis on maternity and domesticity was articulated by Betty Friedan in *The Feminine Mystique* (1963). Women also resented the widespread employment discrimination against them that was documented by the Presidential Commission on the Status of Women's report (1963). Though the 1964 Civil Rights Act barred gender-based discrimination, change was slow in coming. This led to the founding in 1966 of the National Organization of Women (NOW), which grew rapidly and began to lobby for full economic and social equality. By 1967, younger women, disillusioned by the sexism they had encountered in the civil-rights and peace movements, started a women's liberation movement.

F.　Women's Liberation
Militant feminists established women's liberation consciousness-raising sessions, health collectives, and day-care centers and demonstrated for equal rights and legal abortions. In August 1970 the more moderate NOW and the aroused young feminists cooperated in staging the largest women's rights demonstration ever, "the Women's Strike for Equality."

VI.　The Liberal Crusade in Vietnam, 1961–1968
　　A.　Kennedy and Vietnam
Because Kennedy believed in the domino theory as much as Eisenhower did, JFK was determined not to allow the Communist National Liberation Front (NLF), or Vietcong, to win in South Vietnam. He sent large shipments of weapons to the Diem government and greatly increased the number of U.S. military advisers there. But Diem made little headway against the Vietcong, nor would he heed U.S. advice to build support for himself by introducing land or other needed reforms. When a group of South Vietnamese army officers deposed and murdered Diem, Kennedy quickly recognized their regime, hoping it would beat the Vietcong. It didn't, and by the time of Kennedy's assassination, it was becoming clear that the United States would either have to send in many more combat troops or seek a negotiated settlement and withdraw. We do not know which course Kennedy would have taken had he lived.

B.   Escalation of the War
Johnson, who also believed in the domino theory and did not want to give the Republicans grounds for accusing him of being soft on communism, further stepped up U.S. involvement in Vietnam. In February 1964 he had the military prepare plans for air attacks on communist North Vietnam, which was supplying the Vietcong with weapons. In August, claiming that North Vietnamese patrol boats had fired on two U.S. destroyers in the Gulf of Tonkin, Johnson persuaded Congress to pass a resolution authorizing the president to "take all necessary measures." Johnson used the Gulf of Tonkin Resolution to justify massive intervention in Vietnam.

C.   The Endless War
In 1965 Johnson started sustained bombing of North Vietnam and by 1968 had dropped three times more tonnage on it than had been used by all the combatants in World War II. Nonetheless, Hanoi sent more men and supplies to the Vietcong. Therefore, the president took the fateful step of ordering U.S. combat troops to South Vietnam. Some 485,000 draftees were fighting there by 1967, thus Americanizing the war. Still victory eluded us.

D.   Doves Versus Hawks
The Vietnam War polarized the United States as no event since the Civil War had done. Mounting numbers of college students and faculty, intellectuals, clergy, and liberal Democrats resisted the draft, conducted teach-ins, spoke out, and demonstrated against this escalation. They denounced U.S. meddling in an internal struggle in Indochina. They pointed out that the money that this nation was spending annually on the war was draining almost all revenue from Great Society programs and that the draftees sent to fight and die were primarily the poor and disadvantaged. Television coverage of the carnage further eroded support for Johnson's war. On the other hand, "hawks" demanded that the president win a quick and total victory, and, as late as 1968, the majority of Americans still could not accept the idea of a communist victory in Vietnam.

VII. Conclusion
Despite John F. Kennedy's charm and style, he achieved little in the way of domestic reform. After Kennedy's assassination, Lyndon Johnson, responding to a much more activist civil-rights movement, succeeded in getting the lawmakers to pass the civil-rights bill and the tax cut his predecessor had requested. Johnson also pushed through Congress his Great Society program, including federal aid for education, urban renewal, the arts, and health care; immigration reform; protection of the environment; a war against poverty; and a voting rights act. Together these measures were the most thoroughgoing liberal reforms enacted since the New Deal, and they made the United States a more caring and just country. The Great Society program and the hopes for further reform stimulated the ongoing civil-rights movement, and it, in turn, inspired other minorities and women to demand enhanced rights and equality. However, deepening U.S. involvement in Vietnam drained funds and commitment from reform at home before much of a dent had been made in poverty. Disillusioned African-Americans shouted for Black Power, and urban riots broke out. Southern and working-class whites reacted to violence in the cities with even greater resistance to civil rights. As the Vietnam conflict dragged on, Americans divided into hostile camps, and LBJ's presidency and Great Society disintegrated, as did the liberal consensus.

VOCABULARY

The following terms are used in Chapter 28. To understand the chapter fully, it is important that you know what each of them means.

temporize   compromise, delay

charisma	charm, allure, magnetism, special ability to lead
filibuster	to prevent a legislative vote by obstructive tactics, especially by making long speeches
consensus	general agreement
presaged	foreshadowed, forecasted, predicted
pejorative	derogatory; tending to make something seem less worthy than it is

IDENTIFICATIONS

After reading Chapter 28, you should be able to identify and explain the historical significance of each of the following:

Greensboro and other sit-ins, 1960–1961

New Frontier

Clean Air Act, 1963

Peace Corps

détente

J. Edgar Hoover and the FBI

Immigration Act, 1965

National Endowments for the Arts and the Humanities

Thurgood Marshall

Mississippi Freedom Summer Project, 1964

Malcolm X and the Black Muslims

César Chávez, Dolores Huerta, and the United Farm Workers (UFW)

Young Lords

the "pill"

Women's Liberation

SKILL BUILDING: MAPS

On the map of Indochina, locate and explain the importance in U.S. foreign policy of each of the following:

Laos

North Vietnam

South Vietnam

Saigon

Gulf of Tonkin

Hanoi

Danang

South China Sea
Gulf of Siam
Indochina
21°N
19°N
17°N
15°N
13°N
11°N
9°N
103°E
105°E
107°E
111°E

MULTIPLE-CHOICE QUESTIONS

Circle the letter of the item that best completes each statement or answers the question.

1. The U.S. Supreme Court, during the tenure of Chief Justice Earl Warren, made all of the following rulings *except*

   a. requiring states to provide a lawyer at public expense for indigent defendants charged with a felony.

   b. outlawing racial segregation in public schools even if the separate facilities were equal.

   c. overturning the World War II legislation that allowed the government to intern Japanese-Americans.

   d. requiring police to tell a suspect of his or her constitutional rights to remain silent and have a lawyer present during questioning.

2. The Bay of Pigs invasion was

   a. a U.S.-backed attempt by anti-Castro forces to land in Cuba and overthrow the regime there.

   b. the first landing of U.S. marines in South Vietnam and the start of Americanization of that conflict.

   c. the name that southerners applied to the invasion of their region by northern college students and civil-rights activists in the summer of 1964.

   d. an attempt made by the West to supply East Berlin with food after the communists erected the Berlin Wall.

3. The purpose of the 1964 Freedom Summer Project in Mississippi was to

   a. protest the escalation of the Vietnam War.

   b. help and encourage blacks to become registered voters.

   c. force the Interstate Commerce Commission to declare segregated transportation facilities unconstitutional.

   d. persuade the state legislature to ratify the Equal Rights Amendment.

4. Which of these leaders most closely followed the example of Martin Luther King, Jr., in using religion and nonviolent resistance to battle for social justice?

   a. Betty Friedan

   b. César Chávez

   c. Malcolm X

   d. George Wallace

5. In the election of 1964,

   a. both Democrats and Republicans ran candidates who promised to continue and expand the war on poverty.

   b. many liberals still distrusted Lyndon Johnson and therefore voted for Barry Goldwater.

   c. Johnson and the Democrats just barely won over a resurgent Republican party.

   d. the Republican party was captured by its western, southern, and conservative elements.

6. "Hawks" and "doves" divided over the issue of whether the

   a. U.S. government should overthrow the Castro regime in Cuba.

   b. civil-rights movement should use violent acts to protect African-American rights or rely on nonviolent means.

   c. United States should seek total victory in Vietnam or a negotiated settlement.

   d. Warren Court had gone too far in protecting criminals at the expense of their innocent victims.

7. Belief in the domino theory would most likely lead a person to support

    a.   federal intervention in the South to protect freedom riders and other civil-rights activists.
    b.   a test-ban treaty with the Soviet Union to prevent further atmospheric and ocean firing of nuclear weapons.
    c.   U.S. intervention in the Vietnam War to prevent a Vietcong victory.
    d.   appointment of more conservative justices to the Supreme Court to prevent it from falling completely under the influence of Warren liberals.

8. Before his assassination in 1963, John F. Kennedy had succeeded in

    a.   stimulating the U.S. economy with increased military spending.
    b.   getting through Congress a new immigration law that did away with the discriminatory national-origins quota system.
    c.   getting through Congress the most far-reaching voting rights bill since Reconstruction.
    d.   all of the above.

9. The feminist revival in the 1960s was brought about by

    a.   continuing employment discrimination.
    b.   the publication of Betty Friedan's *The Feminine Mystique*.
    c.   the sexism that women activists encountered in the peace and civil-rights movements.
    d.   all of the above.

10. During the last two years of Lyndon Johnson's presidency, the majority of public funds went into

    a.   Medicare and Medicaid.
    b.   the Vietnam War.
    c.   Head Start and other federally assisted educational programs.
    d.   public housing, the Job Corps, and other public-works and employment programs.

11. Which of the following statements about the Black Panther party is correct?

    a.   It demanded a faster pace of racial integration.
    b.   It ran self-help programs in black neighborhoods, but also engaged in shoot-outs with police that ended in the death of many of its members.
    c.   It concentrated on winning more political power for blacks by running candidates for city, state, and national offices, and it had some important electoral victories.
    d.   It carried on the nonviolent, civil disobedience tactics of Martin Luther King, Jr. after he was assassinated.

12. What do books written by Rachel Carson, Michael Harrington, Ralph Nader, and Betty Friedan have in common?

    a.   They all documented and raised the national consciousness about the pervasive racism in American society.
    b.   They all challenged the liberal consensus and paved the way for the "new conservatives," such as William Buckley and the Young Americans for Freedom.
    c.   They all documented evils in American society and helped get legislation passed in the 1960s to correct those problems.
    d.   They were all dismissed by both Presidents Kennedy and Johnson as exaggerated muckraking.

SHORT-ANSWER QUESTIONS

1. Briefly explain the roles played by television in the election of 1960 and in John F. Kennedy's thousand-day presidency.

2. What was the Cuban missile crisis? Why did it almost touch off a nuclear war between the United States and the Soviet Union? How did the two countries pull back from the brink of war? What steps did Kennedy and Khrushchev take to avoid ever coming that close to World War III again?

3. President Kennedy remarked in 1963, "The civil-rights movement should thank God for Bull Connor. He's helped it as much as Abraham Lincoln." Explain the meaning of this statement.

4. How did Martin Luther King, Jr. in his "Letter from a Birmingham Jail" justify his use of nonviolent civil disobedience? What were the circumstances that led to his writing the letter?

5. How and why did President Kennedy deepen U.S. involvement in Vietnam?

6. What were the main provisions of the Civil Rights Act of 1964 and the Voting Rights Act of 1965? What impact did the laws have on the lives of southern African-Americans and politics in the South?

7. Describe four major pieces of legislation or programs that made up President Lyndon B. Johnson's Great Society and war on poverty initiatives.

8. Why in his second term did President Johnson go from electoral triumph to widespread rejection by the American people?

9. According to the Kerner Commission report, what caused the wave of race riots from 1965 through 1968? What did the report recommend to remedy inequality and injustice? Did Congress and President Johnson carry out its recommendations? Why or why not?

10. How did President Johnson convince Congress to pass the Gulf of Tonkin Resolution? What did LBJ mean when he compared the resolution to "grandma's nightshirt—it covered everything"? What did it allow Johnson to do?

ESSAY QUESTIONS

1. Discuss the accomplishments and failures of John F. Kennedy's thousand-day presidency.

2. Martin Luther King, Jr., observed that President Johnson's desire to end poverty and provide economic opportunity for all Americans was "shot down on the battlefields of Vietnam." Do you agree with King's statement? Why or why not?

3. Discuss the development of the 1960s civil-rights movement. What were its successes and its frustrations? How and why did the Black Power movement emerge from it?

4. Discuss the 1960s movements to gain opportunity, equality, and power for women, Mexican-Americans, and Native Americans. Who participated in them? Why? What tactics did they use? What did each movement owe to the civil-rights and Black Power movements?

5. Compare and contrast the United States in the 1950s and in the 1960s. How do you account for the great differences between the two decades?

ANSWERS TO MULTIPLE-CHOICE QUESTIONS

1. c
2. a
3. b
4. b
5. d
6. c
7. c
8. a
9. d
10. b
11. b
12. c

CHAPTER 29

A Time of Upheaval, 1968–1974

OUTLINE AND SUMMARY

I.   Introduction

Chapter 29 deals with the youth movement of the 1960s, the ways in which it attacked the values of the 1950s, and the conservative backlash it produced. That backlash carried Richard Nixon to the White House, where he did much to spearhead a political realignment. Scoring successes in foreign policy, Nixon, the law-and-order advocate, himself violated the laws of the United States. To escape impeachment and conviction, Nixon resigned from the presidency, leaving behind a public thoroughly disillusioned with politics. As you read the chapter, consider these questions: (1) What impact did the student movement and counterculture have on national politics and life between 1968 and 1974? (2) In what ways was 1968 a political turning point? (3) What important changes in U.S. foreign policy did Nixon institute? (4) How did Richard Nixon and other Republicans try to build a new conservative majority and how did their efforts contribute to Nixon's overwhelming reelection in 1972? (5) What were the political and criminal abuses Nixon committed in connection with Watergate that led to calls for his impeachment? (6) What impact did Watergate have on the U.S. political system?

II. The Youth Movement

A.   Introduction

In the 1960s, 8 million Americans were in college, and more than half the population was under thirty years of age. By its very size, this baby-boom generation had a major impact on U.S. society. Most of the young had no quarrel with the system; they just wanted a good job and a secure place in it. A substantial minority of youths were attracted to the New Right, joining organizations like Young Americans for Freedom, admiring Barry Goldwater, and supporting the war in Vietnam.

B.   Toward a New Left

A larger minority were attracted to the New Left revolving around, though not necessarily joining, Students for a Democratic Society (SDS), founded in 1962. Its Port Huron Statement criticized American society and called on youth to build a true "participatory democracy" that valued love and creativity and rejected "materialism, militarism, and racism." The perceived impersonality and bureaucracy of university administrations, the failings of New Frontier and Great Society liberalism, and above all the Vietnam War brought many followers to the movement.

C.   From Protest to Resistance

In 1964, the University of California at Berkeley tried to limit campus political activity, which prompted student Mario Savio to start the Berkeley Free Speech Movement and lead a series of demonstrations and sit-ins joined by thousands of other students. Soon protests spread to colleges all over the country as students demanded that their universities halt research for the military, get rid of compulsory ROTC, admit more minority students, and dozens of other things. The escalation of the Vietnam War and less lenient student draft deferments drew tens of thousands of additional students into the movement. Led by SDS, they staged teach-ins, sit-ins, rallies, marches, and campus takeovers. Chanting "Hell, no, we won't go!" they encouraged young men to burn their draft cards and flee to Canada rather than serve in the armed forces. An antiwar rally in New York's Central Park attracted 500,000 people. The March Against Death in Washington, D.C., in 1969, drew some 300,000 participants. In 1968–1969, student protests broke out in dozens of countries round the world as the young denounced the political institutions and society of their elders.

D. Kent State—Jackson State
In 1970, when President Richard M. Nixon widened the fighting in Southeast Asia with an invasion of Cambodia, a new wave of campus unrest spread across the country. At Kent State University in Ohio, National Guardsmen opened fire on demonstrators, killing four, and at Mississippi's Jackson State College, highway patrolmen shot two students to death. Students condemned Nixon and the repressive violence, but many older citizens turned against the protesters, saying that they got what they deserved for undercutting the president's foreign policy.

E. Legacy of Student Frenzy
Frustrated by its inability to end the war much less remake American society, SDS began to disintegrate. A handful of former members went underground and engaged in terrorism, giving the government a handy excuse for more crackdowns. Other New Left activists drifted into the environmentalist, consumer, antinuclear, and women's movements. Many middle- and working-class people, alarmed by radicalism, began voting for political conservatives by the late 1960s. Still, the New Left did spur broad antiwar sentiment that eventually forced the Nixon administration to extricate itself from Indochina.

III. The Counterculture
A. Introduction
Besides the minority who engaged in radical politics, many young people in the sixties rebelled against accepted middle-class life-styles. Their counterculture rejected competitiveness, the work and success ethic, and responsibility in favor of love, cooperation, freedom, and experimentation with drugs and sex.

B. Hippies and Drugs
Hippie men grew long hair and beards; they and young women wore tie-dyed T-shirts and torn jeans to show their contempt for middle class propriety and materialism. Probably half of all college students smoked marijuana, and a minority tried hallucinogens. Timothy Leary, a former Harvard psychologist, and writer Ken Kesey and followers, the Merry Pranksters, especially recommended the drug LSD as the way to "tune in, turn on, and drop out."

C. Musical Revolution
The decade opened with folk music concerts, proceeded to acid rock and Beatlemania, and in 1969 climaxed with a rock music festival at Woodstock, New York. But by the late 1960s, the counterculture dream of an age of peace and harmony was already turning sour as the haunts of the flower children in San Francisco's Haight-Ashbury and New York's East Village attracted muggers, rapists, and dope peddlers. Senseless acts of violence and murder perpetrated by Charles Manson and his followers and by the Hell's Angels at the Altamont rock concert further tarnished the counterculture.

D. The Sexual Revolution
One part of the counterculture, greater sexual openness and permissiveness, spread well beyond the hippies. The sexual revolution was made possible to a considerable extent by waning fear of unwanted pregnancy. In 1960 the pill became available, and in 1973 the Supreme Court in *Roe* v. *Wade* declared unconstitutional state laws limiting women's right

to an abortion during the first three months after conception. Films and plays became sexually explicit. Live-in arrangements and premarital and extramarital sex were common.

E.   Gay Liberation
Homosexuals organized the Gay Liberation movement and demanded acceptance and equal rights for gays. All of this erotic freedom, however, offended many citizens, who saw these developments as undermining moral decency. By the 1970s they responded by voting for politicians who promised to clean up the smut and protect the family.

IV.   1968: The Politics of Upheaval
A.   The Tet Offensive in Vietnam
On January 31, 1968, the start of Tet, the Vietnamese New Year, the Vietcong and North Vietnamese launched a major offensive, capturing much territory from the South and even staging attacks on the capital, Saigon. U.S. forces eventually repulsed the communists, but the heavy death toll on both sides made growing numbers skeptical about whether we could ever win the conflict at an acceptable cost. By March 1968, 42 percent of Americans described themselves as doves, and many of them looked approvingly on Minnesota's antiwar senator Eugene McCarthy, who had announced that he would enter the upcoming Democratic primaries to challenge Johnson for the presidential nomination.

B.   A Shaken President
After McCarthy did surprisingly well in the New Hampshire primary, a second antiwar candidate entered the race—Robert Kennedy. On March 31, Johnson, finally heeding key Democratic foreign-policy advisers, announced that he was deescalating in Vietnam by halting the bombing in the North. Embittered by the hatred that had developed toward him and doubting his chances against the Kennedy charisma, the president added that he would not seek or accept another term in the White House.

C.   Assassinations and Turmoil
On April 4, 1968, Martin Luther King, Jr. was assassinated. Infuriated African-Americans rioted in Chicago, Washington, D.C., and other cities. In the midst of the national turmoil, Vice President Hubert Humphrey entered the Democratic race. Humphrey received backing from union leaders, Johnson loyalists, and most party officials, who supported the president's Vietnam policies. McCarthy appealed mainly to affluent, educated liberal doves; Kennedy, to the less privileged and various ethnic and racial minorities, as well as peace advocates. On June 5, just hours after he won the California primary, Robert Kennedy was assassinated by a Palestinian refugee, thus removing the best hope for success of the peace forces. In August the Democrats nominated Humphrey, while in the Chicago streets surrounding the convention hall, Mayor Richard Daley's police clubbed antiwar demonstrators. The uproar in Chicago further alarmed many Americans and pushed them into the arms of conservative politicians, promising to restore law and order.

D.   Conservative Resurgence
Richard Nixon, the Republican candidate, made the most of the unrest by promising he could end civil strife; achieve an honorable peace in Vietnam; crack down on radicals; and uphold law and order for the silent majority of hardworking, taxpaying, patriotic Americans. George Wallace, running as a third-party candidate, also appealed to resentful and fearful blue-collar workers, white racists, and people fed up with the counterculture and radicalism.

Wallace captured 14 percent of the vote; Nixon nosed out Humphrey with just over 43 percent. These results indicated that a new conservative coalition had emerged. Fifty-seven percent of the electorate, including much of the old New Deal constituency, had voted for Nixon and Wallace, politicians who repudiated liberal ideals. The new conservative Republican coalition would dominate politics for the rest of the twentieth century. It included a majority of suburbanites, westerners and southerners, and people concerned about traditional values and opposed to racial integration and special government help for the economically disadvantaged.

V. Nixon and World Politics

A. Introduction

Nixon was first elected to Congress from California in 1946 and made a name for himself by accusing Alger Hiss of handing government secrets to the Soviets. He won a Senate seat in 1950, continuing to use his red-baiting tactics. After two terms as Eisenhower's vice-president, he lost the presidential race to Kennedy in 1960 and the governorship of California in 1962. Many thought that would end his political career, but he rebounded to take the Republican nomination and win the presidency in 1968. Nixon and his national security adviser and later secretary of state, Henry Kissinger, believed in realpolitik—that is, making foreign policy moves pragmatically on the basis of power politics and what would advance the national interest, without reference to morality or ideology. They also shared a liking for diplomatic intrigue, hidden from the public.

B. Vietnamization

Nixon and Kissinger decided that the United States must somehow extricate itself from Vietnam. The 1969 Nixon Doctrine pointed to a new course in Asia: henceforth the United States would supply economic and military assistance to countries threatened by communist subversion or invasion, but it would expect them to do the fighting. The need to recall U.S. ground forces from Vietnam was overwhelmingly apparent. Their morale and discipline had snapped, desertions mounted, and frustration led some U.S. soldiers to commit atrocities against Vietnamese civilians, as in My Lai. Nixon began removing U.S. troops from Vietnam, but at the same time he sought "peace with honor" by sending Kissinger to hold secret peace talks with the North Vietnamese. In hope of wringing concessions from the North Vietnamese, Nixon also authorized bombing raids over the North and over their supply lines in neutral Cambodia and Laos.

C. LBJ's War Becomes Nixon's War

The raids did not accomplish their purpose. Hanoi stood its ground, and the bombing touched off a civil war in Cambodia between the Communist Khmer Rouge and pro-U.S. factions. In 1970 the North Vietnamese increased their infiltration of Cambodia, and Nixon, in turn, ordered a joint U.S.–South Vietnamese invasion of that beleaguered country. Nixon also pushed the South Vietnamese into an attack on Laos to destroy communist bases there. The soldiers of the South were routed, and in April 1972 the North mounted a major offensive against Cambodia and the South. Nixon ordered the military to mine North Vietnam's harbors and step up bombing of its supply bases and cities.

D. America's Longest War Ends

The massive bombing finally broke the deadlock in the negotiations that had begun in 1968. In January 1973 the United States and North Vietnam signed the Paris Accords, ending the fighting between them but leaving South Vietnam's future to be settled by the final battles between North and South. The United States' longest war had cost 58,000 dead, 300,000 wounded, and $150 billion. The Vietnamese suffered 2 million casualties, the war had ravaged much of Indochina, and the Communist regime that gained control of the once peaceful Cambodia killed one-third of its people.

E. Détente

Our withdrawal from the war opened the way for détente with China and the U.S.S.R. The falling-out between the two Communist giants also made them receptive to easing tensions with the United States. After two decades in which successive U.S. administrations had refused to recognize the People's Republic of China and had blocked its admission to the United Nations, Kissinger began secret negotiations in 1971, followed by a Nixon trip to China in February 1972, at which Sino-American relations were normalized. In May the president flew to Moscow and signed agreements with the Soviets on trade, technological cooperation, and arms control, including the SALT I pact limiting nuclear missiles. These moves not only improved the world outlook for peace but also enhanced Nixon's image in an election year.

F.   Shuttle Diplomacy

In October 1973 the Middle East was again embroiled in war, as Syria and Egypt attacked Israel. U.S. equipment helped the Israelis to repel the assault and counterattack. In retaliation, the oil-producing Arab states imposed an embargo on shipments of petroleum to the United States and its allies. This led to acute shortages, skyrocketing prices, and rampant inflation in the United States. To ease the fuel crisis and reduce Soviet influence in the Middle East, the Nixon administration tried to cultivate better relations with the Arabs and to mediate between them and Israel. In October 1973 Kissinger began his "shuttle diplomacy," flying from one Middle Eastern capital to another to negotiate peace settlements. He managed to engineer a cease-fire, a withdrawal of Israeli forces from some territories captured in 1973, and an end to the oil embargo. While his efforts successfully blocked Soviet influence in the Middle East, they did not address the Palestinian problem, which continued to threaten peace in the region.

In line with realpolitik, Nixon and Kissinger gave economic and military assistance to any country that they thought important to U.S. financial and strategic interests, especially to countries willing to oppose Soviet influence. This policy often included nations ruled by brutal dictatorships, such as Iran under the shah and the Philippines under Ferdinand Marcos. Nixon also secretly handed the CIA funds to help a military junta overthrow Chile's democratically elected Marxist president, Salvador Allende, and then quickly recognized the military dictator who replaced him.

VI.   Domestic Problems and Divisions

A.   The Nixon Presidency

Nixon's personality contained dark elements that ultimately brought about his downfall. He believed that his enemies, especially the "eastern liberal establishment," were out to get him. Therefore, he must destroy them first.

Early in Nixon's presidency Americans joined together in pride over the 1969 lunar landing and Neil Armstrong's walk on the moon. Nixon also seemed willing at first to follow a moderate course aimed at national reconciliation. He signed into law bills passed by Congress that created the Environmental Protection Agency and the Occupational Safety and Health Administration. Meanwhile many Americans demonstrated increased ecological concern by participating in the first Earth Day in April 1970 and generally favoring conservation, preservation, and other measures to protect the planet. Conservatives decried the cost to business of additional regulations, as well as the increased expenditures that the administration's proposed welfare reform would entail. Thus, Nixon's Family Assistance Plan, guaranteeing a minimal annual income for all Americans, died in the Senate.

B.   A Troubled Economy

Nixon inherited a budget deficit and inflation from the Johnson administration. To combat these, Nixon cut government expenditures and urged the Federal Reserve Board to increase interest rates. Rising unemployment and a recession resulted, and inflation persisted. Worried about the political impact of hard times, the president tried Keynesian economics. In 1971 he deliberately proposed an unbalanced federal budget, and subsequently he devalued the dollar and imposed wage and price ceilings. These policies stimulated the economy and reduced the trade deficit and inflation sufficiently to help get Nixon reelected in 1972. Afterward he ended price and wage controls, and in 1973 inflation and sluggish economic growth (stagflation) resumed.

C.   Law and Order
Nixon used law-enforcement agencies in legal and illegal ways to harass peace advocates, radicals, and his enemies. The Internal Revenue Service paid special attention to tax returns from people in these categories; the FBI and CIA wiretapped their phones and infiltrated their organizations to foment discord and provoke violence. Nixon established the White House "plumbers" to spy on and discredit his opponents. Daniel Ellsberg, who had turned over to the press the secret Pentagon Papers disclosing government lies about U.S. actions in Vietnam, became the plumbers' first target. When the Supreme Court barred Nixon from stopping publication of the papers on the grounds of the First Amendment, the plumbers broke into Ellsberg's psychiatrist's office to look for medical records that might put Ellsberg in a poor light. The Justice Department also indicted him for theft.

D.   The Southern Strategy
Nixon wooed whites tired of civil-rights activism, especially southerners. His administration opposed extension of the 1965 Voting Rights Act and school busing as a means to further integration. The president pushed the Supreme Court toward the right by his appointments of Chief Justice Warren Burger and three other conservatives.

To build a new Republican majority, Nixon also unleashed his vice president, Spiro T. Agnew. Agnew attacked Democrats as "hooligans, hippies, and radical liberals." His speeches apparently swayed some voters because the Republicans suffered minimal losses in the 1970 congressional elections, losing some House members but gaining two Senators.

VII.   The Crisis of the Presidency
A.   The Election of 1972
When the Democrats nominated liberal senator George McGovern for president, they had little chance of winning. Nonetheless, Nixon and his Committee to Reelect the President (CREEP) decided to use every means possible to destroy the opposition, including having the White House plumbers break into Democratic National Committee headquarters in the Watergate complex to install secret wiretaps on the phones. After the burglars were caught, the administration began its attempt to hide the trail to higher-ups. It succeeded long enough to get Nixon overwhelmingly reelected, although the Democrats retained control of Congress.

B.   The Watergate Upheaval
In 1973 the cover-up began to unravel. One of the convicted Watergate burglars confessed that White House aides were involved. Then *Washington Post* reporters Carl Bernstein and Bob Woodward wrote a series of articles exposing CREEP's use of illegal campaign contributions to finance "dirty tricks" against the Democrats. It was finally revealed in 2005 that their main secret source of information was second-in-command of the FBI in 1973, W. Mark Felt. In February 1973 the Senate established a special committee to probe alleged election misdeeds. It heard damaging testimony and, learning that Nixon had secretly taped all conversations held in the Oval Office, demanded that the president turn the recordings over to the committee. Meanwhile Nixon, pretending to cooperate in the investigation, appointed a new attorney general, Elliot Richardson, who chose a special Watergate prosecutor, Archibald Cox. When Cox also requested the tapes, Nixon fired Cox and accepted Richardson's resignation. This "Saturday Night Massacre" prompted the Judiciary Committee to start impeachment proceedings against the president.

C.　A President Disgraced

The administration was further discredited when Vice President Spiro Agnew resigned after pleading no contest to charges of bribe taking and tax evading. House minority leader Gerald Ford replaced Agnew. The president continued to stall on releasing the full, unedited recordings. In July 1974 the Supreme Court ruled that he must do so. The following month he surrendered the subpoenaed tapes, and they revealed that Nixon had personally ordered the Watergate cover-up and had lied about his role for two years. Knowing that he would almost certainly be impeached and convicted, Nixon, on August 9, became the first chief executive in American history to resign, bringing Ford into office as the first nonelected president.

VIII. Conclusion

The baby boomers who participated in the student movement and counterculture of the 1960s desired a more open, democratic, tolerant country, with less materialism and racism, fewer sexual and other inhibitions, and an end to the Vietnam War. To some extent they did move society in the directions they wished, including eventually forcing the United States out of Vietnam. However, they also touched off a backlash among whites frightened by radicalism, black militancy, and the breakdown of law and order and traditional values. Richard Nixon, during his first term as president, removed U.S. forces from Vietnam and improved relations with China and the Soviets, but he also fanned and capitalized on white fears of the youthful counterculture radicals. That combination won him a landslide reelection in 1972. His triumph was short lived because the Watergate break-in and its subsequent investigation revealed the pattern of dirty tricks and criminal acts the White House engaged in to destroy its "enemies." To avoid certain impeachment and conviction, Nixon resigned. Almost fifty members of his administration went to jail, and Gerald Ford became president. Some Americans viewed with pride the way the U.S. political system had weathered the crisis and peacefully transferred power. Others worried about the further erosion of popular trust and belief in their government.

VOCABULARY

The following terms are used in Chapter 29. To understand the chapter fully, it is important that you know what each of them means.

existentialism	the philosophical movement centering on analysis of individual existence
Ethos	basic beliefs and guiding principles
maverick	a nonconformist
impeachment	the charging of a public official, such as the president, with misconduct in office
participatory democracy	a society in which most citizens directly share in government decisions by holding office or making policy
iconoclast	an attacker of cherished beliefs or institutions
hedonism	a way of life devoted to pleasure
monogamy	marriage of one woman with one man
realpolitik	a pragmatic politics (especially as applied to foreign policy) based on advancement of the national interest without concern for ideology or morality

paranoia	a mental disorder in which one mistakenly believes that others have hostile intentions toward him or her
dossier	a file of documents relating to the same matter, subject, or person

IDENTIFICATIONS

After reading Chapter 29, you should be able to identify and explain the historical significance of each of the following:

baby boomers

Young Americans for Freedom

the Beatles and the Rolling Stones

George Wallace

Mayor Richard Daley versus the Yippies

Henry Kissinger

Nixon Doctrine

My Lai massacre

SALT I

Palestine Liberation Organization (PLO)

Occupational Safety and Health Administration (OSHA)

Environmental Protection Agency (EPA)

stagflation

Daniel Ellsberg and the Pentagon Papers

Carl Bernstein and Bob Woodward

the White House "plumbers" and the Watergate break-in and cover-up

Saturday Night Massacre

SKILL BUILDING: MAPS

1. On the map of China and Indochina on the following page, locate and explain the importance in U.S. foreign policy of each of the following:

   South Vietnam

   Saigon

   Danang

   Cambodia

   Laos

   North Vietnam

   Hanoi

   Haiphong

People's Republic of China

Beijing

Sino-Soviet border

2. On the map of the Middle East on the following page, locate and explain the importance in U.S. foreign policy of each of the places listed below:

Syria

Israel

Golan Heights

Egypt

Sinai Peninsula

West Bank

Jerusalem

Jordan

Saudi Arabia

Iran

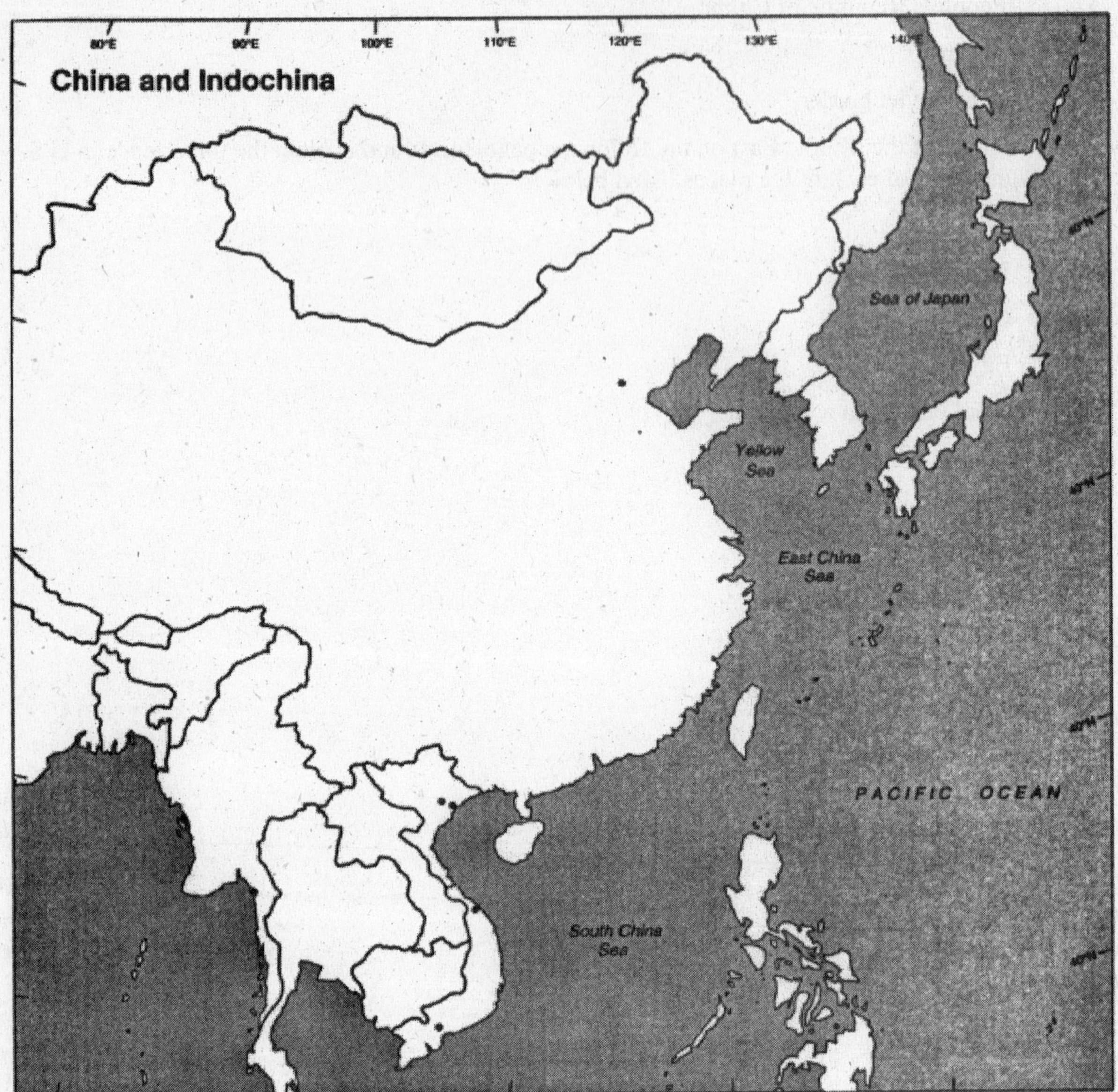

China and Indochina
80°E
90°E
100°E
110°E
120°E
130°E
140°E
Sea of Japan
Yellow
Sea
East China
Sea
PACIFIC OCEAN
South China
Sea

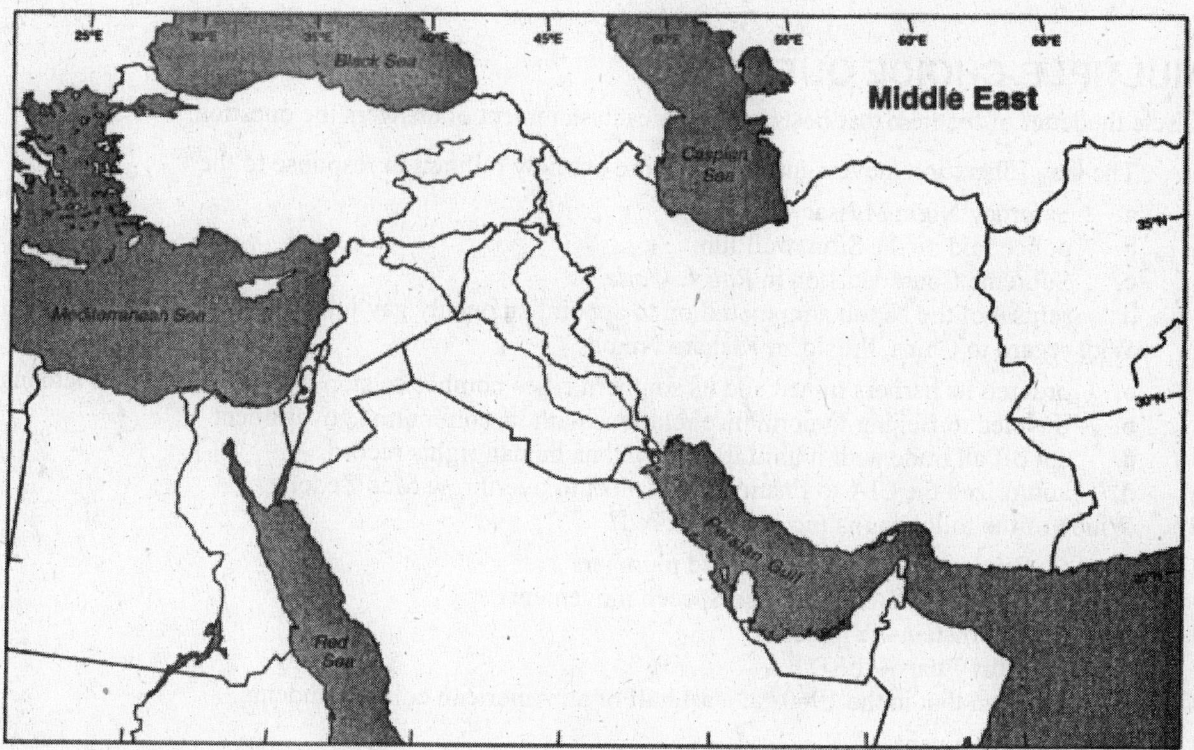

HISTORICAL SOURCES

Authors writing social history often use various cultural artifacts as sources. In Chapter 29 these include the messages on the signs carried by demonstrators, slogans and chants (remembered or learned from films and tapes), songs and music popular during the period, clothing of the time, hairstyles (remembered or seen in photographs), and bumper stickers. Find places in the chapter where each of these artifacts is referred to or quoted. In each case, why is the historian using that source?

Now look at "Beyond America—Global Interactions: The British Invasion." What cultural artifacts associated with the Beatles and other British rock groups are mentioned? How does the author of Chapter 29 analyze the songs, clothing, and looks of the musicians to make his points about the youth counterculture?

The author of Chapter 29 also uses more formal, traditional, historical sources, such as the published reports of congressional investigating committees. For example, on page 913 the author discusses the testimony about wrongdoing in the Nixon White House given before Sam Ervin's committee. That information can be found in U.S. Senate, Select Committee on Presidential Campaign Activities, *Final Report,* 93rd Cong., 2d Sess., 1974. On page 914 the writer summarizes the articles of impeachment against Nixon drawn up by the House Judiciary Committee. The full text of those articles can be read in U.S. Congress, House of Representatives, *Report of the Committee on the Judiciary,* 93rd Cong., 2d Sess., 1974.

MULTIPLE-CHOICE QUESTIONS

Circle the letter of the item that best completes each statement or answers the question.

1. The Gay Liberation movement became more publicly militant in response to the

    a. Saturday Night Massacre.
    b. police raid on the Stonewall Inn.
    c. Supreme Court decision in *Roe* v. *Wade*.
    d. refusal of the Nixon administration to appoint an openly gay jurist to the Supreme Court.

2. With regard to China, President Richard Nixon

    a. ordered its harbors mined and its southern cities bombed to stop it from aiding the Vietcong.
    b. traveled to Beijing to normalize relations with its communist government.
    c. cut off all trade with it until it improved its human rights record.
    d. authorized the CIA to finance secret plots to overthrow Mao Zedong.

3. Which of the following is *incorrectly* paired?

    a. G. Gordon Liddy—White House plumbers
    b. Mario Savio—Berkeley Free Speech movement
    c. Carl Bernstein—Yippies
    d. Timothy Leary—LSD

4. It is estimated that in the 1960s at least half of all American college students

    a. tried marijuana.
    b. burned their draft cards.
    c. became hippies or Yippies.
    d. had to leave their studies for two years to serve in Vietnam.

5. Which of the following facts about the election of 1968 indicates that a new conservative majority had supplanted the long-standing New Deal coalition?

    a. Between them, Nixon and Wallace received a majority of the votes of workers.
    b. Nixon won 43.4 percent of the popular vote.
    c. The great majority of African-Americans voted for Hubert Humphrey.
    d. Almost all union leaders supported Hubert Humphrey.

6. Which of the following did U.S. involvement in Vietnam accomplish?

    a. It prevented the communists from taking power in Cambodia.
    b. It saved South Vietnam from falling under the control of communist North Vietnam.
    c. It stimulated the U.S. economy sufficiently to ensure full employment, business growth, and balanced federal budgets.
    d. None of the above.

7. "That's one small step for man, one giant leap for mankind." This quote refers to

    a. Nixon's decision to resign from the presidency.
    b. the signing of the Paris Accords ending the U.S. presence in Vietnam.
    c. the peaceful inauguration of Gerald Ford after the long nightmare of Watergate.
    d. astronaut Neil Armstrong's walk on the moon.

8. In which of these countries did the Nixon administration help to overthrow a democratically elected Marxist president?

    a. West Germany
    b. Chile
    c. South Korea
    d. Israel

9.   Nixon's southern strategy included all of the following *except*

   a.   opposing school busing to achieve racial integration.
   b.   trying to appoint strict constructionist judges to the federal courts.
   c.   wooing southern African-American votes by strictly enforcing civil-rights laws.
   d.   trying to attract southern white voters to the Republicans by playing down civil rights whenever possible.

10.   Why did John Mitchell, E. Howard Hunt, and G. Gordon Liddy arrange the break-in at the Watergate complex?

   a.   To find information about Daniel Ellsberg that would discredit him in the eyes of the peace movement
   b.   To destroy the Democratic National Committee's files of potential campaign contributors
   c.   To wiretap the telephones of the Democratic National Committee
   d.   All of the above

11.   The police or National Guard did *not* violently attack demonstrators in which of the following places?

   a.   Kent State University
   b.   Jackson State University
   c.   Outside the Chicago Democratic Convention in 1968
   d.   The Spring Mobilization to End the War in New York City in 1967

12.   Which of the following is *inaccurately* identified?

   a.   Warren Burger—nominated for chief justice of the Supreme Court by President Nixon and confirmed by the Senate
   b.   George McGovern—the secret source for much of what Woodward and Bernstein revealed in their articles exposing the Watergate affair
   c.   Spiro Agnew—Nixon's vice president who was forced to resign because of charges of income tax evasion and bribe taking
   d.   Eugene McCarthy—challenged President Johnson in the Democratic primaries in 1968, demanding U.S. withdrawal from Vietnam

SHORT-ANSWER QUESTIONS

1.   What was Students for a Democratic Society (SDS), and what did they say in their Port Huron Statement? How did this New Left movement differ from the Old Left of the 1930s?

2.   What and when was the Tet offensive? What impact did it have on American public opinion about the war in Vietnam?

3.   What were the students at Kent State University protesting in 1970? What happened there? How did students and liberals react? How did the majority of Americans react?

4.   Who were hippies? What was the youth counterculture of the 1960s? What caused it to wane by the 1970s?

5.   What was the sexual revolution of the 1960s and 1970s? What caused it? What brought about a backlash against it by the 1980s?

6.   Explain the roles of Eugene McCarthy, Robert Kennedy, and Hubert Humphrey in the critical election year 1968. What happened inside and outside the Democratic National Convention in Chicago that year? What effect did these events have on the Democrats' chances for victory in November?

7.   Explain what President Nixon meant by the policy of Vietnamization. What other steps did Nixon take to obtain "peace with honor" in Vietnam?

8.   What were the terms of the 1973 Paris Accords between the United States and North Vietnam? Did the Accords bring "peace with honor?"

9.   Discuss Henry Kissinger's "shuttle diplomacy" in the Middle East. What did it accomplish?

10.   How and why did the Nixon administration bring about the overthrow of the Allende government in Chile?

ESSAY QUESTIONS

1.   Discuss the rise and decline of college student radicalism in the period 1960–1970. What caused the radicalism? Who became radicalized? What forms did radical protest take? Why did radical protest wane?

2.   In 1964 Lyndon Johnson was elected president by a landslide. In 1972 Richard Nixon won an equally decisive victory. Yet each man was driven from office in disgrace. Explain the reasons for each one's electoral triumph and subsequent downfall.

3.   Nixon, "who had built his reputation as a staunch Cold Warrior, initiated a new era of détente" with the communist powers. Discuss how and why the president accomplished this.

4.   "While claiming to be the defender of law and order, the Nixon administration committed numerous illegal acts." Write an essay agreeing or disagreeing with this statement, and back up what you say with as many facts as possible.

5.   Some political commentators claimed that "the outcome of Watergate proved that the constitutional system had worked." Others believed that it further eroded trust in government and the ability of presidents to lead effectively. What is your interpretation of the outcome and its impact on the United States?

ANSWERS TO MULTIPLE-CHOICE QUESTIONS

1. b
2. b
3. c
4. a
5. a
6. d
7. d
8. b
9. c
10. c
11. d
12. b

CHAPTER 30

Conservative Resurgence, Economic Woes, Foreign Challenges, 1974–1989

OUTLINE AND SUMMARY

I.   Introduction
Chapter 30 covers U.S. history from Richard Nixon's resignation in 1974 through the presidency of Ronald Reagan, ending in 1989. The chapter develops three main themes: growing conservatism, economic transformations and problems, and the continuing impact of the outside world on life in the United States. As you read this chapter, try to answer these questions: (1) What caused the political conservatism of the period? (2) What were the most important social and economic developments of these years? (3) How successful were the Ford and Carter administrations, and why? (4) What ideas influenced the actions of the Reagan administration? (5) How did world events impact Reagan's two terms as president?

II. Cultural Trends
A.   Personal Pursuits and Diversions
The social activism of the sixties diminished or turned to other causes. The 1960s student radical gave way to the 1970s and 1980s yuppie (young urban professional), preoccupied with personal health, fulfillment, and a consumption life-style. Americans of all ages watched more hours of television and increasingly tuned in to the proliferating cable channels. They also enjoyed the new electronic gadgets: videocassette recorders, compact discs, and personal computers. New musical styles included punk rock and rap or hip hop. Most of the blockbuster movies were escapist entertainment, but a few, such as Robert Altman's *Nashville*, depicted the darker side of American life.

B.   Changing Gender Roles and Sexual Behavior
The number of women working outside the home tripled between 1960 and 1990. Women generally did not earn as much as men and tended to work in gender-segregated occupations, such as nursing, teaching, and retail selling. However, by the 1990s women were beginning to enter middle management, but due to the "glass ceiling," few reached top positions. Also, by the 1990s about 20 percent of lawyers and doctors were female. As more women attended college and pursued careers, the age at which they married went up and the number of children they had went down. By the 1980s the average American family had just 1.6 children. More women engaged in premarital sex at earlier ages than was formerly true, and more lived with men they were not married to. In the 1980s sexual experimentation with multiple partners declined because of the terrible danger of contracting AIDS. By the end of the decade more than 31,000 Americans had died from the disease.

C.   The Persistence of Social Activism
Two social activist movements of the 1960s grew even stronger in the 1970s: environmentalism and feminism. Environmental groups, such as the Sierra Club; the Wilderness Society; and Greenpeace, founded in 1971, all increased their memberships. The anti-nuclear-power campaign of the movement peaked in 1979 after the near-catastrophe at the Three Mile Island plant. A much worse accident at Chernobyl in the Ukraine in 1986 heightened opposition to the building of more nuclear power stations. The women's

movement, also gained new recruits. As of 1975, the National Organization for Women (NOW) had 50,000 members. NOW and other women's groups convinced many states to pass laws against gender bias and got some states to ratify the equal rights amendment. In the late 1970s the women's movement split as moderates disapproved of the tactics of radical feminists and lesbians. Gay men and women became more assertive in the 1970s, coming out of the closet and demanding equal treatment and rights. "Gay Pride" parades in New York City, San Francisco, and Washington, D.C., brought out anywhere from 75,000 to 300,000 marchers. A few openly gay people won seats in state legislatures and Congress. They spearheaded drives for equal rights for homosexuals and lesbians.

D. Grassroots Conservatism
The roots of conservatism go back to the 1950s and early 1960s when William F. Buckley started his journal, *National Review,* and founded Young Americans for Freedom. Barry Goldwater's campaign for president in 1964 foreshadowed the growing power of conservatives in the Republican Party. Phyllis Schlafly began her career as right-wing activist in the 1960s attacking the New Left and the counterculture, and in the following decade, through her Eagle Forum, she kept up a steady denunciation of abortion, gay rights, and the Equal Rights Amendment, which failed to be ratified by the necessary three-fourths of the states. In communities, particularly in the South and the West, conservatives began organizing themselves at the grassroots level. Conservatives, after the *Roe* v. *Wade* decision began a Right-to-Life movement, demanding passage of a constitutional amendment banning abortion. The conservatives were opposed by the women's movement, which championed a woman's right to choose to continue an unwanted pregnancy or not. While public opinion polls indicated the majority of Americans were pro-choice, Congress in 1976 ended Medicaid funding for abortions, denying poor women a choice. Conservatives also convinced Miami and some other cities to repeal ordinances guaranteeing homosexuals' civil rights.

E. Evangelical Protestants Mobilize
Resurgent political and social conservatism was aided and abetted by the burgeoning of evangelical religion. Many evangelical ministers and churches became actively involved in politics. These included Jerry Falwell's Moral Majority, founded in 1979, and Pat Robertson's *700 Club*. The evangelicals were vehemently anticommunist, called for reversals of Supreme Court decisions banning prayer in public schools and permitting abortion, and campaigned for conservative political candidates. Pat Robertson tried unsuccessfully to obtain a Republican nomination for president in 1988.

III. Economic and Social Change in Post-1960s America
A. A Changing Economy
The economy of the 1970s and 1980s was plagued by rampant inflation, almost 14 percent a year by 1980. The doubling of consumer prices between 1970 and 1980 forced many wives into the paid labor force and made taxpayers less willing to support the welfare programs instituted in the 1960s. The family farm continued its long decline, although total farm production increased due to agribusiness. Federal crop subsidy programs accelerated the process of consolidation. Heavy industry in the United States slumped as foreign competitors, with newer machinery and poorly compensated labor, grabbed increasing shares of the domestic market. Indeed, by 1971 the country began having a persistent and worsening trade deficit. U.S. automobile, steel, and other midwestern factories laid off so many workers that the unemployment rate hit 8.5 percent in 1975. As the number of industrial workers decreased, so did union membership, falling from 31 percent of American labor belonging to unions in 1960 to a mere 18 percent by 1985.

B.   The Two Worlds of African-American America
In the 1970s and 1980s the African-American middle class grew in size and made significant advances: 46 percent of African-Americans held white-collar jobs by 1990, and 12 percent of the nation's college students were African-American. However, the plight of the African-American underclass worsened if anything. About one-third of African-Americans were trapped in inner-city slums. There half of all youths dropped out of high school, and 60 percent were unemployed. Drug addiction, violence, illegitimacy, and welfare dependency were prevalent. Attempts to aid disadvantaged African-Americans through affirmative action programs suffered a setback when the Supreme Court, in *Bakke* v. *United States*, struck down quota systems.

C.   Brightening Prospects for Native Americans
In the late 1960s and 1970s Indian militancy brought changes in destructive federal policies. The 1974 Indian Self-Determination Act granted tribes the right to administer government-aid programs and schools on their reservations. Native Americans also won important court cases, including a 1980 award to the Sioux of $107 million for lands in South Dakota wrongfully taken in the nineteenth century. Although Indian pride and rights and tribal ownership of land and businesses were on the rise, Native Americans still struggled with high unemployment, alcoholism, and disease.

D.   New Patterns of Immigration
Since 1965 immigration to the United States has been heavy. Most of the newcomers arrived from the Western Hemisphere (45 percent) and Asia (30 percent). As in the past, the majority of the immigrants were fleeing poverty, but many encountered rough conditions in the United States as well. To stem the tide of illegal immigrants and aid those already in the country, Congress passed the 1986 Immigration Reform and Control Act.

IV.   Years of Malaise: Post-Watergate Politics and Diplomacy, 1974–1981
A.   The Caretaker Presidency of Gerald Ford, 1974–1977
After he became president on August 9, 1974, Gerald Ford pardoned Richard Nixon for "any and all crimes" he might have committed. On domestic issues Ford proved more conservative than his predecessor. He vetoed environmental, social welfare, and federal regulatory bills, but a heavily Democratic Congress overrode him on quite a few. Already troublesome, inflation soared because of an Arab oil embargo and OPEC price increases. Ford responded by calling for voluntary price restraints, which did not work. The Federal Reserve Board's decision to combat inflation by raising interest rates resulted in a severe recession. America's economic woes were compounded by final defeat and humiliation in Vietnam. In April 1975 the South Vietnamese government collapsed, and North Vietnamese communists occupied Saigon, renaming it Ho Chi Minh City.

B.   The Outsider as Insider: President Jimmy Carter, 1977–1981
The Republicans nominated Ford for president in 1976. The Democrats ran a former governor of Georgia, Jimmy Carter. In the aftermath of Watergate, Carter appealed to the nation with his honesty, evangelical Christian faith, and the fact that he was a Washington outsider. Carter, who won in a close race, entered office with no clear political philosophy. In his first year he managed to bring unemployment down by implementing a tax cut and increased public works, but thereafter he showed little inclination to launch social welfare programs that involved federal spending. Having poor relations with Congress, he failed to get it to enact national health insurance or welfare and tax reforms. He did appoint a significant number of women and minority-group members as federal judges.

Environmental issues were important to Carter. In 1980, Congress passed the Alaska Lands Act. In New York's Love Canal housing development, medical researchers found high levels of cancer and birth defects due to industrial pollution. Carter declared the Love Canal a national emergency and signed into law creation of a federal superfund to cleanse the country's most polluted sites, such as Love Canal.

In foreign policy, Carter's record was also mixed. He and his secretary of state, Cyrus Vance, tried to combat human rights abuses in foreign countries, including Chile, Argentina, and South Africa.. They successfully completed negotiations on and got ratification of treaties transferring control of the Panama Canal and Canal Zone to the Panamanians by 1999 and completed normalization of relations with the People's Republic of China. Carter's initial conciliatory stance toward the Soviets turned tough when the U.S.S.R. invaded Afghanistan in 1980. The president then adopted a series of anti-Soviet measures inspired by his hard-line national security adviser, Zbigniew Brzezinski.

C.   The Middle East: Peace Accords and Hostages
Carter's foremost foreign-policy achievement was to invite Egypt's Anwar el-Sadat and Israel's Menachem Begin to Camp David, Maryland, in September 1978. There, with the president's encouragement, the two hammered out an Israeli-Egyptian understanding which was formalized in a treaty in 1979. The Camp David Accords did not end the Arab-Israeli conflict, as Israel continued to build Jewish settlements in occupied Arab territories, the other Arab states refused to talk to Israel, and an Islamic fundamentalist assassinated Sadat.

Carter's worst foreign-policy nightmare also came from the Middle East in 1980, an election year. After Islamic fundamentalists overthrew the United States' ally, the shah of Iran, Carter admitted the cancer-stricken monarch to the United States for treatment. Infuriated Iranians stormed the U.S. embassy in Tehran and took some fifty American hostages. A military rescue attempt failed, and Carter was unable to negotiate their release. Not until Reagan's inauguration did the Iranians let the Americans go.

D.   Troubles and Frustration as Carter's Term Ends
Inflation grew steadily worse largely because of OPEC's repeated price hikes. The Federal Reserve Board countered with ever-higher interest rates, making borrowing so expensive that home building and other industry stagnated. Carter, believing the answer to our woes lay in fuel conservation, created the Department of Energy and proposed to Congress legislation that would penalize waste and reward restraint. Capitol Hill passed only a fraction of what he asked. Americans blamed the austerity-preaching president for the economic mess, and his popularity plunged farther when he was unable to free U.S. hostages held in Iran. When the Democrats renominated Carter in 1980, he had no hope of winning.

V.   The Reagan Revolution, 1981–1984
A.   Roots of the Reagan Revolution
Several things prepared the way for the Reagan revolution. Reagan's promise to end stagflation in the economy with a big tax cut sounded simple and appealing. His promotion of the traditional beliefs in small government, rugged individualism, and unregulated free enterprise resonated better with middle- and working-class whites than the liberal alternatives of big government, social welfare programs, and wars on poverty. Decades of Cold War rhetoric left a deep suspicion of the Soviet Union and communism, and the failure in Vietnam still left a bitter taste. Thus, Americans responded to Reagan's unabashed patriotic anticommunism and reassurances that the nation was as great as ever. A New Right cultural conservatism had emerged in reaction to the social turmoil and sexual revolution of the 1960s. Groups such as Jerry Falwell's Moral Majority and Pat Robertson's Christian Coalition threw their support to right-wing politicians like Reagan, who promised to oppose abortions, gay rights, and other possible threats to family values. The shift of population to the traditionally more conservative Sun Belt also set the stage for Ronald Reagan.

Ronald Reagan, ex-movie actor and General Electric spokesman, former governor of California, and the favorite of conservatives, took the 1980 Republican nomination. In November Reagan swept to victory over Carter and independent candidate John Anderson, and his party gained a majority in the Senate for the first time since 1955. Reagan carried the southern and western states and a majority of the blue-collar vote. Of the old Roosevelt coalition, only African-Americans remained solidly in the Democratic camp.

B.   Reaganomics
Reagan believed that the way to make the economy prosper was to lift government regulation and taxes off the back of business. Between 1981 and 1983, he persuaded Congress to cut income taxes by 25 percent and make up for the lost revenue with drastic reductions in domestic spending. He also appointed persons who shared his commitment to deregulation to head federal agencies. Secretary of the Interior James Watt opened national forest and wilderness areas to private developers. The secretary of transportation rescinded 1970s regulations for reducing air pollution and making cars safer and more efficient. By 1982 the economy was in a deep recession. The unemployment rate reached 10 percent. Minorities and the inner-city poor suffered severely as social welfare programs dried up. The nation also experienced enormous foreign-trade deficits. Because military spending increased rapidly and the sluggish economy resulted in less tax revenue collected, the federal deficit soared. By 1983, with inflation at last licked, the economy began to rebound.

The period 1982–1987 witnessed numerous corporate mergers, many insider-trading and other get-rich-quick schemes, and a great bull market that tripled the average price of stocks. Then, on October 19, 1987, the market crashed, with stocks losing one-fifth of their value. Unlike 1929, however, a depression did not follow.

C.   The "Evil Empire" and Crises in the Middle East
During his first term Reagan was hostile toward the U.S.S.R., calling it an "evil empire." Claiming that the Soviet and Cuban communists were trying to gain footholds in Central America, the administration supported a military junta in El Salvador in its brutal attempts to suppress left-wing rebellion. It also funded and trained the contras in Nicaragua in their efforts to overthrow the pro-Marxist Sandinista government. When Congress banned further military aid for the contras, the White House secretly raised money from private right-wing groups and foreign governments to continue arming them. The president also dispatched marines to Grenada to topple a radical government.

Reagan had no success in bringing peace to the Middle East. In 1982 Israel invaded Lebanon to force the Palestinian Liberation Organization (PLO) out of its stronghold there. As a result of the raid, the PLO withdrew, but civil war between rival Lebanese Christian and Muslim factions heated up. The president sent 2,000 U.S. Marines into Lebanon as part of an international peacekeeping force, but in October 1983 a Muslim terrorist attack killed 239 of the Americans. In 1984 Reagan recalled the remaining men.

D.   Military Buildup and Antinuclear Protest
Reagan launched a huge military buildup. By 1985 the Pentagon's annual budget exceeded $300 billion, almost double what it had been in 1981. Much of the spending went into developing and deploying more nuclear-warhead missiles and other atomic weapons. Alarmed by this buildup, hundreds of thousands of Americans joined the nuclear-freeze movement, seeking a verifiable halt by the superpowers in the manufacture and deployment of nuclear weapons. The 1982 rally of freeze activists and sympathizers in New York City's Central Park drew an enormous crowd, and in the fall of that year freeze resolutions passed in nine states. Reagan responded by starting to build a vast space-based antimissile defense system known as the Strategic Defense Initiative (SDI), nicknamed Star Wars. Opponents of

SDI pointed out its prohibitive cost, its technical implausibility, and the great likelihood of its further escalating the arms race.

E.   Reagan Reelected
In 1984, the Republicans again nominated Reagan and Vice President George Bush. Walter Mondale, the Democratic candidate for president, ran with Representative Geraldine Ferraro, the first woman to appear on the national ticket of a major political party. The Democrats pointed out that Reagan had nearly doubled military spending, aggravated Cold War tensions, produced tremendous federal budget and foreign-trade deficits, drastically curtailed social welfare, and weakened government regulatory agencies. Nonetheless, Reagan remained extremely popular because of his tax cuts, the recovered economy, his appointment of the first woman to the Supreme Court, and his personal charm and courage, especially displayed after he was wounded by a deranged man. Reagan won the election decisively. Soon after the election a group of moderate Democrats, including Arkansas governor Bill Clinton and Tennessee senator Al Gore, founded the Democratic Leadership Council to lead their party to a centrist position, in the hopes of winning subsequent elections.

VI.   Reagan's Second Term, 1985–1989
A.   Supreme Court Appointments, Budget Deficits, and the Iran-Contra Scandal
During Reagan's second term, immigration and tax reform measures passed, but the legacy of Reaganomics—huge budget and foreign-trade deficits—grew worse. With his judicial appointments, Reagan pushed the Supreme Court much further to the right. He elevated conservative Justice William Renquist to chief justice, and named ultraconservative Antonin Scalia and moderate-conservative Anthony Kennedy to the court.

The Iran-contra affair, the worst scandal of the Reagan administration, originated from Middle Eastern problems. Oliver North, a National Security Council aide, in 1985–1986 secretly arranged shipments of U.S. weapons to Iran. Then he diverted money from the sales to the Nicaraguan contras at a time when Congress had forbidden further aid to them. To hide these activities, North shredded incriminating documents requested by investigators. A congressional committee found no proof that Reagan had known of the scheme but criticized him for his casual style of supervision and disregard for the law, which invited such behavior from subordinates. North and others involved were subsequently tried and convicted. North's conviction was overturned in 1991 on technical grounds.

Lesser scandals also marred Reagan's second term. Evidence of bribes and conspiracy in the granting of military contracts surfaced. Reagan's secretary of the interior, James Watt, and attorney general Edwin Meese were accused of influence peddling, which led to the latter's resignation. Despite these and other revelations, the president remained popular.

B.   Reagan's Mission to Moscow
The U.S.S.R., bedeviled by domestic crises, sought an easing of tensions abroad, which was reflected in its willingness to make concessions in its arms control talks with the United States. In 1987 the two superpowers negotiated an agreement to remove 2,500 U.S. and Soviet missiles from Europe. The agreement opened a new era of détente, capped by Reagan's visit to Moscow in May 1988.

C.   The Middle East: Tensions and Terrorism
The Middle East remained a thorny problem. In December 1987 a Palestinian uprising against Israel began, and U.S. efforts to convince Jordan, the Palestinians, and Israel to negotiate failed. The Palestinians and their backers, especially Libya's Colonel Muammar el-Qaddafi, resorted to terrorist attacks against U.S. citizens, including bombing a Pan Am jet in 1988. This cycle of terrorism continued well beyond the 1980s.

D.   Assessing the Reagan Years

Reagan's two terms helped restore a sense of stability to U.S. politics. Inflation was lowered and the economy grew stronger after 1982. But the federal deficit increased and the administration ignored many social issues and long-term economic problems. Many of Reagan's critics dismissed his presidency as filled with nostalgia and self-interest, and claimed that Reagan was little more than an actor reading scripts. Reagan's admirers gave him high marks for reasserting the values of self-reliance and free enterprise and for building the United States' international and military strength.

VII. Conclusion

In the 1970s and 1980s, the United States' political culture became more polarized. On one hand, popular culture provided escapism and many middle-class Americans concentrated on personal pursuits and career goals. But activism did continue in a revived women's movement, a gay rights campaign, and the environmental movement. Conservatives also organized politically. Americans became more divided economically. The poor and many minorities lived in decaying inner cities plagued by crime, drugs, violence, and inadequate public services.

Internationally, Ford, Carter, and Reagan dealt with changing U.S-Soviet relations, which worsened in the late 1970s and early 1980s, but got better in the late 1980s. The Middle East, torn by old conflicts, brought hope, tragedy, and terror to the U.S. abroad, and suggested that the nation was entering a period no less dangerous than the Cold War.

VOCABULARY

The following terms are used in Chapter 30. To understand the chapter fully, it is important that you know what each of them means.

yuppie	a young urban professional
gentrification	the process whereby middle-class people buy run-down housing in poor inner-city neighborhoods and restore it, resulting in the revival of the area but usually pushing out former residents who can no longer afford to live there
evangelical	a form of Christian Protestantism that emphasizes the authority of the Bible and a personal commitment to Christ; eager to share the gospel and convert others
secular	not associated with church or religion, not sacred
malaise	a general feeling of unease
insurgency	a rebellion
panacea	cure-all, universal remedy
junta	a military overthrow of a government by a faction inside a country

IDENTIFICATIONS

After reading Chapter 30, you should be able to identify and explain the historical significance of each of the following:

Bill Gates and Microsoft

Greenpeace

Roe v. *Wade,* right-to-life movement, and pro-choice supporters

National Organization for Women (NOW)

Bakke v *U.S.*

Immigration Reform and Control Act, 1986

American Indian Movement (AIM)

Love Canal

Reaganomics

Secretary of the Interior James Watt and the Sagebrush Revolution

Sandinistas versus contras

Palestine Liberation Organization (PLO)

nuclear-freeze movement

Middle East terrorist attacks and Muammar el-Qaddafi

Mikhail Gorbachev

SKILL BUILDING: MAPS

1. On the map of the Middle East and North Africa that follows, locate and explain the importance to U.S. foreign policy of each of the following:

    Afghanistan

    Israel

    West Bank

    Egypt

    Iran

    Tehran

    Lebanon

    Beirut

    Iraq

    Libya

2. On the map of the Caribbean and Central America on the following page, locate and explain the importance to U.S. foreign policy of each of the following:

    Panama

    Panama Canal Zone

    El Salvador

    Nicaragua

    Honduras

Costa Rica

Cuba

Grenada

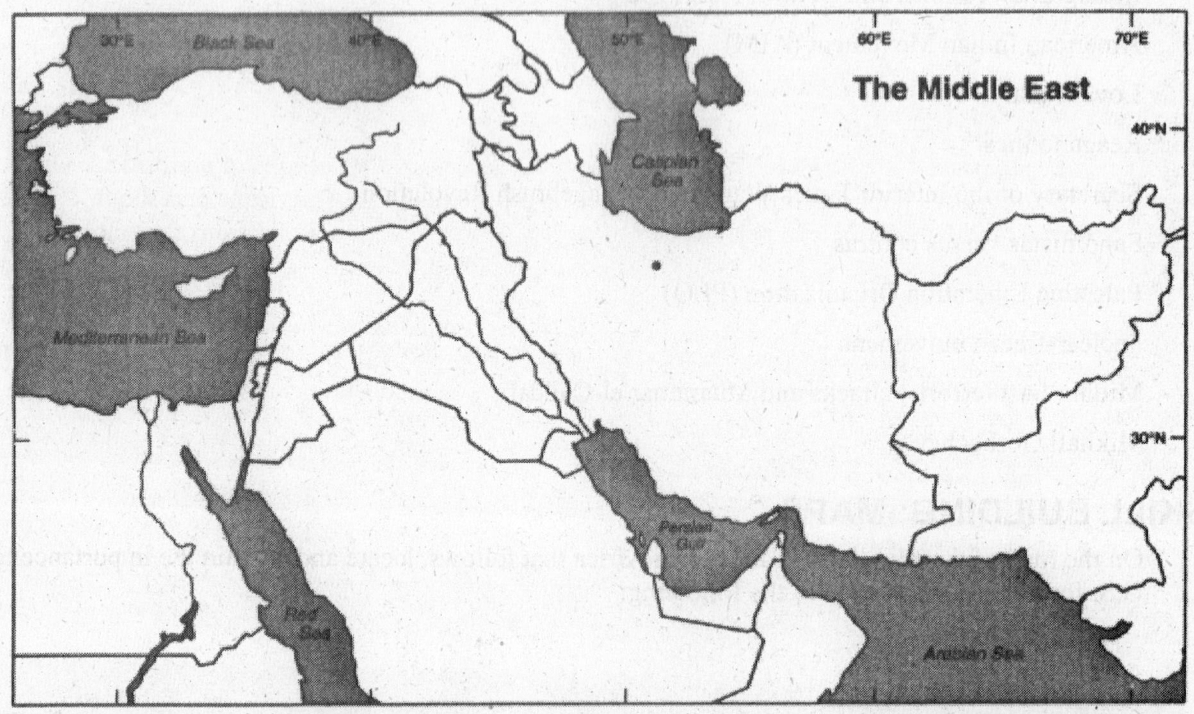

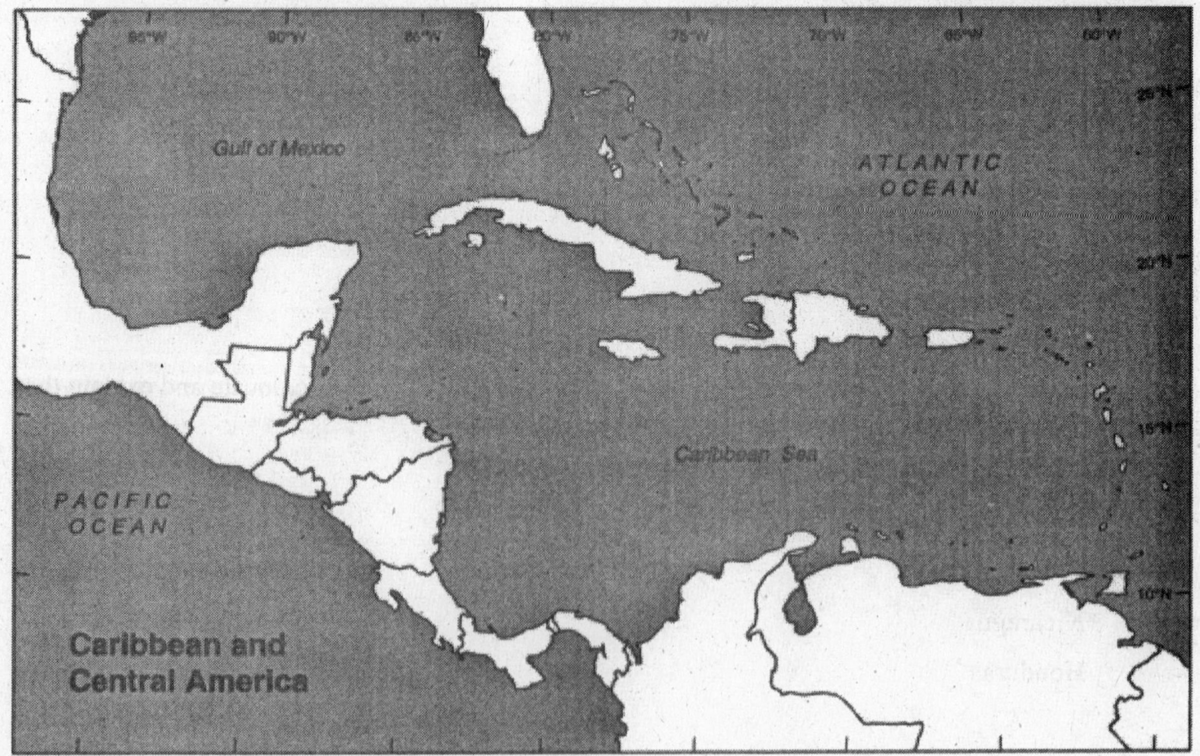

HISTORICAL SOURCES

In Chapter 30 the author has used many of the historical sources we have noted earlier, including data from the U.S. Bureau of the Census. For example, many of the chapter's observations about family patterns, women in the work force, conditions of the black underclass, and ethnic makeup of America's population come from census studies. Look at page 928 where the author makes statements about Hispanics based on Census Bureau estimates. What are these findings? Why can't the historian rely on the accuracy of census figures?

Historians have to use a wide range of sources to assess the successes and failures of a president. On page 933 the author uses public opinion polls to describe the feelings that Americans had about President Carter, and later in the chapter, the author quotes from a newspaper and from a memoir to make conclusions about President Reagan's effectiveness as a leader. What are the dangers of using these types of sources? How would a historian have to be careful when drawing conclusions based on opinion and memory?

MULTIPLE-CHOICE QUESTIONS

Circle the letter of the item that best completes each statement or answers the question.

1. In the 1970s and early 1980s the Federal Reserve Board repeatedly raised interest rates to
   a. stimulate new-home construction.
   b. encourage borrowing for new-plant construction.
   c. combat inflation.
   d. combat unemployment.
2. The only sector of the Roosevelt New Deal coalition who continued through the 1980s to vote consistently for the Democratic presidential candidate was
   a. blue-collar workers.
   b. farmers.
   c. Irish, Polish, and other ethnic Americans.
   d. African-Americans.
3. Which of the following persons is *incorrectly* identified?
   a. Zbigniew Brzezinski—President Carter's national security advisor, who wished to take a hard line toward Russia
   b. Oliver North—President Reagan's chief economic advisor, author of Reaganomics
   c. Sandra Day O'Connor—first woman to sit on the Supreme Court
   d. Geraldine Ferraro—first woman to run for vice president on a major party ticket
4. Three Mile Island is associated with
   a. the Star Wars defense system.
   b. a near-disastrous accident at a nuclear power plant.
   c. gentrification of a rundown area.
   d. the "glass ceiling."
5. Which of the following statements about women in the 1980s is correct?
   a. The majority held paying jobs outside the home.
   b. They were close to achieving equality of pay with men.
   c. Almost half of the lawyers, doctors, and engineers in this country were women.
   d. They were likely to marry at a younger age and have more children than women in the 1950s.

6. The Reagan administration extended military aid and training to the contras in hope that the contras would overthrow a leftist government in

    a. Afghanistan.
    b. Grenada.
    c. Cuba.
    d. Nicaragua.

7. Which of the following statements about evangelical Christians is correct?

    a. They supported the pro-choice movement.
    b. They gave out flowers in airports and city streets.
    c. Most saw the gay and lesbian movement as a collapse of society's morals.
    d. Their political strength disappeared after a series of sexual and financial scandals.

8. Which of the following events happened during Jimmy Carter's presidency?

    a. The inflation rate was finally slowed to 6 percent annually.
    b. The United States invaded Grenada to topple an anti-American left-wing regime.
    c. The Intermediate Nuclear Forces (INF) Treaty was negotiated and ratified.
    d. Treaties transferring control of the Panama Canal and Canal Zone to Panama by 1999 were ratified.

9. Which of these actions was *not* a part of Reaganomics?

    a. Massive cuts in federal spending on domestic programs
    b. Boosting tariff rates to all-time highs to protect U.S. industry from foreign competition and to cut trade deficits
    c. Deregulation of U.S. industry, including banking, the savings-and-loan industry, transportation, and communication
    d. A major cut in federal income taxes

10. Which of the following statements about the Camp David Accords is correct?

    a. Getting Egypt and Israel to negotiate and sign them was President Jimmy Carter's greatest foreign policy achievement.
    b. The signers' promise to respect human rights gave courage to Soviet dissidents.
    c. They were negotiated by Israel and Lebanon under the guidance of President Ronald Reagan.
    d. They were signed by Israel and Jordan and have avoided any conflicts between those two countries since the 1970s.

SHORT-ANSWER QUESTIONS

1. What does the growth of Wal-Mart illustrate about trends in the American economy in the 1970s and 1980s? For what has the company been praised and for what criticized?

2. "[T]he personal computer has grown into a transformative new technology, bringing complex new social and legal issues in its wake." Explain the quote briefly and give at least three examples of how personal computers have transformed American life and/or created new social and legal issues.

3. Describe the new patterns of immigration into the United States that set in after 1965.

4. Which social activist movements of the 1960s continued strongly in the 1970s and 1980s? Why?

5. What was the *Roe* v. *Wade* decision? Why did it prove to be politically divisive throughout the 1980s and early 1990s?

6. How did prospects for Native Americans improve in the late 1960s and 1970s? What impact did the Indian Self-Determination Act (1974) have? What significant problems continued to plague American Indians?

7.   Who was Jesse Jackson? What was his Rainbow Coalition? To whom did he appeal?

8.   What were the troubles that overwhelmed the Carter administration and prevented Carter's reelection?

9.   Explain the Iran-contra affair.

10. Discuss briefly the record of the Reagan administration on environmental issues.

ESSAY QUESTIONS

1.   Discuss the conservative resurgence in America. What caused it? What positions did conservatives take on political, economic, and social issues in the 1970s and 1980s? What role did each of the following play in the conservative resurgence: William F. Buckley; Phyllis Schlafly; Joseph Coors and the Heritage Foundation; and Jerry Falwell, Pat Robertson, and the evangelicals?

2.   Compare and contrast American society and culture in the 1960s with that of the 1970s and 1980s.

3.   Discuss the foreign policies of the United States in Latin America and the Caribbean and the Middle East under the Ford, Carter, and Reagan administrations.

4.   What is meant by the term *Reagan Revolution*? According to Chapter 30, what accounted for the appeal of Ronald Reagan and his policies to the American electorate in the 1980s? What, if anything, have been the lasting effects of Reagan's policies?

5.   Explain how and why U.S.-Soviet relations changed from the late 1970s to 1988.

ANSWERS TO MULTIPLE-CHOICE QUESTIONS

1. c
2. d
3. b
4. b
5. a
6. d
7. c
8. d
9. b
10. a

Beyond the Cold War: Charting a New Course, 1988–2000

OUTLINE AND SUMMARY

I. Introduction

Chapter 31 covers the period from the end of the Cold War, 1988–1989, through the dawn of the twenty-first century. As you read the chapter, consider these questions: (1) What events led to the end of the Cold War and the development of a new relationship between the U.S. and Russia? (2) How well did George W. H. Bush deal with the "new world order" that emerged at the end of the Cold War? (3) What were the domestic policies of Bush, 1989–1993, and of President Clinton, 1993–2001? (4) How did the Clinton administration respond to crises abroad? (5) Which Americans benefited from the economic prosperity of the 1990s and which did not? (6) Why did Americans become even more polarized on political and cultural issues by 2001?

II. The Bush Years: Global Resolve, and Domestic Drift, 1988–1993

A. The Election of 1988

Vice President George Bush captured the Republican nomination, and Massachusetts governor Michael Dukakis beat Jesse Jackson for the top spot on the Democratic ticket. Bush campaigned on Reagan's achievements and painted Dukakis as soft on crime. The governor was unable to articulate a strong vision of the United States' future. Both candidates avoided important issues, resorting instead to photo opportunities and televised spot commercials. Bush won 54 percent of the vote, while the Democrats maintained their majorities in Congress.

B. The Cold War Ends

Soon after Bush's inauguration, Soviet power collapsed. First the Eastern European countries discarded their U.S.S.R.-backed communist regimes. Then East and West Germany reunited, and the Baltic republics declared their independence from Moscow. With our former Cold War adversary clearly no longer a threat, in 1991 President Bush signed another treaty with Gorbachev reducing each country's strategic nuclear arsenal by 25 percent.

Meanwhile Gorbachev's attempts to revive the Soviet economy by introducing some free enterprise alarmed hard-line Communists, who in August 1991 tried to overthrow him. Boris Yeltsin, president of the Russian Republic, and his followers squelched the coup and proclaimed the end of the U.S.S.R. Overwhelmed by the rush of anticommunism and resurgent nationalism, Gorbachev resigned.

President Bush and his secretary of state, James Baker, reacted cautiously to the events in Eastern Europe. Baker tried to see to it that the nuclear arsenal and know-how of the former Soviet republics did not fall into the wrong hands. The United States further cut back its nuclear stockpiles.

Bush abandoned Reagan's intervention in Nicaragua and the long civil war there subsided. However, the United States invaded Panama; toppled its leader, Manuel Noriega; and tried and convicted him for drug selling.

When the economic sanctions of the United States and other countries against the racist white government of South Africa induced it to release Nelson Mandela and drop most apartheid laws, Bush resumed normal trade. The administration refused to impose trade sanctions on China in retaliation for its brutal suppression of prodemocracy demonstrators in Tiananmen Square. The president traveled to Japan in hopes of persuading that prosperous nation to ease the U.S. trade deficit by buying more U.S. products. Little came of his attempt.

C. The Persian Gulf War, 1991

After years of weapons stockpiling, including nuclear and chemical weapons, Saddam Hussein, dictator of Iraq, invaded Kuwait on August 2, 1990. Although the United States had favored Iraq in its earlier war against Iran, President Bush, as well as other world leaders, now saw Hussein as a serious menace. The president, enlisting the support of Congress, the American people, and the United Nations, demanded Iraqi withdrawal from Kuwait. When Hussein did not comply, on January 16, 1991, the United States and other U.N. members began daily bombing raids on Iraqi troops, supply depots, communication centers, and cities. Saddam Hussein retaliated by firing Scud missiles at Israel and Saudi Arabia. The United States tried to intercept these missiles with its Patriot missiles. On February 23, 1991, the U.N. and U.S. ground assault began, and within one hundred hours Kuwait was liberated and Bush declared a cease-fire. U.N. inspectors entered Iraq and began dismantling Hussein's nuclear-weapons plants, but the dictator remained in power, crushing Shiite Muslim and Kurdish uprisings against him.

D. Home-Front Problems and Domestic Policies

Bush inherited economic ills stemming from his predecessor's policies. Savings-and-loan associations collapsed. Deregulation in the Reagan years that permitted savings-and-loan (S&L) associations to extend risky loans and speculate in real estate and other questionable ventures largely caused these disasters. Because deposits in these institutions were federally insured, making good on the losses cost the U.S. taxpayers billions of dollars.

The huge federal deficit produced by Reagan's tax cuts and enormous military spending grew still larger due to the S&L bailout, Gulf War costs, welfare, and Medicare and Medicaid payments. The 1990 package of new taxes and reduced spending failed to stanch the fiscal bleeding. Then, in 1990, recession hit. Sales, housing starts, and tax revenues fell; unemployment climbed. More than 2 million additional Americans sank below the poverty line.

The economic downturn highlighted deep-seated social maladies. Poverty and anger in inner cities worsened and in April 1992 erupted into rioting in Los Angeles and other places. Public schools languished. In 1989, the *Exxon Valdez* oil spill ruined 600 acres of pristine Alaskan coastline, and the Environmental Protection Agency (EPA) pronounced the air in more than one hundred U.S. cities hazardous to breathe. The Bush administration largely ignored these problems. It continued to favor more oil exploration and drilling in Alaska and undermined international treaties on global warming and mining in Antarctica. Bush did, however, sign the 1990 Federal Clean Air Act and the Americans with Disabilities Act, both passed by the Democratic-controlled Congress.

Bush continued Reagan's effort to move the Supreme Court to the right. He nominated David Souter and Clarence Thomas to the high court. The Senate easily confirmed the former but almost rejected the latter because of his questionable judicial qualifications and Anita Hill's charges that he sexually harassed her. As early as 1989, Court decisions reflected the new conservative majority. The justices hedged women's abortion rights, narrowed the interpretation of civil-rights laws, and removed some protections for arrested persons. However, in a five-to-four decision, the Court reaffirmed its earlier *Roe* v. *Wade* stand.

E.   Clinton Versus Bush, and a Third-Party Challenge, 1992
Bush's popularity, at a peak after Operation Desert Storm, plunged with the recession. In 1992 the Democrats nominated Arkansas governor Bill Clinton and Senator Al Gore of Tennessee for president and vice-president, respectively. They promised to promote economic recovery, protect the environment, reform welfare, and create a national health-care system. A Republican convention dominated by the right wing renominated Bush and Quayle. Clinton won with 43 percent of the popular vote to Bush's 38 percent. The strong showing of a third-party candidate, billionaire H. Ross Perot, indicated widespread dissatisfaction with both of the major parties. Perot garnered 19 percent of the vote, the most for any independent since Theodore Roosevelt in 1912. The Democrats retained control of Congress, and the number of women and minority members serving on Capitol Hill grew.

III.   The Clinton Era Begins: Debating Domestic Policy, 1993–1996
A.   Shaping a Domestic Agenda
Clinton dealt with an array of diplomatic problems, but mostly preferred domestic issues to foreign policy. In his domestic program, Clinton aimed particularly to please blue-collar workers and the middle class as well as to advance some of the causes of the 1960s and 1970s, such as feminism and abortion rights. Clinton named many women to cabinet and other top government positions, including Ruth Bader Ginsberg to the Supreme Court and his wife, Hillary Rodham Clinton, to head the Task Force on National Health-Care Reform. The president had only modest success in getting key proposals through Congress. The lawmakers passed the federal spending cuts, tax increases, and the North American Free Trade Agreement with Mexico that Clinton requested, but the legislators rejected his economic-stimulus package (especially when unemployment fell and new jobs increased in 1993–1994 without any spurt of inflation). The health-care plan eventually unveiled by Clinton's task force came under such a barrage of lobbying and partisan attacks that by mid-1994 it had lost most of its support. Nor did Congress accept Clinton's ideas for revamping welfare, which both liberals and conservatives disliked, though for different reasons.

By 1994, allegations of sexual and other misconduct and complaints that he was too eager to please and compromise were seriously eroding Clinton's popularity and effectiveness. More ominous to any liberal or even moderate agenda was the expanding influence of the religious right. Pat Robertson's Christian Coalition mobilized its supporters and by 1994 had gained control of many state Republican Parties.

B.   A Sharp Right Turn, 1994–1996
Frustration with Clinton and his administration led much of the middle class to sympathize with a movement to downsize the federal government and shift power to the states, scrap welfare, and cut taxes and domestic spending. Many of these people also expressed their concern with abortion, pornography, and the supposed collapse of family values. Conservative organizations and special interest groups, such as the Christian Coalition and the National Rifle Association (NRA), funded the campaigns of and rounded up votes for Republicans who favored their agenda.

The improved economy, which should have played into the hands of the Democrats who were in power, won them scant credit because of the stagnation of real income for workers and for the middle class. Newt Gingrich, Republican congressman from Georgia, capitalized on the conservative trend, obtaining the endorsement of fellow Republicans for his Contract with America, which promised to enact what the right wing had been advocating since the days of Barry Goldwater. In the 1994 midterm elections, the

Republicans captured both houses of Congress and many state governorships and legislatures. While the new House Speaker Gingrich led his forces in the effort to legislate their Contract with America, and weakened liberals resisted and compromised, the nation did appear to have taken a significant rightward turn that rejected the social welfare legacy from the Great Society, the New Deal, and running back to the Progressive Eras.

Critics of the federal welfare system charged that it was too expensive and that it undermined the work ethic for relief recipients, creating a permanently dependent underclass. In August 1996, President Clinton signed into law a Republican-passed welfare reform bill that ended the sixty-year-old Aid to Families with Dependent Children (AFDC); allowed states to run their own welfare programs, which were partially funded by federal grants; and strictly limited the number of years anyone could remain on relief.

IV.   The Economic Boom of the 1990s
    A.   An Uneven Prosperity
    The economy boomed in the 1990s because of the personal computer and information technology revolution, rapidly expanding international trade, curtailed inflation, and low interest rates. Stock prices soared often to heights unjustified by the earnings and potentials of the corporations issuing the shares. Almost half of American families invested in these stocks, convinced that was the road to fast wealth. A new round of corporate mergers occurred and profits multiplied. However, the rewards from all this economic activity went almost entirely to those already well-off or rich. While the wealthiest 20 percent of Americans saw their share of national income increase by 13 percent, the average workers' real wages fell. Well-paid industrial jobs kept disappearing; service-sector employment grew. Some service-sector jobs, such as those in information technology, paid handsomely, but required the applicant to have higher education and specialized skills. Unskilled service-sector jobs paid poorly. Since very few workers in the unskilled service sector were unionized (by 2000, only 13.5 percent of labor belonged to unions), they had no bargaining power to improve their wages and conditions. Many corporations, to enhance their profitability, also downsized their payrolls, creating much job insecurity.

    B.   America and the Global Economy
    Economic globalization greatly impacted U.S. foreign policy under the Bush and Clinton administrations. Both presidents urged Japan to buy more U.S. goods to ease this country's trade deficit. Both presidents overlooked China's miserable human rights record and promoted close relations to increase trade. In fact, by 2000, China had become our fourth biggest trading partner, following the first three: Canada, Mexico, and Japan. Again, because of the importance of trade, the Clinton administration granted loan guarantees to Mexico when its peso collapsed and backed IMF loans to a faltering Thailand.

V.   Clinton's Foreign Policy: Defining the United States' Role in a Post–Cold War World
    A.   The Balkans, Russia, and Eastern Europe in the Post-Soviet Era
    The collapse of communism in Eastern and Central Europe unleashed age-old ethnic hatreds. The former Yugoslavia erupted into civil war among Croats, Serbs, and Muslims in Bosnia. In 1995, the Clinton administration brought the heads of the warring factions to Dayton, Ohio. The resulting Dayton Accords imposed a cease-fire and an agreement for governing the province, committing 20,000 U.S. troops to enforce the accords. In 1999, U.S. troops joined a NATO force that occupied Kosovo, in an attempt to halt the ethnic cleansing campaign of Serbia's Slobodan Milosevic. In 2001, Milosevic fell from power. He was tried for war crimes, but died in 2006 before there was an outcome to the trial. With Russia, Clinton signed another arms reduction agreement and backed Russia's admission to the Group of Seven, an organization of the world's leading industrial powers, but Russian-U.S.

relations grew strained when in 1997 NATO admitted three former Soviet allies: Hungary, Poland, and the Czech Republic.

B.   The Middle East: Seeking an Elusive Peace and Combating a Wily Foe
     After hopeful beginnings, Clinton's pursuit of peace in the Middle East failed. In 1993, Israeli and Palestinian leaders had agreed on a timetable for peace at a meeting in Oslo, Norway. However, the bloodshed continued. In 1995, a fanatical Israeli student murdered Israeli Prime Minister Yitzhak Rabin. Benjamin Netanyahu of the hard-line Likud party succeeded Rabin. In July 2000, Clinton invited Yasir Arafat and the new Israeli prime minister, Ehud Barak, to meet at Camp David, but the summit failed to achieve peace. The U.S. also faced another flare-up with Iraq when its leader Saddam Hussein refused to allow UN inspectors to continue their weapons searches.

C.   Nuclear Proliferation, Terrorism, and Peacekeeping Challenges
     In 1968 many countries signed the Nuclear Nonproliferation Treaty, promising not to develop nuclear weapons. India and Pakistan refused to sign and by 1998 both had nuclear bombs. This made their on-going dispute over Kashmir especially dangerous. Communist North Korea, which had signed the treaty, violated its pledge by starting a nuclear development and missile-testing program. In response to U.S. and international pressure and inducements, North Korea agreed to halt the effort, but then resumed work on nuclear bombs and testing missiles.

     Terrorist attacks on Americans by Islamic extremists, many inspired by Osama bin Laden, escalated. These included a 1992 murder of eighteen U.S. soldiers on a peace-keeping mission in Mogadishu, Somalia; a February 1993 bombing at the World Trade Center in New York in which six people died; bombings of U.S. military installations in Saudi Arabia in 1995 and 1996 that killed 24 people; explosions in 1998 at U.S. embassies in Nairobi, Kenya, and Tanzania that killed 220 Americans and local residents; and an attack in 2000 on the U.S. destroyer *Cole* in the harbor of Aden, Yemen, that killed 17 U.S. sailors. Catching and convicting some of the perpetrators and even a U. S. missile strike on a bin Laden terrorist training camp in Afghanistan did not end the problem. As Clinton's secretary of state Madeleine K. Albright stated, the United States is engaged in a "long-term struggle" against terrorism, "the war of the future." Clinton also in 1994 sent U.S. troops into Haiti in support of a UN effort to oust a military junta and return the elected president Jean-Bertrand Aristide to power. This mission essentially failed when ten years later Aristide was again forced into exile amid fighting and violence, which UN peacekeepers sought to quiet.

D.   A New World Order Painfully Emerges
     Hopes that with the end of the Cold War peace would come were dashed in the 1990s. U.S. policy makers found themselves having to respond to many small conflagrations in the Middle East, the Balkans, Asia, and Africa and to combat escalating terrorism instead of concentrating on one enemy. Analysts have pointed to four trends on the international scene since the end of the Cold War: (1) Economic considerations play a major role in the United States' and other nations' foreign policies. (2) The widening gulf between the prosperous industrialized countries and the poverty-ridden populations of the Third World encourage hatreds, resentments and terrorism. (3) Ethnic divisions and religious fundamentalism are on the rise and produce vicious, genocidal violence as in Rwanda in 1994, to which the Clinton administration failed to react. (4) In this complex world the United Nations is struggling to define its part. Public opinion polls indicate most Americans still favor turning to the United Nations for solving international crises despite the organization's weaknesses.

VI. The Clinton Era Ends: Domestic Politics, Impeachment, and a Disputed Election, 1996–2000
   A.   Campaign 1996 and After; Battling Big Tobacco; and Balancing the Budget
        In 1996, Clinton was reelected over his weak Republican challenger, Bob Dole, but the Republicans retained control of Congress. During his second term, Clinton stuck mostly to a middle-of-the-road course, abandoning large-scale programs in favor of modest proposals that appealed to progressives without alienating moderates, such as reducing the national debt, offering tax credits for college tuition, and providing medical care for uninsured children. He did push Capitol Hill to pass tougher federal regulation of tobacco companies, and when the bill failed to pass, he had the Justice Department file suit against the tobacco companies to recover Medicare costs for treating smoking-induced illnesses. In 2005 the courts ruled against the government.

   B.   Scandal Grips the White House
        Clinton's leadership was seriously undermined by a complicated scandal stemming from a sexual harassment lawsuit brought against the president by Paula Jones, dating from his days as governor of Arkansas. Seeking to show a pattern of harassment, Jones's lawyer questioned Clinton about reports he was having an affair with a White House intern, Monica Lewinsky. The president denied the story, but taped conversations indicated otherwise. Independent Counsel Kenneth Starr began investigating whether Clinton had committed perjury, and Clinton publicly admitted to "conduct that was wrong" with Lewinsky. In September 1998, Kenneth Starr found grounds for the impeachment of Clinton, on the basis that he had committed perjury and obstructed justice. The House approved four articles of impeachment and sent them to the Senate for trial. As the trial progressed, Clinton's popularity climbed and most Americans opposed impeachment. The Senate ultimately rejected the charges, and Clinton remained in office, albeit with a tarnished reputation.

   C.   Election 2000: Bush Versus Gore
        In the 2000 presidential election, the Democrats nominated Vice President Al Gore as their candidate, and the Republicans chose George W. Bush, son of former President George H. W. Bush. Despite the strong economy, Gore had image problems. Many Americans preferred Bush as a person, even as they agreed with Gore on issues. Gore won the popular election by 500,000 votes, but in the electoral college the two were so close that the outcome depended on who took Florida's twenty-five electoral votes. Because of a flawed voting system in that state the returns were uncertain for some time after the election. The Florida Supreme Court held that a hand count of all ballots should take place to determine the winner, but Bush's legal team appealed to the U.S. Supreme Court. On December 12, the Supreme Court ruled in a five Republican-appointed justices to four Democratic-appointed judges that the recount should stop. Gore conceded, making George W. Bush the president. The Republicans held on to the House; the Senate was evenly split between the two parties. Former first lady Hillary Rodham Clinton was elected to the Senate from New York, where she joined twelve other women, a record number of female senators.

VII. Cultural Trends at Century's End
   A.   Affluence and a Search for Heroes
        The economic boom of the 1990s created enormous wealth for some Americans. They spent their money conspicuously, on lavish consumer goods. Social critics claimed that a new "winner-take-all" mentality caused those at the top to turn their backs on the larger society. Although some movies did explore the darker side of life, popular entertainment generally celebrated wealth or looked nostalgically to a past where heroes fought real battles over meaningful issues.

B. Outbursts of Violence Stir Concern

The overall crime rate fell during the 1990s due to prosperity, stricter gun control laws, a smaller population of young men, declining use of crack-cocaine, and more offenders sentenced to long jail terms. Nonetheless, the decade was punctuated by horrific acts of violence. Some of these included the shootings at Columbine High School in 1999; the murder of a gay student, Matthew Shepard, in Wyoming; attacks on abortion clinics and doctors who performed abortions; and Timothy McVeigh's and Terry Nichols' bombing of the Murrah Federal Building in Oklahoma City, which claimed the lives of 168 people, 19 of them children.

C. Culture Wars: A Broader View

The culture wars continued in the 1990s, though they usually did not erupt into violence. Christian conservatives and evangelicals stepped up their campaign to save America from its moral decay by demanding a constitutional amendment allowing prayer in public schools, condemning history textbooks for not promoting patriotism and moral values, and attempting to stop equal rights for homosexuals. On the other hand, the Christian Coalition and its allies did not always get their way. Sociologist Alan Wolfe found in his 1998 study that the majority of middle-class Americans favored cultural diversity and tolerance and were "suspicious of extremist positions."

VIII. Conclusion

The dissolution of the U.S.S.R. profoundly changed the international scene. President George H. W. Bush adjusted his foreign policy to the new order well and successfully handled the biggest foreign crisis during his term: Iraq's invasion of Kuwait and the subsequent Persian Gulf War. Bush proved much less able to cope with domestic problems and lost the 1992 election to the Democrat Bill Clinton. During Clinton's first term the defeat of his health-care reform plan and a more conservative national climate led to Republicans gaining majorities in both houses of Congress in 1994. Clinton managed to win a second term in 1998 because he moved right and compromised with the Republicans. For example, he signed a GOP-sponsored welfare measure that dismantled the system put in place by the New Deal in 1935. Clinton was also helped by the booming economy that aided in his balancing the federal budget. The new prosperity did not reach all Americans, however. Displaced industrial workers and inner-city residents saw their share of national income decline. In foreign policy Clinton had a mixed record. He had the United States join in stopping genocidal ethnic violence in the Balkans, but looked the other way in Rwanda. His best efforts to bring peace to the Middle East failed. Political and cultural conflicts continued and intensified in the 1990s. Clinton played into the hands of the conservatives with his sexual indiscretions and cover-up lies. Republicans used these as grounds for impeaching him. Although he was not convicted by the Senate, his reputation suffered. In 2000 the Democrat Al Gore won the election in the popular vote, but lost in the Electoral College to George W. Bush, when a partisan Supreme Court halted the recount of Florida's disputed ballots.

VOCABULARY

The following terms are used in Chapter 31. To understand the chapter fully, it is important that you know what each of them means.

patrician — a person of high birth; person born into the upper classes

apartheid — South Africa's policy of racial separation

ideology — a system of ideas on which economic or political beliefs are based

impeachment	the charging of a public official, such as the president, with misconduct in office
perjury	lying while under oath
partisan	loyal to a particular party; voting along party lines
anecdotal	evidence drawn from stories, rather than from scientifically collected data
apocalyptic	prophesying a final showdown in which the forces of evil are destroyed
pragmatic	a practical approach to problems; open-minded; experimental

IDENTIFICATIONS

After reading Chapter 31, you should be able to identify and explain the historical significance of each of the following:

Mikhail Gorbachev and Boris Yeltsin

James Baker

Nelson Mandela

Tiananmen Square

Saddam Hussein

ozone shield

New Democratic Coalition

Hillary Rodham Clinton and the Task Force on National Health-Care Reform

gays, the military, and "Don't ask, don't tell"

Oklahoma City bombing

Paula Jones, Monica Lewinsky, and Kenneth Starr

ethnic cleansing

Oslo Accords

World Trade Organization

SKILL BUILDING: MAPS

1. On the map of Europe, locate and explain the historic changes that took place in each of the following places in the 1990s:

Estonia

Latvia

Lithuania

Belarus

The Ukraine

Russian Federation

Bosnia

Serbia

Kosovo

2. On the map of the Middle East and North Africa that follows, locate and explain the historic events that occurred in each of the following places in the 1990s:

Kuwait

Iraq

Baghdad

Saudi Arabia

Riyahd

Persian Gulf

Israel

Iran

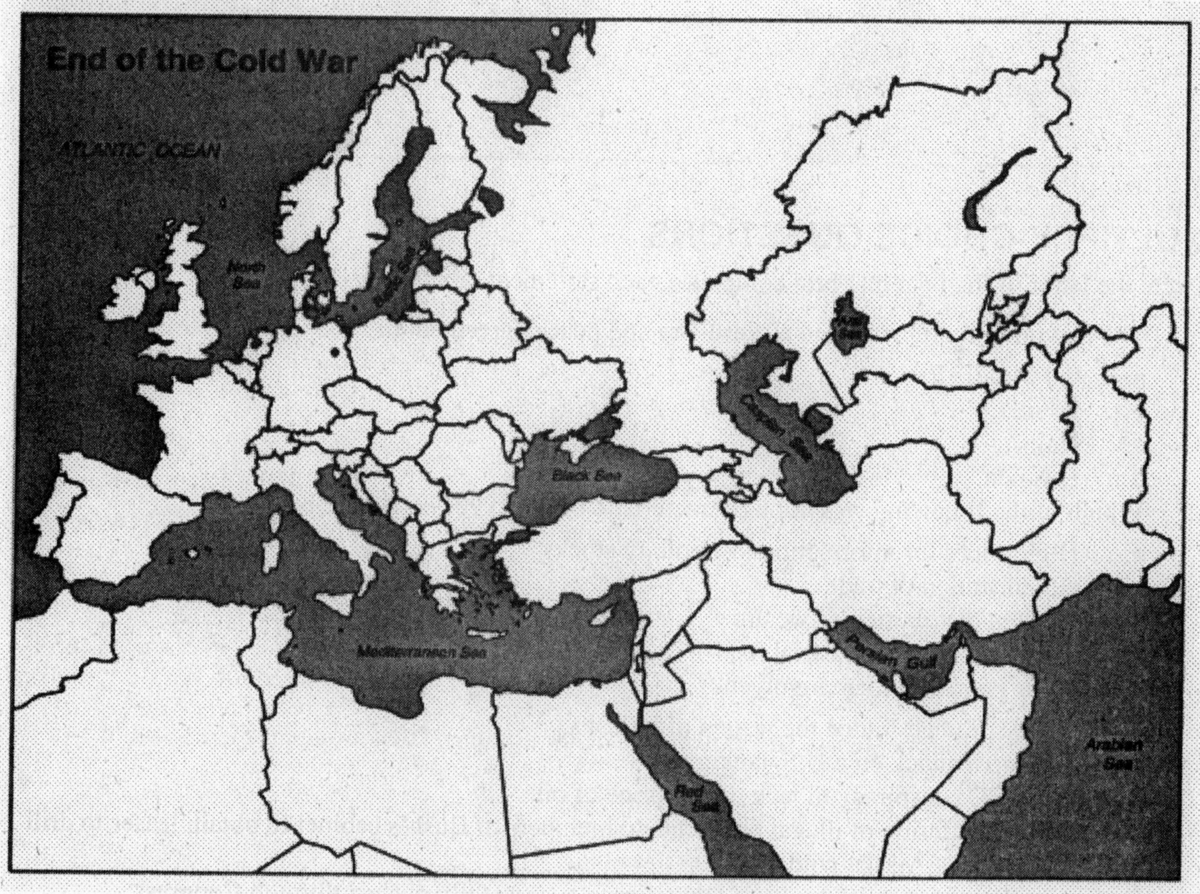

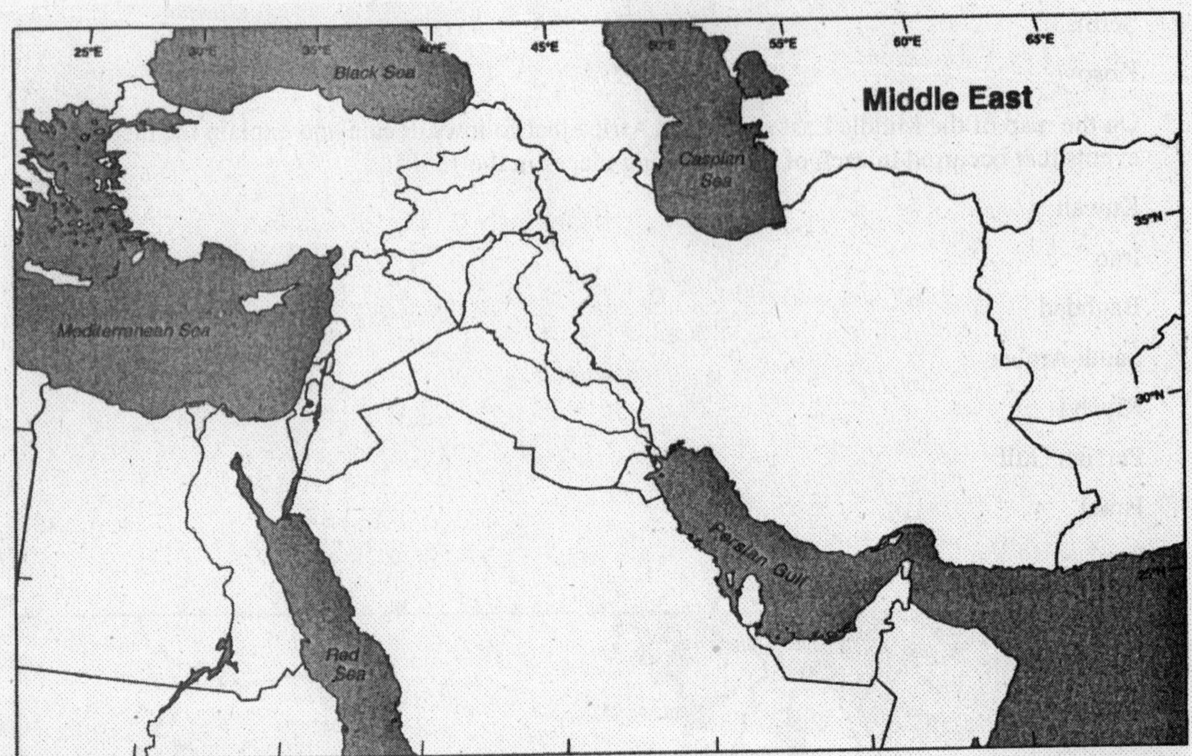

MULTIPLE-CHOICE QUESTIONS

Circle the letter of the item that best completes each statement or answers the question.

1. The Dayton Accords imposed a cease-fire and peace agreement in

   a. the Middle East.
   b. Bosnia.
   c. Haiti.
   d. Rwanda.

2. Which of the following was *not* a characteristic of the 1990s economic boom?

   a. High prices for information technology stocks
   b. Globalization of trade
   c. Uneven distribution of wealth
   d. Rapid growth of industrial jobs

3. The *Exxon Valdez* incident involved

   a. an oil spill that fouled the waters off Alaska.
   b. a terrorist attack on a U.S. tanker.
   c. an OPEC conspiracy to jack up the price of oil.
   d. Exxon's offering of illegal payments to members of Bush's cabinet to obtain leases to drill for oil in the Alaska wilderness.

4. During his first year in office, President Clinton successfully pushed through Congress

   a. a plan for national health-care reform.
   b. spending cuts and tax increases to start reducing the federal budget deficit.
   c. a budget that provided for a much expanded federal-jobs program and other pump-priming measures to stimulate the economy.
   d. a measure opening opportunities for military service to declared homosexuals.

5. Which of the following was most likely to support Newt Gingrich's Contract with America?

    a.   A member of the New Democratic Coalition
    b.   A liberal Democrat
    c.   A member of the Christian Coalition
    d.   An African-American

6. In the 2000 presidential election,

    a.   Gore lost the Electoral College vote when recounting was halted by the Supreme Court.
    b.   Gore and Bush tied the vote, so it was decided by the Senate.
    c.   Bush won the election in a landslide victory.
    d.   Florida's Electoral College votes went to Ralph Nader, causing Gore to lose the election.

7. Which of the following was Clinton *not* accused of?

    a.   Sexual harassment
    b.   Erasing taped evidence
    c.   Perjury
    d.   Obstruction of justice

8. All of the following are women that President Clinton appointed to important federal government positions *except*

    a.   Ruth Bader Ginsberg.
    b.   Madeleine K. Albright.
    c.   Hillary Rodham Clinton.
    d.   Paula Jones.

9. In the 1994 midterm elections,

    a.   the Republicans won majorities in both houses of Congress.
    b.   there was an unusually high voter turnout.
    c.   the Democrats held on to the House but lost the Senate.
    d.   the voters indicated that they wanted more government programs to help the poor and a crackdown on monopolistic corporations.

10. Which of the following statements about the North American Free Trade Agreement (NAFTA) with Mexico is correct?

    a.   It was opposed by business, which feared competition from cheap Mexican imports.
    b.   It was championed by labor as a way to stem illegal immigration from Mexico that was depressing wages in the United States.
    c.   It was negotiated during Bush's administration, but pushed through Congress by President Clinton, who strongly supported it.
    d.   The Democratic-controlled Congress in 1993 rejected it because of fears that it would lead to U.S. companies moving plants to Mexico to take advantage of cheap labor.

11. Which of the following people is *incorrectly* identified?

    a.   H. Ross Perot—President Bush's secretary of state who convinced Israel and the Palestinians to sign the Oslo Accords
    b.   Robert Dole—Republican presidential candidate who lost to Clinton in 1996
    c.   Timothy McVeigh—convicted of and executed for the Oklahoma City bombing
    d.   Joseph Lieberman—Al Gore's running mate in 2000 and first Jewish American to run for vice president on a major party ticket

12. After the first Persian Gulf War, UN inspectors were in Iraq to

    a.   negotiate a peace agreement between Iran and Iraq.
    b.   monitor possible human rights violations against the Kurdish minority.
    c.   oversee democratic elections.
    d.   search for and destroy nuclear, biological, and chemical weapons.

SHORT-ANSWER QUESTIONS

1. Whom did Bush nominate to the Supreme Court, and how did those appointments change the Court?

2. Explain why George H. W. Bush entered the Persian Gulf War. Was he able to obtain international backing for U.S. intervention? Did the United States achieve Bush's objectives in the war?

3. What caused the failure of nearly 600 Saving and Loan Associations (banks) between 1988 and 1990? Why was this failure very costly to U.S. taxpayers?

4. Why was the Welfare Reform Act of 1996 passed? What are its main provisions? How is it a major change in federal welfare policy in place since Franklin D. Roosevelt's New Deal in the 1930s?

5. What is meant by the term *culture wars*? Over what issues were the culture wars fought in the 1990s?

ESSAY QUESTIONS

1. Discuss the most important economic, social, and cultural trends in the 1990s. Which had the greatest impact on American life, and why?

2. The author of Chapter 31 writes, "As president, Bush compiled an uneven record. Internationally, he reacted decisively," but "His domestic record was thin. . . ." Do you agree with this assessment? Why or why not? (Back up your answer with as much evidence about George H. W. Bush's foreign and domestic policies as possible.)

3. Discuss Bill Clinton's presidency. What were his successes and failures domestically and in foreign policy? Why was he impeached, but not convicted? How do you think historians will rank him as a president by 2050? Why?

4. The author of Chapter 31 states, "For better or worse, globalization has become a driving force in our contemporary world." Discuss this statement. In your discussion include the following: a definition of globalization; examples of it in trade, communication, public health, and other areas; why labor, environmentalists, and other progressive groups often protest against it at meetings of the World Trade Organization; and what benefits the majority of economists claim have come from it.

5. America has always been regarded as the land of opportunity for all, yet in 1998 Harvard economist Richard Freeman wrote, "The U.S. has the most unequal distribution of income among the advanced countries—and the degree of inequality has increased more here than in any comparable country." Write an essay exploring why at the end of the twentieth century and the start of the twenty-first this has happened.

ANSWERS TO MULTIPLE-CHOICE QUESTIONS

1. b
2. d
3. a
4. b
5. c
6. a
7. b
8. d
9. a
10. c
11. a
12. d

CHAPTER 32

Global Dangers, Global Challenges, 2001 to the Present

OUTLINE AND SUMMARY

I. Introduction
    Chapter 32 deals with contemporary history, which is still unfolding. It covers the newest wave of immigration that the United States is experiencing and how the nation is adjusting to the recent arrivals. Political, economic, and cultural developments since 2001 are chronicled and, above all, the ramifications of the horrific terrorist attacks of September 11, 2001, are discussed. As you read this chapter and follow events in the news media, try to answer these questions: (1) What demographic and economic trends are having the greatest impact on the United States today? (2) How have the terrorist attacks of 9/11/01 affected the domestic and foreign policies of the country since then? (3) What have been the actions of George W. Bush's administration?

II. America Under Attack: September 11, 2001, and its Aftermath
    A. Introduction
        George W. Bush ran in 2000 as a moderate Republican, but once in office began to follow a hard-line conservative course. He responded to the terrorist attacks of 2001 by organizing a multinational invasion of Afghanistan to root out Osama bin Laden, mastermind of 9/11/01. Subsequently, claiming that Saddam Hussein was also behind the attacks and had weapons of mass destruction, Bush invaded Iraq. At home, the administration signed laws and created new government agencies to beef up homeland security.

    B. The Bush Administration Begins
        Bush, son of a president and grandson of a U. S. senator, pursued a lackluster business career until 1994, when his family connections helped him become governor of Texas and in 2000 win the Republican nomination for president. With the exception of African-Americans Colin Powell, secretary of state, and Condoleezza Rice, national security advisor, most of Bush's appointees were conservative Republicans with close ties to big business. His economic, social, and cultural policies were aimed at pleasing the rich, corporate America, and the religious right, so much so that he began to alienate moderate Republicans and Democrats. By the summer of 2001 his approval ratings hovered around 50 percent, and then came 9/11.

    C. Day of Horror: September 11, 2001
        On September 11, 2001, politics as usual were suspended when terrorists hijacked four planes, flying two of them into the World Trade Center and one into the Pentagon. The other crashed in Pennsylvania after passengers prevented the terrorists from diverting the plane to another target. The death toll was over 3000 and brought home to America the terror attacks that had been mounting overseas. When several people died after opening anonymous letters containing anthrax spores, public anxieties deepened. As the nation mourned, Americans united in a great burst of patriotism, and the country's 6 million Muslims came under suspicion.

D.   Confronting the Enemy in Afghanistan
President Bush blamed the attacks on the Al Qaeda terrorist network, headed by
Osama bin Laden from headquarters in Afghanistan. A tape of bin Laden boasting of
his role confirmed the suspicions. The United States announced a military campaign
to uproot Al Qaeda. On October 7, U.S. forces, supported by troops from Britain,
Canada, and Pakistan, began an offensive in Afghanistan. By December, the United
States claimed victory, though bin Laden remained at large and Taliban fighters dug
into strongholds in the mountains vowing to fight on. Hundreds of other Taliban
fighters were taken as prisoners to Guantanamo Bay in Cuba.

E.   Tightening Home-Front Security
Congress debated airport security and passed legislation requiring all security
personnel to be U.S. citizens. The Justice Department detained hundreds of Middle
Easterners living in the United States and held them without filing charges. Civil
liberties activists criticized this action. In October 2001, Congress passed the USA-
Patriot Act which extended the government's powers to monitor suspects, further
arousing fears that law enforcement could abuse its authority. Nonetheless, Capitol
Hill renewed the law, with some changes, in 2005. In 2002 Congress opened an
investigation into reports that U.S. intelligence agencies had missed clues before the
terrorist attack, and to avoid such weaknesses in the future, Bush and the lawmakers
created a new cabinet-level Department of Homeland Security. The president also
appointed a commission, headed by former New Jersey governor Thomas Kean, to
find out what went wrong and offer suggestions for strengthening national security.
Some of the commission's recommendations were implemented, others ignored.

F.   The Campaign in Iraq, 2003–2004
Starting in 2002, Bush sought to extend the war on terrorism to Iraq. Bush, Vice
President Cheney, and other members of the administration accused Saddam Hussein
of Iraq of aiding and abetting Al Qaeda and possessing nuclear, chemical, and
biological weapons of mass destruction. A group of neoconservative Republicans,
including Paul Wolfowitz and William Kristol, were urging Bush to make preemptive
war on Iraq and remove Saddam. They argued that such a course would spread
democracy and freedom in the Middle East and help bring peace and stability to the
whole region. Skeptics doubted the administration's charges against Iraq, warned a
war there might go on for years, and rather than bringing peace and stability would
produce turmoil, hatreds, and terrorism throughout the Middle East. Despite their
warnings, in October 2002, Congress gave Bush a free hand by voting that the
president should "defend the national security of the United States against the
continuing threat posed by Iraq." The administration made the most of American fears
of terrorism and Iraq in the 2002 midterm elections, winning Republican control of
both houses of Congress. Then, without the support of most of our allies except
British prime minister Tony Blair, the United States launched its war on Iraq in March
2003. In a matter of weeks U.S. troops occupied the country, Saddam was toppled and
in hiding, and on May 1, Bush proclaimed "Mission accomplished." In the months
and years that followed everything went wrong: insurgency, crime, terrorism, and civil
war engulfed Iraq, and the death toll for its people and U.S. troops mounted
relentlessly.

III.   Politics and the Economy in Bush's First Term, 2001–2005
A.   Economic Reverses and Corporate Scandals
In March 2001 the stock market crashed and the economic boom of the 1990s came to
an end. Information technology stocks, which had been terribly inflated, now
plummeted. Hard-pressed companies began to lay off workers and unemployment

rose. Government tax revenues fell, turning the budget surpluses of the Clinton years into mounting deficits for Bush. The Federal Reserve Board repeatedly cut interest rates to stimulate the economy, but economic comeback was slowed by lack of investor confidence. In quick succession, some of the biggest corporations admitted they had overstated their earnings, misled investors, and were now declaring bankruptcy, among them Enron, WorldCom, and Tyco. Investors and employees had lost millions while CEOs and other insiders sold their holdings just before the dire news became public. These scandals were produced by government's deregulation of business and a culture of corporate greed. Congress responded by passing the Sarbanes-Oxley Act, providing for stricter accounting rules and imposing stiffer criminal penalties on corporate executives defrauding investors and others..

B.   The Republican Domestic Agenda
President Bush entered office calling on the lawmakers to pass a huge income tax cut. While his proposal would lower taxes for all Americans, it would give the really big breaks to the wealthy. In May 2001, Congress complied, approving somewhat smaller and less advantageous-to-the-rich tax reductions. Almost immediately, the lost revenue turned Clinton's budget surplus into a burgeoning budget deficit. Despite this problem, the Republican-dominated Congress passed additional tax cuts in 2003 and 2005. The Bush administration drew up and Capitol Hill enacted an energy bill in August 2005 that gave billions of dollars in tax incentives to oil, natural gas, coal, and nuclear power companies and freed them from obeying many environmental-protection regulations. Bush's "No Child Left Behind" educational program involved setting national standards and exams for pupils. Public schools in which students tested poorly would be penalized or even shut down. How well this approach to improving public schools works has yet to be established. To please his religious right supporters, Bush restricted federal funding for stem-cell research, which many scientists believe could produce cures for diseases.

C.   Campaign Finance Reform and the Election of 2004
In 2002, Bush signed into law the McCain-Feingold campaign finance reform act, which banned "soft-money" contributions to political parties. Whether political action committees and lobbyists can find loopholes in the law to continue pouring money into campaigns of their favored candidates remains to be seen. The Democrats chose Senator John Kerry and Senator John Edwards as their candidates for president and vice president, respectively, while the Republicans renominated President Bush and Vice President Cheney in the 2004 election. Though Kerry had voted for the Patriot Act and the use of force against Iraq, he now criticized Bush's conduct of the war and the Patriot Act's menace to civil liberties. Bush defended both the act and the war as necessary to combat terrorism, and the Republicans accused Kerry of "flip flopping." Bush and Kerry also differed on key cultural issues: the death penalty—Bush-pro, Kerry- anti; keeping abortions legal—Kerry-pro, Bush-anti; strict gun control—Kerry-pro, Bush-anti; and gay marriage—Kerry favored leaving the decision to state governments, while Bush proposed a constitutional amendment banning same-sex marriage. Bush won in a close election, and the Republicans strengthened their majorities in both houses of Congress. The election again showed the important roles of organized groups and the Internet in U.S. politics. Liberal groups using the Internet to support progressive candidates and causes included Move On. Org, People for the American Way, and the American Civil Liberties Union. Rallying behind conservative candidates and causes were Pat Robertson's Christian Coalition, James Dobson's Focus on the Family, and others.

IV.   Foreign Policy in a Threatening Era
  A.   The Continuing Struggle in Iraq, Sagging Home-Front Support
        President Bush in January 2005 proclaimed that the United States' mission was to spread democracy and end tyranny in the world and that our intervention in Iraq was one step toward that end. Unfortunately, the reality in Iraq did not match Bush's claims. Iraq was ravaged by suicide bombings, assassinations, kidnappings, attacks on U.S. troops and the Iraqi police force and soldiers we were training, and sectarian violence that was escalating into civil war between Sunnis and Shiites. U.S. efforts to rebuild and restore Iraq's destroyed infrastructure lagged badly due to the continuing fighting and to fraud and overcharging by favored U.S. companies to whom the army gave no-bid contracts, such as Vice President Cheney's old firm, Halliburton. Several elections in Iraq failed to produce a government capable of restoring order or even commanding the allegiance of most citizens. By 2006 an estimated 45,000 Iraqis had died, along with 2,500 GIs. The dismal situation led to waning support for the war at home and calls for our immediate withdrawal, such as that made by Pennsylvania congressional representative Jack Murtha. The antiwar sentiment intensified as evidence surfaced that the Bush administration had deceived the public about Saddam's having weapons of mass destruction and links to al Qaeda and that U.S. soldiers were abusing prisoners in Iraq, Afghanistan, and Guantanamo. Revelations that the Bush administration had authorized the use of torture, wiretapped the phone calls and e-mail of U.S. citizens without obtaining warrants, and defended its right to do these things despite congressional disapproval seriously impaired the president's standing. According to a Harris poll in May 2006, Bush's approval rating had dropped to under 30 percent. As far as achieving a peaceful settlement of the Israeli-Palestinian conflict, Bush scored no more success than he was having in Iraq.

  B.   Nuclear Proliferation Threats
        Bush decided to revive Reagan's antimissile system (Star Wars) even though doing so violated the 1972 ABM treaty with Russia. Putin agreed to the violation and to letting the treaty lapse on the promise that both countries would get rid of two-thirds of their missiles over the next ten years. Serious threats of rogue states developing and using nuclear weapons came from North Korea and Iran. The United States and other nations are trying through diplomacy to persuade these countries to halt their nuclear weapons programs.

  C.   A Widening Trade Gap and China's Growing Power
        During Bush's presidency the trade deficit of the United States grew even larger, over $700 billion in 2005. This was caused by rising prices for the large quantities of oil imported by the U.S.; the burgeoning share of the domestic market for automobiles sold by foreign, especially Japanese, companies; and spiraling increases in imports from China, which had become the fourth biggest economy in the world, exceeded only by the United States, Japan, and Germany. Some U.S. companies complained that China undersold them because Chinese manufacturers paid miserable wages and their government manipulated the value of their currency to make prices low to U.S. consumers. The Bush administration in 2002 tried to help U.S. industry by placing tariffs on steel imports from China and the European Union (EU). However, the tariffs were removed the following year when the EU and other countries threatened to retaliate against U.S. exports. Besides, some U.S. businesses opposed protectionism. Wal-Mart, for example, earns millions selling low-cost Chinese merchandise to U.S. customers, and a number of U.S. companies also profit by having their products made by exploited Chinese workers.

  D.   Environmental Hazards Become a Global Concern

Disasters associated with Three Mile Island, the Love Canal, the *Exxon Valdez*, Chernobyl, and a deadly gas release from a U. S.-owned chemical plant in Bhopal, India (which killed 1700), forced people all over the world to become more concerned about environmental hazards. The U.S. government in the late twentieth and early twenty-first centuries attempted to address some environmental problems. It tried to find a place to dispose of our own and Russia's radioactive waste from nuclear weapons and power plants. The Bush administration is building a nuclear-waste disposal site at Yucca Mountain in Nevada. However, some scientists question the safety of this because the area is subject to earthquakes and water. The Bush administration has refused to cooperate in solving the potentially greatest environmental danger, global warming, which the majority of scientists say is being caused by the burning of fossil fuels. In its energy policies the administration has chosen to dispute and disregard what these scientists claim. Bush also refused to sign the Kyoto Accords, a 2005 international agreement for reducing fossil-fuel emissions that has been endorsed by most nations, except the United States, Australia, India, and China, which happen to be among the worst polluters.

V.   Social and Cultural Trends in Contemporary America
    A.   An Increasingly Diverse People
        A number of demographic trends continued through the 1990s and the beginning of the twenty-first century. The population of the South and West grew disproportionately to that of the Northeast. The aging of the baby-boom generation pushed the median age up, and family patterns and living arrangements changed as the proportion of Americans living in nuclear families declined to about 50 percent by 2004. The nation was also becoming more racially and ethnically diverse as heavy immigration from Asia and Latin America persisted. By 2004, about 12 percent of the U.S. population was foreign born, and Hispanics constituted the biggest minority group.

    B.   Upward Mobility and Social Problems in a Multiethnic Society
        Since 1990, the African-American middle class has made significant advances: median income rose, as did the number of African-American-owned businesses and professionals. Also, more African-Americans moved from North to South than the other way round. However, in the inner cities, chronic problems hung on. Unemployment among ghetto youth rose above 50 percent by 2005. The number of African-American men in prison was disproportionately high. Inner-city African-American women, too, faced problems of drug use, high teen pregnancy rates, and out-of-wedlock births. Native Americans continued to push for the enforcement of nineteenth-century treaties, and Indian-run gambling casinos, while controversial, provided some tribes with substantial income, which they used to support schools, community centers, and social service programs on their reservations. The United States' Hispanic population grew rapidly between 1990 and 2005. This group resists easy generalizations: Mexican Americans are concentrated in the Southwest, while other Hispanics (Puerto Ricans, Cubans, and Central Americans) live mainly in Florida, New York, New Jersey, and Illinois. Some prospered, but others lived in inner-city neighborhoods and faced problems of gangs, drug addiction, and poor education. Many became politically active and lobbied for change. Three-fourths of the United States' 13 million Asian Americans arrived in the United States after 1980. Because they have a high regard for education and strong family networks, many have achieved upward mobility. If current trends persist, demographers predict that by 2050 no single ethnic-racial group will be a majority of the U.S. population. Some Americans have not adjusted well to all of this diversity. As about 1 million

immigrants settled in Los Angeles and New York, respectively, more than 1 million native-born whites moved out of each. There were disputes over making English the official language of the United States, and racial and ethnic hostility of the sort depicted in the movie *Crash* festered.

C. The "New Economy" and the Old Economy
In the late nineteenth century, the U.S. economy transformed from agricultural to industrial, while in the late twentieth and early twenty-first centuries, the economy went from industrial to professional and service based. By 2004, 62 percent of the labor force held white-collar jobs; only 23 percent worked any longer in manufacturing, farming, construction, and transportation. Globalization contributed to this transformation because cheap imported manufactured goods took over the domestic market from U.S.-factory-produced goods. The results proved dire for U.S. blue-collar workers: the big three U.S. automakers between 2000 and 2006 eliminated 140,000 jobs, and comparable cuts occurred in other industries. This, in turn, weakened unions, to which only 12 percent of the work force belonged in 2004, and undermined labor's ability to fight for good wages and benefits. As foreign corporations supplied much of the U.S. market, some of them, such as Toyota, opened plants in the United States and reemployed a portion of the workers that U.S. companies had laid off.

VI. Domestic Policy Since 2004
A. Funding Social Security and Health Care as the Federal Deficit Soars
Conservative Republicans have wanted to end or privatize Social Security since it passed in 1935. Bush proposed a partial privatization, allowing workers to put part of their social-security retirement money in their own investment accounts. The majority of Americans disliked the idea, as well as almost all Democrats and some Republicans, so it was not implemented. The Republican-dominated Congress in 2003 did expand the Medicare program to cover some prescription-drug costs for seniors, but the plan proved extremely complicated and Democrats charged that it did more to enrich drug and heath insurance companies than help older citizens. Meanwhile, the soaring costs for Medicare, Medicaid, and the Iraq war drove the federal deficit to new heights.

B. Hurricane Katrina Tests the Bush Administration
Hurricane Katrina, which hit the Gulf Coast in August 2005, caused some 1,400 deaths. New Orleans was especially hard hit. Inadequate, poorly maintained levees designed to protect the city from the Gulf of Mexico and Lake Pontchartrain, gave way, and the low-lying portions of New Orleans, heavily African-American neighborhoods, flooded. Residents drowned, died waiting for rescuers, lost their homes and all other possessions, were jammed for days in the Superdome without adequate food, water, and sanitary facilities, and some, unable to escape the city on their own, were eventually bussed out at government expense to other cities, such as Houston. The response of municipal, state, and federal governments to the natural disaster proved totally wanting. The Bush administration failed to heed early warnings about impending calamity, and its emergency relief efforts afterward were slow, confused, and marred by fraud and corruption. As of 2006, 60 percent of New Orleans's population had not returned, the most damaged parts of the city were still unrestored, and no one knew if the quickly repaired levees would hold out the water in the next hurricane.

C.   Extending Republican Influence: From the Supreme Court to K Street
In his second term as president, Bush was able to name two more conservative justices to the Supreme Court; John G. Roberts, Jr. replaced Chief Justice Rehnquist, who died in 2005, and Samuel Alito, Jr. took the seat of retiring Sandra Day O'Connor. Hoping there were now enough conservative right-to-life members on the high court to overturn *Roe* v. *Wade,* the South Dakota legislature in 2006 passed a law banning abortion in that state. In the near future the constitutionality of the South Dakota statute will likely be tested in a case that will reach the Supreme Court. Bush and the Republican-controlled Congress were embarrassed by a major scandal involving Washington lobbyist Jack Abramoff and House Speaker Tom DeLay. Under indictment, Abramoff admitted obtaining millions of dollars from corporations and Indian tribes interested in gaining favorable legislation or rulings from Congress and/or the White House and, with the help of DeLay, funneling this money to Republican lawmakers and candidates. DeLay resigned, and other Republicans denied any wrongdoing and distanced themselves from Abramoff as best they could.

D.   Debating Immigration
After 9/11/01, many Americans became alarmed at the estimated 11 million illegal immigrants in the United States. More than three-quarters of the undocumented are from Mexico or other Latin American countries. They have been hired as low-paid laborers by agribusinesses, fast-food chains, construction and landscaping companies, and food-processing plants. Their employers would like to keep these immigrants, claiming they are hard workers and do necessary jobs that Americans will not. Those favoring immigration restriction claim that if the illegal immigrants were not available, employers would have to offer decent wages, and then there would be plenty of Americans who would take the jobs. President Bush proposed a "guest worker" program, allowing foreigners to work briefly in this country and then return home. The House passed a very different bill. It made undocumented immigrants criminals, subject to deportation; called for building a barrier along the Mexican border; and made it a felony for anyone to assist an illegal immigrant. The House bill touched off major protests and demonstrations. The Senate passed a more immigrant-friendly measure, including procedures for eventually converting undocumented aliens in this country to citizens. Bush endorsed the Senate version, but the differences between the two chambers prevented quick passage of any legislation, including action on Bush's "guest worker" proposal.

VII. Conclusion
The 9/11/01 terrorist attacks occurred shortly after George W. Bush was inaugurated. The nation and Congress united behind the president, fully supporting the war in Afghanistan and the passage of the USA-Patriot Act. Initially, Americans, believing the administration's claims that attacking Iraq was also necessary for our security, rallied behind that invasion as well. As the nation watched the situation in Iraq deteriorate and learned about the administration's misleading claims and about scandals and abuses, domestic backing for the war dwindled. On the home front, Bush pushed through tax cuts that most benefited the rich and that soon produced huge budget deficits. The President downplayed the dangers of global warming and refused to sign the Kyoto Accords. Major social trends from the 1990s to 2006 included Americans moving to the South and West, high rates of immigration from Asia and Latin America making greater ethnic diversity, and chronic problems of poverty in the inner cities. The economy continued to shift from industrial to information technology and service based. Bush's second term as president was troubled by burgeoning trade and

federal budget deficits, lobbying and other corruption scandals, ineffective handling of the Hurricane Katrina disaster, and bitter debates over immigration policy.

VOCABULARY

demographic	of or relating to the statistical study of human populations
sectarian	relating to a religious sect or group
paranoid	displaying the traits of a mental disorder in which one mistakenly believes that others have hostile intentions toward him or her
protectionism	the policy of government economic protection of domestic producers from foreign competitors by imposing tariffs or other restrictions on imports
protocol	a preliminary memorandum of diplomatic negotiation or intent
fundamentalist	adhering to a very strict and traditional interpretation of religious texts
nuclear family	a family unit made up of a married mother and father and their children who are minors

IDENITFICATIONS

After reading Chapter 32, you should be able to identify and explain the historical significance of each of the following:

the Taliban

Kean commission report

Saddam Hussein

preemptive war

Nancy Pelosi

Sunni versus Shiite Muslims

Enron Corporation

stem-cell research

bloggers

Halliburton Company

Hamas

"coyotes"

John G. Roberts, Jr.

Samuel Alito, Jr.

Tom DeLay

greenhouse gases

SKILL BUILDING: MAPS

On the map of the Middle East, locate and explain the historic events that occurred in each of the following places since the 1990s:

Israel

Jerusalem

Iraq

Persian Gulf

Pakistan

Afghanistan

Iran

Kabul

Syria

West Bank

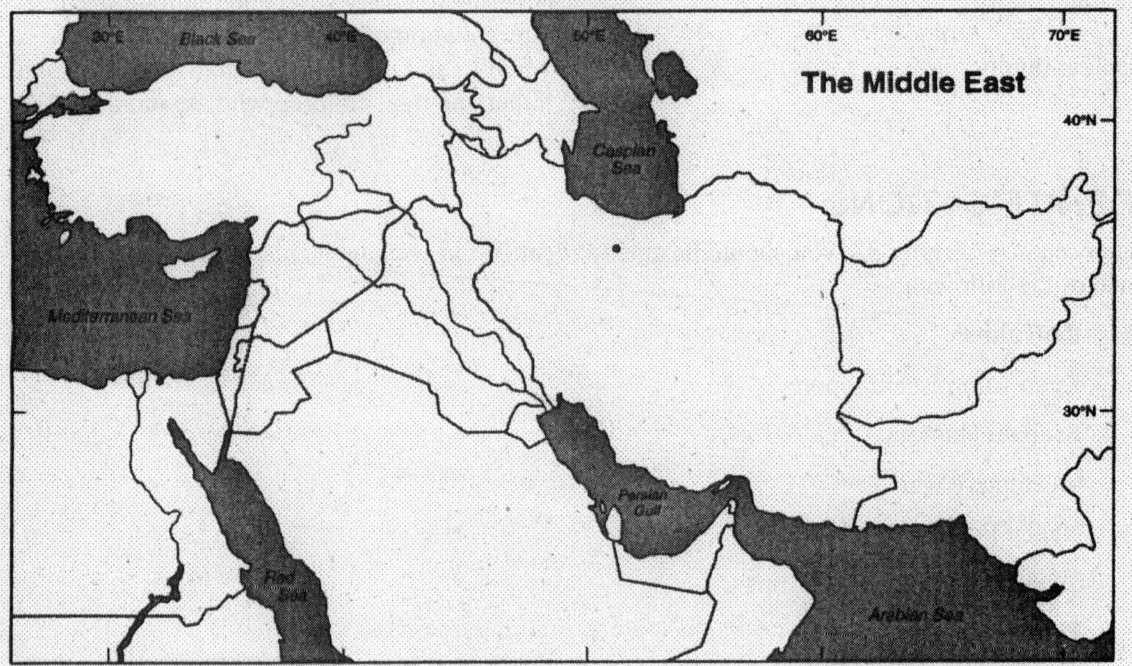

MULTIPLE-CHOICE QUESTIONS

1. As of 2006, the largest minority group in the United States is

    a. Asian
    b. African-American
    c. Middle Eastern–American
    d. Hispanic

2. In 2002 President Bush designated which of the following as the site for depositing radioactive nuclear waste?

    a. Bhopal, India
    b. Three Mile Island, Pennsylvania
    c. Yucca Mountain, Nevada
    d. Chernobyl, Ukraine

3. All of the following groups campaigned heavily for George W. Bush and other conservative candidates *except*

    a. the Christian Coalition.
    b. the American Family Association.
    c. People for the American Way.
    d. Focus on the Family.

4. What do Enron, WorldCom, Adelphia, and Tyco have in common?

    a. The CEOs of all of them were convicted of frauds that ruined their companies and cheated investors and workers.
    b. They were all companies in the information technology field that went bankrupt.
    c. They were all foreign-owned companies that moved into the U.S. market, took over smaller domestic firms, and employed thousands of U.S. workers.
    d. They all ran discount chains that sold cheap foreign imports to millions of American consumers.

5. As of 2004, about what percent of American workers belonged to a labor union?

    a. 40 percent
    b. 25 percent
    c. 6 percent
    d. 12 percent

6. Al Gore's film "An Inconvenient Truth" deals with the dangers posed by

    a. growing economic inequality in the United States.
    b. global warming.
    c. the Bush administration's go-it-alone foreign policy in Iraq.
    d. the failure of public schools to prepare all students for work in our information technology economy.

7. Which of the following does President George W. Bush favor?

    a. Drilling for oil in the Artic National Wildlife Refuge
    b. Expanding stem-cell research
    c. Closing the prison camp for suspected terrorists at Guantanamo Bay
    d. Doubling the amount of federal aid to public schools as a way to implement the No Child Left Behind Act

8.   Bush's domestic policies were designed to appeal to

   a.   moderate Republicans and Reagan Democrats.
   b.   corporate leaders and the religious right.
   c.   environmental activists.
   d.   leaders of the international community.

9.   The 2002 McCain-Feingold campaign finance reform act

   a.   allowed foreign contributors to give money to election campaigns.
   b.   forbid unions and corporations from giving money to candidates.
   c.   banned soft-money contributions to national parties.
   d.   used tobacco settlement money to pay for television ads for each political party.

10.   After the September 11 attacks, the United States engaged in military action against terrorists in which country?

   a.   Iran
   b.   Israel
   c.   Afghanistan
   d.   Korea

SHORT-ANSWER QUESTIONS

1.   Briefly discuss the Bush administration's environmental record.

2.   Who were the neoconservatives, and what were their foreign policy objectives?

3.   Discuss briefly the 2004 elections. Who were the candidates? What were the main issues? What was the outcome? How do you account for the outcome?

4.   Discuss U.S. attempts to prevent nuclear proliferation. How much success has the U.S. had with this effort in North Korea and Iran?

5.   Why was the federal government's response to Hurricane Katrina criticized?

ESSAY QUESTIONS

1.   Discuss what happened to the United States on September 11, 2001, and what impact those events have had on American life and politics ever since.

2.   Discuss the foreign-policy challenges the United States faces in Europe, Asia, and the Middle East. How much has George W. Bush relied on international cooperation to handle these challenges, and how much has he favored a U.S. go-it-alone policy?

3.   The author of Chapter 32 writes, "Nearly all scientists . . . agree that carbon dioxide, methane, and other gases from fossil-fuel combustion in factories, homes, and motor vehicles contribute significantly to global warming." Explain the scientific evidence and technology scientists use to reach this conclusion. What dangers to the world do they predict if these greenhouse gases are not reduced? Have scientists convinced all major governments? Why or why not?

4.   Discuss the major social and cultural trends in contemporary America. What effects are those trends likely to have on America's economy, politics, and culture wars?

5.   Assess how much progress toward full economic, political, and social equality with white, non-Hispanic males each of the following has made by the beginning of the twenty-first century: African-Americans, Hispanics, Asians, Native Americans, and women.

ANSWERS TO MULTIPLE-CHOICE QUESTIONS

1. d
2. c
3. c
4. a
5. d
6. b
7. a
8. b
9. c
10. c

Preparing for the Final Examination

PROLOGUE, CHAPTERS 1 TO 16

As you approach the end of part 1 of your American history course, you may well wonder how you are supposed to remember all those facts for the final. Here are some hints for preparing to take that semester exam: (1) Do not wait until the night before the test (or even the last couple of days prior to it) to start your studying; (2) Review the notes that you have taken on class lectures and assigned readings other than your textbook; (3) Review the chapters of this study guide, rereading carefully the Outline and Summary portion of each; (4) As you do steps 2 and 3, look for issues and themes that seem to come up again and again. History, after all, is about change and continuity over time. Therefore, ask yourself as you review what things about American society changed between the colonial period and the end of Reconstruction and why. On the other hand, which things remained essentially constant or recurred periodically throughout those years? The following sample multiple-choice and essay questions are designed to assist you in pulling together all the facts and seeing more clearly the patterns of change and continuity over the first centuries of American history.

MULTIPLE-CHOICE QUESTIONS

Circle the letter of the item that best completes each statement or answers the question.

1. Which of the following ended slavery everywhere in the United States?

    a.   Lincoln's Emancipation Proclamation
    b.   The Crittenden compromise
    c.   The Thirteenth Amendment
    d.   The Fifteenth Amendment

2. The statement "We hold these truths to be self-evident, that all men are created equal, that they are endowed by their Creator with certain unalienable rights . . ." is found in

    a.   the Declaration of Independence.
    b.   the U.S. Constitution.
    c.   Lincoln's first inaugural address.
    d.   all of the above.

3. Which of the following people is *incorrectly* matched with the reform he or she championed?

    a.   Dorothea Dix—more humane treatment of the mentally ill
    b.   Elizabeth Cady Stanton—women's rights
    c.   Jonathan Edwards—separation of church and state and religious toleration
    d.   William Lloyd Garrison—abolition of slavery

4. The convention held at Seneca Falls, New York, in 1848

    a.   threatened that New England and New York would secede if peace were not made with England immediately.
    b.   launched the feminist movement.
    c.   was the first held by a political party to nominate its candidate for president.
    d.   launched the abolitionist movement.

5.   The forty-ninth parallel became the dividing line between

    a.   northern and southern states.
    b.   American and British parts of the Oregon Territory.
    c.   Kansas and Nebraska
    d.   the Mexican cession and the Louisiana Purchase.

6.   The case of *Commonwealth* v. *Hunt* is significant in the long struggle of

    a.   labor to win recognition of unions and the right to strike.
    b.   women to gain equality in receiving an education.
    c.   the federal government to increase its powers at the expense of the states.
    d.   the abolitionists to end slavery in Washington, D.C.

7.   Which of these statements comes closest to expressing Secretary of the Treasury Alexander Hamilton's views on the proper financial program for the federal government?

    a.   A government should be frugal and avoid a standing debt.
    b.   The government should repudiate the financial obligations incurred by the Continental Congress.
    c.   The federal government should tie the monied classes of the nation to it by selling public securities at attractive rates of interest to them.
    d.   The federal government should encourage the states to pay off their debts quickly by giving them matching grants.

8.   Which of the following statements about the Era of Good Feelings is *incorrect*?

    a.   It was a period of one-party politics.
    b.   During these years the Republicans adopted much of the centralizing nationalism of the old Federalists.
    c.   Congress passed a protective tariff and chartered a new national bank.
    d.   The federal government began an extensive program of federally subsidized transportation improvements.

9.   A typical western farmer in the 1830s and 1840s would probably favor all of the following federal policies *except*

    a.   federal aid for internal improvements.
    b.   renewing the charter of the national bank.
    c.   easy land-purchase terms for squatters.
    d.   the Indian Removal Act of 1830.

10.   The influence of Puritanism was greatest and lasted the longest in

    a.   New France.
    b.   New England.
    c.   New York and Pennsylvania.
    d.   Virginia and Maryland.

11.   During the colonial and Revolutionary War periods, the crop that most shaped the economy and society of the Upper South was

    a.   sugar.
    b.   cotton.
    c.   tobacco.
    d.   wheat.

12. Which of these was a slave uprising?

    a. Bacon's Rebellion
    b. Shays's Rebellion
    c. The Whiskey Rebellion
    d. Nat Turner's rebellion

13. Which of the following statements about slavery in colonial America is correct?

    a. Slavery existed in all thirteen English colonies.
    b. The slave population exceeded the free white population in most of the southern colonies.
    c. British attempts to outlaw slavery in her overseas colonies helped to incite the American Revolution.
    d. The majority of those enslaved were Indians rather than Africans.

14. In the eighteenth century most of the British colonies in America were governed by

    a. the elders of the established church.
    b. a governor, council, and assembly—all elected by the people.
    c. a governor appointed by the crown and an elected assembly dominated by the upper classes.
    d. a proprietor or appointed representatives of the company that had established the colony.

15. Thomas Jefferson was responsible for all of the following *except*

    a. framing the Virginia Statute for Religious Freedom.
    b. drafting the Declaration of Independence.
    c. drafting the U.S. Constitution.
    d. writing the Kentucky resolution.

16. The first systematic statement of the strict versus broad interpretation of the Constitution arose out of the debate over the

    a. tariff.
    b. chartering of a national bank.
    c. barring of slavery from new territory.
    d. purchase of the Louisiana Territory.

17. Which of these describes the Indian policy adopted during the Jacksonian era?

    a. To remove Indians to lands west of the Mississippi River
    b. To establish reservations for Indians in various sections of the country
    c. To force Indians to migrate to territory owned by Mexico
    d. To assimilate the Indians by breaking up the tribes and granting American citizenship to individuals.

18. For white males almost all property qualifications for voting had been abolished

    a. by the end of the American Revolution.
    b. with the ratification of the Constitution and the addition of the Bill of Rights.
    c. by 1800, when Jefferson was elected president.
    d. by the Jacksonian era.

19. The right of the federal courts to declare acts of Congress unconstitutional was first exercised in

    a. *Marbury* v. *Madison.*
    b. *McCulloch* v. *Maryland.*
    c. *Dred Scott* v. *Sandford.*
    d. *Ex parte* Milligan

20. The United States acquired these territories in which chronological order?

    a. Alaska, Florida, Louisiana Territory, Texas, California
    b. Louisiana Territory, Florida, Texas, California, Alaska
    c. Florida, Texas, Louisiana Territory, Alaska, California
    d. Florida, Louisiana Territory, California, Alaska, Texas

21. In the 1840s and 1850s many Americans believed that it was the manifest destiny of the United States to

    a. abolish slavery.
    b. become the world's leading industrial power.
    c. build a mighty overseas empire.
    d. spread its borders from coast to coast.

22. By the eve of the Civil War which groups accounted for roughly 50 percent of the population of cities such as New York, Chicago, St. Louis, and San Francisco?

    a. Italians and Eastern European Jews
    b. Irish and Germans
    c. Polish and Chinese
    d. Scandinavians and Hispanics

23. Which of these led directly to the formation of the Republican Party?

    a. The Compromise of 1850
    b. The Fugitive Slave Law
    c. The Kansas-Nebraska Act
    d. The *Dred Scott* decision

24. Which of these did Lincoln *oppose* in the first year of the Civil War?

    a. Abolishing slavery everywhere in the nation
    b. Compensating the owners of freed slaves
    c. Colonizing freedmen outside the United States
    d. Fighting a war primarily to preserve the Union

25. Many historians believe that Radical Reconstruction was a democratic experiment that failed for all of the following reasons *except*

    a. Congress did not redistribute southern land, and without property the freedmen were too economically vulnerable to hold on to their political rights.
    b. the Republicans were unwilling to continue to use military force to protect blacks and remake southern society.
    c. freedmen failed to understand the responsibilities of citizens and showed little interest in voting and office holding.
    d. Republicans were willing to abandon the last of the Republican Reconstruction governments in 1877 to secure the election of their presidential candidate, Rutherford B. Hayes.

ESSAY QUESTIONS

1. The antebellum years saw the birth and development of the Federalist, Jeffersonian Republican, Democratic, Whig, and Republican parties. Discuss how and why each of these parties began. Who founded each? To which groups did each one mainly appeal? What led to the demise of the Federalist and Whig parties?

2. Each of the following men was in some way involved in the sectional conflict that eventually led to the Civil War: Thomas Jefferson, John C. Calhoun, Daniel Webster, Henry Clay, and Stephen A. Douglas. Discuss the views and activities of these men regarding the sectional conflict.

3. Trace Abraham Lincoln's position on blacks and slavery from the time of the Lincoln-Douglas debates in 1858 to the time of his assassination in 1865. Why did he modify his stands?

4. Discuss the causes of the Civil War. Cite as many facts as possible to back up your analysis.

5. Compare and contrast Andrew Jackson's handling of South Carolina's nullification of federal law in 1832 and James Buchanan's handling of that same state's secession in 1860.

6. Explain the causes of the Mexican War and its impact on sectionalism.

7. Ralph Waldo Emerson once wrote, "There is no strong performance without a little fanaticism in the performance." To what extent could this observation be applied to the abolitionists and other antebellum reformers?

8. In 1820, 1833, and 1850 sectional compromises were agreed to and the Union was preserved. What accommodations were made each time, and why did the attempts to reach one more compromise in 1860–1861 fail?

9. If the enduring vision of America is embodied in the Declaration of Independence's statements about equality and universal rights to justice, liberty, and self-fulfillment, how much progress toward those ideals had blacks and women made by 1877? Back up your evaluation with as many specific facts as possible about the status of blacks and women at the end of Reconstruction.

10. In what respects was the Constitution of the United States as written and ratified in 1787 undemocratic? How was the American political system democratized between 1789 and 1877? What undemocratic features remained to be addressed? Give as many specific examples in your answer as possible.

ANSWERS TO MULTIPLE-CHOICE QUESTIONS

1. c
2. a
3. c
4. b
5. b
6. a
7. c
8. d
9. b
10. b
11. c
12. d
13. a
14. c
15. c
16. b
17. a
18. d
19. a
20. b
21. d
22. b
23. c
24. a
25. c

CHAPTERS 17 TO 32

As you approach the end of your American history course, you may well wonder how you are supposed to remember all those facts for the final. Here are some hints for preparing to take that semester exam. (1) Do not wait until the night before the test (or even the last couple of days prior to it) to start your studying. (2) Review the notes that you have taken on class lectures and assigned readings other than your textbook. (3) Review the chapters of this study guide, rereading carefully the Outline and Summary portion of each. (4) As you do steps 2 and 3, look for issues and themes that seem to come up again and again. History, after all, is about change and continuity over time. Therefore, ask yourself as you review, "What things about American society have changed between the Reconstruction era and 2006 and why?" On the other hand, which things remained essentially constant or recurred periodically throughout those years?

The sample multiple-choice and essay questions that follow are designed to assist you in pulling together all the facts and seeing more clearly the patterns of change and continuity over the last century and a half of American history.

MULTIPLE-CHOICE QUESTIONS

Circle the letter of the item that best completes each statement or answers the question.

1. In which two periods did the federal government make its greatest efforts to protect African-Americans by passing civil-rights laws and constitutional amendments?

    a. The 1920s and 1930s
    b. The administrations of Ronald Reagan and George Bush
    c. Reconstruction and the 1960s
    d. World Wars I and II

2. Which of these was primarily a rural-based reform movement concerned particularly with farmers' economic problems.

    a. The New Frontier
    b. Progressivism
    c. Populism
    d. The Fair Deal

3. The social worker who established Hull House in Chicago was

    a. Harry Hopkins.
    b. Frances Perkins.
    c. Jane Addams.
    d. Jeannette Rankin.

4. Each of these was a muckraking writer whose book helped to secure passage of federal legislation *except*

    a. John Hay.
    b. Upton Sinclair.
    c. Michael Harrington.
    d. Rachel Carson.

5. Oliver H. Kelly, James B. Weaver, William Jennings Bryan, and Henry Wallace were all associated with promoting the interests of which group?

    a. African-Americans
    b. Native Americans
    c. Organized labor
    d. Farmers

6. Which of the following happened to the majority of southern African-Americans in the years between Reconstruction and 1900?

    a. They were driven out of the South by poverty and discrimination.
    b. They became tenants and sharecroppers on land owned by whites.
    c. They got jobs in factories opening in the Midwest and Far West.
    d. They became independent, landowning small farmers.

7. During whose presidency did the United States have the largest trade and federal budget deficits?

    a. Franklin Roosevelt
    b. Lyndon Johnson
    c. Ulysses Grant
    d. George W. Bush

8. All of the following administrations are particularly associated with corruption and wrongdoing in government *except* that of

    a. Ulysses Grant.
    b. Herbert Hoover.
    c. Warren Harding.
    d. Richard Nixon.

9. Which of the wars that the United States fought had the least popular support at home?

    a. Spanish-American War
    b. World War I
    c. World War II
    d. Vietnam War

10. By what year did the majority of the American people live in cities?

    a. 1890
    b. 1920
    c. 1940
    d. 1960

11. In which of these elections was foreign policy *not* an important issue?

    a. 1900
    b. 1916
    c. 1936
    d. 1968

12. After which of these events did women secure the right to vote in national elections?

    a. The Great Depression of the 1930s
    b. Passage of the Equal Rights Amendment in the 1970s
    c. Passage of the Fourteenth Amendment
    d. World War I

13. In which decade did the United States finally get rid of the discriminatory national-origins quota system in our immigration law?

    a. 1970s
    b. 1960s
    c. 1980s
    d. 1920s

14. The elections of 1912, 1924, and 1948 were similar in what way?

    a. In each one there was a third party calling itself Progressive.
    b. In each one the winner received more than 60 percent of the votes.
    c. In each one there was no incumbent running.
    d. Each election was followed immediately by war.

15. Membership in the organized labor movement in the United States increased most rapidly during which decade?

    a. 1890s
    b. 1920s
    c. 1930s
    d. 1990s

16. American armed forces fought against Soviet armies in which of these conflicts?

    a. World War II
    b. Korean War
    c. Vietnam War
    d. None of the above

17. Which of these statements about Native Americans is correct?

    a. Indian tribes lost hundreds of thousands of acres of land to whites under the Dawes Act.
    b. Native Americans resented the Indian Reorganization Act of 1934 because it attempted to suppress Native American culture and force rapid assimilation.
    c. As a result of the termination policy, the great majority of Native Americans live in cities and all reservations have been closed.
    d. None of the above.

18. In which of these periods was the U.S. economy plagued by the highest rates of inflation?

    a. 1875 to 1897
    b. 1900 to World War I
    c. 1920s and 1930s
    d. 1970s and early 1980s

19. All of the following have been used to justify U.S. intervention in Asia *except* the

    a. need to uplift, educate, and teach democracy to backward people.
    b. Good Neighbor policy.
    c. Open Door policy.
    d. domino theory.

20. American literature tended to concern itself more with great social and economic questions and less with the emotional state of the individual during which period?

    a. 1930s
    b. 1950s
    c. 1880s
    d. 1970s and 1980s

21. Which of the following happened after both World War I and World War II?

    a. The Senate rejected treaties permitting the United States to join international organizations created to keep the peace.
    b. There was a heightened fear of internal communism and radicalism and greater attempts to suppress them.
    c. There was a postwar depression.
    d. The party in power during the war was defeated in the next presidential election.

22. All of these people were leaders who opposed the United States' participation in a war being fought in their day *except*

    a. Eugene McCarthy.
    b. Jack Murtha
    c. Eugene Debs.
    d. Theodore Roosevelt.

23. Some critics have blamed Franklin D. Roosevelt for giving in to Soviet domination of eastern Europe at which conference?

    a. Versailles
    b. Potsdam
    c. Yalta
    d. Geneva

24. The treaty granting the United States control over the Panama Canal and Canal Zone was signed and ratified under which president, and the treaty returning control by 1999 to Panama was signed and ratified under which president, respectively?

    a. Theodore Roosevelt and Jimmy Carter
    b. William H. Taft and Richard Nixon
    c. Woodrow Wilson and Lyndon Johnson
    d. William McKinley and Bill Clinton

25. Which of these leaders was the first to gain a mass following among African-Americans?

    a. Booker T. Washington
    b. W. E. B. Du Bois
    c. Marcus Garvey
    d. Malcolm X

26. Three times between 1876 and 2000 men who lost in the popular election for president, but won the majority of votes in the Electoral College entered the White House. These presidents were

    a. Rutherford B. Hayes, Benjamin Harrison, and George W. Bush.
    b. Ulysses S. Grant, Woodrow Wilson, and George W. Bush.
    c. Herbert Hoover, John F. Kennedy, and Ronald Reagan.
    d. Rutherford B. Hayes, John F. Kennedy, and Bill Clinton.

27. In the years since the end of the Cold War, U.S. armed forces have been deployed in all of the following places *except*:

    a. Afghanistan.
    b. Iraq.
    c. Poland.
    d. Somalia.

28. Which of these statements about the economic boom decades of the 1920s and the 1990s is *not* correct?

    a. In both, the benefits of the boom were unequally distributed, with the wealthiest receiving the major share.
    b. In both, new technologies and industries fueled the economic growth.
    c. In both, the real wages of workers rose faster than did corporate profits.
    d. In both, stock prices often soared to levels far above what the shares were worth based on the earnings and prospects of the issuing corporations.

29. In the course of U.S. history two presidents have been impeached, but not convicted. These two were:

    a. Andrew Johnson and Richard Nixon.
    b. Warren G. Harding and Jimmy Carter.
    c. Ronald Reagan and Grover Cleveland.
    d. Andrew Johnson and Bill Clinton.

30. Which event is *not* correctly matched with the presidency during which it occurred?
   a.   Japanese attack on Pearl Harbor—Franklin D. Roosevelt
   b.   Sinking of the *Lusitania*—Theodore Roosevelt
   c.   Cuban missile crisis—John F. Kennedy
   d.   Terrorist attacks on the World Trade Center and Pentagon—George W. Bush

ESSAY QUESTIONS

1. Compare and contrast the old immigrants (pre-1880s), the new immigrants (1880–1920), and the post-1960 immigrants. Who composed each group? Why did each group come? What characteristics did each display? How did each fare in the United States and why?

2. Assess how much progress toward full economic, political, and social equality with whites African-Americans had made by 2006. Back up your assessment with as many specific facts as possible.

3. Pretend that you are a filmmaker working on a forty-five-minute documentary about the changing role of women in American society from Reconstruction to 2006. Which persons, events, trends, and laws would you depict in your movie? Why did you make these particular choices?

4. Discuss the impact of World War I, World War II, and the Vietnam War on American society at home. In your answer consider effects on the economy, women, families, minorities, domestic reform, and civil or constitutional liberties.

5. Compare and contrast the Populist, Progressive, New Deal, and Great Society reform programs. What do you see as the major achievements of each? What do you think were the most serious failures? How much of each of these programs has been dismantled by 2006?

6. Discuss the Latin American policy of the United States from Theodore Roosevelt's corollary to the start of the twenty-first century.

7. Trace federal government policies toward labor and unions from the late nineteenth century to 2002. During which periods has the government been most prolabor? During which periods has government been most hostile to unions? How have the changes in government policy affected the labor movement?

8. Initially the majority of the American people did not wish to enter either World War I or World War II. Yet the United States entered both conflicts. Why?

9. From the late nineteenth century to the present, progressive liberals and conservatives have argued over the proper role of the federal government in the economic and social life of the nation. Explain the positions of each side and the rationales for their positions. Discuss concrete examples of legislation, federal programs, and Supreme Court decisions from 1890 to 2002 that have followed the philosophy of each political camp.

10. Discuss the origins of the Cold War and its impact on U.S. domestic and foreign policy since 1945. When and why did the Cold War end? How has its end affected U.S. foreign policy?

11. How do you define the American dream? Based on your definition, during which period between the 1870s and 2006 has American society come closest to fulfilling your vision? Explain your choice by discussing as many facts about that period as possible.

12. Discuss the preservation, conservation, and environmental movements in the United States from the late nineteenth century to 2006. What environmental issues have these movements addressed at various periods in the past? What are the greatest challenges to the movements as of 2006? What obstacles and opposition have the movements faced? What do you consider the greatest achievements, if any, of these movements?

13. Compare and contrast government actions toward potential domestic enemies of the United States in the 1919–1920 Red Scare, the post–Pearl Harbor years of 1942–1944, the post–World War II McCarthy era (1947–1954), and the post–September 11, 2001, terrorist attacks.

14. Trace the rise of neoconservatism and the radical Right in American politics from the 1950s through 2006. Who in American society has backed the Right? Why?

ANSWERS TO MULTIPLE-CHOICE QUESTIONS

1. c
2. c
3. c
4. a
5. d
6. b
7. d
8. b
9. d
10. b
11. c
12. d
13. b
14. a
15. c
16. d
17. a
18. d
19. b
20. a
21. b
22. d
23. c
24. a
25. c
26. a
27. c
28. c
29. d
30. b